MP

interchange

THIRD EDITION

TEACHER'S EDITION

Jack C. Richards

with Jonathan Hull and Susan Proctor

Interchange Third Edition Teacher's Edition revision prepared by Kate Cory-Wright

CAMBRIDGE UNIVERSITY PRESS
Cambridge, New York, Melbourne, Madrid, Cape Town, Singapore, São Paulo, Delhi, Dubai, Tokyo

Cambridge University Press
32 Avenue of the Americas, New York, NY 10013–2473, USA

www.cambridge.org
Information on this title: www.cambridge.org/9780521601801

First published 2005
10th printing 2010

Interchange Third Edition Teacher's Edition 1 has been developed from *New Interchange* Teacher's Edition 1, first published by Cambridge University Press in 1997.

Printed in Hong Kong, China, by Golden Cup Printing Company Limited

A catalog record for this publication is available from the British Library.

ISBN 978-0-521-60180-1 Teacher's Edition

Art direction, book design, photo research, and layout services: Adventure House, NYC
Audio production: Richard LePage & Associates

Contents

Plan of Book 1

Titles/Topics	Speaking	Grammar
UNIT 1 PAGES 2-7 **Please call me Beth.** Introductions and greetings; names; countries and nationalities	Introducing yourself; introducing someone; checking information; exchanging personal information; saying hello and good-bye	Wh-questions and statements with *be*; questions: *what*, *where*, *who*, and *how*; yes/no questions and short answers with *be*; subject pronouns; possessive adjectives
UNIT 2 PAGES 8-13 **How do you spend your day?** Jobs, workplaces, and school; daily schedules; clock time	Describing work and school; asking for and giving opinions; describing daily schedules	Simple present Wh-questions and statements; question: *when*; time expressions: *at*, *in*, *on*, *around*, *early*, *late*, *until*, *before*, and *after*
PROGRESS CHECK PAGES 14-15		
UNIT 3 PAGES 16-21 **How much is it?** Shopping and prices; clothing and personal items; colors and materials	Talking about prices; giving opinions; discussing preferences; making comparisons; buying and selling things	Demonstratives: *this*, *that*, *these*, *those*; *one* and *ones*; questions: *how much* and *which*; comparisons with adjectives
UNIT 4 PAGES 22-27 **Do you like rap?** Music, movies, and TV programs; entertainers; invitations and excuses; dates and times	Talking about likes and dislikes; giving opinions; making invitations and excuses	Yes/no and Wh-questions with *do*; question: *what kind*; object pronouns; modal verb *would*; verb + *to* + verb
PROGRESS CHECK PAGES 28-29		
UNIT 5 PAGES 30-35 **Tell me about your family.** Families; typical families	Talking about families and family members; exchanging information about the present; describing family life	Present continuous yes/no and Wh-questions, statements, and short answers; quantifiers: *all*, *nearly all*, *most*, *many*, *a lot of*, *some*, *not many*, *a few*, and *few*; pronoun: *no one*
UNIT 6 PAGES 36-41 **How often do you exercise?** Sports, fitness activities, and exercise; routines	Asking about and describing routines and exercise; talking about frequency; discussing sports and athletes; talking about abilities	Adverbs of frequency: *always*, *almost always*, *usually*, *often*, *sometimes*, *hardly ever*, *almost never*, and *never*; questions: *how often*, *how long*, *how well*, and *how good*; short answers
PROGRESS CHECK PAGES 42-43		
UNIT 7 PAGES 44-49 **We had a great time!** Free-time and weekend activities; chores; vacations	Talking about past events; giving opinions about past experiences; talking about vacations	Simple past yes/no and Wh-questions, statements, and short answers with regular and irregular verbs; past of *be*
UNIT 8 PAGES 50-55 **What's your neighborhood like?** Stores and places in a city; neighborhoods; houses and apartments	Asking about and describing locations of places; asking about and describing neighborhoods; asking about quantities	*There is/there are*; *one*, *any*, and *some*; prepositions of place; quantifiers; questions: *how many* and *how much*; count and noncount nouns
PROGRESS CHECK PAGES 56-57		

Pronunciation/Listening	Writing/Reading	Interchange Activity
Linked sounds Listening for names and countries *Self-study*: Listening for personal information	Writing questions requesting personal information "What's in a Name?": Reading about popular names	"Getting to know you": Collecting personal information about classmates
Syllable stress Listening to descriptions of jobs and daily schedules *Self-study*: Listening to a description of a weekly schedule	Writing a biography of a classmate "Why Do You Need a Job?": Reading about people who need jobs	"Common ground": Finding similarities in classmates' daily schedules
Sentence stress Listening to people shopping; listening for items, prices, and opinions *Self-study*: Listening to people discussing clothing options	Writing a comparison of prices in different countries "The World's Online Marketplace™-eBay!": Reading about online shopping	"Flea market": Buying and selling things
Intonation in questions Identifying musical styles; listening for likes and dislikes *Self-study*: Listening to people making invitations	Writing a text message "Christina Aguilera": Reading about a famous entertainer	"What's the question?": Writing and asking questions
Intonation in statements Listening for family relationships *Self-study*: Listening to an interview with a new student	Writing an e-mail about family "The Changing Family": Reading about an American family	"Family facts": Finding out information about classmates' families
Intonation with direct address Listening to people talking about free-time activities; listening to descriptions of sports participation *Self-study*: Listening to a quiz about health and fitness	Writing about favorite activities "Health and Fitness Quiz": Reading about and taking a quiz	"Do you dance?": Finding out about classmates' abilities
Reduction of *did you* Listening to descriptions and opinions of past events and vacations *Self-study*: Listening to a police officer interviewing a possible thief	Writing a postcard "Vacation Postcards": Reading about different kinds of vacations	"Vacation disasters": Describing a terrible vacation
Reduction of *there is/there are* Listening for locations and descriptions of places *Self-study*: Listening for locations in a neighborhood	Writing a roommate wanted ad "The World in One Neighborhood": Reading about a New York City neighborhood	"Neighborhood committee": Making a neighborhood a better place

Titles/Topics	Speaking	Grammar
UNIT 9 PAGES 58-63		
What does she look like? Appearance and dress; clothing and clothing styles; people	Asking about and describing people's appearance; identifying people	Questions for describing people: *What . . . look like*, *how old*, *how tall*, *how long*, and *what color*; modifiers with participles and prepositions
UNIT 10 PAGES 64-69		
Have you ever ridden a camel? Past experiences; unusual activities	Describing past experiences; exchanging information about past experiences and events	Present perfect yes/no and Wh-questions, statements, and short answers with regular and irregular past participles; *already* and *yet*; present perfect vs. simple past; *for* and *since*
PROGRESS CHECK PAGES 70-71		
UNIT 11 PAGES 72-77		
It's a very exciting place! Cities; hometowns; countries	Asking about and describing cities; asking for and giving suggestions; talking about travel and tourism	Adverbs before adjectives; conjunctions: *and*, *but*, *though*, and *however*; modal verbs *can* and *should*
UNIT 12 PAGES 78-83		
It really works! Health problems; medication and remedies; products in a pharmacy	Talking about health problems; asking for and giving advice; making requests; asking for and giving suggestions	Infinitive complements; modal verb *should* for suggestions; modal verbs *can*, *could*, and *may* for requests
PROGRESS CHECK PAGES 84-85		
UNIT 13 PAGES 86-91		
May I take your order? Food and restaurants	Expressing likes and dislikes; agreeing and disagreeing; ordering a meal	*So*, *too*, *neither*, and *either*; modal verbs *would* and *will* for requests
UNIT 14 PAGES 92-97		
The biggest and the best! World geography and facts; countries	Describing countries; making comparisons; expressing opinions; talking about distances and measurements	Comparative and superlative forms of adjectives; questions: *how far*, *how big*, *how high*, *how deep*, *how long*, *how hot*, and *how cold*
PROGRESS CHECK PAGES 98-99		
UNIT 15 PAGES 100-105		
I'm going to a soccer match. Invitations and excuses; leisure-time activities; telephone messages	Talking about plans; making invitations; accepting and refusing invitations; giving reasons; taking and leaving messages	Future with present continuous and *be going to*; messages with *tell* and *ask*
UNIT 16 PAGES 106-111		
A change for the better! Life changes; plans and hopes for the future	Exchanging personal information; describing changes; talking about plans for the future	Describing changes with the present tense, the past tense, the present perfect, and the comparative; verb + infinitive
PROGRESS CHECK PAGES 112-113		
SELF-STUDY		

Pronunciation/Listening	Writing/Reading	Interchange Activity
Contrastive stress Listening to descriptions of people; identifying people *Self-study*: Listening to descriptions of people; identifying styles	Writing an e-mail describing people "Hip-Hop Style": Reading about clothing styles	"Find the differences": Comparing two pictures of a party
Linked sounds Listening to descriptions of events *Self-study*: Listening to a job interview; listening to descriptions of experiences	Writing a letter to an old friend "Taking the Risk": Reading about unusual or dangerous sports	"Lifestyle survey": Finding out about a classmate's lifestyle
Can't and *shouldn't* Listening to descriptions of cities and hometowns; listening for incorrect information *Self-study*: Listening to descriptions of vacation destinations	Writing a magazine article "Greetings from . . . ": Reading about famous cities	"City guide": Creating a guide to fun places in a city
Reduction of *to* Listening to health problems and advice *Self-study*: Listening to advice for a camping trip	Writing a letter to an advice columnist "Rain Forest Remedies?": Reading about natural products as medicine	"Help!": Playing a board game
Stress in responses Listening to restaurant orders *Self-study*: Listening to people talking about restaurant orders	Writing a restaurant review "To Tip or Not to Tip": Reading about tipping customs	"Plan a menu": Creating a menu of dishes
Questions of choice Listening to a TV game show *Self-study*: Listening to people discussing Chiang Mai	Writing an article about a country "Things You Can Do to Help the Environment": Reading about the environment	"How much do you know?": Taking a general knowledge quiz
Reduction of *could you* and *would you* Listening to telephone messages *Self-study*: Listening to telephone messages; identifying errors	Writing unusual favors "Cell Phone Etiquette": Reading about cell phone manners	"Weekend plans": Finding out about classmates' weekend plans
Vowel sounds /ou/ and /ʌ/ Listening to descriptions of changes *Self-study*: Listening to people at a class reunion	Writing a proposal for a class party "Setting Personal Goals": Reading about goals and priorities	"My possible future": Planning a possible future

The new edition

Interchange Third Edition is a fully revised edition of ***New Interchange***, the world's most successful series for adult and young adult learners of English. Written in American English, the course reflects the fact that English is the major language of international communication and is not limited to any one country, region, or culture.

The course has been thoroughly revised to reflect the most recent approaches to language teaching and learning. It remains the innovative series teachers and students have grown to love, while incorporating suggestions from teachers and students all over the world. This edition offers updated content in every unit, additional grammar practice, and more opportunities to develop speaking and listening skills.

SYLLABUS AND APPROACH

Interchange Third Edition uses high-interest themes to integrate speaking, grammar, vocabulary, pronunciation, listening, reading, and writing. There is a strong focus on both accuracy and fluency. The underlying philosophy of the course remains that language is best learned when it is used for meaningful communication.

Topics

The course covers contemporary, real-world topics that are relevant to students' lives (e.g., free time, entertainment). Students have background knowledge and experience with these topics, so they can share opinions and information productively. In addition, cultural information stimulates cross-cultural comparison and discussion.

Functions

A functional syllabus parallels the grammar syllabus in the course. For example, at the same time students learn *Do you . . . ?* questions in Level 1 (e.g., *Do you like jazz?*), they learn how to express likes and dislikes (e.g., *I love it. I can't stand it.*). Throughout the course, students learn useful functions, such as how to introduce themselves, or agree and disagree. Each level presents 50 to 65 functions.

Grammar

Interchange Third Edition has a graded grammar syllabus. Intro Level presents the basic structures for complete beginners, and Level 1 reviews and expands on them. Levels 2 and 3 present more advanced structures, such as passives and conditionals. The course views meaning, form, and use as the three interacting dimensions of language. First, students notice the new grammar in context in the *Conversations* or *Perspectives*. Then they learn and practice using the grammar forms in the *Grammar Focuses*. While they initially practice grammar in a controlled way, students soon move on to freer tasks that lead toward fluency. In other words, students acquire new grammar by using it, and grammar is a means to an end – communicative competence.

Vocabulary

Vocabulary development plays a key role in ***Interchange Third Edition***. Productive vocabulary (vocabulary students are encouraged to use) is presented mainly in *Word Powers* and *Snapshots*. Receptive vocabulary is introduced primarily in *Readings* and *Listenings*. In *Word Powers*, students typically categorize new vocabulary, to reflect how the mind organizes new words. Then they internalize the new vocabulary by using it in a personalized way. Photocopiable *Language summaries* in the Teacher's Edition provide lists of productive vocabulary and expressions for each unit. Each level teaches a productive vocabulary of about 1,000 to 1,300 words.

Speaking

Speaking skills are a central focus of ***Interchange Third Edition***, with an emphasis on natural, conversational language. The *Discussion*, *Role Play*, and *Speaking* exercises, as well as the *Interchange activities*, provide speaking opportunities that systematically build oral fluency. In addition, the *Conversations* illustrate different speaking strategies, such as how to open and close conversations, ask follow-up questions, take turns, and use filler words (e.g., *well*, *you know*, *so*). Moreover, almost all other exercises offer fun, personalized speaking practice and opportunities to share opinions.

Listening

The listening syllabus emphasizes task-based listening activities and incorporates both top-down processing skills (e.g., making predictions) and bottom-up processing skills (e.g., decoding individual words). The *Listening* exercises for all levels provide focus questions or tasks that give students a purpose for listening, while graphic organizers such as charts provide note-taking support. Moreover, most *Conversations* in Levels 1 to 3 provide follow-up listening tasks (e.g., *Listen to the rest of the conversation. What happened?*). Additional listening practice is provided in the Self-study section at the back of the Student's Book.

Reading

In the *Reading* exercises, students read a variety of text types (e.g., newspaper and magazine articles, surveys, letters) for different purposes. For example, they skim the texts for main ideas, scan them for specific information, or read them carefully for details. Then they complete exercises that help develop reading strategies and skills, such as inferencing and guessing meaning from context. They also discuss their opinions about the readings.

Writing

Levels 1 to 3 include a writing syllabus. In the *Writing* exercises, students write a variety of real-world text types (e.g., e-mail messages, postcards, memos). These exercises recycle and review the themes, vocabulary, and grammar in the unit. Students typically look at writing models before they begin writing. They use their experiences and ideas in their writing, and then share their writing with their classmates.

Pronunciation

The pronunciation syllabus focuses on important features of spoken English, such as word stress, intonation, and linked sounds. Every unit includes a *Pronunciation* exercise, the approach being that students benefit most from practicing a little pronunciation on a regular basis. In each unit, students typically notice and then practice a pronunciation feature linked to the new grammar or vocabulary.

CUSTOMIZATION

It's important for teachers to adapt the course materials to the needs, interests, ages, and learning styles of their students. The Teacher's Edition provides numerous additional resources that help teachers tailor their classes for maximum learning and enjoyment. For example, *Games* provide stimulating and fun ways to review or practice skills. In addition, *Fresh ideas* provide stimulating and fun techniques for presenting and reviewing the exercises. Moreover, there are *Photocopiables* for one exercise in every unit, or handouts for innovative supplementary activities.

ASSESSMENT

Interchange Third Edition has a complete and flexible assessment program. The *Progress checks* in the Student's Book encourage students to self-assess their progress in key skill areas after every two units. *Oral quizzes* and *Written quizzes* in the Teacher's Edition provide more formal assessment. In addition, the *Placement and Evaluation Package* is an indispensable tool for placing students at the correct level and regularly evaluating progress.

Student's Book overview

Every unit in ***Interchange Third Edition*** contains two cycles, each of which has a specific topic, grammar point, and function. The units in Level 1 contain a variety of exercises, including a Snapshot, Conversation, Grammar Focus, Pronunciation, Word Power, Discussion (or Speaking/Role Play), Listening, Writing, Reading, and Interchange activity. The sequence of these exercises differs from unit to unit. Here is a sample unit from Level 1.

CYCLE 1 (Exercises 1–7)

Topic: *leisure activities*
Grammar: *simple past*
Function: *talk about the weekend*

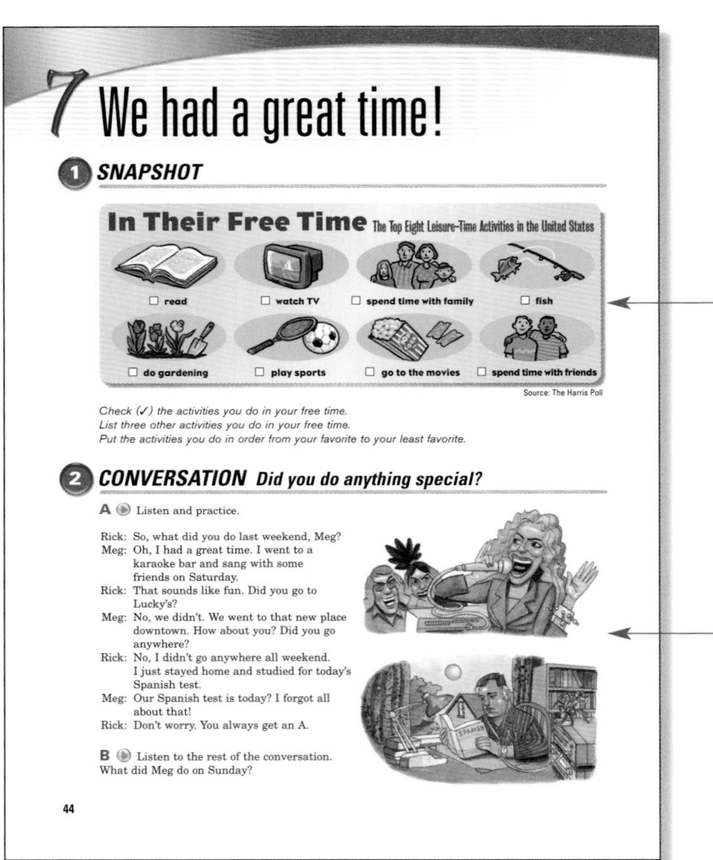

7 We had a great time!

1 SNAPSHOT

In Their Free Time The Top Eight Leisure-Time Activities in the United States

☐ read
☐ watch TV
☐ spend time with family
☐ fish
☐ do gardening
☐ play sports
☐ go to the movies
☐ spend time with friends

Source: The Harris Poll

Check (✓) the activities you do in your free time.
List three other activities you do in your free time.
Put the activities you do in order from your favorite to your least favorite.

2 CONVERSATION Did you do anything special?

A Listen and practice.

Rick: So, what did you do last weekend, Meg?
Meg: Oh, I had a great time. I went to a karaoke bar and sang with some friends on Saturday.
Rick: That sounds like fun. Did you go to Lucky's?
Meg: No, we didn't. We went to that new place downtown. How about you? Did you go anywhere?
Rick: No, I didn't go anywhere all weekend. I just stayed home and studied for today's Spanish test.
Meg: Our Spanish test is today? I forgot all about that!
Rick: Don't worry. You always get an A.

B Listen to the rest of the conversation. What did Meg do on Sunday?

44

SNAPSHOT

- Introduces the unit or cycle topic
- Presents vocabulary for discussing the topic
- Uses real-world information
- Provides personalized guided discussion questions

CONVERSATION

- Provides structured listening and speaking practice
- Introduces the meaning and use of the Cycle 1 grammar in context
- Uses pictures to set the scene and illustrate new vocabulary
- Provides follow-up listening tasks

GRAMMAR FOCUS

- Summarizes the Cycle 1 grammar
- Includes audio recordings of the grammar
- Provides controlled grammar practice in realistic contexts, such as short conversations
- Promotes freer, more personalized speaking practice

PRONUNCIATION

- Provides controlled practice in recognizing and producing sounds linked to the cycle grammar
- Promotes extended or personalized pronunciation practice

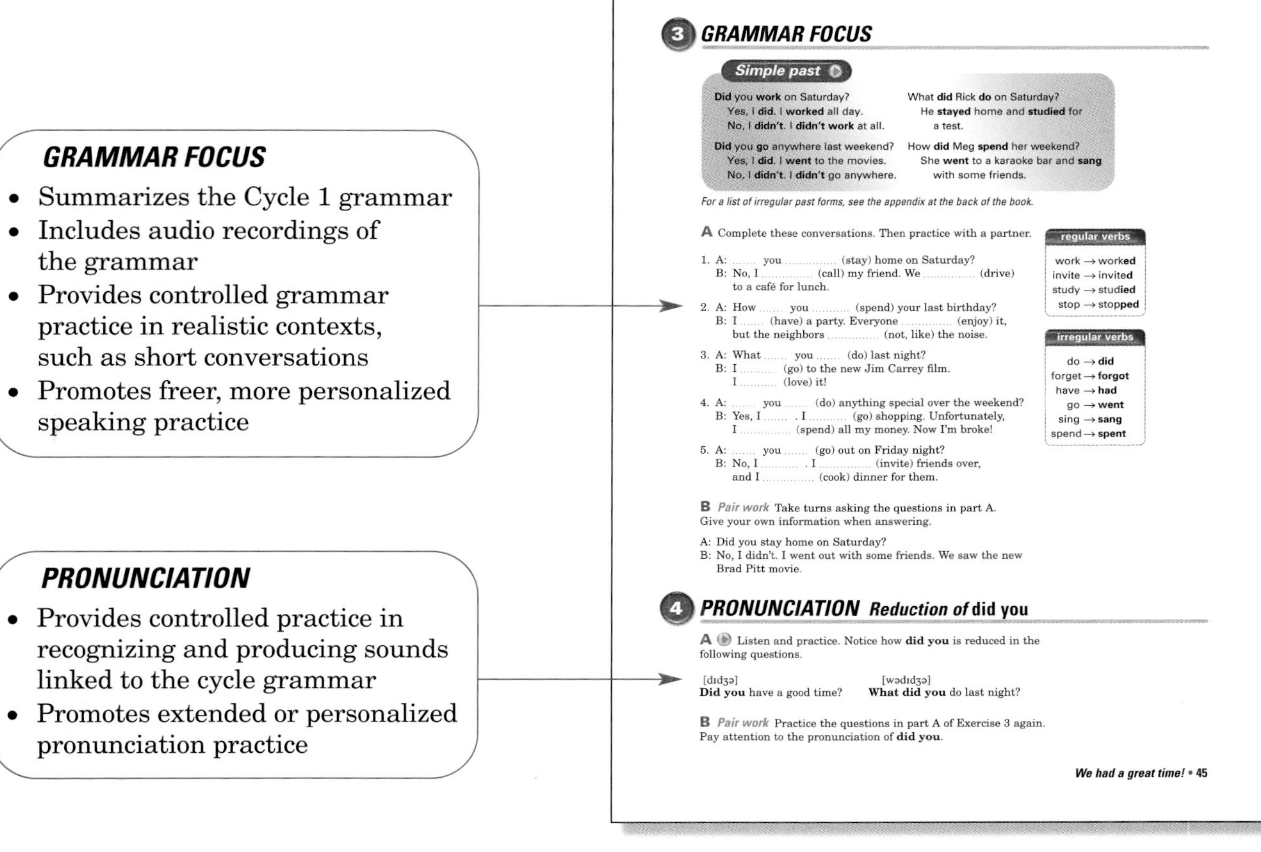

3 GRAMMAR FOCUS

Simple past

Did you **work** on Saturday? Yes, I **did**. I **worked** all day. No, I **didn't**. I **didn't work** at all.	What **did** Rick **do** on Saturday? He **stayed** home and **studied** for a test.
Did you **go** anywhere last weekend? Yes, I **did**. I **went** to the movies. No, I **didn't**. I **didn't** go anywhere.	How **did** Meg **spend** her weekend? She **went** to a karaoke bar and **sang** with some friends.

For a list of irregular past forms, see the appendix at the back of the book.

A Complete these conversations. Then practice with a partner.

1. A: ...... you .... (stay) home on Saturday?
   B: No, I .... (call) my friend. We .... (drive) to a café for lunch.
2. A: How ...... you .... (spend) your last birthday?
   B: I ...... (have) a party. Everyone .... (enjoy) it, but the neighbors .... (not, like) the noise.
3. A: What ...... you ...... (do) last night?
   B: I .... (go) to the new Jim Carrey film. I .... (love) it!
4. A: ...... you ...... (do) anything special over the weekend?
   B: Yes, I .... I .... (go) shopping. Unfortunately, I .... (spend) all my money. Now I'm broke!
5. A: ...... you ...... (go) out on Friday night?
   B: No, I .... I .... (invite) friends over, and I .... (cook) dinner for them.

regular verbs
work → **worked**
invite → **invited**
study → **studied**
stop → **stopped**

irregular verbs
do → **did**
forget → **forgot**
have → **had**
go → **went**
sing → **sang**
spend → **spent**

B *Pair work* Take turns asking the questions in part A. Give your own information when answering.

A: Did you stay home on Saturday?
B: No, I didn't. I went out with some friends. We saw the new Brad Pitt movie.

4 PRONUNCIATION Reduction of did you

A Listen and practice. Notice how **did you** is reduced in the following questions.

[dɪdʒə]
Did you have a good time?

[wədɪdʒə]
What did you do last night?

B *Pair work* Practice the questions in part A of Exercise 3 again. Pay attention to the pronunciation of **did you**.

We had a great time! • 45

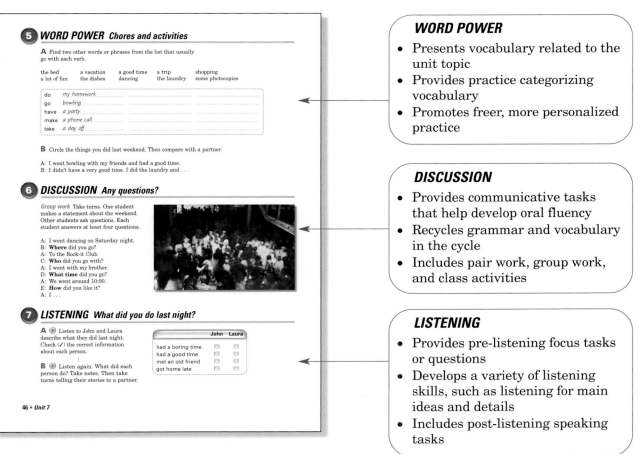

5 WORD POWER Chores and activities

A Find two other words or phrases from the list that usually go with each verb.

the bed
a lot of fun
a vacation
the dishes
a good time
dancing
a trip
the laundry
shopping
some photocopies

do	*my homework*		
go	*bowling*		
have	*a party*		
make	*a phone call*		
take	*a day off*		

B Circle the things you did last weekend. Then compare with a partner.

A: I went bowling with my friends and had a good time.
B: I didn't have a very good time. I did the laundry and . . .

6 DISCUSSION Any questions?

Group work Take turns. One student makes a statement about the weekend. Other students ask questions. Each student answers at least four questions.

A: I went dancing on Saturday night.
B: **Where** did you go?
A: To the Rock-it Club.
C: **Who** did you go with?
A: I went with my brother.
D: **What time** did you go?
A: We went around 10:00.
E: **How** did you like it?
A: I . . .

7 LISTENING What did you do last night?

A Listen to John and Laura describe what they did last night. Check (✓) the correct information about each person.

	John	Laura
had a boring time	☐	☐
had a good time	☐	☐
met an old friend	☐	☐
got home late	☐	☐

B Listen again. What did each person do? Take notes. Then take turns telling their stories to a partner.

46 • *Unit 7*

WORD POWER

- Presents vocabulary related to the unit topic
- Provides practice categorizing vocabulary
- Promotes freer, more personalized practice

DISCUSSION

- Provides communicative tasks that help develop oral fluency
- Recycles grammar and vocabulary in the cycle
- Includes pair work, group work, and class activities

LISTENING

- Provides pre-listening focus tasks or questions
- Develops a variety of listening skills, such as listening for main ideas and details
- Includes post-listening speaking tasks

CYCLE 2 (Exercises 8–14)

Topic: *vacations*
Grammar: *past of* be
Function: *talk about vacations*

CONVERSATION

- Provides structured listening and speaking practice
- Introduces the meaning and use of the Cycle 2 grammar in context
- Uses pictures to set the scene and illustrate new vocabulary
- Introduces useful expressions and discourse features

GRAMMAR FOCUS

- Summarizes the Cycle 2 grammar
- Presents examples from the previous conversation
- Provides controlled grammar practice in realistic contexts

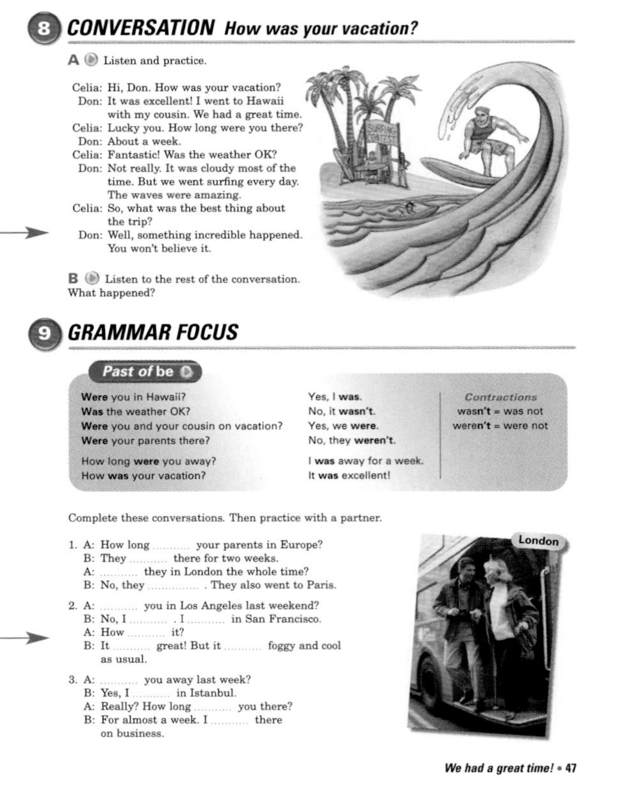

8 CONVERSATION How was your vacation?

A Listen and practice.

Celia: Hi, Don. How was your vacation?
Don: It was excellent! I went to Hawaii with my cousin. We had a great time.
Celia: Lucky you. How long were you there?
Don: About a week.
Celia: Fantastic! Was the weather OK?
Don: Not really. It was cloudy most of the time. But we went surfing every day. The waves were amazing.
Celia: So, what was the best thing about the trip?
Don: Well, something incredible happened. You won't believe it.

B Listen to the rest of the conversation. What happened?

9 GRAMMAR FOCUS

Past of be

		Contractions
Were you in Hawaii?	Yes, I **was**.	**wasn't** = was not
Was the weather OK?	No, it **wasn't**.	**weren't** = were not
Were you and your cousin on vacation?	Yes, we **were**.	
Were your parents there?	No, they **weren't**.	
How long **were** you away?	I **was** away for a week.	
How **was** your vacation?	It **was** excellent!	

Complete these conversations. Then practice with a partner.

1. A: How long .... your parents in Europe?
   B: They .... there for two weeks.
   A: .... they in London the whole time?
   B: No, they .... They also went to Paris.
2. A: .... you in Los Angeles last weekend?
   B: No, I .... I .... in San Francisco.
   A: How .... it?
   B: It .... great! But it .... foggy and cool as usual.
3. A: .... you away last week?
   B: Yes, I .... in Istanbul.
   A: Really? How long .... you there?
   B: For almost a week. I .... there on business.

London

We had a great time! • 47

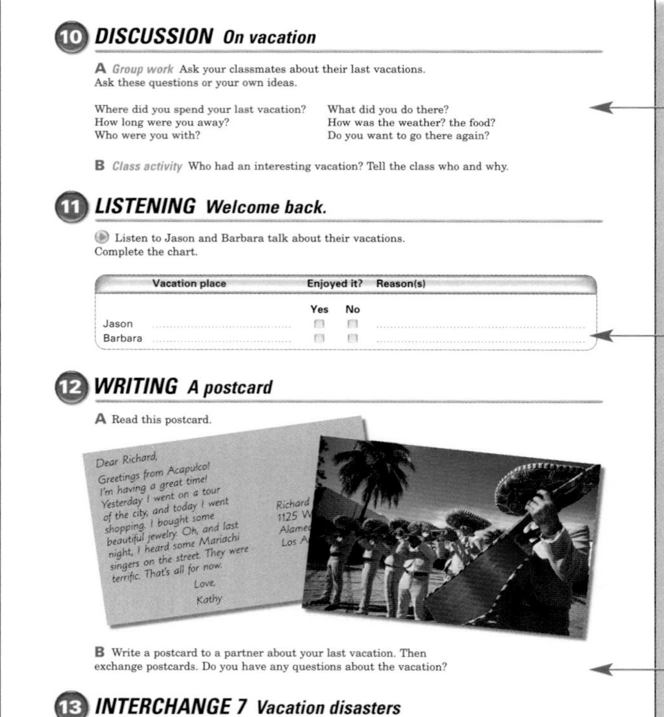

10 DISCUSSION On vacation

A *Group work* Ask your classmates about their last vacations. Ask these questions or your own ideas.

Where did you spend your last vacation?
How long were you away?
Who were you with?
What did you do there?
How was the weather? the food?
Do you want to go there again?

B *Class activity* Who had an interesting vacation? Tell the class who and why.

11 LISTENING Welcome back.

Listen to Jason and Barbara talk about their vacations. Complete the chart.

	Vacation place	Enjoyed it? Yes	No	Reason(s)
Jason		☐	☐	
Barbara		☐	☐	

12 WRITING A postcard

A Read this postcard.

Dear Richard,
Greetings from Acapulco! I'm having a great time! Yesterday I went on a tour of the city, and today I went shopping. I bought some beautiful jewelry. Oh, and last night, I heard some Mariachi singers on the street. They were terrific. That's all for now.
Love,
Kathy

B Write a postcard to a partner about your last vacation. Then exchange postcards. Do you have any questions about the vacation?

13 INTERCHANGE 7 Vacation disasters

Imagine you took a vacation but everything went wrong. Go to Interchange 7.

48 • *Unit 7*

DISCUSSION

- Provides communicative tasks that help develop oral fluency
- Recycles grammar and vocabulary in the cycle
- Includes pair work, group work, and class activities

LISTENING

- Provides pre-listening focus tasks or questions
- Develops a variety of listening skills, such as listening for main ideas and details

WRITING

- Provides a model writing sample
- Develops skills in writing different texts, such as postcards and e-mail messages
- Reinforces the vocabulary and grammar in the cycle or unit

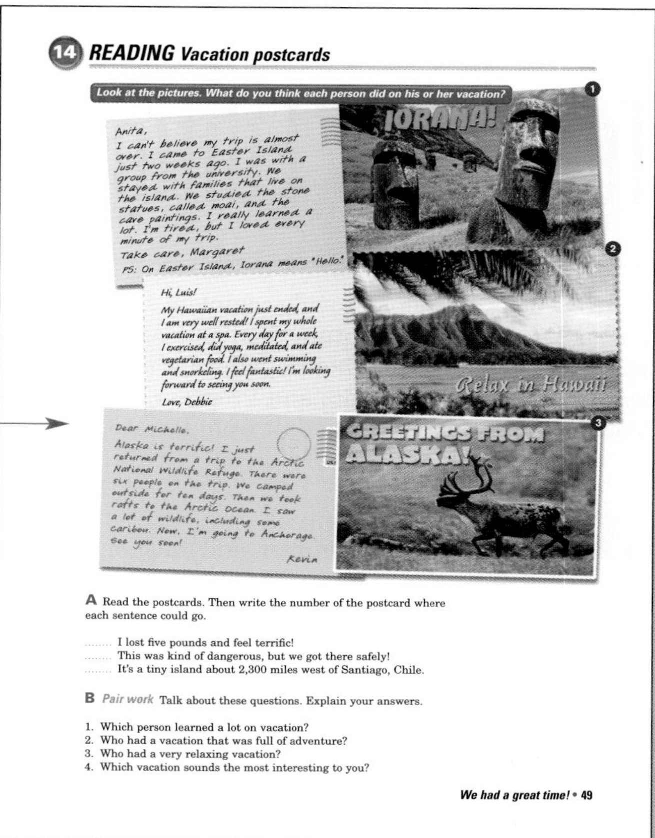

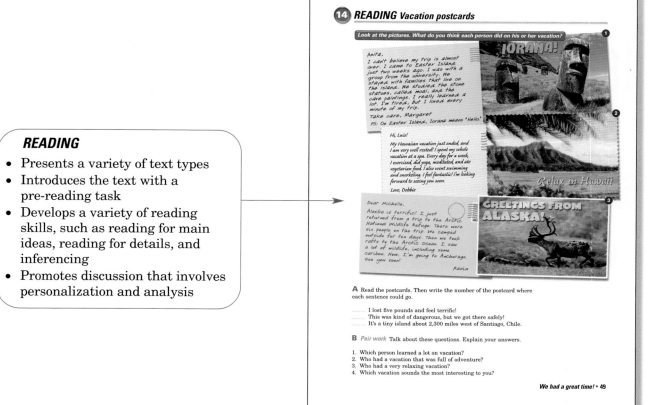

14 READING Vacation postcards

Look at the pictures. What do you think each person did on his or her vacation?

1

Anita,
I can't believe my trip is almost over. I came to Easter Island just two weeks ago. I was with a group from the university. We stayed with families that live on the island. We studied the stone statues, called moai, and the cave paintings. I really learned a lot. I'm tired, but I loved every minute of my trip.
Take care, Margaret
PS: On Easter Island, Iorana means "Hello."

2

Hi, Luis!
My Hawaiian vacation just ended, and I am very well rested! I spent my whole vacation at a spa. Every day for a week, I exercised, did yoga, meditated, and ate vegetarian food. I also went swimming and snorkeling. I feel fantastic! I'm looking forward to seeing you soon.
Love, Debbie

3

Dear Michelle,
Alaska is terrific! I just returned from a trip to the Arctic National Wildlife Refuge. There were six people on the trip. We camped outside for ten days. Then we took rafts to the Arctic Ocean. I saw a lot of wildlife, including some caribou. Now, I'm going to Anchorage. See you soon!
Kevin

A Read the postcards. Then write the number of the postcard where each sentence could go.

.... I lost five pounds and feel terrific!
.... This was kind of dangerous, but we got there safely!
.... It's a tiny island about 2,300 miles west of Santiago, Chile.

B *Pair work* Talk about these questions. Explain your answers.

1. Which person learned a lot on vacation?
2. Who had a vacation that was full of adventure?
3. Who had a very relaxing vacation?
4. Which vacation sounds the most interesting to you?

We had a great time! • 49

READING

- Presents a variety of text types
- Introduces the text with a pre-reading task
- Develops a variety of reading skills, such as reading for main ideas, reading for details, and inferencing
- Promotes discussion that involves personalization and analysis

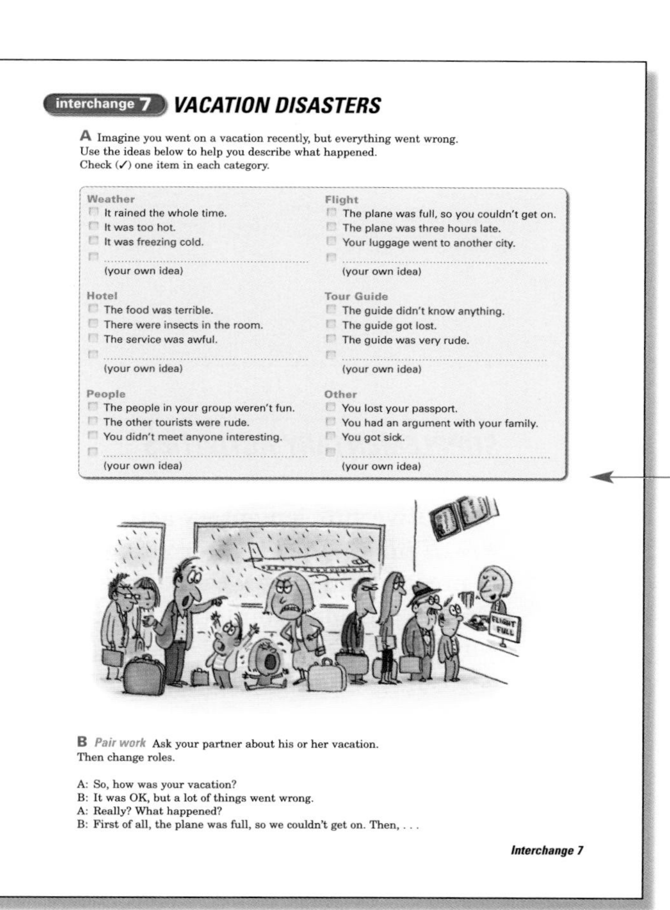

interchange 7 VACATION DISASTERS

A Imagine you went on a vacation recently, but everything went wrong. Use the ideas below to help you describe what happened. Check (✓) one item in each category.

Weather
- It rained the whole time.
- It was too hot.
- It was freezing cold.
- .... (your own idea)

Flight
- The plane was full, so you couldn't get on.
- The plane was three hours late.
- Your luggage went to another city.
- .... (your own idea)

Hotel
- The food was terrible.
- There were insects in the room.
- The service was awful.
- .... (your own idea)

Tour Guide
- The guide didn't know anything.
- The guide got lost.
- The guide was very rude.
- .... (your own idea)

People
- The people in your group weren't fun.
- The other tourists were rude.
- You didn't meet anyone interesting.
- .... (your own idea)

Other
- You lost your passport.
- You had an argument with your family.
- You got sick.
- .... (your own idea)

B *Pair work* Ask your partner about his or her vacation. Then change roles.

A: So, how was your vacation?
B: It was OK, but a lot of things went wrong.
A: Really? What happened?
B: First of all, the plane was full, so we couldn't get on. Then, . . .

Interchange 7

INTERCHANGE ACTIVITY

- Expands on the unit topic, vocabulary, and grammar
- Provides opportunities to consolidate new language in a creative or fun way
- Promotes fluency with communicative activities, such as discussions, information gaps, and games

Teacher's Edition overview

The Teacher's Editions provide complete support for teachers who are using ***Interchange Third Edition***. They contain Oral and Written quizzes, Language summaries, and Workbook answer keys as well as Photocopiables, Fresh ideas, and Games. They also include detailed teaching notes for the units and Progress checks in the Student's Book. Here are selected teaching notes for a sample unit from Level 1.

UNIT PREVIEW

- Previews the topics, grammar, and functions in each unit

TEACHING NOTES

- Includes the ***Learning objectives*** for each exercise
- Provides step-by-step lesson plans
- Suggests ***Options*** for alternative presentations or expansions
- Includes ***Audio scripts***, ***Answers***, and ***Vocabulary*** definitions
- Provides ***TIPs*** that promote teacher training and development

---

We had a great time!

In Unit 7, students discuss daily, leisure, and vacation activities. In Cycle 1, they talk about daily and leisure activities using the simple past with both regular and irregular verbs. In Cycle 2, they talk about vacations using the past tense of be.

Cycle 1, Exercises 1–7

1 SNAPSHOT

Learning objective: learn vocabulary for discussing leisure activities

- Books closed. Ask: "What do you do in your free time?" Help with vocabulary as needed. Write Ss' responses on the board.
- ***Option:*** Ask Ss to guess the top eight leisure activities in the U.S. Later, Ss compare their ideas with the Snapshot.
- Books open. Ask different Ss to read the leisure activities aloud. Point out that these are the top eight leisure activities in the U.S. Elicit or explain any new vocabulary.
- Ask: "Does anything on this list surprise you? What?" Elicit Ss' answers.
- Read and explain the three tasks. Point out that, for the last task, Ss should list the activities starting with their favorite.
- Ss complete the tasks individually. Go around the class and give help as needed.
- Elicit Ss' responses.
- ***Option:*** Use Ss' responses to make a list of the top eight activities for the class.

For a new way to practice the Snapshot vocabulary, try ***Vocabulary Steps*** on page T-154.

2 CONVERSATION

Learning objectives: practice a conversation about weekend activities; see the simple past in context

A *[CD 2, Track 10]*

- Set the scene. Rick and Meg are talking about their weekends. Ask Ss to use the pictures to predict what each person did. Elicit or explain vocabulary in the pictures (e.g., *karaoke*).
- ***Option:*** Ss list all the words they can see in the pictures. Find out who has the most words.
- Books closed. Write these focus questions on the board:
  1. What did Meg do on Saturday?
  2. What did Rick do?
- Play the audio program. Ss listen for the answers. Then elicit the answers. (Answers: 1. She went to a karaoke bar and sang with some friends. 2. He stayed home all weekend and studied for the Spanish test.)
- Books open. Play the audio program again. Ss listen and read silently.
- Ss practice the conversation in pairs. Go around the class and give help as needed.

For a new way to practice this Conversation, try the ***Disappearing Dialog*** on page T-151.

B

- Read the focus question aloud. Ask Ss to guess. Write some of their ideas on the board.
- Play the audio program. Ss work individually. Then go over the answer with the class.

Audio script

RICK: So, Meg, what did you do on Sunday?
MEG: I stayed home in the morning. I just watched TV and read.
RICK: How about in the afternoon?
MEG: Oh, I worked. I have a part-time job at the university bookstore.
RICK: I didn't know you had a job.
MEG: Yeah, I'm a cashier there.

Answer

She stayed home in the morning. She watched TV and read. She went to work in the afternoon.

For more practice talking about last weekend's activities, play the ***Chain Game*** on page T-145.

TIP To help Ss who are weak at listening, write the answers on the board. That way, they can *see* the answers.

T-44

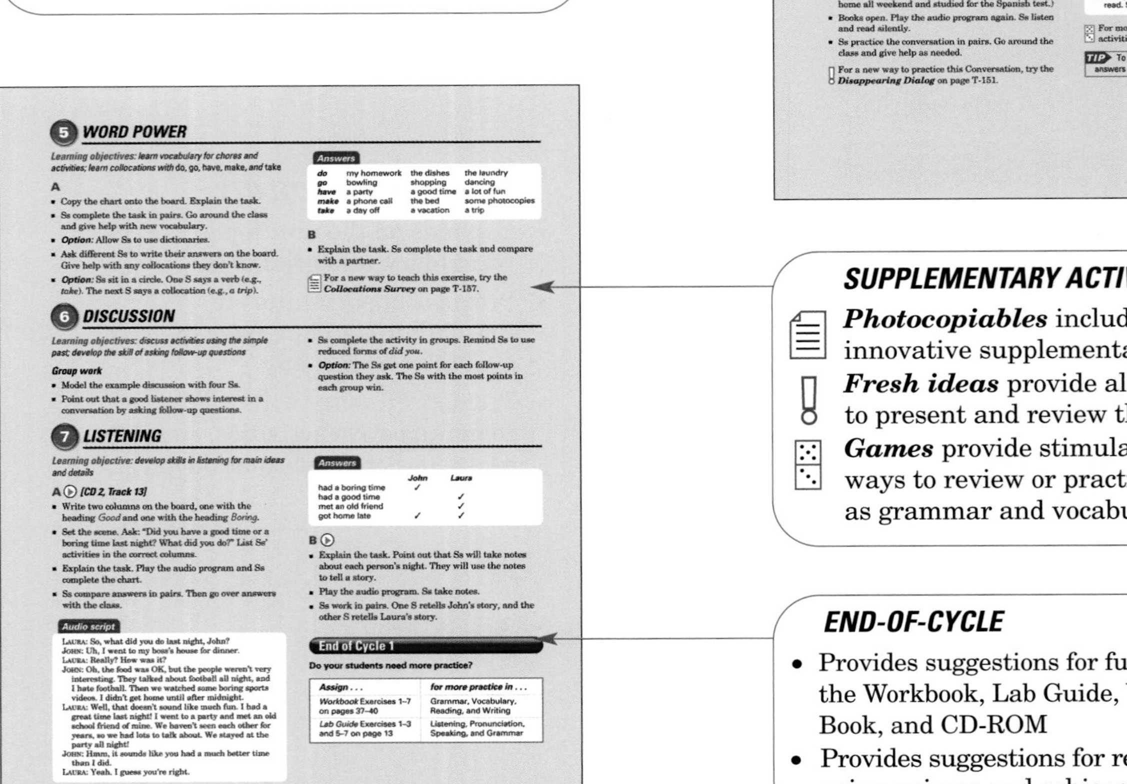

5 WORD POWER

Learning objectives: learn vocabulary for chores and activities; learn collocations with do, go, have, make, *and* take

A

- Copy the chart onto the board. Explain the task.
- Ss complete the task in pairs. Go around the class and give help with new vocabulary.
- ***Option:*** Allow Ss to use dictionaries.
- Ask different Ss to write their answers on the board. Give help with any collocations they don't know.
- ***Option:*** Ss sit in a circle. One S says a verb (e.g., *take*). The next S says a collocation (e.g., *a trip*).

Answers

do	my homework	the dishes	the laundry
go	bowling	shopping	dancing
have	a party	a good time	a lot of fun
make	a phone call	the bed	some photocopies
take	a day off	a vacation	a trip

B

- Explain the task. Ss complete the task and compare with a partner.

For a new way to teach this exercise, try the ***Collocations Survey*** on page T-157.

6 DISCUSSION

Learning objectives: discuss activities using the simple past; develop the skill of asking follow-up questions

Group work

- Model the example discussion with four Ss.
- Point out that a good listener shows interest in a conversation by asking follow-up questions.
- Ss complete the activity in groups. Remind Ss to use reduced forms of *did you*.
- ***Option:*** The Ss get one point for each follow-up question they ask. The Ss with the most points in each group win.

7 LISTENING

Learning objective: develop skills in listening for main ideas and details

A *[CD 2, Track 13]*

- Write two columns on the board, one with the heading *Good* and one with the heading *Boring*.
- Set the scene. Ask: "Did you have a good time or a boring time last night? What did you do?" List Ss' activities in the correct columns.
- Explain the task. Play the audio program and Ss complete the chart.
- Ss compare answers in pairs. Then go over answers with the class.

Audio script

LAURA: So, what did you do last night, John?
JOHN: Uh, I went to my boss's house for dinner.
LAURA: Really? How was it?
JOHN: Oh, the food was OK, but the people weren't very interesting. They talked about football all night, and I hate football. Then we watched some boring sports videos. I didn't get home until after midnight.
LAURA: Well, that doesn't sound like much fun. I had a great time last night! I went to a party and met an old school friend of mine. We haven't seen each other for years, so we had lots to talk about. We stayed at the party all night!
JOHN: Hmm, it sounds like you had a much better time than I did.
LAURA: Yeah. I guess you're right.

Answers

	John	*Laura*
had a boring time	✓	
had a good time		✓
met an old friend		✓
got home late	✓	✓

B

- Explain the task. Point out that Ss will take notes about each person's night. They will use the notes to tell a story.
- Play the audio program. Ss take notes.
- Ss work in pairs. One S retells John's story, and the other S retells Laura's story.

End of Cycle 1

Do your students need more practice?

Assign . . .	***for more practice in . . .***
Workbook Exercises 1–7 on pages 37–40	Grammar, Vocabulary, Reading, and Writing
Lab Guide Exercises 1–3 and 5–7 on page 13	Listening, Pronunciation, Speaking, and Grammar

***We had a great time!* • T-46**

SUPPLEMENTARY ACTIVITIES

Photocopiables include handouts for innovative supplementary activities.

Fresh ideas provide alternative ways to present and review the exercises.

Games provide stimulating and fun ways to review or practice skills such as grammar and vocabulary.

END-OF-CYCLE

- Provides suggestions for further practice in the Workbook, Lab Guide, Video Activity Book, and CD-ROM
- Provides suggestions for regular assessment using quizzes and achievement tests

Course components

Interchange Third Edition is the most complete English language course for adult and young adult learners of English. Here is a list of the core components.

Component	Description
Student's Book with Self-study Audio CD	The Student's Book is intended for classroom use, and contains 16 six-page units. (See the Student's Book overview for a sample unit on pages x-xiii.) Progress checks are provided after every two units, and a Self-study section is included at the back of the book.
Class Audio Program	The Class Audio Cassettes/CDs are intended for classroom use. The program consists of cassettes/CDs with all the audio sections in the Student's Book, such as Conversations, Listenings, Grammar Focuses, and Pronunciations. The program also includes the Student Self-study Audio Cassette/CD.
Teacher's Edition	The interleaved Teacher's Edition includes: • page-by-page notes, with detailed lesson plans, learning objectives, vocabulary glosses, optional activities, and teaching tips • alternative ways to teach the exercises, using Games, Fresh ideas, and Photocopiables • Language summaries of the new vocabulary and expressions in each unit • a complete assessment program, including Oral and Written quizzes • Audio scripts and answer keys for the Student's Book, Workbook, and Quizzes (See the Teacher's Edition overview for sample pages on page xiv.)
Workbook	The six-page units in the Workbook can be used in class or for homework. They follow the same sequence as the Student's Book, and provide students with more practice in grammar, vocabulary, and writing. In addition, Levels 1–3 provide more reading practice.
Placement and Evaluation Package	The package provides three versions of a placement test and four achievement tests for each level of the Student's Book, as well as for *Passages 1* and *2*. The package is composed of a photocopiable testing booklet and two audio CDs.
Video Program	Videos for each level offer dramatized and documentary sequences that reinforce and extend the language presented in the Student's Book. Video Activity Books include step-by-step comprehension and conversation activities, and the Video Teacher's Guides include detailed teaching suggestions.
CD-ROM	Available in PC format, CD-ROMs for Levels Intro, 1, and 2 provide engaging activities for students to do at home or in self-study centers. They include sequences from the Video Program, with over 100 interactive reading, listening, speaking, vocabulary, and grammar activities. They also include progress tests.

For a complete list of components, see the Web site (www.cambridge.org/interchange) or contact your local Cambridge University Press representative.

Frequently asked questions

SNAPSHOT

Q: How long should it take to present and teach the Snapshot?

A: You probably don't need to spend more than 15 minutes. Remember that it's just a warm-up activity.

Q: Should I expect students to learn all the new words in the Snapshot?

A: It's not necessary for students to learn the passive vocabulary in the Snapshots. However, it's a good idea to encourage them to use the productive vocabulary. The productive vocabulary is recycled throughout the unit and listed in the Language summaries at the back of the Teacher's Edition.

CONVERSATION

Q: Is it OK to present the Grammar Focus before the Conversation?

A: Remember that the Conversation is placed first because it introduces the new grammar in context. Also, it illustrates the meaning of the new grammar before the grammar rules are presented. However, you can change the order for variety or if it's more appropriate for your students' learning style.

Q: How helpful is it for students to memorize the Conversation?

A: Students generally benefit more from practicing and expanding on the Conversation than from memorizing it.

PERSPECTIVES

Q: What are Perspectives?

A: Like Conversations, Perspectives introduce the new grammar in context. However, they present the grammar in different ways, such as quotes, surveys, and television or radio shows.

Q: Why aren't there any Perspectives in Levels Intro and 1?

A: The Perspectives typically contain ideas and opinions that serve as starting points for more advanced discussions and debates. Therefore, they are more appropriate for higher levels.

GRAMMAR FOCUS

Q: Should I teach my students more grammar than that in the Grammar Focus box?

A: To avoid overloading students, it's preferable to teach only the grammar in the Grammar Focus box. Then progress to the speaking activities, so that they can apply the rules in communication.

Q: What should I do if my students need more controlled grammar practice?

A: You can assign practice exercises in the Workbook, Lab Guide, Video Activity Book, or CD-ROM for homework. The teaching notes in the Teacher's Edition suggest appropriate assignments for each cycle.

Q: Should I explain the rules to my students or encourage them to guess the rules?

A: Students have different learning styles, so you may want to use different techniques. First, try to involve them in guessing the rules. If they can't guess the rules, then you can explain them.

WORD POWER

Q: How can I help students remember recently taught vocabulary?

A: One way is to spend five minutes of each class reviewing new words. You can also try different vocabulary review techniques from the Fresh ideas and Games in the Teacher's Edition.

LISTENING

Q: What should I do if my students have difficulty understanding the audio program?

A: You can ask students to make predictions before you play the audio program. Then play the audio program a few times, asking students to listen for something different each time. Alternatively, divide the audio program into short sections (e.g., short conversations), stopping the audio program after each section.

Q: My students get very nervous during listening practice. What's the solution?

A: One way is to assure students that they don't need to understand every word. Tell them that they will hear the audio program again. Another option is to have students work collaboratively in pairs or small groups.

SPEAKING ACTIVITIES

Q: My students often have problems understanding my instructions. What am I doing wrong?

A: It is often more helpful to model the activity than to give instructions, especially at lower levels. Model the activity with several students, preferably of different abilities and in different parts of the room.

Q: My students make a lot of errors during pair work and group work. What can I do?

A: Remember that errors are an important part of learning. During fluency-building activities, allow students to practice speaking without interruption and make a list of any errors you hear. Then have the class correct the most common errors at the end of the activity.

READING

Q: How can I teach the Reading sections most effectively?

A: Encourage students to read silently and quickly. When they are skimming or scanning, discourage them from reading aloud, following each sentence with a pencil, or looking up each new word in a dictionary. Also, encourage them to use the discussion questions to share ideas.

PROGRESS CHECKS

Q: The Progress checks are helpful, but I don't have enough time to use them. What can I do?

A: You can use the Progress checks in a variety of ways. For example, you can assign some of the exercises for homework. Alternatively, you can assign students to complete only the Self-assessment section for homework, and then choose exercises related to areas they need to improve.

FLEXIBILITY

Q: The Student's Book doesn't have enough material for my classes. What can I do?

A: Supplement the Student's Book exercises with Photocopiables, Games, and Fresh ideas from the Teacher's Edition or activities from the Web site.

Q: I don't have enough time to complete every exercise. How can I finish them more quickly?

A: Remember that you don't have to complete every exercise in the Student's Book. You can omit selected exercises, such as the Writings, Readings, and Interchange activities.

Authors' acknowledgments

A great number of people contributed to the development of *Interchange Third Edition*. Particular thanks are owed to the following:

The **reviewers** using *New Interchange* in the following schools and institutes – their insights and suggestions have helped define the content and format of the third edition: Gino Pumadera, **American School**, Guayaquil, Ecuador; Don Ahn, **APEX**, Seoul, Korea; teachers at **AUA Language Center**, Bangkok, Thailand; Linda Martinez, **Canada College**, Redwood City, California, USA; Rosa Maria Valencia Rodriguez, **CEMARC**, Mexico City, Mexico; Wendel Mendes Dantas, **Central Universitária**, São Paulo, Brazil; Lee Altschuler, **Cheng Kung University**, Tainan, Taiwan; Chun Mao Le, **Cheng Siu Institute of Technology**, Kaohsiung, Taiwan; Selma Alfonso, **Colégio Arquidiocesano**, São Paulo, Brazil; Daniel de Mello Ferraz, **Colégio Camargo Aranha**, São Paulo, Brazil; Paula dos Santos Dames, **Colegio Militar do Rio de Janeiro**, Rio de Janeiro, Brazil; Elizabeth Ortiz, **COPOL-COPEI**, Guayaquil, Ecuador; Alexandre de Oliveira, **First Idiomas**, São Paulo, Brazil; João Franco Júnior, **2B Idiomas**, São Paulo, Brazil; Jo Ellen Kaiser and David Martin, **Fort Lauderdale High School**, Fort Lauderdale, Florida, USA; Azusa Okada, **Hiroshima Shudo University**, Hiroshima, Japan; Sandra Herrera and Rosario Valdiria, **INACAP**, Santiago, Chile; Samara Camilo Tome Costa, **Instituto Brasil-Estados Unidos**, Rio de Janeiro, Brazil; Eric Hamilton, **Instituto Chileno Norteamericano de Cultura**, Santiago, Chile; **ICNA**, Santiago, Chile; Pedro Benites, Carolina Chenett, Elena Montero Hurtado, Patricia Nieto, and Antonio Rios, **Instituto Cultural Peruano Norteamericano (ICPNA)**, Lima, Peru; Vanclei Nascimento, **Instituto Pentágono**, São Paulo, Brazil; Michael T. Thornton, **Interactive College of Technology**, Chamblee, Georgia, USA; Norma Aguilera Celis, **IPN ESCA Santo Tomas**, Mexico City, Mexico; Lewis Barksdale, **Kanazawa Institute of Technology**, Ishikawa, Japan; Clare St. Lawrence, Gill Christie, and Sandra Forrester, **Key Language Services**, Quito, Ecuador; Érik Mesquita, **King's Cross**, São Paulo, Brazil; Robert S. Dobie, **Kojen English Language Schools**, Taipei, Taiwan; Shoko Miyagi, **Madison Area Technical College**, Madison, Wisconsin, USA; Atsuko K. Yamazaki, **Institute of Technologists**, Saitama, Japan; teachers and students at **Institute of Technologists**, Saitama, Japan; Gregory Hadley, **Niigata University of International and Information Studies**, Niigata, Japan; Tony Brewer and Frank Claypool, **Osaka College of Foreign Languages and International Business**, Osaka, Japan; Chris Kerr, **Osaka University of Economics and Law**, Osaka, Japan; Angela Suzete Zumpano, **Personal Language Center**, São Paulo, Brazil; Simon Banha Jr. and Tomas S. Martins, **Phil Young's English School**, Curitiba, Brazil; Mehran Sabet and Bob Diem, **Seigakuin University**, Saitama, Japan; Lily Beam, **Shie Jen University**, Kaohsiung, Taiwan; Ray Sullivan, **Shibuya Kyoiku Gakuen Makuhari Senior and Junior High School**, Chiba, Japan; Robert Gee, **Sugiyama Jogakuen University**, Nagoya, Japan; Arthur Tu, **Taipei YMCA**, Taipei, Taiwan; Hiroko Nishikage, Alan Hawk, Peter Riley, and Peter Anyon, **Taisho University**, Tokyo, Japan; Vera Berk, **Talkative Idiomas**, São Paulo, Brazil; Patrick D. McCoy, **Toyo University**, Saitama, Japan; Kathleen Krokar and Ellen D. Sellergren, **Truman College**, Chicago, Illinois, USA; Gabriela Cortes Sanchez, **UAM-A**, Mexico City, Mexico; Marco A. Mora Piedra, **Universidad de Costa Rica**, San Jose, Costa Rica; Janette Carvalhinho de Oliveira, **Universidade Federal do Espirito Santo**, Vitoria, Brazil; Belem Saint Martin Lozada, **Universidad ISEC**, Colegio del Valle, Mexico City, Mexico; Robert Sanchez Flores, **Universidad Nacional Autonoma de Mexico**, Centro de Lenguas Campus Aragon, Mexico City, Mexico; Bertha Chela de Rodriguez, **Universidad Simòn Bolìvar**, Caracas, Venezuela; Marilyn Johnson, **Washoe High School**, Reno, Nevada, USA; Monika Soens, **Yen Ping Senior High School**, Taipei, Taiwan; Kim Yoon Gyong, **Yonsei University**, Seoul, Korea; and Tania Borges Lobao, **York Language Institute**, Rio de Janeiro, Brazil.

The **editorial** and **production** team:
David Bohlke, Jeff Chen, Yuri Hara, Pam Harris, Paul Heacock, Louisa Hellegers, Lise R. Minovitz, Pat Nelson, Bill Paulk, Danielle Power, Mary Sandre, Tami Savir, Kayo Taguchi, Louisa van Houten, Mary Vaughn, Jennifer Wilkin, and Dorothy Zemach.

And Cambridge University Press **staff** and **advisors**:
Jim Anderson, Angela Andrade, Mary Louise Baez, Carlos Barbisan, Kathleen Corley, Kate Cory-Wright, Elizabeth Fuzikava, Steve Golden, Cecilia Gomez, Heather Gray, Bob Hands, Pauline Ireland, Ken Kingery, Gareth Knight, Nigel McQuitty, João Madureira, Andy Martin, Alejandro Martinez, Carine Mitchell, Mark O'Neil, Tom Price, Dan Schulte, Catherine Shih, Howard Siegelman, Ivan Sorrentino, Alcione Tavares, Koen Van Landeghem, and Ellen Zlotnick.

CLASSROOM LANGUAGE Student questions

1 Please call me Beth.

1 CONVERSATION Where are you from?

Listen and practice.

David: Hello, I'm David Garza. I'm a new club member.
Beth: Hi. My name is Elizabeth Silva, but please call me Beth.
David: OK. Where are you from, Beth?
Beth: Brazil. How about you?
David: I'm from Mexico.
Beth: Oh, I love Mexico! It's really beautiful.
David: Thanks. So is Brazil!

Beth: Oh, good. Sun Hee is here.
David: Who's Sun Hee?
Beth: She's my classmate. We're in the same math class.
David: Where's she from?
Beth: Korea. Let's go and say hello. Sorry, what's your last name again? Garcia?
David: Actually, it's Garza.
Beth: How do you spell that?
David: G-A-R-Z-A.

2 SPEAKING Checking information

A Match the questions with the responses. Listen and check. Then practice with a partner. Give your own information.

1. I'm sorry. What's your name again? ....
2. What do people call you? ....
3. How do you spell your last name? ....

a. S-I-L-V-A.
b. It's Elizabeth Silva.
c. Everyone calls me Beth.

B *Group work* Introduce yourself with your full name. Use the expressions above. Make a list of names for your group.

A: Hi! I'm Yuriko Noguchi.
B: I'm sorry. What's your last name again? . . .

Please call me Beth.

In Unit 1, students discuss personal information. In Cycle 1, they introduce themselves and others using be *and possessive adjectives. In Cycle 2, they talk about themselves using yes/no questions and short answers with* be.

Cycle 1, Exercises 1–5

CONVERSATION

Learning objectives: *practice a conversation between two people who just met; see statements with* be *and possessive adjectives in context*

> **TIP** To learn your Ss' names, have them make name cards. Each S folds a piece of paper in thirds and writes his or her name on one side. Then they place the name cards on their desks. *David*

[CD 1, Track 1]

- Focus Ss' attention on the picture. Ask: "Where are the people? Who are they? How old are they?" Encourage Ss to make guesses.
- Set the scene. David is a new member of a club for international students. He's meeting Beth for the first time.
- Books closed. Write these questions on the board:
  1. Where is Beth from?
  2. Where is David from?
- Play the first part of the audio program. Elicit Ss' answers. (Answers: 1. Brazil 2. Mexico)
- Write this on the board for the next task:
  First name   *Last name*
  Beth
  David
- Play the first part of the audio program again. Ss listen to find out Beth's and David's last names. Then elicit the answers and write them on the board. (Answers: Silva, Garza)
- Books open. Play the first part of the audio program again. Ss listen and read silently.
- Ss stand up and practice the conversation in pairs. Go around the class and give help as needed.
- ***Option:*** Ss use their own information to practice the first part of the conversation. Before they start, ask Ss to underline the names and countries so they know what information to substitute.
- Ask: "Where is Sun Hee from?" Play the rest of the audio program and elicit the answer. (Answer: Korea)
- Ss practice the conversation in pairs.

For another way to practice this Conversation, try ***Musical Introductions*** on page T-156.

SPEAKING

Learning objectives: *introduce oneself; check information about other people*

A ***[CD 1, Track 2]***

- Explain that sometimes people misunderstand information, so it's important to ask polite questions to check information.
- Have Ss match the questions and responses individually or in pairs. Then play the audio program. Ss listen and check their answers.

Answers

1. b   2. c   3. a

- Play the audio program again. Focus Ss' attention on the intonation of the questions.
- Tell Ss to ask you the questions. Respond with information about yourself. Then Ss use their own information to ask and answer the questions in pairs.
- ***Option:*** Review the letters of the alphabet.

B ***Group work***

- Model the task with a few Ss. Ask them their names. Then check the information before writing it on the board.
- Ss complete the task in small groups.

3 CONVERSATION

Learning objectives: *practice a conversation between three people who just met; see statements with* be *in context*

A [CD 1, Track 3]

- Books closed. Set the scene. Beth is introducing Sun Hee to David. Ask: "What is Sun Hee's last name?" Play the audio program and elicit the answer. (Answer: Park)
- Books open. Focus Ss' attention on the Conversation title. Elicit or explain the meaning of *What's . . . like?* Ask the class: "Where is David from? What's it like?" Ss check answers in the Conversation on page 2. (Answers: Mexico, beautiful)
- Play the audio program again. Ss listen and read the conversation silently. Then they practice it.

For a new way to practice this Conversation, try ***Look Up and Speak!*** on page T-150.

B

- Elicit names of cities in Mexico (e.g., *Mexico City, Acapulco*). Then read the two focus questions.
- Play the audio program. Ss listen to find the answers to the questions. Elicit the answers.

Audio script

SUN HEE: So David, where are you from?
DAVID: I'm from Mexico.
SUN HEE: Really? What city?
DAVID: Mexico City.
SUN HEE: Wow! What's it like there?
DAVID: Oh, it's a very interesting city.
SUN HEE: Is it big?
DAVID: Oh yes. It's big. But I like it a lot.

Answers

David is from Mexico City. It's very interesting and big.

4 PRONUNCIATION

Learning objective: *learn to sound natural by linking words*

[CD 1, Track 4]

- Explain that some English words sound unnatural when pronounced separately. Therefore, native speakers usually link these words.
- Play the audio program. Point out the linked sounds. Ask Ss to practice the sentences.
- ***Option:*** Play the audio program for the Conversation on page 3 again. Then tell Ss to practice linking sounds in selected sentences (e.g., *This is David.*).

5 GRAMMAR FOCUS

Learning objectives: *practice statements with* be*, contractions of* be*, and possessive adjectives; ask and answer questions with* be

[CD 1, Track 5]

***Statements with* be *and contractions of* be**

- Introduce yourself ("I'm . . ."). Explain that it's common to use contractions (e.g., *I'm*) when speaking. Tell Ss to go around the room and introduce themselves.
- Go over the contractions in the Grammar Focus box. Close your thumb and first finger to show how the pronouns + *be* become contractions. For example, your thumb (*you*) and first finger (*are*) contract to become *you're*.

Possessive adjectives

- Explain the difference between subject pronouns and possessive adjectives by writing this on the board:
  I am David. My name is David.
  You are Beth. Your name is Beth.
- Play the audio program for the first Grammar Focus box.

For more practice with possessive adjectives, try the ***Chain Game*** on page T-145.

A

- Ss complete the sentences individually or in pairs. Go over answers with the class.

Answers

1. My name **is** David Garza. I'm from Mexico. **My** family is in Mexico City. My brother **is** a university student. **His** name is Carlos.
2. **My** name is Sun Hee Park. I'm 20 years old. My sister **is** a student here, too. **Our** parents are in Korea right now.
3. I'm Elizabeth, but everyone calls me Beth. **My** last name is Silva. **I'm** a student at City College. My parents **are** on vacation this week. **They're** in Los Angeles.

3 CONVERSATION What's Seoul like?

A Listen and practice.

Beth: Sun Hee, this is David Garza. He's a new club member from Mexico.
Sun Hee: Nice to meet you, David. I'm Sun Hee Park.
David: Hi. So, you're from Korea?
Sun Hee: That's right. I'm from Seoul.
David: That's cool. What's Seoul like?
Sun Hee: It's really nice. It's big and very exciting.

B Listen to the rest of the conversation. What city is David from? What's it like?

4 PRONUNCIATION Linked sounds

Listen and practice. Final consonant sounds are often linked to the vowels that follow them.

I'm‿a new club member. Sun Hee is‿over there. My name‿is‿Elizabeth Silva.

5 GRAMMAR FOCUS

Statements with be; possessive adjectives

Statements with be		Contractions of be	Possessive adjectives
I'**m**	from Mexico.	I'**m** = I am	my
You'**re**	from Brazil.	you'**re** = you are	your
He'**s**	from Japan.	he'**s** = he is	his
She'**s**	a new club member.	she'**s** = she is	her
It'**s**	an exciting city.	it'**s** = it is	its
We'**re**	in the same class.	we'**re** = we are	our
They'**re**	my classmates.	they'**re** = they are	their

A Complete these sentences. Then tell a partner about yourself.

1. My name ...*is*... David Garza. I'm from Mexico. .... family is in Mexico City. My brother .... a university student. .... name is Carlos.
2. .... name is Sun Hee Park. I'm 20 years old. My sister .... a student here, too. .... parents are in Korea right now.
3. I'm Elizabeth, but everyone calls me Beth. .... last name is Silva. .... a student at City College. My parents .... on vacation this week. .... in Los Angeles.

Wh-questions with be

What's your name?	My name's Beth.
Where's your friend?	He's in class.
Who's Sun Hee?	She's my classmate.
What are your classmates **like**?	They're very nice.
Where are you and Luisa from?	We're from Brazil.
How are your classes?	They're really interesting.

B Complete these questions. Then practice with a partner.

1. A: ....*Who's*.... that?
   B: Oh, that's Miss West.
2. A: .... she from?
   B: She's from Miami.
3. A: .... her first name?
   B: It's Celia.
4. A: .... the two students over there?
   B: Their names are Jeremy and Karen.
5. A: .... they from?
   B: They're from Vancouver, Canada.
6. A: .... they like?
   B: They're shy, but very friendly.

C *Group work* Write five questions about your classmates. Then ask and answer the questions.

What's your last name?
Where's Ming from?

6 SNAPSHOT

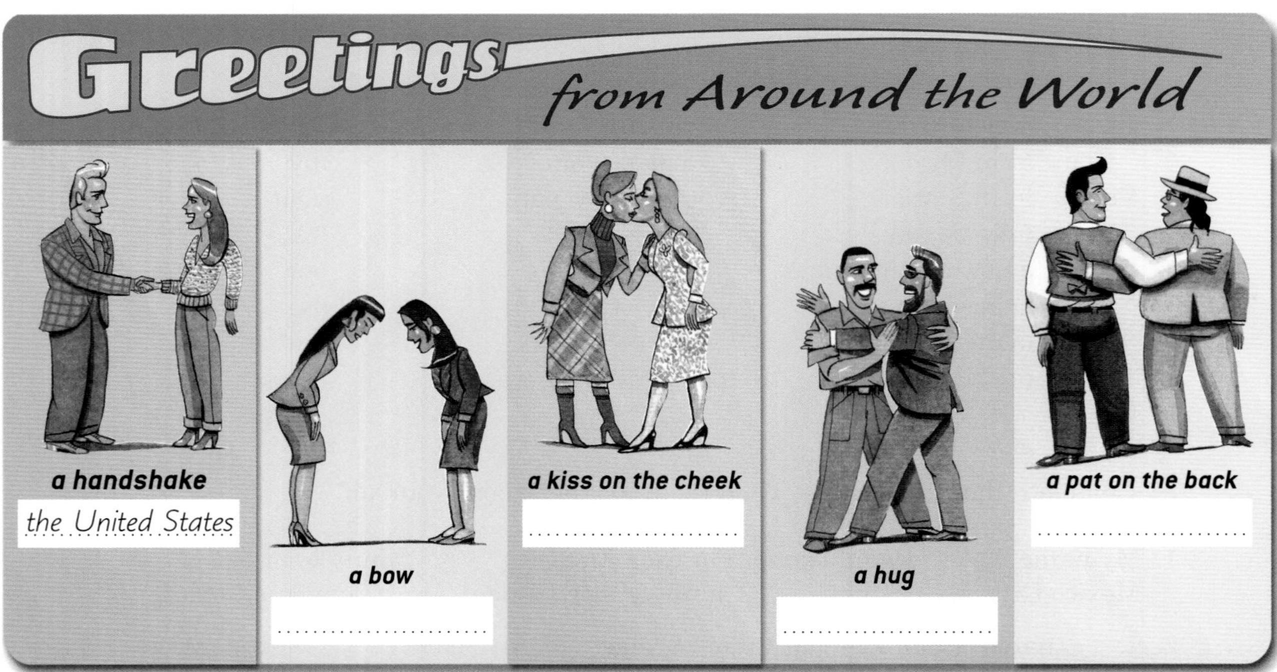

Sources: A World of Difference Institute; *www.brazilbrazil.com*

Which greetings are typical in your county?
Can you write the name of a country for each greeting?
What are other ways to greet people?

Wh-questions with be

- Write these questions and answers on the board:

Questions	*Answers*
What's your name?	*She's my classmate.*
Who's Sun Hee?	*My name's Beth.*
Where are you and Luisa from?	*They're very nice.*
What are your classmates like?	*We're from Brazil.*

- Books closed. Ask Ss to match the questions and answers on the board.
- Books open. Ss check answers with the Grammar Focus box. Answer any questions.
- Play the audio program.
- ***Option:*** Divide the class into two groups. Group A asks the questions and Group B answers. Then change roles.

B

- Ss complete the questions individually. Go over answers with the class.

Answers

1. **Who is** that?/**Who's** that?
2. **Where is** she from?/**Where's** she from?
3. **What is** her first name?/**What's** her first name?
4. **Who are** the two students over there?
5. **Where are** they from?
6. **What are** they like?

- Explain the task. Ss practice the conversations in pairs. Model the task with a strong S and then with another S.
- Ss complete the task individually or in pairs.

C *Group work*

- Explain the task. Elicit possible Wh-questions.
- ***Option:*** Ss look at the Conversations on pages 2 and 3 for examples of Wh-questions with *be*. (Answers: Where are you from? Who's Sun Hee? Where's she from? What's your last name again? What's Seoul like?)
- Ss write five Wh-questions individually. Go around the class and give help as needed.
- Ss work in small groups. They take turns asking and answering their questions.
- Go around the class and write down any errors. Then write the questions or answers with errors on the board. Ss correct the errors as a class.

End of Cycle 1

Do your students need more practice?

Assign . . .	***for more practice in . . .***
Workbook Exercises 1–7 on pages 1–4	Grammar, Vocabulary, Reading, and Writing
Lab Guide Exercises 1–7 on pages 1–2	Listening, Pronunciation, Speaking, and Grammar

Cycle 2, Exercises 6–12

6 *SNAPSHOT*

Learning objective: *learn about greetings used around the world*

- Go around the class, shake Ss' hands, and say "hello" or "hi."
- Focus Ss' attention on the pictures. Point out that a handshake is a common way to greet people in the U.S. and Canada. Read the first question: "Which greetings are typical in your country?" If Ss are from different countries, ask them to demonstrate how they greet people.
- Go over the second and third questions. Ss answer them in pairs or small groups.

Possible answers

a handshake (the United States, Canada, Peru)
a bow (Korea, Japan, Indonesia)
a kiss on the cheek (Brazil, France, Venezuela)
a hug (the United States, Denmark, Egypt)
a pat on the back (Greece, Russia, Mexico)

TIP To encourage Ss to use the Classroom Language on page v of the Student's Book, write the expressions on cards. Then put the cards on the walls.

7 CONVERSATION

Learning objectives: *practice a conversation between two people who know each other; see yes/no questions and short answers with* be *in context*

[CD 1, Track 6]

- Introduce the Conversation title. Ask: "How's it going?" Help Ss with responses (e.g., *fine*, *not bad*).
- Set the scene. A few days after the International Club party, Sun Hee sees David and starts a conversation.
- Write these questions on the board:
  1. Are David's classes interesting this semester?
  2. Are David and Beth in the same chemistry class?
  3. Is Sun Hee on her way to class?
  4. Is Sun Hee free?

Elicit or explain any new vocabulary.

Vocabulary

semester: 15–18 week part of a school year
on . . . way to (a place): going to (a place)
free: not busy

- Books closed. Play the audio program twice. Elicit answers to the questions on the board. (Answers: 1. yes 2. no 3. no 4. yes)
- Books open. Play the audio program again. Ss look at the pictures and read the conversation silently.
- Ss stand up and practice the conversation in pairs.

8 GRAMMAR FOCUS

Learning objective: *practice yes/no questions and short answers with* be

[CD 1, Track 7]

Yes/No questions

- Write several statements with *be* about David and Sun Hee or your own Ss on the board. For example:
  David is a student.
  Julia and Elena are sisters.
- Focus Ss' attention on the statements. Point out that statements begin with a subject + verb.
  David is a student. (David = S, is = V)
  Julia and Elena are sisters. (Julia and Elena = S, are = V)
- ***Option:*** If you don't want to teach the terms *subject* and *verb*, use the numbers 1 and 2 instead.
- Explain that yes/no questions begin with a verb + subject. For example:
  Is David a student? (Is = V, David = S)
  Are Julia and Elena sisters? (Are = V, Julia and Elena = S)
- Ask Ss to change any remaining statements on the board to yes/no questions. Give help as needed.
- Ss study the Grammar Focus box questions.

***Short answers with* be**

- Present the short answers in the Grammar Focus box. Point out that there are two ways of saying "no" for each pronoun, except for *I*.
- Ask yes/no questions with *be* about Ss in the class. Ss respond with short answers.
- Play the audio program. Focus Ss' attention on the stress in short answers (e.g., *Yes, I **am**. No, I'm **not**.*).

A

- Ss complete the conversations individually. Go over answers with the class.

Answers

1. A: **Is** Ms. Gray from the United States?
   B: Yes, she **is**. **She's** from Chicago.
2. A: **Is** English class at 10:00?
   B: No, it **isn't**. **It's** at 11:00.
3. A: **Are** you and Monique from France?
   B: Yes, we **are**. **We're** from Paris.
4. A: **Are** Mr. and Mrs. Tavares American?
   B: No, they **aren't**. **They're** Brazilian.

- Model the first conversation with a strong S and the second conversation with a different S. Then Ss practice the conversations in pairs.

B

- Explain the task. Ss write answers to the questions individually. Then they ask and answer the questions in pairs.

C Group work

- Model the task with the first question. Ss write questions individually. Then they ask their questions.
- ***Option:*** Ss write questions in small groups. Collect the questions and give them to different groups. Ss take turns asking and answering the questions.

7 CONVERSATION How's it going?

Listen and practice.

Sun Hee: Hey, David. How's it going?
David: Fine, thanks. How are you?
Sun Hee: Pretty good. So, are your classes interesting this semester?
David: Yes, they are. I really love chemistry.
Sun Hee: Chemistry? Are you and Beth in the same class?
David: No, we aren't. My class is in the morning. Her class is in the afternoon.
Sun Hee: Listen, I'm on my way to the cafeteria now. Are you free?
David: Sure. Let's go.

8 GRAMMAR FOCUS

Yes/No questions and short answers with be

Are you free?	Yes, I **am**.	No, I'**m not**.
Is David from Mexico?	Yes, he **is**.	No, he'**s not**. / No, he **isn't**.
Is Beth's class in the morning?	Yes, it **is**.	No, it'**s not**. / No, it **isn't**.
Are you and Beth in the same class?	Yes, we **are**.	No, we'**re not**. / No, we **aren't**.
Are your classes interesting?	Yes, they **are**.	No, they'**re not**. / No, they **aren't**.

A Complete these conversations. Then practice with a partner.

1. A: ....*Is*.... Ms. Gray from the United States?
   B: Yes, she .... from Chicago.
2. A: .... English class at 10:00?
   B: No, it .... at 11:00.
3. A: .... you and Monique from France?
   B: Yes, we .... from Paris.
4. A: .... Mr. and Mrs. Tavares American?
   B: No, they .... Brazilian.

B Answer these questions about yourself. If you answer "no," give the correct information. Then ask your partner the questions.

1. Are you from the United States? ....
2. Is your teacher from Canada? ....
3. Is your English class in the morning? ....
4. Are you and your best friend the same age? ....

C *Group work* Write five questions about your classmates. Then take turns asking and answering your questions.

Are Cindy and Brian from Los Angeles?

9 WORD POWER Hello and good-bye

A Do you know these expressions? Which ones are "hellos" and which ones are "good-byes"? Complete the chart. Add expressions of your own.

✓ Bye.
Good morning.
Good night.
Good-bye.
Have a good day.
Hello.

✓ Hey.
Hi.
How are you?
How's it going?
See you later.
See you tomorrow.

Hello	Good-bye
Hey.	*Bye.*

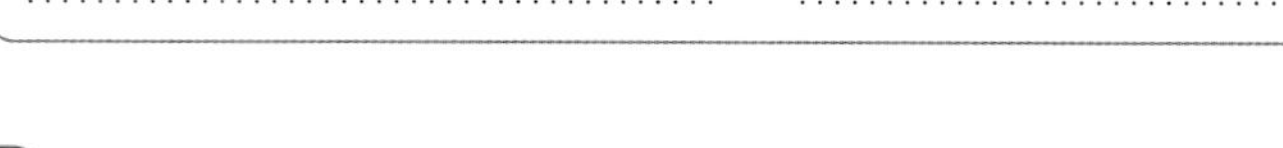

B Match the greetings with the best response.

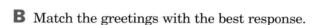

1. Have a good day.
2. Hi. How are you?
3. See you tomorrow.
4. Good morning.

a. Good morning.
b. Thank you. You too.
c. OK. See you.
d. Pretty good, thanks.

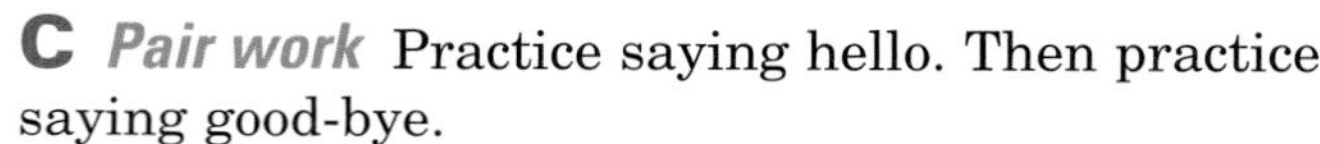

C ***Pair work*** Practice saying hello. Then practice saying good-bye.

A: Hi, Aki. How's it going?
B: Pretty good, thanks. How are you?

10 LISTENING What's your last name again?

Listen to the conversations. Complete the information about each person.

	First name	Last name	Where from?
1.	*Joe*		*the United States*
2.		*Vera*	
3.	*Min Ho*		

11 INTERCHANGE 1 Getting to know you

Find out about your classmates. Go to Interchange 1 at the back of the book.

9 WORD POWER

***Learning objective:** learn different ways to say hello and good-bye*

TIP To show Ss the purpose of an activity, write the learning objective on the board. At the end of the activity, point out what Ss have achieved.

A

- Explain the task. Ss write the expressions they know in the chart.
- Copy the chart from the Student's Book on the board.
- Go over each expression. Then elicit more expressions and have Ss write them in the chart on the board.

Answers

Hello	***Good-bye***
Hey.	Bye.
Good morning.	Good night.
Hello.	Good-bye.
Hi.	Have a good day.
How are you?	See you later.
How's it going?	See you tomorrow
Good afternoon.	*See you.*
Good evening.	*Talk to you later.*

(Note: Additional expressions are italicized.)

B

- Model the first greeting and response with a few Ss.
- Ss match the greetings and responses. Go over answers with the class.

Answers

1. b 2. d 3. c 4. a

C *Pair work*

- Model the conversation with a S.
- Ss practice using expressions from the *Hello* column in part A and responding in pairs. Then they practice using expressions from the *Good-bye* column.

10 LISTENING

***Learning objective:** develop skills in listening for detail*

[CD 1, Track 8]

- Explain the task and the information in the chart. Ask the class: "Where is Joe from? What else do we need to find out about him?"
- Play the first conversation in the audio program. Ss listen to find out Joe's last name.
- Play the rest of the audio program. As Ss listen and complete the chart, draw the chart on the board.
- Elicit answers and have Ss write them in the chart on the board. Do not correct wrong answers.
- Play the audio program again. Stop after each conversation and discuss the answers on the board.

Audio script

1.
MAN: Joe, this is my friend Linda Tanaka. We're in the same English class.
JOE: Hi, Linda. I'm Joseph Miller. Everyone calls me Joe.
LINDA: Nice to meet you, Joe. And what's your last name again?
JOE: It's Miller. M-I-L-L-E-R.
LINDA: Where are you from, Joe?
JOE: I'm from here, the United States – originally from Chicago.
LINDA: Wow! How do you like Chicago?
JOE: Oh, I love it. It's my favorite city.
2.
CLERK: OK, Ms. Vera. Let me just check this information. Is your first name spelled E-L-L-E-N?
ELENA: No, it's not. My first name is Elena. It's spelled E-L-E-N-A.
CLERK: OK. Thanks. And you're from Chile, right?
ELENA: No, I'm not from Chile. I'm from Mexico.
CLERK: Oh, sorry. Mexico. But you are studying English.
ELENA: Actually, I'm not. I'm an engineering student.
CLERK: Engineering. OK. Got it.
3.
MAN: Say, are you In Sook Kim?
IN SOOK: Yes, that's right.
MAN: Is your brother Min Ho Kim?
IN SOOK: Yes, he is!
MAN: Tell me, is Min Ho still here at the university?
IN SOOK: No, he's not. He's at home in Korea.
MAN: Oh, he's in Korea. Is he in school there?
IN SOOK: Yes. He's at Seoul University this semester.

Answers

First name	***Last name***	***Where from?***
Joe	Miller	the United States
Elena	Vera	Mexico
Min Ho	Kim	Korea

11 INTERCHANGE 1

See page T-114 for teaching notes.

12 READING

***Learning objectives:** read and discuss an article about names; develop skills in scanning and reading for detail*

> **TIP** Explain that in real life people read in different ways for different purposes. For example, they read manuals or recipes slowly and in detail, but they skim magazines or scan telephone books more quickly.

- Ask: "What English names do you like? Why?" Elicit answers.
- Focus Ss' attention on the title of the reading. Ask: "What do you think this article is about?" Elicit ideas.
- Ss scan the text quickly to find examples of names. Ask: "Do you know any people with these names? What are they like?"
- Point out that in the last paragraph *Georges* and *Bettys* are simply plurals of *George* and *Betty*. This refers to all people with those names.

A

- Explain the task. Read the statements.
- Ss read the article individually. Then they complete the task. Go over answers with the class.

Answers

True statements: 1, 2, 4, and 5.

B

- Elicit or explain any adjectives from the reading.

Vocabulary

average: like everybody else
creative: making or using new or unusual ideas
athletic: good at sports
nerdy: smart, but without good social skills
old-fashioned: having old ideas; not modern
independent: able to do things without help
adventurous: liking excitement and new things
plain: not very good-looking
ordinary: not special
intelligent: smart

- Explain the task. Give one or two examples.
- Ss complete the task individually. As Ss work, draw the chart on the board.
- Ask Ss who finish first to write their answers in the chart on the board. Then check answers as a class.

Answers

Positive names		*Negative names*	
Jacob	Michael	George	Stanley
Emily	Nicole	Betty	Jane

C *Pair work*

- Ss discuss the questions in pairs.
- ***Option:*** Each pair joins another pair to compare ideas.

For more practice with introductions and the alphabet, play ***Line Up!*** on page T-144. Have Ss line up alphabetically according to first names.

End of Cycle 2

Do your students need more practice?

Assign . . .	*for more practice in . . .*
Workbook Exercises 8–12 on pages 5–6	Grammar, Vocabulary, Reading, and Writing
Lab Guide Exercises 8–11 on page 2	Listening, Pronunciation, Speaking, and Grammar
Video Activity Book Unit 1	Listening, Speaking, and Cultural Awareness
CD-ROM Unit 1	Grammar, Vocabulary, Reading, Listening, and Speaking

12 READING

What's in a Name?

Look at the names in the article. Do you know any people with these names? What are they like?

Your name is very important. When you think of yourself, you probably think of your name first. It is an important part of your identity.

Right now, the two most popular names for babies in the United States are "Jacob" for boys and "Emily" for girls. Why are these names popular? And why are some names unpopular?

Names can become popular because of famous actors, TV or book characters, or athletes. Popular names suggest very positive things. Unpopular names suggest negative things. Surprisingly, people generally agree on the way they feel about names. Here are some common opinions about names from a recent survey.

Boys' names	Girls' names
George: average, boring	**Betty:** old-fashioned, average
Jacob: creative, friendly	**Emily:** independent, adventurous
Michael: good-looking, athletic	**Jane:** plain, ordinary
Stanley: nerdy, serious	**Nicole:** beautiful, intelligent

So why do parents give their children unpopular names? The biggest reason is tradition. Many people are named after a family member. Of course, opinions can change over time. A name that is unpopular now might become popular in the future. That's good news for all the Georges and Bettys out there!

A Read the article. Then check (✓) the statements that are true.

- ☐ 1. Your name is part of your identity.
- ☐ 2. People often feel the same way about a particular name.
- ☐ 3. Boys' names are more popular than girls' names.
- ☐ 4. People are often named after family members.
- ☐ 5. Opinions about names can change.

B According to the article, which names suggest positive things? Which suggest negative things? Complete the chart.

Positive names		Negative names	
....	....	....	....
....	....	....	....

C *Pair work* What names are popular in your country? Why are they popular?

2 How do you spend your day?

1 SNAPSHOT

Source: *The Definitive Guide to the Best and Worst of Everything*

Which jobs are dangerous? Why?
What's your opinion? Which job do you think is the worst?
List three other difficult jobs.

2 WORD POWER

A Complete the word map with jobs from the list.

cashier
chef
✓ company director
✓ dancer
✓ flight attendant
musician
pilot
receptionist
✓ server
singer
tour guide
Web-site designer

Jobs

Office work	Food service	Travel industry	Entertainment business
company director	*server*	*flight attendant*	*dancer*
....	....	....	....
....	....	....	....
....	....	....	....
....	....	....	....

B Add two more jobs to each category. Then compare with a partner.

How do you spend your day?

In Unit 2, students discuss work and school. In Cycle 1, they ask and answer questions about different types of jobs using the simple present. In Cycle 2, they talk about routines and daily schedules using time expressions.

Cycle 1, Exercises 1–6

SNAPSHOT

Learning objective: *talk about bad jobs*

- Books closed. Introduce the topic of jobs. Ask: "Do you have a job? What is it? Do your parents have jobs? What do they do?"
- List three jobs from the Snapshot on the board. Ss guess the worst job. (Answer: lumberjack)
- Books open. Ss compare their ideas with the Snapshot.
- Elicit or explain any new vocabulary.

Vocabulary

salary: money from work
working conditions: the situation at work (e.g., hours, safety, vacation benefits)
security: safety
dangerous: not safe

- Explain the task. Encourage Ss to give reasons for their opinions.
- Ss complete the task in small groups. Go around the class and give help as needed.

WORD POWER

Learning objectives: *learn vocabulary for different jobs; learn ways to categorize jobs*

A

- Ask Ss to look through the vocabulary list. Elicit or explain any new words. Model the pronunciation of new words.

TIP If you don't have enough time to explain new words in class, ask Ss to look them up in a dictionary before class.

- Ss complete the word map individually or in pairs.
- While Ss are working, draw the word map on the board. Ask different Ss to come up and write their answers in the correct category. Go over answers with the class.

TIP To provide variety, check answers in different ways. For example, write each answer on a separate card. Ss post the cards on the board in the correct category.

B

- Present and model the task. Ss write two more jobs for each category. Then they compare with a partner.
- Ask different Ss to add their ideas to the board. Go over answers with the class.

Answers

Office work	***Food service***
company director	server
receptionist	cashier
Web-site designer	chef
secretary	*dishwasher*
sales manager	*host/hostess*
Travel industry	***Entertainment business***
flight attendant	dancer
pilot	musician
tour guide	singer
travel agent	*actor/actress*
hotel manager	*disc jockey*

(Note: Additional examples are italicized.)

To review jobs, play the game ***Simon Says*** on page T-145. For example, if Simon says "Be a singer," Ss act out the job.

To review the vocabulary in this Word Power, try the ***Word Search*** on page T-156.

3 SPEAKING

Learning objective: *talk about jobs and workplaces*

A

- Brainstorm workplaces with the class. Write ideas on the board.
- Ss look at the pictures and describe each person's job (e.g., *She's a salesperson.*). If Ss have difficulty, focus their attention on column A.
- ***Option:*** Ss test each other in pairs. To model, ask: "What's number 1?"
- Explain the task. Ss match the information in columns A, B, and C. Point out that column A lists jobs, column B lists things people do in their jobs, and column C lists prepositional phrases with workplaces. Read the example.
- Ss complete the task individually or in pairs.
- Go around the class and give help as needed.
- Write the first answer on the board. Then ask different Ss to write answers on the board. Go over the answers as a class.

B *Pair work*

- Write these words on the board:

  She's She She works
  He's He He works

- Read the description of a salesperson's job aloud. Then ask a S to describe a chef's job using the words on the board.
- Ss complete the task in pairs. Go around the class and give help as needed.

Answers

She's a salesperson. She sells clothes. She works in a department store.
He's a chef. He cooks food. He works in a restaurant.
He's a flight attendant. He serves passengers. He works for an airline.
She's a carpenter. She builds houses. She works for a construction company.
He's a receptionist. He answers the phone. He works in an office.
She's a nurse. She cares for patients. She works in a hospital.

4 CONVERSATION

Learning objectives: *practice a conversation about jobs; see simple present Wh-questions and statements in context*

A *[CD 1, Track 9]*

- Set the scene. Jason and Andrea are talking about their jobs. Tell Ss to cover the text. Focus their attention on the pictures. Ask: "Who is Jason? What does he do? Who is Andrea? What does she do?" Encourage Ss to guess.

> **TIP** Give Ss (or ask Ss to bring) small cards to cover the text. That way, they can see the picture but not the text. Ask Ss to keep their cards for future classes.

- Play the audio program. Ss listen to check their guesses.
- Write these focus questions on the board:

  True or false?
  1. Andrea loves her job.
  2. Andrea takes people on tours to Asia.
  3. Jason has a full-time job.

- Books closed (or text covered). Play the audio program again. Then check answers to the focus questions. (Answers: 1. true 2. false 3. false)
- Books open (or uncover the text). Play the conversation line by line, giving Ss time to repeat it.
- Ss practice the conversation in pairs.

For a new way to practice this Conversation, try the ***Substitution Dialog*** on page T-151. Have Ss replace the underlined words:

A: What do you do, Andrea?
B: I'm a guide. I take people on tours. And what do you do, Jason?
A: I'm a cashier. I work in a restaurant.

B

- Read the two focus questions aloud. Then play the second part of the audio program. Elicit answers from the class.

Audio script

ANDREA: What do you do, exactly? Do you make hamburgers?
JASON: No, I don't. I just take orders.
ANDREA: And what's it like there? Do you like your job?
JASON: Sure. It's fun. And I get free hamburgers, too!

Answers

He takes orders. He likes his job because it's fun. He gets free hamburgers, too.

3 SPEAKING Work and workplaces

A Look at the pictures. Match the information in columns A, B, and C.

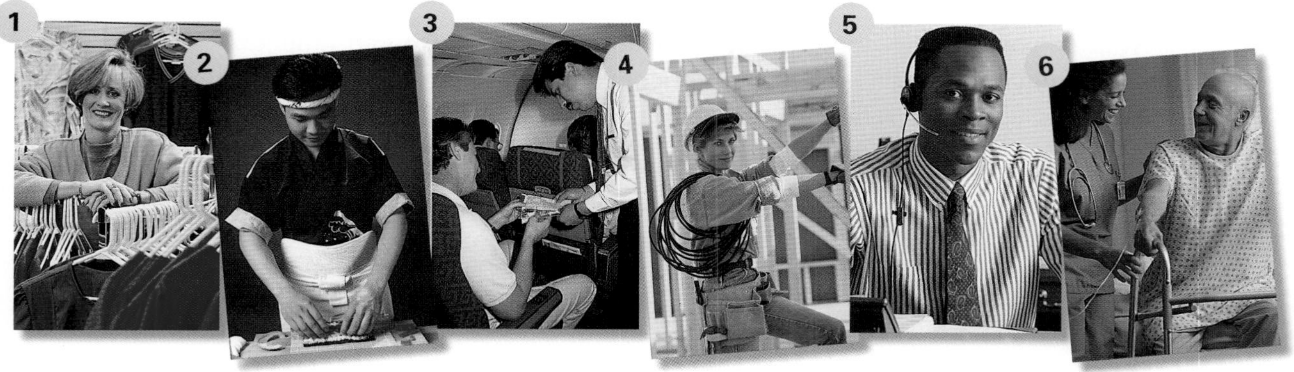

A	*B*	*C*
a salesperson	builds houses	for an airline
a chef	cares for patients	in a restaurant
a flight attendant	answers the phone	for a construction company
a carpenter	cooks food	in a hospital
a receptionist	serves passengers	in a department store
a nurse	sells clothes	in an office

B *Pair work* Take turns describing each person's job.

A: She's a salesperson. She sells clothes. She works in a department store.
B: And he's a chef. He . . .

4 CONVERSATION Where do you work?

A Listen and practice.

Jason: Where do you work, Andrea?
Andrea: I work at Thomas Cook Travel.
Jason: Oh, really? What do you do there?
Andrea: I'm a guide. I take people on tours to countries in South America, like Peru.
Jason: How interesting!
Andrea: Yes, it's a great job. I love it. And what do you do?
Jason: I'm a student, and I have a part-time job, too.
Andrea: Oh? Where do you work?
Jason: In a fast-food restaurant.
Andrea: Which restaurant?
Jason: Hamburger Heaven.

B Listen to the rest of the conversation. What does Jason do, exactly? How does he like his job?

5 GRAMMAR FOCUS

Simple present Wh-questions and statements

		I/You	He/She
What do you **do**?	I'**m** a student, and I **have** a part-time job.	work	works
Where do you **work**?	I **work** at/in a restaurant.	take	takes
Where do you **go** to school?	I **go** to the University of Texas.	study	studies
Where does Andrea **work**?	She **works** at Thomas Cook Travel.	teach	teaches
What does she **do**?	She's a guide. She **takes** people on tours.	do	does
How does she **like** it?	She **loves** it.	go	goes
		have	has

A Complete these conversations. Then practice with a partner.

1. A: What *do* you *do* ?
   B: I'm a full-time student. I study the violin.
   A: And .... do you .... to school?
   B: I .... to the New York School of Music.
   A: Wow! .... do you like your classes?
   B: I .... them a lot.
2. A: What .... Tanya do?
   B: She's a teacher. She .... an art class at a school in Denver.
   A: And what about Ryan? Where .... he work?
   B: He .... for a big computer company in San Francisco.
   A: .... does he do, exactly?
   B: He's a Web-site designer. He .... fantastic Web sites.

B *Pair work* What do you know about these jobs? Complete the chart. Then write sentences about each job.

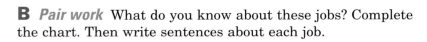

A flight attendant	A doctor	A teacher
▪ *works for an airline*	▪	▪ ....
▪ *assists passengers*	▪	▪ ....
▪ *serves drinks*	▪	▪ ....

A flight attendant works for an airline, assists passengers, and serves drinks.

C *Pair work* Ask your partner questions like these about work and school. Take notes to use in Exercise 6.

What do you do?	Do you study? Where?	How do you like . . . ?
Where do you live?	Do you work? Where?	What's your favorite . . . ?

5 GRAMMAR FOCUS

***Learning objective:** practice simple present Wh-questions and statements*

[CD 1, Track 10]

Simple present statements

- Books closed. Write these sentences on the board, allowing space between lines:
  I'm a guide.
  I work at Thomas Cook Travel.
  I take people on tours.
  I love my job.
- Books open. Ask: "Who said this?" (Answer: Andrea) Ask Ss to describe her job. Write the new version below the original:
  She's a guide.
  She works at Thomas Cook Travel.
  She takes people on tours.
  She loves her job.
- Point out that the verbs for *he*, *she*, and *it* end in *-s*.
- ***Option:*** Repeat the activity with sentences about Jason.

> **TIP** Write the letter *s* on a card. Every time Ss forget to use the final *-s*, hold up the card. Write the word *does* on a separate card for the same purpose.

- Focus Ss' attention on the third column in the Grammar Focus box. Point out the spelling changes that occur with *he/she*.

Simple present Wh-questions

- Draw a chart with five columns on the board. Number the columns from 1 to 5.
- Focus Ss' attention on the Conversation on page 9. Ask Ss to find two questions with the word *do* in part A. Then read the two questions about Jason in part B. Write them in the chart:

1	*2*	*3*	*4*	*5*
Where	*do*	*you*	*work,*	*Andrea?*
What	*do*	*you*	*do*	*there?*
What	*does*	*Jason*	*do,*	*exactly?*
How	*does*	*he*	*like*	*his job?*

- Focus Ss' attention on the questions in the chart and in the Grammar Focus box. Elicit the rule for forming Wh-questions in the simple present:
  Wh- + *do/does* + subject + verb
- Ask Ss the questions in the Grammar Focus box. Ss use their own information for the first three questions.
- Play the audio program. Ss listen and repeat.

A

- Ss complete the task individually. Then they compare answers with a partner.

> **TIP** To build Ss' confidence, have them compare answers in pairs or groups before you check answers as a class.

- Go over answers with the class. Then Ss practice the conversations in pairs.

Answers

1. A: What **do** you **do**?
   B: I'm a full-time student. I study the violin.
   A: And **where** do you **go** to school?
   B: I **go** to the New York School of Music.
   A: Wow! **How** do you like your classes?
   B: I **like** them a lot.
2. A: What **does** Tanya do?
   B: She's a teacher. She **teaches** an art class at a school in Denver.
   A: And what about Ryan? Where **does** he work?
   B: He **works** for a big computer company in San Francisco.
   A: **What** does he do, exactly?
   B: He's a Web-site designer. He **designs** fantastic Web sites.

B *Pair work*

- Explain the task. While Ss complete the task in pairs, copy the chart on the board.
- Ask different Ss to write their answers in the chart on the board.

Possible answers

A flight attendant	***A doctor***	***A teacher***
works for an airline	works in a hospital	works in a school
assists passengers	has an office	teaches classes
serves drinks	cares for patients	helps students

C *Pair work*

- Model the task. Ask a S a few of the questions, and take notes on the board.
- Ss complete the task in pairs. Go around the class and check for use of the simple present.

6 WRITING

Learning objective: *write a biography using the simple present*

A

- Tell Ss to read the model biography silently. Explain any new vocabulary. Point out that the biography does not have the person's name.
- Ss write their biographies. Go around the class and give help as needed.
- ***Option:*** Ss write the biographies for homework.

B *Class activity*

- Collect the biographies and number them. Then pass them around the class. Ss make a numbered list and write their guesses next to each number.
- Elicit Ss' guesses about each biography.
- ***Option:*** Put the numbered biographies on the classroom walls. Ss go around the room with their numbered lists and write their guesses.

End of Cycle 1

Do your students need more practice?

Assign . . .	*for more practice in . . .*
Workbook Exercises 1–6 on pages 7–9	Grammar, Vocabulary, Reading, and Writing
Lab Guide Exercises 1–6 on pages 3–4	Listening, Pronunciation, Speaking, and Grammar

Cycle 2, Exercises 7–12

7 CONVERSATION

Learning objectives: *practice a conversation about daily schedules; see time expressions in context*

A ***[CD 1, Track 11]***

- Point out the title and the picture. Ask: "What is this conversation about?" Elicit ideas.
- Books closed (or text covered). Ask: "What does Helen do?" Play the audio program. Ss listen for the answer. (Answer: She's a TV announcer.)
- Write these questions on the board:
  1. What time does Helen get home at night?
  2. Where does she work?
- Play the audio program again. Ss listen for the answers. (Answers: 1. at midnight 2. on KNTV)
- Books open. Play the audio program again. Ss read the conversation silently. Then they practice in pairs.
- ***Option:*** To review the simple present, ask Ss to describe Helen's daily routine from memory.

B

- Read the two focus questions.
- Play the audio program. Elicit answers from the class.

Audio script

HELEN: And you, Daniel? What's your day like?
DANIEL: Well, right now I'm in school, so I just have a part-time job. But I'm pretty busy. I get up early, around 6:00 A.M. Then I work from 7:00 until 9:00. I go to school and study until 4:00 P.M. Then I work again from 5:00 until 7:00.
HELEN: So what do you do?
DANIEL: I'm a dog walker.
HELEN: A what? What's that?
DANIEL: A dog walker. I take people's dogs for walks. It's great, and it keeps me in shape, too.

Answers

Daniel gets up around 6:00 A.M. He starts work at 7:00.

8 PRONUNCIATION

Learning objective: *notice and use correct syllable stress*

A ***[CD 1, Track 12]***

- Explain that some syllables have more stress. Read the examples, clapping on the stressed syllable.
- Play the audio program. Ss clap on stressed syllables.

B

- Ss complete the chart individually.
- Play the audio program. Ss listen and check their answers. Go over answers with the class.

Answers

● • dancer, pilot, cowboy
● • • company, lumberjack, fisherman
• ● • director, musician, designer

6 WRITING A biography

A Use your notes from Exercise 5 to write a biography of your partner. Don't use your partner's name on the paper; use *he* or *she* instead.

My classmate is a student. She lives near the university. She studies fashion design. She has a part-time job in a . . .

B *Class activity* Pass your biographies around the class. Can you guess who each biography is about?

7 CONVERSATION I start work at five.

A Listen and practice.

Daniel: So, do you usually come to the gym in the morning?
Helen: Yeah, I do.
Daniel: Really? What time do you go to work?
Helen: I work in the afternoon. I start work at five.
Daniel: Wow, that's late. When do you get home at night?
Helen: I usually get home at midnight.
Daniel: Midnight? That *is* late. What do you do, exactly?
Helen: I'm a TV announcer. I do the weather report on KNTV. Don't you recognize me?
Daniel: Oh! You're Helen Black. I love your show! By the way, I'm Daniel. . . .

B Listen to the rest of the conversation. What time does Daniel get up? start work?

8 PRONUNCIATION Syllable stress

A Listen and practice. Notice which syllable has the main stress in these words.

● •	● • •	• ● •
dancer	company	director
....	....	....
....	....	....

B Which stress pattern do these words have? Add them to the columns in part A. Then listen and check.

pilot lumberjack musician designer fisherman cowboy

9 GRAMMAR FOCUS

Time expressions

				Expressing clock time
I get up	**at** 7:00	**in** the morning	**on** weekdays.	7:00
I go to bed	**around** ten	**in** the evening	**on** weeknights.	seven
I leave work	**early**	**in** the afternoon	**on** weekends.	seven o'clock
I get home	**late**	**at** night	**on** Fridays.	7:00 A.M. = 7:00 in the morning
I stay up	**until** midnight	**on** Saturdays.		7:00 P.M. = 7:00 in the evening
I wake up	**before**/**after** noon	**on** Sundays.		

A Complete these sentences with time expressions.

1. I get up .... six .... the morning .... weekdays.
2. I go to bed .... midnight .... weeknights.
3. I start work .... 11:30 .... night.
4. I have lunch .... three .... the afternoon .... Fridays.
5. I stay up .... 1:00 A.M. .... weekends.
6. I have a little snack .... 9:00 .... the evening.
7. I sleep .... noon .... Sundays.

B Rewrite the sentences in part A so that they are true for you. Then compare with a partner.

C *Pair work* Take turns asking and answering these questions.

1. What days do you get up early? late?
2. What are two things you do before 8:00 in the morning?
3. What are three things you do on Saturday mornings?
4. What do you do only on Sundays?

10 LISTENING Daily schedules

A Listen to Rodney, Tina, and Ellen talk about their daily schedules. Complete the chart.

	Job	Gets up at . . .	Gets home at . . .	Goes to bed at . . .
Rodney	*chef*			
Tina		*7:00 A.M.*		
Ellen			*9:00 P.M.*	

B *Class activity* Who do you think has the best daily schedule? Why?

11 INTERCHANGE 2 Common ground

Find out about your classmates' schedules. Go to Interchange 2 at the back of the book.

9 GRAMMAR FOCUS

***Learning objective:** practice time expressions such as prepositions of time and adverbs of time*

[CD 1, Track 13]

Prepositions of time:* at/in/on + *time

- Draw these prepositions and three large circles on the board:

at *in* *on*

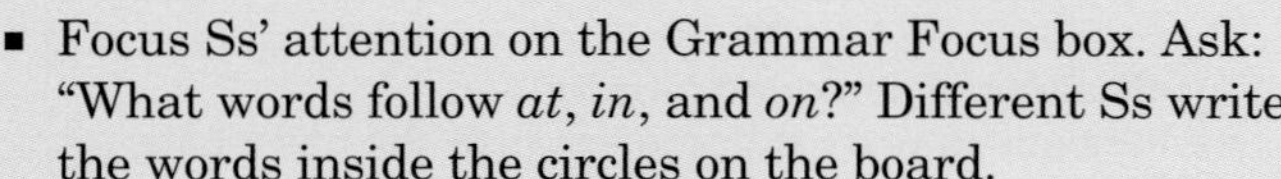

- Focus Ss' attention on the Grammar Focus box. Ask: "What words follow *at*, *in*, and *on*?" Different Ss write the words inside the circles on the board.
- Elicit or explain the rules:
  at + times of day; *night*
  in + parts of day (except *night*)
  on + days of the week

For more practice with prepositions of time, play ***Run For It!*** on page T-148.

Adverbs of time

- Elicit or explain the meanings of *early*, *late*, *around*, *until*, *before*, and *after*. Then play the audio program.

A

- Ss complete the task individually or in pairs.
- Go around the class and give help as needed. Go over answers with the class.

Answers

1. I get up **at** six **in** the morning **on** weekdays.
2. I go **to** bed **at** midnight **on** weeknights.
3. I start work **at** 11:30 **at** night.
4. I have lunch **at** three **in** the afternoon **on** Fridays.
5. I stay up **until** 1:00 A.M. **on** weekends.
6. I have a little snack **at** 9:00 **in** the evening.
7. I sleep **until** noon **on** Sundays.

B

- Model the task. Rewrite one or two sentences on the board so that they are true for you.
- Ss work individually. Then they go over their answers in pairs.

C *Pair work*

- Model the task. First, Ss ask you the questions. Then Ss complete the task in pairs.

10 LISTENING

***Learning objective:** develop skills in listening for specific information*

A [CD 1, Track 14]

- Set the scene. Then play the audio program, stopping after each person talks about his or her schedule. Ss complete the chart individually.
- Play the audio program again.
- Go over answers with the class.

Audio script

TINA: What do you do, Rodney?
RODNEY: I'm a chef.
TINA: Hey, that's great! So, what are your work hours like?
RODNEY: They're OK. I work in the afternoons and evenings. I get up around 9:00 A.M., and I work from 11:00 A.M. until 10:00 P.M. I get home fairly late, about 11:00 P.M. And I'm usually in bed by 1:00 in the morning. And what do you do, Tina?
TINA: Well, I'm an office manager. It's a regular nine-to-five office job, so I get up at 7:00 A.M. and get home around 6:00 P.M. That's OK, though, because I like to go out at night. I go to bed around midnight on weekdays.
RODNEY: What about you, Ellen?
ELLEN: Well, my job is a bit different – I'm a flight attendant. I start work at 6:00 in the morning, so I have to get up before 5:00 A.M.
TINA: Wow! That's too early for me!
ELLEN: Then I often have long flights, so I don't get home until 9:00 at night. But I always go to bed right away – around 10:00.

Answers

	Job	*Gets up at . . .*	*Gets home at . . .*	*Goes to bed at . . .*
Rodney	chef	9 A.M.	11 P.M.	1 A.M.
Tina	office manager	7 A.M.	6 P.M.	midnight
Ellen	flight attendant	5 A.M.	9 P.M.	10 P.M.

B *Class activity*

- Elicit Ss' responses. Then take a class vote.

11 INTERCHANGE 2

See page T-115 for teaching notes.

12 READING

Learning objectives: *read and discuss an article about jobs; develop skills in reading for specific information*

> **TIP** To help Ss focus on the task, tell them not to worry about words they don't understand. Encourage them to keep reading when they see new words.

- Set the scene. A high school student, college student, and new parent need jobs. Ask: "Why do they need jobs?" Elicit ideas and write them on the board.
- Focus Ss' attention on the pictures. Tell Ss to cover the profiles. Ask: "Who is in high school? in college? a new parent?" Encourage Ss to guess.
- Set a time limit of one minute. Ss scan the three profiles quickly to check their guesses. (Answers: Lamar is in high school. Theresa is in college. Kerin is a new parent.)

A

- Explain the task. Tell Ss to guess the meanings of any new words.
- Ss read the article and complete the task. Go over answers with the class.

Answers

1. To save money: Kerin
2. To earn money for college: Theresa
3. To go out on the weekend: Lamar
4. To buy a house: Kerin

- Elicit or explain any new vocabulary.

Vocabulary

experience: the work a person did in the past
quickly: fast
save: to keep for later
take care of: care for
type: to write on a computer
allowance: money parents give children to spend
earn: to receive money for work

B *Pair work*

- Ask Ss to read the article again. Tell them to take notes about each person's schedules and experience.

! For a new way to teach this Reading, try ***Jigsaw Learning*** on page T-152.

- Go over the ads with Ss. Then explain the task. Ask: "What is Theresa's schedule like? What experience does she have? What jobs are good for her? Why?" Elicit ideas from the class.
- Ss choose jobs for Theresa, Kerin, and Lamar in pairs. Make sure Ss explain why.

Possible answers

Theresa has a difficult schedule. She needs a flexible job or an evening job. Grocery store cashier, waitress, and office worker are good jobs for her.
Kerin needs to work at home because she has a baby. She can type and has a computer. Word processor is the best job for her.
Lamar can work afternoons, evenings, and weekends. Grocery store cashier, waiter, and office worker are good jobs for him.

For more practice with daily routines, play ***True or False?*** on page T-148. Have Ss prepare sentences about what they do every day.

End of Cycle 2

Do your students need more practice?

Assign . . .	***for more practice in . . .***
Workbook Exercises 7–12 on pages 10–12	Grammar, Vocabulary, Reading, and Writing
Lab Guide Exercises 7–10 on page 4	Listening, Pronunciation, Speaking, and Grammar
Video Activity Book Unit 2	Listening, Speaking, and Cultural Awareness
CD-ROM Unit 2	Grammar, Vocabulary, Reading, Listening, and Speaking

Evaluation

Assess Ss' understanding of Units 1 and 2 with the quiz on pages T-200 and T-201.

12 READING

Why do you need a job?

Scan the profiles. Who is in high school? Who is in college? Who is a new parent?

These people need jobs. Read about their schedules, experience, and why they need a job.

Theresa Glass

I don't have time to work, but I need a job because college is very expensive. I study art. I have class all day on Monday, Wednesday, and Friday, and on Tuesday and Thursday mornings. I usually study on weekends. I don't have any experience, but I can learn quickly.

Kerin Thomas

My husband and I have a new baby. He makes a good salary, but we don't save very much money. We want to save some money to buy a house. I take care of the baby, so I need a job I can do at home. I know how to type, and I have a computer.

Lamar Andrews

I'm 16 now, and I don't get an allowance from my parents anymore. I need to earn some money because I like to go out on the weekend with my friends. I go to school every day from 9:00 A.M. to 3:30 P.M. My father owns a restaurant, so I know a little about restaurant work.

A Read the article. Why do these people need jobs? Check (✓) the correct boxes.

	Theresa	Kerin	Lamar
1. To save money	☐	☐	☐
2. To earn money for college	☐	☐	☐
3. To go out on the weekend	☐	☐	☐
4. To buy a house	☐	☐	☐

B ***Pair work*** Choose the best job for each person. Explain why.

Art Store Clerk *9:00 A.M. to 5:00 P.M.* *$10 an hour*	**Grocery Store Cashier** *Flexible work hours* *$5.50 an hour*	**Day-care Assistant** *Work with children* *Earn great money*
Waiter/Waitress *Evenings only* *Experience a plus*	**Office Worker** *Nights and evenings* *No experience necessary*	**Word Processor** *Work at home* *Earn up to $20 an hour*

Units 1–2 Progress check

SELF-ASSESSMENT

How well can you do these things? Check (✓) the boxes.

I can	Very well	OK	A little
Introduce myself and another person using statements with *be* (Ex. 1)	☐	☐	☐
Ask questions to check information (Ex. 1)	☐	☐	☐
Exchange information using Wh- and yes/no questions with *be* (Ex. 2)	☐	☐	☐
Ask and answer questions about jobs using the simple present (Ex. 3, 4)	☐	☐	☐
Listen to and understand descriptions of work and school (Ex. 4)	☐	☐	☐
Talk about daily schedules using time expressions (Ex. 5)	☐	☐	☐

1 ROLE PLAY *Introductions*

A *Pair work* You are talking to someone at school. Have a conversation.

A: Hi. How are you?
B: . . .
A: By the way, my name is . . .
B: I'm sorry. What's your name again?
A: . . .
B: I'm . . . . Are you a student here?
A: . . . And how about you?
B: . . .
A: Oh, really? And where are you from?

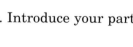

B *Group work* Join another pair. Introduce your partner.

2 SPEAKING *Interview*

Write questions for these answers. Then use the questions to interview a classmate.

1. *What's* .... ? My name is Keiko Kawakami.
2. .... ? I'm from Osaka, Japan.
3. .... ? Yes, my classes are very interesting.
4. .... ? My favorite class is English.
5. .... ? No, my teacher isn't American.
6. .... ? My classmates are very nice.
7. .... ? My best friend is Maria.

Units 1–2 Progress check

SELF-ASSESSMENT

Learning objectives: *reflect on one's learning; identify areas that need improvement*

- Ask: "What did you learn in Units 1 and 2?" Elicit Ss' answers.
- Ss complete the Self-assessment. Encourage them to be honest, and point out they will not get a bad grade if they check (✓) "a little."
- Ss move on to the Progress check exercises. You can have Ss complete them in class or for homework, using one of these techniques:
  1. Ask Ss to complete all the exercises.
  2. Ask Ss: "What do you need to practice?" Then assign exercises based on their answers.
  3. Ask Ss to choose and complete exercises based on their Self-assessment.

1 ROLE PLAY

Learning objectives: *assess one's ability to introduce oneself and another person using statements with* be*; assess one's ability to ask questions to check information*

A *Pair work*

- Read the instructions aloud and focus Ss' attention on the picture. Explain that Ss should pretend they don't know their partners in this role play.
- Model the role play with a S. Explain how to use the conversation cues.
- Ss role-play the conversation in pairs. Encourage Ss to use appropriate body language and gestures, add follow-up questions, and ask for clarification where appropriate.
- ***Option:*** Ss introduce themselves without referring to the example conversation.

B *Group work*

- Each pair joins another pair. Ss introduce their partners to the other pair and ask follow-up questions.

TIP If you don't have enough class time for the speaking activities, assign each S a speaking partner. Then have Ss complete the activities with their partners for homework.

2 SPEAKING

Learning objective: *assess one's ability to exchange information using Wh- and yes/no questions with* be

- Explain the task and model the first question. Ss should consider if the questions are Wh- or yes/no questions.
- Ss work individually to write the seven questions. Point out that there may be more than one correct question for each answer.
- Go over Ss' questions with the class.

Possible answers

1. What's your name?
2. Where are you from?
3. Are your classes interesting?
4. What's your favorite class?
5. Is your teacher American?
6. What are your classmates like?
7. Who is your best friend?

- Ss work in pairs. They take turns using the questions to interview each other. Encourage Ss to add follow-up questions.
- ***Option:*** Each S uses the questions to interview another S.

3 SPEAKING

Learning objective: assess one's ability to ask and answer questions about jobs using the simple present

A

- Explain the task. Then elicit things a receptionist does and write them on the board.
- Ss complete the task individually or in pairs.

B *Group work*

- Ss compare their lists in small groups. Encourage Ss to ask Wh-questions about the jobs (e.g., *What does a receptionist do? Where does a receptionist work?*).
- Go around the class and check Ss' use of the simple present.

LISTENING

Learning objectives: assess one's ability to listen to and understand descriptions of work and school; assess one's ability to ask and answer questions about jobs using the simple present

A [CD 1, Track 15]

- Set the scene. James and Lindsey are talking about work and school at a party.
- Play the audio program once or twice. Ss listen and complete the chart.

Audio script

JAMES: [*doorbell rings*] Hey, Nick. How are you?
NICK: I'm great, James. Welcome to my house. Oh James, this is my friend Lindsey.
JAMES: Hi, Lindsey. It's nice to meet you.
LINDSEY: Nice to meet you, too, James.
[*doorbell rings again*]
NICK: Excuse me.
LINDSEY: So how do you know Nick?
JAMES: Oh, we work in the same office.
LINDSEY: Really? What do you do?
JAMES: I'm a Web-site designer.
LINDSEY: That's exciting! Where do you work?
JAMES: At Central Computers.
LINDSEY: Central Computers, huh? How do you like your job?
JAMES: It's OK. I work late a lot. I usually finish at 10:30, and get home at 11:00.
LINDSEY: That *is* late!
JAMES: Yeah. After work, I usually go to bed right away. What about you? What do you do?
LINDSEY: Oh, I'm a student. I study dance.
JAMES: Wow! Now *that's* exciting! Where do you study?
LINDSEY: At New York Dance.
JAMES: How do you like your classes?
LINDSEY: I love them. I dance all day long. It's wonderful.
JAMES: What do you do after school?
LINDSEY: I have a part-time job. I work in an office.
JAMES: Where is the office?
LINDSEY: Actually, I work in your office! At Central Computers.
JAMES: You do? Well, stop by and say hello sometime.
LINDSEY: OK.

Answers

James	*Lindsey*
Web-site designer	dance student
Central Computers	New York Dance
OK	loves them
goes to bed	works in an office

B *Pair work*

- Explain the task. Ss take turns asking and answering the questions in part A.

SURVEY

Learning objective: assess one's ability to talk about daily schedules using time expressions

A

- Elicit or explain the meaning of *a perfect day*. Model the task by having a S ask you the questions.
- Ss complete the task individually.

B *Pair work*

- Ss take turns describing their perfect day in pairs. Encourage Ss to ask follow-up questions.

WHAT'S NEXT?

Learning objective: become more involved in one's learning

- Focus Ss' attention on the Self-assessment again. Ask: "How well can you do these things now?"
- Ask Ss to underline one thing they need to review. Ask: "What did you underline? How can you review it?"
- If needed, plan additional activities or reviews based on Ss' answers.

3 SPEAKING *What a job!*

A What do you know about these jobs? List three things each person does.

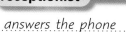

answers the phone
....
....

....
....
....

....
....
....

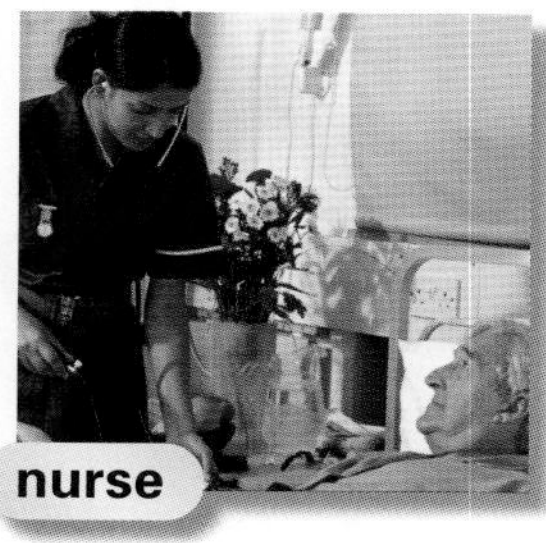

....
....
....

B *Group work* Compare your lists. Take turns asking about the jobs.

4 LISTENING *Work and school*

A Listen to James and Lindsey talk at a party. Complete the chart.

	James	Lindsey
What do you do?	....	....
Where do you work/study?	....	....
How do you like your job/classes?	....	....
What do you do after work/school?	....	....

B *Pair work* Practice the questions in part A. Ask additional questions.

5 SURVEY *My perfect day*

A Imagine your perfect day. Complete the chart with your own answers.

1. What time do you get up? ....
2. What do you do after you get up? ....
3. Where do you go? ....
4. What do you do in the evening? ....
5. When do you go to bed? ....

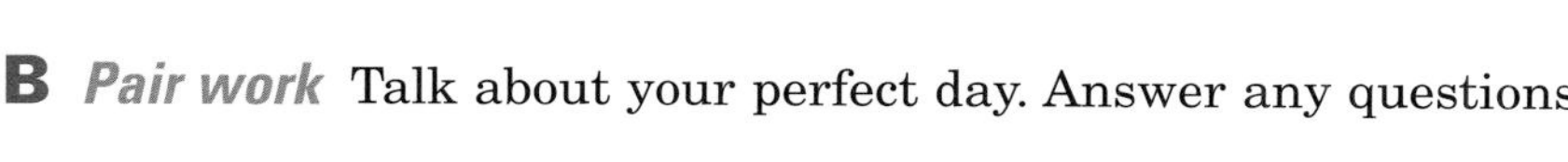

B *Pair work* Talk about your perfect day. Answer any questions.

WHAT'S NEXT?

Look at your Self-assessment again. Do you need to review anything?

3 How much is it?

1 SNAPSHOT

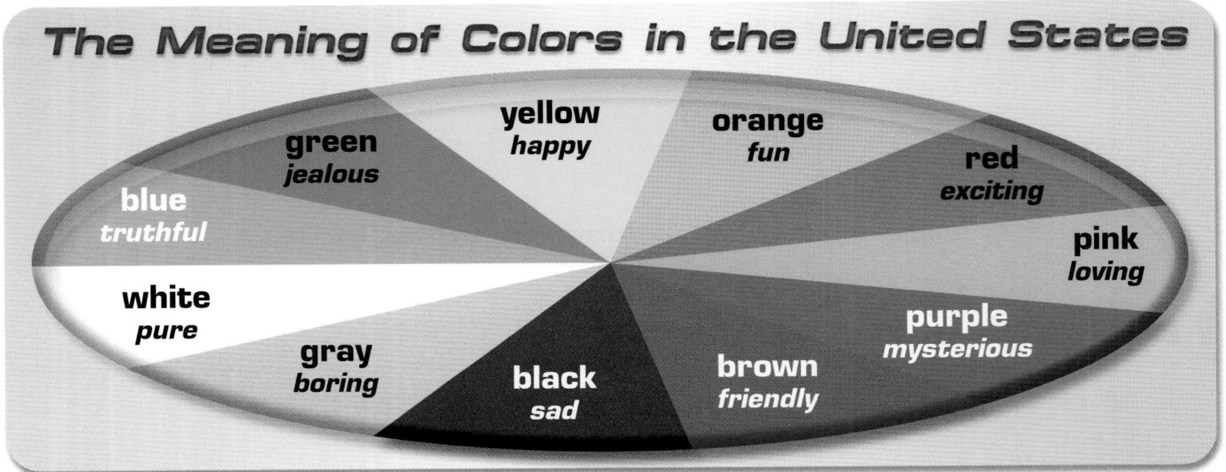

Sources: Based on information from Think Quest; Hewlett-Packard, *The Meaning of Color*

Which words have a positive meaning? Which words have a negative meaning?
What meanings do these colors have for you?
What does your favorite color make you think of?

2 CONVERSATION They're perfect for you.

A Listen and practice.

Steve: Oh, look at those earrings, Maria. They're perfect for you.
Maria: These red ones? I'm not sure.
Steve: No, the yellow ones.
Maria: Oh, these? Hmm. Yellow isn't really a good color for me.
Steve: Well, that necklace isn't bad.
Maria: Which one?
Steve: That blue one right there. How much is it?
Maria: It's $42! That's expensive!
Steve: Hey, let me get it for you. It's your birthday present. Happy birthday!

B Listen to the rest of the conversation. What else do they buy? Who pays for it?

How much is it?

In Unit 3, students discuss money, especially with regard to shopping. In Cycle 1, they talk about prices using demonstratives and the pronouns one/ones. *In Cycle 2, they talk about preferences using comparisons with adjectives.*

Cycle 1, Exercises 1–7

SNAPSHOT

Learning objective: *read about and discuss the meaning of colors*

- Books closed. Ask several Ss: "What is your favorite color?" Write the colors on the board. Help with vocabulary for colors as needed.
- Ask several Ss to choose between pairs of adjectives for colors. For example, ask: "Is red exciting or sad?" "Is white dirty or pure?"
- Books open. Explain that colors have different meanings in different countries. Discuss the meanings in the Snapshot. Elicit or explain any new vocabulary.

Vocabulary

truthful: honest
jealous: unhappy because you want someone's things
mysterious: strange and difficult to understand
friendly: nice to other people; sociable
pure: very clean

- Focus Ss' attention on the first two questions. Draw this chart on the board:

Positive meanings	*Negative meanings*
pure	*sad*

- Ask different Ss to add adjectives from the Snapshot to the chart. Does everyone agree on the placement of *exciting*? of *mysterious*?
- Ss discuss the last two questions in pairs. Allow about five minutes. Then discuss the questions as a class.
- ***Option:*** Select three colors. In pairs or groups, Ss make lists of all the things in the room with those colors.

CONVERSATION

Learning objectives: *practice a conversation about shopping; see demonstratives and* one/ones *in context*

A [CD 1, Track 17]

- To set the scene, focus Ss' attention on the picture. Ask: "Where are they? What are they doing?"
- Write this focus question on the board:
  What color necklace do they buy?
- Books closed (or text covered). Play the audio program. Ss listen for the answer. (Answer: blue)
- ***Option:*** Write these focus questions on the board:
  1. How much is the blue necklace?
  2. Why does Steve buy the necklace?

Then play the audio again. Ss check answers. (Answers: 1. $42 2. It's a birthday present.)

- Books open (or uncover the text). Play the audio program again. Ss listen and read along silently.
- Elicit or explain any new vocabulary.

Vocabulary

I'm not sure.: I don't know.
Hmm: a sound people make when they're thinking
Let me: Allow me to

- Ss practice the conversation in pairs.

! For a new way to practice this Conversation, try the ***Onion Ring*** technique on page T-151.

B

- Read the two focus questions aloud. Then play the audio program. Elicit answers from the class.

Audio script

MARIA: Steve, come and look at this necktie. What do you think?
STEVE: It's a nice tie, but look at the price – $25.
MARIA: Oh, that's not bad. And I want you to have it. Let me get it for you.
STEVE: OK. Sure.

Answers

They buy a tie. Maria pays for it.

3 GRAMMAR FOCUS

***Learning objective:** practice demonstratives and* one/ones

[CD 1, Track 18]

Demonstratives

- Books closed. Point to Ss' things and make statements with *this* and *these* (e.g., "This is Peter's pen. This is Joan's necklace. These are Dan's glasses.").
- Hold some things close to show how we use *this* or *these* for nearby things. Explain that *this* refers to a singular thing, while *these* refers to plurals.
- ***Option:*** Ss place their things in a bag. Each S takes out something and says whose it is (e.g., "This is Mary's pen.").
- Place some thing far away to show how we use *that* and *those*. Ss point to things and make statements (e.g., "That is Bill's book. Those are Mike's keys."). Explain that *that* refers to a singular thing, while *those* refers to plural things.
- To check Ss' understanding of demonstratives and review colors, ask about things in the room (e.g., "What color is this pen? What color are those books?").

One/ones

- Focus Ss' attention on the Conversation on page 16. Ask Ss to find examples of *one* and *ones*.
- For each example, ask: "What noun does *ones* or *one* replace?" (Answers: earrings, necklace) Elicit the rule: *One* replaces a singular noun, and *ones* replaces a plural noun.
- Play the first part of the audio program.

> ***TIP*** To raise awareness of both the meaning and form of a new structure, always link the Grammar Focus to the Conversation.

Prices

- Play the rest of the audio program. Ss repeat the prices. Present additional examples as needed.

For practice in listening for prices, play ***Bingo*** on page T-147 using prices instead of words.

A

- Model the first line of the first conversation.
- Ss complete the task individually. Go over answers with the class.

Answers

1. A: Excuse me. How much **are those** jeans?
   B: Which **ones**? Do you mean **these**?
   A: No, the light blue **ones**.
   B: Oh, **those** are $59.95.
   A: Almost $60! Are you kidding?
2. A: I like **that** backpack over there. How much **is** it?
   B: Which **one**?
   A: The red **one**.
   B: It's $27.49. But **this** green **one** is only $22.25.
   A: OK. Let me see it, please.

- Ss practice the conversations in pairs.
- ***Option:*** Bring in two different pairs of sunglasses, pens, necklaces, or hats. Then Ss practice the conversations again using these things.

B *Pair work*

- Explain the task. Ss work in pairs to choose prices for the sunglasses and cell phones.
- Model the example conversation with a S. Then Ss take turns asking and answering questions about the items. Go around the class to check for the use of demonstratives and *one* or *ones*.
- ***Option:*** If you live in an English-speaking environment, have Ss go to a store to ask the prices of three things in English.
- ***Option:*** Bring in clothing catalogs. Ss use them to practice the conversations.

For a new way to practice this Conversation, try the ***Substitution Dialog*** on page T-151.

For more practice asking for and giving prices, try the ***Price Exchange*** on page T-156.

3 GRAMMAR FOCUS

Demonstratives; one, ones

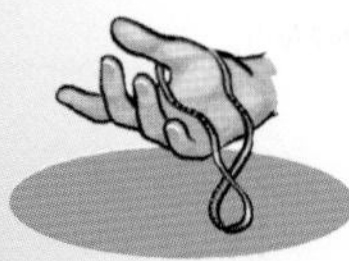

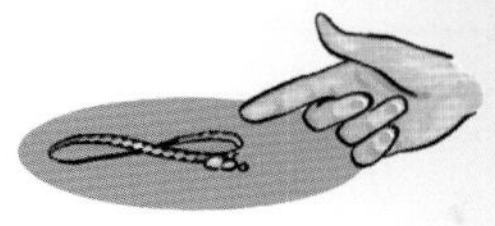

How much is	**this** necklace? **this one**?	**that** necklace? **that one**?	Which **one**? The blue **one**.	It's $42.
How much are	**these** earrings? **these**?	**those** earrings? **those**?	Which **ones**? The yellow **ones**.	They're $18.

prices

$42 = forty-two dollars
$59.95 = fifty-nine ninety-five
OR
fifty-nine dollars and ninety-five cents

A Complete these conversations. Then practice with a partner.

1. A: Excuse me. How much *are those* .... jeans?
   B: Which .... ? Do you mean .... ?
   A: No, the light blue ....
   B: Oh, ... are $59.95.
   A: Almost $60! Are you kidding?

2. A: I like .... backpack over there. How much .... it?
   B: Which .... ?
   A: The red ....
   B: It's $27.49. But .... green .... is only $22.25.
   A: OK. Let me see it, please.

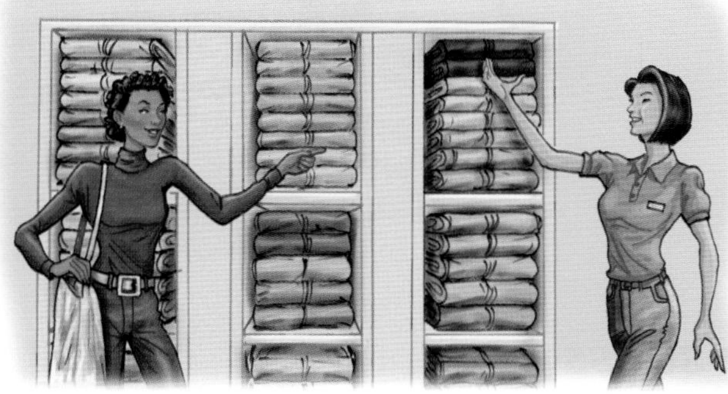

B *Pair work* Add prices to the items. Then ask and answer questions.

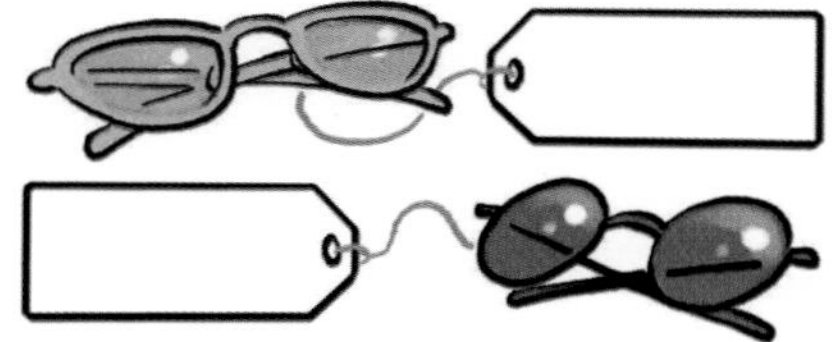

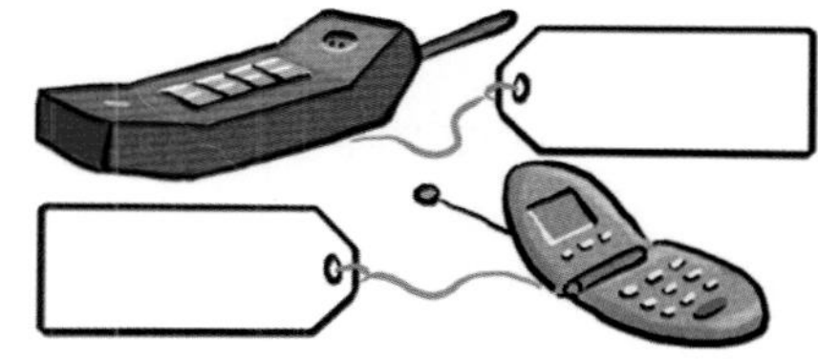

A: How much are these sunglasses?
B: Which ones?
A: The pink ones.
B: They're $86.99.
A: That's expensive!

useful expressions

That's cheap.
That's reasonable.
That's OK/not bad.
That's expensive.

4 LISTENING Look at these!

Listen to Tim and Sandra shopping. Complete the chart.

Item	Price	Do they buy it? Yes	No	Reason
1. in-line skates	....	☐	☐	....
2. cap	....	☐	☐	....
3. sunglasses	....	☐	☐	....
4. watch	....	☐	☐	....

5 ROLE PLAY Can I help you?

A *Pair work* Put items "for sale" on your desk or a table – notebooks, watches, or bags. Use items of different colors.

Student A: You are a clerk. Answer the customer's questions.
Student B: You are a customer. Ask about the price of each item. Say if you want to buy it.

A: Can I help you?
B: Yes. I like these sunglasses. How much are they?
A: Which ones?

B Change roles and try the role play again.

6 PRONUNCIATION Sentence stress

A Listen and practice. Notice that the important words in a sentence have more stress.

Excuse me. They're perfect. I like the blue one. They're not very attractive.

B Practice the conversations in part A of Exercise 3 again. Pay attention to the sentence stress.

7 INTERCHANGE 3 Flea market

See what kinds of deals you can make as a buyer and a seller. Go to Interchange 3.

4 LISTENING

Learning objective: *develop skills in listening for details*

[CD 1, Track 19]

- Set the scene. Tim and Sandra are shopping. They want to know the prices of four things.
- Play the audio program. Ss listen and complete only the *Price* column in their books.
- Play the audio program again. Ss listen to find out if Tim and Sandra buy the things, and their reasons.
- Go over answers with the class.

Audio script

1.
TIM: Look at these! In-line skates. I really want a pair.
SANDRA: But they're pretty expensive. They're $165.
TIM: Oh, yeah. You're right. A hundred and sixty-five dollars is too expensive.
2.
TIM: Here's a great cap for you!
SANDRA: That one? Hmm. Is it expensive?
TIM: Not really. It's only $9.95.
SANDRA: Nine ninety-five is very reasonable. I think I'll take it.
3.
SANDRA: What do you think of those sunglasses? They're only $16.
TIM: They're nice. Try them on.
SANDRA: Oh, no. I think they're too big.
TIM: You're right. They *are* too big.
4.
TIM: I love this watch! Do you like it?
SANDRA: I do. Why don't you get it?
TIM: Hmm, it's pretty expensive. It's $49.99.
SANDRA: That price isn't bad. It's a nice watch.
TIM: Yeah, maybe you're right. I think I'll get it.

Answers

Item	*Price*	*Do they buy it?*	*Reason*
1. in-line skates	$165	no	They're too expensive.
2. cap	$9.95	yes	The price is reasonable.
3. sunglasses	$16	no	They're too big.
4. watch	$49.99	yes	The price isn't bad.

5 ROLE PLAY

Learning objective: *role-play a conversation between a clerk and a customer*

A Pair work

- Place several items of different colors on your desk. Use things such as pens, caps, and notebooks.
- Model the task with a S. You play the clerk and the S plays the customer.
- Ss work in pairs. Tell Ss to ask about the price of more than one item.

B

- Ss change roles and try the role play again.

6 PRONUNCIATION

Learning objectives: *notice sentence stress; learn to sound natural using sentence stress*

A *[CD 1, Track 20]*

- Remind Ss that in each word, one syllable has more stress. Explain that important words in a sentence also have more stress.
- Read the examples, clapping on the stressed words.
- Play the audio program. Ss clap on each stressed word.
- Play the audio program again. Pause for Ss to repeat the sentences, stressing important words.

B

- Ss practice the conversations in part A of Exercise 3 again. Correct Ss' use of sentence stress as needed.

7 INTERCHANGE 3

See pages T-116 and T-117 for teaching notes.

End of Cycle 1

Do your students need more practice?

Assign . . .	*for more practice in . . .*
Workbook Exercises 1–5 on pages 13–15	Grammar, Vocabulary, Reading, and Writing
Lab Guide Exercises 1–5 on page 5	Listening, Pronunciation, Speaking, and Grammar

WORD POWER

Learning objective: *learn vocabulary for clothes and materials*

A

- If possible, bring in one thing made of each material: cotton, rubber, gold, silk, leather, silver, plastic, wool. Write the names of the materials on cards. Put the items on your desk with the cards next to them.
- Say the word for each material. Ss repeat the word.
- Explain the task. Ss work individually to complete the exercise. Go around the class and give help. Make sure that Ss do not add *-s* to the adjectives (e.g., NOT *wool**s** socks, rubber**s** boots*).
- Go over answers with the class.

Answers

1. a **plastic** bracelet	5. a **leather** jacket
2. a **gold** ring	6. a **cotton** shirt
3. a **silk** tie	7. **silver** earrings
4. **wool** socks	8. **rubber** boots

B *Pair work*

- Write the names of the eight things in part A across the top of the board. Ask the question in the book.
- Ask different Ss to write possible materials below each thing on the board. For example, under *socks* they can write *wool*, *cotton*, or *silk*.
- ***Option:*** Use the materials word cards. Ask Ss to place the cards next to other items in the classroom made of these materials.

TIP Ss usually forget about 80 percent of new words after 24 hours. To help them remember more, recycle or review new vocabulary the next class.

C *Class activity*

- Model the conversation with a S.
- Ss make as many statements as possible. Point out that they can use other patterns (e.g., "I am wearing . . .").
- ***Option:*** Ss write four sentences about what they have or what they're wearing on a piece of paper. Collect the papers and read the sentences aloud. Then Ss guess who wrote the sentences.

For more practice with vocabulary for materials, play ***Change Chairs*** on page T-145. Give the first command: "Change chairs if you have a leather jacket."

CONVERSATION

Learning objectives: *practice a conversation about preferences; see comparisons with adjectives in context*

A *[CD 1, Track 21]*

- Elicit ideas and vocabulary based on the picture.
- Set the scene. Sue and Anne are shopping. Ask Ss to listen for answers to these focus questions:
  1. What are they shopping for?
  2. Does Anne buy a leather jacket?
  3. Does Anne buy a wool jacket?
- Books closed. Play the audio program. Then check answers to the focus questions. (Answers: 1. jackets 2. no 3. no)
- Books open. Play the audio program again. Ss listen and read along silently. Elicit or explain any new vocabulary.
- Ss practice the conversation in pairs.

For a new way to teach this Conversation, try ***Say It With Feeling!*** on page T-150.

B

- Read the two focus questions aloud. Then play the audio program. Elicit answers from the class.

Audio script

ANNE: Wow! That jacket is really expensive. I don't want to spend that much money.
SUE: Oh, look. There are some things on sale over there.
ANNE: Oh, you're right. These T-shirts are really nice. And they're cheap, too. I like this one with the bird on it.
SUE: That *is* nice. And the colors are really pretty.
ANNE: Great! I'll take it.

Answers

Anne buys a T-shirt. Sue likes it.

8 WORD POWER Materials

A What are these things made of? Identify each one. Use the words from the list.

cotton	gold	leather	plastic
rubber	silk	silver	wool

1. a ..*plastic*.. bracelet 2. a .... ring 3. a .... tie 4. .... socks

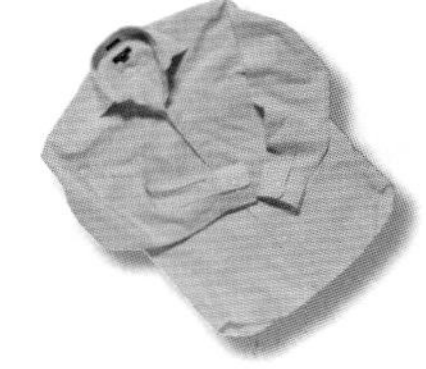
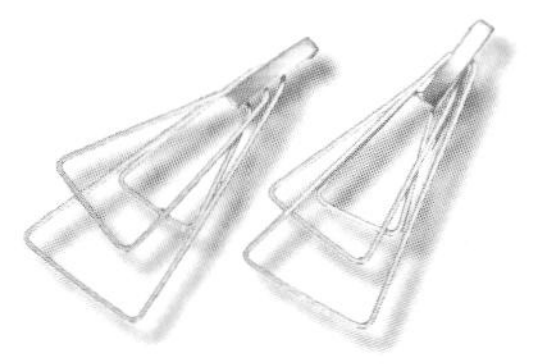

5. a .... jacket 6. a .... shirt 7. .... earrings 8. .... boots

B ***Pair work*** What other materials are the things in part A sometimes made of? Make a list.

C ***Class activity*** Which materials can you find in your classroom?

A: Juan has a leather bag and Ellen has leather shoes.
B: I think Maria has a silk . . .

9 CONVERSATION Which one do you prefer?

A Listen and practice.

Anne: Look! These jackets are really nice. Which one do you prefer?
Sue: I like the wool one better.
Anne: The wool one? Why?
Sue: It looks warmer.
Anne: Well, I like the leather one better. It's more stylish than the wool one.
Sue: Hmm. There's no price tag.
Anne: Excuse me. How much is this jacket?
Clerk: It's $499. Would you like to try it on?
Anne: Uh, no. That's OK! But thanks anyway.
Clerk: You're welcome.

B Listen to the rest of the conversation. What does Anne buy? What does Sue think of it?

10 GRAMMAR FOCUS

Preferences; comparisons with adjectives

Which one do you **prefer**?	That one is **cheaper than** the wool one.	***Spelling***
I **prefer** the leather one.	This one is **nicer than** . . .	cheap → cheaper
Which one do you **like better/more**?	The leather jacket is **prettier than** . . .	nice → nicer
I **like** the leather one **better/more**.	It looks **bigger than** . . .	pretty → prettier
	It's more **stylish than** . . .	big → bigger

For more information on comparatives, see the appendix at the back of the book.

A Complete these conversations. Then practice with a partner.

silk polyester

small medium

cotton wool

1. A: Which dress is .... (pretty), the yellow one or the green one?
   B: Well, the green one is silk. And silk is .... (expensive) polyester.
2. A: Is this blue T-shirt .... (large) the red and white one?
   B: No, the red and white one is .... (big). It's a medium. The blue one is a small.
3. A: Look at these pants! Which ones do you like .... (good)?
   B: I prefer the green cotton ones. They're .... (stylish) the wool ones.

B ***Pair work*** Compare the things in part A. Give your own opinions.

A: Which dress do you like more?
B: I like the yellow one better. The design is nicer.

useful expressions

The color is prettier.
The design is nicer.
The style is more attractive.
The material is better.

11 WRITING Comparing prices

How much do these things cost in your country? Complete the chart. Then compare the prices in your country with the prices in the U.S.

	Price in my country	Price in the U.S.
a newspaper	....	$ .75
a cup of coffee	....	$ 1.00
a CD	....	$17.99
a paperback book	....	$ 7.95

Many things are more expensive in my country than in the United States. For example, a newspaper costs one dollar at home. In the U.S., it's cheaper. It's only 75 cents. A cup of coffee costs . . .

10 GRAMMAR FOCUS

Learning objective: *practice preferences and comparisons with adjectives*

[CD 1, Track 22]

Preferences

- Bring some items to class that are similar (e.g., two rings, two ties, two pens, two T-shirts).
- Focus Ss' attention on the Conversation on page 19. Ask: "Which jackets do Anne and Sue prefer? Why?" Write the answers on the board and underline the words *likes* and *better*:
  Sue likes the wool one better. It looks warmer.
  Anne likes the leather one better. It's more stylish than the wool one.
  Point out that *like better* means *prefer*.
- Hold up two similar items (e.g., two ties). Ask two or three Ss: "Which one do you prefer?" Elicit the response: "I prefer . . ." or "I like . . . better." Repeat with other pairs of items.
- ***Option:*** Use two pairs of similar items to review *ones*.

Comparisons with adjectives

- Underline *warmer* and *more stylish* in the sentences on the board. Then draw two columns on the board, like this:

1	*2*
warmer	*more expensive*
nicer	*more stylish*
prettier	*more beautiful*

TIP To help Ss see the differences in grammar forms, use different colors on the board.

- Point out that column 1 has two one-syllable adjectives (*warm*, *nice*) and one two-syllable adjective that ends in *-y* (*pretty*). The comparative forms of these adjectives end in *-er*.
- Point out that column 2 has adjectives of two or more syllables (e.g., *expensive*). The comparative forms of these start with *more*.
- Elicit more comparative adjectives for both columns. Ask different Ss to write them on the board.
- Point out the spelling rules in the Grammar Focus box. A final *-y* changes to *-i* when we add *-er* (*prett**ier***), and a single vowel + consonant doubles the consonant (*big**ger***).
- Present the irregular forms: *good – better* and *bad – worse*. Then play the audio program.
- Hold up two items again. Ask: "Which . . . do you prefer? Why do you prefer it/them?" Elicit answers.
- ***Option:*** Ask Ss to look back over previous units to find more adjectives. (See pages 7 and 16.) Elicit the comparative forms and ask different Ss to write them in column 1 or 2.

A

- Explain the task. Remind Ss to look at the pictures when answering.
- Ss complete the task individually. Then go over answers with the class.

Answers

1. A: Which dress is **prettier**, the yellow one or the green one?
   B: Well, the green one is silk. And silk is **more expensive than** polyester.
2. A: Is this blue T-shirt **larger than** the red and white one?
   B: No, the red and white one is **bigger**. It's a medium. The blue one is a small.
3. A: Look at these pants! Which ones do you like **better**?
   B: I prefer the cotton ones. They're **more stylish than** the wool ones.

- Ss practice the conversations in pairs.

B *Pair work*

- Focus Ss' attention on the pictures in part A. Model the conversation with a S. Go over the useful expressions.
- Ss work in pairs. They talk about the items, giving their opinions.

For more practice making comparative forms, play ***Tic-Tac-Toe*** on page T-148.

11 WRITING

Learning objective: *write a paragraph comparing prices*

- Have Ss read the directions, chart, and sample paragraph. Allow three minutes.
- Ask: "What does the chart show? What are you going to add to the chart?" (Answers: prices in the U.S., prices in my country)
- Ss work individually. First they complete the chart. Then they write a paragraph comparing prices.
- Ss read each other's paragraphs and make suggestions.
- ***Option:*** Ss write a paragraph in class and then revise it for homework.

12 READING

Learning objectives: *read and discuss an article about Internet shopping; develop skills in scanning and differentiating fact and opinion*

> ***TIP*** To help Ss understand what reading strategy to use, focus their attention on the purpose of the task. For example: "Today we're going to practice differentiating fact from opinion."

- Set the scene. Ask: "How often do you go shopping? Do you like shopping? Do you ever buy things on the Internet?"
- Explain that this article is about a famous Web site called eBay, where people shop online.
- ***Option:*** If Ss have access to the Internet, tell them to look at the eBay Web site before they read.
- Point out the pre-reading questions. Ss guess the answers. Then they scan the text quickly to check their guesses.

Answers

true, true, false

- Elicit or explain any new vocabulary.

Vocabulary

online: using the Internet
marketplace: a place to sell things
bargain: something you get for a good price
member: a person who is part of a group
trade: to buy or sell something
advertisement: words or pictures that try to sell something
traditional: old-fashioned; not new or modern

A

- Explain the task. Ss read the article. Remind Ss not to worry about words they don't know. Ss then answer the questions individually.
- ***Option:*** Ss work in pairs. One S answers questions a–c, while the other S answers questions d–f. Then they share their answers.
- Ss compare answers in pairs or small groups.

Answers

a. over 18 million (paragraph 1)
b. It's easy and friendly, but some people don't like it. (paragraph 3)
c. You put an advertisement for an item on the Web site. People bid for the item. The person who bids the most money buys the item. Then you send the item to the buyer. (paragraph 2)
d. It's an online marketplace. (paragraph 1)
e. You can shop in the United States, Europe, Latin America, China, and many other countries. (paragraph 4)
f. You can buy and sell millions of different things from cars to electronics to musical instruments. (paragraph 2)

B

- Explain the task. Model the first example. First, find the information in the article. (Answer: paragraph 1) Then decide if it is a fact or opinion. (Answer: fact)
- Ss work individually. Go around the class and give help as needed.
- Ss compare answers in pairs. Then go over answers with the class.

Answers

1. fact 2. fact 3. fact 4. opinion 5. opinion

C *Pair work*

- Read the two questions. Then Ss discuss the questions in pairs.
- Discuss the questions as a class.

End of Cycle 2

Do your students need more practice?

Assign . . .	***for more practice in . . .***
Workbook Exercises 6–10 on pages 16–18	Grammar, Vocabulary, Reading, and Writing
Lab Guide Exercises 6–9 on page 6	Listening, Pronunciation, Speaking, and Grammar
Video Activity Book Unit 3	Listening, Speaking, and Cultural Awareness
CD-ROM Unit 3	Grammar, Vocabulary, Reading, Listening, and Speaking

12 READING

The World's Online Marketplace™— eBay!

Check (✓) the statements you think are true. Then scan the article to check your answers.
- ■ *eBay is a place to buy and sell things.*
- ■ *You can make friends on eBay.*
- ■ *Everyone likes eBay.*

1 Do you like shopping online? Do you like finding a bargain or a good buy? Then eBay is for you. eBay is The World's Online Marketplace.™ It's a place to buy and sell almost anything. With over 18 million members, eBay is more popular than any other shopping site on the Internet.

2 People trade millions of different things on eBay's Web site: from cars to electronics to musical instruments. Here's how it works: A member puts an advertisement for an item on the Web site. Other members bid, or offer money, for the item. The person who bids the most money gets to buy the item. Then the seller sends the item to the buyer.

3 "Selling on eBay is easy," says Mike Stacks. He's the owner of a company that sells used computers. And he adds, "I make friends on eBay. I think it's a very friendly place." But some people don't like it. "I think the traditional way to shop is better," says Jenny Feng, a student. "I want to touch things – not see a picture of them."

4 But whether you like it or not, eBay is here to stay. There are now eBay users in the United States, Europe, Latin America, China, and many other countries. Soon, people may be able to shop on eBay anywhere in the world.

A Read the article. Answer these questions. Then write the number of the paragraph where you find each answer.

.... a. How many people use eBay?
.... b. What do people think about eBay?
.... c. How do you sell items on eBay?
.... d. What is eBay?
.... e. Where can you shop on eBay?
.... f. What can you buy and sell on eBay?

B Find these statements in the article. Which are facts? Which are opinions? Check (✓) Fact or Opinion.

	Fact	Opinion
1. It's a place to buy and sell almost anything.	☐	☐
2. eBay is more popular than any other shopping site.	☐	☐
3. The person who bids the most money gets to buy the item.	☐	☐
4. Selling on eBay is easy.	☐	☐
5. The traditional way to shop is better.	☐	☐

C *Pair work* Have you ever shopped online? If so, how was your experience?

4 Do you like rap?

1 SNAPSHOT

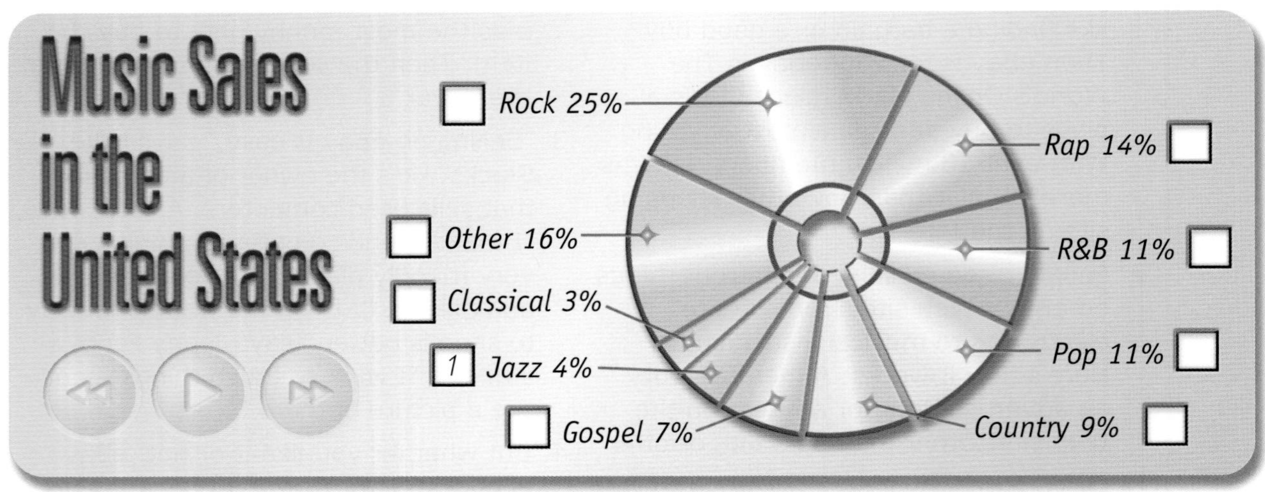

Source: The Recording Industry Association of America, *2002 Consumer Profile*

Listen and number the musical styles from 1 to 8.
Which of these kinds of music are popular in your country?
What other kinds of music are popular in your country?

2 WORD POWER

A Complete the word map with words from the list.

classical	salsa
game shows	science fiction
horror films	soap operas
jazz	talk shows
news	thrillers
pop	westerns

B Add two more words to each category. Then compare with a partner.

C *Group work* Number the items in each list from 1 (you like it the most) to 6 (you like it the least). Then compare your ideas.

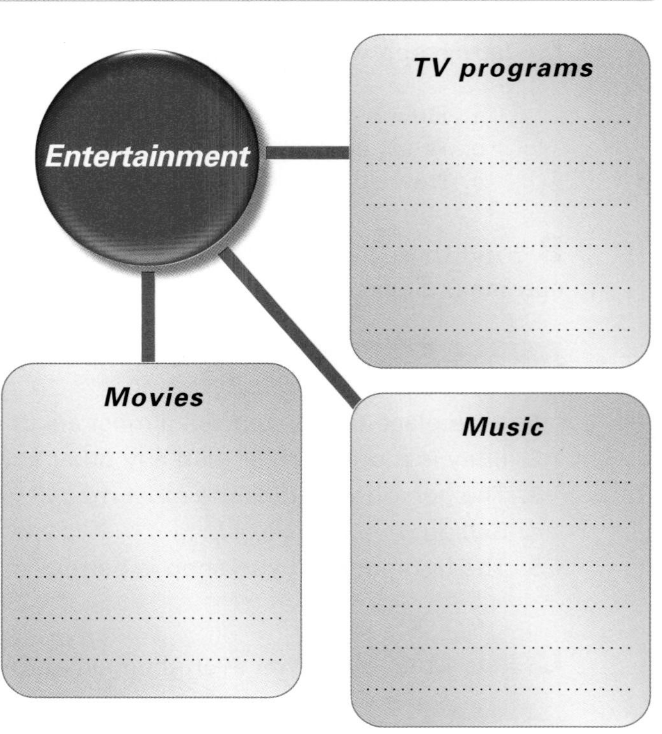

Do you like rap?

In Unit 4, students discuss entertainment and personal likes and dislikes. In Cycle 1, they talk about music using yes/no and Wh-questions with do. *In Cycle 2, they make invitations and excuses using* would *and verb +* to *+ verb.*

Cycle 1, Exercises 1–7

SNAPSHOT

Learning objective: *discuss types of music*

[CD 1, Track 23]

- Books closed. Ask: "What kind of music is popular in your country?" Help with vocabulary as needed. Write answers on the board.
- Books open. Point out the percentage signs. Ask: "What is this symbol called? What does this chart show?" (Answers: percent, music sales in the U.S.)
- Read out the names of the music styles. Ask: "What kind of music is popular in the U.S.? What music is unpopular? Does anything surprise you about the information?" Elicit answers.
- Elicit or explain any new vocabulary.

Vocabulary

rap: music of African-American origin, with rhyming words and a strong beat
R&B: rhythm and blues
country: country-and-western
gospel: a kind of Christian religious music
jazz: a kind of dance music originally popular in the 1920s

- Brainstorm with Ss what the "other" category might include (e.g., *reggae*, *salsa*).
- Explain that Ss will hear eight short pieces of music in different styles. Ss listen and number the musical styles from 1 to 8.
- Play the audio program. Ss complete the task individually. Then they compare answers in pairs.
- ***Option:*** If Ss have difficulty, do the activity with the whole class.

Answers

1. jazz	3. gospel	5. rap	7. rock
2. pop	4. classical	6. country	8. R&B

- Go over the two discussion questions. Ss discuss them in small groups. Then elicit answers from the class.
- ***Option:*** What kind of music does the class like best? Take a poll.

WORD POWER

Learning objective: *learn vocabulary for types of entertainment*

A

- Explain the task. Ss work in pairs or small groups. Allow them to use dictionaries.
- Draw the word map on the board. Ask different Ss to write the answers on the board. Model the pronunciation of the words as you check answers.

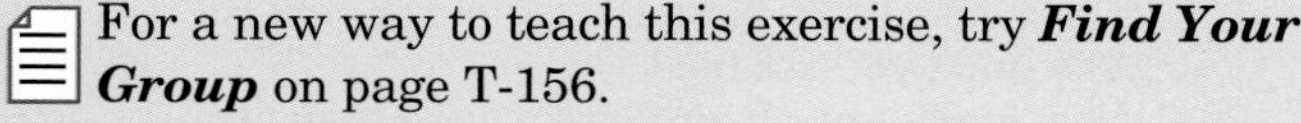
For a new way to teach this exercise, try ***Find Your Group*** on page T-156.

B

- Ss add two more words to each category. Then they compare answers in pairs.
- Ask different Ss to write their new words on the board. Go over their answers and model the pronunciation.

Answers

TV programs	***Movies***	***Music***
game shows	horror films	classical
news	science fiction	jazz
soap operas	thrillers	pop
talk shows	westerns	salsa
cartoons	*adventure*	*reggae*
documentaries	*comedies*	*opera*
sports events	*musicals*	*heavy metal*
reality shows	*drama*	*hip-hop*

(Note: Additional examples are italicized.)

- ***Option:*** To help Ss remember the words in the categories, add names of popular TV programs, movies, and songs or musicians.

C *Group work*

- Explain the task. Ss work individually to rank their items from 1 to 6.
- ***Option:*** Review language for preferences from Unit 3.
- Ss compare their ideas in small groups.

3 CONVERSATION

***Learning objectives:** practice a conversation about likes and dislikes; see yes/no and Wh-questions with* do *in context*

A [CD 1, Track 24]

- Set the scene. Tom and Liz are talking about music. Ask: "Who do you see in the pictures?" (Answers: Eminem, Celine Dion)
- Books closed. Write these statements on the board:
  1. I'm a big fan of Eminem.
  2. I don't know much about rap.
  3. I really like pop music.
  4. I don't like pop music very much.
- Ask: "Who says these things – Liz or Tom?" Play the audio program and Ss listen for the answers. Then elicit the answers. (Answers: 1. Tom 2. Liz 3. Liz 4. Tom)
- Point out the expressions *I'm a big fan of . . . , I really like . . .* , and *I don't like . . . very much.* Ask: "What do you think of Eminem? Celine Dion?"
- Books open. Play the audio program again. Ss listen and read silently.
- Ask these comprehension questions: "Who is Liz's favorite singer? What does Liz think of Eminem?" Elicit Ss' answers. (Answers: Celine Dion. She doesn't know him.)
- Ss practice the conversation in pairs. Go around the class and give help as needed.

For a new way to practice this Conversation, try ***Say It With Feeling!*** on page T-150.

B

- Read the focus questions aloud. Play the audio program once or twice.
- Ss compare answers in small groups. Go over answers with the class.

Audio script

TOM: What about groups, Liz? Who do you like?
LIZ: Oh, I like a lot of different groups. I guess my favorite group is the Beatles.
TOM: The Beatles? You must be kidding!
LIZ: Why? Don't you like them?
TOM: No, I don't. I guess they have some good songs, but I think their music isn't very interesting anymore.

Answers

Her favorite group is the Beatles. No, because he thinks their music isn't very interesting anymore.

GRAMMAR FOCUS

***Learning objective:** practice yes/no and Wh-questions with* do

[CD 1, Track 25]

***Yes/No and Wh-questions with* do**

- Ask Ss to find four questions with *do* or *does* in the Conversation in Exercise 3. Write the questions on the board, in columns:

1	*2*	*3*	*4*	*5*
	Do	*you*	*like*	*rap, Liz?*
	Does	*he*	*play*	*the piano?*
What kind of . . .	*do*	*you*	*like?*	
	Do	*you*	*like*	*her?*

- Focus Ss' attention on the questions on the board. Elicit the rule for forming questions with *do*: Wh-question + *do/does* + subject + verb?
- Elicit new questions from Ss and write them in the columns on the board.
- Point out the language in the Grammar Focus box. Play the audio program for the first and second columns.

Object pronouns

- Go over the object pronouns in the Grammar Focus box. Play the audio program for the third column.
- Ask Ss to find and circle examples of object pronouns in the Conversation in Exercise 3. (Answers: it, him, her) Ask: "What does . . . refer to?" (Answers: it = rap, him = Eminem, her = Celine Dion)

- Explain the task. Model the first answer.
- Ss complete the task individually. Then Ss compare answers with a partner. Go over the answers with the class.

Answers

1. A: **Do** you like science fiction movies?
   B: No, I **don't**. I don't like **them** very much.
2. A: **Do** Jake and Lisa like soap operas?
   B: I think Jake **does**, but I don't know about Lisa. Why don't you ask **her**?
3. A: What **kind** of music **do** Noriko and Ethan like?
   B: They love classical music. Noriko really likes Yo-Yo Ma.
   A: **What does** he play?
   B: The cello. I have his new CD. Let's listen to **it**.

- Ss practice the conversations in pairs.

For a new way to practice yes/no and Wh-questions with *do*, try ***Question Exchange*** on page T-152.

3 CONVERSATION *I really like pop music.*

A Listen and practice.

Tom: Do you like rap, Liz?
Liz: No, I don't like it very much. Do you?
Tom: Yeah, I do. I'm a big fan of Eminem.
Liz: I think I know him. Does he play the piano?
Tom: The piano? No, he doesn't. He's a singer!
Liz: Oh, I guess I don't know much about rap.
Tom: So, what kind of music do you like?
Liz: I really like pop music.
Tom: Who's your favorite singer?
Liz: Celine Dion. I love her voice. Do you like her?
Tom: No, I don't. I don't like pop music very much.

B Listen to the rest of the conversation. Who is Liz's favorite group? Does Tom like that group? Why or why not?

4 GRAMMAR FOCUS

Yes/No and Wh-questions with do

Do you **like** rap?
Yes, I **do**. I like it a lot.
No, I **don't** like it very much.

Does he **play** the piano?
Yes, he **does**.
No, he **doesn't**.

Do they **like** the Beatles?
Yes, they **do**. They love them.
No, they **don't** like them very much.

What kind of music **do** you **like**?
I like rock a lot.

What does he **play**?
He plays the guitar.

Who do they **like**?
They like U2.

Object pronouns
me
you
him
her
it
us
them

Complete these conversations. Then practice with a partner.

1. A: .... you like science fiction movies?
   B: No, I .... I don't like .... very much.
2. A: .... Jake and Lisa like soap operas?
   B: I think Jake .... , but I don't know about Lisa. Why don't you ask .... ?
3. A: What .... of music .... Noriko and Ethan like?
   B: They love classical music. Noriko really likes Yo-Yo Ma.
   A: .... he play?
   B: The cello. I have his new CD. Let's listen to ....

5 PRONUNCIATION *Intonation in questions*

A Listen and practice. Yes/No questions usually have rising intonation. Wh-questions usually have falling intonation.

Do you like pop music? ↗ What kind of music do you like? ↘

B *Pair work* Practice these questions.

Do you like TV?	What programs do you like?
Do you like music videos?	What videos do you like?
Do you play a musical instrument?	What musical instrument do you play?

6 SPEAKING *Entertainment survey*

A *Group work* Write five questions about entertainment and entertainers. Then ask and answer your questions in groups.

Do you like . . . ?
(pop music, TV, movies, plays)
What kinds of . . . do you like?
(music, movies, TV programs)
What do you think of . . . ?
(*The Simpsons*, horror films, gospel music)

B *Group work* Complete this information about your group.

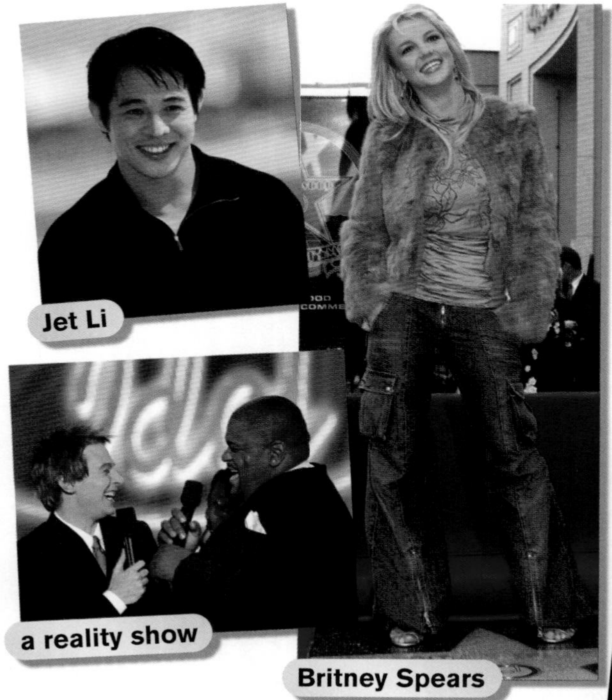
Jet Li
a reality show
Britney Spears

Our Group Favorites

What's your favorite kind of . . . ?

music ....

movie ....

TV program ....

Who's your favorite . . . ?

singer ....

actor ....

actress ....

a horror film
gospel music

C *Class activity* Read your group's list to the class. Then find out the class favorites.

5 PRONUNCIATION

Learning objectives: *notice and use intonation in questions; learn to sound natural when asking questions*

A [CD 1, Track 26]

- Books closed. Use your voice and gestures to demonstrate intonation. Explain that intonation is the rise and fall of the voice.
- Play the audio program. After each question, ask: "Is the voice going up or down?"
- Elicit or explain the rule. Yes/no questions have rising intonation, and Wh-questions have falling intonation.
- Books open. Play the audio program again. Ss repeat the questions. Ask different Ss to read the questions and check their intonation.

> **TIP** If Ss repeat things as a group, it's hard to hear if they are using correct pronunciation or intonation. Therefore, check some individual Ss' pronunciation.

B *Pair work*

- Explain the task. Model the questions using correct intonation.
- Ss work in pairs. Go around the class and check individual Ss' use of intonation.
- ***Option:*** Ss look back at the Conversation on page 23 and mark (with arrows) rising or falling intonation above the questions. Ss then practice the conversation again in pairs, paying special attention to intonation.

SPEAKING

Learning objectives: *talk about entertainment; discuss likes and dislikes*

A *Group work*

- Write two example questions on the board, e.g.:
  Do you like TV?
  What kind of TV programs do you like?
- Ask different Ss to answer the questions.
- Explain the task. Ss work individually to write five questions. Go around the class and give help as needed.
- Ss take turns asking their questions in small groups. Set a time limit of five to seven minutes.
- Go around the class and listen to Ss' responses.
- ***Option:*** Encourage Ss to give longer responses (e.g., *No, I don't, but I love . . . , I'm a big fan of . . . , I prefer . . .*).

B *Group work*

- Ss work in small groups. One S leads the discussion to make sure everybody speaks (e.g., *What's your favorite . . . ? What about you, . . . ? What do you think, . . . ? It's your turn to ask a question.*). Another S records the answers.
- The S who recorded the answers reads the responses, and the group decides the favorites. Then the Ss complete their charts.

> **TIP** Assigning each S in the group a role (e.g., *note-taker, leader, English monitor, reporter*) encourages all Ss to participate.

C *Class activity*

- Write these expressions on the board:
  Our favorite . . . is . . .
  We all like . . .
  We don't agree on . . .
- Explain that Ss can use these expressions to report their group's favorites.
- One S from each group reports the results to the class. Another S from each group writes the results on the board.
- Discuss the favorites as a class.

For more practice with yes/no questions, play ***Twenty Questions*** on page T-145.

7 LISTENING

***Learning objective:** develop skills in listening for detail*

A [CD 1, Track 27]

- Set the scene. Linda is on a game show. The hostess is going to interview three men. Linda will choose one for a date.
- Play the audio program. Pause after every few lines to give Ss time to complete the chart.

> **TIP** If an audio program is long and contains many details, break it into parts. Pause the audio program after each part.

- Ss compare answers in pairs.

Audio script

Hostess: [*applause*] Welcome to *Who's My Date?* Today, Linda is going to meet Bill, John, and Tony. So, let's start with the first question . . . on music. Bill, what kind of music do you like?
Bill: Oh, classical music.
Hostess: Classical. OK. And how about you, John?
John: Well, I like jazz.
Hostess: And you, Tony?
Tony: My favorite music is rock.
Hostess: How about you, Linda?
Linda: Well, I like pop music. I don't like jazz or classical music very much. [*applause*]
Hostess: OK. Now let's talk about movies. Bill, what kind of movies do you like?
Bill: I like thrillers.
Hostess: And how about you, John?
John: Oh, I like westerns.
Hostess: Westerns are good. And how about you, Tony?
Tony: I love horror films.
Hostess: And what about you, Linda?
Linda: I really like horror films, too. [*applause*]
Hostess: And now for question number three. Bill, what kind of TV programs do you like?
Bill: Well, I like to watch news programs.
Hostess: John?
John: Uh, well, you know, I really like talk shows.
Hostess: And Tony, how about you?
Tony: I like game shows a lot.
Hostess: And Linda, what do you like?
Linda: Well, I like talk shows *and* game shows.
Hostess: [*buzzer*] OK! Time is up! Now who's the best date for Linda? [*applause*]

Answers

	Music	*Movies*	*TV programs*
Bill	classical	thrillers	news programs
John	jazz	westerns	talk shows
Tony	rock	horror films	game shows
Linda	pop	horror films	talk shows and game shows

B *Class activity*

- Ss discuss the best date for Linda as a class.

Possible answer

Tony is the best date because he and Linda like horror films and game shows. They all disagree about music.

End of Cycle 1

Do your students need more practice?

Assign . . .	*for more practice in . . .*
Workbook Exercises 1–8 on pages 19–22	Grammar, Vocabulary, Reading, and Writing
Lab Guide Exercises 1–7 on page 7	Listening, Pronunciation, Speaking, and Grammar

Cycle 2, Exercises 8–12

8 CONVERSATION

***Learning objectives:** practice making plans; see* would *and verb +* to *+ verb in context*

A [CD 1, Track 28]

- Ask: "What do you see in the picture?" Then play the audio program. Ss look at the pictures and read the conversation silently.
- Ss practice the conversation in pairs.

B

- Read the focus question aloud. Then play the audio program. Elicit answers from the class.

Audio script

Dave: [*crowd cheering*] Yes! That's *another* goal for the Ducks! That's the Ducks 3, the Frogs 0.
Susan: You really are a Ducks fan, Dave.
Dave: I know. They're my favorite team.
Susan: They're OK, but I like the Frogs a lot better, especially Mario Sanchez.
Dave: He *is* very talented. It's too bad he's not playing today.

Answers

Dave likes the Ducks. Susan likes the Frogs.

7 LISTENING *Who's my date?*

A Listen to four people on a TV game show. Three men want to invite Linda on a date. What kinds of things do they like? What kinds of things does Linda like?

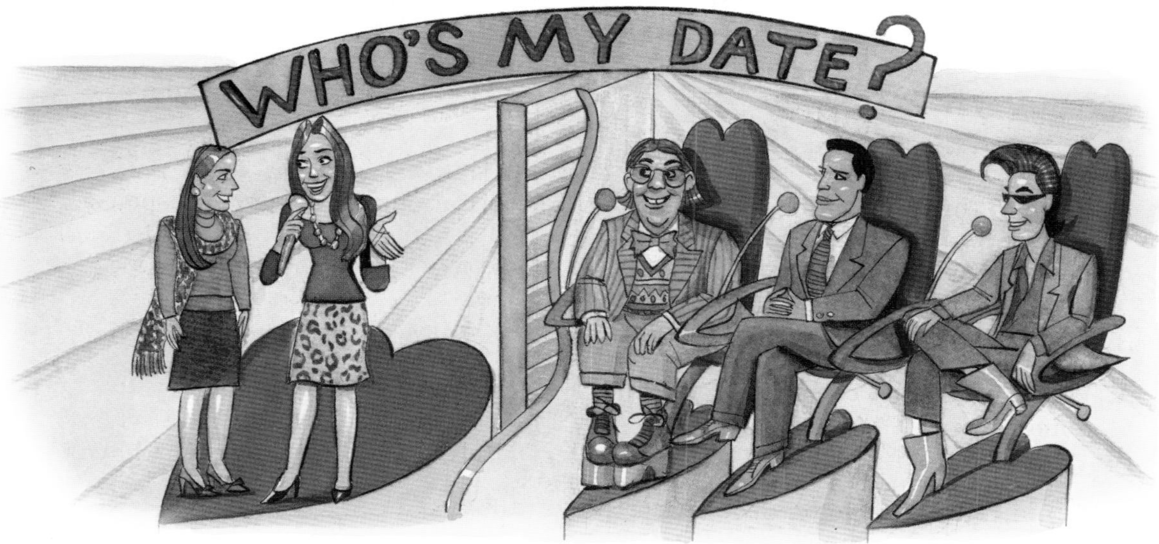

	Music	Movies	TV programs
Bill	*classical*		
John			
Tony			
Linda			

B *Class activity* Who do you think is the best date for Linda? Why?

8 CONVERSATION *An invitation*

A Listen and practice.

Dave: I have tickets to the soccer match on Friday night. Would you like to go?
Susan: Thanks. I'd love to. What time does it start?
Dave: At 8:00.
Susan: That sounds great. So, do you want to have dinner at 6:00?
Dave: Uh, I'd like to, but I have to work late.
Susan: Oh, that's OK. Let's just meet at the stadium before the match, around 7:30.
Dave: OK. Let's meet at the gate.
Susan: That sounds fine. See you there.

B Listen to Dave and Susan at the soccer match. Which team does each person like?

9 GRAMMAR FOCUS

Would; verb + to + verb

Would you **like to go** out on Friday?
Yes, I **would**.
Yes, I'**d love to**. Thanks.
Yes, I'**d** really **like to go**.

Would you **like to go** to a soccer match?
I'**d like to**, but I **have to work** late.
I'**d like to**, but I **need to save** money.
I'**d like to**, but I **want to visit** my parents.

Contraction
I'**d** = I would

A Respond to three invitations. Then write three invitations for the given responses.

1. A: I have tickets to the baseball game on Saturday. Would you like to go?
   B: ....
2. A: Would you like to come over for dinner tomorrow night?
   B: ....
3. A: Would you like to go to a pop concert with me this weekend?
   B: ....
4. A: ....
   ....
   B: Yes, I'd love to. Thank you!
5. A: ....
   ....
   B: Well, I'd like to, but I have to study.
6. A: ....
   ....
   B: Yes, thank you. I'd really like to see it.

B *Pair work* Ask and answer the questions in part A. Give your own responses.

C *Pair work* Think of three things you would like to do. Then invite a partner to do them with you. Your partner asks follow-up questions like these:

When is it?	What time does it start?	When does it end?
Where is it?	Where should we meet?	How should we get there?

10 WRITING A text message

A Text messages are electronic notes. People send them on cell phones. What does this message say?

LIKE 2 C A MOVIE 2NITE?

text message abbreviations

M	= am		L8	= late	
U	= you		W8	= wait	
R	= are		GR8	= great	
C	= see		THX	= thanks	
4	= for		LUV	= love	
2	= to		NITE	= night	

B *Group work* Write a text message to each person in your group. Then exchange messages. Write a response to each message.

11 INTERCHANGE 4 What's the question?

Practice writing and asking questions. Go to Interchange 4.

9 GRAMMAR FOCUS

***Learning objective:** practice* would *and verb +* to *+ verb*

[CD 1, Track 29]

Would

- Refer Ss to the Conversation on page 25. Ask: "How does Dave invite Susan?" Write his question on the board:
  Would you like to go?
- Explain that we use *Would you like to . . . ?* for polite invitations. It is more polite than *Do you want to . . . ?*
- Ask Ss to find Susan's response. Ask: "What does she say?" Write it on the board:
  Thanks. I'd love to.
- Point out that *I'd = I would*. Explain that there are different ways to accept an invitation. Susan uses one. Add two more to the board:
  Yes, I would.
  Yes, I'd really like to (go).
- Play the audio program for the first column in the Grammar Focus box. Ss read silently.

Verb* + to + *verb

- Refer Ss again to the Conversation on page 25. Susan invites Dave to have dinner at 6:00, but he doesn't accept. Ask: "What were his words?" Write them on the board:
  Uh, I'd like to, but I have to work late.
- Explain that we often use the structure *verb* + to + *verb* when making excuses. Focus Ss' attention on the Grammar Focus box. Elicit examples.
- Play the audio program for the second and third columns.

A

- Explain the task. Questions 1–3 require an acceptance or a refusal. Questions 4–6 require an invitation.
- Ss work individually. Go around the class and check their answers. If you notice common problems, stop and go over them with the class.

B *Pair work*

- Explain the task. Ss work in pairs. They take turns asking and answering the questions.

C *Pair work*

- Explain the task. With Ss, brainstorm three things to do. Model inviting a S to do one of those things. Your S partner uses some of the follow-up questions.
- Have Ss first think of three real or imaginary things they would like to do. Then they practice inviting each other. Remind Ss to use *Would you like to . . . ?* and to include follow-up questions.

10 WRITING

***Learning objective:** write and respond to text messages*

A

- Point out that Ss practiced oral invitations. Now they will make text message invitations.

> **TIP** To help Ss see the purpose of what they're learning, always try to link one activity to the next.

- Focus Ss' attention on the text message. Ask Ss to guess its meaning. (Answer: Would you like to see a movie tonight?)
- Discuss abbreviations. Explain that people use the abbreviations because there is very little space on cell phone screens. Elicit the words the text message abbreviations stand for. (Answers: 2 = to, C = see, 2NITE = tonight).
- Ask the class: "Do you ever write text messages? Who do you write to? What do you write about?"

B *Group work*

- Ss work in groups of three. Ss work individually to write a message to the other two Ss in their group.
- Ss exchange messages with the other Ss in the group. They read each message and write a response (e.g., *SOUNDS GR8!*). Then they return the responses. (Note: If Ss can't think of an invitation, encourage them to look at the Grammar Focus or Conversation on page 25 for ideas.)
- ***Option:*** In Ss' responses, they write questions asking for more information. They continue to exchange and return responses, answering questions and asking for more information until they accept or refuse the invitations.
- ***Option:*** If Ss have cell phones, they can practice sending text messages in class or for homework.

11 INTERCHANGE 4

See page T-118 for teaching notes.

12 READING

Learning objectives: *read and discuss an article about a singer; develop skills in scanning a time line*

- Books closed. Draw these diagrams on the board:

CHRISTINA AGUILERA

We know  We'd like to know 

- Ss brainstorm ideas in pairs. If they have difficulty, suggest possible topics (e.g., hit songs, age, nationality). Then Ss come to the board and write things they know or would like to know in the correct diagram. Don't correct Ss if they are wrong. Just correct their language.
- Books open. Point out that the time line shows the history of Christina Aguilera's life.
- Focus Ss' attention on the pictures. Ask different Ss to read the captions aloud.
- Allow Ss two minutes to scan the article quickly and find the dates for the pictures. (Answers: 2002, 1999, 1992) Remind Ss not to read the whole article, but to look quickly for key words (e.g., *Olympics*, *Genie*, *Mickey Mouse*).

For a new way to introduce this Reading, try ***Cloud Prediction*** on page T-154.

A

- Explain the task. Focus Ss' attention on the first event on the time line. Tell Ss to find the sentence in part A that matches this event. (Answer: b)
- Elicit or explain any new vocabulary.

Vocabulary

hit: a very popular song
single: one song
fans: people who love a celebrity
highlights: important events
album: a collection of songs on a CD or cassette
performs: sings or acts
thrilled: very happy and excited
roller-coaster ride: a very exciting time of life, usually with both happy and sad times

- Ss complete the task individually. Go around the class and give help as needed.
- Ss compare answers in pairs. Then go over answers with the class.

Answers

a. 7 e. 4
b. 1 f. 3
c. 8 g. 2
d. 5 h. 6

TIP If your Ss speak languages that have similar vocabulary to English, encourage them to look for cognates, or words with similar forms and meanings (e.g., *generation, success*).

- Focus Ss' attention on the diagrams on the board. Ask: "What did you learn? What do you still want to know? Where can you find this information?"
- ***Option***: Books closed. Ask: "How much can you remember about Christina Aguilera?" Ss work in pairs to list facts.

B *Pair work*

- Read the questions aloud. Ss discuss their favorite musicians in pairs. Then ask Ss to share information with the class.

To review vocabulary from this Reading, play ***Picture It!*** on page T-147.

End of Cycle 2

Do your students need more practice?

Assign . . .	*for more practice in . . .*
Workbook Exercises 9–12 on pages 23–24	Grammar, Vocabulary, Reading, and Writing
Lab Guide Exercises 8–10 on page 8	Listening, Pronunciation, Speaking, and Grammar
Video Activity Book Unit 4	Listening, Speaking, and Cultural Awareness
CD-ROM Unit 4	Grammar, Vocabulary, Reading, Listening, and Speaking

Evaluation

Assess Ss' understanding of Units 3 and 4 with the quiz on pages T-202 and T-203.

12 READING

Christina Aguilera

Scan the article and look at the pictures. In what year did each event take place?

So far, she has multiple hit singles. She has fans of all ages around the world. And many people say she is the best singer of her generation. She is . . . ***Christina Aguilera***.

Here are some highlights of Christina's life and career.

Christina at the Olympics

TIME LINE

- **1980** Christina is born on December 18 in New York.
- **1988** Christina first appears on television in *Star Search* – a television talent show.
- **1992** Christina is on TV in Disney's *New Mickey Mouse Club*, with Britney Spears and Justin Timberlake.
- **1994** Christina records "All I Wanna Do" with Keizo Nakanishi, a Japanese pop star. She tours Japan.
- **1998** Christina sings a song for the Disney movie *Mulan*.
- **1999** Christina has her first big hit – "Genie in a Bottle."
- **2001** Along with other singers, Christina records "Lady Marmalade" for the movie *Moulin Rouge*.
- **2002** Christina performs at the closing ceremonies for the Winter Olympic Games in Salt Lake City, Utah.
- **2004** Christina wins the best female pop vocal Grammy award for "Beautiful."

Christina's first hit – "Genie in a Bottle"

Overall, Christina Aguilera is thrilled by her success. "It's been quite a roller-coaster ride," she laughs. "I simply love [my] job."

So do all Christina's fans.

Christina (second from right) on the *New Mickey Mouse Club*

A Read the article. Then number these sentences from 1 (first event) to 8 (last event).

..... a. She sings at the Winter Olympic Games.
..... b. She is born in New York.
..... c. She wins a Grammy for "Beautiful."
..... d. She records a song for a Disney movie.
..... e. She travels around Japan.
..... f. She works with Britney Spears.
..... g. She is on television for the first time.
..... h. She has her first very successful song.

B ***Pair work*** Who is your favorite musician? What do you know about his or her life?

Units 3–4 Progress check

SELF-ASSESSMENT

How well can you do these things? Check (✓) the boxes.

I can	Very well	OK	A little
Listen to and understand prices and questions with *how much* (Ex. 1)	☐	☐	☐
Ask and answer questions about prices (Ex. 1)	☐	☐	☐
Give opinions using adjectives (Ex. 1, 2)	☐	☐	☐
Talk about preferences and make comparisons with adjectives (Ex. 2)	☐	☐	☐
Ask and answer questions about entertainment using the simple present (Ex. 3)	☐	☐	☐
Make invitations and excuses with *would like to* + verb (Ex. 4)	☐	☐	☐

1 LISTENING Weekend sale

A Listen to a commercial for Dave's Discount Store. Circle the correct prices.

Dave's Discount Store
leather pants
$19 $90
wool pants
$15 $50
silk shirt
$14 $40
cotton shirt
$18 $80
laptop computer
$2,015 $2,050
desktop computer
$1,013 $1,030

B *Pair work* Compare answers. Give your own opinions.

2 ROLE PLAY Shopping trip

Student A: Choose things from Exercise 1 for your family. Ask for Student B's opinion.

Student B: Help Student A choose presents for his or her family.

A: I want to buy a computer for my parents. Which one do you like better?
B: Well. I like the laptop better. It's nicer, and . . .

Change roles and try the role play again.

Units 3–4 Progress check

SELF-ASSESSMENT

***Learning objectives:** reflect on one's learning; identify areas that need improvement*

- Ask: "What did you learn in Units 3 and 4?" Elicit Ss' answers.
- Ss complete the Self-assessment. Encourage them to be honest, and point out they will not get a bad grade if they check (✓) "a little."
- Ss move on to the Progress check exercises. You can have Ss complete them in class or for homework, using one of these techniques:
  1. Ask Ss to complete all the exercises.
  2. Ask Ss: "What do you need to practice?" Then assign exercises based on their answers.
  3. Ask Ss to choose and complete exercises based on their Self-assessment.

1 LISTENING

***Learning objectives:** assess one's ability to listen to and understand prices and questions with* how much; *assess one's ability to ask and answer questions about prices; assess one's ability to give opinions using adjectives*

A [CD 1, Track 30]

- Set the scene. Dave's Discount Store is having a sale today. Ss will hear the prices of six items.
- Play the audio program once or twice. Ss listen and circle the correct price of each item.

Audio script

ANNOUNCER: Come in to Dave's today! Everything is on sale – for one day only. Here are some of our terrific sale prices. First, in the clothing departments, we have great sales on both men's and women's pants. We have leather pants for only $90. That's right! All our stylish leather pants are only $90. And wool pants are on sale for $50. Just $50 for wool pants. Amazing!

But that's not all. Every style and color of shirt is on sale. Designer silk shirts are now only $40. Again, that's $40 for a silk shirt. And cotton shirts are on sale for just $18. Unbelievable!

Finally, in the electronics department, we have a great selection of computers. We have laptop computers for only $2,015. And we have desktop computers for $1,030. A complete computer system for only $1,030. What a deal!

Remember, these prices are for today only, so come in and save at our one-day sale. Get everything you need . . . at Dave's!

B Pair work

- Explain the task. Ss compare prices and give their own opinions about them in pairs. Are the things expensive, reasonable, or cheap?

Answers

leather pants: $90	wool pants: $50
silk shirts: $40	cotton shirts: $18
laptop computers: $2,015	desktop computers: $1,030

2 ROLE PLAY

***Learning objectives:** assess one's ability to give opinions using adjectives; assess one's ability to talk about preferences and make comparisons using adjectives*

- Focus Ss' attention on the pictures in Exercise 1 and explain the task. Students work in pairs. Student A wants to buy presents for his or her family at Dave's Discount Store. Student B is helping Student A choose presents.
- Model the example conversation with a S. Elicit other expressions and comparisons to use in the role plays.
- Ss practice the role play in pairs. Then they change roles. Go around the class and give help as needed.
- ***Option:*** Have Ss give the items different prices, and try the role play again.

3 SURVEY

Learning objective: *assess one's ability to ask and answer questions about entertainment using the simple present*

A

- Ss work individually. They write answers to the questions in the *Me* column.

B *Class activity*

- Explain and model the task. Say: "I usually watch TV at (7:00). When do you usually watch TV?" Ask different Ss until someone gives the same answer.
- Explain that you will write that person's name in the *My classmate* column. Point out that Ss should write a classmate's name only once.
- Ss go around the class and ask questions to complete the activity. Note any grammar, vocabulary, or pronunciation errors.
- ***Option:*** Go over any grammar, vocabulary, or pronunciation errors after Ss complete the activity.

SPEAKING

Learning objective: *check one's ability to make invitations and excuses with* would like to *+ verb*

A

- Explain the task. Then ask a S to read the example invitation in the book.
- Elicit suggestions for other interesting activities and write them on the board.
- Hand out three index cards to each S. Explain the task. Ss write three different invitations individually (one per card). Point out that they should not put their names on the cards.
- Ss complete the task. Go around the class and give help as needed.

B

- Ask different Ss to read the three response cards. Elicit other ways of accepting or refusing an invitation. Encourage Ss to suggest silly or unusual excuses for refusals.
- Hand out three index cards to each S. Explain the task. Ss write one acceptance and two refusals. The acceptance cards should include a question about where or when to meet. Point out that they should not put their names on the cards.
- Ss complete the task. Go around the class and give help as needed.

C *Group work*

- Ss work in small groups. One S collects all the invitation cards, shuffles them, and puts them in a pile.
- A different S collects all the response cards, shuffles them, and puts them in a different pile.
- Explain the task. Each S takes three invitation cards and three response cards. Then they read them silently.
- Model the task. Read an invitation card aloud. Ss accept or refuse the invitation by reading a response card.
- Ss take turns completing the task.

WHAT'S NEXT?

Learning objective: *become more involved in one's learning*

- Focus Ss' attention on the Self-assessment again. Ask: "How well can you do these things now?"
- Ask Ss to underline one thing they need to review. Ask: "What did you underline? How can you review it?"
- If needed, plan additional activities or reviews based on Ss' answers.

3 SURVEY Likes and dislikes

A Write answers to these questions about entertainment.

	Me	My classmate
When do you usually watch TV?	....	....
What kinds of programs do you like?	....	....
Do you like reality shows?	....	....
Do you listen to the radio?	....	....
Who is your favorite singer?	....	....
What do you think of salsa?	....	....
What is your favorite movie?	....	....
What kinds of movies do you dislike?	....	....
Do you like science fiction?	....	....

B ***Class activity*** Find someone who has the same answers. Go around the class. Write a classmate's name only once!

4 SPEAKING What an excuse!

A Make up three invitations to interesting activities. Write them on cards.

I want to see the frog races tomorrow. They're at the park at 2:00. Would you like to go?

B Write three response cards. One is an acceptance card and two are refusals. Think of silly or unusual excuses.

That sounds great! What time do you want to meet?

I'd like to, but I have to wash my cat tomorrow.

I'd love to, but I want to take my bird to a singing contest.

C ***Group work*** Shuffle the invitation cards together and the response cards together. Take three cards from each pile. Then invite people to do the things on your invitation cards. Use the response cards to accept or refuse.

WHAT'S NEXT?

Look at your Self-assessment again. Do you need to review anything?

5 Tell me about your family.

1 WORD POWER Family

A Look at Sam's family tree. How are these people related to him? Add these words to the family tree.

cousin
father
grandmother
niece
sister-in-law
uncle
wife

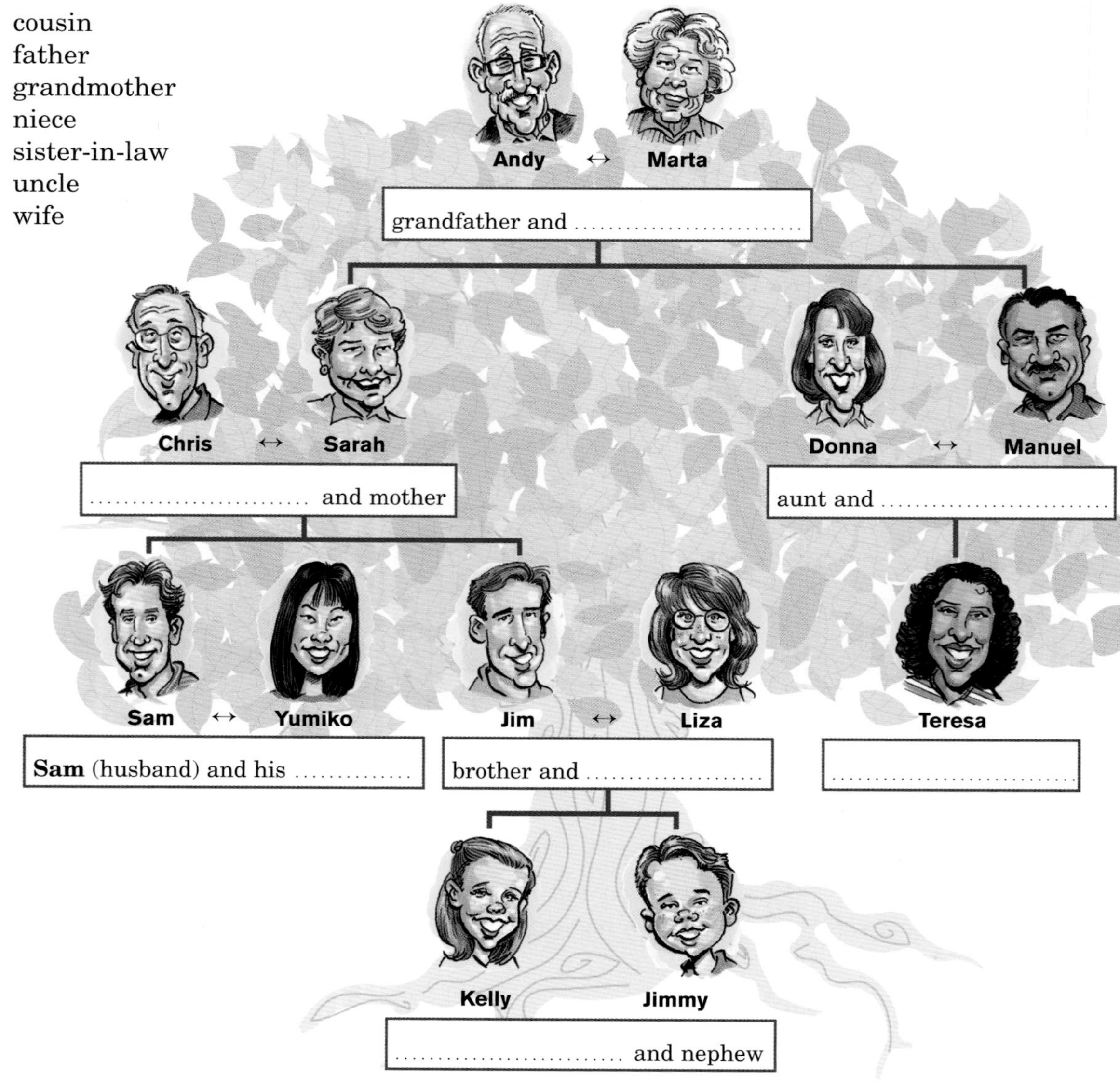

B Draw your family tree (or a friend's family tree). Then take turns talking about your families. Ask follow-up questions to get more information.

For a single person:
There are six people in my family.
I have two brothers and a sister.

For a married person:
There are four people in my family.
We have a son and a daughter.

Tell me about your family.

In Unit 5, students discuss families, typical families, and family life. In Cycle 1, they talk about their own and other families using the present continuous. In Cycle 2, they discuss facts about families using quantifiers.

Cycle 1, Exercises 1–7

WORD POWER

Learning objective: *learn vocabulary for discussing the family*

A

- Write the word *family* in a circle on the board. Then write the words *mother* and *father* around the circle.
- In pairs, Ss brainstorm words for family members and make a list. Then they compare lists with another pair. Go around the class and note the words on their lists.

TIP To avoid teaching words Ss already know, start by asking Ss the words they know. Then teach any remaining vocabulary.

- Ask Ss to find Sam and circle his picture. Then ask: "Who is Yumiko?" (Answer: his wife) Ask Ss to write *wife* under Yumiko's picture and check (✓) *wife* in the vocabulary list.
- Ss complete the exercise in pairs. Go over the answers with the class and check pronunciation.

Answers

grandfather and **grandmother** (Marta)
father (Chris) and mother
aunt and **uncle** (Manuel)
Sam (husband) and his **wife** (Yumiko)
brother and **sister-in-law** (Liza)
cousin (Teresa)
niece (Kelly) and nephew

- As needed, teach other family words (e.g., *great-grandfather*, *great-grandmother*, *grandson*, *granddaughter*, *daughter*, *son*, *stepbrother*, *stepsister*, *only child*, *twins*, *parents*, *ex-wife*, *ex-husband*). Use pictures to present additional vocabulary.
- ***Option:*** For more practice, ask questions about another person in the family tree (e.g., *Donna*). Possible questions include: *Who is Donna's husband? Who is her sister-in-law?*

B

- Explain the task. Ss draw their family trees individually. Point out that single Ss can include their grandparents, parents, brothers, and sisters, while married Ss can include their husband or wife, children, and grandchildren.
- Draw your family tree on the board while Ss complete the task.
- Model the task by describing your own family. Then encourage Ss to ask you questions. If needed, present or review words such as *married*, *single*, *divorced*, *widowed*, or *deceased*.
- Ss complete the task in pairs or small groups. Go around the room and encourage Ss to ask follow-up questions (e.g., *How old is he? What does he do?*).
- Elicit interesting things Ss learned about their partners.
- ***Option***: Ask Ss to bring in pictures of their family. Ss show each other family photos in small groups. Encourage them to add two pieces of information for each photo (e.g., *This is my brother. He's 27, and he's a lawyer.*).

TIP To personalize the class and make the language more meaningful, encourage Ss to bring their own materials to class.

To review the vocabulary of family, try ***Picture Dictation*** on page T-154. Ask Ss to draw a family tree while you say: "Amanda has one brother and one sister. Her brother, Edward, is married to Jean. They have three children. Amanda's sister, Mary, is married to Mike. They have one daughter. Amanda has a husband. His name is Charlie."

For more practice matching words for family members with their meanings, play ***Concentration*** on page T-144.

2 LISTENING

Learning objective: *develop skills in listening for specific information*

[CD 1, Track 32]

- Focus Ss' attention on the pictures. Ask: "How are the people related?" Encourage Ss to make guesses.
- Play the audio program. Ss listen and complete the task. Remind Ss to focus on words for family members.
- Go over answers with the class.

Audio script

1.
Woman: Look at this picture of Michael Douglas. He's my favorite actor.
Man: Yeah, I like his movies. Is that his wife?
Woman: Of course. That's Catherine Zeta-Jones.
Man: Oh, right. She's so beautiful. And a terrific actress.
Woman: They make a nice couple.

2.
Mom: [*music*] Cindy. Cindy!
Cindy: Sorry, Mom. That's my favorite song. Do you know Enrique Iglesias?
Mom: You mean Julio Iglesias? Of course. He's one of my favorite singers.
Cindy: No, no, Enrique Iglesias. Julio is his father.
Mom: Oh, no. I don't think I know him.

3.
Man: What are you reading, Pete?
Pete: I'm reading an article about Francis Ford Coppola. He has a new movie out.
Man: Who?
Pete: Francis Ford Coppola. You know, the director of *The Godfather*. And *The Godfather, Part II*.
Man: Oh, right.
Pete: Do you know who his nephew is? The actor Nicholas Cage.
Man: Really? I didn't know that.

4.
Woman: Look! Here's an article about my favorite movie star, Annette Bening.
Man: I like her, too. She's good in both comedies and dramas. She's married to Warren Beatty, right?
Woman: That's right. In fact, he comes from a talented family. Do you know who Warren Beatty's sister is? Shirley MacLaine!
Man: I don't think I know her.
Woman: Sure you do. She's a movie star, too.

Answers

1. wife 2. father 3. nephew 4. sister-in-law

- Point out that the plural of *sister-in-law* is *sisters-in-law*. Ask Ss for the plural of *brother-in-law*. (Answer: brothers-in-law)

3 CONVERSATION

Learning objectives: *practice a conversation about families; see the present continuous in context*

A [CD 1, Track 33]

- Set the scene. Rita is asking about Sue's family. Focus Ss' attention on the pictures. Ask: "How do you think they are related to Sue?" Elicit ideas.
- Books closed. Explain the task. One S listens for information about the woman and one listens for information about the man. Play the audio program and Ss complete the task.
- Books open. Play the audio program again. Ss listen and read silently.
- Ss practice the conversation in pairs.

B

- Read the two focus questions aloud. Play the audio program once or twice.
- Go over answers with the class.

Audio script

Sue: So, what about your parents, Rita? Where do they live?
Rita: They live in Texas.
Sue: Oh, where in Texas?
Rita: In Austin. It's a small city, but it's very nice.
Sue: Are they still working?
Rita: Oh, yes. My mother is teaching at the university there, and my father is a carpenter.

Answers

They live in Austin, Texas. Her mother teaches at the university, and her father is a carpenter.

4 PRONUNCIATION

Learning objectives: *notice and use intonation in statements; learn to sound natural when making statements*

A [CD 1, Track 34]

- Play the audio program. Point out the falling intonation. Ss repeat the statements. Ask different Ss to say the statements to check their intonation.

B *Pair work*

- Explain the task. Ss work in pairs. Go around the class and check Ss' intonation.

2 LISTENING How are they related?

Listen to four conversations about famous people. How are the people related?

1\. Michael Douglas → Catherine Zeta-Jones ....

2\. Enrique Iglesias → Julio Iglesias ....

3\. Francis Ford Coppola → Nicholas Cage ....

4\. Annette Bening → Shirley MacLaine ....

CONVERSATION Asking about families

A Listen and practice.

Rita: Tell me about your brother and sister, Sue.
Sue: Well, my sister works for the government.
Rita: Oh, what does she do?
Sue: I'm not sure. She's working on a very secret project right now.
Rita: Wow! And what about your brother?
Sue: He's a wildlife photographer.
Rita: What an interesting family! Can I meet them?
Sue: Uh, no. My sister's away. She's not working in the United States this month.
Rita: And your brother?
Sue: He's traveling in the Amazon.

B Listen to the rest of the conversation. Where do Rita's parents live? What do they do?

PRONUNCIATION Intonation in statements

A Listen and practice. Notice that statements usually have falling intonation.

I'm working in Singapore. She's waiting at the bus stop. They're living at home.

B *Pair work* Practice the conversation in Exercise 3 again. Pay attention to the intonation in the statements.

5 GRAMMAR FOCUS

Present continuous

Are you **living** at home now?	Yes, I **am**.	No, **I'm not**.
Is your sister **working** for the government?	Yes, she **is**.	No, she**'s not**. / No, she **isn't**.
Are Ed and Jill **going** to college this year?	Yes, they **are**.	No, they**'re not**. / No, they **aren't**.

Where **are** you **working** now? — **I'm not working**. I need a job.
What **is** your brother **doing** these days? — He**'s traveling** in the Amazon.
Who **are** your parents **visiting** this week? — They**'re visiting** my grandmother.

A Complete these phone conversations using the present continuous.

1

A: Hi, Stephanie. What .... you .... (do)?
B: Hey, Mark. I .... (stand) in an elevator, and it's stuck!
A: Oh, no! Are you OK?
B: Yeah. I – wait! It .... (move) now. Thank goodness!

2

A: Marci, how .... you and Justin .... (enjoy) your shopping trip?
B: We .... (have) a lot of fun.
A: .... your brother .... (spend) a lot of money?
B: No, Mom. He .... (buy) only one or two things. That's all!

B *Pair work* Practice the phone conversations with a partner.

6 DISCUSSION *Is anyone . . . ?*

Group work Ask your classmates about people in their family. What are they doing now? Ask follow-up questions to get more information.

A: Is anyone in your family traveling right now?
B: Yes, my dad is. He's in Korea.
C: What's he doing there?

topics to ask about	
traveling	going to high school or college
living abroad	moving to a new home
taking a class	studying a foreign language

5 GRAMMAR FOCUS

Learning objectives: *practice the present continuous; ask and answer questions using the present continuous*

[CD 1, Track 35]

Simple present vs. present continuous

- Draw this chart on the board:

	Usually	*Right now*
Sue's sister		
Sue's brother		

- Focus Ss' attention on the Conversation on page 31. Ask: "What does Sue's sister do? What is she doing right now?" (Answers: She works for the government. She's working on a secret project.) Complete the chart. Repeat the procedure for Sue's brother.
- Elicit or explain the difference between the two tenses (simple present = habitual actions; present continuous = actions that are happening right now).
- Compare the formation of the two tenses:
  She works. (subject + verb)
  She is working. (subject + *be* + verb + *-ing*)

Present continuous questions and statements

- Focus Ss' attention on the Conversation on page 31. Ask: "Why can't Rita meet Sue's family?" Elicit the answers, and write them on the board:
  Sue's sister is not working in the U.S. this month.
  Sue's brother is traveling in the Amazon right now.
- Focus Ss' attention on the Grammar Focus box. Elicit the rule for forming yes/no and Wh-questions in the present continuous:
  Be + subject + verb + *-ing*?
  (Wh-question) + *be* + subject + verb + *-ing*?
- Ask Ss to underline the time expressions in the Grammar Focus box that show the action is temporary or current: *now*, *this year*, *these days*, *this week*. Add *right now* and *this month*.
- Play the audio program.

A

- Explain the task and model the first question.
- Ss complete the task individually. Encourage Ss to use contractions in statements. Review contractions as needed.
- Ss go over their answers in pairs. Then go over answers with the class.

Answers

1. A: Hi, Stephanie. What **are** you **doing**?
   B: Hey, Mark. I**'m standing** in an elevator, and it's stuck!
   A: Oh, no! Are you OK?
   B: Yeah. I – wait! It**'s moving** now. Thank goodness!
2. A: Marci, how **are** you and Justin **enjoying** your shopping trip?
   B: We**'re having** a lot of fun.
   A: **Is** your brother **spending** a lot of money?
   B: No, Mom. He**'s buying** only one or two things. That's all!

B *Pair work*

- Ss practice the phone conversations.
- ***Option:*** Ss practice the conversations sitting back-to-back or with their cell phones.

For more practice contrasting the simple present with the present continuous, try ***Every Day and Today*** on page T-157.

6 DISCUSSION

Learning objectives: *discuss families using the present continuous; develop the skill of asking follow-up questions*

Group work

- Explain the task and go over the topics in the box. Explain any new vocabulary and elicit other possible discussion topics.
- Model the conversation with one or two Ss. Encourage Ss to add follow-up questions and introduce new topics.
- Give Ss a few minutes to prepare things to say about their families.
- Ss complete the task in small groups. Go around the class and note any common errors. Then go over them with the class.

TIP To help you decide if additional controlled grammar practice is necessary, watch the Ss' performance during the speaking activities.

7 INTERCHANGE 5

See page T-119 for teaching notes.

End of Cycle 1

Do your students need more practice?

Assign . . .	*for more practice in . . .*
Workbook Exercises 1–6 on pages 25–27	Grammar, Vocabulary, Reading, and Writing
Lab Guide Exercises 1–8 on pages 9–10	Listening, Pronunciation, Speaking, and Grammar

Cycle 2, Exercises 8–12

8 SNAPSHOT

Learning objective: *compare and discuss statistics about families in different countries*

- Books closed. Write these questions on the board:
  1. What percentage of homes in the U.S. have three or more televisions?
  a. 41% b. 61% c. 81%
  2. What percentage of families in the U.S. almost always eat dinner together?
  a. 23% b. 43% c. 63%
- Review percentages if needed. Ask Ss to guess the answers to these questions. Then elicit their guesses.
- Books open. Ss read the Snapshot to find the answers. (Answers: 1. a 2. c) Ask: "Who was right? Do these two facts seem positive or negative? Why?"
- Go over the facts about the U.S. Ss then discuss if each fact is positive or negative in small groups.
- Ss write guesses about their own countries in the second column. Then they share and discuss their guesses as a class.

9 CONVERSATION

Learning objectives: *practice a conversation about family size; see quantifiers in context*

A [CD 1, Track 36]

- Ask the class: "How many brothers do you have? How many sisters?" Elicit answers.
- Draw this chart on the board:

	Where from?	*Number of brothers/sisters?*	*Typical?*
1. Mei-li			
2. Marcos			

- Books closed. Set the scene. Marcos and Mei-li are talking about their families.
- Play the audio program. Ss listen for the answers. Ask Ss to complete the chart on the board if they know the answers. Play the audio program again as needed and ask Ss to add to or change the information in the chart. (Answers: 1. China, no brothers or sisters, yes 2. Peru, three brothers and two sisters, no)
- Books open. Play the audio program again. Ss look at the picture and read the conversation silently.
- Ss practice the conversation in pairs.

For a new way to practice this Conversation, try the ***Disappearing Dialog*** on page T-151.

B

- Ask: "Why does Marcos like having a big family?" (Answer: Because he gets lots of birthday presents.)
- Read the focus question aloud. Ask Ss to make predictions and write them on the board.
- Play the audio program. Ss listen to find out if any prediction on the board is correct.

Audio script

MARCOS: So do you like being an only child?
MEI-LI: Of course. I get all my parents' attention. [*laughs*]
MARCOS: Yeah, I share my parents' attention with five other people.
MEI-LI: But sometimes I want a brother or a sister.
MARCOS: Do you ever feel lonely?
MEI-LI: Sure. But it's OK. I have lots of friends.

Answer

She gets all her parents' attention.

7 INTERCHANGE 5 Family facts

Find out about your classmates' families. Go to Interchange 5.

8 SNAPSHOT

Typical Families

	Facts about the United States	Facts about Your Country
In the home	• 41% of homes have three or more televisions. • 63% of families almost always eat dinner together.	• _____ % of homes have three or more televisions. • _____ % of families almost always eat dinner together.
The working family	• 55% of mothers with young children work. • 78% of high school students have jobs.	• _____ % of mothers with young children work. • _____ % of high school students have jobs.
Marriage	• 74% of adults between the ages of 18–35 marry. • 27% of adults between the ages of 18–34 live with their parents.	• _____ % of adults between the ages of 18–35 marry. • _____ % of adults between the ages of 18–34 live with their parents.

Sources: Nielsen Media Research; *Christian Science Monitor*; Families and Work Institute; the U.S. Census Bureau

Which facts seem like positive things? Which seem negative?
What are families like in your country? Write your guesses.
Tell the class your guesses. Do they agree?

9 CONVERSATION *I come from a big family.*

A Listen and practice.

Marcos: How many brothers and sisters do you have, Mei-li?
Mei-li: Actually, I'm an only child.
Marcos: Really?
Mei-li: Yeah, most families in China have only one child nowadays.
Marcos: I didn't know that.
Mei-li: What about you, Marcos?
Marcos: I come from a big family. I have three brothers and two sisters.
Mei-li: Wow! Is that typical in Peru?
Marcos: Not really. A lot of families are smaller these days. But big families are great because you get lots of birthday presents!

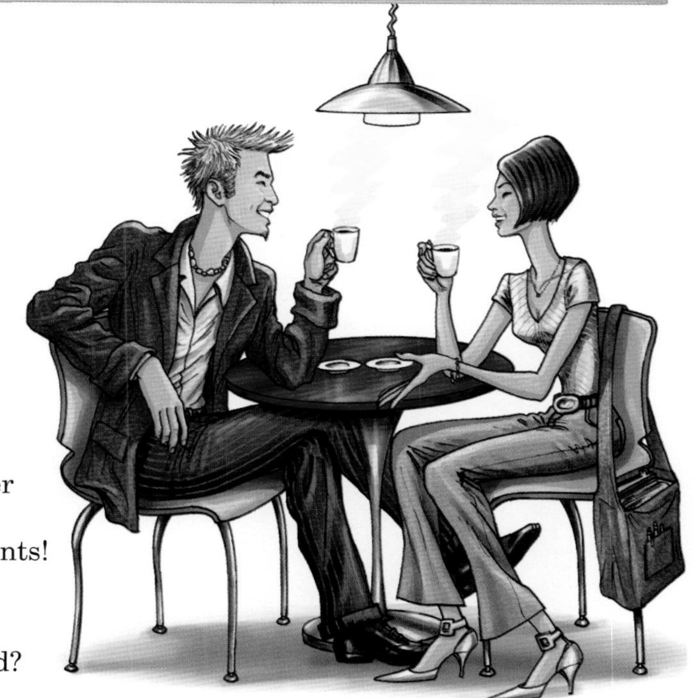

B Listen to the rest of the conversation. What does Mei-li like about being an only child?

10 GRAMMAR FOCUS

Quantifiers

100%	**All** **Nearly all** **Most**	families have only one child.
	Many **A lot of** **Some**	families are smaller these days.
	Not many **A few** **Few**	couples have more than one child.
0%	**No one**	gets married before the age of 18.

A Rewrite these sentences using quantifiers. Then compare with a partner.

1. In China, 50% of women get married by the age of 22.
2. In Australia, 87% of married couples have children.
3. In the United States, 0% of the people vote before the age of 18.
4. Thirty-five percent of the people in Germany live alone.
5. Seventy-eight percent of American high school students have jobs.

B *Pair work* Rewrite the sentences in part A so that they are true about your country.

11 WRITING *An e-mail about your family*

A Write an e-mail to your e-pal about your family.

Dear Young Joon,
Thanks for your e-mail. Now let me tell you about my family. My parents are coffee farmers. Most families here are small. I have one older sister, but I don't have a brother.
My sister's name . . .

B *Group work* Take turns reading your e-mails. Ask questions to get more information.

10 GRAMMAR FOCUS

***Learning objectives:** practice quantifiers; present facts using quantifiers*

[CD 1, Track 37]

- Explain that when people don't know the exact percentage of something, they use words like *most* or *some*. Point out the quantifiers in the Grammar Focus box.
- Explain that all these quantifiers come before plural nouns except one. Ask Ss which one does not. (Answer: no one)
- Play the audio program.
- Ask Ss to find two sentences with quantifiers in the Conversation on page 33. (Answers: Most families in China . . . , A lot of families . . .)
- Ask: "Who is from a big family? Raise your hand." Then elicit a statement about the class that starts with a quantifier (e.g., *Most students in the class are from big families.*). Ask more questions and elicit more statements with quantifiers (e.g., *Are you single? Do you live at home? Are you an only child?*).

A

- Explain the task. Model the first answer.
- Ss rewrite the sentences individually. Point out that more than one quantifier may be possible. Then Ss go over their answers in pairs.
- Go over answers with the class.

Possible answers

1. In China, a lot of women get married by the age of 22.
2. In Australia, nearly all married couples have children.
3. In the United States, no one votes before the age of 18.
4. Some people in Germany live alone.
5. Most American high school students have jobs.

B *Pair work*

- Explain the task and elicit the first answer. Write it on the board.
- Ss complete the task in pairs. Go around the class and give help as needed. Then each pair joins another pair to compare answers.
- ***Option:*** Ss make statements about the facts in the Snapshot on page 33 using quantifiers instead of percentages.

For more practice with quantifiers, play ***Tic-Tac-Toe*** on page T-148.

11 WRITING

***Learning objective:** write an e-mail describing one's family*

A

- Ss describe their family to a partner. Then they read the example e-mail silently.
- Elicit information Ss can include in a description of their family (e.g., names, ages, jobs, where they live). Write all ideas on the board.

For a new way to prepare for this Writing, try ***Mind Mapping*** on page T-154.

- Ss write e-mails about their family. Encourage them to use quantifiers.

B *Group work*

- Ss read each other's e-mails in small groups and ask each other for more information.

12 READING

Learning objectives: *read an article about an American family; develop skills in reading topic sentences*

- Books closed. Ask: "Why do women work outside the home? What happens to the children when both parents work?" Elicit ideas.
- Books open. Read the title and the pre-reading task.
- Explain that the first sentence of a paragraph usually gives you its main idea. This is called a "topic sentence."
- Ss read the topic sentences of the paragraphs. Ask: "Which question from the pre-reading task will the article answer?" (Answer: What happens when both parents work?)

A

- Go over the five questions. Then Ss read the article silently and answer the questions.
- Elicit or explain any new vocabulary.

Vocabulary

housework: work people do to take care of the home, such as cleaning
after-school program: activities for children after school
household chores: work children do to help their parents at home, such as washing the dishes

- Ss compare their answers in groups. Go around the class and give help as needed.
- Go over answers with the class.

Answers

1. Emily and Josh 2. Ben 3. Josh 4. Steve and Josh
5. Judy

B *Pair work*

- Ss complete the task in pairs. Then they share their ideas with the class. Discuss which solutions seem best.

End of Cycle 2

Do your students need more practice?

Assign . . .	***for more practice in . . .***
Workbook Exercises 7–11 on pages 28–30	Grammar, Vocabulary, Reading, and Writing
Lab Guide Exercise 9 on page 10	Listening, Pronunciation, Speaking, and Grammar
Video Activity Book Unit 5	Listening, Speaking, and Cultural Awareness
CD-ROM Unit 5	Grammar, Vocabulary, Reading, Listening, and Speaking

12 READING

The Changing Family

Read the title of the article. Then check (✓) the question you think the article will answer.
- ■ ***Why do women work outside the home?***
- ■ ***What happens when both parents work?***

American families are changing. One important change is that most married women now work outside the home. What happens when both parents work? Read about the Morales family.

Judy and Steve Morales have three children: Josh, 12; Ben, 9; and Emily, 6. Steve is a computer programmer. This year, Judy is working again as a hospital administrator. The family needs the money, and Judy likes her job. Everything is going well, but there are also some problems.

Now that Judy is working, Steve has to help her more with the housework. He doesn't enjoy it.

Judy loves her work, but she feels too tired and busy. She also worries about the children. Judy has to work on Saturdays, so Steve and Judy don't have a lot of free time together.

Emily is having a great time in her after-school program. When Judy comes to pick her up, she doesn't want to leave.

Unfortunately, Ben's school doesn't have an after-school program. Right now, he's spending most afternoons in front of the TV.

Josh is enjoying his new freedom after school. He's playing his music louder and spending more time on the phone. He's also doing a few household chores.

A Read the article. Then answer these questions. Write the names of the family members.

1. Which children are benefiting from Judy working? ....
2. Which child is not benefiting from Judy working? ....
3. Which family member is enjoying more freedom? ....
4. Which family members are doing more housework? ....
5. Which family member feels too busy? ....

B ***Pair work*** What problems are Steve and Judy having? Which do you think is the most serious? Offer some solutions for that problem.

6 How often do you exercise?

1 SNAPSHOT

THE TOP FIVE *SPORTS* AND *FITNESS ACTIVITIES* in the UNITED STATES

SPORTS	FITNESS ACTIVITIES
☐ Basketball	☐ Weight training
☐ Volleyball	☐ Treadmill
☐ Softball	☐ Stretching
☐ Football	☐ Walking
☐ Soccer	☐ Jogging

Source: SGMA International, *Sports Participation in America: 2002 Edition*

Do people in your country enjoy any of these sports or activities?
Check (✓) the sports or fitness activities you enjoy.
Make a list of other sports or activities you do. Then compare with the class.

2 WORD POWER Sports and exercise

A Which of these activities are popular with the following age groups? Check (✓) the activities. Then compare with a partner.

	Children	Teens	Young adults	Middle-aged people	Older people
aerobics	☐	☐	☐	☐	☐
baseball	☐	☐	☐	☐	☐
bicycling	☐	☐	☐	☐	☐
in-line skating	☐	☐	☐	☐	☐
soccer	☐	☐	☐	☐	☐
swimming	☐	☐	☐	☐	☐
tennis	☐	☐	☐	☐	☐
weight training	☐	☐	☐	☐	☐
yoga	☐	☐	☐	☐	☐

B ***Pair work*** Which of the activities above are used with *do*, *go*, or *play*?

do aerobics	*go bicycling*	*play baseball*
....	....	....
....	....	....

How often do you exercise?

In Unit 6, students discuss sports, exercise, and leisure activities. In Cycle 1, they talk about sports and exercise using adverbs of frequency. In Cycle 2, they talk about leisure activities using questions with how and short answers.

Cycle 1, Exercises 1–9

SNAPSHOT

Learning objectives: talk about sports and fitness; learn sports and fitness vocabulary

- Books closed. Introduce the topics of sport and fitness. Ss brainstorm sports and fitness activities. Write Ss' ideas in two columns on the board:

Sports	Fitness activities
volleyball	jogging
soccer	weight training
basketball	walking

TIP To make new vocabulary easy for your Ss to copy, make a vocabulary list on one side of the board. Add new words to the list throughout the class.

- Ask Ss to guess the sports and fitness activities people from the U.S. like best. (Answers: basketball, weight training)
- Books open. Ss look at the Snapshot and compare their guesses. Ask: "Who guessed right?"
- Elicit or explain any new vocabulary. Help Ss with the pronunciation of difficult words (e.g., *weight*, *stretching*). If needed, explain that American football is different from international football. Players use their hands, throw and run with the ball, and wear safety equipment. In the U.S, international football is called *soccer*.

Vocabulary

softball: a sport similar to baseball but with a bigger, softer ball
weight training: lifting weights to become stronger
treadmill: a machine for walking or running
stretching: extending or making your arms and legs longer

- Go over the discussion questions and tasks.
- Ss complete the tasks individually. Go around the class and give help as needed. Then elicit Ss' answers.

WORD POWER

Learning objectives: Discuss types of sports and exercise; learn collocations with do, go, *and* play

A

- Go over the activities in the chart. In pairs, Ss label the pictures with the activities. (Answers: swimming, soccer, tennis, bicycling, baseball, yoga, weight training, aerobics, in-line skating) Give help as needed.
- Explain and model the task. Ask: "What age groups like aerobics?" Point out that there is no correct answer.
- While Ss complete the task individually, write this conversation on the board:
  A: What age groups like (aerobics)?
  B: I think it's popular with (young adults).
  A: I agree. OR *I don't really agree. I think it's popular with (teens).*
- Model the conversation with one or two Ss. Then Ss use the model conversation to compare answers in pairs.

B *Pair work*

- Present the rules for these collocations:
  go + activities ending in *-ing*, except *weight training*
  play + games, such as sports played with a ball
  do + fitness activities and individual exercises
- Ss complete the task in pairs. To check answers, write the verbs *do*, *go*, and *play* on the board. Ask different Ss to write the answers. Give help as needed.

Answers

do	*go*	*play*
aerobics	bicycling	baseball
weight training	in-line skating	soccer
yoga	swimming	tennis

- ***Option:*** Ss circle the activities and sports they enjoy. Then they compare with a partner.

For more practice with sports and exercise vocabulary, play ***Sculptures*** on page T-144.

3 CONVERSATION

***Learning objectives:** practice a conversation about exercise; see adverbs of frequency in context*

A [CD 2, Track 1]

- Use the picture to set the scene. Ask: "Where are Paul and Marie? What are they doing? What do you think they like to do in their free time?"

> **TIP** Use the title and pictures to set the scene. The vocabulary and ideas you elicit will activate Ss' background knowledge and prepare them for the listening.

- Books closed. Write these sentences on the board:
  1. Paul goes in-line skating in his free time.
  2. Marie exercises every day.
  Ask: "Are these sentences true or false?" Play the audio program and elicit the answers. (Answers: 1. true 2. false)
- Elicit or explain any new vocabulary.

Vocabulary

Seriously?: Really?
couch potato: a person who watches a lot of TV and is not very active

- Books open. Play the audio program again. Ss listen and read silently. Ask: "Are you more like Marie or Paul?" Elicit Ss' answers.
- Ss practice the conversation in pairs.

For a new way to practice this Conversation, try the ***Moving Dialog*** on page T-150.

B

- Read the focus question aloud. Ask Ss to make guesses. Write their ideas on the board.
- Play the audio program. Then elicit the answer.

Audio script

MARIE: What else do you like to do, Paul?
PAUL: Well, I like video games a lot. I play them every day. It drives my mom crazy!
MARIE: Hey, I play video games all the time, too.
PAUL: Well, listen, I have some great new games. Why don't we play some after class today?
MARIE: OK!

Answer

He plays video games.

4 GRAMMAR FOCUS

***Learning objectives:** practice adverbs of frequency; ask and answer questions using adverbs of frequency*

[CD 2, Track 2]

Adverbs of frequency

- Write these sentences on the board:
  I ______ get up early.
  I ______ go in-line skating.
  I ______ exercise.
  I ______ just watch TV.
- Ask Ss to find the missing words in the Conversation in Exercise 3 and write them on the board. (Answers: almost always, often, hardly ever, usually) Explain that these are adverbs of frequency. Point out that they go before most verbs. Focus Ss' attention on the second column of the Grammar Focus box.
- On the board write: *I'm always late*. Point out that adverbs of frequency go after the verb *be*.
- Point out the third column. Explain that percentages show how often something happens.
- Now focus Ss' attention on the first column. Ask: "Where do these adverbs go?" (Answer: at the end of a statement or question)
- Play the audio program.

A

- Explain the task. Model the first example. Ss complete the task individually.
- Ss practice the conversations in pairs.

Answers

1. A: Do you **ever** play sports?
   B: Sure. I play soccer **twice a week**.
2. A: What do you **usually** do on Saturday mornings?
   B: Nothing much. **I almost always** sleep until noon.
3. A: Do you **often** do aerobics at the gym?
   B: No, I **hardly ever** do aerobics.
4. A: Do you **always** exercise on Sundays?
   B: No, I **never** exercise on Sundays.
5. A: What do you **usually** do after class?
   B: I go out with my classmates **about three times a week**.

B *Pair work*

- Explain the task. Ss ask and answer the questions in part A in pairs, using their own information.

For more practice with adverbs of frequency, play ***Tic-Tac-Toe*** on page T-148. Write different adverbs of frequency in the nine boxes.

3 CONVERSATION *I hardly ever exercise.*

A Listen and practice.

Marie: You're really fit, Paul. Do you exercise a lot?
Paul: Well, I almost always get up early, and I lift weights for an hour.
Marie: Seriously?
Paul: Sure. And then I often go in-line skating.
Marie: Wow! How often do you exercise like that?
Paul: About five times a week. What about you?
Marie: Oh, I hardly ever exercise. I usually just watch TV in my free time. I guess I'm a real couch potato!

B Listen to the rest of the conversation. What else does Paul do in his free time?

GRAMMAR FOCUS

Adverbs of frequency

How often do you exercise?
I lift weights **every day**.
I go jogging **once a week**.
I play soccer **twice a month**.
I swim about **three times a year**.
I don't exercise very **often/much**.

Do you **ever** watch TV in the evening?
Yes, I **often** watch TV after dinner.
I **sometimes** watch TV before bed.
Sometimes I watch TV before bed.*
I **hardly ever** watch TV.
No, I **never** watch TV.

***Sometimes** *can begin a sentence.*

100%	**always**
	almost always
	usually
	often
	sometimes
	hardly ever
	almost never
0%	**never**

A Put the adverbs in the correct place. Then practice with a partner.

1. A: Do you play sports? (ever)
   B: Sure. I play soccer. (twice a week)
2. A: What do you do on Saturday mornings? (usually)
   B: Nothing much. I sleep until noon. (almost always)
3. A: Do you do aerobics at the gym? (often)
   B: No, I do aerobics. (hardly ever)
4. A: Do you exercise on Sundays? (always)
   B: No, I exercise on Sundays. (never)
5. A: What do you do after class? (usually)
   B: I go out with my classmates. (about three times a week)

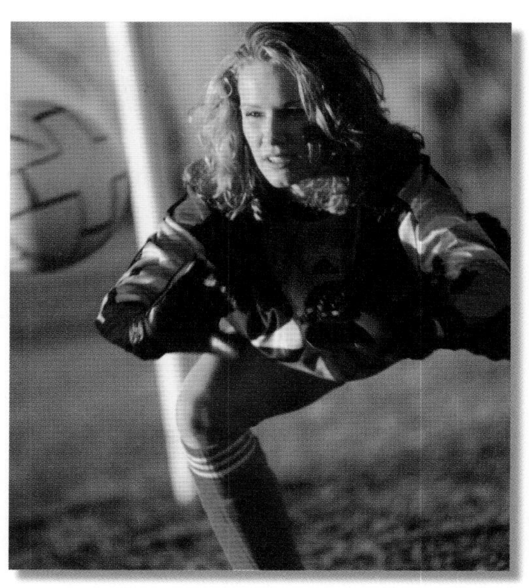

B ***Pair work*** Take turns asking the questions in part A. Give your own information when answering.

5 PRONUNCIATION *Intonation with direct address*

A Listen and practice. Notice these statements with direct address. There is usually falling intonation and a pause before the name.

You're really fit, Paul.   She looks tired, James.   I feel great, Dr. Lee.

B *Pair work* Write four statements using direct address. Then practice them.

6 SPEAKING *Fitness poll*

A *Group work* Take a poll in your group. One person takes notes. Take turns asking each person these questions.

1. Do you have a regular fitness program? How often do you exercise?

2. Do you ever go to a gym? How often do you go? What do you do there?

3. Do you play any sports? Which ones? How often do you play them?

4. Do you ever take long walks? How often? Where do you go?

5. What else do you do to keep fit?

B *Group work* Study the results of the poll. Who in your group has a good fitness program?

7 LISTENING *In the evening*

A Listen to what Ted, Wanda, and Kim like to do in the evening. Complete the chart.

	Favorite activity	How often?
Ted	....	....
Wanda	....	....
Kim	....	....

B Listen again. Who is most similar to you – Ted, Wanda, or Kim?

5 PRONUNCIATION

Learning objectives: *notice intonation with direct address; learn to sound natural when using direct address*

A [CD 2, Track 3]

- Play the audio program. Use gestures to demonstrate falling intonation. Elicit or explain that direct address statements end with falling intonation.
- Play the audio program again. Ss repeat the statements individually.

B *Pair work*

- Explain the task and model it by writing an example statement.
- Ss write four statements in pairs. Then they practice them. Go around the class and check Ss' intonation.

6 SPEAKING

Learning objective: *talk about fitness using* How often *and adverbs of frequency*

A *Group work*

- Focus Ss' attention on the title. Explain that a poll has two parts. First everyone answers the same questions. Then you compare and summarize the answers.
- In small groups, Ss take turns asking each other questions. One S takes notes. Go around the class and give help as needed.

B *Group work*

- Ss compare the results of their poll and decide who has a good fitness program. Then one S in each group reports the information to the class.

7 LISTENING

Learning objective: *develop skills in listening for key words and specific information*

A [CD 2, Track 4]

- Set the scene. Three people are talking about their favorite evening activities. Have Ss brainstorm things people do in the evening.
- Explain the task. Ss listen only for favorite activities and complete the first column in the chart. Write the chart on the board.
- Play the audio program. Ss complete the task individually and compare their answers in pairs. Ask different Ss to write the answers on the board.
- Explain the task. Ss listen only for how often Ted, Wanda, and Kim do the activities. Ss complete the second column.
- Play the audio program again. Ss complete the task individually and compare their answers in pairs. Ask different Ss to write the answers on the board.

TIP If Ss have difficulty understanding the audio program, try to find out where they have difficulty. Replay that part of the program and ask what they hear.

Audio script

WANDA: So, what do you usually do in the evening, Ted?
TED: I exercise a lot. I like to go jogging after work.
KIM: Yeah? How often do you go jogging?
TED: About four or five times a week.
WANDA: Well, I guess you're in great shape.
TED: Thanks!
KIM: You're in great shape, too, Wanda!
WANDA: Oh, thanks, Kim. I usually go to the gym and work out in the evenings. I love it! And I meet a lot of my friends there.
TED: How often do you go?
WANDA: About three times a week, I guess. What about you, Kim? Do you ever work out in the evenings?
KIM: No, I don't exercise very much. I almost always practice my guitar after work. I practice for a couple of hours every night.
TED: Gee, you must be pretty good!

Answers

	Favorite activity	*How often?*
Ted	jogging	about 4–5 times a week
Wanda	working out	about 3 times a week
Kim	practicing the guitar	a couple of hours every night

B

- Play the audio program. Ss listen to find out who is most similar to them. Then they discuss their answers in pairs or small groups.

TIP To encourage Ss to share learning strategies for the Self-study section, hold a class discussion. Ask the class: "When do you do the Self-study exercises? Where do you do them? What helps you improve your listening skills?"

8 DISCUSSION

Learning objective: *discuss sports and athletes using adverbs of frequency*

Group work

- Focus Ss' attention on the picture. Ask: "Who is he? What is he doing?" (Answers: David Beckham, playing soccer)
- Explain that you want Ss to discuss the questions for ten minutes. Point out that it's important to speak fluently, so it's OK to make errors.
- Ss take turns asking and answering the questions in small groups. Go around the class and ask follow-up questions.

For more speaking practice, try ***Famous Athletes*** on page T-157.

9 WRITING

Learning objective: *write about favorite activities using the simple present and adverbs of frequency*

A

- Explain the task. Point out that Ss can write about any favorite activities, not just sports. Ss read the example paragraph silently.
- Ss make notes about favorite activities individually.
- Ss write a paragraph based on their notes. Remind Ss to include one false piece of information.

For a new way to teach this Writing, try ***Pass the Paper*** on page T-153.

B Group work

- Explain the task. Ss read each other's descriptions and write guesses about which activity is false. Then they ask each other to check their guesses.

End of Cycle 1

Do your students need more practice?

Assign . . .	*for more practice in . . .*
Workbook Exercises 1–7 on pages 31–34	Grammar, Vocabulary, Reading, and Writing
Lab Guide Exercises 1–6 on page 11	Listening, Pronunciation, Speaking, and Grammar

Cycle 2, Exercises 10–14

10 CONVERSATION

Learning objectives: *practice a conversation about fitness; see questions with* how *and short answers in context*

A *[CD 2, Track 5]*

- Ss cover the text and look at the picture. Elicit ideas and vocabulary.
- Write this focus question on the board:
  Do Ruth and Keith usually play tennis together?
  Then play the audio program and elicit the answer. (Answer: no)
- Write these focus questions on the board:
  1. How often does Keith do aerobics?
  2. How well does Keith play tennis?
  3. How good is Ruth at tennis?
- Play the audio program again and elicit the answers. (Answers: 1. twice a week 2. pretty well 3. not very good)
- ***Option:*** Have Ss close their eyes as they listen to the audio program.
- Ss read the conversation silently. Then they practice the conversation in pairs.

B

- Read the focus question and ask Ss to guess who wins. Then play the audio program. Ss listen to find the answer.

Audio script

RUTH: Good game, Keith.
KEITH: Thanks. You, too. And congratulations on the win. You play pretty well.
RUTH: Oh, no, not really.
KEITH: How often do you play?
RUTH: Once or twice a year. I'm just lucky today, I guess. Want to play another game?
KEITH: Um . . . sure. After a five-minute break.

Answer

Ruth is the winner.

8 DISCUSSION Sports and athletes

Group work Take turns asking and answering these questions.

Who's your favorite athlete? Why?
Who are three famous athletes in your country?
Do you ever watch sports on TV? Which ones?
Do you ever watch sports live? Which ones?
What are two sports you don't like?
What sport or activity do you want to try?

9 WRITING About favorite activities

A Write about your favorite activities. Include one activity that is false.

I love to exercise! I usually work out every day. I get up early in the morning and go running for about an hour. Then I often go to the gym and do aerobics with some friends. Sometimes I play tennis in the afternoon. I play . . .

B *Group work* Take turns reading your descriptions. Can you guess which information is false?

"You don't play tennis in the afternoon. Right?"

10 CONVERSATION I'm a real fitness freak.

A Listen and practice.

Ruth: You're in great shape, Keith.
Keith: Thanks. I guess I'm a real fitness freak.
Ruth: How often do you work out?
Keith: Well, I do aerobics twice a week. And I play tennis every week.
Ruth: Tennis? That sounds like a lot of fun.
Keith: Oh, do you want to play sometime?
Ruth: Uh, . . . how well do you play?
Keith: Pretty well, I guess.
Ruth: Well, all right. But I'm not very good.
Keith: No problem. I'll give you a few tips.

B Listen to Keith and Ruth after their tennis match. Who's the winner?

11 LISTENING *I'm terrible at sports.*

Listen to Dan, Jean, and Phil discuss sports and exercise. Who is a couch potato? a fitness freak? a sports fan?

a couch potato

a fitness freak

a sports fan

....

12 GRAMMAR FOCUS

Questions with how; *short answers*

How often do you work out?
Every day.
Twice a week.
Not very often.

How long do you spend at the gym?
Thirty minutes a day.
Two hours a week.
About an hour on weekends.

How well do you play tennis?
Pretty well.
About average.
Not very well.

How good are you at sports?
Pretty good.
OK.
Not so good.

A Complete these questions. Then practice with a partner.

1. A: .... at volleyball?
   B: I guess I'm pretty good. I often play on weekends.
2. A: .... spend online?
   B: About an hour after dinner. I like to chat with my friends.
3. A: .... play cards?
   B: Once or twice a month. It's a good way to relax.
4. A: .... type?
   B: Not very well, actually. I need to take a typing class.

B *Group work* Take turns asking the questions in part A. Give your own information when answering.

13 INTERCHANGE 6 *Do you dance?*

Find out what your classmates can do. Go to Interchange 6.

11 LISTENING

Learning objective: *develop skills in listening for details and inferencing*

[CD 2, Track 6]

- Books closed. Set the scene. Three friends (Dan, Jean, and Phil) are talking about sports and exercise. Write the three speakers' names on the board.
- Play the audio program. Ss listen to find out details about each person.
- Ask different Ss to write notes on the board. Point out they can write anything they remember about the speakers.
- Books open. Focus Ss' attention on the pictures and read the captions aloud. Ask: "What do you think each type of person is like?"
- Play the audio program again. Have Ss identify the three people.
- Go over answers with the class. Then ask: "Who are you most like? Why?"

Audio script

JEAN: How good are you at sports, Dan?
DAN: Are you kidding? I'm terrible! But I love to watch sports. I go to football or baseball games all the time. And I buy three or four different sports magazines every week.
JEAN: Wow!
PHIL: Do you like sports, Jean?
JEAN: Oh, yes. I like to exercise. But I don't watch sports very much, and I never buy sports magazines.
PHIL: How much time do you spend exercising?
JEAN: Well, I guess I exercise about two or three hours a day. I do aerobics three times a week, and the other days I go swimming.
PHIL: That's great!
DAN: And what about you, Phil?
PHIL: Oh, I'm too lazy to play sports – I really hate exercising. And I almost never go to any sporting events. In my free time, I like to sit with my feet up and watch my favorite TV shows.

Answers

1. Phil 2. Jean 3. Dan

12 GRAMMAR FOCUS

Learning objective: *practice questions with* how *and short answers*

[CD 2, Track 7]

***Questions with* how**

- Books closed. Write these questions and answers on the board in two columns:

A	B
How often do you work out?	*Pretty well.*
How long do you spend at the gym?	*Twice a week.*
How well do you play tennis?	*Not very good.*
How good are you at sports?	*Two hours a week.*

- Ss match the questions in A with the answers in B. Encourage Ss to guess.
- Books open. Ss check their answers in the Grammar Focus box.
- Focus Ss' attention on the first column of the Grammar Focus box. Elicit or explain the difference between *how often* and *how long* (*how often* = with what frequency, *how long* = in how much time).
- Focus Ss' attention on the second column. Ask: "How are *how well* and *how good* different?" (They have the same meaning, but *good* is an adjective, and *well* is an adverb. Use *how good* with *be* and *how well* with other verbs.)

Short answers

- Point out that it sounds unnatural when people answer with a complete sentence. Therefore, they use short answers.
- Play the audio program.

A

- Explain the task. Ss work individually to complete the questions. Check Ss' work as they finish. Ask Ss with correct questions to write them on the board.
- Ss check answers against the board. Then they practice the conversations in pairs.

Answers

1. A: **How good are you** at volleyball?
2. A: **How long do you** spend online?
3. A: **How often do you** play cards?
4. A: **How well can you** type?

B *Group work*

- Explain the task. Ss take turns asking and answering the questions in small groups.

! For a new way to practice this Conversation, try the ***Onion Ring*** technique on page T-151.

13 INTERCHANGE 6

See page T-120 for teaching notes.

14 READING

***Learning objectives:** read and complete a health and fitness quiz; develop skills in skimming and making inferences*

- Read the title. Ask: "What is this? How is it different from a quiz in class?" Elicit ideas.
- Tell Ss to look over the quiz. Ask: "Where can you find this kind of quiz? What is the quiz about?" (Answers: in a magazine or newspaper, health and fitness)
- Point out the pre-reading question. Then Ss skim the questions in the quiz. Ask Ss to write down the score they think they're going to get.

A

- Explain the task. Read the first question and ask Ss to check (✓) the answer that is true for them.
- Ss read the quiz individually and check (✓) their answers.
- ***Option:*** Ss work in pairs and take turns asking each other the questions. They complete the quiz for each other.
- Go around the class and elicit or explain any new vocabulary.

Vocabulary

nutrition: the food people eat and how it affects their health
meal: breakfast, lunch, or dinner
junk food: food that is not good for you
average: medium; usual
both: two things together
weight: how many pounds or kilos a person is
ideal: desired; perfect

- Ss add up their points. Then they read the *Rate yourself* section.
- Ask: "Are the points the same as you guessed? More than you guessed? Fewer than you guessed? Are you happy with your rating?"
- ***Option:*** Ss give the quiz to friends or family members for homework. Then they share the results in class.

B *Group work*

- Ss compare their scores in small groups. Ask Ss to list five things they can do to improve their health and fitness. Point out that they can use ideas from the quiz.
- Each group joins another group and shares ideas. Then elicit ideas from the groups.

End of Cycle 2

Do your students need more practice?

Assign . . .	*for more practice in . . .*
Workbook Exercises 8–11 on pages 35–36	Grammar, Vocabulary, Reading, and Writing
Lab Guide Exercises 7–9 on page 12	Listening, Pronunciation, Speaking, and Grammar
Video Activity Book Unit 6	Listening, Speaking, and Cultural Awareness
CD-ROM Unit 6	Grammar, Vocabulary, Reading, Listening, and Speaking

Evaluation

Assess Ss' understanding of Units 5 and 6 with the quiz on pages T-204 and T-205.

14 READING

Health and Fitness Quiz

How healthy and fit do you think you are? Skim the questions below. Then guess your health and fitness score from 0 (very unhealthy) to 55 (very healthy).

Your Food and Nutrition	Points
1. How many meals do you eat each day?	
☐ Four or five small meals	5
☐ Three meals	3
☐ One or two meals	0
2. How often do you eat at regular times during the day?	
☐ Almost always	5
☐ Usually	3
☐ Hardly ever	0
3. How many servings of fruits or vegetables do you eat each day?	
☐ Five or more	5
☐ One to four	3
☐ None	0
4. How much junk food do you eat?	
☐ Very little	5
☐ About average	3
☐ A lot	0
5. Do you take vitamins?	
☐ Yes, every day	5
☐ Sometimes	3
☐ No	0

Your Fitness	Points
6. How often do you exercise or play a sport?	
☐ Three or more days a week	5
☐ One or two days a week	3
☐ Never	0
7. Which best describes your exercise program?	
☐ Both weight training and aerobic exercise	5
☐ Either weight training or aerobic exercise	3
☐ None	0
8. How important is your fitness program to you?	
☐ Very important	5
☐ Fairly important	3
☐ Not very important	0

Your Health	Points
9. Which best describes your weight?	
☐ Within 6 pounds (3 kg) of my ideal weight	5
☐ Within 10 pounds (4.5 kg) of my ideal weight	3
☐ More than 12 pounds (5.5 kg) over or under my ideal weight	0
10. How often do you get a physical exam?	
☐ Once a year	5
☐ Every two or three years	3
☐ Rarely	0
11. How often do you sleep well?	
☐ Always	5
☐ Usually or sometimes	3
☐ Hardly ever or never	0

Rate yourself **Total Points** ☐

46 to 55: Excellent job! Keep up the good work!

31 to 45: Good! Your health and fitness are above average.

16 to 30: Your health and fitness are a little below average.

15 or below: You can improve your health and fitness.

A Take the quiz and add up your score. Does your quiz score match your original guess? Do you agree with your quiz score? Why or why not?

B *Group work* Compare your scores. Who is the healthiest and fittest? What can you do to improve your health and fitness?

Units 5–6 Progress check

SELF-ASSESSMENT

How well can you do these things? Check (✓) the boxes.

I can	Very well	OK	A little
Listen to, understand, and describe people's actions (Ex. 1, 2)	☐	☐	☐
Ask and answer questions using the present continuous (Ex. 2, 3)	☐	☐	☐
Describe family life using determiners (Ex. 3)	☐	☐	☐
Describe routines using adverbs of frequency (Ex. 4)	☐	☐	☐
Talk about abilities using *how* questions (Ex. 4)	☐	☐	☐

1 LISTENING What are they doing?

A Listen to people do different things. What are they doing? Complete the chart.

What are they doing?
1. ....
2. ....
3. ....
4. ....

B *Pair work* Compare your answers.

A: In number one, someone is shaving.
B: I don't think so. I think someone is . . .

2 GAME Memory test

Group work Choose a person in the room, but don't say who! Other students take turns asking yes/no questions to guess the person.

A: I'm thinking of someone in the classroom.
B: Is it a woman?
A: Yes, it is.
C: Is she sitting in the front of the room?
A: No, she isn't.
D: Is she sitting in the back?
A: Yes, she is.
E: Is she wearing jeans?
A: No, she isn't.
B: Is it . . . ?

The student with the correct guess has the next turn.

Units 5–6 Progress check

SELF-ASSESSMENT

Learning objectives: *reflect on one's learning; identify areas that need improvement*

- Ask: "What did you learn in Units 5 and 6?" Elicit Ss' answers.
- Ss complete the Self-assessment. Encourage them to be honest, and point out they will not get a bad grade if they check (✓) "a little."
- Ss move on to the Progress check exercises. You can have Ss complete them in class or for homework, using one of these techniques:
  1. Ask Ss to complete all the exercises.
  2. Ask Ss: "What do you need to practice?" Then assign exercises based on their answers.
  3. Ask Ss to choose and complete exercises based on their Self-assessment.

1 LISTENING

Learning objective: *assess one's ability to listen to, understand, and describe people's actions*

A ▶ *[CD 2, Track 8]*

- Explain the task. Ss will hear four sounds of people doing different things. Ss guess what the person is doing and write sentences using the present continuous.
- Model the task. Ask Ss to close their eyes. Then do something that makes a distinctive sound (e.g., write on the board, sharpen your pencil). Ask: "What am I doing?" Ss answer in the present continuous (e.g., *You're writing on the board.*).
- Play the audio program once or twice. Ss listen and complete the chart. Help with vocabulary as needed.

Possible answers

1. Someone is making a drink.
2. Someone is taking a shower and singing.
3. Someone is vacuuming.
4. Someone is sleeping/snoring.

B *Pair work*

- Explain the task. Model the example conversation with a S. Elicit different ways of agreeing and disagreeing.
- Ss compare answers in pairs. Go around the class and check Ss' use of the present continuous.

2 GAME

Learning objectives: *assess one's ability to ask and answer yes/no questions using the present continuous; assess one's ability to describe people's actions*

Group work

- Explain the task. Ss work in small groups. One S chooses a person in the room. The other Ss take turns asking present continuous yes/no questions until they guess the person's identity. The S who guesses correctly has the next turn.
- Model the example conversation. Take the role of Student A and ask other students to take the roles of Students B, C, D, and E.
- Ss play the game in small groups.

3 SURVEY

Learning objectives: *assess one's ability to ask and answer questions using the present continuous; assess one's ability to describe family life using determiners*

A *Group work*

- Explain the task and read the instructions aloud.
- Ss read the questions in small groups. Then, as a group, they add two more yes/no questions about family life. Encourage Ss to use both the simple present and the present continuous.
- Explain the task. Ss take turns asking and answering the questions. They write the number of "yes" and "no" answers in the correct columns. Remind Ss to include their own answers.

B *Group work*

- Explain the task. For each question, Ss add up the number of yes/no responses in their group. Then they write a sentence to describe the group's responses using determiners (e.g., *most*, *some*, *a few*, *all*).
- Ss complete the task in groups. Then they read their sentences to the class.
- ***Option:*** Complete the activity as a class.

DISCUSSION

Learning objectives: *assess one's ability to describe routines using adverbs of frequency; assess one's ability to talk about abilities using* how *questions*

Group work

- Explain the task. Ss choose three questions and check (✓) them individually. Then they ask each other the questions in small groups. When someone answers "yes," the S must add at least one follow-up question, including *how* questions (e.g., *how well*, *how often*, *how good*).
- ***Option:*** Ss think of their own questions beginning with *Do you ever . . . ?*
- Ask four Ss to read the example conversation. Elicit other possible follow-up questions.
- Ss complete the task. Go around the class and check for use of follow-up questions.

WHAT'S NEXT?

Learning objective: *become more involved in one's learning*

- Focus Ss' attention on the Self-assessment again. Ask: "How well can you do these things now?"
- Ask Ss to underline one thing they need to review. Ask: "What did you underline? How can you review it?"
- If needed, plan additional activities or reviews based on Ss' answers.

3 SURVEY Family life

A *Group work* Add two more yes/no questions about family life to the chart. Then ask and answer the questions in groups. Write down the number of "yes" and "no" answers. (Remember to include yourself.)

	Number of yes answers	Number of no answers
1. Are you living with your family?	....	....
2. Do your parents both work?	....	....
3. Do you eat dinner with your family?	....	....
4. Are you working these days?	....	....
5. Are you married?	....	....
6. Do you have any children?	....	....
7.	....	....
8.	....	....

B *Group work* Write up the results of the survey. Then tell the class.

1. In my group, most people are living with their family.
2. A few of their parents both work.

4 DISCUSSION Routines and abilities

Group work Choose three questions. Then ask your questions in groups.

Do you ever . . . ?

- ☐ play computer games
- ☐ listen to English songs
- ☐ chat online
- ☐ do weight training
- ☐ travel to other countries
- ☐ sing karaoke
- ☐ cook for friends
- ☐ go swimming
- ☐ watch old movies

When someone answers "yes," think of other questions you can ask.

A: **Do you ever** play computer games?
B: Yes, I sometimes play them.
C: **What's your favorite** game?
B: I like Star Blaster.
D: **How well** do you play it?
B: Not very well. But I'm getting better.
A: **When** do you play it?
B: I usually play it before bed.
C: **How often** do you play it?
B: Almost every night.

WHAT'S NEXT?

Look at your Self-assessment again. Do you need to review anything?

7 We had a great time!

1 SNAPSHOT

Source: The Harris Poll

Check (✓) the activities you do in your free time.
List three other activities you do in your free time.
Put the activities you do in order from your favorite to your least favorite.

2 CONVERSATION *Did you do anything special?*

A Listen and practice.

Rick: So, what did you do last weekend, Meg?
Meg: Oh, I had a great time. I went to a karaoke bar and sang with some friends on Saturday.
Rick: That sounds like fun. Did you go to Lucky's?
Meg: No, we didn't. We went to that new place downtown. How about you? Did you go anywhere?
Rick: No, I didn't go anywhere all weekend. I just stayed home and studied for today's Spanish test.
Meg: Our Spanish test is today? I forgot all about that!
Rick: Don't worry. You always get an A.

B Listen to the rest of the conversation. What did Meg do on Sunday?

We had a great time!

In Unit 7, students discuss daily, leisure, and vacation activities. In Cycle 1, they talk about daily and leisure activities using the simple past with both regular and irregular verbs. In Cycle 2, they talk about vacations using the past tense of be.

Cycle 1, Exercises 1–7

SNAPSHOT

Learning objective: *learn vocabulary for discussing leisure activities*

- Books closed. Ask: "What do you do in your free time?" Help with vocabulary as needed. Write Ss' responses on the board.
- ***Option:*** Ask Ss to guess the top eight leisure activities in the U.S. Later, Ss compare their ideas with the Snapshot.
- Books open. Ask different Ss to read the leisure activities aloud. Point out that these are the top eight leisure activities in the U.S. Elicit or explain any new vocabulary.
- Ask: "Does anything on this list surprise you? What?" Elicit Ss' answers.
- Read and explain the three tasks. Point out that, for the last task, Ss should list the activities starting with their favorite.
- Ss complete the tasks individually. Go around the class and give help as needed.
- Elicit Ss' responses.
- ***Option:*** Use Ss' responses to make a list of the top eight activities for the class.

For a new way to practice the Snapshot vocabulary, try ***Vocabulary Steps*** on page T-154.

CONVERSATION

Learning objectives: *practice a conversation about weekend activities; see the simple past in context*

A [CD 2, Track 10]

- Set the scene. Rick and Meg are talking about their weekends. Ask Ss to use the pictures to predict what each person did. Elicit or explain vocabulary in the pictures (e.g., *karaoke*).
- ***Option:*** Ss list all the words they can see in the pictures. Find out who has the most words.
- Books closed. Write these focus questions on the board:
  1. What did Meg do on Saturday?
  2. What did Rick do?
- Play the audio program. Ss listen for the answers. Then elicit the answers. (Answers: 1. She went to a karaoke bar and sang with some friends. 2. He stayed home all weekend and studied for the Spanish test.)
- Books open. Play the audio program again. Ss listen and read silently.
- Ss practice the conversation in pairs. Go around the class and give help as needed.

For a new way to practice this Conversation, try the ***Disappearing Dialog*** on page T-151.

B

- Read the focus question aloud. Ask Ss to guess. Write some of their ideas on the board.
- Play the audio program. Ss work individually. Then go over the answer with the class.

Audio script

RICK: So, Meg, what did you do on Sunday?
MEG: I stayed home in the morning. I just watched TV and read.
RICK: How about in the afternoon?
MEG: Oh, I worked. I have a part-time job at the university bookstore.
RICK: I didn't know you had a job.
MEG: Yeah, I'm a cashier there.

Answer

She stayed home in the morning. She watched TV and read. She went to work in the afternoon.

For more practice talking about last weekend's activities, play the ***Chain Game*** on page T-145.

TIP To help Ss who are weak at listening, write the answers on the board. That way, they can *see* the answers.

3 GRAMMAR FOCUS

Learning objective: *practice simple past questions, short answers, and regular and irregular verbs*

[CD 2, Track 11]

***Simple past questions with* did**

- Focus Ss' attention on the Conversation on page 44. Ask Ss to find three questions with *did*. Then write them on the board.

> **TIP** Use a different color for target features (e.g., *did* + verb). This helps Ss visualize the grammar pattern.

- Point out the questions in the Grammar Focus box. Elicit the rules for forming yes/no and Wh-questions in the simple past:

  Did + subject + verb?
  Wh-question + *did* + subject + verb?

- Elicit more examples and write them on the board.
- Play the audio program. Have Ss repeat the questions and responses.

Regular and irregular verbs

- Point out the regular and irregular verbs to the right of part A. Then draw this chart on the board:

Regular verbs	Irregular verbs
work – work<u>ed</u>	have – <u>had</u>
invite – invit<u>ed</u>	go – <u>went</u>

- Focus Ss' attention on the Conversation on page 44 again. Ask Ss to find the simple past forms of *stay* and *study*. (Answers: stayed, studied) Ask a S to write them on the board in the *Regular* column. Then ask Ss to find and circle the simple past of *sing* and *forget*. (Answers: sang, forgot) Ask a different S to write them in the *Irregular* column.
- Have Ss turn to the appendix at the back of the book. Tell them to use this list as needed.
- ***Option:*** Ask Ss to look for patterns in the list of irregular verbs (e.g., *i* → *a*: *sit* → *sat*, *swim* → *swam*, *drink* → *drank*).

> **TIP** Some Ss like to repeat things aloud. Others prefer to mouth words or sentences silently. Help Ss find learning styles they prefer.

A

- Explain the task. Model the first conversation with a strong S. Then model it with a different S.
- Ss complete the task individually. Go over answers with the class.

Answers

1. A: **Did** you **stay** home on Saturday?
   B: No, I **called** my friend. We **drove** to a café for lunch.
2. A: How **did** you **spend** your last birthday?
   B: I **had** a party. Everyone **enjoyed** it, but the neighbors **didn't like** the noise.
3. A: What **did** you **do** last night?
   B: I **went** to the new Jim Carrey film. I **loved** it!
4. A: **Did** you **do** anything special over the weekend?
   B: Yes, I **did**. I **went** shopping. Unfortunately, I **spent** all my money. Now I'm broke!
5. A: **Did** you **go** out on Friday night?
   B: No, I **didn't**. I **invited** friends over, and I **cooked** dinner for them.

- Ss practice the conversations in pairs.

B *Pair work*

- Explain the task. Then model it by asking different Ss to ask you the questions in part A. Give your own responses.
- Point out that Ss can avoid answering a question by saying *I'd rather not say*. They can also make up answers.
- Ss complete the task in pairs.

For more practice with regular and irregular verbs, play ***Bingo*** on page T-147.

4 PRONUNCIATION

Learning objectives: *notice the reduction of* did you; *learn to sound natural when asking* did you *questions*

A *[CD 2, Track 12]*

- Play the audio program. Ss listen for the reduction of *did you*.
- Play the audio program again. Ss practice saying the questions with reductions.
- Tell different Ss to ask the questions. Check their use of reduced forms.

B *Pair work*

- Explain and model the task. Ss complete the task in pairs. Go around the class and check Ss' use of reductions.

3 GRAMMAR FOCUS

Simple past

Did you **work** on Saturday?
Yes, I **did**. I **worked** all day.
No, I **didn't**. I **didn't work** at all.

Did you **go** anywhere last weekend?
Yes, I **did**. I **went** to the movies.
No, I **didn't**. I **didn't** go anywhere.

What **did** Rick **do** on Saturday?
He **stayed** home and **studied** for a test.

How **did** Meg **spend** her weekend?
She **went** to a karaoke bar and **sang** with some friends.

For a list of irregular past forms, see the appendix at the back of the book.

A Complete these conversations. Then practice with a partner.

1. A: .... you .... (stay) home on Saturday?
   B: No, I .... (call) my friend. We .... (drive) to a café for lunch.
2. A: How .... you .... (spend) your last birthday?
   B: I .... (have) a party. Everyone .... (enjoy) it, but the neighbors .... (not, like) the noise.
3. A: What .... you .... (do) last night?
   B: I .... (go) to the new Jim Carrey film. I .... (love) it!
4. A: .... you .... (do) anything special over the weekend?
   B: Yes, I .... I .... (go) shopping. Unfortunately, I .... (spend) all my money. Now I'm broke!
5. A: .... you .... (go) out on Friday night?
   B: No, I .... I .... (invite) friends over, and I .... (cook) dinner for them.

regular verbs

work → work**ed**
invite → invite**d**
study → studi**ed**
stop → stop**ped**

irregular verbs

do → **did**
forget → **forgot**
have → **had**
go → **went**
sing → **sang**
spend → **spent**

B *Pair work* Take turns asking the questions in part A. Give your own information when answering.

A: Did you stay home on Saturday?
B: No, I didn't. I went out with some friends. We saw the new Brad Pitt movie.

4 PRONUNCIATION *Reduction of* did you

A Listen and practice. Notice how **did you** is reduced in the following questions.

[dɪdʒə]
Did you have a good time?

[wədɪdʒə]
What did you do last night?

B *Pair work* Practice the questions in part A of Exercise 3 again. Pay attention to the pronunciation of **did you**.

5 WORD POWER Chores and activities

A Find two other words or phrases from the list that usually go with each verb.

the bed	a vacation	a good time	a trip	shopping
a lot of fun	the dishes	dancing	the laundry	some photocopies

do	*my homework*		
go	*bowling*		
have	*a party*		
make	*a phone call*		
take	*a day off*		

B Circle the things you did last weekend. Then compare with a partner.

A: I went bowling with my friends and had a good time.
B: I didn't have a very good time. I did the laundry and . . .

6 DISCUSSION Any questions?

Group work Take turns. One student makes a statement about the weekend. Other students ask questions. Each student answers at least four questions.

A: I went dancing on Saturday night.
B: **Where** did you go?
A: To the Rock-it Club.
C: **Who** did you go with?
A: I went with my brother.
D: **What time** did you go?
A: We went around 10:00.
E: **How** did you like it?
A: I . . .

7 LISTENING What did you do last night?

A Listen to John and Laura describe what they did last night. Check (✓) the correct information about each person.

	John	Laura
had a boring time	☐	☐
had a good time	☐	☐
met an old friend	☐	☐
got home late	☐	☐

B Listen again. What did each person do? Take notes. Then take turns telling their stories to a partner.

5 WORD POWER

***Learning objectives:** learn vocabulary for chores and activities; learn collocations with* do, go, have, make, *and* take

A

- Copy the chart onto the board. Explain the task.
- Ss complete the task in pairs. Go around the class and give help with new vocabulary.
- ***Option:*** Allow Ss to use dictionaries.
- Ask different Ss to write their answers on the board. Give help with any collocations they don't know.
- ***Option:*** Ss sit in a circle. One S says a verb (e.g., *take*). The next S says a collocation (e.g., *a trip*).

Answers

do	my homework	the dishes	the laundry
go	bowling	shopping	dancing
have	a party	a good time	a lot of fun
make	a phone call	the bed	some photocopies
take	a day off	a vacation	a trip

B

- Explain the task. Ss complete the task and compare with a partner.

For a new way to teach this exercise, try the ***Collocations Survey*** on page T-157.

6 DISCUSSION

***Learning objectives:** discuss activities using the simple past; develop the skill of asking follow-up questions*

Group work

- Model the example discussion with four Ss.
- Point out that a good listener shows interest in a conversation by asking follow-up questions.
- Ss complete the activity in groups. Remind Ss to use reduced forms of *did you*.
- ***Option:*** The Ss get one point for each follow-up question they ask. The Ss with the most points in each group win.

7 LISTENING

***Learning objective:** develop skills in listening for main ideas and details*

A [CD 2, Track 13]

- Write two columns on the board, one with the heading *Good* and one with the heading *Boring*.
- Set the scene. Ask: "Did you have a good time or a boring time last night? What did you do?" List Ss' activities in the correct columns.
- Explain the task. Play the audio program and Ss complete the chart.
- Ss compare answers in pairs. Then go over answers with the class.

Audio script

LAURA: So, what did you do last night, John?
JOHN: Uh, I went to my boss's house for dinner.
LAURA: Really? How was it?
JOHN: Oh, the food was OK, but the people weren't very interesting. They talked about football all night, and I hate football. Then we watched some boring sports videos. I didn't get home until after midnight.
LAURA: Well, that doesn't sound like much fun. I had a great time last night! I went to a party and met an old school friend of mine. We haven't seen each other for years, so we had lots to talk about. We stayed at the party all night!
JOHN: Hmm, it sounds like you had a much better time than I did.
LAURA: Yeah. I guess you're right.

Answers

	John	***Laura***
had a boring time	✓	
had a good time		✓
met an old friend		✓
got home late	✓	✓

B

- Explain the task. Point out that Ss will take notes about each person's night. They will use the notes to tell a story.
- Play the audio program. Ss take notes.
- Ss work in pairs. One S retells John's story, and the other S retells Laura's story.

End of Cycle 1

Do your students need more practice?

Assign . . .	***for more practice in . . .***
Workbook Exercises 1–7 on pages 37–40	Grammar, Vocabulary, Reading, and Writing
Lab Guide Exercises 1–3 and 5–7 on page 13	Listening, Pronunciation, Speaking, and Grammar

CONVERSATION

Learning objectives: *practice a conversation about a vacation; see the past of* be *in context*

A [CD 2, Track 14]

- Books closed. Set the scene. Celia and Don are talking about Don's vacation.
- Write these focus questions on the board:
  1. Did Don enjoy his vacation?
  2. Where did he go?
  3. How long was he there?
- Play the audio program. Elicit Ss' answers to the focus questions. (Answers: 1. yes 2. Hawaii 3. about a week) Go over any expressions Ss don't understand.
- ***Option:*** Add more focus questions to the board, e.g.:
  4. Who did Don go with?
  5. How was the weather?
  6. How were the waves?
  Play the audio program again and check Ss' answers. (Answers: 4. his cousin 5. cloudy 6. amazing)
- Books open. Play the audio program again. Ss listen and read the conversation silently.
- Ss practice the conversation in pairs.

! For a new way to teach this Conversation, try ***Say It With Feeling!*** on page T-150.

B

- Ask Ss to predict what happened. Write their ideas on the board.
- Play the audio program. Ss listen to find out if any prediction was correct.

Audio script

CELIA: So, tell me! What happened?
DON: Well, like I said, I went surfing every day. One day I entered a contest and I won. I got first prize!
CELIA: Wow! Congratulations!
DON: But that's not all. After I won the contest, a man asked me to model for *Hawaiian Surf* magazine. I'm in next month's edition. Can you believe it? A model!

Answer

Don went surfing. He won a contest and a man asked him to model in a magazine.

GRAMMAR FOCUS

Learning objective: *practice the past of* be *in questions and short answers*

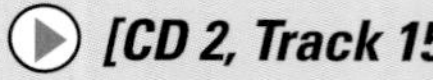

[CD 2, Track 15]

Past of* be *questions

- Write these questions on the board, with *was* or *were* underlined:
  1. Was the weather OK?
  2. What was the best thing about the trip?
  3. How was your vacation?
  4. How long were you there?
- Focus Ss' attention on the Conversation in Exercise 8. Ask Ss to number the questions in the order they appear. (Answer: 3, 4, 1, 2)
- Focus Ss' attention on the underlined words on the board and elicit the rules for yes/no and Wh-questions:

  Was/Were + subject + verb?
  Wh-question + *was/were* + subject + verb?

Was/Were *and contractions*

- Elicit when to use *was* and *were*. Focus Ss' attention on the Grammar Focus box if they aren't sure. Point out that the contraction of *was not* is *wasn't* and *were not* is *weren't*.
- Use the audio program to present the questions, short answers, and contractions.
- Explain the task. Model the first conversation with two Ss.
- Ss complete the task individually. Then Ss practice the conversations in pairs.

Answers

1. A: How long **were** your parents in Europe?
   B: They **were** there for two weeks.
   A: **Were** they in London the whole time?
   B: No, they **weren't**. They also went to Paris.
2. A: **Were** you in Los Angeles last weekend?
   B: No, I **wasn't**. I **was** in San Francisco.
   A: How **was** it?
   B: It **was** great! But it **was** foggy and cool as usual.
3. A: **Were** you away last week?
   B: Yes, I **was** in Istanbul.
   A: Really? How long **were** you there?
   B: For almost a week. I **was** there on business.

8 CONVERSATION How was your vacation?

A Listen and practice.

Celia: Hi, Don. How was your vacation?
Don: It was excellent! I went to Hawaii with my cousin. We had a great time.
Celia: Lucky you. How long were you there?
Don: About a week.
Celia: Fantastic! Was the weather OK?
Don: Not really. It was cloudy most of the time. But we went surfing every day. The waves were amazing.
Celia: So, what was the best thing about the trip?
Don: Well, something incredible happened. You won't believe it.

B Listen to the rest of the conversation. What happened?

9 GRAMMAR FOCUS

Past of be

		Contractions
Were you in Hawaii?	Yes, I **was**.	was**n't** = was not
Was the weather OK?	No, it **wasn't**.	were**n't** = were not
Were you and your cousin on vacation?	Yes, we **were**.	
Were your parents there?	No, they **weren't**.	
How long **were** you away?	I **was** away for a week.	
How **was** your vacation?	It **was** excellent!	

Complete these conversations. Then practice with a partner.

1. A: How long .... your parents in Europe?
   B: They .... there for two weeks.
   A: .... they in London the whole time?
   B: No, they .... They also went to Paris.
2. A: .... you in Los Angeles last weekend?
   B: No, I .... I .... in San Francisco.
   A: How .... it?
   B: It .... great! But it .... foggy and cool as usual.
3. A: .... you away last week?
   B: Yes, I .... in Istanbul.
   A: Really? How long .... you there?
   B: For almost a week. I .... there on business.

10 DISCUSSION On vacation

A *Group work* Ask your classmates about their last vacations. Ask these questions or your own ideas.

Where did you spend your last vacation?
How long were you away?
Who were you with?
What did you do there?
How was the weather? the food?
Do you want to go there again?

B *Class activity* Who had an interesting vacation? Tell the class who and why.

11 LISTENING Welcome back.

Listen to Jason and Barbara talk about their vacations. Complete the chart.

	Vacation place	Enjoyed it? Yes	No	Reason(s)
Jason	....	☐	☐	....
Barbara	....	☐	☐	....

12 WRITING A postcard

A Read this postcard.

Dear Richard,
Greetings from Acapulco!
I'm having a great time!
Yesterday I went on a tour
of the city, and today I went
shopping. I bought some
beautiful jewelry. Oh, and last
night, I heard some Mariachi
singers on the street. They were
terrific. That's all for now.
Love,
Kathy

Richard
1125 W
Alamed
Los A

B Write a postcard to a partner about your last vacation. Then exchange postcards. Do you have any questions about the vacation?

13 INTERCHANGE 7 Vacation disasters

Imagine you took a vacation but everything went wrong. Go to Interchange 7.

10 DISCUSSION

Learning objectives: *discuss vacations using the past tense; develop the skill of retelling a story*

A Group work

- Books closed. Ss work in small groups. Assign different groups the topics *transportation*, *weather*, and *food*. Groups brainstorm words related to the topics.
- Ask a S from each group to write their words on the board. For example:

Transportation	Weather	Food
car, bus	rainy, sunny	good, bad

- Books open. Explain the task and read the example questions. Ask Ss to think of more questions related to vacations. Write their questions on the board.
- Model the task by describing a vacation you took.
- Ss take turns talking about their vacations in small groups. Go around the class and note any errors.
- Write any errors you noted on the board. Ss try to correct them as a class.

TIP It's best not to interrupt Ss during a discussion or fluency activity. Instead, listen and note any errors you hear. Go over the most common ones after the activity.

B Class activity

- Ss in each group vote for the most interesting vacation. Then one S from each group tells the class about it. Encourage other Ss to ask questions.

11 LISTENING

Learning objective: *develop skills in listening for main ideas and details*

[CD 2, Track 16]

- Set the scene. Two friends, Jason and Barbara, are talking about their vacations.
- Play the audio program. Ask Ss to listen to find out their vacation places and if they enjoyed them. They write those answers in the chart.
- Play the audio program again. Ss list the reasons they enjoyed or didn't enjoy their vacations.
- Go over answers with the class.

Audio script

BARBARA: Jason! Hi! Welcome back. You were away last week, right?
JASON: Yeah, I was on vacation.
BARBARA: Where did you go?
JASON: I went to San Francisco.
BARBARA: Nice! How was it?
JASON: Oh, I loved it!
BARBARA: What did you like most about it?
JASON: Well, San Francisco is such a beautiful place. And the weather was actually pretty nice.
BARBARA: Well, that sounds more exciting than my last vacation.
JASON: What did you do, Barbara?
BARBARA: I just stayed home. I don't have enough money to take a trip anywhere.
JASON: Oh, that's too bad.
BARBARA: Oh, not really. I actually enjoyed my vacation. I went to the gym every day, and I lost three pounds.
JASON: Well, that's great. Good for you!

Answers

	Vacation place	Enjoyed it?	Reason(s)
Jason	San Francisco	Yes	beautiful place, nice weather
Barbara	home	Yes	lost 3 pounds

12 WRITING

Learning objectives: *learn postcard-writing skills; use the past tense to write a postcard about a vacation*

A

- Ss read the postcard silently. Elicit or explain any new vocabulary.

B

- Explain the task. Tell Ss to use the questions in Exercise 10 for ideas about the topic.
- Ss write postcards in pairs. Remind Ss to include the greeting, body, signature, and their partner's address. Go around the class and check Ss' work. Then Ss exchange postcards.
- ***Option:*** Bring in real postcards for Ss to use.

! For a new way to teach this Writing, try ***Pass the Paper*** on page T-153.

13 INTERCHANGE 7

See page T-121 for teaching notes.

14 READING

Learning objectives: *read and discuss vacation postcards; develop skills in reading for main ideas and supporting details*

- ***Option:*** Ask Ss to bring in recent vacation photos or postcards. In pairs or small groups, Ss talk about the places.
- Ask Ss to cover the writing on the postcards and look at the pictures. Ask: "Where did each person go on his or her vacation? What do you think he or she did there?" Elicit ideas. Help with vocabulary as needed (e.g., *Easter Island*, *statues*, *caribou*).
- ***Option:*** Bring in a world map and help Ss find Easter Island, Hawaii, and Alaska. Elicit Ss' knowledge about these places.

A

- Explain the task. Remind Ss to try to guess the meanings of any words they don't know.
- Ss read the three postcards silently and complete the task individually. Then they compare answers in pairs or small groups.
- ***Option:*** Ask pairs or groups to find the place in each postcard where the sentences fit best.
- Elicit or explain any new vocabulary.

Vocabulary

statues: stone or clay sculptures that look like people
caves: large underground holes
spa: a health resort; a vacation place where people go to exercise and become healthier
meditated: thought of only one thing, in order to calm one's mind
vegetarian food: food that contains no animal products
snorkeling: swimming with a mask and tube that allows one to breathe underwater
rafts: rubber boats filled with air
wildlife: wild animals and birds

- Go over answers with the class.

Answers

2, 3, 1

B *Pair work*

- Ss answer the questions in pairs. Go around the class and give help as needed.
- To check answers, have pairs share their responses with the class.

Answers

1. Margaret
2. Kevin
3. Debbie
4. Ss' answers will vary.

For a new way to teach this Reading, try ***Jigsaw Learning*** on page T-152.

End of Cycle 2

Do your students need more practice?

Assign . . .	***for more practice in . . .***
Workbook Exercises 8–11 on pages 41–42	Grammar, Vocabulary, Reading, and Writing
Lab Guide Exercises 4 and 8 on pages 13–14	Listening, Pronunciation, Speaking, and Grammar
Video Activity Book Unit 7	Listening, Speaking, and Cultural Awareness
CD-ROM Unit 7	Grammar, Vocabulary, Reading, Listening, and Speaking

14 READING Vacation postcards

Look at the pictures. What do you think each person did on his or her vacation?

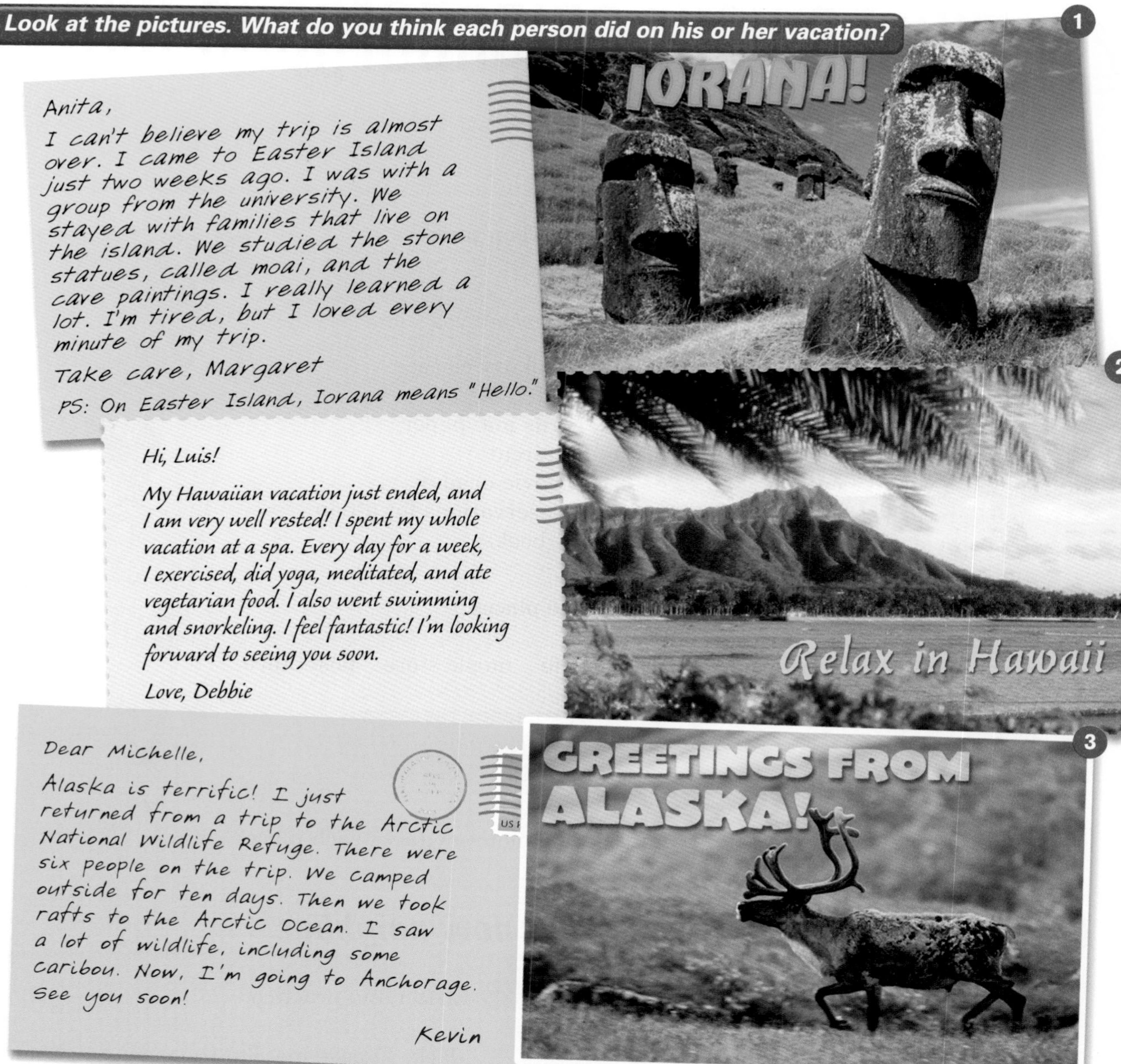

1

Anita,

I can't believe my trip is almost over. I came to Easter Island just two weeks ago. I was with a group from the university. We stayed with families that live on the island. We studied the stone statues, called moai, and the cave paintings. I really learned a lot. I'm tired, but I loved every minute of my trip.

Take care, Margaret

PS: On Easter Island, Iorana means "Hello."

2

Hi, Luis!

My Hawaiian vacation just ended, and I am very well rested! I spent my whole vacation at a spa. Every day for a week, I exercised, did yoga, meditated, and ate vegetarian food. I also went swimming and snorkeling. I feel fantastic! I'm looking forward to seeing you soon.

Love, Debbie

3

Dear Michelle,

Alaska is terrific! I just returned from a trip to the Arctic National Wildlife Refuge. There were six people on the trip. We camped outside for ten days. Then we took rafts to the Arctic Ocean. I saw a lot of wildlife, including some caribou. Now, I'm going to Anchorage. See you soon!

Kevin

A Read the postcards. Then write the number of the postcard where each sentence could go.

.... I lost five pounds and feel terrific!
.... This was kind of dangerous, but we got there safely!
.... It's a tiny island about 2,300 miles west of Santiago, Chile.

B ***Pair work*** Talk about these questions. Explain your answers.

1. Which person learned a lot on vacation?
2. Who had a vacation that was full of adventure?
3. Who had a very relaxing vacation?
4. Which vacation sounds the most interesting to you?

8 What's your neighborhood like?

1 WORD POWER Places

A Match the words and the definitions. Then practice asking the questions with a partner.

What's a . . . ?	*It's a place where you . . . .*
1. barber shop	a. wash and dry clothes
2. laundromat	b. buy food
3. library	c. buy cards and paper
4. stationery store	d. get a haircut
5. travel agency	e. see a movie or play
6. grocery store	f. make reservations for a trip
7. theater	g. borrow books

B *Pair work* Write definitions for these places.

clothing store   drugstore   Internet café   music store   post office

It's a place where you find new fashions. (clothing store)

C *Group work* Read your definitions. Can others guess each place?

2 CONVERSATION *I'm your new neighbor.*

Listen and practice.

Jack: Excuse me. I'm your new neighbor, Jack. I just moved in.
Mrs. Day: Oh. Yes?
Jack: I'm looking for a grocery store. Are there any around here?
Mrs. Day: Yes, there are some on Pine Street.
Jack: Oh, good. And is there a laundromat near here?
Mrs. Day: Well, I think there's one across from the shopping center.
Jack: Thank you.
Mrs. Day: By the way, there's a barber shop in the shopping center, too.
Jack: A barber shop?

What's your neighborhood like?

In Unit 8, students discuss neighborhoods. In Cycle 1, they talk about places using there is/there are *and prepositions of place. In Cycle 2, they talk about neighborhood problems using count and noncount nouns with* how many *and* how much.

Cycle 1, Exercises 1–6

WORD POWER

Learning objective: *learn vocabulary for discussing places in the neighborhood*

A

- Introduce the topic of neighborhoods. Ask: "What places do you need to find in a neighborhood?" Elicit Ss' answers and write them on the board.
- Elicit the names of places Ss see in the picture (e.g., *laundromat, library, barber shop*).
- Model the task. Ask "What's a barber shop?" Tell Ss to say "stop" when you read the correct definition. Read out possible answers (e.g., *It's a place where you wash and dry clothes. It's a place where you buy food.*) until the Ss say "stop."
- Ss match the words and definitions individually. Then go over answers with the class.

Answers

1. d 2. a 3. g 4. c 5. f 6. b 7. e

- Ss take turns asking and answering the questions in pairs. Go around the class and give help as needed.
- ***Option:*** To make the activity more challenging, Ss cover the text and use only the picture to ask and answer questions.
- Go over any errors you noticed, including pronunciation errors.

B *Pair work*

- Present the example definition for *clothing store*. Then elicit more possible definitions from the class (e.g., *It's a place where you buy jeans.*) and write them on the board.
- Ss write definitions for each place in pairs. Go around the class and give help as needed.

Possible answers

Place	***It's a place where you . . . .***
clothing store	find new fashions
drugstore	buy medicine and toiletries
Internet café	send e-mails and surf the net
music store	buy CDs and DVDs
post office	get stamps and mail letters

C *Group work*

- Model the task. Each pair from part B joins another pair. Pairs take turns giving definitions and guessing places.

For a new way to review the vocabulary in this Word Power, try the ***Pair Crossword*** on page T-157.

2 CONVERSATION

Learning objectives: *practice a conversation between neighbors; see* there is/there are *and* one/any/some *in context*

[CD 2, Track 17]

- Books closed. Write this question on the board: *When you move to a new neighborhood, what do you need to find?*
- Elicit answers from the class and write them on the board.
- Set the scene. Jack just moved into a new neighborhood, and he is looking for two things. What are they? Play the audio program.
- Go over answers with the class. (Answer: He's looking for a grocery store and a laundromat.)
- Books open. Elicit information about the picture. Ask: "What other place does Mrs. Day suggest? Why?" Then play the audio program again. Ss listen and find the answers. (Answer: She suggests a barbershop because Jack needs a haircut.)
- Play the audio program again. Ss listen and read the conversation silently.
- Ss practice the conversation in pairs.

GRAMMAR FOCUS

Learning objectives: *ask and answer questions with* there is/there are; *practice using* one, any, *and* some; *practice prepositions of place*

[CD 2, Track 18]

Is there/Are there?

- Before class, write these words on nine large cards:

is	there	a laundromat
one	are	grocery stores
any	some	near/around here

TIP Cards are useful for helping Ss visualize grammar in an active way. They work well with grammar including word order and substitution.

- Focus Ss' attention on the Conversation on page 50. Ask: "What question does Jack ask beginning with *is there*?" Elicit the question. Then ask four Ss to come to the front of the class. Have them stand in line holding up these cards:
  S1: *is* S2: *there*
  S3: *a laundromat* S4: *near/around here*
- Ask: "What question does Jack ask beginning with *are there*?" Elicit the question. Then ask five Ss to stand in line holding up these cards:
  S1: *are* S2: *there* S3: *any*
  S4: *grocery stores* S5: *near/around here*
- Focus Ss' attention on the two questions in the Grammar Focus box. Elicit the rule for forming questions with *is there* and *are there*.
  Is there + *a/an* + singular noun + near/around here?
  Are there + *any* + plural noun + near/around here?

One *and* some

- Ask four Ss to hold up these cards:
  S1: *there* S2: *is*
  S3: *a laundromat* S4: *near/around here*
- Point out that singular nouns such as *a laundromat* can be replaced by *one*. Ask another S to take the card *one* and replace S3.
- Repeat the activity with plural nouns. This time, replace *grocery stores* with *some*.
- Play the audio program.

Prepositions

- Elicit or explain the meaning of the prepositions. Use the map. Ask: "What places are *on* Elm Street?" (Answer: King Plaza Hotel, Frank's Café, Jamison Hotel) Ask Ss about other places using prepositions.
- ***Option:*** For more practice visualizing the prepositions in an active way, ask Ss to stand *across from* each other, *next to* the wall, *near* the board, etc.

A

- Explain the task and read the example questions. Ss write questions individually. Point out that there should be a preposition in each question.
- Ss compare their questions in small groups. They read out their questions and check for grammatical accuracy.
- Go around the class and give help as needed. Ask three or four Ss with correct questions to write them on the board.

Possible answers

All questions should follow these patterns:
Is there + a singular noun + a preposition + a place?
(e.g., *Is there a bank opposite the hotel?*)
Are there any + plural noun + a preposition + a place?
(e.g., *Are there any hotels on Elm Street?*)

B *Pair work*

- Model the task two or three times using the map and the questions on the board:
  T: Is there a pay phone around here?
  S1: Yes, there is. There's one across from the post office.
  T: Are there any gas stations on Maple Avenue?
  S2: No, there aren't. But there are two on Main Street.

TIP To make sure that Ss understand instructions, always model the task at least twice. If possible, model it with different Ss each time.

- Ss take turns asking and answering their questions in pairs. Go around the class and give help as needed.

! For a new way to teach this Grammar Focus, try the ***Picture Dictation*** on page T-154. Describe a town or city center to your Ss. Include streets and places.

3 GRAMMAR FOCUS

There is, there are; one, any, some

Is there a laundromat near here?
Yes, **there is**. There's **one** across from the shopping center.
No, **there isn't**, but there's **one** next to the library.

Are there any grocery stores around here?
Yes, **there are**. There are **some** nice stores on Pine Street.
No, **there aren't**, but there are **some** on Third Avenue.
No, **there aren't any** around here.

Prepositions
on
next to
near/close to
across from/opposite
in front of
in back of/behind
between
on the corner of

A Write questions about these places in the neighborhood map below.

a bank	gas stations	a gym	a laundromat	a post office
a department store	grocery stores	hotels	a pay phone	restaurants

Is there a bank around here?
Are there any gas stations on Main Street?

B ***Pair work*** Ask and answer the questions you wrote in part A.

A: Is there a pay phone around here?
B: Yes, there is. There's one across from the post office.

4 PRONUNCIATION *Reduction of* there is/there are

A Listen and practice. Notice how **there is** and **there are** are reduced in conversation, except for short answers.

Is there a laundromat near here?
Yes, **there is**. **There's** one across from the shopping center.

Are there any grocery stores around here?
Yes, **there are**. **There are** some on Pine Street.

B Practice the questions and answers in part B of Exercise 3 again.

5 SPEAKING *My neighborhood*

Group work Take turns asking and answering questions about places like these in your neighborhood.

a bookstore	a karaoke bar
coffee shops	a library
dance clubs	movie theaters
drugstores	a music store
a gym	a park
an Internet café	restaurants

A: Is there a good bookstore in your neighborhood?
B: Yes, there's an excellent one across from the park.
C: Are there any coffee shops?
B: Sorry, I don't know.
D: Are there any cool dance clubs?
B: I'm not sure, but I think there's one . . .

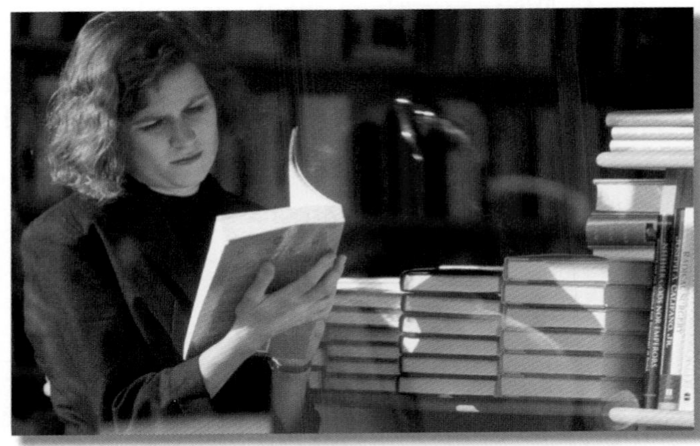

useful expressions

Sorry, I don't know.
I'm not sure, but I think . . .
Of course. There's one . . .

6 LISTENING *What are you looking for?*

A Listen to some hotel guests ask about places to visit in the neighborhood. Complete the chart.

Place	Location	Interesting? Yes	Interesting? No
Hard Rock Cafe	....	☐	☐
Science Museum	....	☐	☐
Aquarium	....	☐	☐

B *Pair work* Which place sounds the most interesting to you? Why?

4 PRONUNCIATION

***Learning objectives:** notice the reduction of* there is/there are*; learn to sound natural when using* there is/there are

A [CD 2, Track 19]

- Play the audio program. Point out the reduced forms. Ask Ss to practice the short conversations using the reductions. Point out that *there is* is often contracted to *there's* in writing, but *there are* is not.

B

- Go over the instructions and model the task.
- Go around the class and give individual feedback on Ss' use of reductions.

TIP It's more important to recognize reductions than to produce them. Don't force Ss to produce reductions if they are not ready.

5 SPEAKING

***Learning objective:** ask and answer questions about neighborhoods using* is there/are there *and* one/any/some

Group work

- Model the task. Ask a S: "Is there a bookstore in your neighborhood?" If the S has difficulty answering, point out the *useful expressions* box for ideas.
- ***Option:*** Point out that people show interest in conversations by adding follow-up questions (e.g., *What's the name of the bookstore? Can you buy used books there?*).
- Ss complete the task in groups. Go around the class and note the Ss' level of fluency.

6 LISTENING

***Learning objective:** develop skills in listening for details*

A [CD 2, Track 20]

- Read out the instructions to set the scene. Then play the audio program. Ss listen and complete the *Location* column in the chart.
- Play the audio program again. Ss listen, decide if the hotel clerk thinks the places are interesting, and check (✓) Yes or No.
- Go over answers with the class.

Audio script

CLERK: Good morning. Can I help you?
GUEST 1: Yes. We need some directions.
CLERK: Sure. What are you looking for?
GUEST 1: Well, first of all, we're looking for the Hard Rock Cafe. How far is it from here?
CLERK: Oh, it's just a few minutes from here – right across from the National Bank.
GUEST 2: The National Bank on Park Avenue?
CLERK: Yes, that's the one.
GUEST 2: Is the Hard Rock Cafe a nice place?
CLERK: Well, I think so. The food is good, and there are some interesting things to look at in the restaurant – like one of Elvis's cars.
GUEST 2: Great! And where is the Science Museum?
CLERK: Well, that's near City Hall.
GUEST 1: Near City Hall. OK, I know where that is. And what's the museum like?
CLERK: Actually, it's not very good. It's small, and there isn't a lot to see there. It's really for young kids.
GUEST 1: Oh, then maybe we won't go there.
GUEST 2: Mmm, one last question – is there an aquarium in the city?
CLERK: Yes, there's a very good one. It's only about six blocks from here. It's in the park next to the train station.
GUEST 2: Oh, next to the train station.
CLERK: Yes. Definitely visit the aquarium.
GUEST 1: Great! Thanks a lot.
CLERK: You're welcome. Have a good day.

Answers

Place	*Location*	*Interesting?*
Hard Rock Cafe	across from the National Bank on Park Avenue	Yes
Science Museum	near City Hall	No
Aquarium	in the park next to the train station	Yes

B Pair work

- Ss discuss the question in pairs.

End of Cycle 1

Do your students need more practice?

Assign . . .	*for more practice in . . .*
Workbook Exercises 1–5 on pages 43–46	Grammar, Vocabulary, Reading, and Writing
Lab Guide Exercises 1–6 on page 15	Listening, Pronunciation, Speaking, and Grammar

Cycle 2, Exercises 7–12

7 SNAPSHOT

Learning objective: *learn vocabulary for talking about problems with neighbors*

- Ask pairs of Ss to brainstorm things that bad neighbors do. Elicit ideas from the class and write them on the board.
- Go over the complaints about neighbors. Elicit or explain new vocabulary.

Vocabulary

complaints: statements people make about problems
barks: makes a loud noise, like a dog
loud: noisy
privacy: state of being alone or without other people
kids: children
garbage: trash

- Ss answer the questions in small groups. Go around the groups and give help as needed.

8 CONVERSATION

Learning objectives: *practice a conversation about a neighborhood; see* how many *and* how much *with quantifiers in context.*

[CD 2, Track 21]

- Elicit information about the picture. Ask: "What is the woman doing? What does the neighborhood look like? Does it look safe?"
- Books closed. Write these focus questions on the board:
  1. *What are Nick and Pam talking about?*
  2. *What happens during the phone call?*
- Play the audio program. Ask Ss to listen for the answers to the focus questions. Then go over the answers. (Answers: 1. Pam's new apartment and neighborhood 2. Pam's car alarm makes a loud noise.)

TIP To reduce anxiety, point out that Ss will hear the audio program several times. Remind them that they aren't expected to understand every word.

- Write these additional focus questions on the board:
  1. *Where is Pam's new apartment?*
  2. *Which floor does she live on?*
  3. *What kind of restaurant is there nearby?*
- Play the audio program again. Elicit Ss' answers. (Answers: 1. downtown 2. the fifth 3. Korean) Then elicit or explain any new vocabulary.

Vocabulary

downtown: the business center of a city
convenient: nearby; easy to find things
parking: places to park the car
safe: not dangerous; without crime
hold on: wait a minute

- Books open. Play the audio program again. Ss listen and read the conversation silently.
- Ss practice the conversation in pairs.
- ***Option:*** Ss continue the conversation in pairs. What happened? Why did the car alarm go off?

! For a new way to practice this Conversation, try the ***Onion Ring*** technique on page T-151.

7 SNAPSHOT

COMMON COMPLAINTS about neighbors

NOISE
"My neighbor's dog barks all night."
"My neighbor always has loud parties."

PRIVACY
"The kids next door always play in my yard."
"My neighbor visits every day. It's too much!"

ANIMAL PROBLEMS
"My neighbor's cats go everywhere."
"My neighbor has six dogs. It's a zoo!"

CLEANLINESS
"My neighbor has garbage in his front yard."
"My neighbor never cuts the grass."

Source: Based on information from *Neighbor Law: Fences, Trees, Boundaries, & Noise*

Do you ever have any of these complaints? Which ones?
What other complaints do you have about neighbors?
What do you do when you have complaints?

8 CONVERSATION *It's pretty safe.*

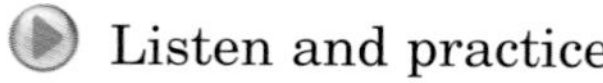

Listen and practice.

Nick: How do you like your new apartment?
Pam: I love it. It's downtown, so it's very convenient.
Nick: Downtown? Is there much noise?
Pam: Oh, no. There isn't any. I live on the fifth floor.
Nick: How many restaurants are there near your place?
Pam: A lot. In fact, there's an excellent Korean place just around the corner.
Nick: What about parking?
Pam: Well, there aren't many parking garages. But I usually find a place on the street.
Nick: Is there much crime?
Pam: No, it's pretty safe. Hold on. That's my car alarm! I'll call you back later.

9 GRAMMAR FOCUS

Quantifiers; how many *and* how much

Count nouns	*Noncount nouns*
Are there **many restaurants**?	Is there **much crime**?
Yes, there are **a lot**.	Yes, there's **a lot**.
Yes, there are **a few**.	Yes, there's **a little**.
No, there are**n't many**.	No, there is**n't much**.
No, there are**n't any**.	No, there is**n't any**.
No, there are **none**.	No, there's **none**.
How many restaurants are there?	**How much** crime is there?
There are ten or twelve.	There's a lot of street crime.

A Write answers to these questions about your neighborhood. Then practice with a partner.

1. Are there many apartment buildings? ....
2. How much traffic is there? ....
3. How many dance clubs are there? ....
4. Is there much noise? ....
5. Are there many pay phones? ....
6. Is there much pollution? ....
7. How many swimming pools are there? ....
8. Is there much parking? ....

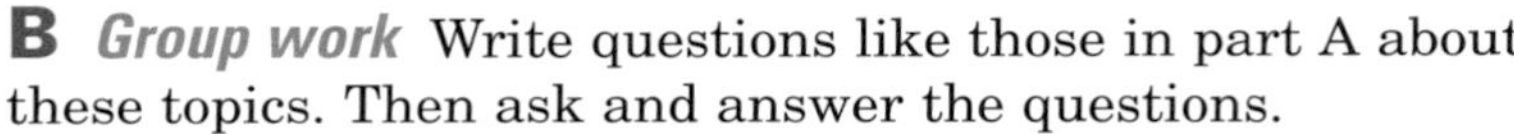

B *Group work* Write questions like those in part A about these topics. Then ask and answer the questions.

cafés crime parks pollution public transportation schools traffic lights

10 INTERCHANGE 8 Neighborhood committee

Make your neighborhood a better place. Go to Interchange 8.

11 WRITING A roommate wanted ad

A Read these bulletin board ads asking for roommates.

Roommates Wanted

Roommate needed to share large 3-bedroom apt. in nice neighborhood. Great park across the street. Only $440 a month! Parking available. Call Sheri or Jen at (352) 555-8381.

Quiet student looking for roommate to share 2-bedroom house near campus. Pets OK. $550 a month plus utilities. E-mail Greg at g.adams@cup.org.

B Now write a "roommate wanted" ad. Use your real name at the end, but you can use a false phone number or e-mail address.

C *Class activity* Put your ads on the bulletin board or wall. Read all the ads and choose one. Then find the person who wrote it. Ask questions to get more information.

9 GRAMMAR FOCUS

Learning objectives: *ask and answer questions with count and noncount nouns; practice using quantifiers*

[CD 2, Track 22]

Count and noncount nouns

- Write this chart on the board:

Count nouns	Noncount nouns
restaurant	traffic
café	parking

- Ask: "Which nouns take a plural *-s* ending?" (Answer: restaurant and café) "Which nouns usually don't take a plural *-s* ending?" (Answer: traffic and parking) Explain that *restaurant* and *café* are count nouns because we can count them (e.g., *one restaurant, two restaurants*). However, we don't count *traffic* or *parking*.

For more practice with count and noncount nouns, play ***Tic-Tac-Toe*** on page T-148.

How many *and* how much

- Focus Ss' attention on the Conversation on page 53. Have Ss underline questions about *noise* and *crime* (e.g., *Is there much noise? Is there much crime?*). Elicit or explain the rules:
  Is there + *much* + noncount noun?
  How much + noncount noun + *is there*?
- Have Ss underline questions with *are there* or *many*. Elicit or explain the rules:
  Are there + *many* + count noun?
  How many + count noun + *are there*?

Quantifiers

- Focus Ss' attention on the Grammar Focus box. Point out that quantifiers are used to describe different amounts of things (e.g., *a lot, a few, any, many, much, none*).
- Ask Ss to look at the Grammar Focus box. Ask "How are *a lot, any*, and *none* similar?" (Answer: They can be used with both count or noncount nouns.)
- Play the audio program.

A

- Model the first question. Ss complete the exercise individually. Then Ss compare their answers in pairs.
- Go over the answers as a class.

Possible answers

1. Yes, there are a lot/many. No, there aren't many/any. No, there are none.
2. There's a lot/a little/none. There isn't much/any.
3. There are a lot/a few/none. There aren't many/any.
4. Yes, there's a lot. No, there isn't any/much. No, there's none/not much.
5. Yes, there are a lot/many. No, there aren't many/any. No, there are none.
6. Yes, there's a lot. No, there isn't any/much. No, there's none/not much.
7. There are a lot/a few/none. There aren't many/any.
8. Yes, there's a lot. No, there isn't any/much. No, there's none/not much.

- Ss ask and answer the questions in pairs.
- ***Option:*** Ss repeat the task with a new partner.

B *Group work*

- Explain and model the task.
- Ss write questions individually. Then they take turns asking and answering the questions in pairs.

10 INTERCHANGE 8

See page T-122 for teaching notes.

11 WRITING

Learning objectives: *read bulletin board ads; write a "roommate wanted" ad*

A

- Ss read the example ads silently. Elicit or explain any new vocabulary.
- Point out written features of an ad (e.g., *apt.* means *apartment*, articles *a/an* and the verb *be* are usually not included).

B

- Explain the task. Ss write their ads individually. Go around the class and give help as needed.

C *Class activity*

- Explain the task. While Ss are asking questions, check for correct use of count and noncount nouns.

12 READING

***Learning objectives:** read an article from a magazine; develop skills in scanning and reading for detail*

- Ss cover the text and look at the pictures. Ask: "What do you think this New York City neighborhood is like?" Elicit ideas from the class.
- Explain the pre-reading task. Point out that Ss should read quickly and focus on the names of countries only. Set a time limit.

TIP When Ss scan an article, set a time limit. This encourages them to read quickly, focusing only on the task.

- Ss silently scan the article and check (✓) the countries that are *not* mentioned. (Answers: Brazil and Japan) Elicit answers from the class. Ask where they found the names of countries. (Answer: first paragraph)

A

- Model the task. Ask Ss to read the first paragraph. Then elicit the main idea.
- Ss read the next two paragraphs and write the paragraph numbers next to the main ideas.

Answers

2, 1, 3

B

- Ss read the article in detail. Elicit or explain any new vocabulary.

Vocabulary

sidewalks: places next to the street where people walk
crowded with: full of
band: a group of musicians
blend: mix
truly: really
are surrounded by: have all around
adopt: begin to use
rents: money people pay to live in apartments
roomy: with lots of space
long-time: for a long time
resident: a person who lives in a place

- Ss complete the exercise. Go over answers with the class.

Answers

inexpensive stores, big apartments, great markets, nice restaurants, many different cultures, good public transportation

C *Pair work*

- Go over the discussion question with the class. Encourage Ss to consider the residents, the businesses, and other neighborhood characteristics. Ss complete the task in pairs.

End of Cycle 2

Do your students need more practice?

Assign . . .	***for more practice in . . .***
Workbook Exercises 6–9 on pages 47–48	Grammar, Vocabulary, Reading, and Writing
Lab Guide Exercises 7–9 on page 16	Listening, Pronunciation, and Speaking
Video Activity Book Unit 8	Listening, Speaking, and Cultural Awareness
CD-ROM Unit 8	Grammar, Vocabulary, Reading, Listening, and Speaking

Evaluation

Assess Ss' understanding of Units 7 and 8 with the quiz on pages T-206 and T-207.

Assess Ss' understanding of Units 1–8 with one of the tests on pages 125–132 of the *Interchange Third Edition/Passages Placement and Evaluation Package.*

12 READING

The World in One Neighborhood

Scan the article. Then check (✓) the countries that are not mentioned.
☐ Brazil ☐ China ☐ India ☐ Japan ☐ Pakistan ☐ Romania ☐ Thailand

1 The sidewalks are crowded with Indian women in colorful traditional dress. A woman on the corner is selling Chinese cakes. A new song from a Romanian band is playing in a restaurant. Is it India? China? Romania? No, it's Astoria, a neighborhood in Queens, New York City. Astoria was once a mostly Greek neighborhood, but the area is changing fast. New residents from India, Pakistan, Thailand, China, and all over the United States are moving in.

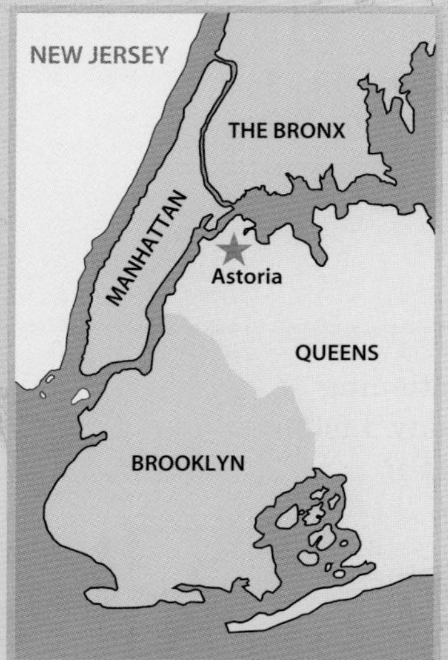

Astoria is a neighborhood in Queens in New York City.

2 The new residents bring many traditions. These traditions blend together to make Astoria truly multicultural. "When people are surrounded by different cultures, they adopt the things that they like," says one resident. "Here in Astoria, it isn't surprising that an Indian woman buys Mexican tortillas from a Korean grocery store. It's one of the things that makes the neighborhood special."

3 It isn't surprising that Astoria is becoming a very popular place to live. The rents are reasonable, the neighborhood is safe, and it has very good public transportation. There are inexpensive stores, many nice restaurants, and good fresh fruit and vegetable markets. And Astoria is a comfortable place to live. Apartments are usually big and roomy. As one long-time resident says, "Why live anywhere else? Astoria has it all."

A Read the article. Then write the number of each paragraph next to its main idea.

.... The new residents make Astoria a multicultural neighborhood.
.... People from all over the world are moving to Astoria.
.... The neighborhood has many good characteristics.

B Check (✓) the things you can find in Astoria.

☐ inexpensive stores ☐ beautiful beaches ☐ many different cultures
☐ big apartments ☐ great markets ☐ interesting old buildings
☐ good schools ☐ nice restaurants ☐ good public transportation

C *Pair work* Do you know of a neighborhood that is similar to Astoria? Describe it.

Units 7–8 Progress check

SELF-ASSESSMENT

How well can you do these things? Check (✓) the boxes.

I can	Very well	OK	A little
Listen to and understand the simple past and past of *be* (Ex. 1)	☐	☐	☐
Describe events using the past tense (Ex. 1)	☐	☐	☐
Ask and answer questions using the simple past (Ex. 2)	☐	☐	☐
Ask and answer questions using the past of *be* (Ex. 2)	☐	☐	☐
Describe the locations of places with *there is/are; one, any, some* (Ex. 3)	☐	☐	☐
Talk about neighborhoods with *how many/much* and quantifiers (Ex. 4)	☐	☐	☐

1 LISTENING Frankie's weekend

A A thief robbed a house on Saturday. A detective is questioning Frankie. The pictures show what Frankie really did on Saturday. Listen to their conversation. Are Frankie's answers true (**T**) or false (**F**)?

1:00 P.M. **T F**

3:00 P.M. **T F**

5:00 P.M. **T F**

6:00 P.M. **T F**

8:00 P.M. **T F**

10:30 P.M. **T F**

B *Pair work* What did Frankie really do? Use the pictures to retell the story.

2 DISCUSSION What can you remember?

A Can you remember what you did yesterday? Check (✓) the things you did. Then add two other things you did.

- ☐ got up early
- ☐ went to class
- ☐ made phone calls
- ☐ went shopping
- ☐ ate at a restaurant
- ☐ did the laundry
- ☐ did the dishes
- ☐ watched TV
- ☐ exercised
- ☐ went to bed late
- ☐ ....
- ☐ ....

B *Group work* Ask questions about each thing in part A.

A: Did you get up early yesterday?
B: No, I didn't. I got up at 10:00. I was very tired.

Units 7–8 Progress check

SELF-ASSESSMENT

***Learning objectives:** reflect on one's learning; identify areas that need improvement*

- Ask: "What did you learn in Units 7 and 8?" Elicit Ss' answers.
- Ss complete the Self-assessment. Encourage them to be honest, and point out they will not get a bad grade if they check (✓) "a little."
- Ss move on to the Progress check exercises. You can have Ss complete them in class or for homework, using one of these techniques:
  1. Ask Ss to complete all the exercises.
  2. Ask Ss: "What do you need to practice?" Then assign exercises based on their answers.
  3. Ask Ss to choose and complete exercises based on their Self-assessment.

1 LISTENING

***Learning objective:** assess one's ability to listen to and understand the simple past and the past of* be

A [CD 2, Track 23]

- Explain the task. Ss listen to a detective ask Frankie questions. They circle **T** if his answers match the pictures and **F** if they don't.
- Play the audio program. Ss complete the task. Then go over answers with the class.

Audio script

DETECTIVE: Hello, Frankie. How was your weekend?
FRANKIE: Oh, it's you, Detective. My weekend? What do you want to know about it?
DETECTIVE: Now just tell the truth. Where were you at 1:00 P.M. on Saturday?
FRANKIE: Ah . . . 1:00 P.M. . . . on Saturday? Well, oh I remember! I was at home. I watched the baseball game on TV. Yeah, the Expos won, four to nothing. It was a great game.
DETECTIVE: OK . . . OK. Where were you at 3:00 P.M.?
FRANKIE: Ah . . . at 3:00? Ah, yeah, I went to my karate class like I always do, every Saturday at 3:00.
DETECTIVE: Karate, huh? Well . . . OK. And what did you do after that? At around 5:00 P.M.?
FRANKIE: Ah, oh, yeah, uh, after karate, I visited some old friends of mine – Tom and Mary Kent, on Front Street.
DETECTIVE: Yeah? Tom and Mary Kent. We'll talk to them. Now Frankie, 6:00. Where were you at 6:00?
FRANKIE: Oh! Gee . . . at 6:00? Well, I went home at 6:00 . . . yeah . . . to . . . uh . . . clean the house.
DETECTIVE: Yeah, yeah, so you cleaned the house. Now listen carefully, Frankie. Where were you at 8:00 on Saturday night?
FRANKIE: Gee . . . at 8:00? Uh . . . oh, yeah . . . I remember now. I was at home. I watched a terrific movie on TV. Yeah . . . it was great!
DETECTIVE: Oh, you watched a movie on TV, did you? And what movie did you watch? What was the name of the movie, Frankie? Huh?
FRANKIE: The movie? The name of the movie. Uh, let me think a minute. It was a fantastic movie.
DETECTIVE: Really?
FRANKIE: No, wait! I remember, it was, uh . . . uh . . . well, it was exciting.
DETECTIVE: OK, OK, Frankie . . .
FRANKIE: . . . and I clearly remember that I went to bed at 10:30, uh, exactly. . . . Yeah. I watched the movie, and I went to bed right after . . . uh . . . the movie. Yeah, boy, I was tired – a long day, like I said.
DETECTIVE: Interesting. Very interesting, Frankie. Come on, Frankie. Let's go down to the police station.
FRANKIE: The police station? Me? Why me? I was at home on Saturday night!
DETECTIVE: Sure, Frankie, sure. [*police siren*]

Answers

T, T, T, T, F, F

B Pair work

- Ss retell the story in pairs.

2 DISCUSSION

***Learning objective:** assess one's ability to ask and answer questions using the simple past tense*

A

- Ss check (✓) the things they did individually yesterday. Then they add two more things.

B Group work

- Ss ask and answer the questions in small groups.

3 SPEAKING

Learning objective: *assess one's ability to describe the locations of places with* there is/are *and* one, any, *and* some

A

- Explain the task. Ss create a neighborhood. They choose five places from the list and add them to *My map*.
- For plurals, tell Ss to be sure to draw two places on their maps.
- Ss complete the task individually.
- Go around the class and give help as needed.

B *Pair work*

- Read the instructions aloud. Ask two Ss to model the example conversation. Explain that Student A draws a café on the corner of Center Street and First Avenue on *My partner's map*. Point out that Ss cannot look at their partner's map.
- Ss take turns asking and answering questions in pairs.
- Tell Ss to ask any additional questions to find the exact location of each place (e.g., *Is it next to the grocery store?*).
- Ss then compare maps. Ask: "Did you draw the places in the correct locations?"

ROLE PLAY

Learning objective: *assess one's ability to talk about neighborhoods with* how many, how much, *and quantifiers*

- Explain the task. Ss work in pairs. Student A is a visitor in Student B's neighborhood. Student A asks questions and Student B answers them.
- Model the example conversation with a S.
- Go over the topics in the box. Explain or elicit any new vocabulary.
- Ss practice the role play in pairs. Then they change roles and practice again.
- Go around the class and check Ss' use of *how many*, *how much*, and quantifiers.

WHAT'S NEXT?

Learning objective: *become more involved in one's learning*

- Focus Ss' attention on the Self-assessment again. Ask: "How well can you do these things now?"
- Ask Ss to underline one thing they need to review. Ask: "What did you underline? How can you review it?"
- If needed, plan additional activities or reviews based on Ss' answers.

3 SPEAKING The neighborhood

A Create a neighborhood. Add five more places to the map labeled "My map." Choose from this list.

a bank   cafés   a dance club   a drugstore   gas stations   a gym   a movie theater

My map

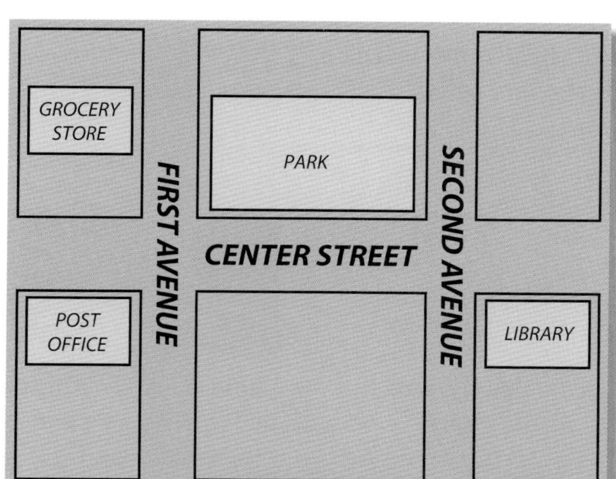

My partner's map

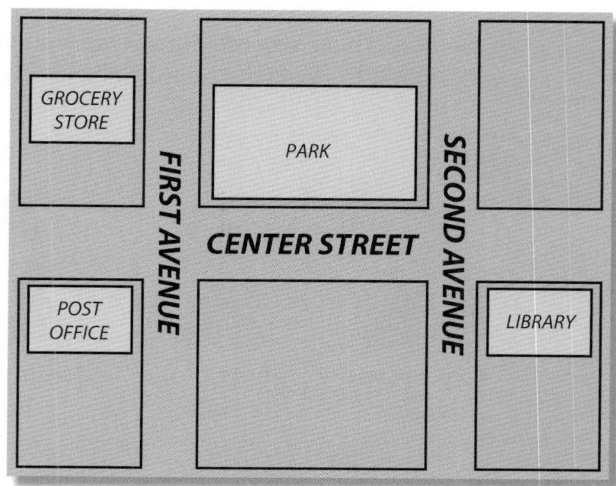

B *Pair work* Ask questions about your partner's map. (But don't look!) Draw the places on the map labeled "My partner's map." When you both finish, compare your maps.

A: Are there any cafés in the neighborhood?
B: Yes, there's one on the corner of Center Street and First Avenue.

4 ROLE PLAY What's it like?

Student A: Imagine you are a visitor in Student B's neighborhood. Ask questions about it.

Student B: Imagine a visitor wants to find out about your neighborhood. Answer the visitor's questions.

A: How much crime is there?
B: There isn't much. It's a very safe neighborhood.
A: Is there much noise?
B: Well, yes, there's a lot. . . .

Change roles and try the role play again.

topics to ask about
- crime
- noise
- parks
- places to shop
- pollution
- public transportation
- schools
- traffic

WHAT'S NEXT?

Look at your Self-assessment again. Do you need to review anything?

What does she look like?

1 WORD POWER Appearance

A Look at these expressions. Can you think of three more words or expressions to describe people? Write them in the box below.

Hair

long brown hair

short blond hair

straight black hair

curly red hair

bald

a mustache and beard

Age

young

middle aged

elderly

Looks

handsome

good-looking

pretty

Height

short

fairly short

medium height

pretty tall

very tall

Other words or expressions

....

....

....

B *Pair work* Choose at least four expressions to describe yourself and your partner. Then compare. Do you agree?

A: You have curly blond hair and a beard. You're young and good-looking.
B: I don't agree. My hair isn't very curly.

Me	My partner
....	....
....	....
....	....
....	....

What does she look like?

In Unit 9, students describe people's appearances. In Cycle 1, they describe people's physical appearances. In Cycle 2, they identify people using modifiers with participles and prepositions to describe what they are wearing or doing.

Cycle 1, Exercises 1–6

WORD POWER

Learning objective: *learn vocabulary for describing people*

A

- Books closed. Explain that Ss will learn ways to describe what people look like. Ask questions about different Ss: "Is he tall or short? Does she have straight or curly hair?"
- ***Option:*** Ask Ss to bring pictures of friends or family members to class. Alternatively, bring magazine pictures of people to class.
- Books open. Focus Ss' attention on the expressions and pictures. Ask them to circle any words they don't know.
- Ask different Ss to read the expressions. Give help with pronunciation as needed. Point out that *handsome* usually refers to men and *pretty* to women, but *good-looking* describes both men and women. Also point out that adverbs such as *fairly* and *pretty* can modify the strength of different descriptions (e.g., *fairly tall, pretty short*).
- Write these headings across the top of the board:
  Hair   Age   Looks   Height   Other
- Ss work in groups. Ask Ss to brainstorm at least three more expressions to describe people. Then ask a S from each group to write their expressions under the correct headings on the board.

Possible answers

Hair: light brown hair, dark brown hair, gray hair, medium length hair, wavy hair, a ponytail
Age: ten, in his or her teens/twenties/thirties, old
Looks: thin, heavy, cute, beautiful, gorgeous
Height: rather short, quite tall
Other: blue eyes, green eyes, dark eyes, brown eyes

TIP Don't give your Ss too much new vocabulary. If they already know the presented vocabulary, add more. If not, add just a few extra words they want to know.

- Explain or elicit the rules for using the new words:
  be + adjective
  have + noun

  Then ask Ss to write *have* or *be* next to the expressions on the board. Stress that we use *be* with age.
- ***Option:*** Ss write sentences about famous people using expressions from the boxes (e.g., *Tom Cruise is handsome.*). Then they read their sentences to their classmates, who agree or disagree.

B *Pair work*

- Ss choose at least four expressions to describe themselves and their partners. They complete the chart individually. Go around the class and give help as needed.
- Ask two Ss to read the example conversation. Elicit other expressions for agreeing or disagreeing (e.g., *That's true. No way!*). Write them on the board.
- Ss compare charts in pairs. Go around the class and give help as needed.
- ***Option:*** Ss work with different partners. This time, they sit back-to-back and describe each other from memory.

! For a new way to review, categorize, or expand on the vocabulary in this Word Power, try ***Mind Mapping*** on page T-154.

2 CONVERSATION

Learning objectives: *practice a conversation between two people describing another person; see descriptions of people in context*

A [CD 2, Track 25]

- Ss cover the text. Ask Ss to describe the people in the picture.
- Write these focus questions on the board:
  1. Who are Randy and Emily talking about?
  2. How does Randy describe her?
  3. How old is she?
- Play the audio program and elicit the answers. (Answers: 1. Randy's new girlfriend 2. She's gorgeous and very tall. She has beautiful red hair. 3. Randy doesn't know.)
- Ss uncover the text. Play the audio program again. Ss listen and read silently.
- Elicit or explain any new vocabulary.

Vocabulary

gorgeous: very beautiful
6 feet 2: 188 centimeters
She won't tell me.: She doesn't want to say.

- Ss practice the conversation in pairs. Go around the class and give help as needed.
- ***Option:*** Ss cover the conversation and look only at the picture. Then they practice the conversation again using their own words.

B

- Read the focus question aloud. Ask Ss to make predictions. Write their predictions on the board.
- Play the audio program. Ss listen for the answer to the focus question.
- Ss compare answers in small groups. Then go over answers with the class. Was anyone's prediction correct?

Audio script

EMILY: She won't tell you her age?
RANDY: No. But I don't care.
EMILY: How old do you think she is?
RANDY: Who knows? I think she's probably in her thirties.
EMILY: And how old are you?
RANDY: I'm 29.
EMILY: Oh, so she's older than you.

Possible answer

Ashley is probably in her thirties. Ashley is older than Randy. Randy doesn't care about Ashley's age.

3 GRAMMAR FOCUS

Learning objectives: *practice describing people; ask and answer questions about appearance*

[CD 2, Track 26]

- Books closed. Write these questions and statements on the board:

1. What does she look like?	*a. It's medium length.*
2. How old is she?	*b. She's gorgeous.*
3. How tall is she?	*c. She's about 32.*
4. How long is her hair?	*d. She's 6 feet 2.*

  Ask Ss to match the questions with the answers.
- Books open. Tell Ss to look at the Grammar Focus box to check their answers.
- Play the audio program.

A

- Explain the task. Read the first question and elicit the question.
- Ss complete the task individually. Then they compare answers in pairs.
- Write the numbers 1 to 7 on the board. Ask different Ss to write the questions on the board. Then go over them as a class.

Answers

1. How old is your brother?
2. How tall are you?
3. What color is Sharon's hair?/What color hair does Sharon have?
4. Does she wear glasses?
5. What does he look like?
6. How long is your sister's hair?
7. What color are your eyes?/What color eyes do you have?

B Pair work

- Explain the task and model the example conversation with a S.
- Ss complete the task in pairs. Go around the class and check Ss' grammar.

For more practice asking questions about appearance, play ***Twenty Questions*** on page T-145.

2 CONVERSATION She's very tall.

A Listen and practice.

Emily: I hear you have a new girlfriend, Randy.
Randy: Yes. Her name's Ashley, and she's gorgeous!
Emily: Really? What does she look like?
Randy: Well, she's very tall.
Emily: How tall?
Randy: About 6 feet 2, I suppose.
Emily: Wow, that *is* tall. What color is her hair?
Randy: She has beautiful red hair.
Emily: And how old is she?
Randy: I don't know. She won't tell me.

B Listen to the rest of the conversation. What else do you learn about Ashley?

3 GRAMMAR FOCUS

Describing people

General appearance	***Age***	***Height***	***Hair***
What does she look like? She's tall, with red hair. She's gorgeous.	How old is she? She's about 32. She's in her thirties.	How tall is she? She's 1 meter 88. She's 6 feet 2.	How long is her hair? It's medium length.
Does he wear glasses? Yes, and he has a beard.	How old is he? He's in his twenties.	How tall is he? He's quite short.	What color is his hair? It's dark/light brown. He has brown hair.

A Write questions to match these statements. Then compare with a partner.

1. .... ? My brother is 26.
2. .... ? I'm 173 cm (5 feet 8).
3. .... ? Sharon has brown hair.
4. .... ? No, she wears contact lenses.
5. .... ? He's tall and very good-looking.
6. .... ? My sister's hair is medium length.
7. .... ? I have dark brown eyes.

B *Pair work* Choose a person in your class. Don't tell your partner who it is. Your partner will ask questions to guess the person's name.

A: Is it a man or a woman?
B: It's a man.
A: How tall is he?
B: . . .

4 LISTENING *Who is it?*

A Listen to descriptions of five people. Number them from 1 to 5.

B Listen again. How old is each person?

5 INTERCHANGE 9 *Find the differences*

Compare two pictures of a party. Go to the back of the book. Student A find Interchange 9A; Student B find Interchange 9B.

6 WRITING *An e-mail describing people*

A Imagine your e-pal is coming to visit you for the first time. You and a classmate are meeting him or her at the airport. Write an e-mail describing yourself and your classmate. (Don't give the classmate's name.)

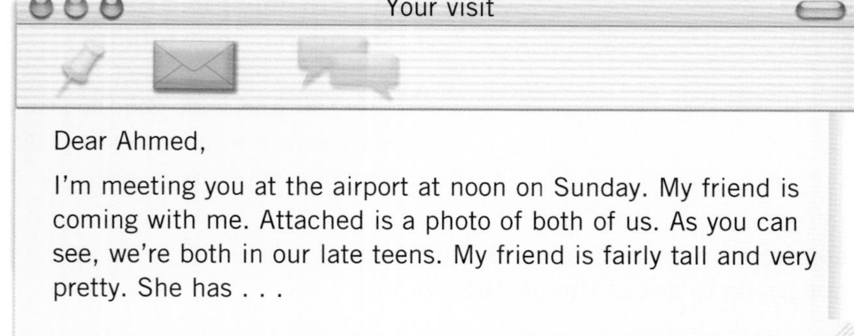
Your visit

Dear Ahmed,

I'm meeting you at the airport at noon on Sunday. My friend is coming with me. Attached is a photo of both of us. As you can see, we're both in our late teens. My friend is fairly tall and very pretty. She has . . .

B *Group work* Read your e-mail to the group. Can they guess the classmate you are describing?

4 LISTENING

Learning objective: develop skills in listening for details

A [CD 2, Track 27]

- Focus Ss' attention on the picture. In pairs Ss brainstorm words or expressions to describe each person. Point out that they should describe the people, not their clothes.
- Each pair joins another pair and compares ideas. Go around the class and give help as needed.
- Explain the task. Tell Ss to listen for key words (e.g., *short*, *glasses*) and not worry about understanding every word.
- Play the audio program. Ss complete the task individually.
- Go over answers with the class.

Audio script

1.
I think Brian's good-looking. He's pretty tall, with dark brown hair and a mustache. He's about 30.
2.
Tina's 18. She's got red hair – shoulder length and very curly – and she always wears interesting glasses, just for fun.
3.
Rosie is pretty tall for her age. She has long blond hair and wears contact lenses. She just turned 10.
4.
Tim's about 23. He's fairly short and a bit heavy. His hair isn't very long.
5.
Alice is very tall, and she's got long black hair. She's around 25. Oh, and she's very slim. She looks like a fashion model.

Answers

2, 4, 1, 5, 3

B

- Ask a S to read the focus question aloud. Then play the audio program. Ss listen for the answers.
- Ss compare answers in pairs. Elicit their answers. Play the audio program again if needed.

Answers

1. 30   2. 18   3. 10   4. 23   5. 25

5 INTERCHANGE 9

See pages T-124 and T-125 for teaching notes.

6 WRITING

Learning objective: learn to write an e-mail describing people

A

- Set the scene. Say: "Imagine an e-pal is visiting you for the first time. You and a classmate are meeting him or her at the airport. How will your e-pal know what you look like?"
- Ask a S to read the model e-mail. Elicit or explain any new words or expressions.
- Explain the task. Each S writes an e-mail describing himself/herself and another classmate. Point out that Ss should not write the name of the classmate.
- ***Option:*** Ss write the e-mail for homework.

B *Group work*

- Explain the task and read the question.
- Ss take turns reading their descriptions in small groups. Their classmates guess who they are describing.

End of Cycle 1

Do your students need more practice?

Assign . . .	*for more practice in . . .*
Workbook Exercises 1–6 on pages 49–52	Grammar, Vocabulary, Reading, and Writing
Lab Guide Exercises 1–4 on page 17	Listening, Pronunciation, Speaking, and Grammar

7 SNAPSHOT

***Learning objective:** talk about clothing styles*

- Books closed. Ask: "What kind of clothing is in fashion now?" Help Ss with vocabulary as needed.
- Write these clothing styles on the board: *classic*, *cool and casual*, and *funky*. Elicit or explain their meanings.

Vocabulary

classic: always fashionable
cool: fashionable at this time
casual: not formal
funky: modern and unusual

- Ss brainstorm examples of clothing for each style.
- Books open. Ss compare their ideas with the Snapshot.
- Ask different Ss to read the questions.
- Ss complete the task individually. Then they compare answers in pairs or small groups. Elicit Ss' answers.
- ***Option:*** Bring fashion magazines to class. Ss discuss which styles are classic, cool and casual, or funky.
- ***Option:*** Assign classes of younger Ss to make their own Snapshots. Ss cut pictures of clothing from fashion magazines, put them on cards, and label the items and styles. Then display the Ss' work.

8 CONVERSATION

***Learning objectives:** practice a conversation between two people at a party; see modifiers with participles and prepositions in context*

A *[CD 2, Track 28]*

- Write these questions on the board:
  1. *Where are these people?*
  2. *What are they doing?*
  3. *What are they wearing?*
  4. *What do they look like?*
- Focus Ss' attention on the picture. Have Ss ask each other the questions about the people in the picture. Then elicit possible answers.
- Set the scene. Raoul comes to a party alone. He meets his friend Liz. She tells him about some people at the party.
- Write these focus questions on the board:
  1. *Where's Maggie?*
  2. *Where's Julia?*
  3. *Does Julia know anyone at the party?*
- Play the audio program once or twice. Elicit Ss' answers to the focus questions. (Answers: 1. She's at a concert. 2. She's standing near the window. 3. No, she doesn't.)
- Play the audio program again. Ss look at the picture and read the conversation silently.
- Elicit or explain any new vocabulary.

Vocabulary

couldn't make it: wasn't able to come

- Ss practice the conversation in pairs.

For a new way to teach this Conversation, try the ***Musical Dialog*** on page T-150.

B

- Explain the task and read the focus question.
- Play the audio program. Ss listen and label the people in the picture individually.
- Ss compare answers in pairs. Then go over answers with the class. Play the audio program again if needed.

Audio script

LIZ: Let's see. Who else is here? Do you know Joe? He's really nice.
RAOUL: No, I don't. Which one is he?
LIZ: He's over there. He's the one wearing white pants and . . .
RAOUL: . . . and a yellow polo shirt?
LIZ: That's right. And then there's Michiko Sasaki. She works with me at the office.
RAOUL: Oh? Which one is Michiko?
LIZ: Oh, she's the very pretty woman in black pants and a green sweater. She's wearing glasses.
RAOUL: Oh, I see her. She's the one talking to Joe, right?
LIZ: Uh-huh.
RAOUL: And who are those two people dancing?
LIZ: Oh, that's my best friend. Her name is Rosa. She's really nice.
RAOUL: Yeah, and she's very attractive in that . . . purple dress.
LIZ: Uh-huh. And she's dancing with John DuPont, her new boyfriend.
RAOUL: John is Rosa's boyfriend?
LIZ: Yeah. Sorry, Raoul. Say, didn't you want to meet Julia?
RAOUL: Uh, I'm sorry, but which one is Julia again?

Answers

(from left to right) Joe, Michiko, Julia, John, Rosa

7 SNAPSHOT

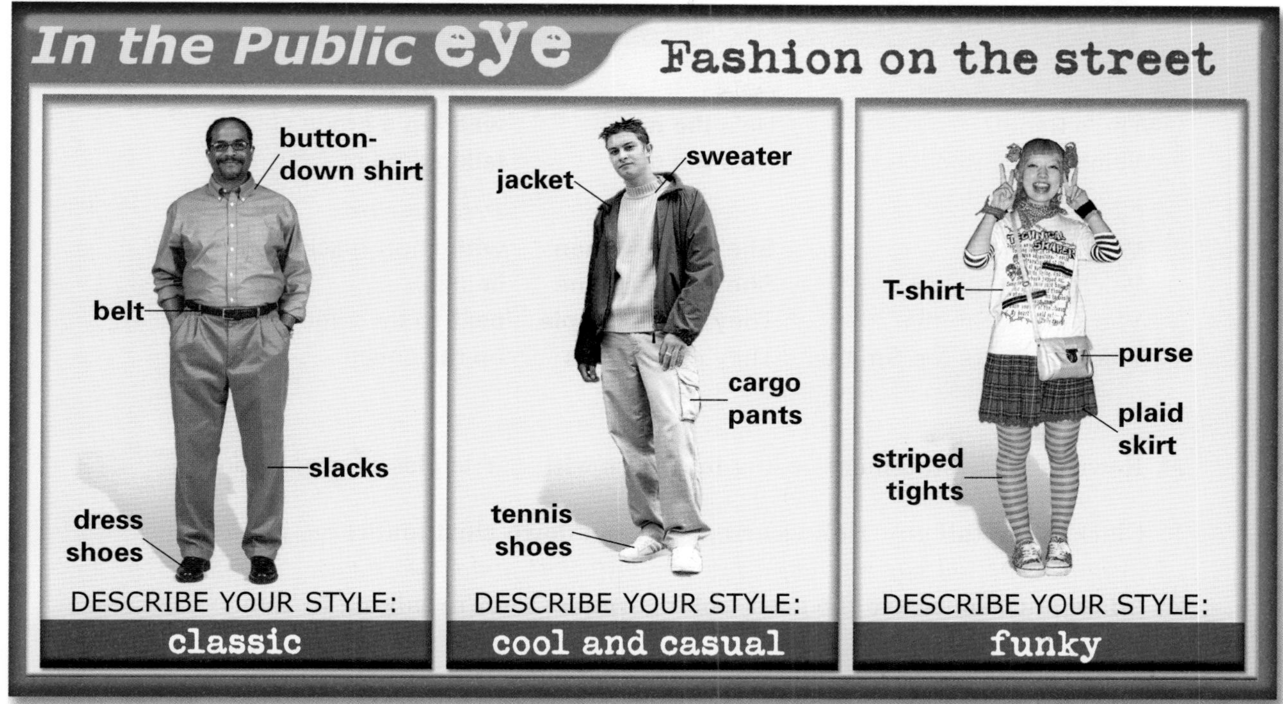

Source: Based on an idea from *Time Out New York*

Which clothing items do you wear almost every day? Circle the items.
What are three more things you like to wear?
What's your style? Is it classic? cool and casual? funky? something else?

8 CONVERSATION Which one is she?

A Listen and practice.

Liz: Hi, Raoul! Good to see you! Where's Maggie?
Raoul: Oh, she couldn't make it. She went to a concert with Alex.
Liz: Oh! Well, why don't you go and talk to Julia? She doesn't know anyone here.
Raoul: Julia? Which one is she? Is she the woman wearing glasses over there?
Liz: No, she's the tall one in jeans. She's standing near the window.
Raoul: Oh, I'd like to meet her.

B Listen to the rest of the conversation. Can you label Joe, Michiko, Rosa, and John in the picture?

9 GRAMMAR FOCUS

Modifiers with participles and prepositions

		Participles
Who's Raoul?	He's **the man**	**wearing** a green shirt.
Which one is Raoul?	He's **the one**	**talking** to Liz.
		Prepositions
Who's Liz?	She's **the woman**	**with** short black hair.
Which one is Julia?	She's **the tall one**	**in** jeans.
Who are the Smiths?	They're **the people**	**next to** the window.
Which ones are the Smiths?	They're **the ones**	**on** the couch.

A Rewrite these statements using modifiers with participles or prepositions.

1. Clark is the tall guy. He's wearing a button-down shirt and cargo pants.
   Clark is the tall guy wearing a button-down shirt and cargo pants.
2. Adam and Louise are the good-looking couple. They're talking to Tom.
   ....
3. Lynne is the young girl. She's in a striped T-shirt and blue jeans.
   ....
4. Jessica is the attractive woman. She's sitting to the left of Antonio.
   ....
5. A.J. is the serious-looking boy. He's listening to his new salsa CD.
   ....

B *Pair work* Complete these questions using the names of people in your class. Then take turns asking and answering the questions.

1. Who's the man sitting next to ....?
2. Who's the woman wearing ....?
3. Who is ....?
4. Which one is ....?
5. Who are the people ....?
6. Who are the ones ....?

10 PRONUNCIATION Contrastive stress in responses

A Listen and practice. Notice how the stress changes to emphasize a contrast.

A: Is Anthony the one wearing the red shirt?
B: No, he's the one wearing the black shirt.

A: Is Judy the woman on the couch?
B: No, Diana is the woman on the couch.

B Mark the stress changes in these conversations. Listen and check. Then practice the conversations.

A: Is Britney the one sitting next to Katy?
B: No, she's the one standing next to Katy.

A: Is Donald the one on the couch?
B: No, he's the one behind the couch.

9 GRAMMAR FOCUS

Learning objective: *practice using modifiers with participles and prepositions*

[CD 2, Track 29]

Modifiers with particles and prepositions

- Write these five sentences on the board:
  1. *He's the man dancing in the living room.*
  2. *She's the one wearing a dress.*
  3. *She's the Japanese woman with dark hair.*
  4. *He's the one in white pants.*
  5. *She's the tall person next to the window.*
- Focus Ss' attention on the Conversation on page 61. Ss identify each person in pairs.
- Go over the answers as a class. (Answers: 1. John 2. Rosa 3. Michiko 4. Joe 5. Julia)
- Explain the form of a present participle (verb + *-ing*). Then elicit the participles in the sentences on the board (*dancing* and *wearing*) and underline them.
- Elicit the prepositions in the sentences on the board (*with*, *in*, and *next to*) and circle them.
- Focus Ss' attention on the Grammar Focus box. Point out that *one* replaces *man* or *woman* and *ones* refers to people.
- Play the audio program. Answer any remaining questions.

A

- Explain the task and ask two Ss to read the example statement and rewritten statement.
- Ss complete the task individually. Then they compare answers in pairs.
- Ask different Ss to write the answers on the board. Then go over them with the class.

Answers

1. Clark is the tall guy wearing a button-down shirt and cargo pants.
2. Adam and Louise are the good-looking couple talking to Tom.
3. Lynne is the young girl in a striped T-shirt and blue jeans.
4. Jessica is the attractive woman sitting to the left of Antonio.
5. A.J. is the serious-looking boy listening to his new salsa CD.

B *Pair work*

- Explain the task. Ss complete the task using the names of classmates.
- Ss complete the task individually. Go around the class and give help as needed.
- Ss take turns asking and answering their questions in pairs. Go around the class and note any grammar errors.
- ***Option:*** For more practice, Ss change partners and complete the task again.

10 PRONUNCIATION

Learning objectives: *notice changes in stress; learn to sound natural when using contrastive stress*

A [CD 2, Track 30]

- Play the audio program. Ss listen for the stressed words.
- Focus Ss' attention on the conversations. Point out that people use more stress when they correct information. Ask: "What words does Student B stress?" (Answers: black, Diana)
- Play the audio program again. Ss listen and clap when they hear the stressed words.

B

- Focus Ss' attention on the conversations. Ask them to mark the words they think Student B will stress.
- Play the audio program. Ss check and correct their guesses.
- Check answers as a class. Then Ss practice the conversations in pairs.

Answers

(Contrastive stress is in boldface.)
1. A: Is Britney the one sitting next to Katy?
   B: No, she's the one **standing** next to Katy.
2. A: Is Donald the one on the couch?
   B: No, he's the one **behind** the couch.

- ***Option:*** Ask Ss to write questions about classmates or classroom objects with incorrect information (e.g., *Is the teacher the one sitting in the back? Is your backpack the one on the floor?*). Then Ss ask each other the questions in pairs. Go around the class and check their use of contrastive stress.

! For a new way to teach this Pronunciation, try ***Walking Stress*** on page T-152.

11 READING

***Learning objectives:** read and discuss an article about hip-hop fashions; develop skills in scanning and reading for detail*

- Books closed. Write *Hip-Hop Style* on the board. Ask Ss to write down words related to this expression in pairs. If Ss don't know anything about the expression, ask them to write questions they have about it. Elicit Ss' answers and questions.
- Books open. Ss read the pre-reading question, and scan the article to find three fashions.

Possible answers

loose-fitting street clothes, baggy pants, sweatshirts, hiking boots, baseball caps, jackets with sports logos, expensive athletic shoes

A

- Ss read the article silently. Ask Ss to guess the meanings of any words they don't know.

TIP Encourage Ss to guess the meaning of a new word by looking at the part of speech, its position in the sentence, and the context.

- Explain the task and model the first example. Ss find the words in italics in the article. Then they match each word with its meaning.
- Ss complete the task individually. Then they compare their answers in pairs.
- ***Option:*** Ss work in groups of three. Each S matches two words with their meanings. Then Ss share answers as a group.
- Go over answers with the class.

Answers

1. a 2. c 3. d 4. f 5. b 6. e

- Elicit or explain any remaining vocabulary.

Vocabulary

common look: a similar appearance
hot style: a fashion that is popular right now
backward: opposite to the usual direction
logos: pictures or designs that companies use as symbols
African-American kids: related to American children of African origin
Detroit and Chicago: large cities in the midwestern U.S.
thanks to: because of
teens: teenagers
performers: entertainers

- Ask Ss what they learned or found interesting in the article.
- ***Option:*** Ss find the topic of each paragraph. (Answers: 1. the hip-hop look 2. how the look became popular 3. who wears the look and why)

B

- Ask different Ss to read the six questions. Then Ss read the article again and answer the questions.
- Go over answers with the class.

Possible answers

1. It is a type of urban music with a heavy beat.
2. They are loose-fitting street clothes.
3. They began in Detroit and Chicago.
4. They became popular more than 20 years ago.
5. Because hip-hop music videos and movies became popular.
6. Because a lot of hip-hop performers wear them.

C *Pair work*

- Ss discuss the questions in pairs. Then elicit their ideas.

For a new way to teach the vocabulary in this Reading, try ***I Think I Know*** on page T-158.

End of Cycle 2

Do your students need more practice?

Assign . . .	*for more practice in . . .*
Workbook Exercises 7–11 on pages 52–54	Grammar, Vocabulary, Reading, and Writing
Lab Guide Exercises 5–8 on page 18	Listening, Pronunciation, Speaking, and Grammar
Video Activity Book Unit 9	Listening, Speaking, and Cultural Awareness
CD-ROM Unit 9	Grammar, Vocabulary, Reading, Listening, and Speaking

11 READING

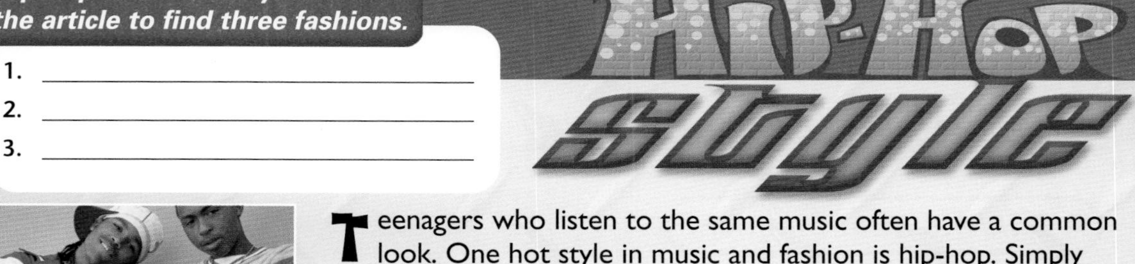

What hip-hop fashions do you know? Scan the article to find three fashions.

1. ______________________
2. ______________________
3. ______________________

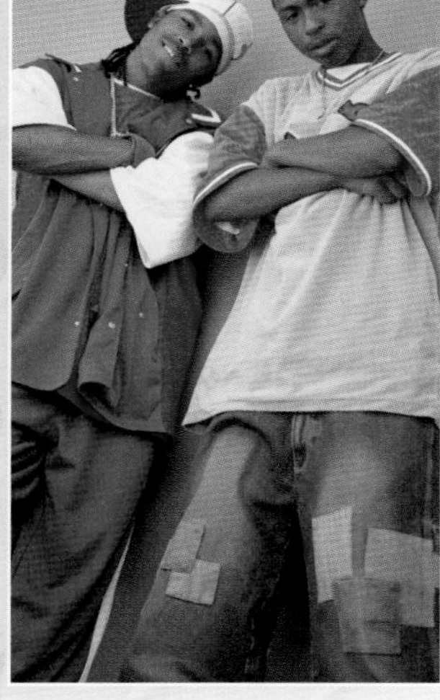

Teenagers who listen to the same music often have a common look. One hot style in music and fashion is hip-hop. Simply put, hip-hop is a type of urban music with a heavy beat. Typical hip-hop fashions are loose-fitting street clothes. The style includes baggy pants, sweatshirts, hiking boots, baseball caps (usually worn backward), jackets with sports logos, and expensive athletic shoes. In the hip-hop style, boys and girls often dress the same way.

African-American kids in Detroit and Chicago first made hip-hop fashions trendy more than 20 years ago. They wore baggy street clothes to dance clubs. Then North American and European bands also began wearing this style. Thanks to the popularity of music videos and movies, hip-hop soon became an international fashion sensation.

Teens around the world, from Britain to South Africa to Japan, now wear hip-hop clothing. Seventeen-year-old Melanie Borrow, of Manchester, England, says, "My pride and joy in life are my Levi's jeans." In the United States, teens spend a lot of money on hip-hop fashions. David Bowen, 17, of Evanston, Illinois, has five pairs of hiking boots, each costing around $100. David says, "They're popular because a lot of hip-hop performers wear them."

A Read the article. Find the words in *italics* in the article. Then match each word with its meaning.

.... 1. *look*	a. appearance
.... 2. *urban*	b. popular trend; hit
.... 3. *beat*	c. from big cities
.... 4. *loose-fitting*	d. musical rhythm
.... 5. *sensation*	e. something to be proud of
.... 6. *pride and joy*	f. very large; baggy

B Answer these questions.

1. What is hip-hop music? ....
2. What are hip-hop fashions? ....
3. Where did hip-hop fashions begin? ....
4. When did hip-hop fashions become popular? ....
5. Why did hip-hop become a fashion sensation? ....
6. Why are hiking boots popular? ....

C ***Pair work*** Which hip-hop fashions do you like? Which do you dislike?

10 Have you ever ridden a camel?

1 SNAPSHOT

A Guide to Entertainment **Fun things to do**

sing in a karaoke bar	go to an Internet café	try mountain biking	go ice-skating	see a live concert

Source: *Time Out Magazine: The Obsessive Guide to Impulsive Entertainment*

Which activities have you tried?
Which activities would you like to try? Why?
Make a list of other activities you would like to try. Then compare with the class.

2 CONVERSATION A visit to New Orleans

A Listen and practice.

Jan: It's great to see you, Todd. Have you been in New Orleans long?
Todd: Just a few days. I'm really excited to be here.
Jan: I can't wait to show you the city. Have you been to a jazz club yet?
Todd: Yeah, I've already been to one.
Jan: Oh. Well, how about a riverboat tour?
Todd: Uh, I've already done that, too.
Jan: Have you ridden in a streetcar? They're a lot of fun.
Todd: Actually, that's how I got here today.
Jan: Well, is there anything you want to do?
Todd: You know, I really just want to take it easy. My feet are killing me!

B Listen to the rest of the conversation. What do they plan to do tomorrow?

Have you ever ridden a camel?

In Unit 10, students talk about past experiences. In Cycle 1, they talk about recent activities using the present perfect, already, *and* yet. *In Cycle 2, they discuss experiences from the recent and distant past using the present perfect and simple past,* for, *and* since.

Cycle 1, Exercises 1–3

SNAPSHOT

Learning objective: *talk about fun activities to do*

- Books closed. Explain that this unit is about fun and unusual activities. Elicit fun or unusual activities Ss like to do and write them on the board.
- Books open. Ss look at the Snapshot and compare their ideas. Elicit or explain any new vocabulary.

Vocabulary

karaoke bar: a place where people sing along with recorded popular music
live concert: a concert that is happening while you watch it; not a recorded concert

- Point out that this information is from an entertainment guide, a book that lists things to do. Ask: "Do any of these activities surprise you? Why?" Elicit Ss' answers.
- Explain the task and read the questions.
- Ss discuss the questions in small groups. Go around the class to give help as needed. Then elicit Ss' answers to the first two questions.
- ***Option:*** Ss send a "messenger" to another group to report their original group's answers.

2 CONVERSATION

Learning objectives: *practice a conversation between two people in New Orleans; see the present perfect in context*

A ***[CD 2, Track 31]***

- Books closed. Ask: "Where is New Orleans? What music is famous there? What festival is famous there?" (Answers: Louisiana, jazz, Mardi Gras)
- Books open. Set the scene. Todd is visiting New Orleans. His friend Jan wants to show him the city.
- Draw this chart on the board:

Activities	Yes	No
1. Go to a jazz club		
2. Do a riverboat tour		
3. Ride a streetcar		
4. Relax		

  Ask Ss to copy the chart.
- Explain the task. Ss listen to the audio program and check (✓) *Yes* if Todd has done the activities and *No* if he hasn't.
- Play the audio program and Ss complete the task. Then elicit their answers. (Answers: 1. yes 2. yes 3. yes 4. no)
- Play the audio program again. Ss listen and read along silently.
- Ask these comprehension questions: "When did Todd arrive in New Orleans? How did he get to the café?" Elicit Ss' answers. (Answers: a few days ago, by streetcar)
- Elicit or explain any new vocabulary.

Vocabulary

I can't wait to: I'm excited about; I'm looking forward to
riverboat: a large passenger boat that travels on a river
streetcar: a passenger train that goes along city streets
take it easy: relax
My feet are killing me!: My feet really hurt!

- Ss practice the conversation in pairs.

B

- Explain the task and read the focus question.
- Play the audio program. Ss listen for the answer individually. Then elicit the answer.

Audio script

JAN: So let's just stay here and relax. I know you're tired.
TODD: Thanks, Jan. But we can plan something for tomorrow.
JAN: Great! Have you been to the zoo?
TODD: No, I haven't. But I've heard it's good. Let's go there in the afternoon.
JAN: OK.
TODD: Say, have you been to the French market? I'd love to go there, too.
JAN: Actually, I've never been there.
TODD: You're kidding! And how many years have you lived in New Orleans? We have to go there.

Answer

They plan to go to the zoo and the French market.

3 GRAMMAR FOCUS

Learning objectives: *practice the present perfect with* already *and* yet*; ask and answer questions using the present perfect with regular and irregular past participles*

[CD 2, Track 32]

Present perfect

- Focus Ss' attention on the Conversation on page 64. Ask: "What has Todd done in New Orleans?" Elicit Ss' answers and write them on the board:

		been	*to a jazz club.*
He	*has*	*done*	*a riverboat tour.*
		ridden	*in a streetcar.*

- Ask: "When did he do these things?" (Answer: sometime in the past few days)
- Explain that these sentences are in the present perfect. We use this tense with past actions when the exact time is not important.
- Draw this time line on the board:

  TODD ARRIVED *jazz club* *NOW*

  |__________x__________|

  Explain that Todd has been to a jazz club sometime in the past few days. We don't know the exact time, and it's not important.
- Say: "Imagine that Todd has been to three jazz clubs this week." Draw two more x's on the time line and say: "Todd has been to a jazz club three times this week."
- Focus Ss' attention on the Grammar Focus box. Elicit or explain the rules for forming present perfect statements and yes/no questions:
  Subject + *has/have* + past participle.
  Has/have + subject + past participle?
- Point out the placement of *yet* and *already* and explain the meaning. *Yet* goes at the end of present perfect questions and at the end of negative statements. *Already* goes before the past participle and means "earlier than expected."
- Play the audio program and answer any questions.

A

- Explain the task and read the first answer. Then ask different Ss and elicit their answers. If needed, point out the expressions *once*, *twice*, and *three times*.
- Call on Ss to read the regular and irregular past participles. Then point out the list of irregular past participles in the appendix.
- Ss complete the task individually and compare answers in pairs. Then ask different Ss to write their answers on the board.

Possible answers

1. I've cleaned the house once/twice this week./
   I haven't cleaned the house this week.
2. I've made my bed every day/three times this week./
   I haven't made my bed this week.
3. I've cooked dinner every day/four times this week./
   I haven't cooked dinner this week.
4. I've done laundry once/twice this week./
   I haven't done laundry this week.
5. I've washed the dishes once/five times this week./
   I haven't washed the dishes this week.
6. I've gone grocery shopping once/twice this week./
   I haven't gone grocery shopping this week.

B

- Explain the task and model the first conversation with a S.
- Ss complete the task individually. Encourage Ss to use contractions in their answers. Go around the class and give help as needed. Then elicit Ss' answers.

Answers

1. A: **Have** you **done** much exercise this week?
   B: Yes, I**'ve** already **been** to aerobics class four times.
2. A: **Have** you **played** any sports this month?
   B: No, I **haven't had** the time.
3. A: How many movies **have** you **been** to this month?
   B: Actually, I **haven't seen** any yet.
4. A: **Have** you **been** to any interesting parties recently?
   B: No, I **haven't gone** to any parties for quite a while.
5. A: **Have** you **called** any friends today?
   B: Yes, I**'ve** already **made** three calls.
6. A: How many times **have** you **gone** out to eat this week?
   B: I**'ve eaten** at fast-food restaurants a couple of times.

C *Pair work*

- Ss take turns asking and answering the questions in part B in pairs.

For more practice with present perfect questions, play ***Hot Potato*** on page T-147.

End of Cycle 1

Do your students need more practice?

Assign . . .	*for more practice in . . .*
Workbook Exercises 1–3 on pages 55–56	Grammar, Vocabulary, Reading, and Writing
Lab Guide Exercises 1–5 on page 19	Listening, Pronunciation, Speaking, and Grammar

3 GRAMMAR FOCUS

Present perfect; already, yet

The present perfect is formed with the verb **have** *+ the past participle.*

Have you **been** to a jazz club?	Yes, I**'ve been** to several.	No, I **haven't been** to one.
Has she **ridden** in a streetcar?	Yes, she**'s ridden** in one.	No, she **hasn't ridden** in one.
Has he **called** home lately?	Yes, he**'s called** twice this week.	No, he **hasn't called** in months.
Have they **eaten** dinner yet?	Yes, they**'ve** already **eaten**.	No, they **haven't eaten** yet.

Contractions

I**'ve** = I have	he**'s** = he has	we**'ve** = we have	have**n't** = have not
you**'ve** = you have	she**'s** = she has	they**'ve** = they have	has**n't** = has not
	it**'s** = it has		

For a complete list of irregular past participles, see the appendix at the back of the book.

A How many times have you done these things in the past week? Write your answers. Then compare with a partner.

1. clean the house
2. make your bed
3. cook dinner
4. do laundry
5. wash the dishes
6. go grocery shopping

I've cleaned the house once this week.

OR

I haven't cleaned the house this week.

regular past participles

call → call**ed**
hike → hik**ed**
jog → jog**ged**
try → tri**ed**

irregular past participles

be → **been**
do → **done**
eat → **eaten**
go → **gone**
have → **had**
make → **made**
ride → **ridden**
see → **seen**

B Complete these conversations using the present perfect. Then practice with a partner.

1. A: *Have* you *done* much exercise this week? (do)
   B: Yes, I .... already .... to aerobics class four times. (be)
2. A: .... you .... any sports this month? (play)
   B: No, I .... the time. (have)
3. A: How many movies .... you .... to this month? (be)
   B: Actually, I .... any yet. (see)
4. A: .... you .... to any interesting parties recently? (be)
   B: No, I .... to any parties for quite a while. (go)
5. A: .... you .... any friends today? (call)
   B: Yes, I .... already .... three calls. (make)
6. A: How many times .... you .... out to eat this week? (go)
   B: I .... at fast-food restaurants a couple of times. (eat)

C *Pair work* Take turns asking the questions in part B. Give your own information when answering.

4 CONVERSATION Actually, I have.

A Listen and practice.

Peter: I'm sorry I'm late. Have you been here long?
Mandy: No, only for a few minutes.
Peter: Have you chosen a restaurant yet?
Mandy: I can't decide. Have you ever eaten Moroccan food?
Peter: No, I haven't. Is it good?
Mandy: It's delicious. I've had it several times.
Peter: Or how about Thai food? Have you ever had green curry?
Mandy: Actually, I have. I lived in Thailand as a teenager. I ate it a lot there.
Peter: I didn't know that. How long did you live there?
Mandy: I lived there for two years.

B Listen to the rest of the conversation. Where do they decide to have dinner?

5 GRAMMAR FOCUS

Present perfect vs. simple past

Use the present perfect for an indefinite time in the past.
Use the simple past for a specific event in the past.

Have you ever **eaten** Moroccan food?	Yes, I **have**. I **ate** it once in Paris. No, I **haven't**. I**'ve** never **eaten** it.
Have you ever **had** green curry?	Yes, I **have**. I **tried** it several years ago. No, I **haven't**. I**'ve** never **had** it.

A Complete these conversations. Use the present perfect and simple past of the verbs given and short answers. Then practice with a partner.

1. A: .... you ever .... in a karaoke bar? (sing)
   B: Yes, I .... I .... in one on my birthday.
2. A: .... you ever .... something valuable? (lose)
   B: No, I .... But my brother .... his camera on a trip once.
3. A: .... you ever .... a traffic ticket? (get)
   B: Yes, I .... Once I .... a ticket and had to pay $50.
4. A: .... you ever .... a live concert? (see)
   B: Yes, I .... I .... U2 at the stadium last year.
5. A: .... you ever .... late for an important appointment? (be)
   B: No, I .... But my sister .... 30 minutes late for her wedding!

B *Pair work* Take turns asking the questions in part A. Give your own information when answering.

CONVERSATION

Learning objectives: *practice a conversation about types of food; see the present perfect and simple past in context*

A [CD 2, Track 33]

- Set the scene. Peter and Mandy are discussing where to eat dinner. Elicit ideas and vocabulary from the picture.
- Write this focus question on the board:
  What does Peter learn about Mandy?
- Books closed. Play the audio program and Ss listen for the answer. (Answer: She lived in Thailand for two years as a teenager.)
- Books open. Play the audio program again. Ss read the conversation silently.
- Ss practice the conversation in pairs.

For a new way to practice this Conversation, try the ***Moving Dialog*** on page T-150.

B

- Explain the task and read the focus question. Encourage Ss to make predictions.
- Play the audio program. Ss listen for the answer. Then elicit the answer from the class.

Audio script

PETER: So what about dinner? I'm hungry!
MANDY: Have you tried Sakura? They have excellent sushi.
PETER: Actually, I had Japanese food for lunch.
MANDY: Well, should we have Italian food? Café Roma is a great place, and it isn't far.
PETER: That's fine with me. I love Italian food.

Answer

They decide to have dinner at Café Roma.

GRAMMAR FOCUS

Learning objectives: *practice the present perfect and simple past; practice using expressions with* for *and* since

[CD 2, Track 34]

Present perfect

- Write these questions on the board:
  1. Has Peter ever eaten Moroccan food?
  2. Has Mandy ever had green curry?
- Focus Ss' attention on the Conversation in Exercise 4 and elicit the answers. (Answers: 1. No, he hasn't. 2. Yes, she has.)
- Ask a few *Have you ever* questions around the class (e.g., "Have you ever eaten Moroccan food? Have you ever eaten green curry?"). Elicit Ss' answers.
- Write this on the board:
  Have you ever eaten green curry?
  (No,) I've never eaten green curry.
- Point out that *ever* means "at any time in your life." We use it in present perfect questions, but not in answers. *Never* means "not ever," and we use it in present perfect statements.

Simple past

- Ask: "When did Mandy eat green curry?" Then elicit possible answers (e.g., She ate it several years ago/in 2002/as a teenager.).
- Focus Ss' attention on the Grammar Focus box. Point out that we use the simple past to talk about a specific event in the past.
- Point out that we pronounce *ever* with a lot of stress and *have* with little stress. Then play the audio program.

A

- Explain the task and model the first conversation with a S.
- Ss complete the task individually. Go around and encourage Ss to use contractions in short answers.
- Elicit the answers. Then Ss practice with a partner.

Answers

1. A: **Have** you ever **sung** in a karaoke bar?
   B: Yes, I **have**. I **sang** in one on my birthday.
2. A: **Have** you ever **lost** something valuable?
   B: No, I **haven't**. But my brother **lost** his camera on a trip once.
3. A: **Have** you ever **gotten** a traffic ticket?
   B: Yes, I **have**. Once I **got** a ticket and had to pay $50.
4. A: **Have** you ever **seen** a live concert?
   B: Yes, I **have**. I **saw** U2 at the stadium last year.
5. A: **Have** you ever **been** late for an important appointment?
   B: No, I **haven't**. But my sister **was** 30 minutes late for her wedding!

B *Pair work*

- Explain the task. Then Ss complete it in pairs.

For more simple past/present perfect practice, try the ***Question Game*** on page T-158.

For and since

- Write this on the board:
  I lived in Thailand for two years.
  I've lived in Thailand for two years.
- Elicit or explain the difference. The first sentence is in the simple past. It means "I lived in Thailand in the past, but I don't live in Thailand now." The second sentence is in the present perfect. It means "I moved to Thailand two years ago and I still live in Thailand now."
- Focus Ss' attention on the two expression boxes. Ask: "When do we use *for*? When do we use *since*?"
- Elicit or explain that we use *for* with periods of time and *since* with points in time. Elicit other expressions that go with *for* (e.g., *a day/a week/a year*), and *since* (*yesterday/last week/2 P.M.*).
- Play the audio program.

C

- Explain the task and model the first sentence. Then Ss complete the task individually. Go over answers with the class.

Answers

1. for	3. since	5. for	7. for
2. for	4. for	6. since	8. since

For more practice with *for* and *since*, play ***Run For It!*** on page T-148.

D *Pair work*

- Explain the task and ask the first question. Elicit different answers with *for* and *since*.
- Ss complete the task in pairs. Go around the class and note any errors. Then write the errors on the board and correct them with the class.

6 PRONUNCIATION

Learning objective: *learn to sound natural by linking final /t/ and /d/ sounds in verbs with the vowels that follow*

A *[CD 2, Track 35]*

- Explain the task. Focus Ss' attention on the linked sounds in the example conversations. Then play the audio program.

B *Pair work*

- Explain and model the task. Elicit the linked sounds in the answers (i.e., *cut it*, *tasted it*, *tried it*, *brought it*, *read it*). Ask Ss to repeat the linked sounds.
- Ss work in pairs. They ask and answer the questions. Go around the class and check their use of linked sounds.

7 LISTENING

Learning objective: *develop skills in listening for main ideas*

[CD 2, Track 36]

- Ask: "What's the most interesting thing you've done recently?" Elicit Ss' answers.
- Set the scene and explain the task. Clarice and Karl are talking about interesting things they've done recently. Ss listen to find out where they went and why they liked it.
- Play the audio program. Ss complete the first column of the chart individually. While they listen, draw the chart on the board. Then elicit the answers and ask Ss to write the answers on the board.
- Play the audio program again. Ss complete the second column of the chart individually. Then elicit the answers and ask different Ss to write them on the board.

Audio script

KARL: So, Clarice, what have you been up to lately?
CLARICE: Oh, well, . . . I tried a new restaurant last week. The Classical Café. Have you ever been there?
KARL: No, I haven't. What's it like?
CLARICE: It's wonderful! The food is great, and the prices are reasonable. But the most interesting thing is the waiters. They sing.
KARL: The waiters sing? You're kidding!
CLARICE: No, they're really terrific.
KARL: I've got to go there.
CLARICE: Yeah, you should, Karl. And what about you? Have you done anything interesting lately?
KARL: Oh, well, I went mountain climbing last month.
CLARICE: Really? I've never done that.
KARL: Well, I was in Switzerland.
CLARICE: You went mountain climbing in Switzerland?
KARL: Yeah. It was really exciting! Of course it was dangerous, but I enjoyed it a lot.
CLARICE: Wow! I'm impressed!

Possible answers

	Where they went	*Why they liked it*
Clarice	to the Classical Café	food is great; prices are reasonable; waiters sing
Karl	mountain climbing in Switzerland	really exciting

- ***Option:*** Ask Ss: "Who had a more interesting time, Clarice or Karl? Why?"

For *and* since

How long **did** you **live** in Thailand?	I **lived** there **for** two years. It was wonderful.
How long **have** you **lived** in Miami?	I**'ve lived** here **for** six months. I love it here. I**'ve lived** here **since** last year. I'm really happy here.

C Complete these sentences with *for* or *since*.

1. Pam was in Central America .... a month last year.
2. I've been a college student .... almost four years.
3. Hiroshi has been at work .... 6:00 A.M.
4. I haven't gone to a party .... a long time.
5. Josh lived in Venezuela .... two years as a kid.
6. My parents have been on vacation .... Monday.
7. Natalie was engaged to Danny .... six months.
8. Pat and Valeria have been best friends .... high school.

expressions with *for*

two weeks
a few months
several years
a long time

expressions with *since*

6:45
last weekend
1997
elementary school

D *Pair work* Ask and answer these questions.

How long have you had your current hairstyle?
How long have you studied at this school?
How long have you known your best friend?
How long have you been awake today?

6 PRONUNCIATION *Linked sounds*

A Listen and practice. Final /t/ and /d/ sounds in verbs are linked to the vowels that follow them.

A: Have you cooked lunch yet?
B: Yes, I've already cooked‿it. (/t/)

A: Have you ever tried Cuban food?
B: Yes, I tried‿it once in Miami. (/d/)

B *Pair work* Ask and answer these questions. Use *it* in your responses. Pay attention to the linked sounds.

Have you ever cut your hair?
Have you ever tasted goat cheese?
Have you ever tried Korean food?
Have you brought your dictionary today?
Have you read the latest Harry Potter book yet?

7 LISTENING *I'm impressed!*

Listen to Clarice and Karl talk about interesting things they've done recently. Complete the chart.

	Where they went	Why they liked it
Clarice	....	....
Karl	....	....

8 WORD POWER Activities

Find two phrases in the list to go with each verb. Add another phrase for each verb. Then write the past participle forms of the verbs.

an appointment	a camel	herbal tea	iced coffee	a sports car	your cell phone
a bicycle	a class	a hill	a mountain	a truck	your keys

climb			
drink			
drive			
lose			
miss			
ride			

9 SPEAKING Have you ever . . . ?

A *Group work* Ask your classmates questions about some of the things in Exercise 8 or your own ideas.

A: Have you ever ridden a camel?
B: Yes, I have.
C: Really? Where were you?

B *Class activity* Tell the class one interesting thing you learned about a classmate.

10 WRITING A letter to an old friend

Write a letter to someone you haven't seen for a long time. Include three things you have done since you last saw that person. Then exchange letters with a partner and write a response to it.

Dear Hector,

How have you been? We last saw each other at our high school graduation, right? What have you done since then? I started college three years ago. I really like my classes, so far. I've been on a girls' soccer team for . . .

11 INTERCHANGE 10 Lifestyle survey

Is your lifestyle easygoing and relaxed, or busy and fast-paced? Go to Interchange 10 at the back of the book.

8 WORD POWER

Learning objective: *learn collocations for activities with* climb, drink, drive, lose, miss, *and* ride

- Explain the task. Ss find two phrases in the list that go with each verb. Model the first example (*climb + a hill/a mountain*). Then elicit other words or phrases that go with climb (e.g., *the stairs*).
- Elicit or explain any new vocabulary. Point out that we use *lose* when we have something but then can't find it; however, we use *miss* when we don't get to or go to something.
- Ss complete the task in pairs. While they work, draw the chart on the board. Then go around the class and give help as needed.
- ***Option:*** Allow Ss to use their dictionaries.
- Elicit Ss' answers. Ask different Ss to write their answers on the board.

Answers

climb	a hill	a mountain	*the stairs*
drink	herbal tea	iced coffee	*soda*
drive	a sports car	a truck	*a car*
lose	your cell phone	your keys	*your glasses*
miss	an appointment	a class	*the bus*
ride	a bicycle	a camel	*a horse*

(Note: Possible additional phrases are italicized.)

- Elicit the past participle forms of the verbs. (Answers: climbed, drunk, driven, lost, missed, ridden)

For more practice with these collocations, play ***Concentration*** on page T-144. Ss match the verb and a phrase to make collocation.

9 SPEAKING

Learning objective: *talk about past experiences using the present perfect and collocations*

A Group work

- Write these expressions on the board:
  Really? Wow! I'm impressed! You're kidding!
  Point out that we use these expressions to show interest or surprise. Model how to say them. Ss repeat.
- ***Option:*** Ss find more examples of responses in previous conversations. Practice them as a class.
- Explain the activity and model the example conversation with two Ss. Focus Ss' attention on the picture and ask: "Where was she?" Encourage Ss to make guesses.
- Elicit other follow-up questions and write them on the board.
- Ss complete the activity in small groups. Go around the class and encourage Ss to ask follow-up questions.
- ***Option:*** Ss get one point for each follow-up question they ask. The S in each group with the most points wins.

B Class activity

- Ss share things they learned about their classmates with the class.

10 WRITING

Learning objective: *write a letter to an old friend using the present perfect and simple past*

- Ask the class: "Who haven't you seen in a long time?" Elicit Ss' answers.
- Explain the task. Then Ss read the example letter silently.
- Ss write their letters individually. Remind Ss to check their use of present perfect and simple past.
- Ss exchange letters in pairs. They imagine they are the "old friend" and write a response.

11 INTERCHANGE 10

See page T-123 for teaching notes.

12 READING

***Learning objectives:** read and discuss interviews about risky sports; develop skills in skimming and reading for specific information*

- Books closed. Write *Risky Sports* on the board. Elicit or explain that *risky* means "dangerous."
- Ss brainstorm risky sports in small groups. Then ask different Ss to write them on the board.

TIP To prepare Ss for a Reading, ask Ss to brainstorm things they already know about the topic.

- Books open. Read the pre-reading task. Elicit ideas from the pictures.
- Ss skim the interviews and complete the task.

Answers

1. scuba diving 2. hang gliding 3. mountain climbing

A

- Elicit, explain, or ask Ss to look up new vocabulary.

Vocabulary

accident: something bad that happens unexpectedly
upside down: with the top at the bottom
lived through: experienced
challenge: something that requires much mental or physical work
overcoming: fighting successfully against
bubbles: pockets of air in a liquid
rare: unusual
explore: look around; discover

TIP To avoid confusing Ss, only pre-teach the words they need to complete the task. They can look up the other words later.

- Explain the task. Ss read the interviews and complete the chart. Then go over the answers with the class.

Possible answers

	Sport	*What they enjoy*	*The danger(s)*
1. Jenny	hang gliding	flying like a bird	strong wind
2. Tom	mountain climbing	the challenge, overcoming danger	thin air, storms, bad weather
3. Ray	scuba diving	exploring another world	the bends

B *Pair work*

- Explain the task and read the discussion questions. Ss discuss the questions in pairs.

End of Cycle 2

Do your students need more practice?

Assign . . .	*for more practice in . . .*
Workbook Exercises 4–10 on pages 56–60	Grammar, Vocabulary, Reading, and Writing
Lab Guide Exercises 6–9 on page 20	Listening, Pronunciation, Speaking, and Grammar
Video Activity Book Unit 10	Listening, Speaking, and Cultural Awareness
CD-ROM Unit 10	Grammar, Vocabulary, Reading, Listening, and Speaking

Evaluation

Assess Ss' understanding of Units 9 and 10 with the quiz on pages T-208 and T-209.

12 READING

Taking the Risk

Look at the pictures and skim the interviews. Then write the name of the sport next to each picture.

1 ....

2 ....

3 ....

Sports World magazine recently spoke with Jenny Adams, Tom Barker, and Ray Lee about risky sports.

SW: Hang gliding is a dangerous sport, Jenny. What do you enjoy about it, and have you ever had an accident?

Jenny: No, I've never been hurt. Maybe I've been lucky. Sometimes the wind can be too strong. Once, my glider turned upside down and I almost crashed, but I parachuted away just in time. Actually, I've always felt that hang gliding is very safe. And it's amazing to be able to fly like a bird.

SW: Tom, you've been mountain climbing for years now. What are some of the dangers you've experienced?

Tom: When you're high up on a mountain, the conditions are hard on the human body. The air is thin, and you get tired. I've lived through storms and bad weather. But I like the challenge and I like overcoming danger. That's why I do it.

SW: Ray, have you ever experienced any dangers while scuba diving?

Ray: Luckily, I haven't. But people can get the bends if they come up too quickly from deep under water. Bubbles form in the blood. The bends can be serious, and can even cause death. But the condition is rare. Diving isn't really that dangerous. And the great thing is that it lets you explore another world.

A Read the interviews. Then complete the chart.

	Sport	What they enjoy	The danger(s)
1. Jenny	....	....	....
2. Tom	....	....	....
3. Ray	....	....	....

B *Pair work* Would you like to try any of these sports? Why or why not?

Units 9–10 Progress check

SELF-ASSESSMENT

How well can you do these things? Check (✓) the boxes.

I can	Very well	OK	A little
Ask about and describe people's appearance (Ex. 1)	☐	☐	☐
Identify people using modifiers with participles and prepositions (Ex. 2)	☐	☐	☐
Answer questions using the present perfect with *already* and *yet* (Ex. 3)	☐	☐	☐
Listen to and understand descriptions of past experiences and events (Ex. 4)	☐	☐	☐
Ask and answer questions using the present perfect and simple past (Ex. 4)	☐	☐	☐
Use *how long, for,* and *since* with the present perfect (Ex. 5)	☐	☐	☐

1 ROLE PLAY Missing person

Student A: One of your classmates is lost. You are talking to a police officer. Answer the officer's questions and describe your classmate.

Student B: You are a police officer. Someone is describing a lost classmate. Ask questions to complete the form. Can you identify the classmate?

Change roles and try the role play again.

MISSING PERSON'S REPORT

NAME: ______________________ # 78439122475

HEIGHT: ________ WEIGHT: ________ AGE: ________

EYE COLOR		HAIR COLOR	
☐ BLUE	☐ BROWN	☐ BLONDE	☐ BROWN
☐ GREEN	☐ HAZEL	☐ RED	☐ BLACK
		☐ GRAY	☐ BALD

CLOTHING: ______________________

GLASSES, ETC: ______________________

2 SPEAKING Which one is . . . ?

A Look at this picture. How many sentences can you write to identify the people?

Amy and T.J. are the people in sunglasses.
They're the ones holding hands.

B ***Pair work*** Close your books. Who do you remember? Take turns asking about the people.

A: Which one is Bill?
B: I think Bill is the guy sitting . . .

Units 9–10 Progress check

SELF-ASSESSMENT

Learning objectives: *reflect on one's learning; identify areas that need improvement*

- Ask: "What did you learn in Units 9 and 10?" Elicit Ss' answers.
- Ss complete the Self-assessment. Encourage them to be honest, and point out they will not get a bad grade if they check (✓) "a little."
- Ss move on to the Progress check exercises. You can have Ss complete them in class or for homework, using one of these techniques:
  1. Ask Ss to complete all the exercises.
  2. Ask Ss: "What do you need to practice?" Then assign exercises based on their answers.
  3. Ask Ss to choose and complete exercises based on their Self-assessment.

1 ROLE PLAY

Learning objective: *assess one's ability to ask about and describe a person's appearance*

- Read the instructions aloud and explain the task. Student A makes a report about a lost classmate and Student B completes the *Missing person's report*. Point out that Student A should not give the name of the classmate. Then Student B guesses the identity of the lost classmate.
- Go over the information in the report. Elicit different things S can write in the report.
- Write this example conversation on the board:

  A: Excuse me, Officer. Can you help me? One of my classmates is lost.
  B: Sure. Um, is the person a man or a woman?
  A: A woman.
  B: OK. I need to know her age. How old is she?
  A: I think she's 19 or 20.
  B: All right. And how tall is she?

  Model the conversation with a S. The S is person A and you are person B. Whenever the S gives additional information, pretend to write it in the report.
- Ss complete the task in pairs. Then Student B looks around the room and identifies the lost classmate.
- Set a time limit of about three minutes. Then Ss change roles. Go around the class and give help as needed.

> **TIP** If you don't have enough class time for the speaking activities, assign each S a speaking partner. Then have Ss complete the activities with their partners for homework.

2 SPEAKING

Learning objective: *assess one's ability to identify people using modifiers with participles and prepositions*

A

- Focus Ss' attention on the picture. Ask a S to read the example sentence.
- Ss write sentences about each person individually.
- ***Option:*** Go around the class and check Ss' work.

Possible answers

Kate is the woman/one holding a drink/in jeans.
Louisa is the woman/one sitting on the sofa/in boots.
Bill is the man/one eating something/in a black shirt.
Amy and T.J. are the people/ones holding hands/in sunglasses.

B *Pair work*

- Write the names *Kate*, *Louisa*, *Bill*, and *Amy and T.J.* on the board.
- Books closed. Explain the task. Ss ask questions about the people on the board in pairs (e.g., *Which one is Bill?*). They answer using their memory of the picture. If they have difficulty, they can look at their sentences.
- Model the example conversation with a few Ss. Elicit different ways Ss can answer.
- Ss complete the task.

3 SPEAKING

Learning objective: assess one's ability to answer questions using the present perfect with already *and* yet

A

- Explain the task. Ss imagine they are preparing for three situations. Read the situations and the example.
- Ss list four things they need to do for each situation.

B Pair work

- Explain the task. Ss exchange lists. Student A asks Student B what he or she has done in each situation. Student B gives responses using *already* or *yet*.
- Ss complete the task in pairs.

4 LISTENING

Learning objectives: assess one's ability to listen to and understand descriptions of past experiences and events; assess one's ability to ask and answer questions using the present perfect and simple past

A [CD 2, Track 37]

- Set the scene. Jamie is on a cruise and is talking to someone about things she has done.
- Go over the chart and explain any new vocabulary. Then play the audio program. Ss complete the task.

Audio script

MAN: Are you enjoying the cruise, Jamie?
JAMIE: Oh, yes, very much. Actually, I won a contest and this cruise was the prize.
MAN: That's fantastic! Hey, I've always wondered something about contests. The cruise left from Miami, so how did they get you there? Did they fly you there?
JAMIE: No, I live in Miami, so I didn't have to travel at all. I've never flown on a plane. But I did get to stay in an expensive hotel in Miami for a day.
MAN: That's nice.
JAMIE: Yeah, it was. Oh, and I saw Madonna there. She was in the same hotel.
MAN: Madonna? Really? Did you meet her?
JAMIE: No, in fact, I've never met a famous person. But I think she smiled at me.
MAN: Cool.
JAMIE: Yeah. And I got to enjoy the hotel activities. I even tried windsurfing.
MAN: Sounds fun.
JAMIE: Yeah, it was. But I did something stupid. I took my wallet with me and almost lost it. I'm always very careful with my wallet, and have never lost it. It almost fell into the ocean. Luckily, I caught it.
MAN: That *was* lucky! Well, it sounds like you've really enjoyed this trip.
JAMIE: For the most part. I mean, I've been a little seasick, but I'll remember this trip forever. I've even kept a diary this whole time so I can tell my friends all about it.
MAN: I'm sure they'll love that. Well, enjoy the rest of the cruise.
JAMIE: Thanks. I will.

Answers

won a contest, stayed in an expensive hotel, gone windsurfing, been seasick, kept a diary

B Group work

- Ss take turns asking about the events in part A in small groups.

5 SURVEY

Learning objective: assess one's ability to use how long, for, *and* since *with the present perfect*

A

- Ss complete the *My answers* column individually. Point out that they should use *for* or *since*.

B Class activity

- Model the task. Ask several Ss the first question until one gives the same answer. Explain that you will write that S's name in the *Classmate's name* column.
- Ss go around the room and complete the task.

WHAT'S NEXT?

Learning objective: become more involved in one's learning

- Focus Ss' attention on the Self-assessment again. Ask: "How well can you do these things now?"
- Ask Ss to underline one thing they need to review. Ask: "What did you underline? How can you review it?"
- If needed, plan additional activities or reviews based on Ss' answers.

3 SPEAKING Reminders

A Imagine you are preparing for these situations. Make a list of four things you need to do for each situation.

Your first day of school is in a week.
You are moving to a new apartment.
You are going to the beach.

To do list: first day of school
1. buy school supplies

B *Pair work* Exchange lists. Take turns asking about what has been done. When answering, decide what you have or haven't done.

A: Have you bought school supplies yet?
B: Yes, I've already gotten them.

4 LISTENING What have you done?

A Jamie is on a cruise. Listen to her talk about things she has done. Check (✓) the correct things.

- ☐ won a contest
- ☐ flown in a plane
- ☐ stayed in an expensive hotel
- ☐ met a famous person
- ☐ gone windsurfing
- ☐ lost her wallet
- ☐ been seasick
- ☐ kept a diary

B *Group work* Have you ever done the things in part A? Take turns asking about each thing.

5 SURVEY How long . . . ?

A Write answers to these questions using *for* and *since*.

How long have you . . . ?	My answers	Classmate's name
owned this book	....	....
studied English	....	....
known your best friend	....	....
lived in this town or city	....	....
been a student	....	....

B *Class activity* Go around the class. Find someone who has the same answers.

WHAT'S NEXT?

Look at your Self-assessment again. Do you need to review anything?

11 It's a very exciting place!

1 WORD POWER *Adjectives*

A *Pair work* Match each word in column A with its opposite in column B. Then add two more pairs of adjectives to the list.

A	*B*
1. beautiful	a. boring
2. cheap	b. crowded
3. clean	c. dangerous
4. interesting	d. expensive
5. quiet	e. noisy
6. relaxing	f. polluted
7. safe	g. stressful
8. spacious	h. ugly
9.	i. ....
10.	j. ....

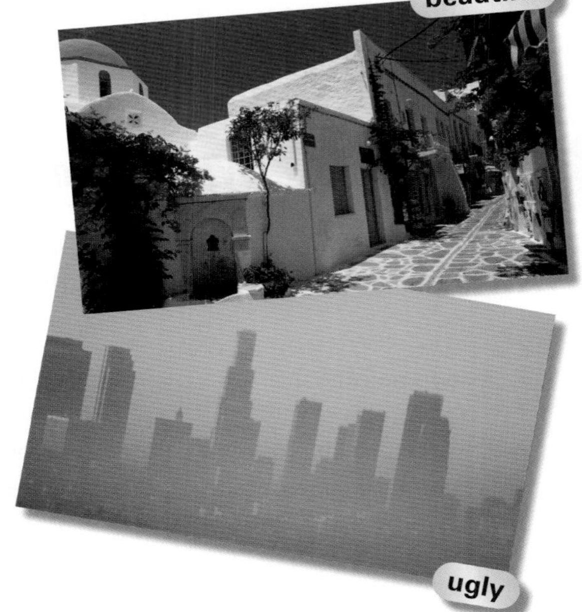
beautiful
ugly

B *Pair work* Choose two places you know. Describe them to your partner using the words in part A.

2 CONVERSATION *It's a fairly big city.*

A Listen and practice.

Eric: So where are you from, Carmen?
Carmen: I'm from San Juan, Puerto Rico.
Eric: Wow, I've heard that's a really nice city.
Carmen: Yeah, it is. The weather is great, and there are some fantastic beaches just outside the city.
Eric: Is it expensive there?
Carmen: No, it's not very expensive. Prices are pretty reasonable.
Eric: How big is the city?
Carmen: It's a fairly big city, but it's not *too* big.
Eric: It sounds perfect to me. Maybe I should plan a trip there sometime.

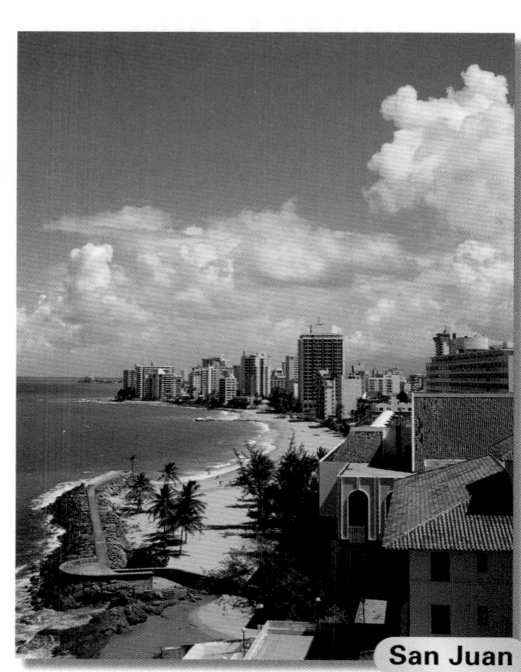
San Juan

B Listen to the rest of the conversation. What does Carmen say about entertainment in San Juan?

It's a very exciting place!

In Unit 11, students talk about hometowns, cities, and countries. In Cycle 1, they talk about their hometowns using adverbs, adjectives, and conjunctions. In Cycle 2, they discuss popular vacation places using can *and* should.

Cycle 1, Exercises 1–5

1 WORD POWER

Learning objective: *learn vocabulary for describing places*

A *Pair work*

- Elicit adjectives that describe cities (e.g., *beautiful, ugly*) and write them on the board.
- Ss check (✓) the adjectives they listed. Then they read the other words silently.
- Elicit words Ss don't understand or know how to pronounce. Explain or pronounce these words.
- Explain the task and elicit the first example. Then Ss complete the matching task in pairs.
- Go over answers with the class.

Answers

1. h 2. d 3. f 4. a 5. e 6. g 7. c 8. b

- Pairs now add two more sets of opposites. Ss may use their dictionaries if they wish. Go over possible answers.

Possible answers

modern/traditional large/small hot/cold

- Ask Ss to write the new adjectives in their notebooks and check (✓) the ones that describe their city or town.

For more practice matching opposite adjectives, play ***Concentration*** on page T-144.

B *Pair work*

- Ss choose two cities or towns from any country and describe them in pairs. Encourage them to use the adjectives in part A.

2 CONVERSATION

Learning objectives: *practice a conversation about a city; see adverbs before adjectives, and conjunctions, in context*

A *[CD 3, Track 1]*

- Books closed. Set the scene. Eric is asking Carmen about her hometown of San Juan, Puerto Rico.
- Ask: "What do you know about Puerto Rico? Where is it? What's it like?"
- Write this on the board:
  1. Weather: OK or great?
  2. Beaches: polluted or fantastic?
  3. Prices: reasonable or expensive?
- Play the audio program. Ss listen to the audio program to find the answers. Then they compare answers with a partner.
- Go over the answers with the class. (Answers: 1. great 2. fantastic 3. reasonable)
- Books open. Play the audio program again. Ss listen and read silently. Then they practice the conversation in pairs. Go around the class and give help as needed.

For a new way to teach this Conversation, try the ***Disappearing Dialog*** on page T-151.

B

- Explain the task and read the focus question.
- Play the audio program. Ss listen for the answer. Then they compare answers in small groups. Go over the answer with the class.

Audio script

ERIC: So what kinds of things are there to do in San Juan?
CARMEN: Well, there are a lot of nightclubs. Puerto Ricans love to dance.
ERIC: I'm not much of a dancer. Anything else?
CARMEN: Well, a lot of people enjoy going out to eat. There are some excellent restaurants in Old San Juan. They're popular with both locals and tourists.
ERIC: Now that sounds good. I love to eat!

Possible answer

There are a lot of nightclubs and some excellent restaurants.

- ***Option:*** Ask Ss: "Would you like to visit San Juan? Why or why not?"

3 GRAMMAR FOCUS

Learning objectives: *practice using adverbs before adjectives; write sentences using conjunctions*

[CD 3, Track 2]

Adverbs before adjectives

- Focus Ss' attention on the Conversation on page 72. Ask: "What has Eric heard about San Juan?" (Answer: *It's really nice*.) Then ask: "How big is San Juan?" (Answer: *It's fairly big*.)
- Explain that sometimes we use adverbs like *very*, *really*, and *fairly* to modify adjectives.
- Ask Ss to find more examples of adverbs that modify adjectives in the Conversation and underline them (e.g., <u>*very*</u> *expensive*, <u>*pretty*</u> *reasonable*, <u>*too*</u> *big*). Elicit other adverbs.
- Focus Ss' attention on the adverbs box. Point out that they are organized from the most to the least.
- Focus Ss' attention on the Grammar Focus box. Point out the position of the adverb and elicit the rule:
  X *is* adverb + adjective.
  X *is a/an* adverb + adjective + noun.
- Explain that *too* means "more than you want," so we usually use it with negative adjectives (e.g., *too bad*, NOT *too nice*). Also, we cannot use *too* with an adverb + adjective + noun (e.g., *too expensive*, NOT *a too expensive city*).
- Play the audio program.
- ***Option:*** Focus Ss' attention on part B of the Word Power on page 72. Ss describe a city again, using adverbs + adjectives.

A

- Explain the task. Ss match the questions with the answers.
- Go over answers with the class. Then Ss practice the conversations in pairs.

Answers

1. c 2. d 3. a 4. b

For practice asking questions about cities, play ***Twenty Questions*** on page T-145.

Conjunctions

- Focus Ss' attention on the first sentence in the second Grammar Focus box. Ask: "Are *exciting* and *nice* positive or negative?" (Answer: Both are positive.)
- Point out that we use *and* to connect two positive or two negative ideas. Elicit a sentence with two negative ideas (e.g., *The city is ugly, and the weather is terrible.*). Ask: "What punctuation comes before *and*?" (Answer: a comma)
- Focus Ss' attention on the other three sentences. Ask: "Are they positive + positive, negative + negative, or positive + negative?" (Answer: positive + negative) Explain that we use *but*, *though*, and *however* to connect a positive idea with a negative idea.
- Tell Ss to look at the position of *but*, *though*, and *however*. Ask: "How are *though* and *however* different from *but*?" (Answer: *But* is in the middle of the sentence. *Though* and *however* are at the end.)
- Ask: "What punctuation comes before each conjunction?" (Answer: a comma) Point out that *and* and *but* connect two complete sentences.
- Play the audio program.

B

- Explain the task and model the first answer. Ss complete the task individually. Go around the class and check Ss' use of punctuation.
- Ask different Ss to write their answers on the board. Go over answers with the class.

Answers

1. Taipei is very nice, and everyone is extremely friendly.
2. The streets are crowded. It's easy to get around, though.
3. The weather is nice. Summers get pretty hot, however.
4. Shopping is great, but you have to bargain in the markets.
5. The food is delicious, and it's not too expensive.
6. It's an amazing city, and I love to go there.

C *Group work*

- Write these topics on the board:
  People *Food* *Shopping*
  Weather *Crime* *Things to do*
- Explain the task and ask a S to read the example conversation. Point out that Ss can discuss the topics on the board.
- Ss complete the task. Ask Ss to guess the false statement in each description.
- Go around the class and note any errors. Then write them on the board and ask Ss to correct them.

TIP To check if Ss have understood the grammar, write their errors on the board. Then ask Ss to correct them.

3 GRAMMAR FOCUS

Adverbs before adjectives

San Juan is **really** nice.
It's **fairly** big.
It's not **very** expensive.

It's a **really** nice city.
It's a **fairly** big city.
It's not a **very** expensive place.

It's **too** noisy and it's **too** crowded for me.

adverbs

extremely
very
really
pretty
fairly
somewhat

A Match the questions with the answers. Then practice the conversations.

1. What's Seoul like?
   Is it an interesting place? ....
2. Do you like your hometown?
   Why or why not? ....
3. What's Sydney like?
   I've never been there. ....
4. Have you ever been to
   São Paulo? ....

a. Oh, really? It's beautiful and very clean. It has a great harbor and beautiful beaches.
b. Yes, I have. It's an extremely large and crowded place, but I love it. It has excellent restaurants.
c. Yes. It has amazing shopping, and the people are pretty friendly.
d. Not really. It's too small, and it's really boring. That's why I moved away.

Conjunctions

It's an exciting city, **and** the weather is nice.
It's a big city, **but** it's not too big.

It's a big city. It's not too big, **though**.
It's a big city. It's not too big, **however**.

B Choose the correct conjunctions and rewrite the sentences.

1. Taipei is very nice. Everyone is extremely friendly. (and / but)
   ....
2. The streets are crowded. It's easy to get around. (and / though)
   ....
3. The weather is nice. Summers get pretty hot. (and / however)
   ....
4. Shopping is great. You have to bargain in the markets. (and / but)
   ....
5. The food is delicious. It's not too expensive. (and / though)
   ....
6. It's an amazing city. I love to go there. (and / however)
   ....

C *Group work* Describe three cities or towns in your country. State two positive and one negative feature for each.

A: Lima is very exciting and there are a lot of things to do, but it's too cold.
B: The weather in Shanghai is . . .

4 LISTENING My hometown

Listen to Joyce and Nicholas talk about their hometowns.
What do they say? Check (✓) the correct boxes.

	Big?		Interesting?		Expensive?		Beautiful?	
	Yes	No	Yes	No	Yes	No	Yes	No
1. Joyce	☐	☐	☐	☐	☐	☐	☐	☐
2. Nicholas	☐	☐	☐	☐	☐	☐	☐	☐

5 WRITING A magazine article

A Imagine you work for an airline magazine. Think of an interesting place for tourists to visit in your country and write a short article.

East meets West

Istanbul is a very interesting city in western Turkey. It's special for several reasons. First, it has some wonderful mosques. The Blue Mosque is extremely beautiful, and no visitor should miss it. Allow plenty of time to visit this very amazing place. Second, the city has a lot of . . .

B *Pair work* Exchange papers and read each other's articles. Which place sounds the most interesting?

6 SNAPSHOT

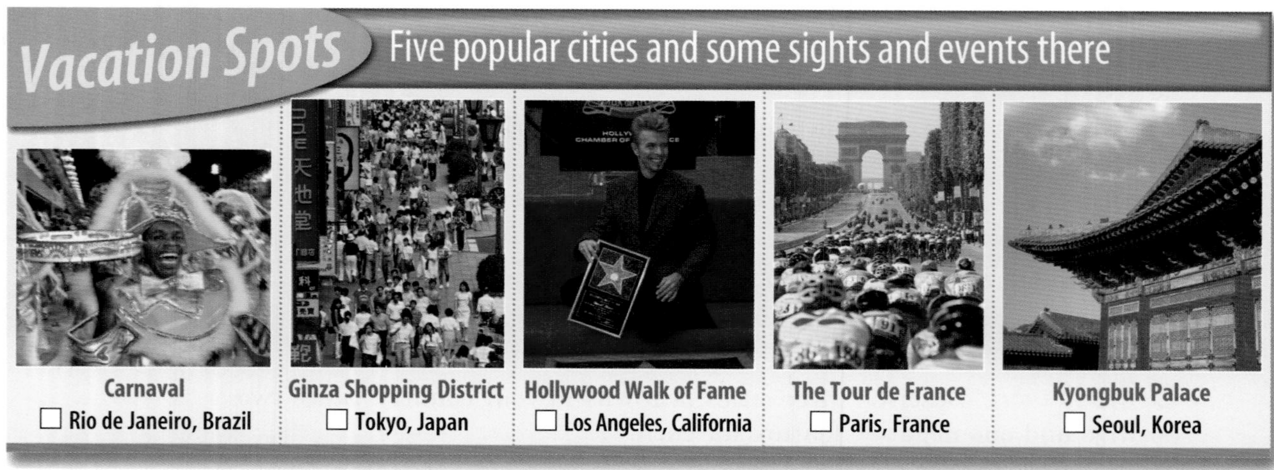

Vacation Spots
Five popular cities and some sights and events there
Carnaval
☐ Rio de Janeiro, Brazil
Ginza Shopping District
☐ Tokyo, Japan
Hollywood Walk of Fame
☐ Los Angeles, California
The Tour de France
☐ Paris, France
Kyongbuk Palace
☐ Seoul, Korea

Source: *www.fodors.com*

Check (✓) the places you would like to visit.
What three other places in the world would you like to visit? Why?
Put the places you would like to visit in order from most interesting to least interesting.

4 LISTENING

Learning objective: *develop skills in listening for details*

[CD 3, Track 3]

- Books closed. Set the scene. Joyce and Nicholas are talking about their hometowns. Ask: "Do Joyce and Nicholas like their hometowns?" Play the audio program and Ss listen for the answer. (Answer: Joyce doesn't like her hometown, but Nicholas likes his.)
- Books open. Explain the task. Play the audio program and Ss complete the chart.
- Ss compare answers in pairs. Then go over answers.

Audio script

1.
WOMAN: So tell me about your hometown, Joyce.
JOYCE: Well, it's a really small town.
WOMAN: What's it like there?
JOYCE: Oh, I think it's boring.
WOMAN: Really? Why?
JOYCE: Well, there's nothing to do. No good restaurants. No nightlife.
WOMAN: Oh, that's too bad. But small towns are pretty inexpensive to live in.
JOYCE: Well, yeah, it is really cheap. And lots of people love it there because it's very pretty.
WOMAN: Yeah?
JOYCE: Uh-huh. It has great scenery – lots of mountains and rivers, lakes and trees. . . .
WOMAN: Well, I don't know, Joyce. It sounds like a great place.
2.
WOMAN: Do you come from a big city, Nicholas?
NICHOLAS: Yeah, I guess. It's pretty big.
WOMAN: So there's a lot to do there?
NICHOLAS: Yeah. It's a really fun place. It has some cool art museums and great theaters and restaurants.
WOMAN: Really? How are the prices? Is it expensive?
NICHOLAS: I guess so. Food costs a lot in the supermarket and in restaurants. And apartments! The rents are very high.
WOMAN: And what's it like there? What does it look like?
NICHOLAS: Well, it's very clean, and it's really pretty, too. There are lots of parks and trees right in the center of the city.

Answers

	Big?	*Interesting?*	*Expensive?*	*Beautiful?*
1. Joyce	no	no	no	yes
2. Nicholas	yes	yes	yes	yes

For a new way to practice listening for adverbs, try ***Stand Up, Sit Down*** on page T-151.

5 WRITING

Learning objective: *write an article about a place using adverbs before adjectives, and conjunctions*

A

- Explain the task. Then Ss look at the picture and read the example article silently.
- Point out that travel articles often have a lot of descriptive adjectives and adverbs. Ask Ss to underline the adjectives and adverbs.
- Ss write their article in class or for homework.
- ***Option:*** Ss use the Internet to research information and download pictures to include in their articles.

B *Pair work*

- Explain the task. Ss complete the task in pairs.

End of Cycle 1

Do your students need more practice?

Assign . . .	*for more practice in . . .*
Workbook Exercises 1–6 on pages 61–64	Grammar, Vocabulary, Reading, and Writing
Lab Guide Exercises 1–3 on page 21	Listening, Pronunciation, Speaking, and Grammar

Cycle 2, Exercises 6–13

6 SNAPSHOT

Learning objective: *talk about popular vacation spots*

- Books closed. Write the five countries from the Snapshot on the board. Ask: "Which country would you like to visit? Why?"
- Books open. Ss read the Snapshot. Elicit or explain any new vocabulary.

Vocabulary

Walk of Fame: a famous area where the names of many celebrities are on the sidewalk
Tour de France: a famous bicycle race

- Explain the tasks. Ss complete the tasks individually. Then they discuss their answers in small groups.

7 CONVERSATION

Learning objectives: *practice a conversation about Mexico City; see modal verbs* can *and* should *in context*

A [CD 3, Track 4]

- Books closed. Set the scene. Two friends are talking about a city. Ask: "What city is it?" Play the first part of the audio program and Ss listen for the answer. (Answer: Mexico City)
- Write these focus questions on the board:
  1. What's a good time to visit Mexico City?
  2. What's the weather like there?
  3. How many places does Elena recommend?
- Play the rest of the audio program. Then elicit Ss' answers to the questions on the board. (Answers: 1. anytime 2. always nice 3. three)
- Books open. Play the audio program again and Ss read the conversation silently. Elicit or explain any new vocabulary.

Vocabulary

And what else?: Is there anything more?
you shouldn't miss: you should see

- Ss practice the conversation in pairs.

For a new way to practice this Conversation, try the ***Scrambled Dialog*** on page T-158.

B

- Explain the task and read the focus questions. Play the audio program. Elicit Ss' answers.

Audio script

ELENA: Where are you from again, Thomas?
THOMAS: I'm from Toronto, Canada.
ELENA: Oh! I've always wanted to go there. What's it like? What can you do there?
THOMAS: Well, there's a lot to do. But visitors should definitely spend some time in the museums. The museums there are great!

Answers

He's from Toronto, Canada. You should definitely visit the museums.

- ***Option:*** Ss discuss if they prefer to visit Mexico City or Toronto. Ask them to give reasons.

8 GRAMMAR FOCUS

Learning objectives: *practice conversations using* can *and* should*; ask and answer questions using* can *and* should

[CD 3, Track 5]

Can *and* should

- Focus Ss' attention on the Conversation in Exercise 7. Ask: "How does Thomas ask for advice about Mexico City?" Write his question on the board:
  Can you tell me a little about Mexico City?
- Ask: "How does Elena suggest when to go? How does she suggest what to see?" Elicit the answers and write them on the board:
  You can go anytime.
  You should definitely visit . . .
  You shouldn't miss the . . .
- Point out that *can* and *should* are modals. They show a speaker's attitude or "mood." People use *can* and *should* to ask for and give advice.
- Elicit or explain the rule for using *can* and *should* in Wh-questions and statements:
  Wh-question + modal + subject + verb?
  Subject + modal (+ *not*) verb.
  Point out that modals do not take a final *-s*.
- Focus Ss' attention on the Grammar Focus box and play the audio program.

A

- Explain the task and model the first conversation with a S. Ss complete the task individually.
- Go over answers with the class. Then Ss practice the conversations in pairs.

Answers

1. A: I **can't** decide where to go on my vacation.
   B: You **should** go to India. It's my favorite place to visit.
2. A: I'm planning to go to Bogotá next year. When do you think I **should** go?
   B: You **can** go anytime. The weather is nice all year.
3. A: **Should** I rent a car when I arrive in Cairo? What do you recommend?
   B: No, you **should** definitely use the subway. It's fast and efficient.
4. A: Where **can** I get some nice jewelry in Bangkok?
   B: You **shouldn't** miss the weekend market. It's the best place for bargains.
5. A: What **can** I see from the Eiffel Tower?
   B: You **can** see all of Paris, but in bad weather you **can't** see anything.

B *Pair work*

- Explain the task and read the questions. Ss complete the task individually. Then they compare answers in pairs.
- Elicit answers from the class.

7 CONVERSATION What should I see there?

A Listen and practice.

Thomas: Can you tell me a little about Mexico City?
Elena: Sure I can. What would you like to know?
Thomas: Well, what's a good time to visit?
Elena: I think you can go anytime. The weather is always nice.
Thomas: Oh, good! And what should I see there?
Elena: Well, you should definitely visit the National Museum and go to the Palace of Fine Arts.
Thomas: And what else?
Elena: Oh, you shouldn't miss the Pyramid of the Sun. It's very interesting.
Thomas: It all sounds really exciting!

the Palace of Fine Arts

the Pyramid of the Sun

B Listen to the rest of the conversation. Where is Thomas from? What should you do there?

8 GRAMMAR FOCUS

Modal verbs can and should

What **can** I do in Mexico City?	What **should** I see there?
You **can** see the Palace of Fine Arts.	You **should** visit the National Museum.
You **can't** visit some museums on Mondays.	You **shouldn't** miss the Pyramid of the Sun.

A Complete these conversations using *can*, *can't*, *should*, or *shouldn't*. Then practice with a partner.

1. A: I .... decide where to go on my vacation.
   B: You .... go to India. It's my favorite place to visit.
2. A: I'm planning to go to Bogotá next year. When do you think I .... go?
   B: You .... go anytime. The weather is nice all year.
3. A: .... I rent a car when I arrive in Cairo? What do you recommend?
   B: No, you .... definitely use the subway. It's fast and efficient.
4. A: Where .... I get some nice jewelry in Bangkok?
   B: You .... miss the weekend market. It's the best place for bargains.
5. A: What .... I see from the Eiffel Tower?
   B: You .... see all of Paris, but in bad weather you .... see anything.

B *Pair work* Write answers to these questions about your country. Then compare with a partner.

What time of year should you go there?
What are three things you can do there?
Can you buy anything special?
What shouldn't a visitor miss?

9 PRONUNCIATION *Can't and shouldn't*

A Listen and practice these statements. Notice how the *t* in **can't** and **shouldn't** is not strongly pronounced.

You can'**t** go shopping on Sundays.
You shouldn'**t** swim at the beaches.
You can'**t** get a taxi easily at night.
You shouldn'**t** miss the night markets.

B *Class activity* Are any of the above statements true about your city or town?

10 LISTENING *Three countries*

A Listen to speakers talk about Japan, Argentina, and Italy. Complete the chart.

	Capital city	What visitors should see or do
1. Japan		
2. Argentina		
3. Italy		

B Listen again. One thing about each country is incorrect. What is it?

11 SPEAKING *Interesting places*

Group work Has anyone visited an interesting country or place in your country? Find out more about it. Start like this and ask questions like the ones below.

A: I visited Chile once.
B: Really? What's the best time of year to visit?
A: You can go anytime. I went in March.
C: What's the weather like then?

What's the best time of year to visit?
What's the weather like then?
What should tourists see and do there?
What special foods can you eat?
What's the shopping like?
What things should people buy?
What else can visitors do there?

Santiago, Chile

12 INTERCHANGE 11 *City guide*

Make a guide to fun places in your city. Go to Interchange 11.

9 PRONUNCIATION

Learning objective: *learn to sound natural when using* can't *and* shouldn't

A [CD 3, Track 6]

- Books closed. Play the audio program. Ask: "What do you notice about the pronunciation of *t* in *can't* and *shouldn't*?" (Answer: It is not strongly pronounced.)
- Books open. Play the audio program again. Ss listen and repeat. Go around the class and check their pronunciation of *can't* and *shouldn't*.

B *Class activity*

- Read the question and elicit answers from the class.

10 LISTENING

Learning objective: *develop skills in listening for details*

A [CD 3, Track 7]

- Books closed. Write *Japan*, *Argentina*, and *Italy* in large circles on the board. Ask: "What do you know about these countries?" Elicit Ss' answers and ask different Ss to make notes around the circles on the board.
- Explain the task. Ss listen for more information about these countries. Play the audio program, pausing after each country. Ask different Ss to come up and add notes to the board.
- Books open. Explain the task. Play the audio program again and Ss complete the chart individually. Then they compare answers in pairs. Elicit answers from the class.

Audio script

1.
Japan has several big islands and many smaller islands. The capital city is Tokyo. The highest mountain in Japan is called Mount Everest. There are many beautiful Buddhist temples in Japan. And visitors should try Japanese food, especially sashimi, which is raw fish.

2.
Argentina is a large country in South America. The capital city is Buenos Aires. The people all speak French. People visiting Buenos Aires shouldn't miss the downtown area. Many interesting people gather in this area. Argentina is also a good place to buy leather.

3.
Italy is a country in southern Europe, on the Atlantic Ocean. The country is shaped like a boot. It's famous for its excellent food. Everyone should try the pizza there. It's also famous for its art and old buildings, especially in the capital city of Rome. Visitors shouldn't miss that!

Answers

	Capital city	What visitors should see or do
1. Japan	Tokyo	go to temples; eat Japanese food especially sashimi
2. Argentina	Buenos Aires	see the downtown area; buy leather
3. Italy	Rome	try pizza; see art and old buildings; visit Rome

B

- Explain the task and read the focus question. Play the audio program, and Ss listen for the answers. Then elicit the correct answers.

Answers

1. Japan's highest mountain is Mount Fuji, not Everest.
2. Argentinians speak Spanish, not French.
3. Italy is on the Mediterranean Sea, not the Atlantic Ocean.

TIP To increase Ss' confidence and sense of achievement, play the audio program again at the end of the activity.

11 SPEAKING

Learning objective: *talk about vacations using* can, can't, should, *and* shouldn't

Group work

- Explain the task and ask three Ss to read the example conversation. Go over the discussion questions.
- ***Option:*** Brainstorm additional discussion questions with the class. Write them on the board.
- Ss complete the activity in small groups. Go around the class and encourage Ss to ask follow-up questions.

12 INTERCHANGE 11

See page T-126 for teaching notes.

13 READING

Learning objectives: *read and discuss e-mail messages; develop skills in predicting and reading for specific information*

- Books closed. Write these questions on the board:
  1. When on vacation, do you ever write to people?
  2. Do you send e-mails, letters, or postcards?
  3. Who do you write to?
  4. What do you write about?
  Ss discuss the questions in pairs. Then elicit their answers.
- Books open. Write *Buenos Aires*, *Prague*, and *Shanghai* on the board. Then read the pre-reading question. Ss complete the task individually.
- Ss scan the article to check their guesses.

Answers

Holly: Prague
Stan: Shanghai
Melinda: Buenos Aires

- Ask Ss to underline any new vocabulary and look it up before class. Elicit or explain any words Ss cannot find.

Vocabulary

castle: a large building where kings and other rulers lived
ancient: from a long time ago; very old
ballet: a classical European dance that tells a story
locals: people who live in a place
cruise: a pleasure trip on a large boat
tango: a Latin-American ballroom dance
canals: long, narrow waterways for boat travel
delta: an area of land where a river divides into smaller rivers before it flows into the sea

For a new way to teach the vocabulary in this Reading, try ***Vocabulary Mingle*** on page T-153.

A

- Explain the task and go over the activities in the chart. Tell Ss to only check (✓) the cities first. Model the first example. Tell Ss to look quickly through the e-mails for words related to *go shopping*. Ss complete the task individually.
- Tell Ss to look through the e-mails in detail for specific examples. Ss complete the task individually. Then they go over answers in pairs.
- Ask different Ss to write their answers on the board, using sentences with *can* (e.g., You can go shopping at the Bund in Shanghai.).

Answers

Activity	*Prague*	*Shanghai*	*Buenos Aires*	*Specific examples*
1. go shopping		✓	✓	the Bund, Calle Florida
2. see old buildings	✓	✓		1930s buildings, Prague Castle
3. see dancing	✓		✓	World Dance Festival, tango
4. attend a festival	✓	✓		Dragon Boat and World Dance Festival
5. take a boat trip		✓	✓	night cruise, sail on the canals

B *Pair work*

- Read the discussion questions. Ss discuss them in pairs.

For a new way to practice reading for specific information, try the ***Reading Race*** on page T-152.

End of Cycle 2

Do your students need more practice?

Assign . . .	*for more practice in . . .*
Workbook Exercises 7–10 on pages 65–66	Grammar, Vocabulary Reading, and Writing
Lab Guide Exercises 4–9 on page 22	Listening, Pronunciation, Speaking, and Grammar
Video Activity Book Unit 11	Listening, Speaking, and Cultural Awareness
CD-ROM Unit 11	Grammar, Vocabulary, Reading, Listening, and Speaking

13 READING Greetings from . . .

Look at the pictures from three e-mail messages. What place do you think each person is visiting?

Holly: ______ Stan: ______ Melinda: ______

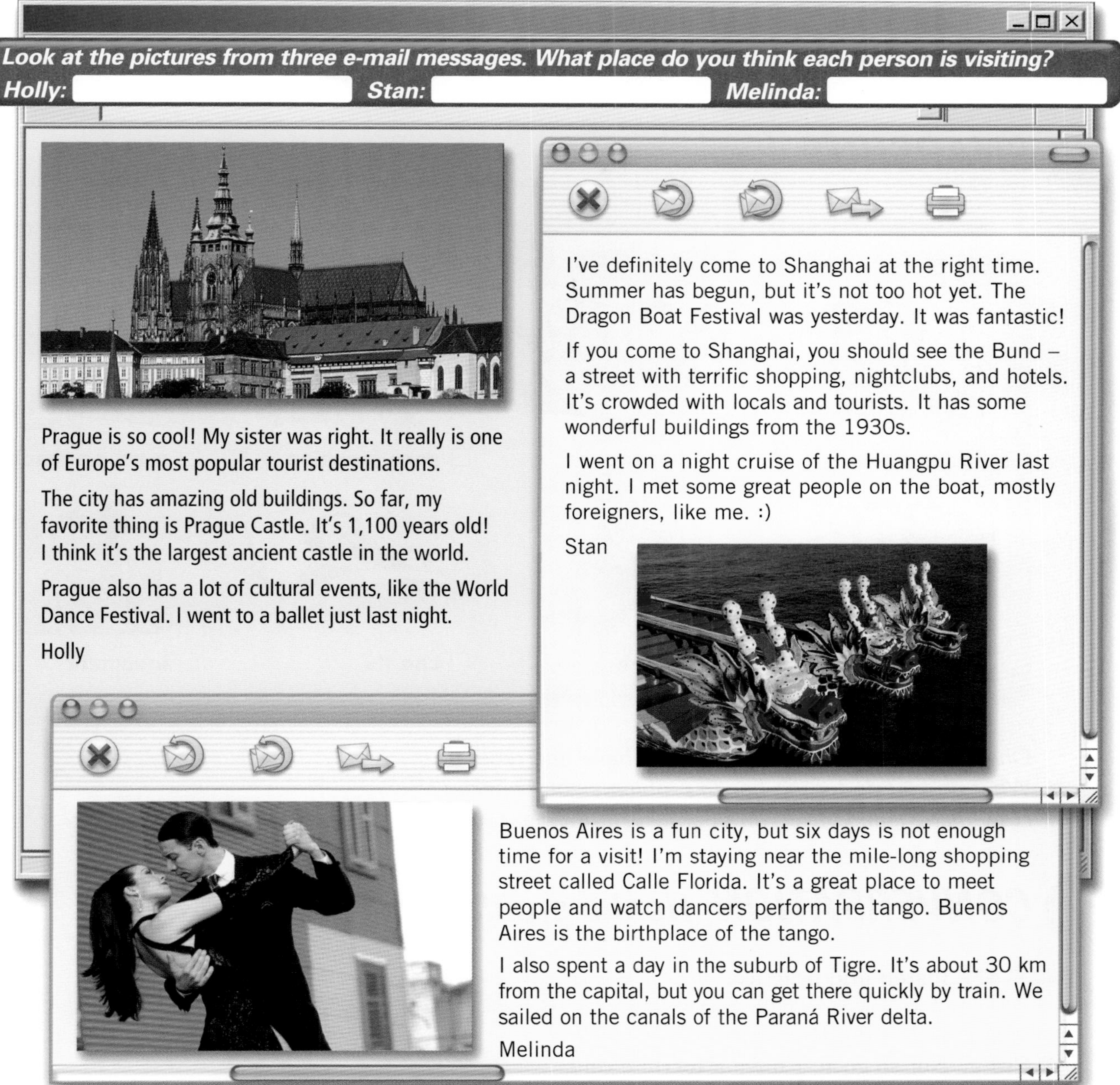

Prague is so cool! My sister was right. It really is one of Europe's most popular tourist destinations.

The city has amazing old buildings. So far, my favorite thing is Prague Castle. It's 1,100 years old! I think it's the largest ancient castle in the world.

Prague also has a lot of cultural events, like the World Dance Festival. I went to a ballet just last night.

Holly

I've definitely come to Shanghai at the right time. Summer has begun, but it's not too hot yet. The Dragon Boat Festival was yesterday. It was fantastic!

If you come to Shanghai, you should see the Bund – a street with terrific shopping, nightclubs, and hotels. It's crowded with locals and tourists. It has some wonderful buildings from the 1930s.

I went on a night cruise of the Huangpu River last night. I met some great people on the boat, mostly foreigners, like me. :)

Stan

Buenos Aires is a fun city, but six days is not enough time for a visit! I'm staying near the mile-long shopping street called Calle Florida. It's a great place to meet people and watch dancers perform the tango. Buenos Aires is the birthplace of the tango.

I also spent a day in the suburb of Tigre. It's about 30 km from the capital, but you can get there quickly by train. We sailed on the canals of the Paraná River delta.

Melinda

A Read the e-mails. Check (✓) the cities where you can do these things. Then complete the chart with examples from the e-mails.

Activity	Prague	Shanghai	Buenos Aires	Specific examples
1. go shopping	☐	☐	☐	....
2. see old buildings	☐	☐	☐	....
3. see dancing	☐	☐	☐	....
4. attend a festival	☐	☐	☐	....
5. take a boat trip	☐	☐	☐	....

B *Pair work* Which city would you most like to visit? Why?

12 It really works!

1 SNAPSHOT

Source: National Center for Health Statistics

Check (✓) the health problems you have had recently.
What do you do for the health problems you checked?
How many times have you been sick in the past year?

2 CONVERSATION Health problems

A Listen and practice.

Joan: Hi, Craig! How are you?
Craig: Not so good. I have a terrible cold.
Joan: Really? That's too bad! You should be at home in bed. It's really important to get a lot of rest.
Craig: Yeah, you're right.
Joan: And have you taken anything for it?
Craig: No, I haven't.
Joan: Well, it's sometimes helpful to eat garlic soup. Just chop up a whole head of garlic and cook it in chicken stock. Try it! It really works!
Craig: Yuck! That sounds awful!

B Listen to advice from two more of Craig's co-workers. What do they suggest?

It really works!

In Unit 12, students talk about health. In Cycle 1, they talk about health problems and give advice using infinitive complements. In Cycle 2, they ask for advice and give suggestions about health care products using the modal verbs can, could, and may.

Cycle 1, Exercises 1–6

1 SNAPSHOT

Learning objectives: *learn vocabulary for common health problems; talk about health problems*

- Books closed. Elicit common health problems from the class and write them on the board.
- Books open. Ss compare their ideas with the Snapshot. Explain any new vocabulary, using gestures if needed.
- Explain the tasks. Ss complete the tasks in small groups. Go around the class and give help as needed.
- Ask the class: "How many of you have had a headache recently? Raise your hands." Ask about each health problem. Count the number of Ss who have had each one.

! For a new way to practice the vocabulary in this Word Power, try ***Vocabulary Steps*** on page T-154. Ss rank the health problems according to most/least serious or most/least common.

2 CONVERSATION

Learning objectives: *practice a conversation about health problems; see infinitive complements in context*

A [CD 3, Track 8]

- Ss cover the text and look at the picture. Elicit or explain vocabulary (e.g., *tissues*). Ask: "What health problem do you think Craig has? How do you know?"
- Play the first part of the audio program. Ss listen to check the answer. (Answer: a cold)
- Write this focus question on the board: *What does Joan suggest for Craig's cold?*
- Play the audio program and ask Ss to listen for the answer. Elicit the answer. (Answer: garlic soup)
- Elicit or explain any new vocabulary.

Vocabulary

get a lot of rest: relax or sleep a lot
have you taken anything for it?: have you taken any medicine?
chop up: cut into small pieces
chicken stock: the liquid from chicken soup
Yuck!: an expression of dislike, especially about food

- Play the audio program again. Ss listen and read silently.
- Ss practice the conversation in pairs. Go around the class and give help as needed.

TIP To encourage Ss to look at each other while practicing Conversations, ask them to stand up and face each other. This also makes the conversation more active and natural.

B

- Read the task and focus question. Ask Ss to make predictions. Write their ideas on the board.
- Play the audio program. Ss listen for the answers individually. Then elicit answers from the class.

Audio script

1.
CRAIG: [*coughs*]
WOMAN: That cold sounds pretty bad, Craig!
CRAIG: Yeah, it is. Don't get too close.
WOMAN: Well, you know, it's important to drink a lot of liquids. I have some herbal tea. Let me make you a cup.
CRAIG: Oh, OK. That sounds good.
2.
MAN: How's that cold, Craig?
CRAIG: Not so good. [*sneezes*] I've still got it.
MAN: Oh, too bad. Well, listen, it's a good idea to take some cold medicine. And you should go home and take a long, hot bath.
CRAIG: You're right. Maybe I should. Thanks for the advice.

Answers

The woman suggests herbal tea. The man suggests cold medicine. He also says Craig should go home and take a long, hot bath.

3 GRAMMAR FOCUS

Learning objectives: *practice using infinitive complements; ask for and give advice using infinitive complements*

[CD 3, Track 9]

- Books closed. Write these sentences on the board:
  You should get a lot of rest.
  You should eat garlic soup.
- Point out that these sentences give suggestions with *should*. We can also give suggestions with infinitive complements. Cross out the words *You should* and replace them with *It's important to* and *It's helpful to.*
- Books open. Focus Ss' attention on the Grammar Focus box. Elicit the rule for forming infinitive complements:
  It's important/helpful/a good idea to + verb.
- Focus Ss' attention on the Conversation on page 78. Ask Ss to underline the two examples of infinitive complements.
- Play the audio program.
- ***Option:*** Present additional positive infinitive complements (e.g., *It's useful to, It's best to, It's essential to*) and also negative infinitives (e.g., *It's important* ***not*** *to, It's best* ***not*** *to*).

A

- Explain the task. Ss read the problems and advice silently. Use the picture or gestures to explain new vocabulary (e.g., *a sore throat, a fever, a toothache, a burn*).
- Read the first problem. Elicit different pieces of advice.
- Ss complete the task individually. Then go over answers with the class.

Possible answers

1. a, c, d, i, j	3. b, d, e, g, i	5. g, h, j	7. b, f, i, j
2. a, d, i, j	4. c, d, g, i, j	6. d, g, j	8. c, d, g, i, j

B *Group work*

- Explain the task. Then model the example conversation with two Ss.
- Ss take turns giving advice in small groups. Go around the class and check their use of infinitive complements.

TIP Use your fingers to help Ss self-correct their errors. For example, if the error is in the fourth word in a sentence, show four fingers and point to the fourth finger.

C

- Explain the task and elicit endings for the first example. Write them on the board.
- Ss complete the task individually. Go around the class and give help as needed.

For a new way to practice the vocabulary in this Grammar Focus, try ***Mime*** on page T-148.

4 PRONUNCIATION

Learning objectives: *notice the reduction of* to*; learn to sound natural when using* to *in conversation*

A *[CD 3, Track 10]*

- Model the reduction of *to*. Then play the audio program. Ss listen for the reduction of *to*.
- Play the audio program again. Ss take turns practicing the conversation in pairs.

TIP If you are concerned about your pronunciation and intonation, always use the audio program to present material.

B *Pair work*

- Explain the task. Ss work in pairs. They ask for and give advice using their sentences from part C of Exercise 3. Ask a few pairs of Ss to model the task.
- Ss complete the task in pairs. Go around the class and check their reduction of *to*. Then elicit the most popular advice for each problem.

3 GRAMMAR FOCUS

Infinitive complements

What should you do for a cold?	**It's important**	to get a lot of rest.
	It's sometimes helpful	to eat garlic soup.
	It's a good idea	to take some vitamin C.

A Look at these health problems. Choose several pieces of good advice for each problem.

Problems	*Advice*
1. a sore throat	a. take some vitamin C
2. a cough	b. put some ointment on it
3. a backache	c. drink lots of liquids
4. a fever	d. go to bed and rest
5. a toothache	e. put a heating pad on it
6. a bad headache	f. put it under cold water
7. a burn	g. take some aspirin
8. the flu	h. see a dentist
	i. see a doctor
	j. get some medicine

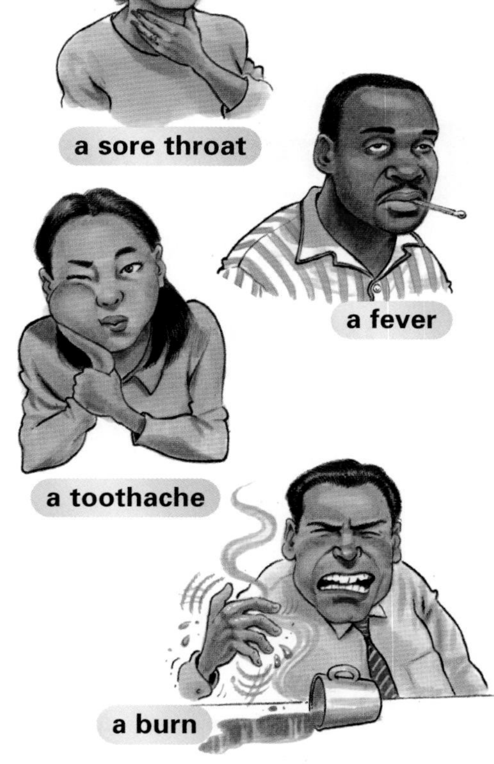

B *Group work* Talk about the problems in part A and give advice. What other advice do you have?

A: What should you do for a sore throat?
B: It's a good idea to get some medicine from the drugstore.
C: Yes. And it's important to drink lots of liquids and . . .

C Write advice for these problems. (You will use this advice in Exercise 4.)

a cold   sore eyes   a sunburn   sore muscles

For a cold, it's a good idea to . . .

4 PRONUNCIATION Reduction of to

A Listen and practice. In conversation, **to** is often reduced to /tə/.

A: What should you do for a fever?
B: It's important **to** take some aspirin. And it's a good idea **to** see a doctor.

B *Pair work* Look back at part C of Exercise 3. Ask for and give advice about each health problem. Pay attention to the pronunciation of **to**.

5 DISCUSSION *Difficult situations*

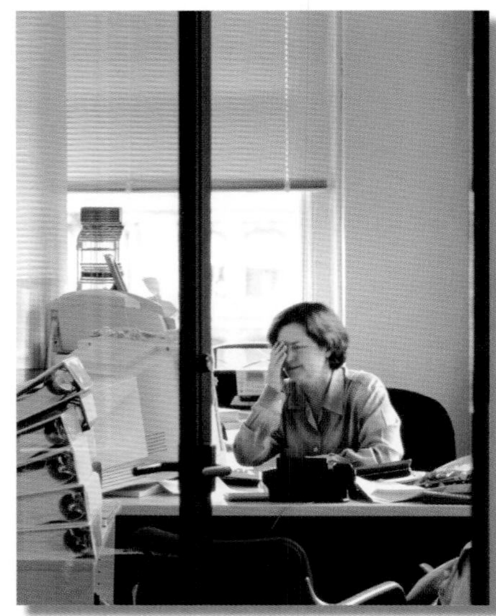

A *Group work* What do you do in these situations? Think of three suggestions for each situation.

What do you do when . . . ?

you feel very stressed
you have an argument with a friend
it's 2:00 A.M. and you can't sleep
someone standing near you faints
you need to study but you can't concentrate

A: What do you do when you feel very stressed?
B: I think it's important to breathe deeply.
C: Yes, and it's sometimes helpful to . . .

B *Class activity* Have any of the above situations happened to you recently? Share what you did with the class.

6 INTERCHANGE 12 *Help!*

Play a board game. Go to Interchange 12.

7 WORD POWER *Containers*

A Use the words in the list to complete these expressions. Then compare with a partner.

bag	jar
bottle	pack
box	stick
can	tube

1. a .... of toothpaste
2. a .... of aspirin
3. a .... of bandages
4. a .... of shaving cream
5. a .... of tissues
6. a .... of face cream
7. a .... of cough drops
8. a .... of deodorant

B *Pair work* What is one more thing you can buy in each of the containers above?

"You can buy a bag of breath mints."

C *Pair work* What are the five most useful items in your medicine cabinet?

5 DISCUSSION

Learning objective: *discuss difficult situations using infinitive complements*

A *Group work*

- Books closed. Ask: "What should you do when you forget someone's name?" Elicit Ss' answers, encouraging them to use *should* or infinitive complements.
- Books open. Explain the task and ask different Ss to read the example situations. Elicit or explain any new vocabulary. Then ask three Ss to read the example conversation.
- Ss discuss the situations in small groups. Go around the class and write down any errors you hear.
- Write the most common errors on the board. Ask Ss to correct them in pairs.

For a new way to practice this Discussion, try the ***Onion Ring*** technique on page T-151.

B *Class activity*

- Read the question to the class. Elicit Ss' answers. Encourage Ss to ask follow-up questions.

6 INTERCHANGE 12

See page T-127 for teaching notes.

End of Cycle 1

Do your students need more practice?

Assign . . .	*For more practice in . . .*
Workbook Exercises 1–4 on pages 67–69	Grammar, Vocabulary, Reading, and Writing
Lab Guide Exercises 1–5 on page 23	Listening, Pronunciation, Speaking, and Grammar

Cycle 2, Exercises 7–13

7 WORD POWER

Learning objective: *learn vocabulary for containers*

A

- Books closed. Write the names of the various products from the Word Power on the board. Ask Ss which ones they use. Elicit or explain any new vocabulary.
- ***Option:*** Bring some of the products to class (e.g., a toothbrush, deodorant). Elicit the vocabulary.

TIP To teach the vocabulary for small everyday objects bring the actual objects to class.

- Books open. Focus Ss' attention on the picture. Elicit or present the words for containers.
- Ss complete the task individually.
- Go over answers with the class. Point out that we don't stress the word *of*.

Answers

1. a **tube** of toothpaste
2. a **bottle** of aspirin
3. a **box** of bandages
4. a **can** of shaving cream
5. a **pack** of tissues
6. a **jar** of face cream
7. a **bag** of cough drops
8. a **stick** of deodorant

B *Pair work*

- Explain the task and ask a S to read the model sentence. Point out that Ss can include any items (e.g., foods).
- Ss work in pairs. Then Ss write their ideas on the board.

Possible answers

1. a bag of breath mints/potato chips/rice
2. a bottle of vitamins/shampoo/juice
3. a box of herbal tea/cereal/candy
4. a can of hair spray/foot spray/soda
5. a jar of coffee/mayonnaise/jam
6. a pack of lozenges/gum/mints
7. a stick of gum/butter
8. a tube of ointment/hand cream/hair gel

C *Pair work*

- Read the question. Ss complete the task in pairs.

For a new way to review the vocabulary in this Word Power, try ***Picture Completion*** on page T-158.

8 CONVERSATION

Learning objectives: *practice a conversation between a pharmacist and a customer; see modal verbs for requests and suggestions in context*

A [CD 3, Track 11]

- Books closed. Ask: "Where do you think the speakers are?" Play the audio program and Ss listen for the answer. Elicit the answer. (Answer: a pharmacy)
- Books open. Ss cover the text. Elicit the containers in the picture. Then ask: "What does the woman buy?" Encourage Ss to guess. Then play the audio program and elicit the answers. (Answers: a box of cough drops, some lotion, and three bottles of multivitamins)
- Ask: "What three problems does the woman talk about?" Play the audio program again and Ss listen for the answers. Elicit the answers. (Answers: a cough/cold, dry skin, no energy.)
- ***Option:*** Ss work in two groups. Group A listens for the problems the woman talks about. Group B listens for the things she buys. Then they share information.
- Ss uncover the text. Ss read the conversation silently.
- Ss stand and practice the conversation in pairs. Encourage them to role-play the conversation, as if they are in a pharmacy.

! For a new way to practice this Conversation, try ***Say It With Feeling!*** on page T-150.

B

- Write these phrases on the board:
  tired eyes   *a backache*   *insomnia*
- Ask: "What problem does the customer have?" Play the audio program. Ss listen to find the answer. (Answer: a backache)
- Explain the task and read the focus question. Then play the audio program again. Elicit the answer.

Audio script

CUSTOMER: Excuse me.
PHARMACIST: Yes? How can I help you?
CUSTOMER: Um, what do you suggest for a backache?
PHARMACIST: Well, you should take some aspirin. And it's a good idea to use a heating pad.
CUSTOMER: Oh, and where are the aspirin?
PHARMACIST: They're in aisle five. Right over there.

Answer

He wants some aspirin.

GRAMMAR FOCUS

Learning objective: *practice conversations using modal verbs for requests and suggestions*

[CD 3, Track 12]

- Explain that it's impolite to say *Give me* or *I want* when asking for things in a store. People usually make requests using modal verbs such as *can*, *could*, and *may*.
- Focus Ss' attention on the Conversation in Exercise 8. Ask: "How did Mrs. Webb ask for things?" Ask Ss to underline the examples. (Answers: *Could I have . . . ? . . . what do you suggest? Can you suggest . . . ? May I have . . . ?*)
- Focus Ss' attention on the example questions in the first column of the Grammar Focus box. Point out that the first question (*Can/May I help you?*) is an offer of help. The other three questions are requests for help. Explain that people can use *can*, *could*, and *may* to make a request, but *may* is the most formal.
- Elicit the rule for questions with modals:
  Modal + subject + verb?
- Focus Ss' attention on the three ways to make suggestions in the second column. Ask Ss to find examples in the Conversation in Exercise 8 and underline them twice.
- Play the audio program.
- Explain the task and model the first conversation with a S.
- Ss complete the task individually. Then they compare answers in pairs.

Possible answers

1. A: **Can/May** I help you?
   B: Yes. **Can/Could/May** I have something for itchy eyes?
   A: Sure. I **suggest** a bottle of eye drops.
2. A: What do you **have/suggest** for sore muscles?
   B: You **should** try this ointment. It's excellent.
   A: OK. I'll take it.
3. A: **Can/Could/May** I have a box of bandages, please?
   B: Here you are.
   A: And what do you **have/suggest** for insomnia?
   B: **Try** some of this herbal tea. It's very relaxing.
   A: OK. Thanks.

- Ss practice the conversations in pairs.

! For a new way to practice the conversations in this Grammar Focus, try the ***Substitution Dialog*** on page T-151. Ss replace the health problems and suggestions with ideas of their own.

8 CONVERSATION What do you suggest?

A Listen and practice.

Pharmacist: Hi. May I help you?
Mrs. Webb: Yes, please. Could I have something for a cough? I think I'm getting a cold.
Pharmacist: Well, I suggest a box of these cough drops.
Mrs. Webb: Thank you. And what do you suggest for dry skin?
Pharmacist: Try some of this new lotion. It's very good.
Mrs. Webb: OK. And one more thing. My husband has no energy these days. Can you suggest anything?
Pharmacist: He should try some of these multivitamins. They're excellent.
Mrs. Webb: Great! May I have three large bottles, please?

B Listen to the pharmacist talk to the next customer. What does the customer want?

9 GRAMMAR FOCUS

Modal verbs can, could, may *for requests; suggestions*

Can/May I help you?	What do you suggest/have for dry skin?
Can I have a box of cough drops?	Try some of this lotion.
Could I have something for a cough?	I suggest some ointment.
May I have a bottle of aspirin?	You should get some skin cream.

Complete these conversations with the verbs *can*, *could*, *may*, *have*, *try*, *suggest*, or *should*. Then compare and practice with a partner.

1. A: .... I help you?
   B: Yes. .... I have something for itchy eyes?
   A: Sure. I .... a bottle of eye drops.
2. A: What do you .... for sore muscles?
   B: You .... try this ointment. It's excellent.
   A: OK. I'll take it.
3. A: .... I have a box of bandages, please?
   B: Here you are.
   A: And what do you .... for insomnia?
   B: .... some of this herbal tea. It's very relaxing.
   A: OK. Thanks.

10 LISTENING *Try this!*

A Listen to four people talk to a pharmacist. Check (✓) each person's problem.

1. ☐ The man's feet are sore.
   ☐ The man's feet are itchy.
2. ☐ The woman can't eat.
   ☐ The woman has an upset stomach.
3. ☐ The man has difficulty sleeping.
   ☐ The man is sleeping too much.
4. ☐ The woman burned her hand.
   ☐ The woman has a bad sunburn.

B Listen again. What does the pharmacist suggest for each person?

11 ROLE PLAY *Can I help you?*

Student A: You are a customer in a drugstore. You need:

something for low energy
something for the flu
something for a backache
something for dry skin
something for an upset stomach

Ask for some suggestions.

Student B: You are a pharmacist in a drugstore. A customer needs some things. Make some suggestions.

Change roles and try the role play again.

12 WRITING *A letter to an advice columnist*

A Read these letters to an advice columnist.

Dear Fix-it Fred,

I have a problem and need your advice. What do you suggest for losing weight? My friends say I look fine, but I don't think so. I've tried several diets, but they just don't work for me. I'm desperate! Can you please help?

Not Slim Jim

Dear Fix-it Fred,

Several months ago, I moved to another town to start college. I call my boyfriend back home every weekend. Now he says the distance is too great and we should break up. I want to stay together. What do you suggest?

Heartbroken

B Now imagine you want some advice about a problem. Write a short letter to an advice columnist. Think of an interesting way to sign it.

C *Group work* Exchange letters. Read and write down some advice at the bottom of each letter. Then share the most interesting letter and advice with the class.

10 LISTENING

***Learning objective:** develop skills in listening for specific information*

A [CD 3, Track 13]

- Set the scene and explain the task. Then play the audio program. Ss listen for the answers.

Audio script

1.
PHARMACIST: Can I help you?
MAN: Yes, I'd like something for my feet. I went on a long hike yesterday and my feet are really sore.
PHARMACIST: I see. Why don't you try some of this ointment? You can put it on at night. It's very good for sore feet. I use it myself, actually.
2.
WOMAN: Excuse me. I'm looking for something for a stomachache.
PHARMACIST: I see. How long have you had this problem?
WOMAN: For a few days, and it's getting worse.
PHARMACIST: I'll give you some pills to take for a few days. They should help. Take two of these, three times a day, with meals.
3.
PHARMACIST: Can I help you?
MAN: Yes. I just came back from London on a long flight, and I'm having trouble sleeping.
PHARMACIST: We have several things for that, including sleeping pills. But I suggest you try some of this herbal tea. It's very good for jet lag. Drink some before you go to bed at night.
MAN: Thanks. I'll try it. I don't like taking sleeping pills.
4.
PHARMACIST: Good morning. What can I do for you?
WOMAN: Um, I need something for a burn. I burned my hand a little when I was cooking last night. Look here.
PHARMACIST: Oh, yes. I'll give you some cream for it. After you put on the cream, place a bandage over it for a few days. You should be fine.
WOMAN: Thanks.

- Go over answers with the class.

Answers

1. The man's feet are sore.
2. The woman has an upset stomach.
3. The man has difficulty sleeping.
4. The woman burned her hand.

B

- Explain the task and read the focus question. Then play the audio program and Ss listen for the answers.
- Ss go over their answers in pairs. Then go over answers with the class.

Answers

1. ointment
2. pills
3. herbal tea
4. cream and a bandage

11 ROLE PLAY

***Learning objective:** role-play a conversation between two people in a drugstore*

- Set the scene and explain the task. Ss work in pairs. Student A is a customer in a drugstore, and Student B is a pharmacist. The customer asks for five things and the pharmacist makes suggestions.
- ***Option:*** If Ss need help getting started, refer them to the first few lines of the Conversation on page 81.
- Ss complete the role play in pairs.
- Ss change roles. Go around the class and take notes on their grammar, pronunciation, fluency, and ideas.

For a new way to teach this Role Play, try ***Time Out!*** on page T-153.

12 WRITING

***Learning objectives:** write a letter to an advice columnist using modal verbs for requests; write a response using suggestions*

A

- Ask: "Do you ever read advice columns? Do you like them? Why or why not?"
- Ss read the example letters silently. Elicit or explain any new vocabulary.

B

- Explain the task. Ss complete the task individually in class or for homework.

C *Group work*

- Explain the task. Then Ss complete the task in small groups.

13 READING

***Learning objectives:** read and discuss an article about the rain forest; develop skills in predicting, skimming, and understanding the sequence of information*

- Read the pre-reading question. Tell Ss to look at the title, pictures, and captions. Elicit Ss' predictions. (Answer: finding health remedies in the rain forest)

! For a new way to practice predicting, try ***Cloud Prediction*** on page T-154.

A

- Explain the task. Tell Ss to skim the article for the answer. Point out that they shouldn't worry about any new vocabulary.
- Allow about three minutes for Ss to complete the task. Then Ss check the best description of the article. Elicit the answer.

Answer

1

- Point out that this way of ordering information is common in many magazine articles.

B

- Present or ask Ss to look up key vocabulary from the reading.

TIP To save time, have Ss look up the vocabulary in a dictionary before class. To encourage peer teaching, assign each S a few words to look up. Then have them teach each other the words in class.

Vocabulary

rain forest: a tropical forest
medicinal: related to medicine
jungle: a tropical forest with many trees and plants
bleeding: losing blood
sources: places where things come from
researchers: people who study something
searching: looking for
produced: made; created

- Explain the task. Then answer the first question and identify the paragraph as a class.
- Ss complete the task individually and compare answers in pairs. Go around the class and check their answers. Help Ss with pronunciation as needed.

Answers

Par. 3 (from his grandmother)
Par. 5 (medical researchers)
Par. 2 (medicinal plants)
Par. 6 (none)
Par. 4 (about 50 percent)

- ***Option:*** Ss read the article again and underline any words they still don't know. Explain the words.

C *Group work*

- Ss discuss the question in small groups. Go around the class and help with vocabulary as needed. Then elicit Ss' answers. (Possible answers: They're a source of oxygen, wood, rubber, and food. They're a home for many animals.)

End of Cycle 2

Do your students need more practice?

Assign . . .	*for more practice in . . .*
Workbook Exercises 5–8 on pages 70–72	Grammar, Vocabulary, Reading, and Writing
Lab Guide Exercises 6–7 on page 23	Listening, Pronunciation, Speaking, and Grammar
Video Activity Book Unit 12	Listening, Speaking, and Cultural Awareness
CD-ROM Unit 12	Grammar, Vocabulary, Reading, Listening, and Speaking

Evaluation

Assess Ss' understanding of Units 11 and 12 with the quiz on pages T-210 and T-211.

13 READING

Rain Forest Remedies?

Look at the title, pictures, and captions. What do you think the article is about?

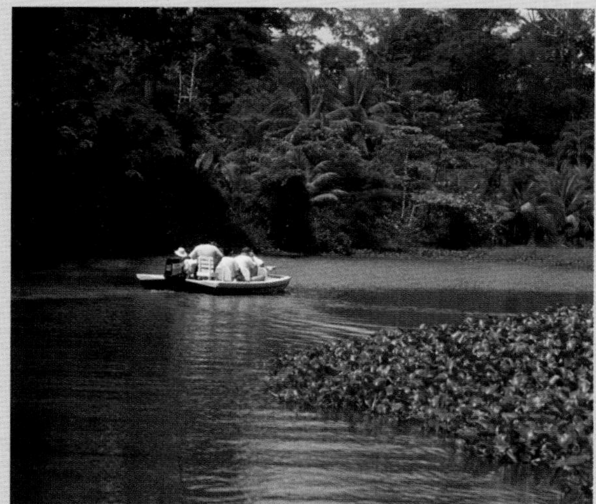

Carol Maxwell writes a column on health. Recently, she took a trip to Tortuguero National Park in Costa Rica.

1 Rodrigo Bonilla turns off the motor of the boat. We get off the boat and follow him along the path into the rain forest. Above us, a monkey with a baby hangs from a tree.

2 On this hot January day, Rodrigo is not looking for wild animals, but for medicinal plants – plants that can cure or treat illnesses. Medicinal plants grow in rain forests around the world.

3 Rodrigo is Costa Rican. He learned about jungle medicine from his grandmother. He shows us many different plants, such as the broom tree. He tells us that parts of the broom tree can help stop bleeding.

4 People have always used natural products as medicine. In fact, about 50 percent of Western medicines, such as aspirin, come from natural sources. And some animals eat certain kinds of plants when they are sick.

5 This is why medical researchers are so interested in plants. Many companies are now working with local governments and searching the rain forests for medicinal plants.

6 So far, the search has not produced any new medicines. But it's a good idea to keep looking. That's why we are now here in the Costa Rican rain forest.

A broom tree

A Read the article. Then check (✓) the best description of the article.

- ☐ 1. The article starts with a description and then gives facts.
- ☐ 2. The article gives the writer's opinion.
- ☐ 3. The article starts with facts and then gives advice.

B Answer these questions. Then write the number of the paragraph where you find each answer.

.... Where did Rodrigo learn about jungle medicine?
.... Who is interested in studying medicinal plants?
.... What is Rodrigo looking for in the rain forest?
.... How many new medicines have come from Rodrigo's search?
.... How many Western medicines come from natural sources?

C *Group work* Can you think of other reasons why rain forests are important?

Units 11–12 Progress check

SELF-ASSESSMENT

How well can you do these things? Check (✓) the boxes.

I can	Very well	OK	A little
Listen to and understand descriptions of cities (Ex. 1)	☐	☐	☐
Describe places using adjectives, adverbs, and conjunctions (Ex. 1, 2)	☐	☐	☐
Ask questions about cities and hometowns (Ex. 2)	☐	☐	☐
Ask for and give suggestions with *can* and *should* (Ex. 2, 3)	☐	☐	☐
Ask for and give advice using infinitive complements (Ex. 3, 4)	☐	☐	☐
Give suggestions on a variety of problems (Ex. 4)	☐	☐	☐

1 LISTENING *I'm from Honolulu.*

A Listen to Jenny talk about Honolulu. What does she say about these things? Complete the chart.

1. size of city	**3.** prices of things ....
2. weather	**4.** most famous place ....

B Write sentences comparing Honolulu with your hometown. Then discuss with a partner.

Honolulu isn't too big, but Seoul is really big.

2 ROLE PLAY *My hometown*

Student A: Imagine you are planning to visit Student B's hometown. Ask questions using the ones in the box or your own questions.

Student B: Answer Student A's questions about your hometown.

A: What's your hometown like?
B: It's quiet but fairly interesting. . . .

some questions

What's your hometown like?
How big is it?
What's the weather like?
Is it expensive?
What should you see there?
What can you do there?

Change roles and try the role play again.

Units 11–12 Progress check

SELF-ASSESSMENT

Learning objectives: *reflect on one's learning; identify areas that need improvement*

- Ask: "What did you learn in Units 11 and 12?" Elicit Ss' answers.
- Ss complete the Self-assessment. Encourage them to be honest, and point out they will not get a bad grade if they check (✓) "a little."
- Ss move on to the Progress check exercises. You can have Ss complete them in class or for homework, using one of these techniques:
  1. Ask Ss to complete all the exercises.
  2. Ask Ss: "What do you need to practice?" Then assign exercises based on their answers.
  3. Ask Ss to choose and complete exercises based on their Self-assessment.

1 LISTENING

Learning objectives: *assess one's ability to listen to and understand descriptions of cities; assess one's ability to describe places using adjectives, adverbs, and conjunctions*

A [CD 3, Track 14]

- Set the scene and explain the task. Jenny is talking about Honolulu, her hometown. Ss listen and write the size of the city, weather, prices of things, and most famous place in their chart.
- Play the audio program once or twice. Ss listen and complete the chart.

Audio script

MAN: So, you're from Hawaii, Jenny.
JENNY: That's right.
MAN: Where in Hawaii?
JENNY: I'm from Honolulu – on the island of Oahu.
MAN: Wow! Honolulu! That's a fairly big city, isn't it?
JENNY: No, not really. It's not too big.
MAN: The weather is great, though. Right?
JENNY: Oh, yes. It is. It's very comfortable the whole year. Warm, but not too hot.
MAN: I've heard that Honolulu is an expensive city. Is that true?
JENNY: Well, yes, it is pretty expensive. Rents are high and food is expensive, too. That's because everything comes in by plane from the mainland.
MAN: What's that beach in Honolulu?
JENNY: Well, the most famous place in Honolulu is probably Waikiki Beach. That's where all the tourists go.
MAN: Yeah, that's it. Waikiki Beach.

- Go over answers with the class.

Answers

1. not too big
2. very comfortable; warm, but not too hot
3. pretty expensive
4. Waikiki Beach

B

- Explain the task. Ss write sentences comparing Honolulu with their hometown. Point out the conjunction, adjectives, and adverbs in the example.
- Ss write sentences individually. Then they compare their sentences in pairs.

2 ROLE PLAY

Learning objectives: *assess one's ability to describe places using adjectives, adverbs, and conjunctions; assess one's ability to ask questions about cities and hometowns; assess one's ability to ask for and give suggestions with* can *and* should

- Explain the task. Ss work in pairs. Student A is planning to visit Student B's hometown, and asks questions about it. Student B answers the questions.
- Go over the possible questions. Model the example conversation with a S.
- Ss practice the role play in pairs. Then they change roles and practice again. Go around the class and give help as needed.

3 DISCUSSION

Learning objectives: *assess one's ability to ask for and give suggestions using* can *and* should*; assess one's ability to ask for and give advice using infinitive complements*

A *Group work*

- Explain the task and model the example conversation with two Ss.
- Ss write advice and remedies for the problems individually. Go around the class and give help as needed.
- Ss compare their ideas in small groups. Encourage Ss to use expressions of advice (e.g., *it's useful to*, *it's helpful to*, *you should*).
- Go around the room and check Ss' use of infinitive complements.

B *Group work*

- Read the questions and explain the task.
- Ss discuss the questions in small groups. Encourage them to add follow-up questions.

SPEAKING

Learning objectives: *assess one's ability to ask for and give advice using infinitive complements; assess one's ability to give suggestions on a variety of problems*

A *Group work*

- Set the scene. The three problems are from an advice column.
- Ss read the problems silently. Then elicit or explain any new vocabulary.
- Explain the task. In small groups, Ss suggest advice for each problem and choose the best advice. Model the example conversation with two Ss.
- Ss complete the task.

B *Class activity*

- Ask different Ss to read their group's advice.

WHAT'S NEXT?

Learning objective: *become more involved in one's learning*

- Focus Ss' attention on the Self-assessment again. Ask: "How well can you do these things now?"
- Ask Ss to underline one thing they need to review. Ask: "What did you underline? How can you review it?"
- If needed, plan additional activities or reviews based on Ss' answers.

3 DISCUSSION Medicines and remedies

A *Group work* Write advice and remedies for these problems. Then discuss your ideas in groups.

a stomachache

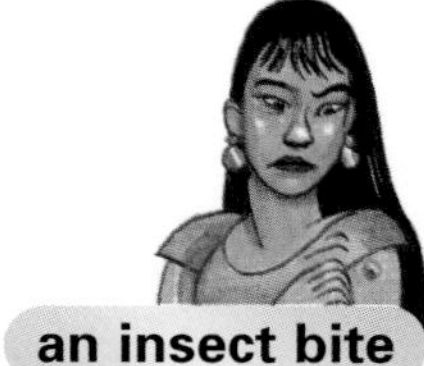
an insect bite

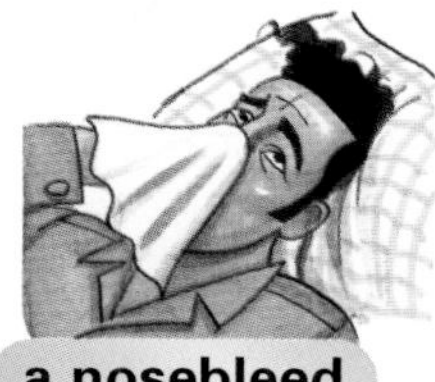
a nosebleed

the hiccups

For a stomachache, it's a good idea to . . .

A: What can you do for a stomachache?
B: I think it's a good idea to buy a bottle of antacid.
C: Yes. And it's helpful to drink herbal tea.

B *Group work* What health problems do you visit a doctor for? go to a drugstore for? use a home remedy for? Ask for advice and remedies.

4 SPEAKING Advice column

A *Group work* Look at these problems from an advice column. Suggest advice for each problem. Then choose the best advice.

I'm visiting the United States. I'm staying with a family while I'm here. What small gifts can I get for them?

My doctor says that I'm not in good shape. I need to lose about four and a half kilos (10 pounds). What can I do?

Our school wants to buy some new gym equipment. Can you suggest some good ways to raise money?

A: I think she should give them some flowers.
B: That's a good idea. Or she can bring chocolates.
C: I suggest . . .

B *Class activity* Share your group's advice for each problem with the class.

WHAT'S NEXT?

Look at your Self-assessment again. Do you need to review anything?

13 May I take your order?

1 SNAPSHOT

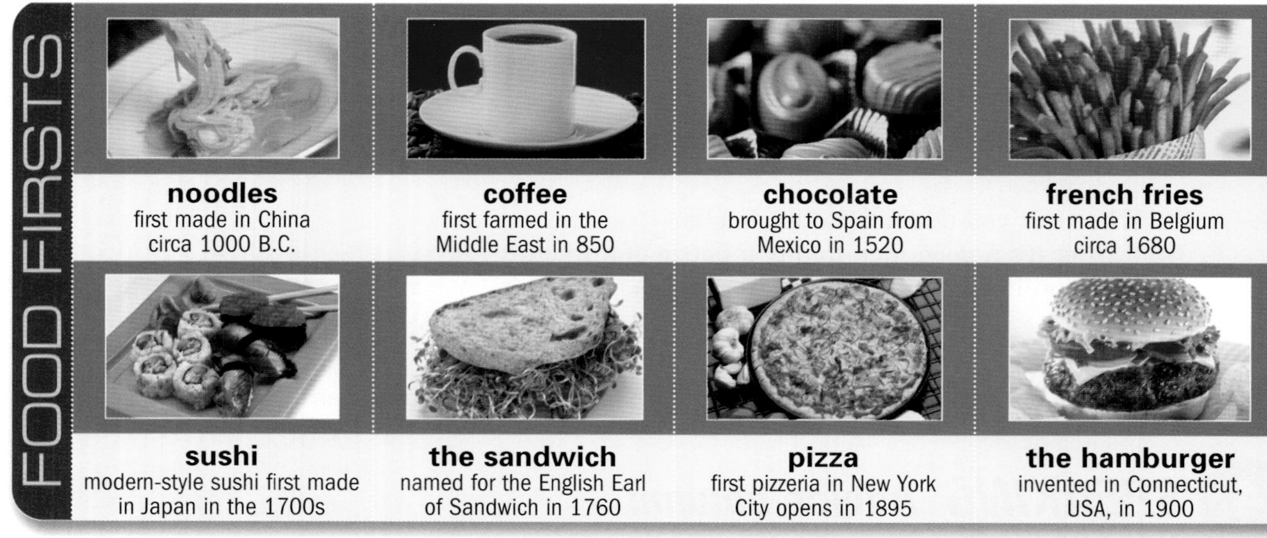

FOOD FIRSTS
noodles
first made in China circa 1000 B.C.
coffee
first farmed in the Middle East in 850
chocolate
brought to Spain from Mexico in 1520
french fries
first made in Belgium circa 1680
sushi
modern-style sushi first made in Japan in the 1700s
the sandwich
named for the English Earl of Sandwich in 1760
pizza
first pizzeria in New York City opens in 1895
the hamburger
invented in Connecticut, USA, in 1900

Sources: *New York Public Library Book of Chronologies*; *www.digitalsushi.net*; *www.belgianfries.com*

What are these foods made of?
Put the foods in order from your favorite to your least favorite.
What are three other foods you enjoy?

2 CONVERSATION *Going out for dinner*

A Listen and practice.

Jeff: Say, would you like to go out to dinner tonight?
Bob: Sure. Where do you want to go?
Jeff: Well, what do you think of Indian food?
Bob: I love it, but I'm not really in the mood for it today.
Jeff: Yeah. I'm not either, I guess. It's a bit spicy.
Bob: Hmm. How do you like Japanese food?
Jeff: Oh, I like it a lot.
Bob: I do, too. And I know a nice Japanese restaurant near here – it's called Iroha.
Jeff: Oh, I've always wanted to go there.
Bob: Terrific! Let's go!

B Listen to the rest of the conversation.
What time do they decide to have dinner?
Where do they decide to meet?

May I take your order?

In Unit 13, students talk about food. In Cycle 1, they agree and disagree about food preferences using so, too, neither, and either. In Cycle 2, they order food at a restaurant using the modal verbs would and will.

Cycle 1, Exercises 1–4

SNAPSHOT

***Learning objectives:** read about the origins of popular foods; talk about favorite foods*

- Books closed. Write these foods on the board:

noodles	*sushi*
coffee	*the sandwich*
chocolate	*pizza*
french fries	*the hamburger*

  Ask Ss to guess where each food item is from.
- Books open. Ss check their answers with the Snapshot.
- Ask different Ss to read the facts. Elicit or explain any new vocabulary.

Vocabulary

circa: around
B.C.: before Christ
farmed: grown
earl: a British man of high social rank

- Point out that the Earl of Sandwich's real name was John Montague, and he loved to play cards. He created the first sandwich so he could eat neatly during card games.
- Ask: "Does any information in the Snapshot surprise you?" Elicit Ss' answers.
- Explain the tasks. Then Ss complete the tasks in pairs. Go around the class and give help as needed.

CONVERSATION

***Learning objectives:** practice a conversation between two people deciding where to go for dinner; see* so, too, neither, *and* either *in context*

A [CD 3, Track 16]

- Books closed. Set the scene. Jeff and Bob are discussing where to go for dinner. Write these focus questions on the board:
  1. What two kinds of food do they talk about?
  2. What kind of food do they decide to eat?
- Play the audio program. Then elicit the answers. (Answers: 1. Indian and Japanese 2. Japanese)
- Books open. Play the audio program again. Ss listen and read silently.
- Elicit or explain any new vocabulary.

Vocabulary

I'm not in the mood for: I don't really want
a bit: a little
spicy: with a hot or strong flavor, like pepper or curry

- Ss practice the conversation in pairs. Then ask Ss to role-play the conversation for the class.

! For a new way to practice this Conversation, try ***Say It With Feeling!*** on page T-150.

B

- Explain the task and read the focus questions. Then play the audio program. Elicit the answers.

Audio script

JEFF: So, do you want to eat early or late?
BOB: Let's eat early. Then maybe we can go to a movie afterward.
JEFF: Good idea! Why don't we have dinner around 6:00?
BOB: Six is good. And where do you want to meet?
JEFF: Let's meet at the restaurant, OK?
BOB: Yeah, that's fine with me.

Answers

They decide to have dinner around 6:00 P.M. They decide to meet at the restaurant.

3 GRAMMAR FOCUS

Learning objective: *practice agreeing and disagreeing using* so, too, neither, *and* either

[CD 3, Track 17]

- Focus Ss' attention on the Grammar Focus box. Ask: "Which column has positive statements? Which column has negative statements?" (Answers: The first column has positive statements, and the second column has negative statements.)

So *and* too

- Focus Ss' attention on the first column. Point out that we can use *so* or *too* to agree with a positive statement.
- Write these responses on the board:
  So do I. *So am I.* *So can I.*
  Ask: "When do we use each response?" Elicit or explain the rule. (Answer: The verb in each response matches that of the sentence before it.)
- Focus Ss' attention on the difference between *so* and *too*. Point out that *so* is at the beginning of the response and *too* is at the end:
  So + *do/am/can* + *I*.
  I + *do/am/can* + ***too***.
- Ask Ss to find responses in the first column that disagree with positive statements. (Answers: *Really? I don't like it very much. / Oh, I'm not. / Really? I can't.*)
- Play the audio program for the first column.
- ***Option:*** Drill *So do I, So am I*, or *So can I* responses. Read a list of ten positive statements to the class (e.g., *I live near here. I am smart. I can speak English.*). Ss respond chorally and then individually.

Neither *and* either

- Focus Ss' attention on the second column of the Grammar Focus box. Elicit the rules for agreeing with a negative statement:
  Neither + *do/am/can* + *I*.
  *I do**n't**/I'm **not**/I ca**n't** **either***.
- Point out different ways to disagree with negative statements (e.g., *Oh, I like it a lot. / Really? I am.*).
- Play the audio program for the second column.
- ***Option:*** Drill *Neither do I, Neither am I*, or *Neither can I* responses. Read a list of ten negative statements to the class (e.g., *I don't like fish ice cream. I'm not hungry. I can't cook French food.*). Ss respond chorally and then individually.

A

- Ask different Ss to read the adjectives describing food. Help with pronunciation as needed.
- Explain the task. Ss write responses to show agreement with the statements. Point out that each statement has two correct responses.
- Read the first two statements and elicit Ss' responses. Write correct responses on the board.
- Ss complete the task individually. Then they compare answers in pairs. Go over answers with the class.

Possible answers

1. Neither am I./I'm not either.
2. So can I./I can, too.
3. So do I./I do, too.
4. Neither can I./I can't either.
5. Neither do I./I don't either.
6. So am I./I am, too.
7. So am I./I am, too.
8. Neither do I./I don't, either.
9. So do I./I do, too.
10. Neither can I./I can't either.

B *Pair work*

- Explain the task. Ss work in pairs. They take turns reading the statements in part A and responding with their own opinions.
- Go around the class and check Ss' use of grammar.

For more practice, play ***Concentration*** on page T-144. Ss match cards with the same meaning (e.g., *So do I.* and *I do, too.*).

C

- Elicit different ways to say *I like* and *I don't like*. Write them on the board:

I like	*I don't like*
I really like	*I don't really like*
I'm in the mood for	*I'm not in the mood for*
I like . . . very much.	*I don't like . . . very much.*
I'm crazy about	*I'm not crazy about*
I love	*I hate*

- Explain the task. Model the first example by writing two sentences on the board.
- Ss complete the task individually. Don't ask Ss to compare statements at this time. They will do this in Exercise 4.

3 GRAMMAR FOCUS

So, too, neither, either

I like Japanese food a lot.
So do I./I do, **too**.
Really? I don't like it very much.

I'm crazy about dessert.
So am I./I am, **too**.
Oh, I'm not.

I can eat really spicy food.
So can I./I can, **too**.
Really? I can't.

I don't like greasy food.
Neither do I./I don't **either**.
Oh, I like it a lot.

I'm not in the mood for Indian food.
Neither am I./I'm not **either**.
Really? I am.

I can't stand fast food.
Neither can I./I can't **either**.
Oh, I love it!

healthy greasy salty rich spicy delicious bland

A Write responses to show agreement with these statements. Then compare with a partner.

1. I'm not crazy about French food. ....
2. I can eat any kind of food. ....
3. I think Mexican food is delicious. ....
4. I can't stand greasy food. ....
5. I don't like salty food. ....
6. I'm in the mood for something spicy. ....
7. I'm crazy about Korean food. ....
8. I don't enjoy rich food very much. ....
9. I always eat healthy food. ....
10. I can't eat bland food. ....

B *Pair work* Take turns responding to the statements in part A again. Give your own opinion when responding.

C Write statements about these things. (You will use the statements in Exercise 4.)

1. two kinds of food you like
2. two kinds of food you can't stand
3. two kinds of food you are in the mood for

4 PRONUNCIATION *Stress in responses*

A Listen and practice. Notice how the last word of each response is stressed.

I do, too.	So do I.	I don't either.	Neither do I.
I am, too.	So am I.	I'm not either.	Neither am I.
I can, too.	So can I.	I can't either.	Neither can I.

B *Pair work* Take turns reading the statements you wrote in part C of Exercise 3. Pay attention to the stress in your responses.

5 WORD POWER *International dishes*

A Complete the chart. Then add one more word to each category.

beef curry	sweet and sour shrimp	mushroom omelet
tuna sushi	grilled salmon	stir-fried tofu
fried bananas	lamb kebabs	chicken burrito

Meat	Seafood	Vegetarian
....	....	....
....	....	....
....	....	....
....	....	....

B *Group work* Which dishes have you tried? Which would you like to try?

6 CONVERSATION *Ordering a meal*

A Listen and practice.

Waiter: May I take your order?
Customer: Yes. I'd like the lamb kebabs.
Waiter: All right. And would you like a salad?
Customer: Yes, I'll have a mixed green salad.
Waiter: OK. What kind of dressing would you like? We have blue cheese and vinaigrette.
Customer: Blue cheese, please.
Waiter: And would you like anything to drink?
Customer: Yes, I'd like a large iced tea, please.

B Listen to the waiter talk to the next customer. What does the customer order?

4 PRONUNCIATION

Learning objectives: *notice stress in responses; learn to sound natural when responding with* so, too, neither, *and* either

A ▶ *[CD 3, Track 18]*

- Explain the task. Then play the audio program. Point out the stress by clapping your hands on the last word of each response.
- Play the audio program again. Ss listen and practice.

B *Pair work*

- Explain the task. Then Ss complete the task in pairs. Go around the class and check Ss' pronunciation.

For a new way to practice this Pronunciation, try ***Bubble Cards*** on page T-159.

End of Cycle 1

Do your students need more practice?

Assign . . .	*for more practice in . . .*
Workbook Exercises 1–3 on pages 73–75	Grammar, Vocabulary, Reading, and Writing
Lab Guide Exercises 1–4 on page 24	Listening, Pronunciation, Speaking, and Grammar

Cycle 2, Exercises 5–12

5 WORD POWER

Learning objective: *learn vocabulary for discussing international dishes*

A

- Explain the task and model the pronunciation of the international dishes. Explain any new vocabulary.
- Ss complete the chart individually.
- Draw the chart on the board. Ask different Ss to complete the chart.

Answers

Meat	***Seafood***	***Vegetarian***
beef curry	tuna sushi	fried bananas
lamb kebabs	sweet and sour shrimp	mushroom omelet
chicken burrito	grilled salmon	stir-fried tofu
chicken sate	*paella*	*vegetable curry*
hot dog	*ceviche*	*spinach lasagna*

(Note: Possible answers are italicized.)

B *Group work*

- Ss discuss the questions in small groups.

6 CONVERSATION

Learning objectives: *practice a conversation between a waiter and a customer; see modal verbs* would *and* will *for requests in context*

A ▶ *[CD 3, Track 19]*

- Ss cover the text. Elicit ideas and vocabulary from the picture. Ask: "What kind of restaurant is this? What kinds of food do they serve?"
- Set the scene. A waiter is taking a customer's order. Write this summary sentence on the board:
  The customer orders lamb/chicken kebabs, a salad with blue cheese/vinaigrette dressing, and an iced coffee/tea.
- Play the audio program. Ss listen for the correct answers. Ask different Ss to circle the correct answers on the board. (Answers: lamb, blue cheese, tea)
- Ss uncover the text. Play the audio program again. Ss listen and read silently.
- Ss practice the conversation in pairs.

B ▶

- Explain the task and read the focus question. Then play the audio program. Elicit the answer.

Audio script

WAITER: Are you ready to order?
WOMAN: Yes, I think so. I'd like a cheeseburger, please.
WAITER: Would you like today's special, a cheeseburger and fries?
WOMAN: Uh, no fries for me. But I'll take a small potato salad.
WAITER: OK. Anything to drink?
WOMAN: Yeah. I'll have a large iced coffee, please.
WAITER: And how about some dessert. We have pie, cake, and ice cream.
WOMAN: No, thanks. I'm trying to watch my weight.

Answers

a cheeseburger, a small potato salad, and a large iced coffee

7 GRAMMAR FOCUS

Learning objective: *practice conversations using modal verbs* would *and* will *for requests*

[CD 3, Track 20]

***Modal verbs* would *and* will**

- Write these sentences on the board:
  1. What kind of dressing do you want?
  2. And do you want anything to drink?
  3. I want a mixed green salad.
  4. I want a large iced tea, please.

  Explain that people don't usually say *want* in formal situations.
- Focus Ss' attention on the Conversation on page 88. Ss find and underline sentences and questions with the same meaning as those on the board. Ask different Ss to write them on the board. (Answers: 1. What kind of dressing would you like? 2. And would you like anything to drink? 3. I'll have a mixed green salad. 4. I'd like a large iced tea, please.)
- Focus Ss' attention on the Grammar Focus box. Elicit the structure for making Wh- and yes/no questions with *would*:
  Wh-question + *would* + subject + verb?
  Would + subject + verb?
  Point out that the word *would* does not have strong stress.
- Elicit or explain that we can order in a restaurant with *I'd like* or *I'll have*. Point out the contractions. Play the audio program.
- Explain the task and model the first two lines of the conversation. Ss complete the conversation individually. Then they compare answers in pairs.
- Go over answers by asking different Ss to read the conversation.

Answers

WAITRESS: What **would** you like to order?
CUSTOMER: **I'll** have the fried chicken.
WAITRESS: **Would** you like rice or potatoes?
CUSTOMER: Potatoes, please.
WAITRESS: What kind of potatoes would you **like**? Mashed, baked, or french fries?
CUSTOMER: **I'd** like mashed potatoes.
WAITRESS: OK. And **would** you like anything to drink?
CUSTOMER: I guess **I'll** have a cup of coffee.
WAITRESS: Would you **like** anything else?
CUSTOMER: No, that**'ll** be all for now, thanks.

Later

WAITRESS: Would you **like** dessert?
CUSTOMER: Yes, **I'd** like ice cream.
WAITRESS: What flavor **would** you like?
CUSTOMER: Hmm. **I'll** have chocolate, please.
WAITRESS: OK. I'll bring it right away.

! For a new way to practice the conversations in this Grammar Focus, try the ***Substitution Dialog*** on page T-151. Ss replace the food and drink items with their own ideas.

8 ROLE PLAY

Learning objective: *role-play a conversation between a customer and a waiter or waitress in a coffee shop*

- Ss work in pairs. Set the scene and explain the task. Student A is a customer in a coffee shop. Student B is a waiter or waitress. Student A orders lunch and Student B takes the order. If possible, Student A sits at a table and Student B stands. Model the pronunciation of the things if needed.
- Model taking the order with a S. Show how to add follow-up questions (e.g., *Would you like dressing on your salad? Would you like anything else?*). Ss complete the role play in pairs.
- Provide useful feedback. Then ask Ss to change roles and use their own information. Go around the class and encourage Ss to ask follow-up questions.
- ***Option:*** Ss complete the role play in small groups. One S is the waiter/waitress and the other Ss are customers.

TIP To make role plays more authentic, bring props to class. For example, in a restaurant role play you can bring real menus, pens, and notepads.

! For a new way to practice this Role Play, try ***Time Out!*** on page T-153.

7 GRAMMAR FOCUS

Modal verbs would *and* will *for requests*

What **would** you **like**?	I'**d like** the lamb kebabs. I'**ll have** a small salad.	***Contractions*** I'**ll** = I will I'**d** = I would
What kind of dressing **would** you **like**?	I'**d like** blue cheese, please. I'**ll have** vinaigrette.	
What **would** you **like** to drink?	I'**d like** an iced tea. I'**ll have** coffee.	
Would you **like** anything else?	Yes, please. I'**d like** some water. No, thank you. That'**ll be** all.	

Complete this conversation. Then practice with a partner.

Waitress: What .... you like to order?
Customer: I .... have the fried chicken.
Waitress: .... you like rice or potatoes?
Customer: Potatoes, please.
Waitress: What kind of potatoes would you .... ? Mashed, baked, or french fries?
Customer: I .... like mashed potatoes.
Waitress: OK. And .... you like anything to drink?
Customer: I guess I .... have a cup of coffee.
Waitress: Would you .... anything else?
Customer: No, that .... be all for now, thanks.

Later

Waitress: Would you .... dessert?
Customer: Yes, I .... like ice cream.
Waitress: What flavor .... you like?
Customer: Hmm. I .... have chocolate, please.
Waitress: OK. I'll bring it right away.

8 ROLE PLAY *In a coffee shop*

Student A: You are a customer in a coffee shop.
This is what you want to order for lunch:

spaghetti and meatballs
a tomato and cucumber salad
an iced tea with lemon
a slice of cheesecake

Student B: You are the waiter or waitress.
Take your customer's order.

Change roles and try the role play again.
Use your own ideas.

9 LISTENING *Let's order.*

A Listen to Rex and Hannah order in a restaurant. What did each of them order? Fill in their check.

Phil's Diner No. 399825

Thank You! Total

B Listen to the rest of the conversation. Circle the two items that the waiter forgot to bring.

10 INTERCHANGE 13 *Plan a menu*

Create a menu of dishes to offer at your very own restaurant. Go to Interchange 13.

11 WRITING *A restaurant review*

A Have you eaten out at a restaurant recently? How was it? Write a review of the restaurant for a local newspaper.

Last week, I had lunch at Luigi's, a new Italian restaurant in my neighborhood. I ordered a green salad and a cheese pizza. The pizza was excellent, but the salad wasn't very good. The lettuce wasn't very fresh. For dessert, I had chocolate cake and a cappuccino. The cake was rich and delicious, and the . . .

B ***Group work*** Take turns reading your reviews to the group. Is there a restaurant you would like to try?

9 LISTENING

Learning objective: *develop skills in listening for details*

A [CD 3, Track 21]

- Set the scene and explain the task. Point out the picture and ask "What foods and drinks do you see?"
- Play the audio program. Ss fill in the check individually.
- Ss compare answers in pairs. Play the audio program again if needed. Then go over answers with the class.

For a new way to practice this Listening, try ***Prediction Bingo*** on page T-146.

Audio script

WAITER: Hi. May I take your order?
REX: Yes. I'll have a cup of coffee.
WAITER: Cream and sugar?
REX: Oh, yes, please.
WAITER: And you?
HANNAH: I'd like a chicken sandwich. And I'll have some chips . . . oh, you call them french fries here. Right. I'll have some french fries, please.
WAITER: All right. One coffee with cream and sugar and a chicken sandwich with french fries. Uh, anything else?
HANNAH: Yes, I'd like an iced tea, please.
WAITER: One iced tea. Thank you.
REX: Oh, wait a minute! What kind of desserts do you have?
WAITER: Well, we have pie, cake, ice cream, chocolate mousse . . .
REX: Oooo! What kind of pie do you have?
WAITER: I think today we have apple, cherry, lemon . . .
REX: Hmm, I think I'll have a piece of apple pie with my coffee. How about you, Hannah?
HANNAH: Oh, maybe I'll have a piece later . . . or . . . I'll have some of yours! [*laughs*]
WAITER: Then it's one coffee, one apple pie, one chicken sandwich, an order of french fries, and an iced tea. Right?
REX: Yes, thank you.
HANNAH: Thanks.

Answers

Rex's order: coffee with cream and sugar, a piece of apple pie
Hannah's order: a chicken sandwich, french fries, iced tea

B

- Ask: "Has a waiter or waitress ever made a mistake with your order? What happened?" Elicit Ss' answers.
- Play the audio program. Ss complete the task individually. Then go over answers with the class.

Audio script

HANNAH: Oh, here comes our waiter!
REX: Yeah, I wondered what took so long.
WAITER: Whew! Here you are!
HANNAH: Uh, I ordered french fries with my chicken sandwich, and you brought me . . . yuck! . . . mashed potatoes with gravy!
WAITER: Oh, you ordered french fries?
HANNAH: Yes.
WAITER: Well, then, OK.
REX: Uh, and could I have the apple pie I ordered?
WAITER: What apple pie? Did you order apple pie?
REX: Uh-huh, yeah, I did, with my coffee. Remember?
WAITER: Really? Gee, how did I forget that?
HANNAH: Uh, can I ask you a question?
WAITER: Yes?
HANNAH: How long have you been a waiter?
WAITER: Who me? Oh, uh, today is my first day. [*all laugh*] Well, I'll get your apple pie and the french fries right away. Sorry about that.
REX: Oh, that's OK.
HANNAH: Yeah, thanks. Good luck.
WAITER: Thanks.

Answers

He forgot to bring the french fries and apple pie.

10 INTERCHANGE 13

See page T-128 for teaching notes.

11 WRITING

Learning objective: *write a restaurant review*

A

- Explain the task. Ss discuss the questions in pairs. Then they read the example review silently.
- Ss complete the task individually in class or for homework.

For a new way to teach this Writing, try ***Mind Mapping*** on page T-154.

B *Group work*

- Explain the task. Ss read their reviews in small groups. Then they choose a restaurant they would like to try.
- ***Option:*** Put the reviews on the walls around the class. Ss read them and choose one they would like to try.

12 READING

Learning objectives: *read and discuss an article about tipping in the United States; develop skills in scanning and guessing meaning from context*

- Focus Ss' attention on the picture. Ask: "Who are the people on the left? What do they want? Elicit Ss' answers and explain new vocabulary. (Answers: They are a chef, parking valet, maid, barber, taxi driver, waiter, and bellhop. They all want a tip.)
- Explain that this article is about tipping in the U.S. Ss read the first paragraph silently. Ask: "Where do Americans usually give tips?" (Answers: in restaurants, airports, hotels, and hair salons)
- Explain the task and read the pre-reading questions. Ss scan the article for the answers.
- Go over answers with the class. Ask: "What helped you find the answers?" (Answer: The jobs are in boldface.)

Answers

Someone who carries your suitcase: $1 or $2 for each suitcase
Someone who parks your car: $1
Someone who serves you in a fast-food restaurant: nothing

- ***Option:*** Ask Ss if they think each tip is reasonable, too little, or too much.

! For a new way to teach this Reading, try Running Dictation on page T-153. Use the first paragraph only.

A

- Explain the task. Encourage Ss to guess the answers by choosing the meaning of each word that best fits the sentence in the article.
- Ss complete the task individually. Then they compare answers in pairs.
- Go over answers with the class. Elicit or explain any new vocabulary.

Vocabulary

slang: informal spoken language
service: help that someone gives a customer
size: amount
parking valets: restaurant or hotel employees who park your car for you
bellhops: hotel employees who carry your bags for you
guidelines: general rules about how to do something
porters: people who carry your bags for you at an airport or railway station
service providers: people in the service industry

Answers

1. regular pay for a job
2. happy or satisfied
3. change according to
4. a way of acting
5. act toward
6. courtesy

B

- Explain the task. Point out that Ss must do some math to complete the task. Ss complete the task individually and compare answers in pairs.
- Ask different Ss to write the answers on the board. Then ask the class to correct the answers if needed.

Answers

1. at least $4.50
2. ✓
3. ✓
4. at least $7
5. at least $3.10

C *Group work*

- Ss discuss the questions in small groups. Then they share their information with the class.

End of Cycle 2

Do your students need more practice?

Assign . . .	*for more practice in . . .*
Workbook Exercises 4–8 on pages 76–78	Grammar, Vocabulary, Reading, and Writing
Lab Guide Exercises 5–8 on page 24	Listening, Pronunciation, Speaking, and Grammar
Video Activity Book Unit 13	Listening, Speaking, and Cultural Awareness
CD-ROM Unit 13	Grammar, Vocabulary, Reading, Listening, and Speaking

12 READING

To Tip or Not to Tip?

Scan the article. How much should you tip someone in the United States who: carries your suitcase at a hotel? parks your car? serves you in a fast-food restaurant?

The word *tip* comes from an old English slang word that means *to give*. It's both a noun and a verb. Americans usually tip people in places like restaurants, airports, hotels, and hair salons.

People who work in these places often get paid low wages. A tip shows that the customer is pleased with the service.

Sometimes it's hard to know how much to tip. The size of the tip usually depends on the service. People such as parking valets or bellhops usually get smaller tips. The tip for people such as taxi drivers and waiters or waitresses is usually larger. Here are a few guidelines for tipping in the United States:

Airport porters or hotel bellhops: $1 or $2 for carrying each suitcase
Parking valets: $1 for parking a car
Hotel door attendants: $1 or $2 for getting a taxi
Hotel maids: $1 to $5 per night
Taxi drivers: 15 percent of the bill; more if they help you with bags
Waiters and waitresses: 15 to 20 percent of the bill (There is no tipping in fast-food restaurants.)
Barbers or hairstylists: 15 percent of the bill

When you're not sure about how much to tip, do what feels right. You don't have to tip for bad service. And you can give a bigger tip for very good service. Remember, though, your behavior is more important than your money. Always treat service providers with respect.

A Read the article. Find the words in *italics* in the article. Then check (✓) the meaning of each word.

1. *wages*	☐ regular pay for a job ☐ tips received for a job	4. *behavior*	☐ a way of acting ☐ a way of feeling
2. *pleased*	☐ happy or satisfied ☐ annoyed or bothered	5. *treat*	☐ ignore ☐ act toward
3. *depend on*	☐ be the same as ☐ change according to	6. *respect*	☐ courtesy ☐ rudeness

B Check (✓) the statements that describe appropriate tipping behavior. For the other items, what is acceptable?

☐ 1. Your haircut costs $30. You love it. You tip the stylist $2.
☐ 2. A porter at the airport helps you with three suitcases. You tip him $6.
☐ 3. Your fast-food meal costs $8. You don't leave a tip.
☐ 4. You stay in a hotel for a week. You leave a $5 tip for the hotel maid.
☐ 5. Your taxi ride costs $14. The driver carries your bag. You tip him $3.

C *Group work* Is tipping customary in your country? Do you like the idea of tipping? Why or why not?

14 The biggest and the best!

1 WORD POWER *Geography*

A Label the picture with words from the list. Then compare with a partner.

a. beach
b. desert
c. forest
d. hill
e. island
f. lake
g. mountain
h. ocean
i. river
j. valley
k. volcano
l. waterfall

B *Pair work* What other geography words can you think of? Do you see any of them in the picture above?

C *Group work* Try to think of famous examples for each item in part A.

A: A famous beach is Waikiki in Hawaii.
B: And the Sahara is a famous . . .

The biggest and the best!

In Unit 14, students talk about world geography. In Cycle 1, they talk about geography using the comparative and superlative forms of adjectives. In Cycle 2, they discuss distances, measurements, and places using questions with how.

Cycle 1, Exercises 1–7

WORD POWER

Learning objective: *learn vocabulary for discussing geography*

A

- ***Option:*** Bring in a world map, globe, or atlas to class.
- Explain that this unit is about world geography.
- Explain the task. Ss label the picture with words from the list. Go around the class and give help as needed.
- Ss compare their pictures in pairs. Elicit or explain any new vocabulary or pronunciation.

Answers

(from left to right)
b, g, i, j, k, c, f, d, e, a, l, h

B *Pair work*

- Ss brainstorm to see how many words they can think of that relate to geography. Ask different Ss to write their words on the board under these headings:
  Water-related words *Land-related words*
  Climate-related words *Other*
- Go over the words and ask Ss to copy them into their vocabulary notebooks.

Possible answers

Water-related: sea, stream, coast, pond, coral reef
Land-related: continent, plateau, canyon, rain forest
Climate-related: weather, storm, rain, snow, cloud, fog
Other: country, city, town, village

TIP Create a Vocabulary Box. As a new word is taught, a S writes the word on a slip of paper and puts it in the box. Review words as a warm-up activity in future classes, or use them in games.

- ***Option:*** Review vocabulary with ***Odd Man Out***. List geography words, and ask Ss to find which word is different from the others (e.g., *hill*, *mountain*, *volcano*, *ocean*; ocean is the only water-related word).

C *Group work*

- Explain the task. Read the example conversation. Point out that the words *Mount* and *Lake* come before the name (e.g., ***Mount*** *Fuji*, ***Lake*** *Victoria*). The other terms come after the name (e.g. *Waikiki* ***Beach***, *the Nile* ***River***, *the Sahara* ***Desert***).
- Ss work in small groups to think of other examples. Ask groups to share their examples with the class.
- Point out that seas, rivers, and mountain ranges (but not most lakes) use the definite article (e.g., *the Black Sea*, *the Rhine River*, *the Himalayas*), but bring this up only if Ss ask you.

Possible answers

beach – Waikiki, Copacabana, Bondi
desert – Sahara, Atacama, Gobi
forest – Black Forest, Sherwood Forest
hill – Capitol Hill, Bunker Hill, Beverly Hills
island – Puerto Rico, Java, Hokkaido
lake – Titicaca, Superior, Baikal
mountain – Aconcagua, Everest, Kilimanjaro
ocean – Atlantic, Indian, Arctic
river – Amazon, Rhine, Mekong
valley – Silicon, Loire, Death
volcano – Cotopaxi, Etna, Pinatubo
waterfall – Angel Falls, Iguaçú Falls, Niagara Falls

! For a new way to practice this vocabulary, try ***Picture Dictation*** on page T-154. Describe a scene similiar to the one in the picture.

2 CONVERSATION

Learning objectives: *practice a conversation about geography; see comparisons with adjectives in context*

A [CD 3, Track 22]

- Set the scene. Mike is asking Wendy some questions from a geography quiz. Point out that Wendy gets some answers wrong.
- Play the audio program. Ss listen to Wendy's answers and underline them in the conversation.
- Ask: "How many questions do you think Wendy got right? One? Two? Three? All four?"

B

- Play the audio program. Ss listen for the correct answers.
- Ask: "How many answers did Wendy get right?" (Answer: two)

Audio script

MIKE: So let's see how you did on this quiz. The first question: Which is larger, China or Canada? You said . . .
WENDY: Canada.
MIKE: And you're right! Both are large, but Canada *is* larger. Next: What's the longest river in the Americas? You said the Mississippi. Sorry, no. It's the Amazon.
WENDY: Oh, of course.
MIKE: This next question I didn't know. Monaco *is* more crowded than Singapore.
WENDY: So I got it right? I just guessed.
MIKE: And finally, you said that Bogotá is the highest capital city in South America.
WENDY: Yeah, I remember hearing that somewhere.
MIKE: Sorry, Wendy, but you're wrong. La Paz in Bolivia is the highest.
WENDY: Really? Gee, I guess I didn't do so well – two right but two wrong!

Answers

Canada, Amazon, Monaco, La Paz

GRAMMAR FOCUS

Learning objective: *ask and answer questions using comparisons with adjectives*

[CD 3, Track 23]

Comparative and superlative forms of adjectives

- Focus Ss' attention on the Conversation in Exercise 2. Ask Ss to identify the first two questions that compare things. (Answers: Which country is larger, China or Canada? What's the longest river in the Americas?)
- Ask Ss to make sentences comparing two things in their country (e.g., *mountains*, *rivers*, *cities*). If necessary, review comparative adjectives using Exercise 10 in Unit 3.
- Draw a chart on the board, like this:

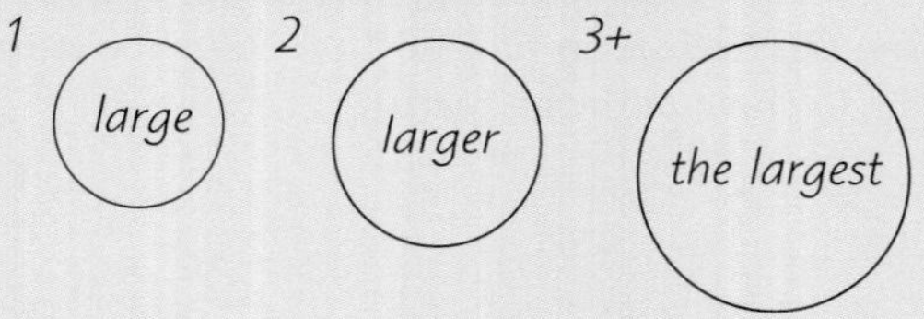

- Explain the reasons for the numbers 1, 2, 3+ (e.g., *3+ is used when we are comparing three or more things*).
- Elicit or explain the rules for forming the superlative:
  1. use the definite article (e.g., ***the*** *largest country*)
  2. when the adjective has only one syllable or two syllables ending in y, use: *the* + adjective + *-est* + noun (e.g., *the long**est** river, the pretti**est** lake*)
  3. when the adjective has two or more syllables, use: *the most* + adjective + noun (e.g., *the **most** crowded country*)
- Refer Ss to the appendix at the back of the book for spelling rules. Go over with the class.
- Give Ss a list of adjectives. Ask them to write the comparative and superlative words in the circles on the board.
- Point to the examples in the Grammar Focus box. Play the audio program.

A

- Go over the task. Ss complete the sentences individually. Then they ask and answer the questions in pairs.
- Elicit the Ss' answers.

Answers

1. Which country is **smaller**, Monaco or Vatican City?
2. Which waterfall is **higher**, Niagara Falls or Angel Falls?
3. Which city is **more crowded**, Hong Kong or Cairo?
4. Which lake is **larger**, the Caspian Sea or Lake Superior?
5. Which is **the highest**: Mount Aconcagua, Mount Everest, or Mount Fuji?
6. What is **the longest** river in the world, the Nile or the Amazon?
7. Which city is **the most expensive**: Tokyo, Moscow, or Hong Kong?
8. What is **the deepest** ocean in the world, the Pacific or the Atlantic?

(Note: Answers to questions are underlined.)

B *Class activity*

- Explain the task. Ss write four questions and take turns asking them around the class.
- ***Option:*** Ss practice the conversation from Exercise 2 using their own questions.

2 CONVERSATION Which is larger?

A Listen and practice.

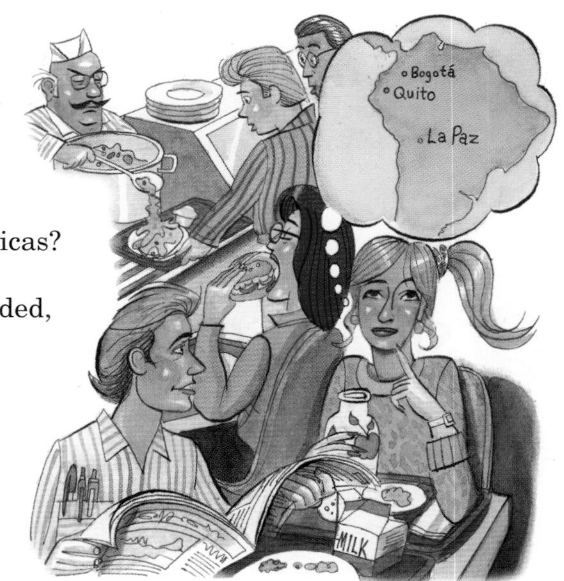

Mike: Here's a geography quiz in the paper.
Wendy: Oh, I love geography. Ask me the questions.
Mike: Sure, first question. Which country is larger, China or Canada?
Wendy: I know. Canada is larger than China.
Mike: OK, next. What's the longest river in the Americas?
Wendy: Hmm, I think it's the Mississippi.
Mike: Here's a hard one. Which country is more crowded, Monaco or Singapore?
Wendy: I'm not sure. I think Monaco is more crowded.
Mike: OK, one more. Which South American capital city is the highest: La Paz, Quito, or Bogotá?
Wendy: Oh, that's easy. Bogotá is the highest.

B Listen to the rest of the conversation. How many questions did Wendy get right?

3 GRAMMAR FOCUS

Comparisons with adjectives

Which country is **larger**, Canada or China?
Canada is **larger than** China.

Which city has **the largest** population: Tokyo, Mexico City, or São Paulo?
Tokyo has **the largest** population of the three.

What is **the most beautiful** mountain in the world?
I think Mount Fuji is **the most beautiful.**

Adjective	*Comparative*	*Superlative*
long	longer	the longest
dry	drier	the driest
big	bigger	the biggest
famous	more famous	the most famous
beautiful	more beautiful	the most beautiful
good	better	the best
bad	worse	the worst

For more information on comparatives and superlatives, see the appendix at the back of the book.

A Complete questions 1 to 4 with comparatives and questions 5 to 8 with superlatives. Then ask and answer the questions.

1. Which country is .... , Monaco or Vatican City? (small)
2. Which waterfall is .... , Niagara Falls or Angel Falls? (high)
3. Which city is .... , Hong Kong or Cairo? (crowded)
4. Which lake is .... , the Caspian Sea or Lake Superior? (large)
5. Which is .... : Mount Aconcagua, Mount Everest, or Mount Fuji? (high)
6. What is .... river in the world, the Nile or the Amazon? (long)
7. Which city is .... : Tokyo, Moscow, or Hong Kong? (expensive)
8. What is .... ocean in the world, the Pacific or the Atlantic? (deep)

B *Class activity* Write four questions like those in part A about your country or other countries. Then ask your questions around the class.

4 PRONUNCIATION *Questions of choice*

Listen to the intonation in questions of choice. Then practice the questions in part A of Exercise 3 again.

Which city is bigger, Bangkok or Beirut?

Which country is the most interesting: Korea, Brazil, or Greece?

SPEAKING *Our recommendations*

Group work Imagine these people are planning to visit your country. What would they enjoy doing? Agree on a recommendation for each person.

Molly

"I really like quiet places where I can relax, hike, and enjoy the views. I can't stand big crowds."

Rod

"I love to eat in nice restaurants, go dancing, and stay out late at night. I don't like small towns."

Teresa

"My favorite activity is shopping. I love to buy gifts to take home. I don't like modern shopping malls."

A: Molly should go to . . . because it has the best views in the country, and it's very quiet.
B: Or what about . . . ? I think the views there are more beautiful.
C: She also likes to hike, so . . .

6 LISTENING *Game show*

Three people are on a TV game show. Listen and check (✓) the correct answers.

1. ☐ the Statue of Liberty
   ☐ the Eiffel Tower
   ☐ the Panama Canal
2. ☐ Taipei 101
   ☐ the Jin Mao Building
   ☐ the Petronas Towers
3. ☐ gold
   ☐ butter
   ☐ feathers
4. ☐ the U.S.
   ☐ China
   ☐ Canada
5. ☐ India
   ☐ Russia
   ☐ China
6. ☐ Australia
   ☐ Argentina
   ☐ Brazil

4 PRONUNCIATION

Learning objective: *learn to sound natural when asking questions of choice*

[CD 3, Track 24]

- Point out that intonation changes in questions of choice. Play the audio program.
- ***Option:*** Model the intonation by humming. Ss repeat.
- Focus Ss' attention on part A of Exercise 3. Explain the task. Model the first question.
- Ss work in pairs. They take turns asking the questions. Give feedback on individual Ss' intonation.

5 SPEAKING

Learning objective: *give visitors recommendations using comparisons with adjectives*

Group work

- Set the scene. Ss imagine that three people are planning to visit their country.
- Ask a S to read Molly's statement. Elicit recommendations from the class. Ask: "Where do you think Molly should go? What should she do?"
- Model the example conversation with two Ss.

TIP Discussions are difficult for many Ss. Allow Ss time to plan what they are going to say.

- Ss from the same countries work in groups if possible. They discuss where the visitors should go and why. Go around the class and give help as needed.
- ***Option:*** Ss form new groups. Each new group should contain one S from the original group. Ss exchange information and ideas about Molly, Rod, and Teresa.

6 LISTENING

Learning objective: *develop skills in listening for details*

[CD 3, Track 25]

- Set the scene. Explain that Ss are going to hear three people on a TV game show.
- Write these focus questions on the board:
  1. *Which is the ____________ ?*
  2. *What is the ____________ building in the world?*
  3. *Which is the ____________ ?*
  4. *Which country is the ____________ ?*
  5. *Which country has the ____________ population?*
  6. *Which is the ____________ ?*
- Play the audio program. Ss listen for the game show questions and fill in the blanks. (Answers: oldest, tallest, heaviest, largest, largest, smallest)
- Play the audio program again. Ss check their answers.
- Ss go over the answers in pairs. Then go over answers with the class.

Audio script

Hostess [*music and applause*] Our contestants this evening are Jack, Susan, and Jonathan. And now, contestants, let's get right to our first question. Question number one: Which is the oldest: the Statue of Liberty, the Eiffel Tower, or the Panama Canal? [*buzzer*] Jack?

Jack: The Statue of Liberty is the oldest. They built it in 1886. They didn't build the Eiffel Tower until 1889, and the Panama Canal until 1914.

Hostess: That's correct! [*applause*] Question number two: What is the tallest building in the world? Is it Taipei 101, the Jin Mao Building in Shanghai, or the Petronas Towers in Kuala Lumpur? [*buzzer*] Susan.

Susan: The Taipei 101 building is the tallest.

Hostess: That's right! [*applause*] Question number three: Which is the heaviest: a pound of gold, a pound of butter, or a pound of feathers? [*buzzer*] Jonathan.

Jonathan: They all weigh the same.

Hostess: Yes! [*applause*] Question number four: Which country is the largest: the U.S., China, or Canada? Nobody knows? Does anybody want to guess? [*buzzer*] Jack.

Jack: Uh . . . China is the largest. [*audience laughs*]

Hostess: No, sorry!

Jack: Oh, shoot!

Hostess: [*buzzer*] Jonathan.

Jonathan: Canada is the largest.

Hostess: Correct! [*applause*] Question number five: Which country has the largest population: India, Russia, or China? [*buzzer*] Susan.

Susan: China has the largest.

Hostess: Very good! [*applause*] Question number six: Which is the smallest: Australia, Argentina, or Brazil? [*buzzer*] Susan.

Susan: Argentina is the smallest of the three.

Hostess: That's right! [*applause and music*] OK, contestants, the winner is . . .

Answers

1. the Statue of Liberty
2. Taipei 101
3. They all weigh the same.
4. Canada
5. China
6. Argentina

7 INTERCHANGE 14

See page T-129 for teaching notes.

Assign . . .	*for more practice in . . .*
Workbook Exercises 1–5 on pages 79–82	Grammar, Vocabulary, Reading, and Writing
Lab Guide Exercises 1–5 on page 25	Listening, Pronunciation, Speaking, and Grammar

End of Cycle 1

Do your students need more practice?

Cycle 2, Exercises 8–12

SNAPSHOT

Learning objectives: *read a world geography test; talk about geographic facts*

- Books closed. As a warm-up, ask some questions about items in the Snapshot (e.g., *What's the most popular country to visit in the world?*). Ss guess the answers in teams.
- Books open. Explain the task. Ss read the Snapshot. They check (✓) the facts they think are true and check their guesses at the bottom of the Snapshot. Then they answer questions about their own country.
- Ss work in pairs. Help Ss with vocabulary.
- Ask: "Does anything surprise you about the facts? What?" Have a brief class discussion.
- ***Option:*** Ss underline all the superlative forms of adjectives in the Snapshot. (Answers: most popular, greatest, deepest, longest, busiest, most isolated)

CONVERSATION

Learning objectives: *practice a conversation about distances and measurements; see questions with* how *in context*

A ▶ [CD 3, Track 26]

- Books closed. Ask: "What do you know about New Zealand? What would you like to know about New Zealand?" Ss work in small groups to discuss the questions.
- Play the audio program. Ss listen for information about New Zealand.
- ***Option:*** If any of the Ss' questions were not answered, tell them to find out the answers for the next class.
- Write these focus questions on the board:
  1. Where is Scott going next year?
  2. Where is Beth from?
  3. How far is Auckland from Sydney?
- Books open. Play the audio program again. Ss read the conversation silently. They write down the answers. (Answers: 1. Australia 2. Auckland, New Zealand 3. about 2,000 kilometers)
- Ss practice the conversation in pairs.

! For a new way to practice this Conversation, try ***Look Up and Speak!*** on page T-150.

B ▶

- Write the following on the board:

great beaches	*coral reef*	*surfing*
boating and sailing	*waterfalls*	*jet boating*
volcanoes	*good skiing*	*deserts*

- Play the audio program. Ss listen to find the things mentioned in the conversation.
- Elicit answers from around the class. Then have a brief follow-up discussion. Ask: "Would you like to visit New Zealand? Why or why not?"

Audio script

SCOTT: Tell me a little more about New Zealand, Beth.
BETH: Well, it has some great beaches. There are some excellent surfing beaches in the North Island.
SCOTT: Well, I don't really like surfing, but I love boating.
BETH: Really? You can go boating in Auckland. It's one of the most popular places for sailing. And you should definitely try jet boating in the South Island.
SCOTT: Oh, I'd love to do that! It sounds really exciting.
BETH: It is. And there's good skiing in New Zealand. Lots of people go there to ski.
SCOTT: It sounds perfect for me. Now I have to go!

Answers

New Zealand is famous for great beaches, surfing, boating, sailing, jet boating, and skiing.

7 INTERCHANGE 14 How much do you know?

You probably know more than you think you do! Take a quiz.
Go to Interchange 14.

8 SNAPSHOT

TEST YOUR WORLD KNOWLEDGE

- ☐ **France** is the most popular country to visit. It has about 76 million visitors a year.
- ☐ **China** has the greatest number of stores in the world. There are over 19 million stores.
- ☐ **Lake Baikal** in Russia is the deepest lake on earth. It's 1,637 meters (5,371 feet) deep.
- ☐ **Tokyo Disneyland** is the world's most popular amusement park. It has over 25 million visitors a year.
- ☐ The longest nonstop flight is from **New York to Singapore**. It's 18 hours long.
- ☐ The busiest airport in the world is **London Heathrow**, with over 55 million passengers a year.
- ☐ **Canada** has the longest coastline of any country on earth. It's 243,792 kilometers (151,485 miles) long.
- ☐ **Easter Island** is the world's most isolated island. It's about 3,700 kilometers (2,300 miles) from the South American continent.

All the facts are true.

Source: *The Top 10 of Everything*

Check (✓) the facts that you think are true. Then check your answers at the bottom of the Snapshot.

What is the largest city in your country? the most popular city to visit? the busiest airport?

9 CONVERSATION Distances and measurements

A Listen and practice.

Scott: I'm going to Australia next year. Aren't you from Australia, Beth?
Beth: Actually, I'm from New Zealand.
Scott: Oh, I didn't know that. So what's it like there?
Beth: Oh, it's beautiful. It has lots of farms, and it's very mountainous.
Scott: Really? How high are the mountains?
Beth: Well, the highest one is Mount Cook. It's about 3,800 meters high.
Scott: Hmm. How far is New Zealand from Australia?
Beth: Well, I live in Auckland, and Auckland is about 2,000 kilometers from Sydney.
Scott: Well maybe I should visit you next year, too!

Mount Cook

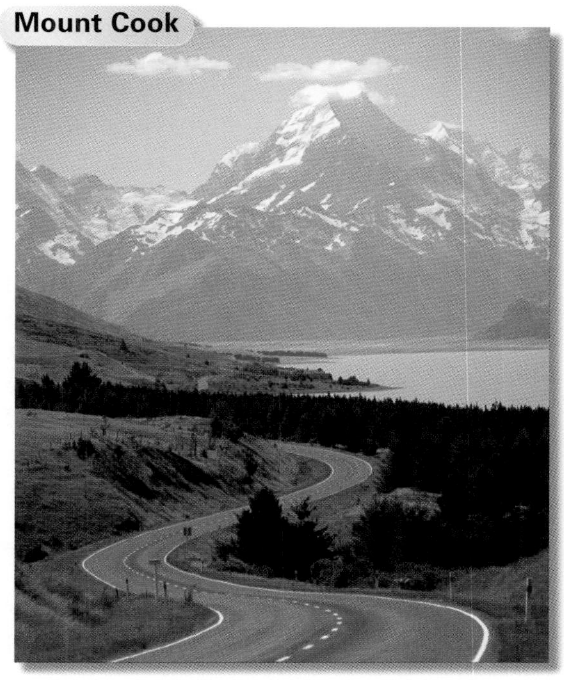

B Listen to the rest of the conversation. What else is New Zealand famous for?

10 GRAMMAR FOCUS

Questions with *how*

How far is New Zealand from Australia?	It's about 2,000 kilometers.	(1,200 miles)
How big is Singapore?	It's 648 square kilometers.	(250 square miles)
How high is Mount Cook?	It's 3,740 meters **high**.	(12,250 feet)
How deep is the Grand Canyon?	It's about 1,900 meters **deep**.	(6,250 feet)
How long is the Mississippi River?	It's about 5,970 kilometers **long**.	(3,710 miles)
How hot is Auckland in the summer?	It gets up to about 23° Celsius.	(74° Fahrenheit)
How cold is it in the winter?	It goes down to about 10° Celsius.	(50° Fahrenheit)

A Write the questions to these answers. Then practice with a partner.

1. A: ....?
   B: Angel Falls is 979 meters (3,212 feet) high.
2. A: ....?
   B: California is about 403,970 square kilometers (155,973 square miles).
3. A: ....?
   B: The Nile is 6,670 kilometers (4,145 miles) long.
4. A: ....?
   B: Washington, D.C., gets up to about 32° Celsius (90° Fahrenheit) in the summer.

B *Group work* Think of five questions with *how* about places in your country or other countries you know. Ask and answer your questions in groups.

11 WRITING *An article*

A Write an article for a country's Web site. Include general information about the country and recommend the best places to visit.

Korea's Best Kept Secret

Korea is one of the most interesting countries in the world. There is a fascinating mix of both ancient and modern in this small northeast Asian country. It's famous for its beautiful landscape, rich culture, and delicious food. One of the most popular places to visit is Jeju Island, located off the southern coast. This unique island is . . .

Jeju Island, Korea

B *Pair work* Read your partner's article. Ask questions to get more information. Does the article make you want to visit that country?

10 GRAMMAR FOCUS

Learning objective: *ask and answer questions with* how

[CD 3, Track 27]

How + *adjective*

- ***Option:*** Find out which systems Ss are familiar with for distances (e.g., *meters and kilometers* or *feet and miles*) and for temperature (*Celsius* or *Fahrenheit*). Use the most suitable system during the class.
- Write this on the board:

How far is NZ from Australia?	*It's 3,740 meters high.*
How big is Singapore?	*It's 1,900 meters deep.*
How high is Mount Cook?	*It's about 2,000 kilometers.*
How deep is the Grand Canyon?	*It's 648 square kilometers.*

- Ask Ss to match the questions with the correct answers. Ss check their answers in the Grammar Focus box.
- Point out the use of *how* + adjective (e.g., *how far*, *how big*) in questions. Elicit more examples. Ask Ss to write them on the board in visual form:

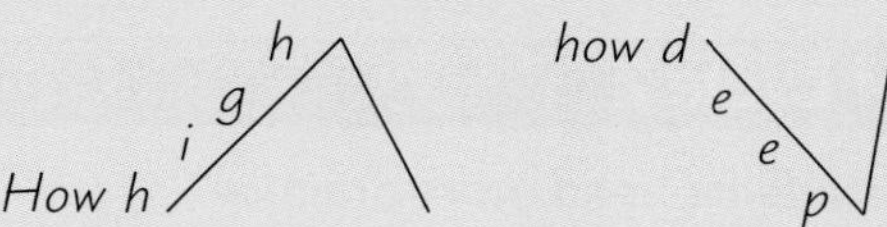

TIP Visual and spatial Ss find structures and vocabulary easier to remember if they store the language in a pictorial form.

- Focus Ss' attention on the answers in the Grammar Focus box. Ask: "What is different about *high*, *deep*, and *long*?" (Answer: They are repeated in the answer.)
- Use the audio program to present the questions and answers.
- ***Option:*** Give your Ss practice with large numbers by having them repeat the answers line by line.

A

- Explain the task. Ss complete the task individually. Check Ss' answers before they work in pairs to practice the conversations.

Answers

1. How high is Angel Falls?
2. How big is California?
3. How long is the Nile?
4. How hot is Washington, D.C., in the summer?

B *Group work*

- ***Option:*** Ss can find facts in advance of this activity from the Internet, an atlas, or a guidebook.
- Explain the task. Elicit an example question. Ss write five questions with *how*.
- Ss work individually to write the questions. Go around the class and give help as needed.
- Ss ask and answer questions in groups.
- ***Option:*** Organize the class into teams and prepare a class game show using the Ss' questions.

11 WRITING

Learning objective: *write an article for a Web site using recommendations, numbers, and comparisons with adjectives*

A

- ***Option:*** Ss check the Internet or other sources for information about a country. Tell Ss to look at real examples of country Web sites.
- Explain the task. Ss write about the country and places to visit.
- Ss read the example article silently. Elicit the topics included in the article.
- Ss choose a country to write about. Brainstorm with the class details to include in the articles (e.g., location, landscape, food, language, cities, culture, and people).
- Ss compose their first drafts. Then ask Ss to correct their grammar and spelling after writing the content.
- ***Option***: Ss prepare attractive Web site articles and display them on the wall for others to read.

B *Pair work*

- Explain the task. Ss work in pairs. They exchange articles and read them silently. Then the reader asks questions to get more information (e.g., *What else is it famous for?*).
- Encourage Ss to give each other helpful peer feedback. Then Ss revise their articles.

For a new way to correct errors, try ***Error Correction*** on page T-159.

12 READING

***Learning objectives:** read and discuss an article about the environment; develop skills in recognizing sources and understanding details*

- Books closed. Write these questions on the board:
  Do you like to take long showers? How long do you spend in the shower?
  Do you usually walk, ride a bicycle, take public transportation, or use a car?
- Ss discuss the questions in pairs.
- Books open. Explain that this article is about the environment. Ss look at the pictures and decide which show environmental problems and which show solutions. Help Ss with vocabulary.

Answers

problems: 1, 4, 5, 8
solutions: 2, 3, 6, 7

A

- Explain the task. Ss read the article. Then they guess where the article is from. (Answer: a magazine) Ask: "How do you know? What clues tell you the answer?" (Answer: photos, design, title)
- Elicit or explain any new vocabulary.

Vocabulary

SUVs: sport utility vehicles
vehicles: machines used for transporting people or things
acid rain: drops of water containing harmful chemicals as a result of burning substances such as coal and oil
tuned up: adjusted so it works as effectively as possible
fluorescent: giving off a very bright light when electricity or other waves go through it
throws away: disposes of; gets rid of
landfills: places where large amounts of garbage are buried
over and over again: repeatedly
disposable products: things that can be thrown away after being used
recycled: collected and treated to be used again
"low-flow" showerhead: a device that controls or restricts the movement of water
leaky: allowing water to escape, even when turned off

B

- Explain the task. Read aloud the first statement in part B. Ask: "Where should we look for advice about this?" (Answer: the section about water) Ask a S to describe how to find the answer. Ask another S to write the advice on the board.
- Ss continue the task individually. Go over answers with the class.

Possible answers

1. Stephanie should buy a low-flow showerhead and take shorter showers.
2. Ralph should turn down the heat during the day.
3. Matt should think before he buys it.
4. Stuart should walk or bicycle to work.
5. Sheila should buy fluorescent bulbs and remember to turn lights off.

C *Group work*

- Ss work in groups to discuss the question. Go around the class and give help as needed.
- Groups share their suggestions with the class. Groups choose a S to write their suggestions on the board.

Possible answers

Buy products that have the recycling symbol on them.
Plant trees, instead of cutting them down.
Learn how people are helping the environment.
Support existing environmental groups.
Don't leave the water on when brushing your teeth.

End of Cycle 2

Do your students need more practice?

Assign . . .	*for more practice in . . .*
Workbook Exercises 6–8 on pages 83–84	Grammar, Vocabulary, Reading, and Writing
Lab Guide Exercises 6–8 on page 25	Listening, Pronunciation, Speaking, and Grammar
Video Activity Book Unit 14	Listening, Speaking, and Cultural Awareness
CD-ROM Unit 14	Grammar, Vocabulary, Reading, Listening, and Speaking

Evaluation

Assess Ss' understanding of Units 13 and 14 with the quiz on pages T-212 and T-213.

12 READING

Things You Can Do to Help the Environment

Look at the pictures. Which show environmental problems? Which show solutions?

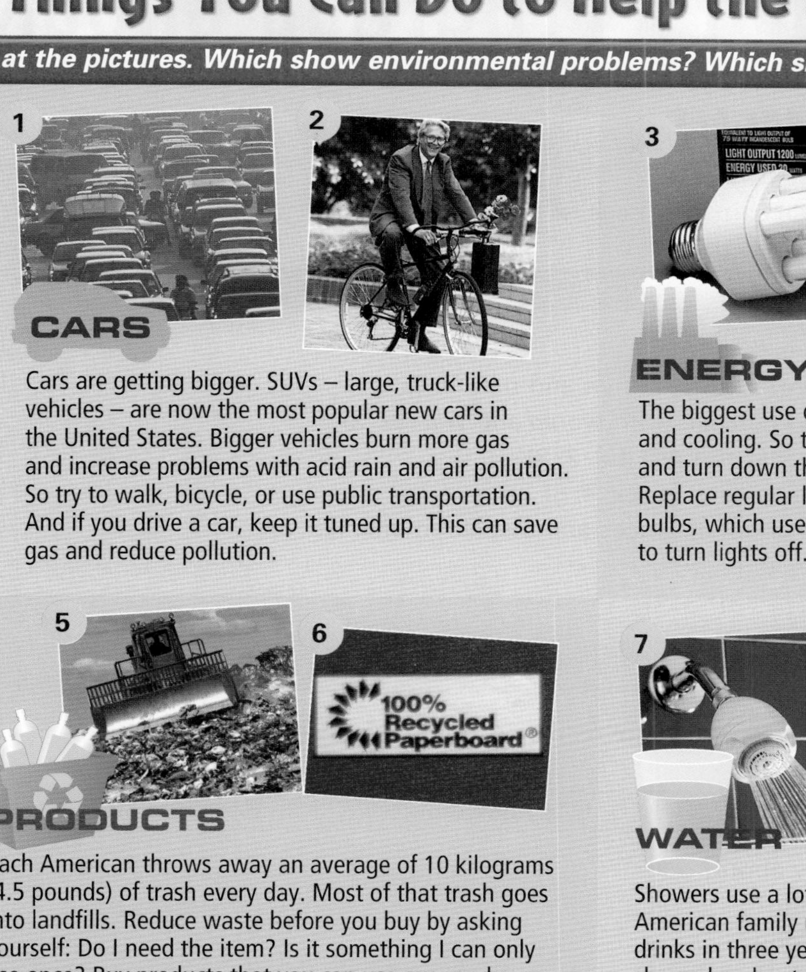

CARS

Cars are getting bigger. SUVs – large, truck-like vehicles – are now the most popular new cars in the United States. Bigger vehicles burn more gas and increase problems with acid rain and air pollution. So try to walk, bicycle, or use public transportation. And if you drive a car, keep it tuned up. This can save gas and reduce pollution.

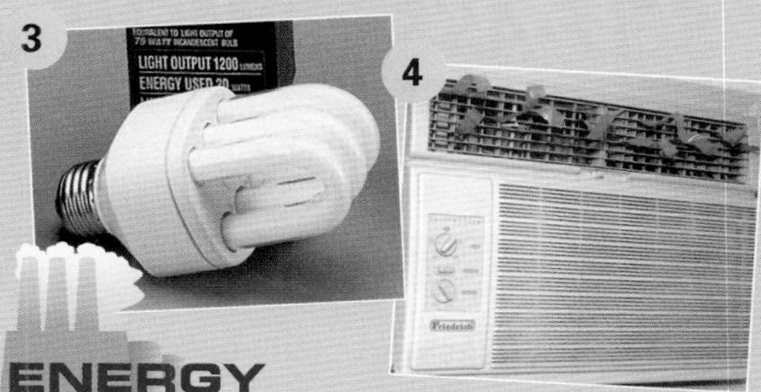

ENERGY

The biggest use of home energy is for heating and cooling. So turn up your air conditioner and turn down the heat, especially at night. Replace regular light bulbs with fluorescent bulbs, which use less energy. And remember to turn lights off.

PRODUCTS

Each American throws away an average of 10 kilograms (4.5 pounds) of trash every day. Most of that trash goes into landfills. Reduce waste before you buy by asking yourself: Do I need the item? Is it something I can only use once? Buy products that you can use over and over again. If you use disposable products, choose those made from recycled materials.

WATER

Showers use a lot of water. In one week, a typical American family uses as much water as a person drinks in three years! Buy a special "low-flow" showerhead or take shorter showers. This can cut water use in half. Also, fix any leaky faucets.

A Read the article. Where do you think it is from? Check (✓) the correct answer.

☐ a textbook ☐ an encyclopedia ☐ a magazine ☐ an advertisement

B Read these statements. Then write the advice from the article that each person should follow.

1. Stephanie always takes long showers in the morning. ....
2. In the winter, Ralph keeps the heat turned up all day. ....
3. Matt buys a newspaper every day, but never reads it. ....
4. Stuart drives to work, but his office is near his home. ....
5. Sheila leaves the lights on at home all the time. ....

C ***Group work*** What other ways do you know about to help the environment?

Units 13–14 Progress check

SELF-ASSESSMENT

How well can you do these things? Check (✓) the boxes.

I can	Very well	OK	A little
Express likes and dislikes (Ex. 1)	☐	☐	☐
Agree and disagree using *so, too, either,* and *neither* (Ex. 1)	☐	☐	☐
Listen to and understand requests with *would* and *will* (Ex. 2)	☐	☐	☐
Make requests using *would* and *will* (Ex. 2, 3)	☐	☐	☐
Make comparisons with adjectives (Ex. 4, 5)	☐	☐	☐
Ask questions with *how* about distances and measurements (Ex. 5)	☐	☐	☐

1 SURVEY *Food facts*

A Answer these questions. Write your responses under the column "My answers."

	My answers	Classmate's name
What food are you crazy about?	....	....
What food can't you stand?	....	....
Do you like vegetarian food?	....	....
Can you eat very rich food?	....	....
What restaurant do you like a lot?	....	....
How often do you go out to eat?	....	....

B *Class activity* Go around the class. Find someone who has the same opinions or habits.

A: I'm crazy about Korean food.
B: I am, too./So am I. OR Oh, I'm not. I'm crazy about . . .

2 LISTENING *In a restaurant*

Listen to six requests in a restaurant. Check (✓) the best response.

1. ☐ Yes. This way, please.
   ☐ Yes, please.
2. ☐ No, I don't.
   ☐ Yes, I'll have tea, please.
3. ☐ I'd like a steak, please.
   ☐ Yes, I would.
4. ☐ I'll have a cup of coffee.
   ☐ Italian, please.
5. ☐ Carrots, please.
   ☐ Yes, I will.
6. ☐ Yes, I'd like some water.
   ☐ No, I don't think so.

Units 13–14 Progress check

SELF-ASSESSMENT

***Learning objectives:** reflect on one's learning; identify areas that need improvement*

- Ask: "What did you learn in Units 13 and 14?" Elicit Ss' answers.
- Ss complete the Self-assessment. Encourage them to be honest, and point out they will not get a bad grade if they check (✓) "a little."
- Ss move on to the Progress check exercises. You can have Ss complete them in class or for homework, using one of these techniques:
  1. Ask Ss to complete all the exercises.
  2. Ask Ss: "What do you need to practice?" Then assign exercises based on their answers.
  3. Ask Ss to choose and complete exercises based on their Self-assessment.

SURVEY

***Learning objectives:** assess one's ability to express likes and dislikes; assess one's ability to agree and disagree using* so, too, either, *and* neither

A

- Ss write answers to the questions in the *My answers* column individually.

B *Class activity*

- Explain the task. Then model the example conversation with a few Ss. Point out that the S begins the conversation by making a statement.
- Elicit how to make statements from the remaining questions in the chart.
- Explain that Ss write the name of a classmate with the same opinion or habit in the *Classmate's name* column. Then they move on and talk to another classmate.
- Ss complete the task. Encourage them to respond with expressions of agreement or disagreement (e.g., *So am I. Oh, I'm not.*).
- Go around the class and note any grammar, vocabulary, or pronunciation errors.

LISTENING

***Learning objectives:** assess one's ability to listen to and understand requests with* would *and* will*; assess one's ability to make requests using* would *and* will

[CD 3, Track 28]

- Explain the task. Ss listen to restaurant requests and check (✓) the correct responses.
- Play the audio program once or twice. Ss complete the task individually.
- Go over answers with the class.

Audio script

1. Could I have a table for two, please?
2. Can I get you anything to drink?
3. What would you like for dinner?
4. What kind of dressing would you like?
5. What vegetable would you like?
6. Would you like dessert?

Answers

1. Yes. This way, please.
2. Yes, I'll have tea, please.
3. I'd like a steak, please.
4. Italian, please.
5. Carrots, please.
6. No, I don't think so.

3 ROLE PLAY

***Learning objective:** assess one's ability to make requests using* would *and* will

- Set the scene and explain the task. Ss work in pairs. Student A is a waiter or waitress in a restaurant and Student B is a hungry customer. Student B orders a meal and Student A writes the order on the check.
- Ss practice the role play in pairs. Then they change roles.
- Go around the class and check Ss' use of *would* and *will*.

SPEAKING

***Learning objective:** assess one's ability to make comparisons with adjectives*

A Pair work

- Explain the task and read the example fact and question.
- Ss write six facts and six related Wh-questions in pairs. Encourage Ss to use comparisons with adjectives.

B Group work

- Explain the task. Each pair joins another pair. Ss take turns asking and answering their questions. Tell each pair to write down how many questions the other pair answers correctly.
- Ss complete the task in groups. Go around the class and check Ss' use of comparisons with adjectives. Then ask which pair got the most correct answers.
- ***Option:*** Ask Ss to share their facts. Find out who has the most unusual facts.

GAME

***Learning objectives:** assess one's ability to make comparisons with adjectives; assess one's ability to ask questions with* how *about distances and measurements*

A

- Explain the task and ask different Ss to read the example statements.
- Point out that all the statements can be answers for Wh- or *how* questions. Elicit possible questions (e.g., *How far is your house from the school? Which ocean is bigger, the Pacific or the Atlantic? Who has the longest hair in our class?*).
- Ss complete the task. Go around the class and give help as needed.

B Class activity

- Explain the task and model the example conversation with a S.
- Ss play the game as a class.

WHAT'S NEXT?

***Learning objective:** become more involved in one's learning*

- Focus Ss' attention on the Self-assessment again. Ask: "How well can you do these things now?"
- Ask Ss to underline one thing they need to review. Ask: "What did you underline? How can you review it?"
- If needed, plan additional activities or reviews based on Ss' answers.

3 ROLE PLAY What would you like?

Student A: Imagine you are a waiter/waitress and Student B is a customer. Take his or her order and write it on the check.

Student B: Imagine you are a hungry customer and can order anything you like. Student A is a waiter/waitress. Order a meal.

Change roles and try the role play again.

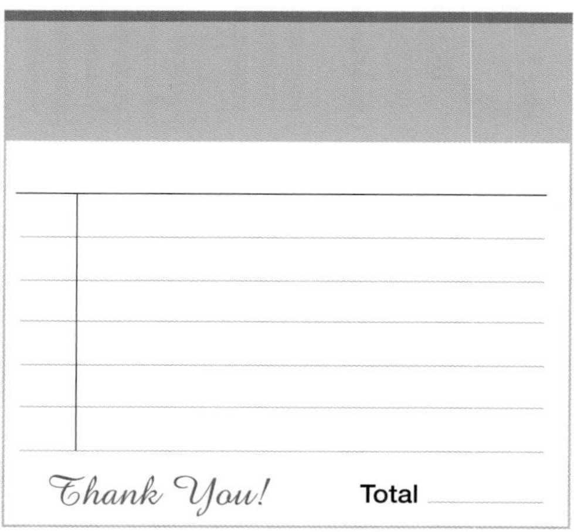

SPEAKING City quiz

A ***Pair work*** Write down six facts about your city using comparatives or superlatives. Then write six Wh-questions based on your facts.

1. The busiest street is Market Drive.
What's the busiest street in our city?

B ***Group work*** Join another pair. Take turns asking the other pair your questions. How many can they answer correctly?

GAME What's the question?

A Think of three statements that can be answered with *how* questions or Wh-questions with comparatives and superlatives. Write each statement on a separate card.

B ***Class activity*** Divide into Team A and B. Shuffle the cards together. One student from Team A picks a card and reads it to a student from Team B. That student tries to make a question for it.

A: The Pacific Ocean is bigger than the Atlantic Ocean.
B: Which ocean is bigger, the Pacific or the Atlantic?

Keep score. The team with the most correct questions wins.

It's about four kilometers from my house to the school.

The Pacific Ocean is bigger than the Atlantic Ocean.

Ana has the longest hair in our class.

WHAT'S NEXT?

Look at your Self-assessment again. Do you need to review anything?

15 I'm going to a soccer match.

1 SNAPSHOT

Making EXCUSES

Some common excuses for not accepting an invitation

- ☐ I can't. My parents are visiting from out of town.
- ☐ I'm busy that night.
- ☐ I'm sorry. I can't find a babysitter.
- ☐ I'm not feeling well.
- ☐ I have to work.
- ☐ I just got a new puppy. I have to stay home with it.
- ☐ I have class that night.
- ☐ My favorite TV show is on that night.
- ☐ I have to get up early the next morning.

I'm sorry. I have to wash my hair that night.

Sources: *www.excuses.co.uk*; interviews with people aged 18–45

Have you ever used any of these excuses? Have you ever heard any of them?
Which are good excuses and which are bad excuses? Check (✓) the good ones.
What other excuses can you make for not accepting an invitation?

2 CONVERSATION *Making plans*

A Listen and practice.

Lynn: Say, Miguel, what are you doing tonight? Do you want to go bowling?
Miguel: I'd love to, but I can't. I'm going to a soccer match with my brother.
Lynn: Oh, well maybe some other time.
Miguel: Are you doing anything tomorrow? We could go then.
Lynn: Tomorrow sounds fine. I'm going to work until five.
Miguel: So let's go around six.
Lynn: OK. Afterward, maybe we can get some dinner.
Miguel: Sounds great.

B Listen to the rest of the conversation. When are they going to have dinner? Who are they going to meet after dinner?

I'm going to a soccer match.

In Unit 15, students talk about activities and plans. In Cycle 1, they discuss future activities and plans using the present continuous, be going to, *and time expressions. In Cycle 2, they leave messages using* tell *and* ask.

Cycle 1, Exercises 1–6

1 SNAPSHOT

Learning objective: *read and talk about common excuses for not accepting an invitation*

- Books closed. Write the following excuses on the board. Ask Ss to guess what this Snapshot is about. Elicit or explain that these are all excuses.
  I'm sorry, I can't. *I'm busy that night.*
  I have to work. *I'm too tired.*
- Books open. Call on Ss to read the excuses.
- Elicit or explain any new vocabulary.

Vocabulary

babysitter: a person who takes care of someone else's baby or child for a short time
puppy: a young dog

- Explain the tasks. For the second task, ask Ss to imagine they are having a party, but some people can't come. Tell Ss to check (✓) the excuses they would find acceptable.
- Ss work in pairs to complete the tasks. Go around the class and give help as needed.
- Ask Ss for feedback on the second task. Which excuses are rude? Which ones are acceptable?
- Elicit Ss' ideas for the third task (e.g., *I have a headache.*).

2 CONVERSATION

Learning objectives: *practice a conversation between two people making plans; see future with present continuous and* be going to *in context*

A ▶ [CD 3, Track 30]

- Ask Ss to look at the picture and invent a story about the two people. To guide Ss, ask: "Who are they? Where are they? What is their relationship? What is she asking him? What is he saying?"

For more practice with vocabulary, play ***Picture It!*** on page T-147.

- Set the scene. Lynn and Miguel are co-workers. Lynn is asking Miguel out on a date.
- Books closed. Write these focus questions on the board:
  1. What is Lynn inviting Miguel to do?
  2. Why can't Miguel go?
  3. When are they going to meet?
- Play the audio program. Then elicit the answers. (Answers: 1. go bowling 2. He's going to a soccer match that night. 3. tomorrow night)
- Books open. Play the audio program again. Ss listen and read along silently.

For a new way to practice this Conversation, try ***Say It With Feeling!*** on page T-150.

B ▶

- Read the focus questions aloud. Ask Ss to guess the answers. Write some of their ideas on the board.
- Play the audio program. Ss work individually. Then go over answers with the class.

Audio script

LYNN: After we're done bowling, do you want to go to The Chinese Palace for dinner?
MIGUEL: Sure. I love their food. We can go around 8:00. That's not too late. You know, maybe Jason can join us.
LYNN: Yeah. Hey Jason, what are you doing tomorrow night? Do you want to join Miguel and me for dinner? We're going to The Chinese Palace at 8:00.
JASON: I have to work till 8:30. But why don't I meet you afterward?
MIGUEL: That'd be great, Jason.

Answers

They're going to have dinner at 8:00. Jason is going to meet them afterward.

- ***Option:*** Have a brief class discussion. Ask: "Do young people go on dates in your country? Where do people usually go on dates? Do you think it's OK for co-workers to date? Why or why not?"

3 GRAMMAR FOCUS

Learning objective: *practice using future with the present continuous and* be going to

▶ ***[CD 3, Track 31]***

Present continuous with future meaning

- Focus Ss' attention on the Conversation on page 100. Write these sentences on the board:
  Lynn: What _____ you _____ tonight?
  Miguel: _____ you _____ anything tomorrow?
- Call on Ss to fill in the blanks. (Answers: are/doing, Are/doing) Ask: "Do you recognize this tense?"
- Explain that earlier we used this tense to talk about what is happening right now. Now we are going to use it to talk about the future.
- Point to the first column in the Grammar Focus box. Elicit the rule for forming the present continuous: Question: (Wh) + *be* + subject + verb + *-ing* + ? Statement: Subject + *be* + verb + *-ing*.

Be going to

- Explain that we can also use *be going to* + verb for future plans. Focus Ss' attention on the second column in the Grammar Focus box.
- Draw a calendar for the week, and point to today's date. Ask questions like these:
  T: Are you going to do anything on Friday? (*pointing to Friday*)
  S1: Yes. I'm going to study.
  T: What about you, Pablo? What are you doing on Friday?
- Play the audio program. Ask Ss to repeat or mouth the words as they hear them.

A

- Explain the task. Model the first answer in both columns.
- Ss complete the conversations individually. Ask early finishers to write their answers on the board.

Answers

1. What **are** you **doing** tonight? Would you like to go out?
2. **Are** you **doing** anything on Friday night? Do you want to see a movie?
3. We**'re having** friends over for a barbecue on Sunday. Would you and your parents like to come?
4. **Are** you **staying** in town next weekend? Do you want to go for a hike?

a. I**'m going to be** here on Saturday, but not Sunday. Let's try and go on Saturday.
b. Well, my father **is going to visit** my brother at college. But my mother and I **are going to be** at home. We'd love to come!
c. Sorry, I can't. I**'m going to work** overtime tonight. How about tomorrow night?
d. Can we go to a late show? I**'m going to stay** at the office till 7:00.

B

- Explain the task. Ss match the invitations to the responses. Go over answers with the class.

Answers

1. c 2. d 3. b 4. a

- Ss practice the invitations in pairs.

4 WORD POWER

Learning objective: *learn vocabulary for discussing leisure activities*

A

- Explain the task. Model with several words from the list.
- Ss work in pairs. Go around the class, giving help with vocabulary.
- Ss add one more example to each category. To check answers, write the word map on the board.

Answers

Friendly gatherings	***Spectator sports***
barbecue	baseball game
beach party	basketball game
birthday party	golf tournament
picnic	tennis match
dinner party	*soccer match*
wedding	*football game*

Live performances	
comedy act	dance performance
play	rock concert
ballet	*opera*

(Note: Additional examples are italicized.)

B *Pair work*

- Explain the task. Model the example conversation with a S.
- Ss talk about the activities in pairs. Go around the class and give help as needed.

To review the vocabulary in this Word Power, play ***Vocabulary Tennis*** on page T-147.

3 GRAMMAR FOCUS

Future with present continuous and be going to

With present continuous	*With be going to + verb*	*Time expressions*
What **are** you **doing** tonight?	What **is** she **going to do** tomorrow?	tonight
I'**m going** to a soccer match.	She'**s going to work** until five.	tomorrow
Are you **doing** anything tomorrow?	**Are** they **going to go** bowling?	on Friday
No, I'm not.	Yes, they are.	this weekend
		next week

A Complete the invitations in column A with the present continuous used as future. Complete the responses in column B with *be going to*.

A

1. What .... you .... (do) tonight? Would you like to go out?
2. .... you .... (do) anything on Friday night? Do you want to see a movie?
3. We .... (have) friends over for a barbecue on Sunday. Would you and your parents like to come?
4. .... you .... (stay) in town next weekend? Do you want to go for a hike?

B

a. I .... (be) here on Saturday, but not Sunday. Let's try and go on Saturday.
b. Well, my father .... (visit) my brother at college. But my mother and I .... (be) home. We'd love to come!
c. Sorry, I can't. I .... (work) overtime tonight. How about tomorrow night?
d. Can we go to a late show? I .... (stay) at the office till 7:00.

B Match the invitations in column A with the responses in column B. Then practice with a partner.

4 WORD POWER

A Complete the word map with phrases from the list. Then add one more example to each category.

barbecue	dance performance
baseball game	golf tournament
basketball game	picnic
beach party	play
birthday party	rock concert
comedy act	tennis match

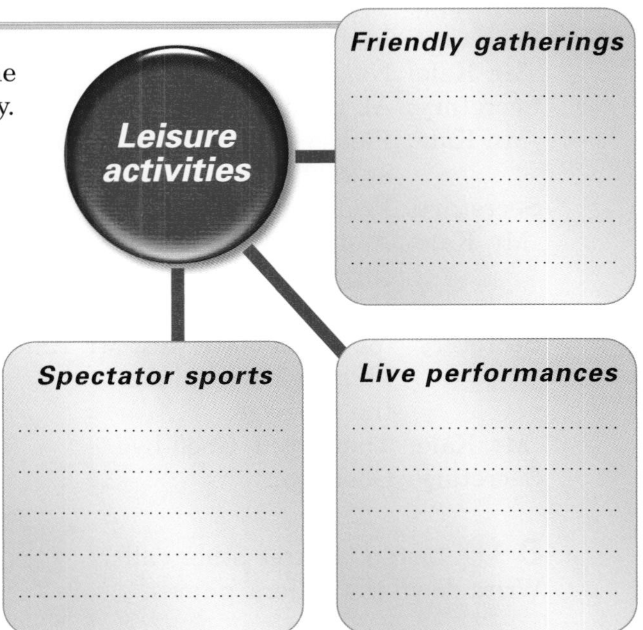

B *Pair work* Are you going to do any of the activities on the chart? When are you doing them? Talk with a partner.

A: I'm going to see a tennis match.
B: Really? Who's playing?

5 ROLE PLAY *Accept or refuse?*

Student A: Choose an activity from Exercise 4 and invite a partner to go with you. Be ready to say where and when the activity is.

A: Say, are you doing anything on . . . ?
Would you like to . . . ?

Student B: Your partner invites you out. Either accept the invitation and ask for more information, or say you can't go and give an excuse.

Accept	*Refuse*
B: OK. That sounds fun. Where is it?	B: Oh, I'm sorry, I can't. I'm . . .

Change roles and try the role play again.

6 INTERCHANGE 15 *Weekend plans*

Find out what your classmates are going to do this weekend. Go to Interchange 15.

7 CONVERSATION *Can I take a message?*

A Listen and practice.

Secretary: Good morning, Parker Industries.
Mr. Kale: Hello. May I speak to Ms. Graham, please?
Secretary: I'm sorry. She's not in. Can I take a message?
Mr. Kale: Yes, please. This is Mr. Kale.
Secretary: Is that G-A-L-E?
Mr. Kale: No, it's K-A-L-E.
Secretary: All right.
Mr. Kale: Please tell her our meeting is on Friday at 2:30.
Secretary: Friday at 2:30.
Mr. Kale: And could you ask her to call me this afternoon? My number is (646) 555-4031.
Secretary: (646) 555-4031. Yes, Mr. Kale. I'll give Ms. Graham the message.
Mr. Kale: Thank you. Good-bye.
Secretary: Good-bye.

B Listen to three other calls. Write down the callers' names.

5 ROLE PLAY

Learning objective: *role-play a conversation between two people making plans*

- Divide the class into groups A and B. Ask Student Bs to look at the excuses in the Snapshot on page 100 while you explain the task to Student As.
- Explain the task to Student As. Model the example questions. Elicit additional questions that Ss can use to invite someone out (e.g., *What are you doing on . . . ? Are you busy on . . . ?*). Write these cues on the board for Student As to use in their invitations:
  activity/event　　*day/date/time*　　*place*
- While Student As plan their invitations, explain the task to Student Bs. Model how to accept or refuse an invitation. Elicit more examples from Ss (e.g., *Wow! That sounds great! Thanks, I've really wanted to do that!*).
- Model the role play with Ss. Show Ss how to elaborate and use their own words.
- Ss work in pairs to do the role play. Remind Ss to use the cues in the book and on the board.
- Provide feedback. Then Ss change roles and do the activity again.

6 INTERCHANGE 15

See page T-130 for teaching notes.

End of Cycle 1

Do your students need more practice?

Assign . . .	***for more practice in . . .***
Workbook Exercises 1–7 on pages 85–88	Grammar, Vocabulary, Reading, and Writing
Lab Guide Exercises 1–4 on page 26	Listening, Pronunciation, Speaking, and Grammar

Cycle 2, Exercises 7–13

7 CONVERSATION

Learning objectives: *practice a conversation between two people talking on the phone; see messages with* tell *and* ask *in context*

A ▶ *[CD 3, Track 32]*

- Ask Ss to cover the text. Have Ss describe the picture. Then ask: "Have you ever taken a message? Who for? Where?"
- Write this focus question on the board:
  What are Mr. Kale's two messages for Ms. Graham?
- Play the audio program. Then elicit the answers. (Answers: The meeting is on Friday at 2:30. Call him this afternoon.)
- Ask Ss to uncover the text. Play the audio program again. Ss read the conversation silently, paying attention to how the telephone numbers are said.
- Ss practice the conversation in pairs. Tell Ss to sit back-to-back.

For a new way to teach this Conversation, try ***Hear the Differences*** on page T-159.

B ▶

- Explain the task. Ss listen to find out the names of the three callers. Play the audio program.
- Elicit answers from around the class.

Audio script

SECRETARY: [*phone rings*] Good morning, Parker Industries.
MR. LEE: Hello. May I speak to Ms. Graham, please?
SECRETARY: I'm sorry, she's not in. Can I take a message?
MR. LEE: Yes, this is Tom Lee. Can you ask her to call me back? She has the number.
SECRETARY: Of course, Mr. Lee.

SECRETARY: [*phone rings*] Good morning, Parker Industries.
MS. BROWN: Hello. Is Ms. Graham there?
SECRETARY: I'm afraid she's not in. Can I take a message?
MS. BROWN: Yes, this is Susan Brown. Please have her call me back as soon as possible. The number is 555-9037.
SECRETARY: Yes, Ms. Brown. I'll give her the message.

SECRETARY: [*phone rings*] Good morning, Parker Industries.
KELLY: Hi. Is Mom there? This is Kelly.
SECRETARY: Oh hi, Kelly. How's it going?
KELLY: Pretty good.
SECRETARY: Listen, your mom isn't here right now, but I'll tell her you called.
KELLY: OK.

Answer

Tom Lee, Susan Brown, Kelly

8 GRAMMAR FOCUS

Learning objective: *practice writing and giving messages with* tell *and* ask

[CD 3, Track 33]

Tell *with statements*

- Focus Ss' attention on the "statement" part of the Grammar Focus box. Ask these four questions:
  1. "What is the message?" (The meeting is on Friday.)
  2. "Do we use *tell* or *ask* with statements?" (*tell*)
  3. "Does the message change when we use *tell*?" (no)
  4. "What are three ways to ask someone to relay a message?" (Please tell x . . . . / Could you tell him/her . . . ? / Would you tell him/her . . . ?)
- Elicit the rule for forming messages with a statement:
  Tell + person + *(that)* + the statement.

Ask *with requests*

- Repeat the above steps for requests with the "request" part of the Grammar Focus box.
  1. "What is the message?" (Call me this afternoon.)
  2. "Do we use *tell* or *ask* with requests?" (*ask*)
  3. "Does the message change when we use *ask*?" (no, but we use *to*)
  4. "What are three ways to ask someone to relay a message?" (Please ask x . . . . / Could you ask him/her . . . ? / Would you ask him/her . . . ?)
- Elicit the rule for forming messages with a request:
  Ask + person + *to* + the request.
- Focus Ss' attention on the Conversation on page 102. Ask: "What structures does Mr. Kale use when he gives his two messages?" (Answers: Please tell her . . . . Could you ask her to . . . ?)
- Use the audio program to present the language.
- Present messages 1–6. Elicit or explain any new vocabulary (e.g., *pick up*, *canceled*, *hockey*). Model the first sentence with Ss, using the cue given.
- Ss complete the task individually.
- ***Option:*** If Ss have difficulty with the patterns for *tell* and *ask,* ask them to read each message and find the *ask* examples (2, 4, 6). Ask Ss "Is this a request?"
- Ss compare messages in pairs. Then elicit and check Ss' answers around the class.

Answers

1. Could you tell Joel (that) the movie is at 7:00?
2. Would you ask Mitch to pick me up at home around 4:00?
3. Please tell Eva (that) the concert on Saturday is canceled.
4. Would you ask Jim to bring the tickets for the hockey game tonight?
5. Would you tell Ann (that) the museum opens at 10:00 tomorrow morning?
6. Please ask Jerry to meet us in front of the cafeteria at 12:15.

WRITING

Learning objective: *write a note asking someone to pass on messages with* tell *and* ask

Pair work

- Explain the task. Ask Ss to read the example message silently. Using the example message, demonstrate with a S.

  The writer's tasks:
  1. The writer writes a note to his or her partner. The note should include at least two messages to other people in the class.
  2. Then the writer gives the written message to his or her partner.

  The partner's tasks:
  1. The partner reads the note and then gets up to tell the messages to the two people named in the note.
  2. The partner goes to the first person in the note and tells the writer's message. Then the partner goes to the second person in the note and tells the writer's other message.

TIP For long instructions, it helps to write them on the board so Ss can follow them as the activity develops.

- Ss write their notes individually. Remind Ss to include messages for two other people. Encourage Ss to write interesting or unusual messages.
- Give Ss five to ten minutes to write their messages.
- ***Option:*** Assign this writing task for homework.
- Ss exchange their notes with a partner. Then everyone gets up to deliver each message.

8 GRAMMAR FOCUS

Messages with tell and ask

Statement	*Messages with a statement*
The meeting is on Friday.	**Please tell Ann (that)** the meeting is on Friday. **Could you tell her (that)** the meeting is on Friday? **Would you tell her (that)** the meeting is on Friday?
Request	***Messages with a request***
Call me this afternoon.	**Please ask him to** call me this afternoon. **Could you ask him to** call me this afternoon? **Would you ask him to** call me this afternoon?

Look at the message slips. Ask someone to pass on these messages. Use the words in parentheses. Then compare with a partner.

1. Joel – The movie is at 7:00.
   (could) *Could you tell Joel the movie is at 7:00?*
2. Mitch – Pick me up at home around 4:00.
   (would)
3. Eva – The concert on Saturday is canceled.
   (please)
4. Jim – Bring the tickets for the hockey game tonight.
   (would)
5. Ann – The museum opens at 10:00 tomorrow morning.
   (would)
6. Jerry – Meet us in front of the cafeteria at 12:15.
   (please)

9 WRITING Unusual favors

Pair work Think of unusual messages for three people in your class. Write a note to your partner asking him or her to pass on the messages.

Dear Su Hee,
It's my birthday tomorrow. Could you please tell Ms. King that I want to have a party during class? Also, could you ask Steve to buy a birthday cake? Thanks.
Juan

10 PRONUNCIATION *Reduction of* could you *and* would you

A Listen and practice. Notice how **could you** and **would you** are reduced in conversation.

[cʊdʒə]
Could you tell Matt the meeting is at 5:00?

[wʊdʒə]
Would you ask him to pick me up at 4:30?

B Practice these questions with reduced forms.

Could you tell them I'll be late?
Would you ask her to be on time?
Could you ask her to return my dictionary?
Would you tell him there's a picnic tomorrow?

11 LISTENING *Taking a message*

Listen to telephone calls to Mr. Lin and Ms. Carson. Write down the messages.

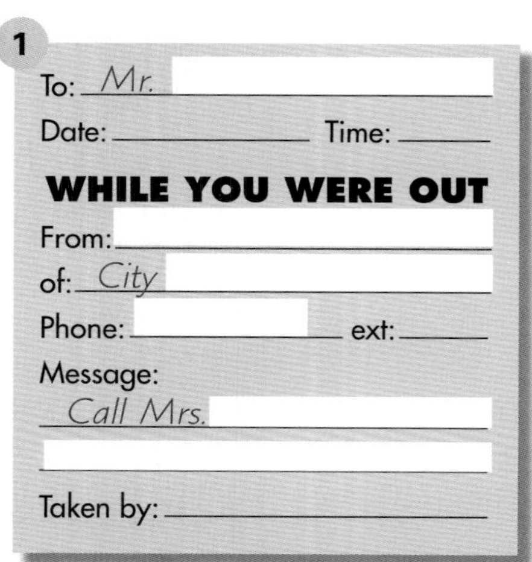
1
To: Mr.
Date: ______ Time: ______
WHILE YOU WERE OUT
From: ______
of: City
Phone: ______ ext: ______
Message:
Call Mrs.
Taken by: ______

2
To: Wendy
Date: ______ Time: ______
WHILE YOU WERE OUT
From: ______
of: National
Phone: ______ ext: ______
Message:
Taken by: ______

12 ROLE PLAY *Who's calling?*

Student A: Call your friend Andrew to tell him this:

There's a party at Ray's house on Saturday night.
Ray's address is 414 Maple St., Apt. 202.
Pick me up at 8:00 P.M.

Student B: Someone calls for your brother Andrew. He isn't in. Take a message for him.

useful expressions

May I speak to . . . ?
Sorry, but . . . isn't here.
Can I leave a message?
Can I take a message?
I'll give . . . the message.

Change roles and try another role play.

Student A: Someone calls for your sister Janet. She isn't in. Take a message for her.

Student B: Call your friend Janet to tell her this:

There's no class next Friday afternoon.
The class is going to a movie at Westwood Theater.
Meet us in front of the theater at 4:30.

10 PRONUNCIATION

Learning objective: *notice the reduced forms of* could you *and* would you

A ▶ ***[CD 3, Track 34]***

- Play the audio program. Model the consonant sounds *d* + *y* in *could you* and *would you*. Ss repeat.
- Call on different Ss to try the reductions.

B

- Read out the four questions for the class. Ask Ss to repeat.

! For a new way to practice this Pronunciation, try ***Walking Stress*** on page T-152.

11 LISTENING

Learning objective: *develop skills in listening for details*

▶ ***[CD 3, Track 35]***

- Explain the task. Point out the different parts of the message slips.
- Play the audio program. Ss listen and write down the messages. Then Ss compare answers with a partner.
- Play the audio program again. Break up the two listenings into smaller segments. Pause after every few lines to give Ss time to complete the messages.

Audio script

1.

RECEPTIONIST: [*phone rings*] Good afternoon, MBI. May I help you?
MRS. PARIS: Hello. I want to speak to Mr. Lin, please.
RECEPTIONIST: I'm sorry. Mr. Lin is in a meeting right now. Would you like to leave a message?
MRS. PARIS: Yes, please. This is Mrs. Paris of City Car Center.
RECEPTIONIST: Mrs. Paris. Is that P-A-R-I-S?
MRS. PARIS: Yes, that's right. Please ask him to call me at the City Car Center before 3:30 this afternoon. It's very important.
RECEPTIONIST: All right. And your number, please?
MRS. PARIS: 555-3290.
RECEPTIONIST: 555-3290?
MRS. PARIS: That's it.
RECEPTIONIST: OK. I'll ask him to call you before 3:30, Mrs. Paris.
MRS. PARIS: Thank you. Good-bye.
RECEPTIONIST: Good-bye.

2.

RECEPTIONIST: [*phone rings*] This is Software Systems. Good morning.
SAM: Good morning. May I speak to Ms. Carson, please?
RECEPTIONIST: Hmm . . . do you mean Mrs. Carter?
SAM: No, Carson, Ms. Wendy Carson. She's new there.
RECEPTIONIST: Let me check. Oh, yes, let me try to connect you. Hold on. [*phone rings three times*] I'm sorry. There's no answer. May I take a message?
SAM: Yes. Would you please ask her to call Sam at First National Bank?
RECEPTIONIST: Sam . . . at First National Bank.
SAM: The number is 555-1187, extension 313.
RECEPTIONIST: 555-1187, extension 313?
SAM: That's right.
RECEPTIONIST: OK. I'll give her the message.
SAM: Thanks so much. Bye.
RECEPTIONIST: Good-bye.

- Call on Ss to write their answers on the board.

Answers

1. To: Mr. **Lin**
   from: **Mrs. Paris**
   of: City **Car Center**
   Phone: **555-3290**
   Message: Call Mrs. **Paris before 3:30 this afternoon. Important!**
2. To: Wendy **Carson**
   from: **Sam**
   of: **First** National **Bank**
   Phone: **555-1187** ext. **313**
   Message: **Call Sam at the bank.**

12 ROLE PLAY

Learning objective: *role-play a conversation between two people talking on the phone*

- Divide the class into pairs and assign A/B roles. Explain the roles and go over the A/B cues.
- Model the role play with a S. Have Ss sit back-to-back. Change roles if necessary.
- ***Option:*** Before starting the activity, tell Ss to reread the Conversation on page 102. Or Ss can listen again to the audio program in Exercise 11 to review phone etiquette. Ask Student As to find expressions callers use and Student Bs to find expressions secretaries use.
- Ss do the first role play, sitting back-to-back. Provide feedback after they finish.
- Explain the second role play and go over the A/B cues. Pairs do the new role play.

TIP To maintain interest, it's best to ask only one pair to demonstrate the role play to the class.

13 READING

Learning objectives: *read and discuss an article about cell phone etiquette; develop skills in scanning, summarizing, and recognizing point of view*

- Books closed. To set the scene, ask Ss to brainstorm things that cell phone users do that are dangerous or rude (e.g., *They talk too loudly. They take calls in movie theaters.*).
- Books open. Call on a S to read the title aloud. Elicit or explain that *etiquette* means "manners."
- Tell Ss to read the cell phone article quickly. Ask Ss to find the answers to the pre-reading questions. (Answers: It's not OK to use a cell phone in a movie theater. It's not OK to use a cell phone in a restaurant if there is a sign saying "turn off cell phones." It's not OK to use a cell phone on the street if you talk loudly or if you don't watch where you're going.)

A

- Explain the task. Ss read the article silently. Remind Ss to try to guess the meanings of any words they don't know.
- Elicit or explain any new vocabulary.

Vocabulary

happens: occurs; takes place
day-to-day: ordinary; regular
loudmouth: a person who talks too noisily or too much
management: the people in charge of a business or company
take care of: deal with; handle
take calls: answer the phone

! For a new way to teach the vocabulary in this Reading, try ***Vocabulary Mingle*** on page T-153.

- Ss complete the summary. Then go over answers with the class.
- ***Option:*** If the summary seems too difficult for your Ss, include the words in a cloud summary on the board, like this:

Answers

Many people talk too **loudly** on cell phones. While you **can't** control their behavior, you can follow a few simple rules. For example: turn **off** your phone in public places, speak **softly** on phone calls, and **never** take a phone call in a movie theater.

B

- Ask the following question: "Is the writer against cell phones, for cell phones, or for cell phones only if they're used in a way that doesn't bother other people?"
- Elicit examples in the article that show the writer's opinion.
- Explain the task. Ss imagine they are the writer of the article. They check (✓) the sentences the writer would agree with.
- Ss complete the task individually. Then they compare answers with a partner.
- Go over answers with the class.

Answers

The writer would probably agree with 3, 6, 7, 8.

C *Pair work*

- Explain the task. Ss work in pairs. They discuss which opinions they agree or disagree with and why.

End of Cycle 2

Do your students need more practice?

Assign . . .	***for more practice in . . .***
Workbook Exercises 8–11 on pages 89–90	Grammar, Vocabulary, Reading, and Writing
Lab Guide Exercises 5–8 on page 26	Listening, Pronunciation, Speaking, and Grammar
Video Activity Book Unit 15	Listening, Speaking, and Cultural Awareness
CD-ROM Unit 15	Grammar, Vocabulary, Reading, Listening, and Speaking

13 READING

Cell Phone Etiquette

Scan the article. Is it OK to use a cell phone in a movie theater? in a restaurant? on the street?

What do you do in a situation like this? You're eating dinner with friends at a nice restaurant. You're having a great time when a phone rings at the table next to you. A man takes out his phone and starts talking loudly about problems he's having with his girlfriend. He talks for almost ten minutes! This happens all the time – on buses, in restaurants, everywhere!

Many people find cell phones useful in their day-to-day lives. But we've all sat next to someone talking too loudly on a cell phone. You may want to tell the loudmouth to end the conversation, but let the management take care of noisy customers. You can only control your own behavior. Here are a few rules:

- Off means off! Respect the rules of restaurants and other public places. If a sign says "turn off cell phones," don't use your phone.
- Keep private conversations private! Speak softly and for a short time. Try to move away from other people.
- Lights off, phone off! Never take calls in a theater or at the movies.
- Pay attention! Talking on a cell phone while driving is dangerous. And watch where you're going when you're walking down the street and talking on the phone.

As more people use cell phones, things are only going to get worse. So, the next time you're getting ready to make a call, stop and consider the people around you.

A Read the article. Then complete the summary with information from the article.

Many people talk too .... on cell phones. While you .... control their behavior, you can follow a few simple rules. For example: turn .... your phone in public places, speak .... on phone calls, and .... take a phone call in a movie theater.

B Check (✓) the statements the writer would probably agree with.

- [ ] 1. You should never use a cell phone in public.
- [ ] 2. Cell phone users are very rude people.
- [ ] 3. Turn off your cell phone if someone asks you to.
- [ ] 4. You should challenge people who talk too loudly on cell phones.
- [ ] 5. It's OK to talk on the phone while driving a car.
- [ ] 6. You can use a cell phone in public if you speak quietly.
- [ ] 7. Don't shout into the phone.
- [ ] 8. Don't stand close to other people when you are using a cell phone.

C *Pair work* Do you agree with the writer's opinions? Why or why not?

16 A change for the better!

1 SNAPSHOT

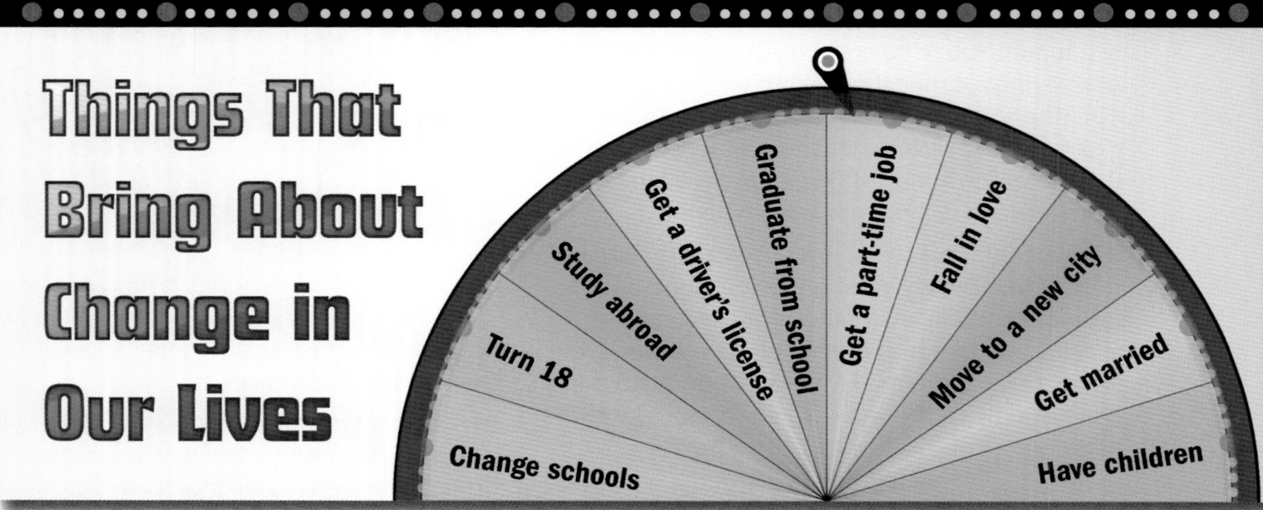

Source: Based on interviews with people between the ages of 16 and 50

Which of these events are important changes? Which are small changes?
Have any of these things happened to you recently?
What other things bring about change in our lives?

2 CONVERSATION Catching up

A Listen and practice.

Diane: Hi, Kerry. I haven't seen you in ages. How have you been?
Kerry: Pretty good, thanks.
Diane: Are you still in school?
Kerry: No, not anymore. I graduated last year. And I got a job at Midstate Bank.
Diane: That's great news. You know, you look different. Have you changed your hair?
Kerry: Yeah, it's shorter. And I wear contacts now. Oh, and I've lost weight.
Diane: Well, you look fantastic!
Kerry: Thanks, so do you. And there's one more thing. Look! I got engaged.
Diane: Congratulations!

B Listen to the rest of the conversation. How has Diane changed?

A change for the better!

In Unit 16, students talk about changes in a person's life. In Cycle 1, they discuss changes using the comparative and the present, past, and present perfect tenses. In Cycle 2, they talk about plans for the future using verb + infinitive.

Cycle 1, Exercises 1–5

1 SNAPSHOT

Learning objective: *read and talk about things that change our lives*

- Books closed. Write the unit title on the board. Elicit or explain the meaning of "a change for the better" and also "a change for the worse." Explain that this unit is about important changes in our lives.
- Ss brainstorm things that change our lives (e.g., *get married*, *have a child*, *change schools*). Help with vocabulary as needed.
- Books open. Ss compare their ideas with those in the Snapshot.
- Elicit or explain any new vocabulary.

Vocabulary

abroad: in a foreign country
driver's license: a document that proves you are legally allowed to drive a car
graduate: complete your studies

- Explain the tasks. Ss discuss the questions in pairs or small groups. Remind Ss they don't have to share personal information. They can respond by saying "I prefer not to talk about that."
- Have a brief class discussion about changes that have occurred in Ss' lives.

2 CONVERSATION

Learning objectives: *practice a conversation between two people catching up; see descriptions of changes in context*

A *[CD 3, Track 36]*

- Set the scene. Two old friends run into each other and "catch up" on changes in their lives.
- Books closed. Play the audio program. Ask: "Has Kerry's life changed for the better or for the worse?" (Answer: for the better)
- Write these focus questions on the board:
  True or false?
  1. Kerry is still in school.
  2. Her hair is shorter than before.
  3. She got married.
- Play the audio program again. Then elicit the answers. (Answers: 1. false 2. true 3. false) For the false ones, ask Ss what really happened.
- Books open. Play the audio program again. Ss listen and read along silently. Elicit or explain any new vocabulary.

Vocabulary

contacts: short for contact lenses
got engaged: formally agreed to marry someone

For a new way to practice this Conversation, try ***Say It With Feeling!*** on page T-150.

- Ss practice the conversation in pairs. Go around the class and give help as needed.
- ***Option:*** Ss write their own conversation, based on the one in the book. They practice the new conversation in pairs.

B

- Play the audio program once or twice. Ss listen to find out how Diane has changed.
- Ss compare answers in small groups. Then go over answers with the class.

Audio script

KERRY: So tell me, Diane, what have you been up to?
DIANE: Well, let's see. I've changed jobs.
KERRY: Really? You don't work at the hospital anymore?
DIANE: No, I left last year. I'm still a nurse, but I work in a private clinic. My job is less stressful now.
KERRY: Do you still live downtown?
DIANE: Oh, no. I moved to a new place. I'm in the suburbs now. I live in Parkview, just outside the city.
KERRY: Parkview? That's where I live! That means we're neighbors!

Possible answer

Diane changed jobs, works now in a private clinic, and moved to the suburbs.

GRAMMAR FOCUS

Learning objective: *practice describing changes with the present tense, the past tense, the present perfect, and comparatives*

[CD 3, Track 37]

- ***Option:*** Ask Ss to bring in some old photos that show how they have changed. Ss can show each other their photos and discuss them.
- Write these four categories on the board:
  Present tense *Present perfect*
  Past tense *Comparative*
- Focus Ss' attention on the Conversation on page 106. Ask Ss to find examples in each category. Call on Ss to write them on the board.
- ***Option:*** Divide the class into four groups and assign each group a different tense.

Possible answers

Present tense
Are you still in school?
That's great news.
You look different.
I wear contacts now.

Present perfect
I haven't seen you in ages.
How have you been?
Have you changed your hair?
I've lost weight.

Past tense
I graduated last year.
I got a job.
I got engaged.

Comparative
It's shorter.

- Play the audio program to present the grammar. Then ask Ss to describe the changes to the man in the picture (e.g., *He wears different clothes now. He has grown taller. His hair is shorter now.*).
- ***Option:*** If needed, review the tenses. For the past tense, see Unit 7; for the present perfect, see Unit 10; and for comparatives, see Unit 14.

A

- Explain the task. Ss check (✓) true statements and correct any false statements. Put this example on the board:
  ✓1. I've changed my hairstyle.
  2. I dress differently now. *I dress the same.*
- Ss complete the task individually. Go around the class and give help as needed.

B *Pair work*

- Explain the task. Then Ss work in pairs to compare their part A responses. Ask the class: "Who has changed in similar ways?"

C *Group work*

- Explain the task. Ss work individually. They write five sentences describing other changes in their lives.
- Ss work in groups to compare answers. Allow about five minutes for discussion. Remind Ss to decide who in the group has changed the most.

LISTENING

Learning objective: *develop skills in listening for details*

[CD 3, Track 38]

- Set the scene. Linda and Scott are looking through a photo album and discussing how they have changed over the years.
- Play the audio program. Ss listen and take notes on three changes they hear. Go over answers with the class.

Audio script

LINDA: What are you looking at, Scott?
SCOTT: Oh, just one of our photo albums.
LINDA: Oh, look – it's our wedding picture.
SCOTT: Yeah. Just think, we'll be celebrating our fifth wedding anniversary this month.
LINDA: Yeah, and I remember we didn't get along so well when we first met. But a year later, we fell in love and got married.
SCOTT: And here's a picture of our honeymoon. Wow! We sure look different now, don't we?
LINDA: Yes. My hair is much shorter now. And you've gained a little weight. You were always too thin. Oh, and look. Here's a picture of the day we brought Maggie home from the hospital.
SCOTT: She's so cute. And now we have two kids. Who would have guessed?
LINDA: Yeah. We're just lucky that they look like me.

Possible answers

They didn't get along when they first met.
They're married now.
Linda's hair is shorter.
Scott has gained weight.
They have two kids now.

For a new way to teach this Listening, try ***Photo Identification*** on page T-159.

3 GRAMMAR FOCUS

Describing changes

With the present tense	*With the present perfect*
I'**m not** in school anymore.	I'**ve lost** weight.
I **wear** contacts now.	I'**ve changed** jobs.
With the past tense	*With the comparative*
I **got** engaged.	My hair is **shorter** now.
I **moved** to a new place.	My job is **less stressful**.

A How have you changed in the last five years? Check (✓) the statements that are true for you. If a statement isn't true, give the correct information.

- [ ] 1. I've changed my hairstyle.
- [ ] 2. I dress differently now.
- [ ] 3. I've lost weight.
- [ ] 4. I moved into my own apartment.
- [ ] 5. I got married.
- [ ] 6. I'm more outgoing than before.
- [ ] 7. I don't go to many parties anymore.
- [ ] 8. My life is easier now.

B *Pair work* Compare your responses in part A. Have you changed in similar ways?

C *Group work* Write five sentences describing other changes in your life. Then compare in groups. Who in the group has changed the most?

4 LISTENING Memory lane

Linda and Scott are looking through a photo album. Listen to their conversation. How have they changed? Write down three changes.

Changes
....
....
....

5 WORD POWER

A Complete the word map with phrases from the list. Then add two more examples to each category.

dye my hair
gain weight
get a bank loan
get a credit card
grow a beard
improve my English vocabulary
learn a new sport
learn how to dance
open a savings account
start a new hobby
wear contact lenses
win the lottery

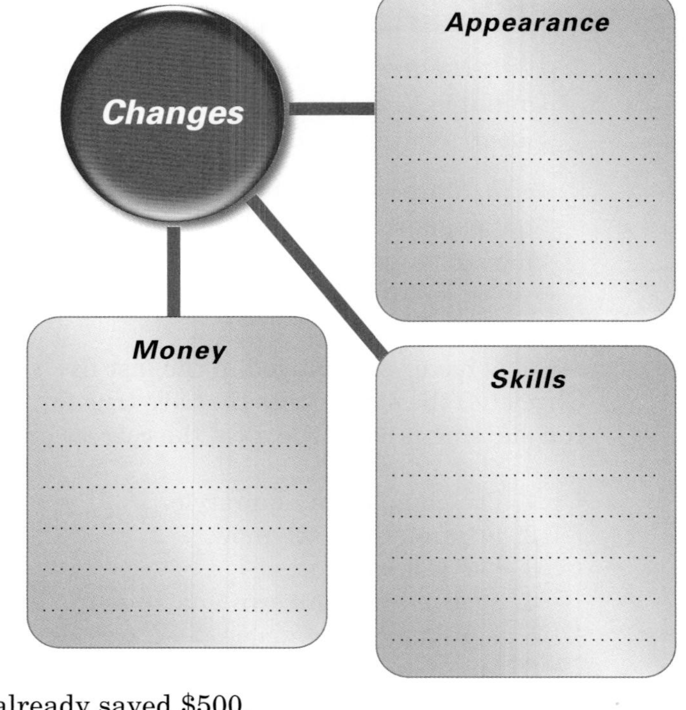

B *Pair work* Have you changed in any of these areas? Tell your partner about a change in each category.

A: I opened a savings account last year. I've already saved $500.
B: I got my first credit card last month. Can I borrow . . . ?

6 CONVERSATION Planning your future

A Listen and practice.

Alex: So what are you going to do after graduation, Susan?
Susan: Well, I've saved some money, and I think I'd really like to travel.
Alex: Lucky you. That sounds exciting!
Susan: Yeah. Then I plan to get a job and my own apartment.
Alex: Oh, you're not going to live at home?
Susan: No, I don't want to live with my parents – not after I start to work.
Alex: I know what you mean.
Susan: What about you, Alex? Any plans yet?
Alex: I'm going to get a job *and* live at home. I'm broke, and I want to pay off my student loan!

B Listen to the rest of the conversation. What kind of job does Alex want? Where would Susan like to travel?

5 WORD POWER

***Learning objective:** learn vocabulary for discussing changes*

A

- Explain the task. Ss complete the word map with phrases from the list.
- Call on Ss to read the phrases. Explain any vocabulary.
- Ss complete the word map. Remind them to add two more examples to each category.
- Draw the word map on the board. Ask Ss to write answers and add more examples to each category.

Answers

Appearance	**Money**	**Skills**
dye my hair	get a bank loan	improve my English vocabulary
gain weight	get a credit card	learn a new sport
grow a beard	open a savings account	learn how to dance
wear contact lenses	win the lottery	start a new hobby
lose weight	*get a mortgage*	*learn how to paint*
dress better	*support a charity*	*take an art class*

(Note: Additional examples are italicized.)

B *Pair work*

- Explain the task. Elicit additional responses and write them on the board.
- Ss discuss their changes in each category.

End of Cycle 1

Do your students need more practice?

Assign . . .	*for more practice in . . .*
Workbook Exercises 1–5 on pages 91–93	Grammar, Vocabulary, Reading, and Writing
Lab Guide Exercises 1–3 on page 27	Listening, Pronunciation, Speaking, and Grammar

Cycle 2, Exercises 6–12

6 CONVERSATION

***Learning objectives:** practice a conversation between two people planning their futures; see verb + infinitive in context*

A [CD 3, Track 39]

- Have Ss cover the text. Use the picture to set the scene. Ask: "What's happening? What do you think they are discussing?" Elicit ideas.
- Write this chart on the board (without the answers). Ask Ss to listen for three future plans for each person.

  Future plans
  Susan *travel, get a job, get her own apartment*
  Alex *get a job, live at home, pay off his student loan*
- Play the audio program. Ss write their answers. Ss compare answers in pairs. Then go over answers with the class.
- Have Ss uncover the text. Play the audio program again. Ss read the conversation silently.
- Elicit or explain any new vocabulary.

Vocabulary

graduation: the ceremony at which a person who has completed a course of study gets a diploma
I'm broke: I don't have any money.
pay off: make the final payment for something
student loan: money given to a student but which must be paid back after graduating

- Ss practice the conversation in pairs.

B

- Play the audio program. Ss listen to find out the answers to the focus questions.
- Elicit answers from around the class.

Audio script

SUSAN: What kind of job are you looking for?
ALEX: Well, I've thought a lot about it, and I'd like to do computer programming. So I hope to get a job with a big computer company.
SUSAN: That sounds really interesting.
ALEX: Yeah, I've got an interview next week.
SUSAN: Well, good luck!
ALEX: And where do you plan to travel to, Susan?
SUSAN: Well, I'd like to travel around the United States a bit. There are so many places that I've never seen.
ALEX: Well, please send me a lot of postcards while you're away.
SUSAN: All right, I will. And I hope you get the job.
ALEX: Me, too!

Possible answers

Alex wants a job as a computer programmer with a big company. Susan wants to travel around the U.S.

7 GRAMMAR FOCUS

Learning objectives: *practice using verb + infinitive; ask and answer questions about the future using verb + infinitive*

[CD 3, Track 40]

- Books closed. Write these sentences on the board:
  Susan: I'd really ______ ______ travel.
  Susan: I ______ ______ get a job and my own apartment.
  Susan: I don't ______ ______ live with my parents.
  Alex: I'm ______ ______ get a job and live at home.
- Books open. Focus Ss' attention on the Conversation on page 108. Call on Ss to find the answers and to fill in the blanks on the board. (Answers: like to, plan to, want to, going to)
- Ask Ss to look at the Grammar Focus box.
- Ask: "What do these structures have in common? What other structures follow this pattern?" (Answers: All are verb + infinitive; *hope to*, *would like to*)
- Play the audio program. Then have Ss make sentences of their own (e.g., *I don't plan to get married this year.*).

For more practice with verb + infinitive, play ***Line Up!*** on page T-144. Ss line up according to the age when they hope to marry, how many children they hope to have, etc.

A

- Explain the task. Tell Ss to write true information about themselves. Encourage Ss to use each verb from the Grammar Focus box at least once.
- Ss work individually to complete the sentences. Remind Ss to add two more statements for numbers 7 and 8. Go around the class and give help. (Note: Don't check Ss' answers until the end of part B.)
- ***Option:*** Tell Ss to look at the photos. As a class, discuss the aspects of people's lives that the photos represent (e.g., *families*, *working parents*, *getting married*, *becoming successful*).

B *Pair work*

- Ss work in pairs to discuss their responses. Tell pairs to check (✓) the statements on their lists that are the same and to put an X next to the ones that are different.
- Elicit some "same" and "different" responses from pairs.

C *Group work*

- Explain the task. Call on Ss to read the questions. Check for correct intonation.
- Ss work in small groups. They take turns asking and answering the questions. Tell Ss to ask the questions in any order they want. Also encourage Ss to ask follow-up questions and to respond to group members' plans.
- ***Option:*** Ss earn one point for every follow-up question they ask.

8 PRONUNCIATION

Learning objective: *notice the difference between the vowel sounds /ou/ and /ʌ/*

A [CD 3, Track 41]

- Explain that words spelled with *o* are pronounced in different ways in English. Point out the two examples in the book.
- Play the audio program and let Ss listen to the two sounds and practice.
- Elicit more words that contain the two sounds (e.g., *lot*, *job*, *grow*, *oh*).
- ***Option:*** If Ss are having problems, ask them to find words spelled with *o* in the unit. Say the words, and ask Ss which have the /ou/ sound, which have the /ʌ/ sound, and which have some other sound.

For more practice with this Pronunciation, play ***Bingo*** on page T-147.

B

- Explain the task. Model the first word.
- Play the audio program. Ss check (✓) the sound they hear.
- ***Option:*** Ss first check (✓) the sound they think is represented by the letter *o*. Then play the audio program. Ss check if their guesses were right or wrong.
- Check Ss' answers on the board.

Answers

/ou/	both	cold	home	over
/ʌ/	come	honey	money	mother

- ***Option:*** Ss work in pairs. They write a conversation with at least five words from part A or B. Then Ss practice the conversation.

TIP Each week, select a "sound of the week" and focus specifically on that (or, in this case, the two sounds).

7 GRAMMAR FOCUS

Verb + infinitive

What **are** you **going to do** after graduation?

I'**m** (not) **going to get** a job right away.
I (don't) **plan to get** my own apartment.
I (don't) **want to live** with my parents.

I **hope to get** a new car.
I'**d like to travel** this summer.
I'**d love to move** to a new city.

A Complete these statements so that they are true for you. Use information from the grammar box. Then add two more statements of your own.

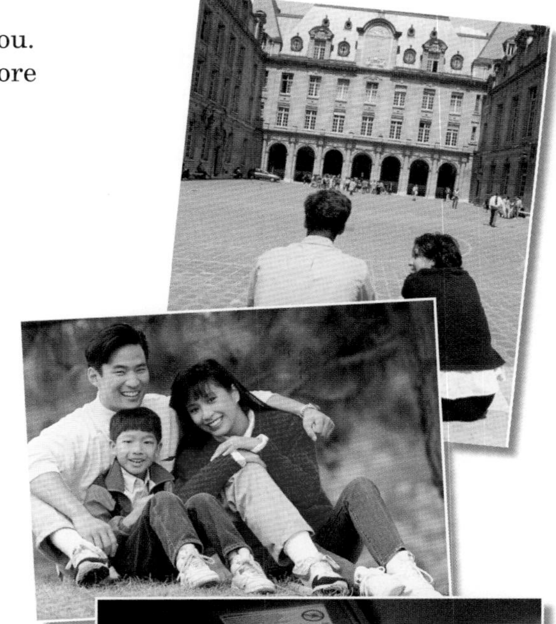

1. I .... study abroad.
2. I .... live with my parents.
3. I .... get married.
4. I .... have a lot of kids.
5. I .... make a lot of money!
6. I .... become very successful.
7. ....
8. ....

B *Pair work* Compare your responses with a partner. How are you the same? How are you different?

C *Group work* What are your plans for the future? Take turns asking and answering these questions.

What are you going to do after this English course is over?
Do you plan to study here again next year?
What other languages would you like to learn?
What countries would you like to visit? Why?
Do you want to get a (new) job in a few years?
What kind of future do you hope to have?

8 PRONUNCIATION *Vowel sounds /oʊ/ and /ʌ/*

A Many words spelled with *o* are pronounced /oʊ/ or /ʌ/. Listen to the difference and practice.

/oʊ/ =	don't	smoke	go	loan	own	hope
/ʌ/ =	month	love	some	does	young	touch

B Listen to these words. Check (✓) the correct pronunciation.

	both	cold	come	home	honey	money	mother	over
/oʊ/	☐	☐	☐	☐	☐	☐	☐	☐
/ʌ/	☐	☐	☐	☐	☐	☐	☐	☐

9 INTERCHANGE 16 *My possible future*

Imagine you could do anything, go anywhere, and meet anybody.
Go to Interchange 16.

10 SPEAKING *A class party*

A *Group work* Make plans for a class party.
Talk about these things and take notes.

Date	Transportation	Responsibilities
Time	Activities	Entertainment
Place	Food and drinks	Cost (if any)

A: When are we going to have our party?
B: I'd like to have it on Saturday. What do you think?
C: That sounds fine. Let's plan to have it in the afternoon so we can . . .

B *Class activity* Read each other's plans.
Then choose the best party plan.

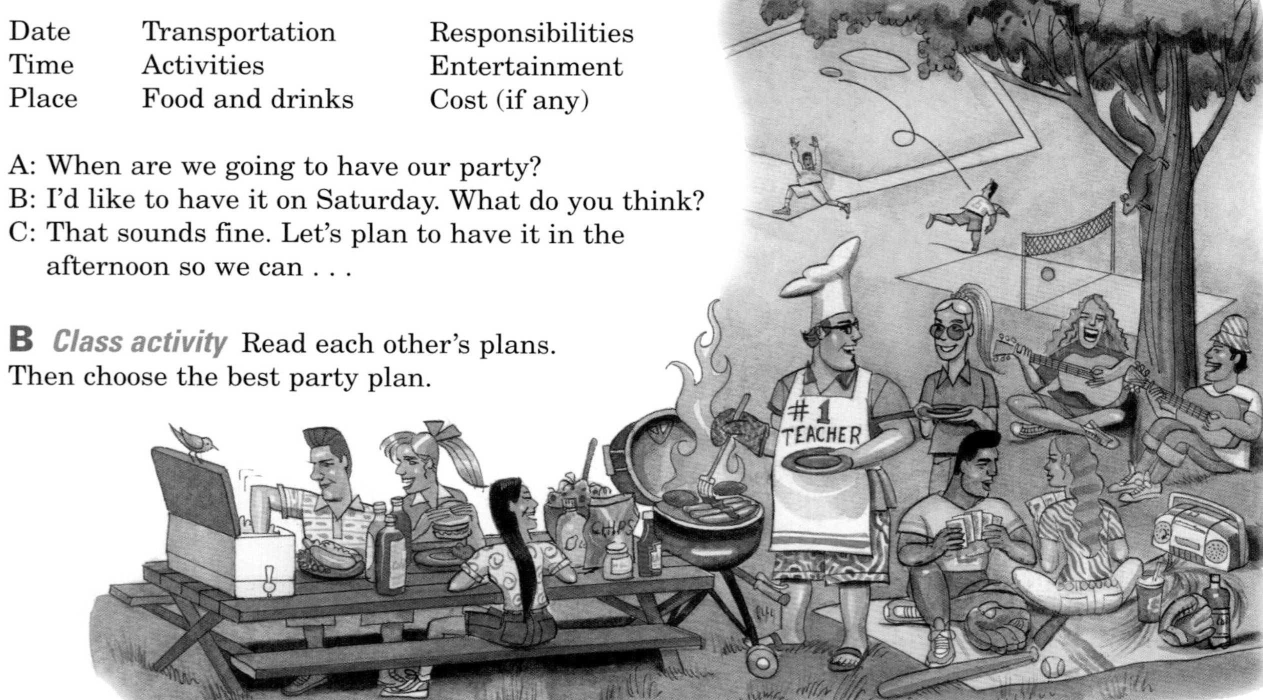

11 WRITING *A proposal*

A *Group work* Work with your same group from Exercise 10.
As a group, write a proposal for the class party.

Baseball Fun in the Sun!

1. Date and Time: We'd like to have our end-of-the-class party next Saturday, on June 18th, from 12:00 – 4:00 P.M.

2. Place: We plan to meet at City Park near the baseball field. If it rains, meet on Sunday at the same time and place.

3. Transportation: We can take the bus to the park. Go to . . .

B *Class activity* Present your proposal to the class. Each person in your group should present a different part.

9 INTERCHANGE 16

See page T-131 for teaching notes.

10 SPEAKING

Learning objective: *talk about plans for a class party using verb + infinitive*

A Group work

- Explain the task. Ss make plans for a class party. Go over the issues they need to think about (e.g., *date*, *time*, *place*, *transportation*). Model the conversation with two Ss.
- Encourage Ss to use a variety of verb + infinitive forms.
- Ss work in small groups to discuss their plans. Set a time limit of about ten minutes. Tell groups to choose one person to take notes.

If you notice that you always monitor groups in the same order (e.g., you always start at the front of the class), change your routine. Try starting from another direction so that some Ss do not get ignored.

B Class activity

- Explain the task. Ss take turns reading each other's plans. Then they choose the best party plan.
- ***Option:*** Ss can report their plans orally to the class, or they can write them down in a proposal. (See Exercise 11, Writing.) If Ss report orally, make sure all Ss have a role in the reporting. If Ss write reports, pass the proposals around or put them on the walls.
- Take a vote. Who has the best party plan? As a class, discuss whether Ss really want to have a party.

11 WRITING

Learning objective: *learn how to write a proposal using verb + infinitive.*

A Group work

- Explain the task. Ask Ss to read the example proposal silently. Ss write a similar proposal, based on their discussion in Exercise 10.
- Ss form the same small groups as in Exercise 10. They write their proposal for an end-of-the-class party. Go around the groups and give help as needed.

B Class activity

- Explain the task. Each S in the group chooses a different section (e.g., *date and time*, *place*) to present to the class.
- Groups take turns presenting their ideas to the class. While a group presents its proposal, the other groups take notes so that they can vote afterward.
- ***Option:*** After Ss vote on the best proposal, have the party!

12 READING

Learning objectives: *read and discuss an article about setting personal goals; develop skills in recognizing audience and reading for specific information*

- Go over the pre-reading question. Ask Ss to scan the article to find the headings. (Note: The headings are in red.)
- Ss read the headings individually. Then pairs discuss which aspects of their lives they would like to improve.

A

- Explain the task. Ss read the article silently. Remind Ss to try to guess the meanings of any words they don't know.
- Ask: "Who do you think the article was written for?" Go over the answer with the class.

Answer

people who are looking for direction

- Elicit or explain any remaining new vocabulary.

Vocabulary

setting personal goals: choosing specific objectives for what you would like to do or change in your life
technique: a way of doing something that involves planning
fields: areas of activity or interest
community service: work done without payment to help others
acquire: obtain; gain
achieve: accomplish; reach
realistic: likely to happen in the future; reasonable
manageable: easy or possible to deal with; controllable
adjust: change slightly
reflect: show; express

B

- Read aloud the questions in part B. Then ask Ss to look for the answers. (Encourage Ss to look for the information quickly, without reading the whole article again.) Give Ss a time limit.
- Ss compare answers in pairs or groups. Have the Ss who finish first write their responses on the board.

Answers

1. People set personal goals because they need more direction in life.
2. Top athletes and successful businesspeople in all fields set personal goals.
3. You should divide your goals into steps because one big goal is more manageable to achieve in small tasks.
4. It is important to adjust your goals because your goals can change with time.

C *Pair work*

- Explain the task. Ss work in pairs to discuss personal goals and the steps they will take to achieve them.
- ***Option:*** Draw this diagram on the board. Label the circles (from outside to in): five-year goal, one-year goal, three-month goal, one-month goal. Label the center circle "Major Goal." Ss copy the diagram and complete it. Then they discuss the goals in pairs.

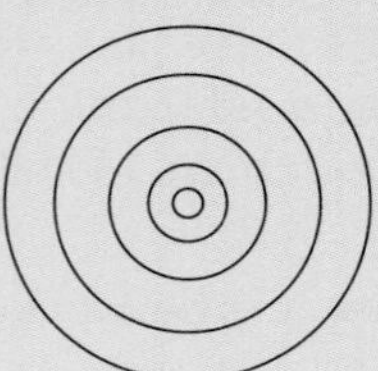

End of Cycle 2

Do your students need more practice?

Assign . . .	*for more practice in . . .*
Workbook Exercises 6–10 on pages 94–96	Grammar, Vocabulary, Reading, and Writing
Lab Guide Exercises 4–8 on page 27	Listening, Pronunciation, Speaking, and Grammar
Video Activity Book Unit 16	Listening, Speaking, and Cultural Awareness
CD-ROM Unit 16	Grammar, Vocabulary, Reading, Listening, and Speaking

Evaluation

Assess Ss' understanding of Units 15 and 16 with the quiz on pages T-214 and T-215.

Assess Ss' understanding of Units 9–16 with one of the tests on pages 133–142 of the *Interchange Third Edition/Passages Placement and Evaluation Package.*

12 READING

Setting Personal Goals

Look at the headings in the article. Which of these areas of your life would you like to change or improve?

We often hear people say, "I need more direction in my life." Setting personal goals can give your life a sense of direction. It's a technique used by top athletes and successful business people in all fields. Before you set personal goals, think about what you want to achieve with your life.

Try to set goals in some of the following categories:

- **Career** – What level do you want to reach in your career?
- **Community service** – Do you want to help make the world a better place?
- **Creative** – Do you want to achieve any artistic goals?
- **Education** – Is there any knowledge you want to acquire? What information will you need to achieve it?
- **Family** – What kind of relationship do you want with your husband, wife, children, and other family members?
- **Financial** – How much money do you want to earn?
- **Physical** – Are there any athletic goals you want to achieve?
- **Recreation** – How do you want to enjoy yourself?

Write down your goals and think about them carefully. Are they realistic? When will you be able to achieve them?

To help make the process more manageable, divide your goals into smaller tasks. For example, if you want to reach a major goal in ten years, set a five-year goal, a one-year goal, a three-month goal, and a one-month goal.

Remember, your goals can change with time. Adjust them regularly to reflect this growth in your personality. Be sure your goals are things you hope to achieve, not what your parents, spouse, family, or employers want.

A Read the article. Who do you think the article was written for? Check (✓) the correct answer.

People who . . .

☐ have very clear goals ☐ are looking for direction ☐ don't care about their future

B Answer these questions.

1. Why do people set personal goals? ....
2. What kinds of people set personal goals? ....
3. Why should you divide your goals into steps? ....
4. Why is it important to adjust your goals? ....

C *Pair work* What are your personal goals? What steps will you take to achieve them?

Units 15–16 Progress check

SELF-ASSESSMENT

How well can you do these things? Check (✓) the boxes.

I can	Very well	OK	A little
Discuss future plans using the present continuous and *be going to* (Ex. 1)	☐	☐	☐
Invite another person to do something (Ex. 2)	☐	☐	☐
Accept invitations, refuse invitations, and make excuses (Ex. 2)	☐	☐	☐
Listen to and understand messages with *tell* and *ask* (Ex. 3)	☐	☐	☐
Ask about and describe changes using a variety of tenses and forms (Ex. 4)	☐	☐	☐
Talk about hopes and wishes using verb + infinitive (Ex. 5)	☐	☐	☐

1 DISCUSSION The weekend

A *Group work* Find out what your classmates are doing this weekend. Ask for two details about each person's plans.

Name	Plans	Details
....	....	....
....	....	....
....	....	....

A: What are you going to do this weekend?
B: I'm seeing a rock concert on Saturday.
C: Which band are you going to see?

B *Group work* Whose weekend plans sound the best? Why?

2 ROLE PLAY Inviting a friend

Student A: Invite Student B to one of the events from Exercise 1. Say where and when it is.

Student B: Student A invites you out. Accept and ask for more information, or refuse and give an excuse.

Change roles and try the role play again.

Units 15–16 Progress check

SELF-ASSESSMENT

***Learning objectives:** reflect on one's learning; identify areas that need improvement*

- Ask: "What did you learn in Units 15 and 16?" Elicit Ss' answers.
- Ss complete the Self-assessment. Encourage them to be honest, and point out they will not get a bad grade if they check (✓) "a little."
- Ss move on to the Progress check exercises. You can have Ss complete them in class or for homework, using one of these techniques:
  1. Ask Ss to complete all the exercises.
  2. Ask Ss: "What do you need to practice?" Then assign exercises based on their answers.
  3. Ask Ss to choose and complete exercises based on their Self-assessment.

1 DISCUSSION

***Learning objective:** assess one's ability to discuss future plans using the present continuous and* be going to

A *Group work*

- Explain the task. Ss work in groups of four. Each S writes the names of the other three Ss in the first column. Ss then ask each other about their weekend plans. Encourage them to ask follow-up questions to find out details.
- Ss complete the task. Go around the class and check their use of the present continuous and *be going to*.

B *Group work*

- Explain the task. Ss discuss the questions in groups and share their results with the class.

2 ROLE PLAY

***Learning objectives:** assess one's ability to invite another person to do something; assess one's ability to accept invitations, refuse invitations, and make excuses*

- Elicit different ways to make invitations, accept invitations, refuse invitations, and make excuses. Write them on the board.
- Explain the task. Ss work in pairs. Student A invites Student B to an event from Exercise 1. Student B accepts or refuses.
- Model the role play with a S.
- Ss complete the role play in pairs. Then they change roles and practice again. Go around the class and give help as needed.

3 LISTENING

***Learning objective:** assess one's ability to listen to and understand messages with* tell *and* ask

[CD 3, Track 42]

- Set the scene and explain the task. Ss will hear two telephone calls. They listen and write the name of the person the message is for, the caller, and the message.
- Play the audio program once or twice. Ss listen and complete the messages.

Audio script

1.
MAN: [*phone rings*] Hello.
LISA: Hi. Could I speak to Paul, please?
MAN: I'm sorry. Paul is not home right now. May I take a message?
LISA: Oh, um. Sure. This is Lisa. Would you tell him to meet me at the theater at 7:00? The play starts at 7:30.
MAN: Meet Lisa at the theater at 7:00. The play is at 7:30. Got it.
LISA: Thanks. Bye.
MAN: Bye-bye.

2.
MAN: [*phone rings*] Hello.
ANN: Hi. Brian?
MAN: No, sorry. Brian isn't here right now. Can I take a message?
ANN: Yes, thanks. Do you have a pencil?
MAN: Yeah. Go ahead.
ANN: OK. This is Ann. Could you tell him that I'm still at the barbecue? Please ask him to pick me up here. Not at home.
MAN: You're still at the barbecue. He should pick you up there. Not at home.
ANN: That's it. Thanks.
MAN: No problem.

- Go over answers with the class.

Possible answers

1. Message for: **Paul**
   Caller: **Lisa**
   Message: **Play is at 7:30. Meet her at theater at 7:00.**
2. Message for: **Brian**
   Caller: **Ann**
   Message: **Pick her up at barbecue, not at home.**

4 SURVEY

***Learning objective:** assess one's ability to ask about and describe changes using a variety of tenses and forms*

A Class activity

- Explain the task and go over the chart. Explain any new vocabulary. Then elicit how to make questions with the phrases in the chart (e.g., *Did you get your hair cut last week?*).
- Set a time limit of about ten minutes. Ss complete the task. Go around the class and note any grammar or vocabulary errors.

B Class activity

- Ss compare their information as a class. Ask: "Who has changed the most?'

5 SPEAKING

***Learning objective:** assess one's ability to talk about hopes and wishes using verb + infinitive*

- Ss check (✓) the goals they want to accomplish individually. Then they add two more goals.
- Explain the task. Each S chooses one goal. Then they plan how to achieve the goal in pairs.
- Model the example conversation with a S. Then Ss complete the task in pairs. Go around the class and check their use of verb + infinitive.

WHAT'S NEXT?

***Learning objective:** become more involved in one's learning*

- Focus Ss' attention on the Self-assessment again. Ask: "How well can you do these things now?"
- Ask Ss to underline one thing they need to review. Ask: "What did you underline? How can you review it?"
- If needed, plan additional activities or reviews based on Ss' answers.

3 LISTENING Telephone messages

Listen to the telephone conversations. Write down the messages.

1

Message for: ____________________
Caller: ____________________
Message: ____________________
____
____
____

2

Message for: ____________________
Caller: ____________________
Message: ____________________
____
____
____

4 SURVEY Changes

A *Class activity* Go around the class and find this information. Write a classmate's name only once! Ask follow-up questions.

Find someone who	Name
1. got his or her hair cut last week	....
2. doesn't wear glasses anymore	....
3. has changed schools recently	....
4. is thinner than he or she was before	....
5. got married last year	....
6. has started a new hobby	....
7. is happier these days	....
8. goes out more often these days	....

last week

this week

B *Class activity* Compare your information. Who in the class has changed the most?

5 SPEAKING Setting goals

Check (✓) the goals you have and add two more. Then choose one goal. Plan how to accomplish it with a partner.

- ☐ own my own computer
- ☐ move to a new city
- ☐ have more free time
- ☐ have more friends
- ☐ get into a good school
- ☐ travel a lot more
- ☐ live a long time
- ☐ ....
- ☐ ....

A: I'd like to travel a lot more.
B: How are you going to do that?

WHAT'S NEXT?

Look at your Self-assessment again. Do you need to review anything?

Interchange activities

interchange 1

***Learning objective:** find out more about classmates in interviews*

A *Class activity*

- As a warm-up, stand next to different Ss. For each S, ask the class: "What is his/her name? Where is he/she from?"
- Ask Ss to look at the picture. If needed, explain that Eminem is a popular rap singer who uses just one name.
- Go over the questions in the chart. Help Ss with vocabulary and pronunciation. If necessary, review hobbies and the months of the year.
- Explain the task. Model the questions with a S. Point out that Ss will interview three classmates.
- Ss complete the task. Go around the class and give help as needed. Write down any grammar or vocabulary errors and go over them after Ss complete the task.

B *Group work*

- Explain the task. Go over the questions and review the vocabulary if needed.
- Ss discuss the questions as a group.
- ***Option:*** Elicit interesting information that Ss found out about their classmates.

Interchange activities

interchange 1 *GETTING TO KNOW YOU*

A *Class activity* Go around the class and interview three classmates. Complete the chart.

	Classmate 1	Classmate 2	Classmate 3
What's your first name?			
What's your last name?			
Where are you from?			
When's your birthday?			
What are your hobbies?			

B *Group work* Compare your information in groups. Then discuss these questions.

Who . . . ?

has an interesting first name
has a common last name
has the same name as a famous person
is not from a big city
has the next birthday
has an unusual hobby

Interchange 1

interchange 2 COMMON GROUND

A *Class activity* Answer these questions about yourself. Then interview four classmates.

Names:	Me				
What time do you . . . ?	**Times**				
get up during the week					
get up on weekends					
have breakfast					
leave for work or school					
get home from work or school					
have dinner					
go to bed during the week					
go to bed on weekends					

B *Pair work* Whose schedule is the most like yours? Tell your partner.

A: Keiko and I have similar schedules. We both get up at 6:00 and have breakfast at 7:00.
B: I leave for work at 7:30, but Jeff leaves for school at . . .

useful expressions

We both . . . at . . .
We . . . at different times.
My schedule is different from my classmates' schedules.

Interchange 2

interchange 2

Learning objective: *find out more about classmates using a survey about schedules*

A Class activity

- Focus Ss' attention on the pictures at the bottom of the page. Ask: "What does the woman do every day? What time does she do each thing?"
- Go over any new vocabulary in the chart. Teach or review how to write times.
- Explain the first part of the task. Ask Ss: "What time do you get up during the week?" Ss complete the first line in the *Me* column. Then they complete the rest of the column individually. Allow about three minutes. Go around the class and give help as needed.
- Explain the rest of the task. Ss go around the class and interview four classmates. They write each classmate's name at the top of the column and ask the questions in the chart. They write a time for each response.
- Model the task with a S.

TIP At beginning levels, sometimes instructions are difficult to understand. It is much more effective to *model* the task than to explain it.

- Set a time limit of about 15 minutes. Then Ss complete the task. Go around the class and give help as needed. Write down any errors you hear for Ss to correct later.

B Pair work

- Explain the task. Go over the useful expressions and model the example conversation.
- Ss complete the task in pairs. Encourage them to explain why.
- Elicit answers from the class.

interchange 3

***Learning objectives:** ask for and give prices; practice bargaining*

A

- Point out the title. Explain that a *flea market* is a place where people sell used things. Sellers have an "asking price," but people bargain.
- Ask: "Are there flea markets in your country? Do people bargain for better prices?" Encourage discussion.
- Focus Ss' attention on the pictures on both pages. Ask: "What do you see here? What are these people doing?"
- Divide the Ss into pairs and assign pages A and B. Explain the task.
- Focus Ss' attention on the TV. Ask: "What is a good price for a used TV?" Tell Ss with page A to choose an "asking price" and write it down. Then focus Ss' attention on the painting. Ask: "What is a good price for the painting?" Tell Ss with page B to choose an "asking price" and write it down.
- Ss work individually to make up prices for the remaining four items.

TIP If Ss have difficulty with a specific task, try a different grouping for the task. For example, have them work in small groups instead of pairs.

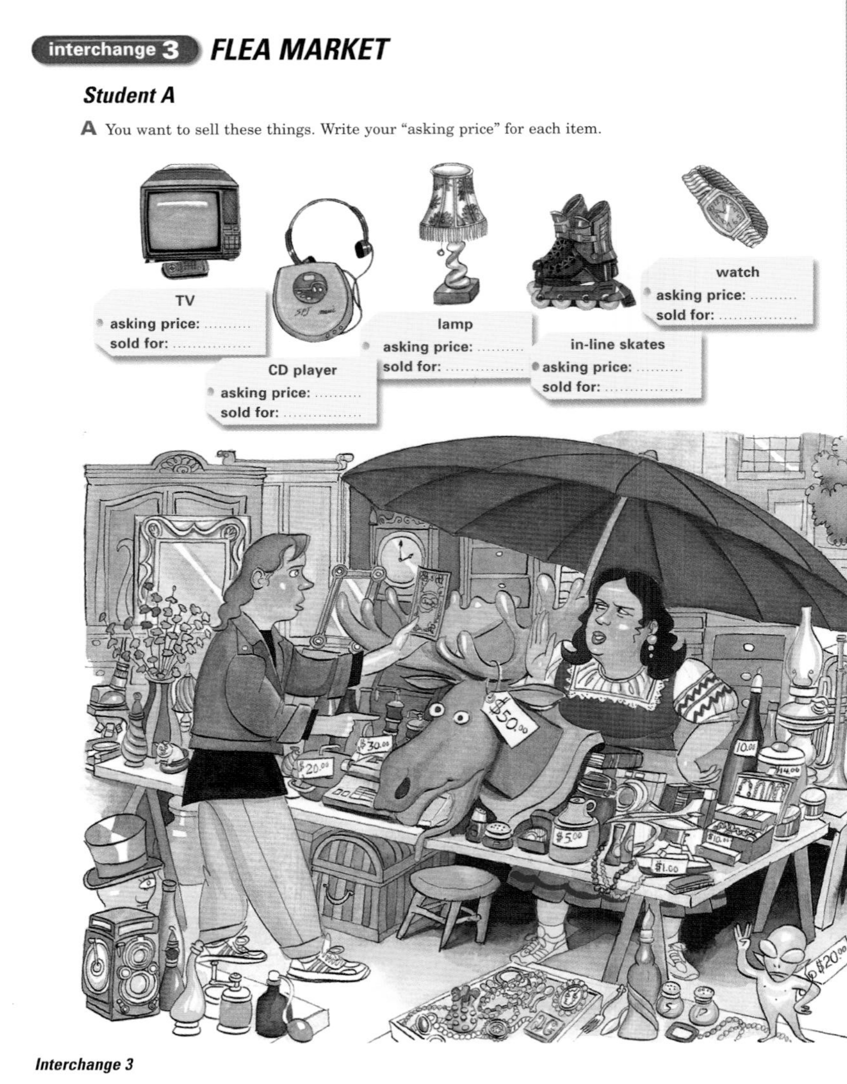

Interchange 3

B *Pair work*

- Explain the task. Ss work in pairs. Student As and Bs take turns as buyer and seller. The buyers choose three things they want to buy from their partner's page. Buyers decide on a good price for each thing.
- Model the example conversation with a few Ss, showing that A is the buyer and B is the seller. Remind the class to vary the conversation and to bargain.
- Give Ss a time limit of about ten minutes. Explain that partners need to take turns starting the conversation so that each S is both buyer and seller.
- Continue until both partners buy and sell at least three things. Tell the Ss to write down the prices they bought the things for.
- Go around the class and give help as needed.
- ***Option:*** Ask a pair of Ss to perform their role play for the class. Alternatively, Ss can change partners and try the activity again.

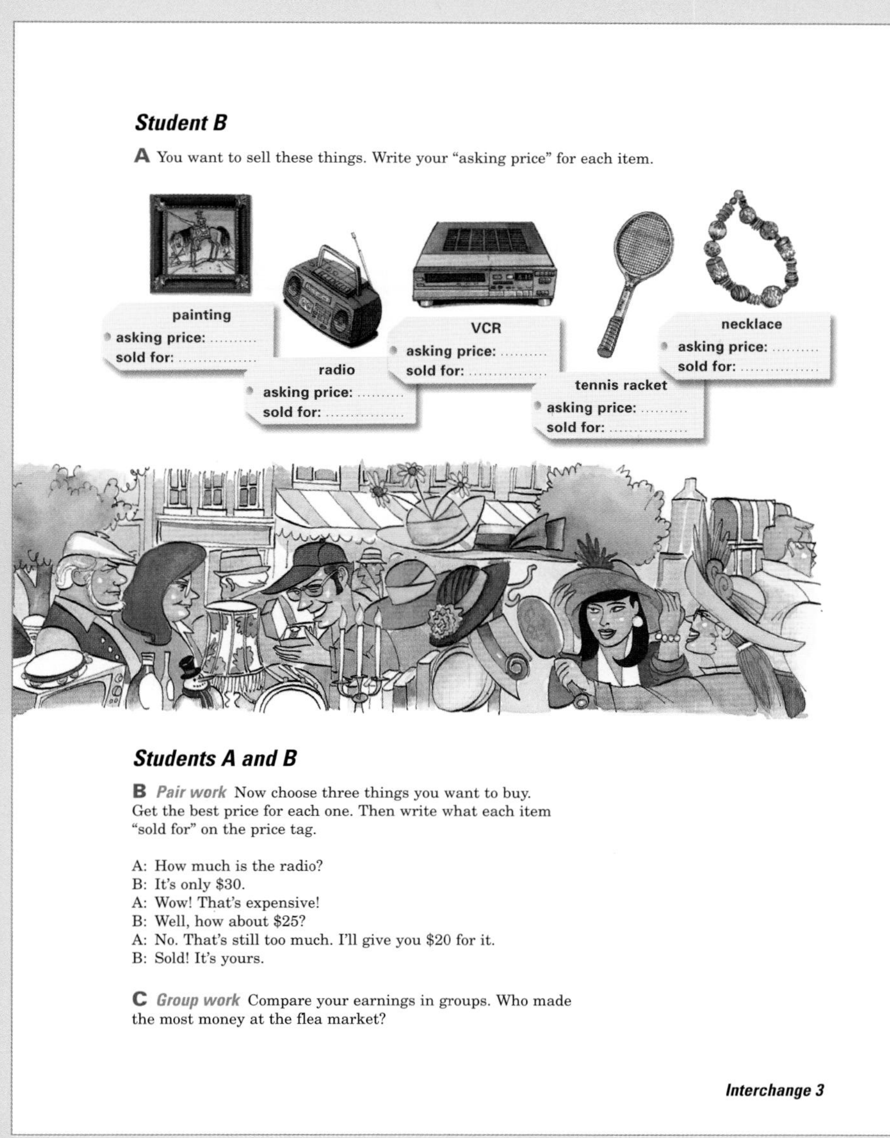

Student B

A You want to sell these things. Write your "asking price" for each item.

painting
asking price: ....
sold for: ....

radio
asking price: ....
sold for: ....

VCR
asking price: ....
sold for: ....

tennis racket
asking price: ....
sold for: ....

necklace
asking price: ....
sold for: ....

Students A and B

B *Pair work* Now choose three things you want to buy. Get the best price for each one. Then write what each item "sold for" on the price tag.

A: How much is the radio?
B: It's only $30.
A: Wow! That's expensive!
B: Well, how about $25?
A: No. That's still too much. I'll give you $20 for it.
B: Sold! It's yours.

C *Group work* Compare your earnings in groups. Who made the most money at the flea market?

Interchange 3

- ***Option:*** Ss make a list of six to eight things to sell at a flea market. They can also bring in two or three things and role-play a sale at a flea market.

C *Group work*

- Ss look at the "sold for" part of their page and add up the amount of money they made individually.
- Ss work in small groups. They tell each other what they sold and at what price.
- Ss compare how much money they earned. Who made the most money?

interchange 4

Learning objective: *speak more fluently about favorite music, TV programs, and Web sites*

A

- Explain the task. Ss read the answers and then write the questions. Elicit the first question: *When do you listen to the radio?* Ss write that question.
- Ss complete the task individually.

B *Pair work*

- Explain the first part of the task. Ss compare their questions in pairs. Then go over answers as a class.

Possible answers

When **do you listen to the radio**?
When **do you watch TV**?
What **is your favorite radio station**?
Do **you have a favorite Web site**?
What **is your favorite TV program**?
What kind **of sports do you like to watch**?

- Explain the second part of the task. Remind Ss to use their own information and encourage them to ask follow-up questions.
- Go around the class and check Ss' grammar and intonation. Write down any errors you notice.
- ***Option:*** When Ss finish, they ask and answer the questions with a different partner.
- Write the questions or sentences with errors on the board. Ask Ss to correct the errors in pairs. Then elicit their answers.

interchange 4 ***WHAT'S THE QUESTION?***

A Look at these answers. Then complete the questions.

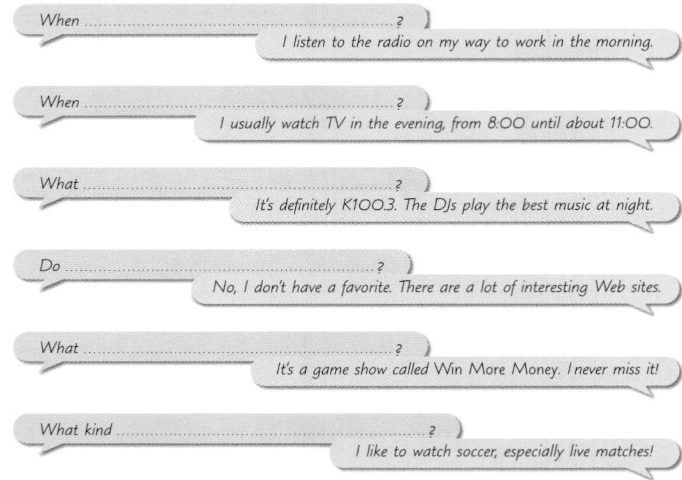

When .... ?
I listen to the radio on my way to work in the morning.
When .... ?
I usually watch TV in the evening, from 8:00 until about 11:00.
What .... ?
It's definitely K100.3. The DJs play the best music at night.
Do .... ?
No, I don't have a favorite. There are a lot of interesting Web sites.
What .... ?
It's a game show called Win More Money. I never miss it!
What kind .... ?
I like to watch soccer, especially live matches!

B ***Pair work*** Compare your completed questions with a partner. Then ask and answer the questions. Answer with your own information.

A: When do you listen to the radio?
B: I listen to the radio in the evening.
A: What do you listen to?

game show

soccer match

Interchange 4

interchange 5 ***FAMILY FACTS***

A *Class activity* Go around the class and find this information.
Write a classmate's name only once. Ask follow-up questions of your own.

Find someone	Name
1. who is an only child **"Do you have any brothers or sisters?"**	....
2. who has more than two brothers **"How many brothers do you have?"**	....
3. who has more than two sisters **"How many sisters do you have?"**	....
4. whose brother or sister is living abroad **"Are any of your brothers or sisters living abroad? Where?"**	....
5. who lives with his or her grandparents **"Do you live with your grandparents?"**	....
6. who has a great-grandparent still living **"Is your great-grandmother or great-grandfather still living?"**	....
7. who has a family member with an unusual job **"Does anyone in your family have an unusual job?"**	....
8. whose mother or father is studying English **"Is either of your parents studying English? Where?"**	....

B *Group work* Compare your information in groups.

Interchange 5

interchange 5

Learning objective: *gain fluency asking questions about classmates' families*

A *Class activity*

- Focus Ss' attention on the pictures. Point out that they show three different families. Ask: "What can you tell me about each family?"
- Go over the chart and explain the task.
- Model the first question with several Ss. Ask the question until you find a S who is an only child. Write that S's name in the *Name* column.
- Elicit possible follow-up questions for the first question. Write them on the board.
- Point out that Ss can make up responses or say "Sorry, I'd rather not say" if they don't want to give true information.
- Set a time limit of 10 to 15 minutes. Ss complete the activity.
- Go around the room and encourage Ss to move around and talk to other classmates. Note any errors, such as question formation.

B *Group work*

- Ss compare their answers in small groups. Then elicit interesting things they learned about their classmates.
- Go over any errors you noticed in part A and ask Ss to correct them.

interchange 6

Learning objective: *speak more fluently about leisure activities*

A *Class activity*

- Focus Ss' attention on the picture. Ask: "What is a talent show?" Elicit ideas. If needed, explain that it is a contest in which people sing, dance, or play an instrument.
- Explain the task. Ss ask each other who does these activities, how often they do them, and how well they do them. Point out that Ss must try to find one person who does each thing. Also, they cannot use the same name twice.
- Model the task with a S at the front of the class, using the example conversation.
- Set a time limit of 10 to 15 minutes. Ss go around the room and complete the activity.

B *Group work*

- Explain the task. Tell Ss to imagine the class is participating in a talent show. Ss choose three people from the class to enter in the contest. Ask: "What will each person do in the contest? Why?"
- Model the conversation with two Ss. Then Ss complete the task in small groups.
- Ask the groups to share and explain their choices with the class.

interchange 6 *DO YOU DANCE?*

A *Class activity* Does anyone in your class do these things? How often and how well do they do them? Go around the class and find one person for each activity.

Activity	Name	How often?	How well?
dance			
play the guitar			
sing			
draw			
paint			
do karate			

A: Do you dance?
B: Yes, I do.
A: How often do you go dancing?
B: Every weekend.
A: And how well do you dance?
B: Actually, not very well. But I enjoy it!

B *Group work* Imagine your class is participating in a talent show. Who would you enter in the contest? Choose three people from your class. Explain your choices.

A: Let's enter Adam in the talent show.
B: Why Adam?
A: Because he dances very well.
C: Yes, he does. And Yvette is very good at playing the guitar. Let's enter her, too!

Interchange 6

interchange 7 *VACATION DISASTERS*

A Imagine you went on a vacation recently, but everything went wrong. Use the ideas below to help you describe what happened. Check (✓) one item in each category.

Weather
- [ ] It rained the whole time.
- [ ] It was too hot.
- [ ] It was freezing cold.
- [ ] .... (your own idea)

Flight
- [ ] The plane was full, so you couldn't get on.
- [ ] The plane was three hours late.
- [ ] Your luggage went to another city.
- [ ] .... (your own idea)

Hotel
- [ ] The food was terrible.
- [ ] There were insects in the room.
- [ ] The service was awful.
- [ ] .... (your own idea)

Tour Guide
- [ ] The guide didn't know anything.
- [ ] The guide got lost.
- [ ] The guide was very rude.
- [ ] .... (your own idea)

People
- [ ] The people in your group weren't fun.
- [ ] The other tourists were rude.
- [ ] You didn't meet anyone interesting.
- [ ] .... (your own idea)

Other
- [ ] You lost your passport.
- [ ] You had an argument with your family.
- [ ] You got sick.
- [ ] .... (your own idea)

B ***Pair work*** Ask your partner about his or her vacation. Then change roles.

A: So, how was your vacation?
B: It was OK, but a lot of things went wrong.
A: Really? What happened?
B: First of all, the plane was full, so we couldn't get on. Then, . . .

Interchange 7

interchange 7

Learning objective: *speak more fluently about vacation disasters*

A

- Books closed. As a class, ask Ss to brainstorm things that can go wrong on vacations (e.g., *airline loses your luggage, the food isn't good, the hotel is terrible*). Write their ideas on the board.
- Books open. Focus Ss' attention on the family in the picture. Elicit things that might be wrong with their vacation. Add these ideas to the board.
- Explain the task. Ss imagine they went on vacation and everything went wrong. They check (✓) an item for each category or write their own ideas. Set a time limit of about ten minutes.

B *Pair work*

- Explain the task. Model the conversation with a S.
- Ss take turns asking questions about vacations in pairs. Go around the class and suggest follow-up questions and more detailed responses as needed.
- ***Option:*** Ask different Ss to share their vacation stories with the class. The class votes for the worst vacation.

interchange 8

Learning objective: *discuss neighborhood improvements as part of a neighborhood planning committee*

A

- Focus Ss' attention on the vocabulary in the chart. Ask them to underline any words they don't know. Elicit or explain the meanings.

Vocabulary

youth center: a building with recreational facilities for teenagers
botanical garden: a large garden with many plants
video arcade: a place where people play video games
ice-skating rink: a place with an ice floor for ice-skating or hockey
skateboard park: an outdoor area where people can skateboard

- ***Option:*** To practice quantifiers, Ss ask and answer questions about the facilities in their city (e.g., *Are there many swimming pools? No, there aren't any. / Yes, there are a few.*).
- Model the task. Ask: "How important are public libraries for a community? Why?" Elicit responses from the class. Then ask Ss to check (✓) *Very important*, *Somewhat important*, or *Not important*. Point out that there is no correct answer.
- Ss complete the task individually. Encourage them to think of reasons for their choices.

B *Group work*

- Set the scene. Ss imagine they are on a neighborhood planning committee. The community has no recreational facilities. They want to provide some facilities, but they don't have much money. Ss decide which *three* things are most important and why.
- Model the example conversation with two Ss. Then Ss work in small groups. They discuss recreational facilities and decide which three are most important. Set a time limit of about ten minutes.
- Ask one S in each group to report the facilities they chose and the reasons for them.

interchange 8 *NEIGHBORHOOD COMMITTEE*

A How important are these recreational facilities for your community? Check (✓) your opinions.

Recreational facility	Very important	Somewhat important	Not important
a public library	☐	☐	☐
a youth center	☐	☐	☐
a botanical garden	☐	☐	☐
a video arcade	☐	☐	☐
an amusement park	☐	☐	☐
an ice-skating rink	☐	☐	☐
an in-line skating path	☐	☐	☐
a zoo	☐	☐	☐
a skateboard park	☐	☐	☐
a swimming pool	☐	☐	☐
an Internet café	☐	☐	☐

B *Group work* Imagine you are on a neighborhood planning committee. Your community currently has no recreational facilities. Agree on the three most important facilities.

A: A youth center is very important because young people need a place to go.
B: I don't agree. I think that . . . is more important because . . .
C: I agree with Marta. A youth center should be one of our choices.

Interchange 8

interchange 10 *LIFESTYLE SURVEY*

A *Pair work* What kind of lifestyle does your partner have: easygoing and relaxed or busy and fast-paced? Interview your partner using this survey.

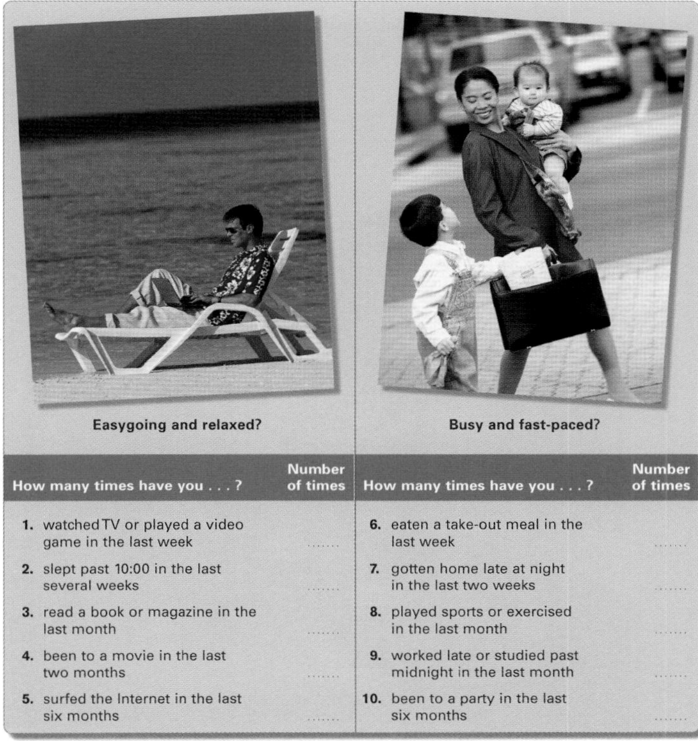

Easygoing and relaxed?		Busy and fast-paced?	
How many times have you . . . ?	**Number of times**	**How many times have you . . . ?**	**Number of times**
1. watched TV or played a video game in the last week	....	**6.** eaten a take-out meal in the last week	....
2. slept past 10:00 in the last several weeks	....	**7.** gotten home late at night in the last two weeks	....
3. read a book or magazine in the last month	....	**8.** played sports or exercised in the last month	....
4. been to a movie in the last two months	....	**9.** worked late or studied past midnight in the last month	....
5. surfed the Internet in the last six months	....	**10.** been to a party in the last six months	....

B *Group work* Tell the group what you think your partner's lifestyle is like and why.

"Mario's lifestyle is busy and fast-paced. He hardly ever has time to watch TV, read a book, or go to the movies. He studies a lot, and he often eats take-out meals. He also . . . "

Interchange 10

interchange 10

Learning objective: *interview a partner about his or her lifestyle*

A *Pair work*

- Focus S's attention on the two pictures. Then write *easygoing and relaxed* and *busy and fast-paced* on the board. Explain that these are different lifestyles. Elicit different activities and write them on the board under each lifestyle.
- Explain the task. Then Ss read the questions silently. Elicit or explain any new vocabulary.
- Model the activity by asking a S the first interview question. Show where to write the number of times.
- Ss complete the activity in pairs. Go around the class and give help as needed.
- ***Option:*** To make Ss listen more carefully, tell them to ask the questions in a different order.

B *Group work*

- Explain the task and ask a S to read the example response.
- ***Option:*** Use the two pictures to elicit model responses from the class. For example, say: "This man has an easygoing and relaxed lifestyle. He really enjoys reading. In fact, he has read four novels in the past month! He also . . ."
- Ss use their surveys to make notes about their partner's lifestyle.
- In groups, Ss take turns talking about their partner's lifestyle.
- Ask the class: "Who has an easygoing and relaxed lifestyle? Why? Who has a busy and fast-paced lifestyle? Why?" Elicit Ss' answers.

interchange 9A/B

Learning objective: *speak more fluently about differences in people's appearances*

A *Pair work*

- Ss work in pairs. One S looks at Interchange 9A and the other S looks at Interchange 9B.
- Explain the task. Both Ss have pictures of a party, but there are some differences in the pictures. Ss ask each other questions to find the differences without looking at their partner's picture.
- Ask different Ss to read the questions at the top of the page. Point out that Ss can use these questions to find the differences.
- Model the task with one pair. Ask: "What is Dave wearing in Picture 1? in Picture 2?" Elicit answers. (Answers: Student A: "In Picture 1, Dave's wearing a blue shirt." Student B: "In Picture 2, he's wearing a white shirt.")

> **TIP** With information gap activities, tell Ss to sit across from their partners and put a textbook between them. That way, they can hear each other but not see each other's pictures.

- Ss complete the task in pairs. Go around the class and give help as needed.

interchange 9A ***FIND THE DIFFERENCES***

Student A

A *Pair work* How many differences can you find between your picture here and your partner's picture? Ask questions like these to find the differences.

How many people are standing / sitting / wearing . . . / holding a drink? Who?
What color is . . . 's T-shirt / sweater / hair?
Does . . . wear glasses / have a beard / have long hair?
What does . . . look like?

B *Class activity* How many differences are there in the pictures?

"In picture 1, Dave's T-shirt is . . . . In picture 2, it's . . . "

Interchange 9A

B *Class activity*

- Tell pairs to look over their answers (i.e., the differences between the two pictures) and to choose one to write on the board. Encourage them to come to the board quickly by making it a rule that no answer can be written twice.
- To check the answers written on the board, ask the pair who wrote an answer to read it aloud for the class. Then find out if other Ss agree. If they do agree, go on to the next answer until all of them have been checked. If Ss don't agree, ask the class to look at both pictures again to check it.

interchange 9B FIND THE DIFFERENCES

Student B

A *Pair work* How many differences can you find between your picture here and your partner's picture? Ask questions like these to find the differences.

How many people are standing / sitting / wearing . . . / holding a drink? Who?
What color is . . . 's T-shirt / sweater / hair?
Does . . . wear glasses / have a beard / have long hair?
What does . . . look like?

Picture 2

B *Class activity* How many differences are there in the pictures?

"In picture 1, Dave's T-shirt is . . . . In picture 2, it's . . . "

Interchange 9B

Possible answers

1. In Picture 1, Dave is wearing a blue shirt. In Picture 2, he's wearing a white shirt.
2. In Picture 1, Anna's hair is long. In Picture 2, it's short.
3. In Picture 1, Anna is sitting. In Picture 2, she's standing.
4. In Picture 1, Kate's sweater is orange. In Picture 2, it's purple.
5. In Picture 1, Fiona has curly red hair. In Picture 2, she has straight brown hair.
6. In Picture 1, Patrick doesn't have a mustache or beard. In Picture 2, he has a mustache and beard.
7. In Picture 1, Neil is standing. In Picture 2, he's sitting.
8. In Picture 1, Neil is wearing glasses. In Picture 2, he isn't.
9. In Picture 1, Neil has a drink. In Picture 2, he doesn't have a drink.
10. In Picture 1, there are three gifts on the table. In Picture 2, there are two gifts on the table.

interchange 11

***Learning objective:** speak more fluently about cities by discussing a guide found on a city's Web site*

A

- Ask: "Where are some different places to find out information about a city?" Elicit Ss' answers.

> **TIP** To get Ss' attention, give them instructions from different places. Sometimes give them from the back of the classroom; other times give them from the middle of the classroom.

- Explain the task. Ss make a city guide for a Web site. Have them choose a city they know well or a city they want to learn about.
- Go over the questions and chart. Point out that this guide is from a city's Web site. Elicit or explain any new vocabulary.

Vocabulary

souvenirs: things you buy to help you remember a place you visit
inexpensive: cheap
historical sights: important places in a city's or country's past
bargain clothing stores: stores that have cheap clothes
free: costing no money

- Ss complete the guide individually in class or for homework.

B *Group work*

- Explain the task. Ask different Ss to read the questions aloud. Then elicit additional questions and ask a S to write them on the board.
- Ss compare their city guides in small groups. (If possible, Ss should work with classmates who wrote about different cities.)
- Go around the class and encourage Ss to ask follow-up questions.

---

interchange 11 ***CITY GUIDE***

A Where can you get information about a city? buy souvenirs? see historical sights? Complete the city guide with information about a city of your choice.

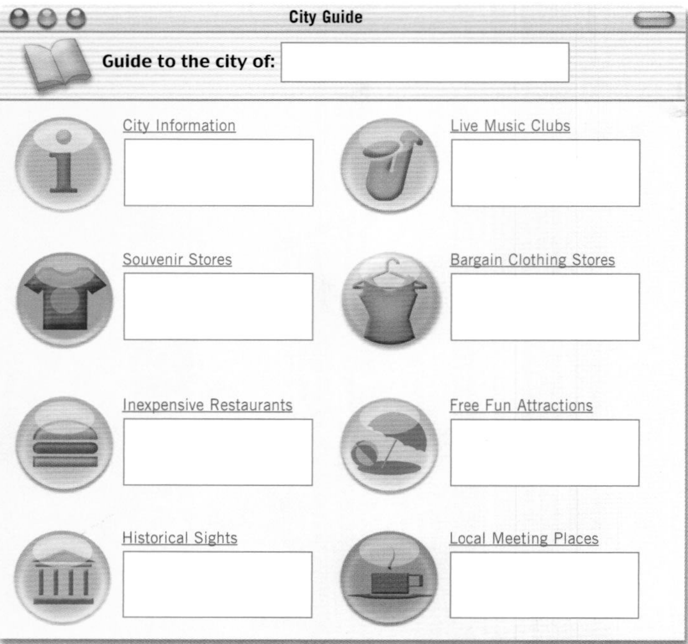

City Guide
Guide to the city of:
City Information
Live Music Clubs
Souvenir Stores
Bargain Clothing Stores
Inexpensive Restaurants
Free Fun Attractions
Historical Sights
Local Meeting Places

B *Group work* Compare your city guide in groups. Ask these questions and your own questions. Add any additional or interesting information to your guide.

Where can you get information about your city?
Where's a good place to buy souvenirs?
Where's an inexpensive place to eat?
What historical sights should you visit?
Where's the best place to hear music?
Where's a cheap place to shop for clothes?
What fun things can you do for free?
Where's a popular place to meet?

Interchange 11

interchange 12 HELP!

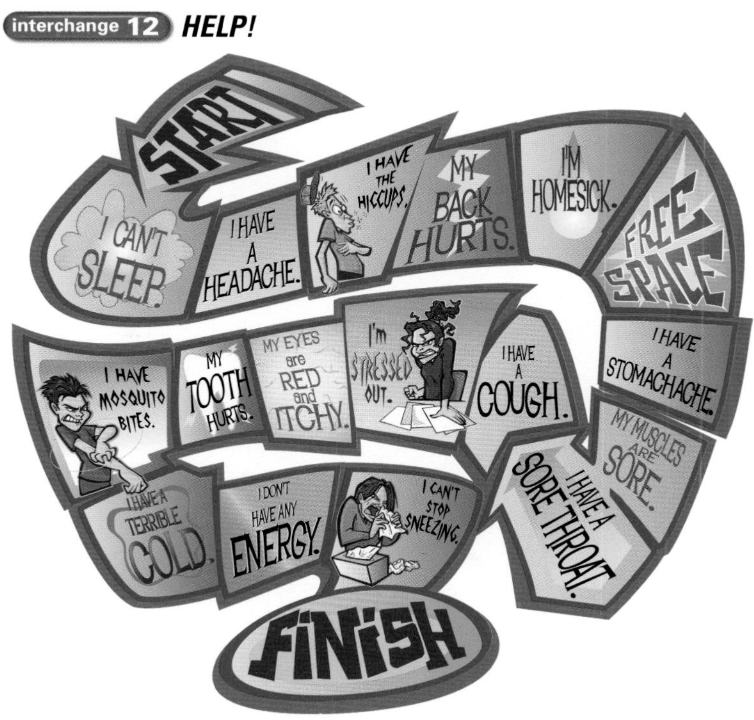
START
I CAN'T SLEEP.
I HAVE A HEADACHE.
I HAVE THE HICCUPS.
MY BACK HURTS.
I'M HOMESICK.
FREE SPACE
I HAVE A STOMACHACHE.
MY MUSCLES ARE SORE.
I HAVE A SORE THROAT.
I CAN'T STOP SNEEZING.
I DON'T HAVE ANY ENERGY.
I HAVE A TERRIBLE COLD.
I HAVE MOSQUITO BITES.
MY TOOTH HURTS.
MY EYES are RED and ITCHY.
I'm STRESSED OUT.
I HAVE A COUGH.
FINISH

A *Group work* Play the board game. Follow these instructions.

1. Use small pieces of paper with your initials on them as markers.
2. Take turns by tossing a coin:
   If the coin lands face up, move two spaces.
   If the coin lands face down, move one space.
3. When you land on a space, ask two others in your group for advice.

A: I have a terrible headache. Akira, what's your advice?
B: Well, it's important to get a lot of rest.
A: Thanks. What about you, Jason? What do you think?
C: You should take two aspirin. That always works for me.

useful expressions
I think it would be useful to . . .
One thing you could do is . . .
It's a good idea to . . .
It's important to . . .
You should . . .

B *Class activity* Who gave the best advice in your group? Tell the class.

Interchange 12

interchange 12

Learning objective: *speak more fluently about health problems and medical advice by playing a board game*

A *Group work*

- Focus Ss' attention on the board game and read the instructions. Show Ss how to write their initials on small pieces of paper and use them as markers.
- ***Option:*** Ss can use other small items as markers (e.g., pen caps or erasers).
- Show Ss how to toss a coin. Point out which side is face up and which side is face down.
- Have different Ss read the problems in each space. Then ask three Ss to model the example conversation.
- Show how to play the game with a group of three Ss.

TIP In low-level classes, it is more effective to model a game or activity than to explain it.

- Ss play the game in small groups. Go around the class and encourage Ss to use the expression in the useful expressions box.

B *Class activity*

- Read the question. Elicit information from each group. Encourage them to give examples.

interchange 13

***Learning objective:** discuss and create a menu for a new restaurant*

A *Group work*

- Write these words on the board:
  soups *salads* *main dishes*
  desserts *beverages*
- In small groups, Ss discuss their favorite dishes in each category. Then elicit their answers and write them on the board.
- Set the scene and explain the task. Explain that a *kid's menu* has dishes children like. They are usually cheaper and smaller than dishes on the regular menu. Elicit possible dishes for this menu.
- Ss complete the task in small groups. Go around the class and give help with vocabulary, spelling, or prices.

B *Group work*

- In the same groups, Ss choose a name for their restaurant and write it at the top of the menu. To help Ss think of ideas, ask these questions: "Where is the restaurant? What's special about it?"

C *Class activity*

- Collect each group's menu. Then put them around the class so each group can see the other groups' menus.
- Read the instructions and explain the task. Ss go around the class and compare the menus. Then they write a name of the restaurant next to each phrase.
- Elicit answers from the class. Encourage Ss to explain their reasons.

interchange 13 *PLAN A MENU*

A *Group work* Imagine you are opening a new restaurant. Create a menu of dishes you'd like to offer. Then write the prices.

Today's Special

Soups

Salads

Main Dishes

Kids' Menu

Desserts

Beverages

B *Group work* Choose a name for your restaurant. Write it at the top of the menu.

C *Class activity* Compare your menus. Which group has . . . ?

the most interesting menu
the most typical menu
the healthiest menu
the cheapest prices
the best name for a restaurant

Interchange 13

interchange 14 HOW MUCH DO YOU KNOW?

A *Pair work* Take turns asking and answering these questions. Check (✓) the answer you think is correct for each question.

World Knowledge Quiz

1. Which animal lives the longest?	☐ a whale	☐ an elephant	☐ a tortoise
2. Which one is the tallest?	☐ an elephant	☐ a giraffe	☐ a camel
3. Which of these is the heaviest?	☐ the brain	☐ the heart	☐ the liver
4. Which planet is the coldest?	☐ Neptune	☐ Saturn	☐ Pluto
5. Which one is the biggest?	☐ Jupiter	☐ Earth	☐ Mars
6. Which metal is the heaviest?	☐ gold	☐ silver	☐ aluminum
7. Which country is the driest?	☐ Egypt	☐ Peru	☐ Chile
8. Which one is closest to the equator?	☐ Malaysia	☐ Colombia	☐ India
9. Which place is the wettest?	☐ Kauai, Hawaii	☐ Bogor, Indonesia	☐ Manaus, Brazil
10. Which place is the hottest?	☐ Al 'Aziziyah, Libya	☐ Death Valley, the U.S.	☐ Alice Springs, Australia

Correct answers

1. a tortoise 2. a giraffe 3. the liver 4. Pluto 5. Jupiter 6. gold 7. Egypt 8. Colombia 9. Kauai, Hawaii 10. Al 'Aziziyah, Libya

How many did you get correct?

10 Perfect! Brilliant! You should be a teacher.
6–9 Very good! Do you watch lots of TV game shows?
2–5 Just OK. How often do you go to the library?
0–1 Oh, dear. You should never be on a quiz show.

B *Pair work* Write your own quiz. Then ask the questions to another pair.

Interchange 14

interchange 14

Learning objective: *speak more fluently about general knowledge facts by asking and answering quiz questions*

A Pair work

- Write these subjects on the board:

  biology *geography*
  science *history*
  chemistry *foreign languages*

- As a warm-up, ask: "Do you watch quiz shows on TV? How well would you do with these subjects?" Encourage discussion.
- Explain the task. Model the first question with its three choices.
- Call on Ss to read the questions and the three choices. (It's best not to explain new words at this time as this might give away the answer.)
- Model this possible conversation with a S:

  T: Which animal lives the longest, a whale, an elephant, or a tortoise?
  S: I think a whale lives the longest.
  T: Hmm. I think a tortoise lives the longest.
  S: I don't agree. I think a whale lives the longest.
  T: OK, I guess we disagree here. So I'll check the *tortoise* and you check the *whale*. We'll find out later who got the correct answer for this one.
  S: Now it's my turn. Let's go on to question 2. Which one . . . ?

- Ss work in pairs. Ss take turns asking and answering the questions. Tell Ss to cover the answers.
- Allow five to ten minutes for the activity. When time is up, pairs check their answers in the "correct answers" box, total their scores, and read the description of the scores.

B Pair work

- Explain the task. Ss work in pairs to write their own quiz. Ask them to include an answer key and score chart.
- Each pair joins another pair. Ss take turns asking and answering the other pair's questions.

interchange 15

***Learning objective:** speak more fluently about plans for the weekend*

A *Class activity*

- As a warm-up, ask: "What are you doing this weekend?"
- ***Option:*** Let the class ask you about your weekend plans.
- Ask Ss to look at the items in the chart. Elicit or explain any new vocabulary. Call on Ss to form the questions from the phrases (e.g., *Are you going to go to an amusement park this weekend?*).
- Model by asking different Ss: "Are you going to visit relatives this weekend?" When a S says "no," go on to the next person until you find someone who says "yes." Write that person's name in the chart, and ask at least two follow-up questions. Write the details in the *Notes* column.
- Ask two Ss to model the conversation.
- Model how to react to hearing about someone's plans (e.g., *Really? That sounds great! Wow! That sounds like fun!*). Ss practice the expressions.
- Ss move around the class to do the activity.

TIP It's best not to interrupt Ss during a fluency exercise. For this type of activity, communication of real information is more important than grammatical or lexical accuracy.

- After the activity, go over any common errors.

B *Pair work*

- Ss work in pairs to discuss the questions.

---

interchange 15 WEEKEND PLANS

A *Class activity* What are your classmates' plans for the weekend? Go around the class and find people who are going to do these things. For each question, ask for further information.

Find someone who is going to	Name	Notes
go to an amusement park		
stay out late		
visit relatives		
practice English		
rent a video or DVD		
study for a test		
exercise		
go shopping		

A: Linda, are you going to go to an amusement park this weekend?
B: Yes, I am, actually.
A: What are you going to do there?
B: I'm going to go on the roller-coaster.

B *Pair work* Compare your information with a partner. Who is going to do something fun? physical? serious?

Interchange 15

interchange 16 MY POSSIBLE FUTURE

A Complete this chart with information about yourself.

My possible future	
What are two things you plan to do next year?	....
What are two things you aren't going to do next year?	....
What is something you hope to buy in the next year?	....
What would you like to change about your appearance?	....
What is a place you want to visit someday?	....
What is a city you would like to live in someday?	....
What kind of job would you like to have?	....
What career goals do you hope to achieve?	....
What famous person would you like to meet?	....

B *Group work* Compare your information in groups. Be prepared to explain the future you have planned.

A: What are two things you plan to do next year?
B: Well, I'm going to take a cooking class and I'm also going to go to Italy.
C: Oh, really? What part of Italy are you going to visit?
B: I'm not sure yet! What about you? What are two things you plan to do next year?

Interchange 16

interchange 16

Learning objective: *speak more fluently about possibilities for the future*

A

- Focus Ss' attention on the picture. Elicit what kind of dreams and plans the woman has.
- Explain the task. Ss answer each question in the chart with information about themselves.
- ***Option:*** Have Ss ask you the questions in the chart. Reply with your own information. If there are any problems with pronunciation or intonation of questions, review briefly.
- Ss complete the chart individually. Go around the class and give help as needed.

B *Group work*

- Explain the task. Model the example conversation with Ss.
- Ss form groups and take turns explaining their possible future plans.
- ***Option:*** Ask each group to choose the most interesting or unusual future plans that someone talked about. Then that S tells the rest of the class about his or her plans.

Units 1–16 Self-study

1 WHERE ARE YOU FROM?

A Listen to two conversations. Check (✓) the countries the people talk about.

☐ Argentina ☐ Australia ☐ Brazil ☐ France ☐ Italy ☐ Turkey ☐ Uruguay

B Listen again. Answer the questions.

1. What is Robert's nickname? ....
2. Where is Robert from? ....
3. What is Sandra's last name? ....
4. Where is Sandra from? ....

2 I'M REALLY BUSY!

A Listen to Steve and Eun Ha talk after class. When does Steve do each thing? Check (✓) the days.

DAILY PLANNER	Monday	Tuesday	Wednesday	Thursday	Friday	Times
go to work	☑	☐	☐	☐	☐	3:30
take a computer class	☐	☐	☐	☐	☐	______
work as a tour guide	☐	☐	☐	☐	☐	______
go to English class	☐	☐	☐	☐	☐	______

B Listen again. Write the start times for each activity.

3 I WANT TO LOOK NICER.

A Listen to Josh and Anne get ready for a party. Check (✓) the clothes they mention.

☐ black pants
☐ cotton shirt
☐ jeans
☐ leather jacket
☐ silk shirt
☐ silk sweater
☐ wool jacket
☐ wool sweater

B Listen again. What does Josh wear? Circle the correct picture.

4 WOULD YOU LIKE TO GO?

A Listen to three people invite friends to events and activities. Complete the chart with the events, days, and times.

	Event/Activity	Day	Time	Do they accept?
1. Cam and Marla	....	....	....	☐ Yes ☐ No
2. Lucy and Chris	....	....	....	☐ Yes ☐ No
3. Ed and Joanna	....	....	....	☐ Yes ☐ No

B Listen again. Do the friends accept? Check (✓) Yes or No.

5 A NEW STUDENT

A Listen to an interview for an article in a student newspaper. Does Akemi have a large family? ☐ Yes ☐ No

B Listen again. Correct the nine mistakes in the article.

Akemi Takayama is a new student. She is from Japan. Her parents are living in ~~Tokyo~~ Kobe. Her brother lives in Osaka. Her sister is studying the violin in Miami. Akemi has seven aunts and uncles. They are living in Japan. One niece and nephew are traveling in the U.S. They are visiting Akemi this week. Akemi has a lot of cousins in Australia. A few of her cousins are in Mexico. Akemi is studying French. Please welcome Akemi to our school!

6 TAKE A QUIZ!

A Listen to the questions. Write the activities you hear.

ARE YOU A COUCH POTATO? FIND OUT NOW!

Activities			
1. exercise	a. two hours	b. an hour	c. twenty minutes
2. play tennis	a. yes, often	b. yes, sometimes	c. no, never
3.	a. once a week	b. once a month	c. four times a year
4.	a. five days a week	b. twice a week	c. hardly ever
5.	a. yes, often	b. yes, sometimes	c. no, never
6.	a. very well	b. pretty well	c. not very well
7.	a. three times a week	b. once a week	c. hardly ever
8.	a. pretty good	b. OK	c. terrible

If you answered: *Mostly As*: Slow down . . . you could be a fitness and sports fanatic! *Mostly Bs*: You exercise often, but not enough. *Mostly Cs*: Be careful! You may be a couch potato!

B Now take the quiz! Listen again. Circle your responses.

7 COMPUTER THIEF!

A Listen to a police officer interview Mike Doe. Number the events of each day from 1 to 5 in the order they happened.

Date: March 3
Name: Mike Doe

Saturday
___ He went shopping.
___ He watched TV.
_1_ He worked.
___ He walked home.
___ He cooked dinner at home.

Sunday
___ He stopped at the office.
___ He went to bed.
___ He did laundry.
___ He spent time at the park.
___ He walked home and watched DVDs.

B Listen again. Do you think Mike took the computer? Why or why not?

8 I'M LOST.

A Listen to people ask for the location of the places below. Where do you think they are? ☐ the city center ☐ a small town ☐ the suburbs

B Listen again. Draw the places on the map.

post office, grocery store, bookstore, café (2)

travel agency, music store, laundromat, pay phone (3)

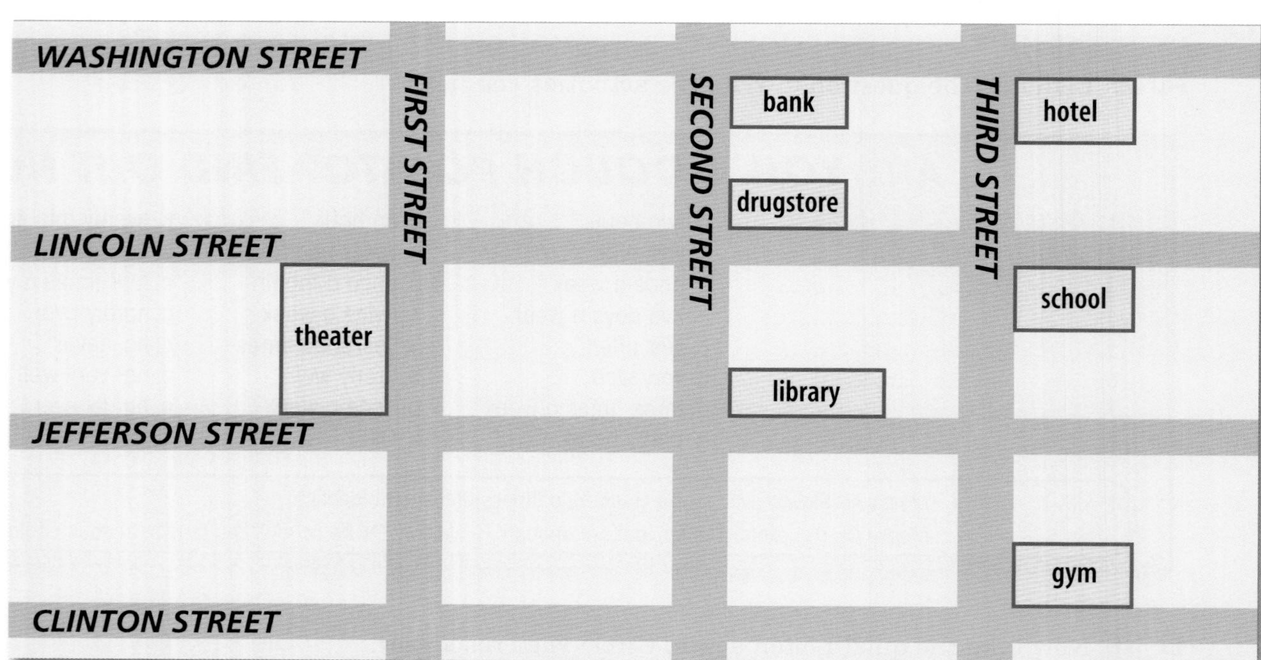

9 I CAN'T FIND HER.

A Listen to the descriptions. Match the names with the pictures.

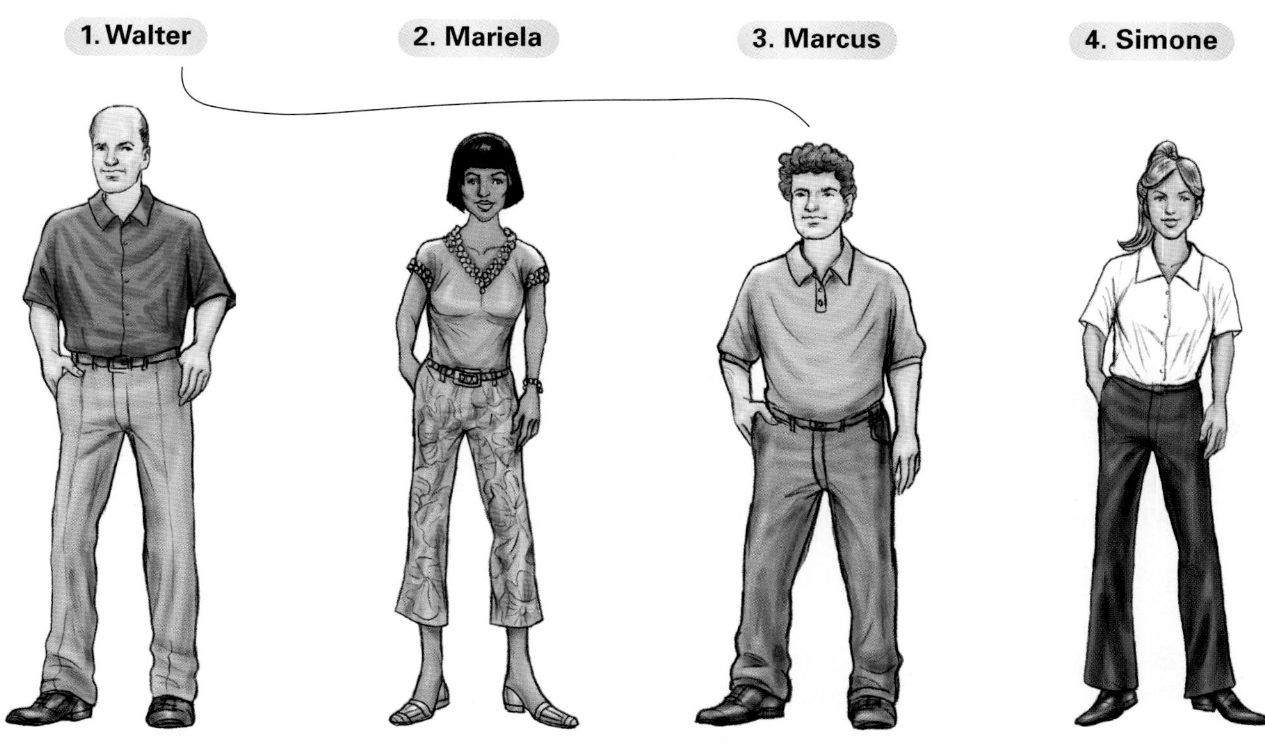

B Listen again. What is each person's style? Write the correct word.

Walter: casual   Mariela: ....   Marcus: ....   Simone: ....

10 HAVE YOU EVER . . . ?

A Listen to Katie and Phil interview for a job on a new adventure TV show. What countries have they visited? Write **K** for Katie and **P** for Phil.

.... Brazil .... China .... Korea .... Singapore
.... Chile .... Japan .... Peru .... Thailand

B Listen again. Check (✓) the answers. Who do you think will get the job?

	Katie		Phil	
	Yes	No	Yes	No
1. Have they ever driven a sports car?	☐	☐	☐	☐
2. Have they ever sung karaoke?	☐	☐	☐	☐
3. Have they eaten different kinds of foods?	☐	☐	☐	☐
4. Have they been camping?	☐	☐	☐	☐
5. Have they ridden an elephant?	☐	☐	☐	☐

11 PLAN MY VACATION!

A Listen to Charles help Maya plan her vacation. What cities has Charles visited? ☐ London ☐ Cairo ☐ New Orleans

B Listen again. What is each city like? Complete the chart.

	Cost	Size	Weather
London	....	....	....
Cairo	....	....	....
New Orleans	....	....	....

12 WHAT SHOULD WE TAKE?

A Listen to Dana and Hilary plan for a camping trip. What problems do they talk about?

1. headache 2. .... 3. .... 4. .... 5. .... 6. ....

B Listen again. Match the problems to these items. Write the number in the box.

☐ 

☐ 

1 

☐ 

☐ 

☐ 

13 I CAN'T EAT SPICY FOOD.

A Listen to two people in a restaurant talk about their orders. Cross out the things they did *not* order.

B Listen again. Why didn't they order certain foods? For each thing you crossed out, write the reason next to it.

Eastern Palace

sweet and sour chicken	
tofu curry	
grilled tuna	
fried rice with vegetables	
lamb kebabs	
green salad	
Total	

14 CHIANG MAI IT IS!

A Listen to Kai and Nina talk about where to teach in Thailand. Check (✓) True or False for each statement.

What's Chiang Mai like?	True	False
1. Chiang Mai is larger than Bangkok.	☐	☐
2. Chiang Mai is near the ocean.	☐	☐
3. The region around Chiang Mai is famous for hiking.	☐	☐
4. The highest mountain near Chiang Mai is 5,000 feet high.	☐	☐
5. Chiang Mai is wettest in the winter.	☐	☐
6. Bangkok is 400 miles from Chiang Mai.	☐	☐

B Listen again. For the statements you marked false, write the correct information.

15 I CAN'T, BECAUSE . . .

Listen to these telephone messages. There are two errors in each message. Correct the errors.

Ann –
Kelly from ~~yoga class~~ school called. They are playing baseball at 7 P.M. tomorrow. Please call before 5:00 if you are going to play.

Robin,
Martin called. Would you please tell Dave to be at the picnic on Thursday? Afterward, they are going to discuss the beach party.

16 PAST, PRESENT, OR FUTURE

A Listen to Ricki and Will talk at a class reunion. Write *past*, *present*, or *future* below each picture.

1. past 2. .... 3. .... 4. .... 5. .... 6. ....

B Listen again. What does Ricki hope to do in the future? Correct these false statements.

1. She'd like to start working soon.
2. She'd like to open a restaurant.
3. She hopes to work in an office.
4. She plans to get a loan from her parents.

Self-study audio scripts

1 Where are you from?

A Listen to two conversations. Check the countries the people talk about.

CARMEN: Hello. I'm Carmen da Silva.
BOBBY: Nice to meet you, Carmen, I'm Robert Kincaid. Everyone calls me Bobby.
CARMEN: Where are you from, Bobby?
BOBBY: I'm from Sydney, Australia.
CARMEN: Cool. I hear that's a great place.
BOBBY: Yeah, it's fun. How about you, Carmen? Where are you from?
CARMEN: I'm from Brazil.
BOBBY: Where in Brazil?
CARMEN: I'm from Porto Alegre.
BOBBY: Oh, yeah, near Uruguay. How interesting!

DAVE: Hey, Mario, who's that over there?
MARIO: That's Sandra Lagna. She's in my English class.
DAVE: Lagna?
MARIO: L-A-G-N-A. She's from Italy, like me.
DAVE: Wow! Is she from Milan?
MARIO: No, she's not. She's from Florence.
DAVE: Oh. What's she like?
MARIO: She's really interesting. Why don't you go talk to her?

B Listen again. Answer the questions.

2 I'm really busy!

A Listen to Steve and Eun Ha talk after class. When does Steve do each thing? Check the days.

EUN HA: Hi, Steve! How's it going?
STEVE: OK, I guess. I'm just so busy in the evenings!
EUN HA: What do you do after class?
STEVE: Well, I go to work on Mondays and Tuesdays at 3:30.
EUN HA: You have a job, too? Where do you work?
STEVE: I'm a receptionist at the Kings Hotel. I work late and get home around 11:00.
EUN HA: Wow! That's a long day!
STEVE: Yeah. Then on Wednesdays and Fridays I take a computer class at 7:00 P.M.
EUN HA: Another class?
STEVE: Yeah, but that's not all. On Thursdays I work as a tour guide for the university. I start at 9:00 A.M. and work until 5:00.
EUN HA: And you have English class with me at noon on Tuesdays, Wednesdays, and Fridays! You really *are* busy!

B Listen again. Write the start times for each activity.

3 I want to look nicer.

A Listen to Josh and Anne get ready for a party. Check the clothes they mention.

JOSH: I don't know what to wear to the party.
ANNE: Well, how about jeans and a cotton shirt?
JOSH: No, I want to look nicer.
ANNE: OK, what about your black pants and a silk shirt?
JOSH: That sounds better. But it's cold tonight.
ANNE: So, wear your wool sweater.
JOSH: Which one?
ANNE: The red one.
JOSH: I like the blue one better. Do you think it looks OK?
ANNE: Yes, the blue one is nice.
JOSH: OK, and I'll bring my leather jacket, too.
ANNE: Good idea. Now hurry! We're late!

B Listen again. What does Josh wear? Circle the correct picture.

4 Would you like to go?

A Listen to three people invite friends to events and activities. Complete the chart with the events, days, and times.

1. CAM: Hey, Marla, would you like to see a kung fu movie with me on Wednesday?
MARLA: Um . . .
CAM: There's a 6:00 show.
MARLA: Sorry, Cam. I don't like kung fu movies very much.
CAM: Oh, what kind of movies do you like?
MARLA: I prefer science fiction.

2. LUCY: Chris, there's a really good jazz group playing downtown. Do you like jazz?
CHRIS: Yes, I do. I love jazz!
LUCY: Would you like to go?
CHRIS: Sure! When is the show?
LUCY: It's Thursday at 8:30.
CHRIS: Great. Thanks a lot!

3. ED: Hey, Joanna, do you like R&B?
JOANNA: Sure. I like it a lot.
ED: I have tickets to a concert this weekend. Would you like to go?
JOANNA: Yes, I would. But . . . when is the concert?
ED: It's on Saturday at 3:00.
JOANNA: Oh no, I have to work Saturday afternoon.
ED: Well, maybe some other time.

B Listen again. Do the friends accept? Check Yes or No.

5 A new student

A Listen to an interview for an article in a student newspaper. Does Akemi have a large family?

MAX: Welcome to our school, Akemi!
AKEMI: Thank you.
MAX: Akemi, are your parents living in Japan now?
AKEMI: Yes, they are. They live in Kobe.
MAX: What about the rest of your family?
AKEMI: Well, my brother and I are living here in Los Angeles. My sister is going to school in Tokyo. She is studying the piano.
MAX: Do you have any aunts and uncles?
AKEMI: Yes, I have five. They are living in Japan. But one aunt and uncle are traveling in the U.S. They are visiting me this week.
MAX: What about your cousins?
AKEMI: I have a lot of cousins in Japan. A few of my cousins are going to school in the U.S.
MAX: What are they studying?
AKEMI: They are studying English, like me!

B Listen again. Correct the nine mistakes in the article.

6 Take a quiz!

A Listen to the questions. Write the activities you hear.

WOMAN: Are you a couch potato? Find out now!

1. How long do you usually exercise every day?
2. Do you ever play tennis?
3. How often do you swim?
4. How often do you go to the gym?
5. Do you ever go jogging?
6. How well do you ride a bicycle?
7. How often do you do aerobics?
8. How good are you at yoga?

B Now take the quiz! Listen again. Circle your responses.

7 Computer thief!

A Listen to a police officer interview Mike Doe. Number the events of each day from 1 to 5 in the order they happened.

OFFICER: OK, Mr. Doe. Did you take a desktop computer from your office over the weekend?
MIKE: A desktop computer? Of course not!
OFFICER: Tell me then, how did you spend your weekend?
MIKE: Let's see. I worked at the office Saturday morning.
OFFICER: Were there other people at your office on Saturday?
MIKE: No, there weren't. I was alone. I left at 2:00.
OFFICER: What did you do after that?
MIKE: I went shopping with a friend, and then I walked home alone.
OFFICER: Was anyone at home with you?
MIKE: No. I live alone.
OFFICER: What did you do Saturday night?
MIKE: I cooked dinner at home. And then I watched TV.
OFFICER: Did you go anywhere on Sunday?
MIKE: Well, I did laundry in the morning. Then around 1:00 I spent some time with friends at the park.
OFFICER: How long were you there?
MIKE: About an hour. Then I stopped at the office for a minute.
OFFICER: You were at the office again on Sunday? Did anyone see you there?
MIKE: Yes. My boss was there.
OFFICER: Then what did you do?
MIKE: I walked home and watched some DVDs. Then I went to bed.
OFFICER: I see, Mr. Doe. You can go now. Thank you for your time.

B Listen again. Do you think Mike took the computer? Why or why not?

8 I'm lost.

A Listen to people ask for the location of the places below. Where do you think they are?

1. MAN: Excuse me. I'm looking for the post office.
WOMAN: There's one on the corner of Lincoln and Third Street. It's next to the hotel.

2. WOMAN: Is there a travel agency near here?
MAN: Yeah, there's one on Second Street. It's between Washington and Lincoln, across from the bank.

3. MAN: Where can I find a grocery store?
WOMAN: There's one between Lincoln and Jefferson, on First Street. It's opposite the theater.

4. WOMAN: Are there any music stores around here?
MAN: Yeah, there's one on Jefferson, between Second and Third, next to the library.

5. MAN: Where can I find a good bookstore?
WOMAN: There's one on the corner of Clinton and Third, across from a gym.

6. WOMAN: I'm looking for a laundromat. Is there one nearby?
MAN: There's one on Second Street, between the bank and a drugstore.

7. WOMAN: Is there a café in the neighborhood?
MAN: Sure, there are a couple. There's one on Third Street, across from the post office. There's another one on Lincoln, behind the theater.

8. MAN: Where can I find a pay phone?
WOMAN: There are a lot nearby. There's one on Jefferson, across from the library. There's another next to the gym on Third Street. And there's another one on Third Street next to the school.

B Listen again. Draw the places on the map.

9 I can't find her.

A Listen to the descriptions. Match the names with the pictures.

1. WOMAN: Hey, where's Walter?
MAN: Who's Walter?
WOMAN: He's a friend from yoga class.
MAN: What does he look like?
WOMAN: He's short, with curly brown hair. He's usually casually dressed.
MAN: Is he the one in jeans, talking to Sarah?
WOMAN: Oh, yes. That's Walter. Come on. I'll introduce you.

2. MAN: Hey, Joe, which woman is your girlfriend?
JOE: Hmm. I don't see Mariela. She's wearing black pants and a white shirt. She's very classic.
MAN: How tall is she?
JOE: She's about medium height, with straight blond hair.
MAN: How long is her hair?
JOE: It's pretty long.
MAN: Oh, there she is, on the couch. Let's go and say hello.

3. MAN: I think Marcus is here. Do you see him?
WOMAN: Who's Marcus?
MAN: He's my brother.
WOMAN: What does he look like?
MAN: He's pretty tall, with red hair. He's a little bald.
WOMAN: What is he wearing?
MAN: He always wears a red shirt. He's very casual.
WOMAN: I think I see him, over there.
MAN: Yeah, that's him!

4. WOMAN 1: I can't find Simone.
WOMAN 2: Simone, hmm. Which one is Simone?
WOMAN 1: She's the woman with short black hair. You talked to her before, remember?
WOMAN 2: How tall is she?
WOMAN 1: She's really tall and wears funky clothes.
WOMAN 2: Oh, right! I remember. I saw her in the kitchen, talking to Joe.

B Listen again. What is each person's style? Write the correct word.

10 Have you ever . . . ?

A Listen to Katie and Phil interview for a job on a new adventure TV show. What countries have they visited? Write **K** for Katie and **P** for Phil.

MAN: Katie, Phil, you're both interviewing for the position of host for our new reality TV show, right?
KATIE/PHIL: That's right/Yes.
MAN: OK, well this job requires a lot of travel and knowledge of the world. Have you traveled to many places?
KATIE: Yes, I have. I've been all over Asia.
PHIL: I've been to Asia and South America.
MAN: Katie, where have you been in Asia?
KATIE: Well, I've been a few times: once to China, once to Thailand, and twice to Japan.
MAN: You've never been to Korea?
KATIE: No, I haven't.
PHIL: I have. And I've been to China, Japan, and Singapore.
MAN: What about South America? Have you been to Peru?
PHIL: I've never been to Peru, but I lived in Chile for a summer when I was in high school. From there I traveled to Brazil.
MAN: Now, our show is a little crazy, so it's important for you to know how to do different kinds of things. Have you ever driven a sports car?
KATIE: A sports car? Um, no, I haven't.
PHIL: I have.
MAN: Have you ever sung karaoke?
KATIE: Yes, I went to a lot of karaoke bars in Japan.
PHIL: Uh . . . no. I don't like karaoke.
MAN: Have you eaten many different kinds of food?
PHIL: No, not really.
KATIE: Yes, I've tried many exotic foods, mostly in Thailand. I love Japanese food, too.
MAN: Have you ever been on a camping trip in the mountains?
KATIE: Yes, I hiked in China for three days, and I've been camping here in the U.S.
PHIL: Uh, no, I've never been camping.
MAN: And have you ever ridden an elephant?
KATIE: Yes, in Thailand!
PHIL: Well, no. I'm, uh, afraid of elephants.
MAN: OK, that's all, Katie and Phil. Thank you for your time. We'll be in touch with you soon.

B Listen again. Check the answers. Who do you think will get the job?

11 Plan my vacation!

A Listen to Charles help Maya plan her vacation. What cities has Charles visited?

MAYA: Charles, you travel a lot, right? Do you want to help me plan my vacation? I have one week.
CHARLES: Sure. But you don't have a lot of time, so I suggest you stay in one place. Then you can visit all the museums and sights.
MAYA: I see. Well, what about London?
CHARLES: London is great, but it's *very* expensive. It's also very big.
MAYA: Do you think it will be too hot?
CHARLES: No, the weather is OK there. It's pretty cool.
MAYA: OK, so how about Cairo? I've heard it's really cheap.
CHARLES: Yeah, it is, but it's so crowded! It's extremely big and it's very hot.
MAYA: Oh. Well, what about New Orleans then?
CHARLES: New Orleans is somewhat expensive, but not too much.
MAYA: Is it a big city?
CHARLES: It's fairly small, so it's pretty easy to walk around. But it's hot and humid there.
MAYA: Hmm. I can't decide. I need to think about this some more.

B Listen again. What is each city like? Complete the chart.

12 What should we take?

A Listen to Dana and Hilary plan for a camping trip. What problems do they talk about?

DANA: Hey, Hilary, what else should we pack for our camping trip?
HILARY: Well, I think it's important to have a first-aid kit.
DANA: A first-aid kit? Really?
HILARY: Sure. It's important to be prepared for anything. We should take a bottle of aspirin. We could get a headache.
DANA: OK. Should we take anything for cuts? I always get cut when I camp.
HILARY: Let's take a tube of ointment.
DANA: Good idea.
HILARY: What else? Oh, it's good to bring cough drops in case someone gets a cold.
DANA: OK. And what about sore muscles? We'll be hiking a lot.
HILARY: We should take this lotion. I've used it before and it really works.
DANA: Should we take sunscreen? I don't want to get a sunburn.
HILARY: Definitely.
DANA: And what about insomnia?
HILARY: Insomnia? I think we'll sleep very well. But I suggest a book to read, just in case.
DANA: OK, that's it then. Wait a minute! There isn't any space for our clothes!

B Listen again. Match the problems to these items. Write the number in the box.

13 I can't eat spicy food.

A Listen to two people in a restaurant talk about their orders. Cross out the things they did *not* order.

NANCY: Hmm, what would you like to eat, Warren? Look, there's sweet and sour chicken, your favorite.
WARREN: I'm not in the mood for chicken tonight. I think I'll have the tofu curry.
NANCY: Oh, I don't know what to order.
WARREN: You could try the grilled tuna.
NANCY: I'm not crazy about seafood.
WARREN: Well, there's fried rice with vegetables.
NANCY: That's too greasy.
WARREN: What about the lamb kebabs? I love lamb.
NANCY: So do I. Hmm. That sounds good. I think I'll have the kebabs, then, and a green salad.
WARREN: Great, Nancy. Let's order. I'm starving!

B Listen again. Why didn't they order certain foods? For each thing you crossed out, write the reason next to it.

14 Chiang Mai it is!

A Listen to Kai and Nina talk about where to teach in Thailand. Check True or False for each statement.

NINA: Hey, Kai, you're from Thailand, right?
KAI: Yeah.
NINA: You know, I've applied to teach English there and I want to ask your opinion.
KAI: Sure, go ahead.
NINA: What are the largest cities in Thailand?
KAI: Well, Bangkok is the biggest, of course. There's also Chiang Mai. It's a lot smaller.
NINA: I've heard that the area around Chiang Mai is interesting. It's near the ocean, right?
KAI: No, it's in the mountains. It's the most famous place in Thailand for hiking.
NINA: I love to hike! How high are the mountains?
KAI: I think the highest is around 2,600 meters.
NINA: Wow. That's about 8,500 feet. And how hot is it in the summer?
KAI: Well, up in the mountains, it's not so bad, maybe 24 degrees Celsius during the day.
NINA: What about rain?
KAI: Summer is the rainy season, and it's wettest from June through October. Then it's drier for the rest of the year.
NINA: And how far is Chiang Mai from Bangkok?
KAI: Oh, about 400 miles. It takes a whole day on the train, but the countryside is beautiful.
NINA: It sounds perfect. I think I've decided, then. Chiang Mai it is!

B Listen again. For the statements you marked false, write the correct information.

15 I can't, because . . .

Listen to these telephone messages. There are two errors in each message. Correct the errors.

ANNE: [*recording*] Hi, this is Anne. Leave me a message! [*beep*]
KELLY: Hi, Anne, this is Kelly from school. We're playing baseball at 7:00 P.M. tonight. Can you find a babysitter? Please call me before 5:00 to tell me if you are going to play. Thanks! [*beep*]

ROBIN: [*recording*] Hello, this is Robin Hall. Please leave a message after the beep. [*beep*]
MARTIN: Robin, this is Martin. Would you please tell Dave to be sure he's at the company picnic on Tuesday? Afterward, we're going to discuss the company business plan. Thank you. [*beep*]

16 Past, present, or future

A Listen to Ricki and Will talk at a class reunion. Write past, present, or future below each picture.

WILL: Ricki! It's good to see you! You look great!
RICKI: Thanks, Will. I've changed a lot, haven't I?
WILL: You sure have. Your hair is much shorter now. And you don't wear glasses anymore.
RICKI: Yeah, I wear contact lenses now.
WILL: And I heard you have a new baby.
RICKI: Yeah, I got married five years ago, and I had my daughter six months ago. Her name is Ellen. My life is much busier now.
WILL: I can imagine. And are you still living in Miami?
RICKI: No, my husband changed jobs about a year ago, and we moved to New York last summer.
WILL: That's great. Are you working?
RICKI: No, not yet. But I'd love to start again in a few years. You know, when Ellen is older. We'd like to move to the country when she's ready for school.
WILL: Yeah. Well, what do you plan to do?
RICKI: You know, I'd like to open a travel agency. And I hope to work from home.
WILL: How are you going to do it?
RICKI: To start, I plan to get a bank loan. And right now, my husband is helping me find information on the Internet.

B Listen again. What does Ricki hope to do in the future? Correct these false statements.

Self-study answer key

1

A Australia, Brazil, Italy, Uruguay

B 1. Bobby 2. Sydney, Australia 3. Lagna 4. Florence, Italy

2

A/B

	M	*Tu*	*W*	*Th*	*F*	*Times*
go to work	✓	✓				3:30
take a computer class			✓		✓	7:00
work as a tour guide				✓		9:00
go to English class		✓	✓		✓	12:00

3

A black pants, cotton shirt, jeans, leather jacket, silk shirt, wool sweater

black pants	jeans	silk shirt
cotton shirt	leather jacket	wool sweater

B the third picture

4

A/B

	Event/ Activity	*Day*	*Time*	*Accept?*
Cam and Marla	movie	W	6:00	No
Lucy and Chris	jazz group	Th	8:30	Yes
Ed and Joanna	R&B concert	Sa	3:00	No

5

A Yes

B

1. ~~Tokyo~~ Kobe
2. ~~Osaka~~ Los Angeles
3. ~~the violin~~ the piano
4. ~~Miami~~ Tokyo
5. ~~seven~~ five
6. ~~niece and nephew~~ aunt and uncle
7. ~~Australia~~ Japan
8. ~~Mexico~~ the U.S.
9. ~~French~~ English

6

A

1. exercise
2. play tennis
3. swim
4. go to the gym
5. go jogging
6. ride a bicycle
7. do aerobics
8. yoga

B Answers will vary.

7

A

Saturday
2 He went shopping.
5 He watched TV.
1 He worked.
3 He walked home.
4 He cooked dinner at home.

Sunday
3 He stopped at the office.
5 He went to bed.
1 He did laundry.
2 He spent time at the park.
4 He walked home and watched DVDs.

B (Possible answer) Mike didn't take the computer. He was at the office twice but walked home both times. A desktop computer is too heavy to carry home.

8

A (Possible answer) the city center

B (See script to check answers.)

9

A/B Walter: third person (casual)
Mariela: fourth person (classic)
Marcus: first person (casual)
Simone: second person (funky)

10

A Katie: China, Japan, Thailand
Phil: Brazil, Chile, China, Japan, Korea, Singapore

B

	Katie		*Phil*	
	Yes	*No*	*Yes*	*No*
1. Have they ever driven a sports car?		✓	✓	
2. Have they ever sung karaoke?	✓			✓
3. Have they eaten different kinds of foods?	✓			✓
4. Have they been camping?	✓			✓
5. Have they ridden an elephant?	✓			✓

11

A London, Cairo, and New Orleans

B

	Cost	*Size*	*Weather*
London	very expensive	very big	OK, pretty cool
Cairo	really cheap	extremely big	very hot
New Orleans	somewhat expensive	fairly small	quite hot and humid

12

A/B

1. a headache (aspirin)
2. cuts (ointment)
3. a cold (cough drops)
4. sore muscles (lotion)
5. a sunburn (sunscreen)
6. insomnia (a book)

13

A/B ~~sweet and sour chicken~~ (He's not in the mood for chicken.)
~~grilled tuna~~ (She's not crazy about seafood.)
~~fried rice with vegetables~~ (It's too greasy.)

14

A/B

1. False (Bangkok is larger than Chiang Mai.)
2. False (Chiang Mai is in the mountains.)
3. True
4. False (The highest mountain is 8,500 feet.)
5. False (It's wettest from June through October.)
6. True

15

Message for Anne
~~yoga class~~ school
~~tomorrow~~ tonight

Message for Robin
~~Thursday~~ Tuesday
~~beach party~~ business plan

16

A

1. past
2. present
3. past
4. present
5. future
6. future

B

1. She'd like to start working in a few years.
2. She wants to open a travel agency.
3. She hopes to work from home.
4. She plans to get a bank loan.

Games

How can you create a fun and lively atmosphere in the classroom?

Games provide stimulating ways to practice a variety of skills, including vocabulary, grammar, speaking, and listening. Classic and innovative games, such as Twenty Questions, Hot Potato, and Change Chairs, add enjoyment to learning. Depending on the teacher's goals, games can be used as a warm-up, as additional practice, or as a review.

These 20 Games can be adapted for use with different skills and with different levels. Unlike the Photocopiables, handouts are not usually required.

Games	Use to practice	Use with
1. Kim's Game	Vocabulary	Intro Level
2. Line Up!	Vocabulary, Grammar, Speaking	Levels Intro - 1
3. Sculptures	Vocabulary, Grammar	Levels Intro - 1
4. Concentration	Vocabulary, Grammar	Levels Intro - 1
5. Simon Says	Vocabulary, Listening	Levels Intro - 1
6. Change Chairs	Vocabulary, Listening	Levels Intro - 1
7. Chain Game	Vocabulary, Grammar, Listening	Levels Intro - 2
8. Twenty Questions	Grammar, Speaking, Listening	Levels 1 - 2
9. Ask the Right Question	Grammar	Levels 2 - 3
10. Split Sentences	Grammar	Levels 2 - 3
11. Just One Minute	Speaking, Listening	Levels 2 - 3
12. Prediction Bingo	Listening, Reading	Level 3
13. Bingo	Listening, Vocabulary	All levels
14. Hot Potato	Grammar, Speaking	All levels
15. Picture It!	Vocabulary	All levels
16. Vocabulary Tennis	Vocabulary	All levels
17. Run For It!	Grammar	All levels
18. Mime	Vocabulary, Grammar	All levels
19. Tic-Tac-Toe	Vocabulary, Grammar, Pronunciation	All levels
20. True or False?	Grammar, Speaking, Listening	All levels

1 KIM'S GAME

Aim: *Improve Ss' ability to remember vocabulary.*
Level: *Intro*
Preparation: *Bring objects (or pictures of objects) to class.*
Comment: *Use to review vocabulary.*

- Put the objects on your desk and cover them.
- Explain the task. Uncover the objects and ask Ss to look at them for three minutes. Then cover them. In pairs, Ss list the objects they remember. Set a three-minute time limit.
- Ss complete the task.
- Uncover the objects. The pair with the most correct words wins.

Variation 1: Write words on the board. Then erase them.

Variation 2: Put a picture with a lot of details on your desk. Ss use a specific structure (e.g., *there is/ there are*, prepositions of place) to write sentences about the objects.

2 LINE UP!

Aim: *Give Ss practice using a variety of skills in an active way.*
Levels: *Intro and 1*
Preparation: *None*
Comment: *Use to review vocabulary and practice grammar and speaking.*

- Review or teach these expressions: *You're in front of / behind me.*
- Write a question on the board. For example: *What time do you get up?*
- Explain the task. Ss go around the class and ask each other the question on the board. Then they stand in line according to the answers (e.g., in time order). Point out that the board is the beginning and the other end of the classroom is the end (e.g., of the day).
- Model the task with a few Ss.
- Explain that when two answers are the same, Ss stand in alphabetical order of their first names.
- Ss complete the task.
- Ask Ss to explain their position in line. For example: "I'm number 1. I get up at 5:00."

Variations: Use this game to practice the alphabet (e.g., *What's your last name?*), dates (e.g., *When's your birthday?*), lengths of time (e.g., *How long do you sleep each night?*), and structures (e.g., *How many phone calls have you made today?*).

Acknowledgment: *Idea adapted from* The Grammar Activity Book *by Bob Obee, Cambridge University Press.*

3 SCULPTURES

Aim: *Give Ss practice reviewing vocabulary in an active way.*
Levels: *Intro and 1*
Preparation: *List vocabulary you want to review.*
Comment: *Use to review vocabulary and grammar.*

- Divide the class into teams of three.
- Explain the task. Whisper an activity to one S (e.g., *play soccer*). This S whispers the activity to the other Ss on his or her team. The team has one minute to form a sculpture that illustrates the activity (e.g., S1 pretends to kick a ball, S2 pretends to be a goalkeeper). The other teams guess the activity. The first team to guess correctly gets a point.
- Model the task with one team.
- Play the game until you use all the vocabulary. The team with the most points wins.

Variation 1: Use this game to review vocabulary such as household chores, celebrations, or entertainment.

Variation 2: Ask Ss to use specific grammar structures when guessing the activity (e.g., present continuous, simple past).

4 CONCENTRATION

Aim: *Give Ss practice reviewing vocabulary and grammar in a fun way.*
Levels: *Intro and 1*
Preparation: *Make one set of cards for each group of Ss. Two cards in each set match (e.g., word + picture, word + definition, word + opposite).*
Comment: *Use to review vocabulary and grammar.*

- Ss work in groups of four. Give each group a set of cards. Ask the Ss to put all their cards face down on a desk.
- Explain the task. Ss take turns choosing two cards, turning them over, and saying the words. If the two cards match, they keep the pair of cards and take another turn. If the cards don't match, they put them face down again, and the next S takes a turn.
- Model the task with one group.
- Ss play the game. The S in each group with the most cards wins.

Variation: After Ss match cards, they use the word in a sentence with a specific verb tense (e.g., simple present).

5 SIMON SAYS

Aim: *Give Ss active practice developing listening skills.*
Levels: *Intro and 1*
Preparation: *None*
Comment: *Use to review vocabulary and practice listening.*

- Ss stand up.
- Explain the task. Give an instruction. If you start the instruction with "Simon says" (e.g., "Simon says touch your toes."), Ss follow the instruction. If you give the instruction without "Simon says" (e.g., "Touch your toes."), Ss do nothing.
- Explain that Ss sit down if they follow the instruction when you don't say "Simon says." They also sit down if they do the wrong action (e.g., they touch their knees instead of their toes).
- Model the game with a few instructions.
- Play the game. The last student standing wins.

Variation 1: Use this game to review action verbs (e.g., *sing*, *swim*) or sports (e.g., *play tennis*).

Variation 2: The winning S stands at the front of the class and gives the instructions for the next game.

6 CHANGE CHAIRS

Aim: *Review vocabulary and improve listening in an active way.*
Levels: *Intro and 1*
Preparation: *None*
Comment: *Use with classes of six or more Ss to review vocabulary and improve listening.*

- Ask Ss to move their chairs in a circle, facing the center. Stand in the middle.
- Explain the task. Give an instruction that starts with "Change chairs" (e.g., "Change chairs if you are wearing jeans."). All Ss wearing jeans stand up and change chairs.
- Model the task a few times.
- Ask one S to stand up. Take away his or her chair.
- Explain the task. The S without a chair stands in the center and gives the next instruction (e.g., "Change chairs if you have one brother."). This time, the S in the center also tries to sit down. The S left without a chair stands in the center and gives the next instruction.
- Model the task.
- Ss play the game.

Variation: Use this game to review specific categories of vocabulary (e.g., clothes, hobbies).

7 CHAIN GAME

Aim: *Give Ss listening practice while reviewing vocabulary.*
Levels: *Intro, 1, and 2*
Preparation: *None*
Comment: *Use to review vocabulary and practice grammar and listening.*

- Ss sit in circles in small groups.
- Explain the task. S1 makes a sentence. S2 repeats the sentence and adds to it. S3 repeats S2's sentence and adds to it. For example:
  S1: Last weekend I went dancing.
  S2: Last weekend I went dancing and read a book.
  S3: Last weekend I went dancing, read a book, and . . .
  Ss continue until a S can't remember what to say. Then the next S continues the sentence.
- Point out that the information in the sentence can be false.
- Model the game with one group.
- Ss play the game.

Variations: Use this activity to review specific groups of vocabulary, such as food (e.g., *I like . . .*), clothes (e.g., *I went to the store and I bought . . .*), or family members (e.g., *Tonight I'm going to call . . .*).

8 TWENTY QUESTIONS

Aim: *Give Ss practice asking yes/no questions.*
Levels: *1 and 2*
Preparation: *None*
Comment: *Use to practice grammar, speaking, and listening.*

- Ss work in small groups.
- Explain the task. One S in each group thinks of a famous person. The other Ss ask yes/no questions to guess the person. For example: "Is it a man? Is he a singer? Is he from Canada?" The S only answers "yes" or "no." The S who correctly guesses the person gets a point and thinks of the next famous person.
- Model the task. Think of a famous person and the class asks yes/no questions.
- Ss play the game. The S in each group with the most points wins.

Variation 1: Write famous people's names on pieces of paper (one name per paper, one paper per S). Attach the papers to the Ss' backs. Ss go around the room and ask yes/no questions to guess the name (e.g., "Am I a man?").

Variation 2: Use this game to practice present tense (e.g., *Is she an actress?*), past tense (e.g., *Was she an actress?*), or infinitives and gerunds (e.g., *Is it used to send information? Is it used for sending information?*).

9 ASK THE RIGHT QUESTION

Aim: *Give Ss practice making Wh-questions.*
Levels: *2 and 3*
Preparation: *Bring three index cards for each S.*
Comment: *Use to practice grammar.*

- Write this statement on the board:
  Evan's a chef at Ricky's Restaurant.
- Elicit Wh-questions that the statement could answer (e.g., "Where does Evan work? What does Evan do? Who's the chef at Ricky's Restaurant?").
- Give each S three index cards. Ss write one statement on each card that could answer several Wh-questions. Go around the class and give help as needed.
- Collect all the cards and mix them up. Then divide the class into two teams (A and B).
- Explain the game. S1 from Team A chooses a card and reads the statement aloud. S1 from Team B makes a Wh-question for it. If the question is correct, Team B gets a point. If it is not correct, S1 from Team A makes a Wh-question. If the question is correct, Team A gets a point. Then S2 from Team B chooses a card.
- Model the game a few times.
- Play the game until you use all the cards. The team with the most points wins.

10 SPLIT SENTENCES

Aim: *Help Ss understand complex sentences.*
Levels: *2 and 3*
Preparation: *Write ten complex sentences and split them in half. Make sets of the split sentences (one per three Ss). Put each set in an envelope.*
Comment: *Use to practice grammar.*

- Model the task with split sentences.
  For example:

If I found a wallet,	*I would call the police.*
If I saw a ghost,	*I would scream.*
If I were rich,	*I would share my wealth.*

- Ss work in teams of three. Give each group a set of split sentences.
- Ask each group to match the split sentences.
- Ss complete the task.
- The first team to match the split sentences correctly wins.

Variations: Use this game to practice specific complex structures, such as conditionals, passives, two-part verbs, and tag questions.

11 JUST ONE MINUTE

Aim: *Help Ss develop oral fluency and listening skills.*
Levels: *2 and 3*
Preparation: *Bring a clock or watch with a second hand to class.*
Comment: *Use to practice speaking and listening.*

- Write a topic on the board (e.g., customs, food, transportation).
- Explain the game. Ss work in pairs. S1 talks about the topic for one minute. Point out that S1 cannot repeat ideas, change the topic, or hesitate for more than five seconds. S2 listens for repetition, topic changes, or hesitations. After one minute, say, "Stop!" If S1 talked without any repetition, topic changes, or hesitations, he or she gets a point.
- Play the game. S2 tells S1 about any repetition, topic changes, or hesitations. If there are none, S1 gets a point.
- The Ss in each pair change roles. Write another topic on the board and S2 talks for one minute.
- Play the game with a few more topics. The S in each pair with the most points wins.

Variation 1: Write several topics on the board. S1 chooses a topic from the board.

Variation 2: At the end of each game, a S chooses the next topic.

12 PREDICTION BINGO

Aim: *Give Ss practice predicting the content of an audio program or text.*
Level: *3*
Preparation: *None*
Comment: *Use to practice listening or reading.*

- Tell Ss the topic of the audio program they will listen to or the text they will read (e.g., our lives in the future).
- Explain the task. Each S draws a bingo card with nine squares. Ss predict content words (i.e., nouns, verbs, adjectives) related to the topic individually. Then they write one word in each square.
  For example:

robots	*cell phones*	*computers*
school	*work*	*cars*
money	*travel*	*time*

- Ss listen to the audio program or read the text. When Ss hear or see a word that's on their bingo card, they circle it.
- The S with the most circled words wins.

Variation: Ss make bingo cards in pairs. Then they exchange cards with another pair.

BINGO

Aim: *Help Ss improve listening and vocabulary in a fun way.*
Levels: *All*
Preparation: *Prepare a list of at least 15 words you want to review.*
Comment: *Use to practice listening and vocabulary.*

- Tell Ss to draw a bingo card on a piece of paper:

- Read and spell each word on your list. Then make a sentence with it. For example, say: "Family. F-A-M-I-L-Y. There are three people in my family."
- Ss listen and write each word in a different square on their bingo cards. Point out that they can write the words in any order.
- Play the game. Read out the words from your list in a different order. As you read each word aloud, spell it and use it in a sentence. Ss circle the words on their cards. (Note: Cross the words off your list, so you can check Ss' cards later.) The first S to circle all the words in one row shouts "Bingo!" If the words are correct, the student wins.

Variation 1: Use this game to review vocabulary, the alphabet, sounds, numbers, or grammar (e.g., verb forms).

Variation 2: Instead of reading out the word, read out a definition. For example, when you say "This is the opposite of *hot*," Ss circle *cold*.

14 HOT POTATO

Aim: *Give Ss practice asking and answering questions.*
Levels: *All*
Preparation: *Write questions on ten pieces of paper (one per paper). Then wrap the papers around each other to make a paper ball. Bring music and a cassette or CD player to class.*
Comment: *Use to practice grammar and speaking.*

- Ss sit in a circle.
- Explain the game. While you play music, Ss throw the paper ball to each other. When you stop the music, the S holding the ball takes off the outside piece of paper, reads the question, and answers it. Then start the music and the Ss throw the paper ball again.
- Model the game, then play the game until Ss answer all ten questions.

Variation: Use this game to practice specific structures (e.g., present perfect, passives, and conditionals).

15 PICTURE IT!

Aim: *Help Ss understand vocabulary in a visual way.*
Levels: *All*
Preparation: *Make sets of vocabulary cards (one per four Ss). Put each set in an envelope.*
Comment: *Use to review vocabulary.*

- Ss work in groups of four. Give each group a set of cards.
- Explain the rules. One S in each group chooses a card and draws a picture of the word on a piece of paper. The other Ss try to guess the word. The first S to guess the word correctly gets a point and chooses the next card.
- Point out that the S drawing the picture cannot write numbers or letters, talk, or make gestures.
- Model the task by drawing a picture of a word on the board. The class guesses the word.
- Play the game until Ss use all the cards. The S in each group with the most points wins.

Variation: Use one set of cards. Divide the class into two teams (A and B). One S from Team A chooses a card and draws the picture on the board. The Ss in Team A have two minutes to guess the word. If they guess correctly, Team A gets a point. Repeat with Team B and continue until Ss use all cards. The team with the most points wins.

16 VOCABULARY TENNIS

Aim: *Help Ss review categories of words in a fun way.*
Levels: *All*
Preparation: *None*
Comment: *Use to review vocabulary.*

- Divide the class into two teams (A and B).
- Explain the game. Call out a category (e.g., jobs). Team A "serves" by saying a word in that category (e.g., teacher). Team B "returns the serve" by saying a different word from that category (e.g., nurse). The teams take turns saying words from the category.
- The game continues until one team can't think of any more words. The other team gets a point.
- Call out a different category (e.g., colors, furniture, leisure activities, adjectives) and play the game again.
- The team with the most points wins.

Variation: Bring a balloon to class. Teams A and B stand on opposite sides of the room. When Team A says a word, it "serves" the balloon to Team B. Team B must say a different word before the balloon reaches its side of the room. If Team B doesn't say a word or drops the balloon, Team A gets a point.

17 RUN FOR IT!

Aim: *Help Ss practice prepositions of time.*
Levels: *All*
Preparation: *Prepare a list of sentences with missing prepositions. Write each missing preposition on a separate card and post the cards around the classroom walls.*
Comment: *Use to practice grammar.*

- Divide Ss into two teams (A and B). Assign each member of the teams a number (e.g., S1, S2).
- Read out the first sentence without saying the preposition (e.g., "I always get up BLANK 6 A.M. on weekdays."). S1 from each team runs to find the card containing the missing preposition. The first S to reach the correct card gets a point for his or her team.
- Play the game until you use all the sentences. The team with the most points wins.

Variation 1: Use this game to review prepositions of place or time, modals, and auxiliaries (e.g., *do*, *did*, *have*).

Variation 2: If Ss cannot move freely around the room, they can point to the correct wall.

18 MIME

Aim: *Help Ss personalize and review vocabulary and grammar in an active way.*
Levels: *All*
Preparation: *Make sets of vocabulary cards (one per four Ss). Put each set in an envelope.*
Comment: *Use to review vocabulary and grammar.*

- Ss work in groups of four. Give each group a set of cards.
- Explain the rules. One S in each group chooses a card and mimes the activity (e.g., wash your hair, watch a comedy on TV). The first S to guess the activity correctly keeps the card and chooses the next one.
- Point out that Ss cannot speak while they are miming words.
- Ss continue until they use all the cards. The S with the most cards wins.

Variation 1: Use this game to review specific structures, such as present continuous (e.g., *She is washing her hair.*) or simple past vs. past continuous (e.g., *He was cooking when the phone rang.*).

Variation 2: Ss make sets of vocabulary cards in small groups. Then they exchange cards with another group, and mime the activities on the new cards.

19 TIC-TAC-TOE

Aim: *Help Ss review words in a fun way.*
Levels: *All*
Preparation: *Make a list of words you want to review.*
Comment: *Use to review vocabulary and practice grammar and pronunciation.*

- Draw a chart with nine squares on the board. Write one word in each square. For example:

know	give	think
fall	feel	buy
catch	sing	swim

- Divide the class into two teams (X and O).
- Explain the game. Team X chooses a word on the board (e.g., *buy*) and uses it in a specific way (e.g., changes the verb tense or uses it in a sentence). If the answer is correct, replace the word *buy* with an X. If the answer is incorrect, Team O tries to give the correct answer. If Team O's answer is correct, replace the word *buy* with an O. If neither team gives the correct answer, tell Ss the answer. Then replace the word *buy* with a different word.
- Play the game. The first team to get a straight line of three Xs or Os (across, down, or diagonally) wins.

Variation: Use this game to review question words (e.g., *what*, *where*) modals (e.g., *would*, *could*), adverbs of frequency, pronunciation (e.g., pronunciation of words, rhyming words), and vocabulary.

20 TRUE OR FALSE?

Aim: *Give Ss practice using grammar in a personalized way.*
Levels: *All*
Preparation: *None*
Comment: *Use to practice grammar, speaking, and listening.*

- Each S writes six statements about themselves. Three statements are true and three are false. For example:
  I can sing really well.
  I have three sisters.
- Explain the game. Ss take turns reading their statements aloud in small groups. The other Ss guess which statements are true and which are false. Ss get one point for each correct guess.
- Ss play the game. The S in each group with the most points wins.

! Fresh ideas

How can you tailor your classes to your students' needs, learning styles, and ages?

Fresh ideas provide innovative ways to teach a variety of exercises in the Student's Book. Techniques such as Disappearing Dialog, Onion Ring, and Jigsaw Learning make classes livelier, more interactive, and more varied. Depending on the exercise, these techniques can either supplement or replace the suggestions in the page-by-page teaching notes.

These 20 Fresh ideas can be adapted for use with different exercises and with different levels. Unlike the Photocopiables, handouts are not usually required.

Fresh ideas	Use with	Use with
1. Look Up and Speak!	Conversations	All levels
2. Say It With Feeling!	Conversations	All levels
3. Moving Dialog	Conversations	All levels
4. Musical Dialog	Conversations	All levels
5. Substitution Dialog	Conversations, Grammar Focuses	All levels
6. Disappearing Dialog	Conversations, Grammar Focuses	All levels
7. Onion Ring	Conversations, Discussions	All levels
8. Stand Up, Sit Down	Listenings	All levels
9. Walking Stress	Pronunciations	All levels
10. Question Exchange	Grammar Focuses	All levels
11. Reading Race	Readings, Perspectives	All levels
12. Jigsaw Learning	Readings, Listenings	Levels 1 - 3
13. Running Dictation	Readings, Perspectives	Levels 1 - 3
14. Vocabulary Mingle	Readings, Perspectives	Levels 1 - 3
15. Time Out!	Role Plays	Levels 1 - 3
16. Pass the Paper	Writings	Levels 1 - 3
17. Mind Mapping	Writings, Word Powers	Levels 1 - 3
18. Picture Dictation	Snapshots, Word Powers	Levels 1 - 3
19. Vocabulary Steps	Snapshots, Word Powers	All levels
20. Cloud Prediction	Conversations, Listenings, or Readings	All levels

1 LOOK UP AND SPEAK!

Aim: *Encourage Ss to look at their partners while practicing Conversations.*
Levels: *All*
Preparation: *None*
Comment: *Use with Conversations.*

- Point out that it's important to look at your partner when speaking.
- Explain the task. Ss work in pairs. S1 looks briefly at the first line of the conversation and tries to remember it. Then S1 looks up at S2 and says the line. S2 looks briefly at the next line of conversation, tries to remember it, and then looks up and says it.
- Model the task with one or two Ss.
- Ss complete the task in pairs.

Note: This technique works best when Ss stand up and face each other. It's a useful way to help Ss develop eye contact while speaking.

2 SAY IT WITH FEELING!

Aim: *Improve Ss' pronunciation, intonation, and understanding of a Conversation in an enjoyable way.*
Levels: *All*
Preparation: *None*
Comment: *Use with Conversations.*

- Explain the task. Ss listen to the audio program, focusing on the speakers' intonation and emotions (e.g., anger, surprise).
- Play the audio program. Ask Ss to repeat selected phrases with the correct intonation. Encourage them to exaggerate the intonation. They can also add gestures, if appropriate.
- Ss practice the conversation in pairs, using lots of intonation. Then they change roles and practice again.

Option: Ask pairs of Ss to perform the conversation in front of the class. The class votes for the best performance.

3 MOVING DIALOG

Aim: *Give Ss more speaking practice with different Ss.*
Levels: *All*
Preparation: *None*
Comment: *Use with Conversations.*

- Explain the task. Ss stand in two lines (A and B), facing each other. Then they practice the conversation.
- When you clap, the Ss in line A all move one step to their right. One S at the end of line A will not have a partner. He or she runs quickly to the beginning of line A.
- Ss practice the conversation with new partners.
- Continue as many times as needed.

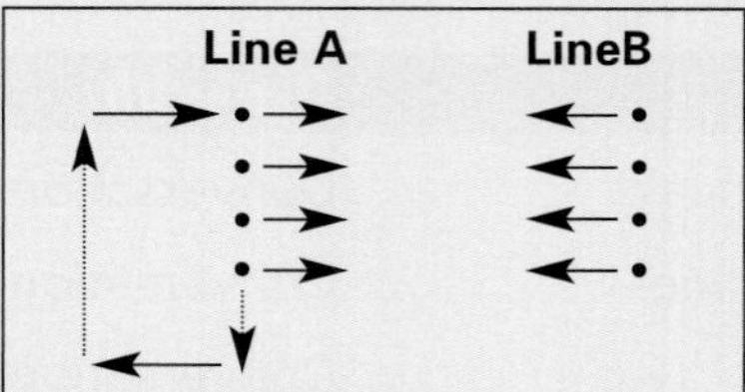

4 MUSICAL DIALOG

Aim: *Give Ss conversation practice in a natural and fun setting.*
Levels: *All*
Preparation: *Bring party music and a cassette or CD player to class.*
Comment: *Use with Conversations that could take place at a party (e.g., introductions, invitations, or discussions about childhood, daily routines, or families).*

- Explain the task. Ss move around the room while you play music. When you stop the music, they begin conversations with the S closest to them. They use the conversation in the Student Book as a model, substituting information about themselves.
- Model the task with one or two Ss.
- Play the party music. Stop the music every 20 or 30 seconds for Ss to complete the task.
- Continue as many times as needed.

Variation: Play the music without stopping. When you turn up the volume, Ss shout to begin conversations with the Ss closest to them.

5 SUBSTITUTION DIALOG

Aim: *Give Ss controlled practice with new structures.*
Levels: *All*
Preparation: *Choose four to six words or phrases to substitute.*
Comment: *Use with Conversations or Grammar Focus exercises that involve conversations.*

- After completing the Conversation or Grammar Focus conversation, tell Ss to underline and number the words or phrases you chose. For example:
  Customer: I'd like a hamburger (1), please.
  Waiter: All right. And would you like a salad (2)?
- Write substitutions for the underlined words on the board. For example:
  (1) a chicken sandwich/some french fries/ . . .
  (2) some soup/an appetizer/ . . .
- Explain the task. Ss practice the conversation twice using the substitutions on the board. Then they practice it using their own ideas.
- Model the task. Then Ss complete the task in pairs.

6 DISAPPEARING DIALOG

Aim: *Give Ss confidence using new vocabulary and grammar.*
Levels: *All*
Preparation: *None*
Comment: *Use with Conversations or Grammar Focus exercises that involve conversations.*

- After completing the Conversation or Grammar Focus conversation, write all or part of it on the board.
- Explain the task. Ss work in pairs. They take turns practicing the conversation on the board repeatedly. As they practice, gradually erase words from the board.
- Ss practice the conversation. Erase one word per line each time they practice. For example:
  A: Good morning. How are you?
  B: I'm just fine. Thank you. . . .
  becomes
  A: Good morning. ______ are you?
  B: I'm just fine. ______ you. . . .
- Erase more words. Gradually Ss will be able to practice the conversation without support.

Variation: Divide the class into two teams. One S from each team reads the conversation while you erase the words. When a S can't remember a word, the other team gets a point. The team with the most points wins.

7 ONION RING

Aim: *Give Ss more practice speaking with different Ss.*
Levels: *All*
Preparation: *None*
Comment: *Use with Conversations or Discussions.*

- Divide the class into two groups, A and B.
- The groups stand in two circles, one inside the other. Ss in Group A bring their books and make a circle around the classroom, facing inward. Ss in Group B bring their books and make an inside circle. Each S in Group B faces a S from Group A.

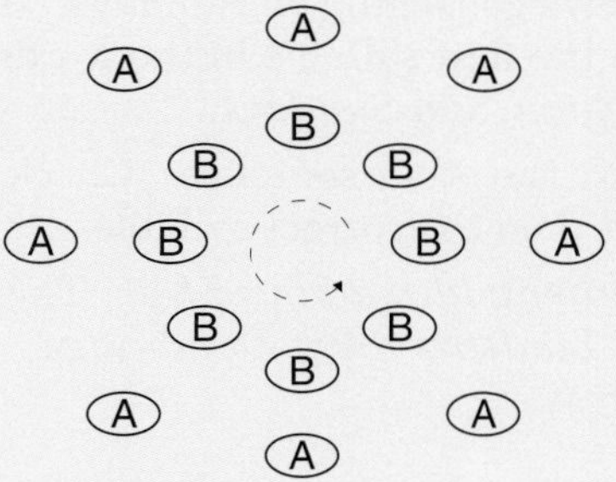

- Explain the task. Ss practice the conversation in pairs. When you say "Change!," Ss in Group B move to the left and practice the conversation with new partners from Group A.
- Ss practice the conversation. Call out "Change!" when most Ss complete the conversation.

Variation: Only Ss in Group A bring their books. Ss in Group B improvise the conversation.

8 STAND UP, SIT DOWN

Aim: *Focus Ss' attention on listening for specific sounds.*
Levels: *All*
Preparation: *None*
Comment: *Use with Listenings.*

- Ss complete the Listening exercises.
- Explain the task. Ss listen to the audio program again, focusing on a specific sound (e.g., [θ]). They stand up and sit down whenever they hear the sound.
- Model the task. Play a little of the audio program and demonstrate when to stand up and sit down.
- Play the audio program. Ss carry out the task.

Variation 1: Ss can also listen for other things, such as verb tenses (e.g., simple past), times, prices, pronouns, numbers, days, or types of words.

Variation 2: Divide the class into two groups (A and B). Each group listens for a different thing (e.g., Group A listens for [θ] and Group B listens for [ð]; Group A listens for simple past and Group B listens for past continuous).

9 WALKING STRESS

Aim: *Raise Ss' awareness of sentence stress in an active and fun way.*
Levels: *All*
Preparation: *None*
Comment: *Use with Pronunciations that focus on sentence stress.*

- Play the audio program. Focus Ss' attention on the sentence stress.
- Explain the task. Ss stand up and move to a place where they can move freely. Then model the task. Say: "I always go jogging on Sundays." Step forward on the first syllable in the words *always*, *jogging*, and *Sundays*.
- Read or play the other sentences. Check that Ss walk forward on the correct syllables.

Acknowledgment: *Idea adapted from* The Standby Book *by Seth Lindstromberg, Cambridge University Press.*

10 QUESTION EXCHANGE

Aim: *Give Ss practice making and answering questions.*
Levels: *All*
Preparation: *Write one verb or phrase for each S on pieces of paper.*
Comment: *Use with Grammar Focuses that involve questions.*

- After presenting the Grammar Focus, write the grammar structure on the board. For example:
  How often do you ________ ?
- Give each S a piece of paper with a different verb or phrase (e.g., *play sports*).
- Explain the task. Ss go around the room and find a partner. They take turns asking and answering questions using the structure on the board and the word or phrase on their piece of papers. For example:
  How often do you play sports?
  Then Ss exchange papers and find a new partner.
- Model the task with one or two Ss.
- Ss complete the task. Continue until Ss exchange papers with most of their classmates.
- Elicit interesting answers from the class.

Option: Encourage Ss to ask follow-up questions.

Acknowledgment: *Idea adapted from* Teaching Multilevel Classes *by Natalie Hess, Cambridge University Press.*

11 READING RACE

Aim: *Give Ss practice reading for specific information.*
Levels: *All*
Preparation: *Photocopy and enlarge the text. Cut the copy into paragraphs and post the paragraphs around the classroom walls. Prepare and copy a handout with 6 to 12 comprehension questions about the text (one handout per S).*
Comment: *Use with Readings or Perspectives that have several short texts.*

- Books closed. Distribute the handout and explain the task. Ss go around the class with their handouts, scan the texts, and answer the questions. The first S to correctly answer all the questions wins.
- Model the task with the first question. Then Ss complete the task.
- Ss check their answers by reading the texts in their Student's Books.

12 JIGSAW LEARNING

Aim: *Give Ss practice using all four skills in a collaborative way.*
Levels: *1, 2, and 3*
Preparation: *None*
Comment: *Use with Readings or Listenings that can be divided into three or four short texts.*

- Draw a chart on the board. List the texts at the top and things you want Ss to find on the left. For example:

	Text A	Text B	Text C
Topic			
Problem			

  Ss copy the chart on a piece of paper.
- Divide the class into three groups (A, B, and C).
- Explain the task. Ss complete the chart for their group only. For example, Group A only reads Text A and completes column A.
- Ss complete the task.
- Divide the class into new groups of three. Each group has one S each from groups A, B, and C. Ss share information to complete their charts.

Variation for Listenings: Bring three audio programs and cassette or CD players to class. Ss listen to the audio program in three groups and complete the column for their group. Then they form new groups and share their information.

13 RUNNING DICTATION

Aim: *Give Ss practice using all four skills in a collaborative way.*
Levels: *1, 2, and 3*
Preparation: *Photocopy and enlarge several copies of the text. Post the copies around the classroom walls.*
Comment: *Use with Readings or Perspectives.*

- Books closed. Ss work in pairs.
- Explain the task. S1 from each pair goes to the wall and memorizes part of the text. Then S1 comes back and dictates the information to S2, and S2 writes it down.
- Point out that Ss cannot shout across the room or remove the copies from the walls. When you call out "Change!," Ss change roles.
- Ss complete the task. The first pair to finish wins.
- Books open. Ss check their spelling.

14 VOCABULARY MINGLE

Aim: *Encourage Ss to find the meaning of unknown words.*
Levels: *1, 2, and 3*
Preparation: *None*
Comment: *Use with Readings or Perspectives.*

- Explain the first task. Ss read the text. When they find a word they don't know, they underline it with a straight line. If they think they know the meaning but are not sure, they underline it with a squiggly line.
- Ss complete the task individually.
- Explain the second task. Ss take their books and go around the room. They ask each other the meanings of the words they don't know or aren't sure of.
- Model the task with one or two Ss:
  T: What does *large* mean?
  S1: It means "big."
  T: Thanks.
- Ss complete the task.
- Help Ss with any remaining words they don't know.

Variation: Ss sit in small groups and ask each other the meanings of new words.

15 TIME OUT!

Aim: *Help students develop fluency and confidence.*
Levels: *1, 2, and 3*
Preparation: *None*
Comment: *Use with Role Plays.*

- Divide Ss into groups of six. Two Ss (S1 and S2) are the actors. The other four Ss help the actors.
- Explain the task. S1 and S2 perform the role play using the instructions in their Student's Books. If they don't know what to say or can't remember a word, they call "Time Out!" The role play stops and they ask the Ss in their group for help. They can also ask the other Ss in the group to replace them.
- Ss continue the role play until all Ss are actors.

Variation 1: S1 and S2 can bring in other Ss as new characters.

Variation 2: Ss can create new situations based on the role play.

Acknowledgment: *Idea adapted from* Strategic Interaction *by Robert J. Di Pietro, Cambridge University Press.*

16 PASS THE PAPER

Aim: *Help Ss generate ideas and plan compositions.*
Levels: *1, 2, and 3*
Preparation: *None*
Comment: *Use with Writings.*

- Before beginning their compositions, Ss work in groups of five or six. Ask Ss to write their name in the top right-hand corner of a blank piece of paper.
- Explain the task. Ss write a question related to the composition topic on their piece of paper (e.g., *Where did you go?*). Then they pass their paper to the right, and take the paper from their left. Each time Ss receive a paper, they write one question and pass the paper to the right.
- Ss complete the task. They continue until there are ten questions on each paper.
- Ss find their original papers, read the questions, and circle four or five they want to answer.
- Ss number the questions in the order they plan to answer them. Then they write their compositions.

17 MIND MAPPING

Aim: *Help Ss generate ideas and plan their compositions.*
Levels: *1, 2, and 3*
Preparation: *None*
Comment: *Use with Writings or Word Powers.*

- Write the composition theme (e.g., holidays) in a large circle on the board. Then elicit topics related to the theme and write them in smaller circles around the theme. For example:

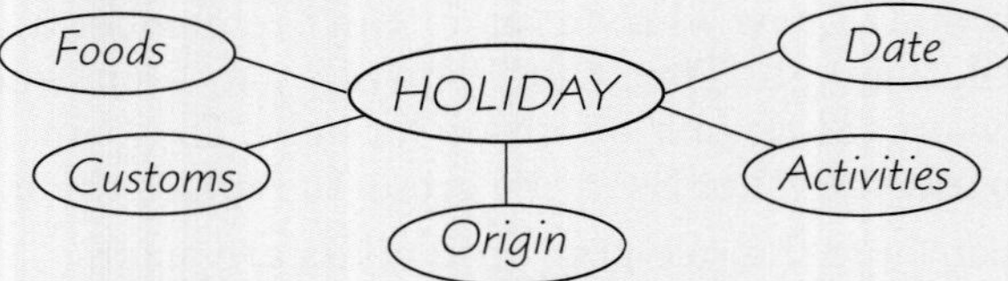

- Elicit words or phrases related to each topic. Write them in circles around the topics.
- Explain the task. Ss choose three topics to write about. They number them in the order they want to write about them.
- Brainstorm possible opening and closing sentences for the compositions.
- Ss write their compositions, using an opening sentence, three topics, and a conclusion.

Variation for Word Powers: Use the first two steps of this technique to review, categorize, and expand on vocabulary from Word Powers.

18 PICTURE DICTATION

Aim: *Develop Ss' vocabulary and listening skills.*
Levels: *1, 2, and 3*
Preparation: *None*
Comment: *Use with Snapshots and Word Powers that have pictures with a lot of details (e.g., clothes, maps, furniture).*

- Teach or review prepositional phrases of place (e.g., *in the middle, on the right / left, at the top / bottom, in the top / bottom right-hand / left-hand corner*).
- Explain the task. Ss work in pairs. S1 looks at the picture and S2 has a blank piece of paper. S1 describes the picture. S2 listens and draws it.
- Ss complete the task. Then they compare their drawings with the picture in the Student's Book.

Option: Describe a picture, and the class draws it.

Variation: Photocopy the picture and post it on the wall. S1 from each pair goes to the wall and returns to S2. S1 describes the picture to S2, and S2 draws it.

19 VOCABULARY STEPS

Aim: *Help Ss review and personalize vocabulary in a category.*
Levels: *All*
Preparation: *Choose four to six words in a category.*
Comment: *Use with Snapshots or Word Powers.*

- After presenting the Snapshot or Word Power, write the words you chose on the board. For example, if the category is *seasons*, write the words *spring*, *summer*, *fall*, and *winter*. Then draw steps on the board:

- Explain the task. Ss rank the words individually according to a criterion (e.g., favorite). They write their favorite at the top of the steps and their least favorite at the bottom of the steps.
- Ss complete the task. Then they compare their answers in pairs.

Variation 1: Ask Ss to rank vocabulary using different criteria. For example: sports (most fun, most popular), things (most useful, most expensive), foods (tastiest, healthiest), or jobs (most difficult, most dangerous).

Variation 2: Ask higher-level Ss to rank the words collaboratively in small groups.

Acknowledgment: *Idea adapted from* Five-Minute Activities *by Penny Ur and Andrew Wright, Cambridge University Press.*

20 CLOUD PREDICTION

Aim: *Develop Ss' ability to predict content from key words.*
Levels: *All*
Preparation: *List six to ten key words from the text.*
Comment: *Use with Conversations, Listenings, or Readings.*

- Write the key words on the board, inside a large cloud.
- Explain the task. Ss work in pairs. They use the key words on the board to predict the main ideas of the Conversation or Listening.
- Point out that all predictions are acceptable.
- Ss complete the task. Elicit Ss' predictions.
- Ss listen to the audio program and check their predictions.

Variation for Readings: After eliciting predictions, Ss read the text and check their predictions.

Photocopiables

Where can you find interesting, easy-to-use handouts for your classes?

Photocopiables provide varied ways to teach specific exercises in the Student's Book, and include activities such as word searches, information gaps, and board games. Depending on the exercise, these materials can either supplement or replace the suggestions in the page-by-page teaching notes.

There are 16 Photocopiables, one for each unit. Each activity includes a Photocopiable. Handouts can be found at the end of this section.

Units	*Exercises*	*Photocopiables*
1. Please call me Beth.	Conversation on page 2	Musical Introductions
2. How do you spend your day?	Word Power on page 8	Word Search
3. How much is it?	Grammar Focus on page 17	Price Exchange
4. Do you like rap?	Word Power on page 22	Find Your Group
5. Tell me about your family.	Grammar Focus on page 32	Every Day and Today
6. How often do you exercise?	Discussion on page 39	Famous Athletes
7. We had a great time!	Word Power on page 46	Collocations Survey
8. What's your neighborhood like?	Word Power on page 50	Pair Crossword
9. What does she look like?	Reading on page 63	I Think I Know
10. Have you ever ridden a camel?	Grammar Focus on page 66	Question Game
11. It's a very exciting place!	Conversation on page 75	Scrambled Dialog
12. It really works!	Word Power on page 80	Picture Completion
13. May I take your order?	Pronunciation on page 88	Bubble Cards
14. The biggest and the best!	Writing on page 96	Error Correction
15. I'm going to a soccer match.	Conversation on page 102	Hear the Differences
16. A change for the better!	Listening on page 107	Photo Identification

❶ MUSICAL INTRODUCTIONS

Aim: *Give Ss practice introducing themselves in a party-like situation.*
Preparation: *Make one copy of Photocopiable 1 for every four Ss. Cut the copies into four cards. Bring party music and a cassette or CD player to class.*
Comment: *Use after the Conversation on page 2.*

- Give one card to each S.
- Explain the task. While you play the music, Ss move around the room, dancing or walking. When you stop the audio program, Ss introduce themselves to the people closest to them.
- Point out that Ss can use the model conversation on their cards to guide them, but they should substitute the italicized words with their own information.
- Model the task with a S.
- Ss complete the task. Continue as long as needed.

❷ WORD SEARCH

Aim: *Give Ss a review of words for different jobs.*
Preparation: *Make one copy of Photocopiable 2 for every two Ss.*
Comment: *Use after the Word Power on page 8.*

- Ss work in pairs. Give one handout to each pair.
- Point out that there are 15 jobs in the word search. The jobs appear in the Snapshot or the Word Power. The jobs can go across, down, or diagonally. Point out the word *cashier* as an example.
- Explain the task. Ss find the jobs in pairs and circle them. Then they write them on the lines.
- Ss complete the task. The pair that finds all the words first wins. Then elicit the answers.

Answers

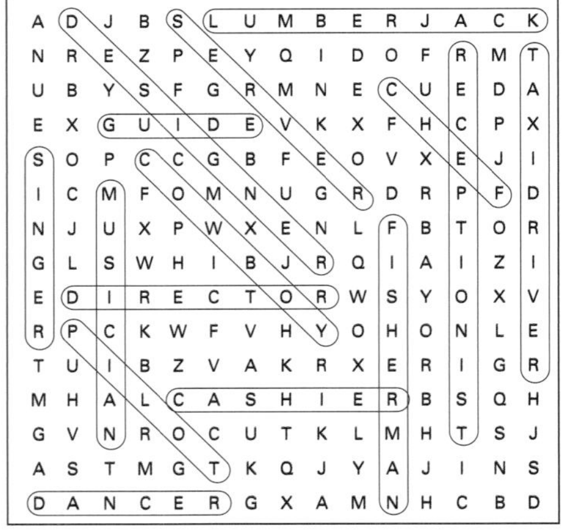

❸ PRICE EXCHANGE

Aim: *Give Ss practice asking* how much is/are . . .? *in an information gap activity.*
Preparation: *Make one copy of Photocopiable 3 for every two Ss. Cut the copies in half.*
Comment: *Use after the Grammar Focus on page 17.*

- Ss work in pairs. Give Picture A to S1 and Picture B to S2 of each pair. Point out that they cannot look at each other's pictures.
- Set the scene. Pictures A and B show the same items, but some things in each picture don't have prices. Teach or review any new vocabulary.
- Explain the task. S1 and S2 take turns asking the prices of these things. Model the task with a S:
  T: How much are the pencils?
  S: They're $2.15.
- Ss complete the task. Then they look at each other's pictures to check their answers.

❹ FIND YOUR GROUP

Aim: *Give Ss practice categorizing vocabulary in an active way.*
Preparation: *Make one copy of Photocopiable 4 for every 12 Ss. Cut the copies into 12 cards.*
Comment: *Use with classes of 12 or more Ss in place of parts A and B of the Word Power on page 22.*

- On the board write:
  Movies *Music* *TV programs*
- Give each S a card. Explain that the words on the cards are from the categories on the board.
- Explain the task. Ss go around the class and find the Ss with words from the same category. Then they sit down as a group.
- Model the task with a few Ss.
  T: My word is "thrillers." They're a kind of movie.
  S: Mine is "westerns." They're in the same category.
  OR
  Mine is "pop." It's in a different category.
- Ss complete the task until they are all in groups.
- Elicit the words in each category. Ss check answers on page T-22.

Option: After Ss complete the activity, they brainstorm more words for their categories.

5 EVERY DAY AND TODAY

Aim: *Give Ss practice visualizing the difference between simple present and present continuous.*
Preparation: *Make one copy of Photocopiable 5 and cut it into 12 pictures. Enlarge the pictures.*
Comment: *Use after the Grammar Focus on page 32.*

- Hold up the picture of the doctor. Ask questions to elicit simple present answers: "Where does she work? What does she do every day?" (Possible answers: She works in a hospital. She sees patients every day.)
- Hold up the picture of the doctor studying French. Ask questions to elicit present continuous answers: "What's she wearing? What's she doing?" (Possible answers: She's wearing a T-shirt, jeans, and earrings. She's studying French.)
- Repeat the procedure with the other pictures.

Option: After completing the Grammar Focus, Ss write simple present and present continuous sentences about the pictures in small groups.

Acknowledgment: *Idea adapted from* Pictures for Language Learning *by Andrew Wright, Cambridge University Press.*

6 FAMOUS ATHLETES

Aim: *Give Ss practice asking and answering questions in an information gap activity.*
Preparation: *Make one copy of Photocopiable 6 for every three Ss. Cut the copies in three.*
Comment: *Use after the Discussion on page 39.*

- Ss work in groups of three. Give Chart A to S1, Chart B to S2, and Chart C to S3. Point out that they cannot look at each other's charts.
- Explain the task. Ss ask and answer questions to complete their charts. Elicit questions they can ask: "What sport does he/she play? Where is he/she from? Where does he/she live now? What interesting fact do you know about him/her?"
- Ss complete the task.
- Ss look at each other's charts to check their information.

Option: After they complete the task, Ss role-play interviews with the sports personalities in the chart (or with different sports personalities). One S is the sports personality and the other two Ss are interviewers.

7 COLLOCATIONS SURVEY

Aim: *Give Ss practice using collocations in a class survey.*
Preparation: *Make one copy of Photocopiable 7 for every S.*
Comment: *Use before the Word Power on page 46.*

- Give each S a handout. Teach or review the time expressions.
- Ss work in pairs. They take turns asking each other questions to complete the survey. Model the task with a S:
  T: When was the last time you went shopping?
  S: Yesterday morning.
  T: OK, I'm writing "Yesterday morning."
- Ss complete the survey in pairs.
- Elicit Ss' answers. Ask: "Who went shopping this morning? yesterday?"
- Ss move on to part A of the Word Power, using the collocations in their survey for help.

Variation: Ss go around the room and ask a different S each question. They write each S's name and answer.

8 PAIR CROSSWORD

Aim: *Give Ss practice reviewing vocabulary and definitions collaboratively.*
Preparation: *Make one copy of Photocopiable 8 for every two Ss. Cut the copies in half.*
Comment: *Use after the Word Power on page 50.*

- Divide the class into two groups (A and B). Give Part A of the handout to Group A and Part B to Group B.
- Explain that Group A has all the across words of the puzzle and Group B has all the down words. Ss write clues for their words as a group. For example, a clue for the word *library* is *a place where you borrow books*.
- Ss complete the task in groups. Go around the class and give help as needed.
- Divide Ss into pairs with one S from Group A and one S from Group B. Point out that they cannot look at each other's crossword puzzle.
- Ss take turns reading their clues aloud and guessing the words. They use the words to complete the puzzle.
- Model the task with a S:
  T: What's the clue for one across?
  S: It's a place where you borrow books.
- Ss complete the task. Go around the class and give help as needed.
- Ss look at their partner's crossword puzzle to check their answers.

9 I THINK I KNOW

Aim: *Help Ss learn the meanings of new words collaboratively.*
Preparation: *Make one copy of Photocopiable 9 for every two Ss. Cut the copies in half.*
Comment: *Use before the Reading on page 63.*

- Give each S a handout. Explain the task. Ss check (✓) the appropriate column for each word (*I know* if they know the meaning, *I think I know* if they think they know the meaning, or *I don't know* if they don't know the meaning).
- Ss complete the task individually.
- Ss work in groups. Ss explain the words they know to each other. As they learn the meanings of new words, they move their check marks to the left.
- Elicit or explain any words Ss don't know.

Acknowledgment: *Idea adapted from* The Standby Book *by Seth Lindstromberg, Cambridge University Press.*

10 QUESTION GAME

Aim: *Give Ss practice using simple past and present perfect.*
Preparation: *Make one copy of Photocopiable 10 for every four Ss. Bring one die and four markers for every group.*
Comment: *Use after the Grammar Focus on page 66.*

- Ss work in groups of four. Give each group a handout, a die, and four markers. Teach or review any new vocabulary.
- Model the game with one group. Ss put their markers on Start. S1 rolls the die and moves his or her marker the number of squares indicated on the die. Then S1 uses the words in the square to make a simple past or present perfect question. For example, S1 uses the words *ever be late for a test* to make a present perfect question (i.e., *Have you ever been late for a test?*).
- If a S lands on a blank square he or she loses a turn.
- Point out that Ss can move the marker in any direction. Also, they must say the questions, not write them. If the question is correct, the S writes his or her initials in that square. Then S2 takes a turn.
- Monitor the class and give help as needed. The game ends when all the squares have initials. The S with the most initialed squares wins.

Option: When Ss finish, they ask each other the questions. Encourage them to ask follow-up questions.

Acknowledgment: *Idea adapted from* The Grammar Activity Book *by Bob Obee, Cambridge University Press.*

11 SCRAMBLED DIALOG

Aim: *Familiarize Ss with an audio script before they listen to it.*
Preparation: *Make one copy of Photocopiable 11 for every two Ss. Cut the copies into strips and put them in envelopes.*
Comment: *Use before the Conversation on page 75.*

- Ss work in pairs. Give each pair an envelope.
- Set the scene and explain the task. Two friends are talking about Mexico City. Ss arrange the strips to form the conversation. Ask: "What is the first sentence?" (Answer: *Can you tell me a little about Mexico City?*)
- Ss complete the task in pairs.
- Play the audio program. Ss listen and check the order of their conversations.

Option: After they listen to the audio program, Ss practice the conversation using information about a different city. See the instructions for ***Substitution Dialog*** on page T-151.

12 PICTURE COMPLETION

Aim: *Give Ss listening practice as they review vocabulary.*
Preparation: *Make one copy of Photocopiable 12 for every two Ss. Cut the pages in half.*
Comment: *Use after the Word Power on page 80.*

- Give the Ss Part A of the handout.
- Teach or review these words: *top shelf*, *middle shelf*, *bottom shelf*; *on the right*, *on the left*, *in the middle*; *on the right-hand side*, *on the left-hand side*. Check Ss' understanding by asking them to point to different parts of the picture. For example, say: "Point to the left-hand side of the top shelf. Point to the middle shelf."
- Explain and model the task. As you describe the contents of the cabinet, Ss draw them in the picture. Point out that they can use simple sketches. Say: "On the left-hand side of the top shelf, there are two bags of cough drops." The Ss draw the pictures.
- Use Part B of the handout (the Answer key) to describe the rest of the contents, while Ss draw them.
- Ss compare their pictures in pairs. Then give Ss Part B of the handout for them to check their answers.

Option: After Ss complete the activity, they draw pictures of medicine cabinets with different contents. Then they take turns describing and drawing their medicine cabinets in pairs.

13 BUBBLE CARDS

Aim: *Give Ss practice using syllable stress in responses.*
Preparation: *Make one copy of Photocopiable 13 for every 15 Ss. Cut the copies into two sets of cards (responses and bubbles). Put the response cards and bubble cards in separate envelopes.*
Comment: *Use after the Pronunciation on page 88.*

- Give each Ss one response card and one bubble card (with "TOP" at the top). Explain that the bubbles represent the syllables in a sentence, and the big bubble represents the syllable with the most stress in the sentence.
- Teach or review these expressions: *Read your response. Hum your bubble card. That matches. That doesn't match.*
- Explain the task. Ss go around the room and match their bubble card with a response card. Then they make a short conversation that includes the response. For example:
  A: I hate bananas.
  B: So do **I**.
- Ss complete the task. Each time Ss match cards, replace their cards with new ones.

Variation: Use these sets of cards to play ***Concentration***. See the instructions on page T-144.

Acknowledgment: *Idea adapted from* The Standby Book *by Seth Lindstromberg, Cambridge University Press.*

14 ERROR CORRECTION

Aim: *Give Ss practice correcting written errors in pairs.*
Preparation: *Make one copy of Photocopiable 14 for every two Ss. Cut the copies in half.*
Comment: *Use after the Writing on page 96.*

- Give half the class Worksheet A and half the class Worksheet B. Explain that six sentences on each worksheet have grammar mistakes. Ss write *C* if the sentence is correct and *NC* if it is not correct.
- Ss complete the task individually.
- Ss work in pairs. One has Worksheet A and one has Worksheet B. They compare sentences and decide which one is correct. (For each sentence, one S has the correct sentence.)
- Go over answers with the class.

Answers

Correct answers in A: 1, 3, 5, 6, 9, 12
Correct answers in B: 2, 4, 7, 8, 10, 11

Acknowledgment: *Idea adapted from* Grammar Games *by Mario Rinvolucri, Cambridge University Press.*

15 HEAR THE DIFFERENCES

Aim: *Give Ss practice listening for errors.*
Preparation: *Make one copy of Photocopiable 15 for every three Ss. Cut the copies in three.*
Comment: *Use with the Conversation on page 102.*

- Books closed. Give each S a handout. Ss read the conversation silently.
- Explain the task. When you play the audio program, Ss listen for differences between the audio recording and the handout. When they hear a difference, they circle and correct it.
- Play the audio program three times. The first time, Ss circle the errors. The second time, Ss correct the errors. The third time, they check their corrections.
- Books open. Ss read the conversation to check their answers.

Option: Pairs practice the conversation sitting back-to-back.

16 PHOTO IDENTIFICATION

Aim: *Give Ss practice matching descriptions with pictures.*
Preparation: *Make one copy of Photocopiable 16 for every two Ss.*
Comment: *Use with the Listening on page 107.*

- Ss work in pairs. Give one handout to each pair.
- Set the scene and explain the task. Scott and Linda are looking through a photo album. Ss listen to the audio program and check (✓) the pictures that appear in their photo album.
- Play the audio program and Ss complete the task.
- Play the audio program again and Ss check their answers.

Answers

Pictures checked: top right, bottom left, bottom right

- Ss move on to the Listening on page 107.

Option: Ss listen to the audio program and take notes about how Scott and Linda have changed. Then they role-play the conversation in pairs.

PHOTOCOPIABLE 1 Musical Introductions

A: Hello. I'm *David Garza*.

B: Hi! My name is *Elizabeth Silva*, but please call me *Beth*.

A: Nice to meet you, *Beth*.

B: Nice to meet you, too. Where are you from, *David*?

A: I'm from *Mexico*. How about you?

B: I'm from *Brazil*.

A: Hello. I'm *David Garza*.

B: Hi! My name is *Elizabeth Silva*, but please call me *Beth*.

A: Nice to meet you, *Beth*.

B: Nice to meet you, too. Where are you from, *David*?

A: I'm from *Mexico*. How about you?

B: I'm from *Brazil*.

A: Hello. I'm *David Garza*.

B: Hi! My name is *Elizabeth Silva*, but please call me *Beth*.

A: Nice to meet you, *Beth*.

B: Nice to meet you, too. Where are you from, *David*?

A: I'm from *Mexico*. How about you?

B: I'm from *Brazil*.

A: Hello. I'm *David Garza*.

B: Hi! My name is *Elizabeth Silva*, but please call me *Beth*.

A: Nice to meet you, *Beth*.

B: Nice to meet you, too. Where are you from, *David*?

A: I'm from *Mexico*. How about you?

B: I'm from *Brazil*.

PHOTOCOPIABLE 2 Word Search

Jobs

A	D	J	B	S	L	U	M	B	E	R	J	A	C	K
N	R	E	Z	P	E	Y	Q	I	D	O	F	R	M	T
U	B	Y	S	F	G	R	M	N	E	C	U	E	D	A
E	X	G	U	I	D	E	V	K	X	F	H	C	P	X
S	O	P	C	C	G	B	F	E	O	V	X	E	J	I
I	C	M	F	O	M	N	U	G	R	D	R	P	F	D
N	J	U	X	P	W	X	E	N	L	F	B	T	O	R
G	L	S	W	H	I	B	J	R	Q	I	A	I	Z	I
E	D	I	R	E	C	T	O	R	W	S	Y	O	X	V
R	P	C	K	W	F	V	H	Y	O	H	O	N	L	E
T	U	I	B	Z	V	A	K	R	X	E	R	I	G	R
M	H	A	L	C	A	S	H	I	E	R	B	S	Q	H
G	V	N	R	O	C	U	T	K	L	M	H	T	S	J
A	S	T	M	G	T	K	Q	J	Y	A	J	I	N	S
D	A	N	C	E	R	G	X	A	M	N	H	C	B	D

cashier

PHOTOCOPIABLE 3 Price Exchange

Picture A

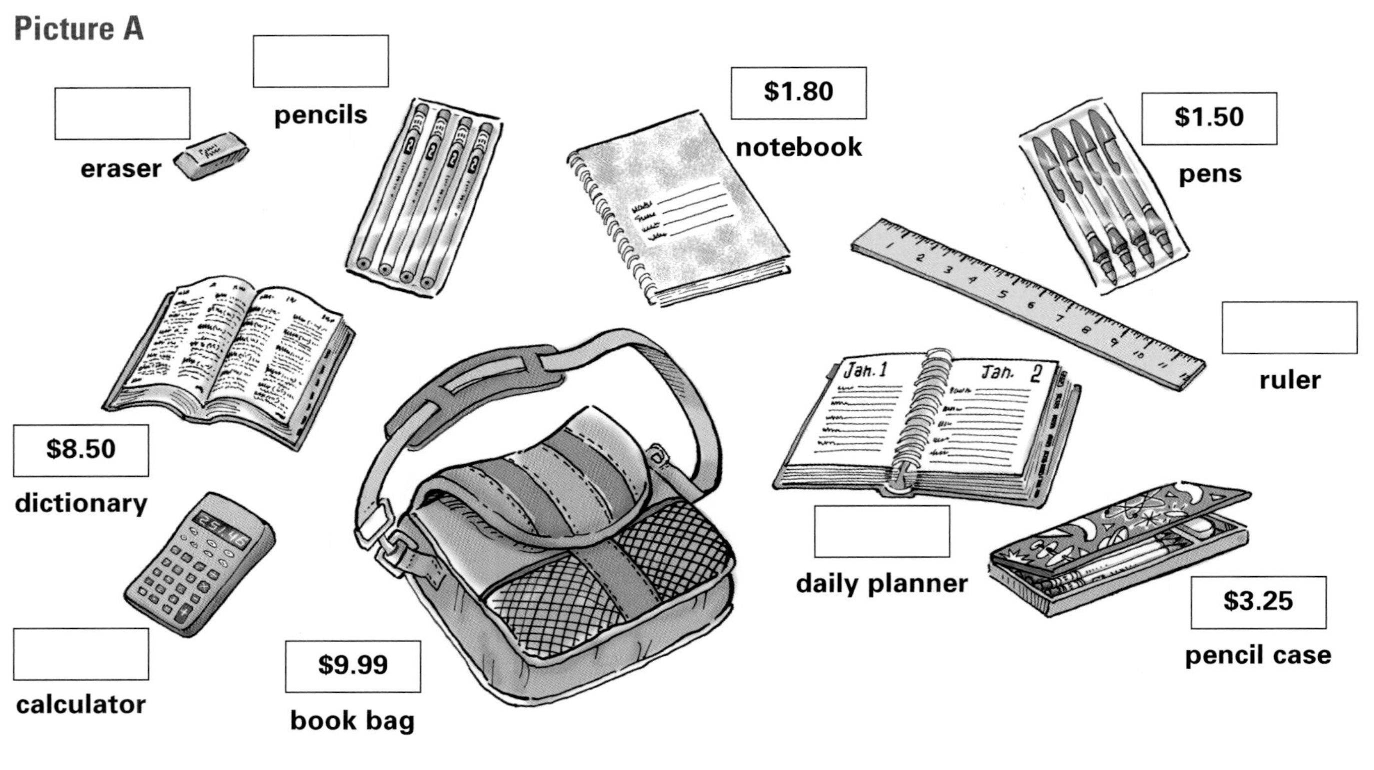

Picture B

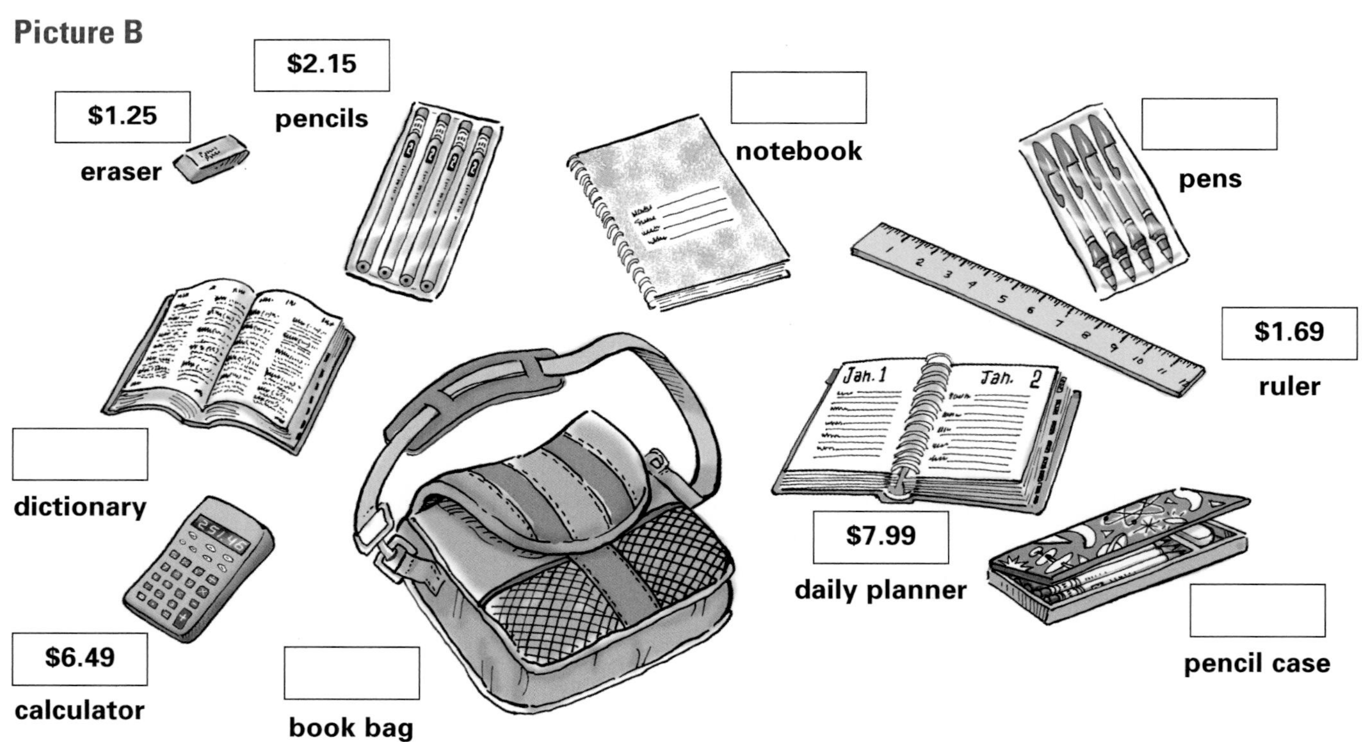

PHOTOCOPIABLE 4 Find Your Group

thrillers	**westerns**	**horror films**
soap operas	**talk shows**	**science fiction**
game shows	**news**	**jazz**
classical	**pop**	**salsa**

PHOTOCOPIABLE 5 Every Day and Today

PHOTOCOPIABLE 6 Famous Athletes

Chart A	 Ronaldo	 Anna Kournikova	 Yao Ming
Sport			*basketball*
Where from	*Brazil*		
Where now			*the U.S.*
Interesting fact		*Her favorite color is black.*	

Chart B	 Ronaldo	 Anna Kournikova	 Yao Ming
Sport	*soccer*		
Where from		*Russia*	
Where now	*the U.S.*		
Interesting fact			*His teammates call him "Dynasty."*

Chart C	 Ronaldo	 Anna Kournikova	 Yao Ming
Sport		*tennis*	
Where from			*China*
Where now		*Italy*	
Interesting fact	*His son's name is Ronald.*		

PHOTOCOPIABLE 7 Collocations Survey

When was the last time you . . . ?	*Time expression*
went shopping	
did your homework	
had a lot of fun	
went dancing	
made photocopies	
did the laundry	
had a party	
took a day off	
did the dishes	
made a phone call	
took a trip	
made the bed	
took a vacation	
went bowling	
had a good time	

time expressions	
this morning	last weekend
this afternoon	last week
yesterday morning	last month
yesterday afternoon	last summer
yesterday evening	last year
last night	in 2003

PHOTOCOPIABLE 8 Pair Crossword

Part A

Across

1. A library
   is a place where
4. A café
5. Houses
7. A theater
9. A drugstore
10. A bank
12. Post offices

Part B

Down

2. A restaurant
   is a place where
3. A laundromat
5. Hotels
6. Museums
8. A rest room
10. A bookstore
11. A school

PHOTOCOPIABLE 9 I Think I Know

	I know	*I think I know*	*I don't know*
1. hip-hop			
2. typical			
3. street clothes			
4. baggy pants			
5. sweatshirt			
6. hiking boots			
7. baseball cap			
8. backward			
9. sports logo			
10. athletic shoes			
11. trendy			
12. performer			

	I know	*I think I know*	*I don't know*
1. hip-hop			
2. typical			
3. street clothes			
4. baggy pants			
5. sweatshirt			
6. hiking boots			
7. baseball cap			
8. backward			
9. sports logo			
10. athletic shoes			
11. trendy			
12. performer			

Did you . . . ?/Have you . . . ?

		ever see a ghost		cook last weekend		
	see a movie last week		sleep late last Sunday		ever cut your own hair	
call home lately		get up early last Sunday		use a computer yesterday		go shopping lately
	play any sports this month		ever run in a race		write any e-mails yesterday	
make your bed yesterday morning		ever appear on TV	**START**	eat out lately		ever ride a motorcycle
	ever get a traffic ticket		ever be late for a test		take a vacation last year	
ever fall asleep in class		eat lunch yet		ever meet a celebrity		watch TV last night
	ever try Indian food		go to a party last Saturday		visit a foreign country last year	
		go to bed early last night		do much exercise this week		

PHOTOCOPIABLE 11 Scrambled Dialog

Can you tell me a little about **Mexico City**?

And what else?

Well, you should definitely visit **the National Museum** and go to **the Palace of Fine Arts**.

Well, what's a good time to visit?

Oh, good! And what should I see there?

Sure I can. What would you like to know?

It all sounds really **exciting**!

Oh, you shouldn't miss **the Pyramid of the Sun**. It's very **interesting**.

I think you can go **anytime**. The weather is **always nice**.

PHOTOCOPIABLE 12 Picture Completion

Part A

Part B

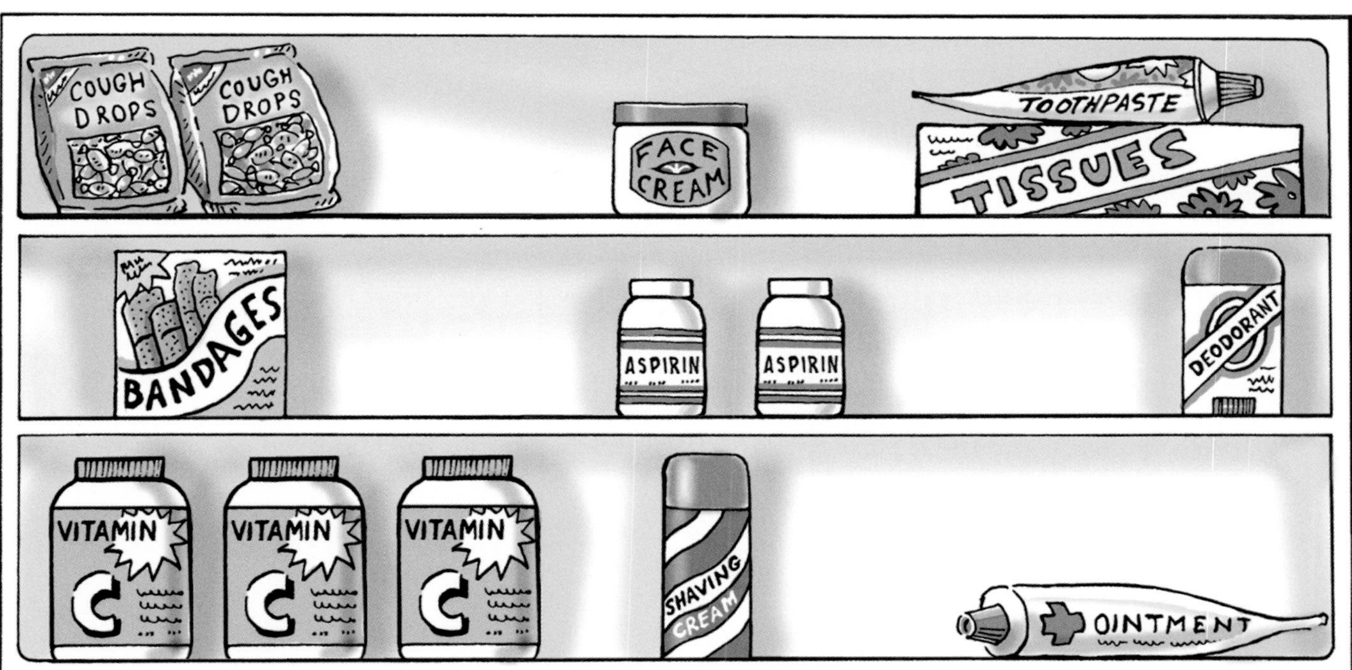

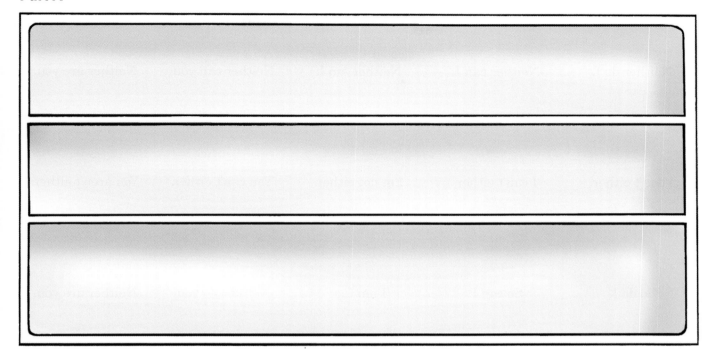

PHOTOCOPIABLE 13 Bubble Cards

Response cards

Neither do I.	Neither can I.	Neither am I.	Neither can you.	Neither are you.
I don't either.	I can't either.	I'm not either.	You can't either.	You aren't either.
So do I.	So can I.	I am too.	Neither do you.	Neither are you.

Bubble cards

(TOP) 	(TOP) 	(TOP) 	(TOP) 	(TOP) 
(TOP)	(TOP) 	(TOP) 	(TOP) 	(TOP) 
(TOP)	(TOP)	(TOP)	(TOP)	(TOP) 

PHOTOCOPIABLE 14 Error Correction

Worksheet A

_____ **1.** Thailand has many beautiful beaches.
_____ **2.** The cathedral has 500 years.
_____ **3.** Many foreigners come in December.
_____ **4.** Much of the tourists are American.
_____ **5.** Bali has the most beautiful beaches in the world.
_____ **6.** New Orleans has the best carnival in North America.
_____ **7.** The weather is more good in the summer.
_____ **8.** The Grand Canyon is about 1,900 deep meters.
_____ **9.** The most famous attraction is Sugar Loaf mountain.
_____ **10.** Every year, thousands of tourists are visiting Hawaii.
_____ **11.** Tokyo is more larger than Kobe.
_____ **12.** People like to visit our country.

Worksheet B

_____ **1.** Thailand have many beautiful beaches.
_____ **2.** The cathedral is 500 years old.
_____ **3.** Much foreigners come in December.
_____ **4.** Many of the tourists are American.
_____ **5.** Bali has the more beautiful beaches in the world.
_____ **6.** New Orleans has the most good carnival in North America.
_____ **7.** The weather is better in the summer.
_____ **8.** The Grand Canyon is about 1,900 meters deep.
_____ **9.** The more famous attraction is Sugar Loaf mountain.
_____ **10.** Every year, thousands of tourists visit Hawaii.
_____ **11.** Tokyo is larger than Kobe.
_____ **12.** People likes to visit our country.

PHOTOCOPIABLE 15 Hear the Differences

Secretary: Good morning, Parker Industries.
Mr. Kale: Hello. May I speak to Mr. Graham, please?
Secretary: I'm sorry. He's not in. Can I take a message?
Mr. Kale: Yes, please. This is Mr. Kale.
Secretary: Is that C-A-L-E?
Mr. Kale: No, it's K-A-L-E.
Secretary: All right.
Mr. Kale: Please tell him our meeting is on Friday at 12:30.
Secretary: Friday at 12:30.
Mr. Kale: And could you ask her to call me tomorrow afternoon? My number is (646) 555-4013.
Secretary: (646) 555-4013. Yes, Mr. Kale. I'll give Mr. Graham the message.
Mr. Kale: Thank you. Good-bye.
Secretary: Good-bye.

Secretary: Good morning, Parker Industries.
Mr. Kale: Hello. May I speak to Mr. Graham, please?
Secretary: I'm sorry. He's not in. Can I take a message?
Mr. Kale: Yes, please. This is Mr. Kale.
Secretary: Is that C-A-L-E?
Mr. Kale: No, it's K-A-L-E.
Secretary: All right.
Mr. Kale: Please tell him our meeting is on Friday at 12:30.
Secretary: Friday at 12:30.
Mr. Kale: And could you ask her to call me tomorrow afternoon? My number is (646) 555-4013.
Secretary: (646) 555-4013. Yes, Mr. Kale. I'll give Mr. Graham the message.
Mr. Kale: Thank you. Good-bye.
Secretary: Good-bye.

Secretary: Good morning, Parker Industries.
Mr. Kale: Hello. May I speak to Mr. Graham, please?
Secretary: I'm sorry. He's not in. Can I take a message?
Mr. Kale: Yes, please. This is Mr. Kale.
Secretary: Is that C-A-L-E?
Mr. Kale: No, it's K-A-L-E.
Secretary: All right.
Mr. Kale: Please tell him our meeting is on Friday at 12:30.
Secretary: Friday at 12:30.
Mr. Kale: And could you ask her to call me tomorrow afternoon? My number is (646) 555-4013.
Secretary: (646) 555-4013. Yes, Mr. Kale. I'll give Mr. Graham the message.
Mr. Kale: Thank you. Good-bye.
Secretary: Good-bye.

PHOTOCOPIABLE 16 Photo Identification

Unit 1 Language summary

Vocabulary

Nouns
birthday
bow
brother
cafeteria
chemistry
city
class
classmate
club
English
family
friend
hobby
member
name
parents
person
semester
sister
teacher
student
university
vacation
year

Pronouns
Subject pronouns
I
you
he
she
it
we
they

Titles
Miss
Mr.
Mrs.
Ms.

Adjectives
Possessives
my
your
his
her
its
our
their

Other
beautiful
big
common
cool
exciting
famous
friendly
good
interesting
new
next
nice
old
same
shy
unusual

Articles
a
an
the

Verbs
am
are
has
is
love

Adverbs
Responses
no
yes

Other
actually
here
(over) there
not
now
really (+ adjective)
too (+ adjective)
very (+ adjective)

Prepositions
at (10:00/City College)
from (Seoul/Korea)
in (the morning/the same class)
on (my way to . . .)

Conjunctions
and
but
or

Expressions

Saying hello
Hi.
Hey.
Hello.
Good morning.
How are you?/How's it going?
(I'm) fine, thanks.
Pretty good.
OK.

Saying good-bye
Bye.
Good-bye.
See you later.
See you tomorrow.
Have a good day.
Good night.

Exchanging personal information
What's your name?
I'm . . . ./My name is . . . .
What's your first/last name?
It's . . . .
What are your hobbies?
My hobbies are . . . .
When's your birthday?
It's . . . .
What's . . . like?
He's/She's/It's . . . .
What are . . . like?
They're . . . .
Where are you from?
I'm/We're from . . . .

Introducing someone
This is . . . ./These are . . . .
Nice to meet you.

Asking about someone
Who's that?
That's . . . .
His/Her name is . . . .
Who are they?
They're . . . .
Their names are . . . and . . . .
Where's your friend?
He's/She's . . . .

Thanking someone
Thanks.
Thank you.

Checking information
Sorry, what's your name again?
It's . . . .
How do you spell . . . ?
What do people call you?
Everyone calls me . . . .
Please call me . . . .

Making suggestions
Let's . . . .

Apologizing
(I'm) sorry.

Agreeing
That's right.
OK.
Sure.

Unit 2 Language summary

Vocabulary

Nouns

Jobs/Professions

(TV) announcer
carpenter
cashier
chef
company director
construction worker
cowboy
dancer
doctor
fisherman
flight attendant
lumberjack
musician
nurse
pilot
receptionist
salesperson
server
singer
taxi driver
tour guide
Web-site designer

Types of jobs

entertainment business
food service
office work
travel industry

Workplaces

airline
(computer) company
department store
hospital
office
restaurant
school
university

Other

breakfast
clothes
country
dinner
drink
food
house
job
music
passenger
patient
phone
schedule
snack
thing
time
weather report
work

Adjectives

bad
better
dangerous
different
difficult
fantastic
full-time
great
part-time
similar
worse
worst

Verbs

answer
assist
build
care for
cook
design
do
get (home)
get up
go (to bed/to school/to work)
have (a job/lunch)
leave (work/for work)
like
live
recognize
sell
serve
sleep
sound (interesting)
spend (your day)
start
stay up
study
take
teach
wake up
watch
work (in an office/for an airline)

Adverbs

Responses

yeah

Other

a lot
early
exactly
home
late
only
usually

Prepositions

around/about (10:00/noon)
after (midnight)
at (7:00/night/midnight)
at (a travel agency/a fast-food restaurant)
before (noon)
during (the week)
in (a hospital/an office)
in (the morning/the afternoon/the evening)
like (Peru)
on (weekdays/Fridays)
until (midnight)

Expressions

Talking about work/school

What do you do (exactly/there)?
  I'm a/an . . . .
Where do you work?
  I work in/at/for . . . .
How do you like your job/classes?
  I like it/them a lot.
  I love it/them.
Where do you go to school?
  I go to . . . .
What's your favorite . . . ?
  My favorite . . . is . . . .

Asking for more information

What time . . . ?
Which . . . ?
Why?

Talking about daily schedules

How do you spend your day?
  Well, I . . . .
What time do you go to work/school?
  I go to work/school at . . . .
When do you get home?
  I usually get home at . . . .

Expressing interest

Oh?
Oh, really?
Really?
How interesting!

Expressing surprise

Oh!
Wow!

Starting a sentence

Well, ...
By the way, ...

Unit 3 Language summary

Vocabulary

Nouns

Clothes and jewelry

backpack
bag
boots
bracelet
cap
dress
earrings
in-line skates
jacket
jeans
necklace
ring
shirt
socks
sunglasses
tie
T-shirt
watch

Materials*

cotton
gold
leather
plastic
polyester
rubber
silk
silver
wool

Other

CD
cell phone
cent
clerk
coffee
cost
cup
customer
design
dollar
flea market
item
lamp
notebook
newspaper
paperback book
painting
(CD) player
(birthday) present
price
tennis racket
radio
style
(price) tag
VCR

Pronouns

one
ones

Adjectives

Colors

black
blue
brown
gray
green
orange
pink
purple
red
white
yellow

Other

attractive
boring
cheap
each
expensive
fun
happy
jealous
large
light
loving
medium
mysterious
perfect
pretty
pure
reasonable
sad
small
stylish
truthful
warm

Verbs

Modal

can

Other

ask
buy
help
let (me) + verb
look (= seem)
look at
mean
pay (for)
prefer
say
see
sell (for)
think (of)
try on
want to (+ verb)

Adverbs

almost
else
more
right there

*Names of materials can be used as nouns or adjectives.

Expressions

Talking about prices

How much is this/that necklace?
It's . . . .
That' s not bad.
How much are these/those earrings?
They're . . . .
That's expensive.

Comparing

The silk dress is prettier/ more expensive than the polyester dress.

Getting someone's attention

Excuse me.
Look!
Look at . . . .
Oh, ...

Offering help

Can I help you?

Identifying things

Which one?
The blue one.
Which ones?
The yellow ones.

Talking about preferences

Which one do you prefer?
I prefer the . . . one.
Which ones do you like better/more?
I like the . . . one better/more.

Making and declining an offer

Would you like to . . . ?
Uh, no. That's OK.

Thanking someone

Thanks anyway.
You're welcome.

Expressing doubt

Hmm.
I'm not sure.
Uh, ...

Expressing surprise

Are you kidding?

Unit 4 Language summary

Vocabulary

Nouns
Movies
horror film
science fiction
thriller
western
TV programs
game show
news
soap opera
talk show
Music*
classical
country
gospel
jazz
pop
R&B (rhythm and blues)
rap
rock
salsa

Musical instruments
cello
guitar
piano
Entertainers
actor
actress
group
singer
Other
concert
date
fan
(baseball) game
gate
kind (of)
(soccer) match
(text) message
(electronic) note
play
stadium
ticket
video
voice

Pronouns
Object pronouns
me
you
him
her
it
us
them

Verbs
Modal
would
Other
come
have to (+ verb)
go out
guess
know
listen to
meet
miss
need to (+ verb)
play (an instrument)
see
save
send
study
think
visit
win

Adverbs
especially
just
never
pretty (+ adjective)
still
tomorrow
(not) very much

Prepositions
about (it)
for (dinner)
with (me)
from . . . until/till . . .

*Names of musical styles can be used as nouns or adjectives.

Expressions

Talking about likes and dislikes
Do you like . . . ?
Yes, I do. I like . . . a lot./
I love . . . .
No, I don't. I don't like . . .
very much.
What kind of . . . do you like?
What do you think of . . . ?
Who's/What's your favorite . . . ?

Inviting someone
Would you like to . . . ?
Do you want to . . . ?
Accepting an invitation
Yes, I would.
Yes, I'd love to.
Yes, I'd really like to.
Refusing an invitation
I'd like to, but I have to . . . .
I'd like to, but I need to . . . .
I'd like to, but I want to . . . .

Asking about events
When is it?
Where is it?
What time does it start?
Where should we . . . ?

Unit 5 Language summary

Vocabulary

Nouns

Family/Relatives
aunt
brother
children
cousin
dad
daughter
father
grandfather
grandmother
grandparents
great-grandfather
great-grandmother
great-grandparent
husband
mom
mother
nephew
niece
sister
sister-in-law
son
uncle
wife

Other
adult
age
bus stop
college
couple
elevator
e-mail
family tree
fact
foreign language
government
money
only child
people
percent
(wildlife) photographer
project
teenager
shopping trip
television
women

Pronouns

anyone
no one

Adjectives

Quantifiers
all
nearly all
most
many
a lot of/lots of
some
not many
a few
few

Other
dear (+ name)
married
secret
single
stuck
typical
unmarried
young

Verbs

eat
enjoy
get (married)
marry
move
spend (money)
stand
tell
travel
vote
wait

Adverbs

Time expressions
(almost) always
right now
this week/month/year
these days

Other
abroad
alone
away
together

Prepositions

between (the ages of . . . and . . .)
by (the age of . . .)
of

Conjunction

because

Expressions

Asking about family
Tell me about your family.
How many people are there in your family?
  There are . . . people in my family.
  We have . . . son(s) and . . . daughter(s).
How many brothers and sisters do you have?
  I have . . . brother(s) and . . . sister(s).
  I'm an only child.

Exchanging information about the present
Are you living at home?
  Yes, I am./No, I'm not.
Where are you working now?
  I'm working . . . .
Is anyone in your family . . . right now?
  Yes, my . . . is . . . .

Expressing interest
What an interesting . . . .

Expressing relief
Thank goodness!

Unit 6 Language summary

Vocabulary

Nouns

Sports and fitness activities

aerobics
baseball
basketball
bicycling
football
in-line skating
jogging
karate
running
soccer
softball
stretching
swimming
tennis
treadmill
volleyball
walking
weight training
yoga

Other

athlete
country
couch potato
fitness freak
free time
gym
sports fanatic
talent show
tip

Pronoun

nothing

Adjectives

average
fit
good at (something)
middle-aged
real
regular
tired

Verbs

chat
dance
draw
enter
exercise
keep
lift weights
paint
play (cards/a sport)
relax
sing
spend (time)
take (a walk)
type
work out

Adverbs

Frequency

always
almost always
usually
often
sometimes
hardly ever
almost never
never
every . . .
once a . . .
twice a . . .
three times a . . .
not very often/much

Other

online*
sometime
then

Prepositions

in (my free time/great shape)
for (a walk)
like (that)

*Can also be an adjective

Expressions

Talking about routines

How often do you . . . ?
Every . . . .
Once/Twice/Three times a . . . .
Not very often.
Do you ever . . . ?
Yes, I always/often/sometimes . . . .
No, I never/hardly ever . . . .
How long do you spend . . . ?
Two hours a day./Thirty minutes a day.

Talking about abilities

How well do you . . . ?
Pretty well./About average.
Not very well.
How good are you at . . . ?
Pretty good./OK.
Not very good.

Asking for more information

What else . . . ?

Expressing surprise/disbelief

Seriously?

Agreeing

All right.
No problem!

Unit 7 Language summary

Vocabulary

Nouns
argument
bowling
city
dishes
flight
food
gardening
homework
hotel
insect
karaoke bar
laundry
luggage
neighbor
noise
party
passport
photocopy
(air)plane
room
service
surfing
test
tourist
trip
vacation
waves
weather

Pronouns
anything
anybody
something

Adjectives
amazing
awful
broke
cloudy
cold
cool
excellent
foggy
freezing
full
hot
incredible
lost
lucky
rude
sick
terrible
special
terrific
whole

Verbs
believe
call
cook
drive
fish
forget
happen
hear
invite
make (a phone call)
rain
read
stay (home)
stop
take (a day off)
worry
wrong

Adverbs
Time expressions
again
all day/night/weekend
as usual
last night/Saturday/weekend
most of the time
the whole time
today
yesterday

Other
also
anywhere
downtown
first of all
unfortunately

Prepositions
on (business/vacation/a trip)
over (the weekend)

Expressions

Asking about past activities
Did you go anywhere last weekend?
How did you spend . . . ?
What did you do . . . ?
Where did you . . . ?
What time did you . . . ?
Who did you . . . with?
How long were you . . . ?

Giving opinions about past experiences
How did you like . . . ?/How was . . . ?
It was . . . ./I really enjoyed it.
What was the best thing about . . . ?
Was the . . . OK?

Unit 8 Language summary

Vocabulary

Nouns

Neighborhood/ Recreational facilities

amusement park
apartment (building)
aquarium
avenue
bank
barber shop
bookstore
(botanical) garden
campus
clothing store
dance club
drugstore
gas station
grocery store
gym
hotel
ice-skating rink
in-line skating path
Internet café
laundromat
(public) library
movie theater
(science) museum
music store
park
pay phone
post office
restaurant
shopping center
skateboard park
stationery store
swimming pool
theater
traffic light
(public) transportation
travel agency
video arcade
youth center
zoo

Other

ad(vertisement)
(car) alarm
animal
bedroom
card
cat
choice
cleanliness
complaint
crime
dog
door
fashion
floor
garbage
grass
haircut
kid
parking
pet
pollution
privacy
reservation
roommate
utilities
yard

Adjectives

available
convenient
fancy
loud
quiet

Verbs

agree
bark
borrow
call back
cut
dry
find
hold on
look for
share
wash

Adverbs

Responses

of course

Other

everywhere
in fact
too (= also)

Prepositions

on
next to
near(by)
close to
across from
opposite
in front of
in back of
behind
between
on the corner of

Conjunction

so

Expressions

Defining a place

What's a . . . ?
  It's a place where you . . . .

Asking for and giving locations

Is there a/an . . . near here?
  Yes, there is. There's one . . . .
  No, there isn't, but there's one . . . .
Are there any . . . around here?
  Yes, there are. There are some . . . .
  No, there aren't, but there are some . . . .
  No, there aren't any . . . around here.

Asking about quantities

Are there many . . . ?
  Yes, there are a lot.
  Yes, there are a few.
  No, there aren't many.
  No, there aren't any.
  No, there are none.
Is there much . . . ?
  Yes, there's a lot.
  Yes, there's a little.
  No, there isn't much.
  No, there isn't any.
  No, there's none.

Unit 9 Language summary

Vocabulary

Nouns
appearance
beard
centimeter
contact lenses
couple
e-pal
eye
feet
girlfriend
glasses
guy
hair
height
length
looks
man
meter
mustache
picture
sweater
window
woman

Adjectives
bald
blond
casual
classic
curly
dark
elderly
funky
good-looking
gorgeous
handsome
long
medium
middle aged
serious-looking
short
straight
tall

Verbs
describe
hold
learn
sit
suppose
wear

Adverbs
fairly (+ adjective)
quite (+ adjective)

Prepositions
in (a T-shirt/jeans/his twenties)
on (the couch)
to (the left of)
with (red hair)

Expressions

Asking about appearance
What does she look like?
  She's tall.
  She has red hair.
How old is she?
  She's about 32.
  She's in her thirties.
How tall is she?
  She's 1 meter 88.
  She's 6 feet 2.
How long is her hair?
  It's medium length.
What color is her hair?
  It's light brown.
What color are her eyes?
  They're dark green.
Does he wear glasses?
  Yes, he does./No, he doesn't.

Identifying someone
Who's Raoul?
  He's the man wearing a green shirt/talking to Liz.
Which one is Julia?
  She's the one in jeans/near the window.

Making suggestions
Why don't you . . . ?

Unit 10 Language summary

Vocabulary

Nouns
appointment
(mountain) biking
camel
(goat) cheese
curry
dictionary
elementary school
hairstyle
hill
key
(herbal) tea
lifestyle
magazine
(take-out) meal
riverboat tour
streetcar
truck
wedding

Adjectives
awake
busy
current
easygoing
engaged
fast-paced
iced
important
latest
live (concert)
relaxed
several
valuable

Verbs
choose
clean
climb
cut
decide
hike
kill
lose
read
ride
surf (the Internet)
take (it easy)
taste
try

Adverbs
already
ago
lately
past
recently
yet

Prepositions
for (a while/two weeks/several years)
since (6:45/last week/elementary school)

Expressions

Talking about past experiences
Have you ever . . . ?
Have you . . . recently/lately . . . this week?
  Yes, I have./No, I haven't.
Have you . . . yet?
  Yes, I have. I've (already) . . . .
  No, I haven't. I haven't . . . (yet).
How many times have you . . . ?
  I've . . . once/twice/several times.
How long have you lived here?
  I've lived here for/since . . . .
How long did you live there?
  I lived there for . . . .

Expressing uncertainty
I can't decide.

Apologizing
I'm sorry (I'm late).

Unit 11 Language summary

Vocabulary

Nouns
attraction
bargain
beach
event
(city) guide
harbor
hometown
information
sight
souvenir
spot
subway
summer
taxi
town
visitor

Pronoun
you (= anyone)

Adjectives
best
clean
crowded
delicious
efficient
fast
historical
local
inexpensive
noisy
polluted
safe
spacious
stressful
ugly

Verbs
Modal
should

Other
arrive
get around
move away
plan to (+ verb)
recommend
rent
use

Adverbs
anytime
definitely
easily
extremely (+ adjective)
maybe
somewhat (+ adjective)

Prepositions
outside (the city)
about (Mexico City)

Conjunctions
however
though

Expressions

Describing something
What's . . . like?
It's . . . and . . . .
It's . . . , but (it's not) . . . .
It's . . . . It's not (too) . . . , though.
It's . . . . It's not (too) . . . , however.

Asking for information
Can you tell me about . . . ?

Talking about advisability
What can you do . . . ?
You can . . . .
You can't . . . .
Can I . . . ?
Yes, you can./No, you can't.

Asking for and giving suggestions
What should I . . . ?
You should . . . .
You shouldn't . . . .
Should I . . . ?
Yes, you should./No, you shouldn't.

Unit 12 Language summary

Vocabulary

Nouns

Health problems
backache
burn
cold
cough
dry skin
fever
flu
headache
hiccups
insomnia
itchy eyes
mosquito bites
sore eyes/muscles/throat
stomachache
sunburn
toothache
upset stomach

Containers
bag
bottle
box
can
jar
pack
stick
tube

Pharmacy items
aspirin
bandages
breath mints
cough drops
deodorant
eye drops
face cream
heating pad
lotion
multivitamin
ointment
shaving cream
tissues
toothpaste
vitamin C

Other
advice
back
chicken stock
dentist
energy
garlic
hand
head
idea
liquid
muscle
rest
throat
tooth

Adjectives
helpful
homesick
itchy
stressed (out)

Verbs

Modals
could
may

Other
burn
chop up
concentrate
faint
get (a cold)
hurt
rest
put
see (a doctor/a dentist)
suggest
sneeze
take (medicine/
  something for . . .)
work (= succeed)

Prepositions
in (bed)
under (cold water)

Expressions

Talking about health problems
How are you?
  Not so good. I have . . . .
That's too bad.

Offering and accepting assistance
Can/May I help you?
  Yes, please.
Can/Could/May I have . . . ?

Asking for and giving advice
What should you do . . . ?
  It's important/helpful/a good idea to . . . .
What do you suggest/have for . . . ?
  Try/I suggest/You should . . . .

Expressing dislike
Yuck!

Agreeing
You're right.

Unit 13 Language summary

Vocabulary

Nouns

Food and beverages

banana
bean
beef
bread
burrito
cake
cappuccino
(blue) cheese
chicken
chocolate
cucumber
(main) dish
dessert
dressing
flavor
french fries
hamburger
ice cream
kebab
lamb
lemon
lettuce
meat
meatball
mushroom
noodle
omelet
pizza
potato
rice
salad
salmon
sandwich
seafood
shrimp
soup
sushi
tofu
tomato
tuna
vinaigrette
water

Other

coffee shop
menu
order
review
waiter
waitress

Adjectives

baked
bland
fresh
fried
greasy
grilled
healthy
international
mashed
mixed
rich
salty
sour
spicy
stir-fried
sweet
vegetarian

Verbs

Modals

will
would

Other

bring
order
take (an order)

Adverbs

a bit (+ adjective)
either
neither
tonight

Preposition

with (lemon)

Expressions

Expressing feelings

I'm (not) crazy about . . . .
I'm (not) in the mood for . . . .
I can't stand . . . .

Agreeing and disagreeing

I like . . . .
  So do I./I do, too.
I don't like . . . .
  Neither do I./I don't either.
I'm crazy about . . . .
  So am I./I am, too.
I'm not in the mood for . . . .
  Neither am I./I'm not either.
I can . . . .
  So can I./I can, too.
I can't . . . .
  Neither can I./I can't either.

Ordering in a restaurant

May I take your order?
What would you like (to . . .)?
  I'd like/I'll have a/an/the . . . .
What kind of . . . would you like?
  I'd like/I'll have . . . , please.
Would you like anything else?
  Yes, please. I'd like . . . .
  No, thank you. That'll be all.

Unit 14 Language summary

Vocabulary

Nouns

Geography
capital
coastline
desert
earth
forest
island
lake
ocean
planet
river
sea
view
valley
volcano
waterfall
world

Distances and measurements
degree (Celsius/Fahrenheit)
kilometer
meter
(square) mile

Other
airport
farm
gift
knowledge
metal
million
number
population
quiz
winter

Adjectives
deep
far
hard
high
isolated
mountainous
wet
worse

Verbs
get up (to)
go down (to)

Adverb
next year

Prepositions
in (the summer/the world/the Americas)
of (the three)
on (the island/earth)
from . . . to . . .

Expressions

Talking about distances and measurements
How far is . . . from . . . ?
It's about . . . kilometers/miles.
How big is . . . ?
It's . . . square kilometers/miles.
How high is . . . ?
It's . . . meters/feet high.
How deep is . . . ?
It's . . . meters/feet deep.
How long is . . . ?
It's . . . kilometers/miles long.
How hot is . . . in the summer?
It gets up to . . . degrees.
How cold is . . . in the winter?
It goes down to . . . degrees.

Making comparisons
Which country is larger, . . . or . . . ?
. . . is larger than . . . .
Which country is the largest: . . . , . . . , or . . . ?
. . . is the largest of the three.
Which country has the largest . . . ?
. . . has the largest . . . .
What is the most beautiful . . . in the world?
I think . . . is the most beautiful.

Unit 15 Language summary

Vocabulary

Nouns

Leisure activities

(comedy) act
barbecue
(dance) performance
gathering
hockey game
picnic
(golf) tournament
rock concert

Other

address
babysitter
DVD
excuse
favor
invitation
meeting
message
relative
request
roller coaster
statement
puppy

Adjectives

canceled
physical

Verbs

accept
give
open
pick (someone) up
practice
refuse
return
speak

Adverbs

afterward
on time
overtime

Expressions

Talking about plans

What are you doing tonight?
  I'm going . . . .
Are you doing anything tonight?
  Yes, I am. I'm . . . .
  No, I'm not.
What is she going to do tomorrow?
  She's going . . . .
Are they going to . . . ?
  Yes, they are.

Apologizing and giving reasons

I'd love to, but I can't. I . . . .
Sorry, but I have to . . . .

Making a business call

Hello. May I speak to . . . ?
  . . . 's not in. Can I take a message?
Yes, please. This is . . . . Would you
  ask . . . to call me?
This is . . . .
  I'll give . . . the message.

Leaving and taking messages

Can/May I take a message?
  Please tell . . . (that) . . . .
  Please ask . . . to . . . .
  Would/Could you tell . . . to . . . ?
  Would/Could you ask . . . to . . . ?

Unit 16 Language summary

Vocabulary

Nouns
(savings) account
(photo) album
credit
card
career
change
course
future
goal
graduation
(driver's) license
life
(bank/student) loan
lottery
responsibility
skill
vocabulary
weight

Adjectives
broke
outgoing
own
successful

Verbs
achieve
become
bring about
catch up
change
dress
dye
fall (in love)
gain
graduate
grow
hope (+ verb)
improve
pay off
take (the bus)
win

Adverbs
anymore
differently
less
someday

Prepositions
in (ages/a few years)
into (my own apartment)

Expressions

Describing changes
You've really changed!
I'm not in school anymore.
I wear contact lenses.
I got engaged.
I moved to a new place.
I've lost weight.
I've changed jobs.
My hair is shorter now.
My job is less stressful.

Talking about future plans
I'm (not) going to . . . .
I (don't) plan/want to . . . .
I hope to . . . .
I'd like/love to . . . .

Expressing congratulations
Congratulations!

Oral quizzes

The questions found in the Question bank (pages T-194 to T-197) may be used to assess students' mastery of the material presented in *Interchange Third Edition*, Level 1. Each set of questions covers material from one unit.

When to give a quiz

- Oral quizzes may be given before or after Ss take the written quiz.
- Ask Ss the appropriate questions after the class has completed two units of material.
- Alternatively, questions may be asked after Ss have completed three or more units.

Before giving a quiz

- Photocopy the oral quiz scoring sheet – one for each S in the class.
- Depending on the number of Ss to be quizzed and the amount of time needed to assess each one, schedule about 20–30 minutes of a class period for the quiz.
- Become familiar with the aspects of speaking that the quiz measures (i.e., comprehension, fluency, grammar, vocabulary, and pronunciation).
- Tell the Ss that they are going to have an oral quiz. Explain that the goal is to answer questions and talk about the topics in the unit.
- Review vocabulary from the unit and prepare a list of words to include in the oral quiz. For specified questions, hold up or point at objects to indicate what Ss will describe or discuss.

How to give a quiz

- Point out that the purpose of the quiz is not for Ss to compete for the highest score; rather, the quiz will inform Ss (and the teacher) about how well they learned the material and what material, if any, may need extra review and practice.
- Tell Ss that they are not allowed to use their Student's Books or dictionaries during the quiz.
- When asking yes/no questions, it is often best to choose information that will elicit a negative answer. This will allow a follow-up question, or lead the S to provide the correct information.
- When selecting from among the questions provided, don't feel it's necessary to ask them all. You may also include questions and follow-up prompts of your own.
- It's often useful to vary the sequence of the questions you ask so that other Ss don't know exactly what to expect.
- The most effective (but time-consuming) way to use this quiz is to ask questions to one S at a time. When necessary, ask follow-up questions to encourage fuller answers. Try to help Ss feel like equal partners in the interaction, rather than feeling as if they are being interviewed or quizzed.
- Encourage Ss to ask questions to you or to other classmates. For specified questions, name or gesture toward a S or group of Ss. For example, tell the S: "Now ask me . . . " or "Now ask David . . . ."

Alternative presentation

- Choose questions to ask a group of two or three Ss. Be prepared to score Ss simultaneously, using a separate oral quiz scoring sheet for each S.

How to score a quiz

- Assign each S a number from 0 to 5 for each of the five areas. Reserve 0 for Ss who fail to take the quiz. Using this system, a maximum score of 25 points is possible by adding scores in each area.
- As Ss are assessed based on what is taught in a particular unit, they could get the maximum score on the oral quiz. This suggests that a S has mastered the content, structures, and vocabulary specific to that unit. Although some aspects of language (e.g., pronunciation) are not unit-specific, the scores should be based on the kind of speech and communication modeled in the unit.
- If a letter grade system is useful to the teacher and the Ss, this scoring system can be used:

  23–25 = A or Excellent
  20–22 = B or Very Good
  17–19 = C or Good
  16 or below = Needs improvement
- To keep quiz results in one place, use the form on page T-199 to record Ss' scores.
- If the results of the oral quiz are used with the results of the written quiz, add the scores together and divide by two.
- In addition to a numeric score, it's very important to provide Ss with written comments, including positive feedback. Praise Ss on their strengths and suggest areas for improvement.

Oral quiz scoring sheet

Name: ______________________

Date: ______________________

Score: ______________________

		Poor	Fair	Good	Very good	Excellent
Comprehension	0	1	2	3	4	5
Fluency	0	1	2	3	4	5
Grammar	0	1	2	3	4	5
Vocabulary	0	1	2	3	4	5
Pronunciation	0	1	2	3	4	5

General comments

Suggestions for improvement

Comprehension = ability to understand questions and respond appropriately
Fluency = ability to speak quickly, naturally, and without many pauses
Grammar = ability to use correct grammar and sentence structures
Vocabulary = ability to understand and use vocabulary words and phrases
Pronunciation = ability to use correct stress, rhythm, and intonation patterns

Question bank

Unit 1 Please call me Beth.

Hello/Hi. Good morning/afternoon/evening. How are you?

What's your first/last name? What's your first/last name, again? How do you spell that?

Where are you from? Where's [classmate] from? Are you and [classmate] from [country]?

How are your classes? What are your classmates like?

Are you and [classmate] in the same class? Are your classes interesting?

Is your English class in the morning? Are you free after class?

Unit 2 How do you spend your day?

What do you do? Where do you work? Where do you go to school?

Do you like your classes? What's your favorite class?

How do you like your classmates?

Where does [classmate] work/go to school? What about [other classmate]? What does he/she do, exactly? How does he/she like it?

Describe your daily routine. What do you do early in the morning? What do you do in the afternoon? What do you do late at night? What do you do on weekends?

When do you usually get up/come to school/have lunch/get home/go to bed?

What time is your English class? What time is it right now?

Ask me about my job. *or* Ask [classmate] about his/her job or classes.

Unit 3 How much is it?

(***Note:*** *Bring a variety of objects or pictures of objects to class. Add prices.*)

How much is this/that? (*Indicate object.*) What color is it? / Is it cotton/gold/leather/plastic/rubber/silk/silver/wool?

How much are these/those? (*Indicate objects.*) What color are they? What material are they made of?

Which one do you prefer/like better? (*Indicate objects.*) Why? Which one is cheaper/prettier/nicer/better/more stylish/more expensive?

Which ones do you prefer/like better? (*Indicate objects.*) Why? Which ones are cheaper/prettier/nicer/better/more stylish/more expensive?

Ask me about my clothing preferences. *or* Ask [classmate] about his/her clothing preferences.

Unit 4 Do you like rap?

What kinds of music do you like? Do you like [type of music]?

What do you think of [name of singer/group/musician]? Who's your favorite?

What kinds of TV programs do you like? Do you like [type of TV show]?

What do you think of [name of popular TV program]?

What kinds of movies do you like? Do you like [type of movie]?

What do you think of [name of recent movie]?

Would you like to go to [event] with me this weekend? Why or why not?

Would you like to [activity] with me this weekend?

Ask me about music/TV shows/movies. *or* Ask [classmate] about music/TV shows/movies.

Unit 5 Tell me about your family.

Do you come from a big/small family? How many brothers and sisters do you have?

Are you living at home now? Where are you working/studying?

Tell me about your family. Is your [family member] working for [company name]?

What is your [family member] doing these days?

Is anyone in your family [activity] right now?

Are [classmates] studying English this year?

How many of your friends are single/married? (*Elicit quantifiers.*)

How many of your classmates are good at English? (*Elicit quantifiers.*)

Ask me about my family. *or* Ask [classmate] about his/her family.

Unit 6 How often do you exercise?

How often do you [activity]?

What do you do every day/once a week/twice a month/three times a year?

What do you usually do on [day of the week] mornings/afternoons/evenings?

Do you ever [activity] on [day of the week] mornings/afternoons/evenings?

Do you always [activity] at night?

Do you ever play/watch sports? How often?

Do you often read magazines/books/newspapers? What kinds? Which ones?

How long do you spend at the gym/at school/in class/online every day?

How well do you play [sport or game]?

How good are you at [sport, game, or activity]?

Ask me about my daily routine. *or* Ask [classmate] about his/her daily routine.

Unit 7 We had a great time!

How did you spend yesterday? Where did you go? Did you have a good time?

What did you do last weekend? Did you [activity]?

Did you go out on Friday night? Did you meet any friends? When did you go to bed?

Did you work on Saturday/Sunday? What time did you get up? Was the weather OK?

What was the best thing about your weekend?

Did you see a movie last week? What did you see? How did you like it?

Did you [activity] last month? Were your classmates with you? Who was with you?

Where did you spend your last vacation? How long were you there? Who were you with? What did you do there? How was the weather? How was the food?

Ask me about my last vacation. *or* Ask [classmate] about his/her weekend or last vacation.

Unit 8 What's your neighborhood like?

What's a [place name]?

Is there a [place name] in your neighborhood?

Is there a [place name] near here? Where is it?

Are there any [place names] in your neighborhood?

Are there any [place names] in this neighborhood? Where is one near here?

Is there much crime/noise/parking/pollution/public transportation/traffic in your neighborhood? How much is there?

Are there many schools/traffic lights/parking garages/pay phones in your neighborhood? How many are there around here? Where is one?

Ask me about my neighborhood. *or* Ask [classmate] about his/her neighborhood.

Unit 9 What does she look like?

(***Note:*** *Bring in pictures of people from a magazine to class. Add names.*)

What does [name] look like?
How long is his/her hair? What color is his/her hair? What color are his/her eyes?

Does [name] wear glasses? How old is [name]? How tall is [name]?

Does [name] wear contact lenses/have curly blond hair/have a beard?

Is [male name] handsome/middle-aged/very tall?

Is [female name] pretty/elderly/fairly short?

Who/Which one is [name]? Who's the man/woman/one [participle or preposition + . . .]?

Which ones are [two names]? Who are the ones [participle or preposition + . . .]?

Is [name] the man/woman/one [participle or preposition + . . .]?

Are [two names] the men/women/ones [participle or preposition + . . .]?

Ask me about [classmate's] appearance. *or* Ask [classmate] about my appearance.

Unit 10 Have you ever ridden a camel?

Have you been to [place]? How many times?

Have you ever eaten [type of cuisine]?

Have you ever [activity]? When did you . . . ?

Have you [activity] yet today? Have you [activity] lately/recently?

How many times have you [activity] this week?

Has your [family member] called you this week?

Has your [family member or friend] had a vacation this year?

Where have you lived for six months or more?

How long have you lived in this [town or city]? How long did you live in [town or city]?

How long were you in elementary/high school?

How long have you studied English?

How long have you been here today?

How long have you had that [object]?

Ask me about what I've done recently. *or* Ask [classmate] about what he/she has done recently.

Unit 11 It's a very exciting place!

What's your hometown like? How big is it? Is it [adjective]? Are there any [attractions]? What's the weather like in the [season]?

What's the shopping like in your hometown? What are the prices like? What can you do in the evenings? How about the weekends?

What shouldn't I miss in your hometown? What should I see there? What can't I do there? Is [attraction] open every day? How much does it cost?

What's the public transportation like in this [town or city]? Should I take the buses? Should I rent a car?

Ask me about my hometown. *or* Ask [classmate] about his/her hometown.

Unit 12 It really works!

How are you? How are you feeling today?

What should you do for [health problem]?

What do you do when you can't sleep/feel very stressed/can't concentrate?

What can you buy in a [name of container]?

Imagine you have [health problem] and I'm a pharmacist. Ask me for something.

Unit 13 May I take your order?

(***Note:*** *Bring in a restaurant menu to class or use the menu in Interchange 13.*)

May I take your order?

What would you like? Would you like a/some [food]?

What would you like to drink?

Would you like dessert?

Would you like anything else?

Imagine you're a waiter/waitress. Take my order. *or* Take [classmate's] order.

I love [food] a lot./I'm in the mood for [food]./I can eat [food]. How about you?

I don't like [food]./I'm not crazy about [food]./I can't stand [food]. How about you?

Unit 14 The biggest and the best!

Which country is larger, [country 1] or [country 2]?

Which city has the largest population: [city 1], [city 2], or [city 3]?

Which is the most beautiful city/country/mountain in the world?

Who is more famous, [actor 1] or [actor 2]?

Which is the best place for a vacation: the beach, an island, or the mountains?

How far is your home from school?

How big is your hometown?

About how high is [mountain]? How deep is [canyon]? How long is [river]?

How hot/cold is it here in the summer?

Think of two or three places. Ask questions comparing them.

Unit 15 I'm going to a soccer match.

What are you doing tonight? Are you going to see a baseball game/go to a rock concert/have a picnic?

Are you going out or having dinner at home? What are you going to eat?

What is [classmate] doing tonight? Ask him/her.

What are you doing tomorrow? Are you having friends over? Who are you inviting?

What are you going to do this weekend? Are you going to [activity]?

What are your friends going to do this weekend? Are they going to [activity]?

Think of some unusual favors. Ask me to pass them on. (*Elicit* Please/Could you/Would you + tell/ask . . . ?)

Unit 16 A change for the better!

Can you tell me about some recent changes in your life?

Have you changed jobs/gotten a raise/moved to a new apartment/won the lottery?

Are you more [adjective] than before? Is your life more/less stressful now?

How have your friends or family members changed recently?

How have I changed since the beginning of this course?

What are you going to do after this course? Do you want to [activity]?

Do you hope to travel abroad? Why or why not?

Do you plan to continue learning English? Why or why not?

Would you like to take a vacation somewhere? Where?

What is something interesting you'd love to do?

Ask me about my future plans. *or* Ask [classmate] about his/her future plans.

Written quizzes

The following eight quizzes may be used to assess students' mastery of the material presented in *Interchange Third Edition*, Level 1. Each quiz covers two units. These quizzes will inform the teacher about what material needs to be reviewed and give Ss a sense of accomplishment.

When to give a quiz

- Give the appropriate quiz after the class has completed two units and the accompanying Progress check.
- Alternatively, quizzes may be given before Ss complete the Progress check. This may help Ss know what material to review.

Before giving a quiz

- Photocopy the quiz – one for each S in the class.
- Schedule about 20–30 minutes of a class period for the quiz.
- Locate and set the recorded part A for the quiz listening section on the Class Audio Cassette or Audio CD.
- Tell Ss that they are going to have a "pencil and paper" quiz. Suggest that they prepare by reviewing the appropriate units and unit summaries. Ss should pay particular attention to the Conversations, Grammar Focus points, and Word Power exercises. Tell Ss that the quiz will also contain a short listening section and a short reading passage.

How to give a quiz

- Point out that the purpose of the quiz is not for Ss to compete for the highest score; rather, the quiz will inform Ss (and the teacher) about how well they learned the material and what material, if any, may need extra review and practice.
- On the day of the quiz, hand out one photocopy of the quiz to each S.
- Encourage Ss to take about five minutes to look through the quiz, without answering any of the items. Make sure Ss understand the instructions.
- Tell Ss that they are not allowed to use their Student's Books or dictionaries during the quiz.
- Tell Ss that about five minutes of the quiz time will be used for the listening section (part A). This is the first section of the quiz; however, it is up to the teacher to decide whether to give the listening section at the beginning or end of the time.
- To help Ss use their time efficiently and to finish on time, write the total time for the quiz on the board before beginning the quiz:
  Total time: 30 minutes
- After the quiz begins, revise the time shown on the board every five minutes or so to tell the class how much time is left.
- When giving the listening section of the quiz, direct the class to part A and go over the instructions. Advise Ss just to listen the first time they hear the audio recording, and then to listen and mark their answers during the second playing. Then play the audio recording straight through twice, without stopping or pausing.

Alternative presentation

- If the teacher does not wish to use the class time for the quiz, tell Ss to complete the whole quiz at home except for part A, the listening section. Advise the Ss to complete the quiz at home in 30 minutes and not to use their Student's Books or dictionaries. During the preceding or following class, take five minutes to play the audio recording and complete part A.

How to score a quiz

- Either collect the quiz and use the Quiz answer key to score it, or go over the answers with the class while allowing each S to correct his or her own quiz. Alternatively, tell the Ss to exchange quizzes with a partner and correct each other's answers as the teacher elicits or reads the answers aloud.
- Each quiz has a total score of 25 points (25 correct answers are possible at 1 point each). If a letter grade system is useful to the teacher and the Ss, this scoring system can be used:

  23–25 = A or Excellent
  20–22 = B or Very Good
  17–19 = C or Good
  16 or below = Needs improvement
- To keep quiz results in one place, use the form on page T-199 to record Ss' scores.
- If the results of the written quiz are being used with the results of the oral quiz, add the scores together and divide by two.

Class quiz scoring sheet

Students' Names	Units 1-2	Units 3-4	Units 5-6	Units 7-8	Units 9-10	Units 11-12	Units 13-14	Units 15-16	Total
1.									
2.									
3.									
4.									
5.									
6.									
7.									
8.									
9.									
10.									
11.									
12.									
13.									
14.									
15.									
16.									
17.									
18.									
19.									
20.									
21.									
22.									
23.									
24.									
25.									
26.									
27.									
28.									
29.									
30.									

Units 1–2 quiz

Name: ____________________

Date: ____________________

Score: ____________________

A Lucy, Michael, and Sylvie are talking. Listen and check (✓) the correct answers.

1. Sylvie is
   - ☐ Lucy's friend.
   - ☐ from Toronto.
   - ☐ Michael's classmate.
2. Sylvie's last name is
   - ☐ Marso.
   - ☐ Marceau.
   - ☐ Marcoe.
3. Lucy's math teacher is
   - ☐ pretty great.
   - ☐ very interesting.
   - ☐ really good.
4. They are all
   - ☐ in the cafeteria.
   - ☐ in the same school.
   - ☐ in the same chemistry class.

B Complete the conversations. Use the correct form of *be*.

1. A: Where __________ you from, Teresa?
   B: I'm from Mexico City. How about you?
2. A: __________ David in your class this semester?
   B: Yes. We're in the same Spanish class.
3. A: What __________ your math class like?
   B: It's really interesting, and the teacher's great!
4. A: __________ Maria and Brian from Canada?
   B: No, from England.

C Circle the correct word.

1. A: Nice to meet you, Rich. And what's (**his** / **their** / **your**) last name, again?
   B: (**Her** / **My** / **Its**) last name is Parker. It's nice to meet you, too.
2. A: This is my new friend, Elizabeth. Everyone calls (**me** / **them** / **her**) Beth.
   B: Hi, Beth. We're the Johnsons. (**Your** / **His** / **Our**) first names are Frank and Judy.

D Complete the conversations.

1. A: Where __________ you work?
   B: I work in a restaurant. I'm a chef.
2. A: What __________ he do, exactly?
   B: He's a pilot for Global Airlines.
3. A: Where does she __________ to school?
   B: She goes to the University of Colorado.

E Correct the mistake in each set of sentences.

Example: He's a ~~chef~~ *carpenter*. He works for a construction company. He builds houses.

1. Carmen is a salesperson. She works for an airline. She serves drinks to passengers.
2. I work for World Travel. I'm a receptionist. I take people on tours.
3. Sam and Jerry are in the entertainment business. They play music. They are servers.

F Complete the sentences with *at*, *in*, *late*, *on*, or *until*.

1. I sleep ____________ 10:00 on weekdays.
2. John gets home ____________ at night on weekends.
3. They have lunch ____________ Saturdays around 1:00 P.M.

G Read the e-mail. Then check (✓) the correct answers.

Hi, Ernesto!

In your e-mail message, you asked me: "What do I do every day?"

Well, I'm a student at the University of Michigan. I really like my classes. I study computer science and Chinese. I go to school around 8:00 in the morning on weekdays. Around noon, I have lunch with some classmates. On Mondays and Fridays, I work out in the gym before my classes. And in the late afternoon, on Tuesdays and Thursdays, my friend Daniel and I have part-time jobs. We work in the school cafeteria. And I study in the library every weeknight until about 2:00 A.M. I'm a full-time student, and I don't have time to watch TV.

And what do you do? Send me another e-mail, please!

Your new e-friend,

Chris

1. Ernesto is Chris's
   - ☐ classmate.
   - ☐ new friend.
   - ☐ best friend.
2. Chris is a
   - ☐ part-time teacher.
   - ☐ full-time student.
   - ☐ TV announcer.
3. Daniel
   - ☐ works in the library.
   - ☐ exercises every day.
   - ☐ is Chris's friend.
4. On Tuesdays and Thursdays, Chris
   - ☐ writes to Ernesto.
   - ☐ works with Daniel.
   - ☐ doesn't study at the library.

Units 3–4 quiz

Name: ____________________

Date: ____________________

Score: ____________________

A Ann and Ben are talking in a clothing store. Listen and check (✓) the correct answers.

1. Ben prefers the
   - ☐ green shirts.
   - ☐ red shirts.
   - ☐ blue shirts.
2. The blue shirts are
   - ☐ $25.
   - ☐ $29.
   - ☐ $41.
3. The green shirts are made of
   - ☐ polyester.
   - ☐ silk.
   - ☐ cotton.
4. Ben's size is
   - ☐ large.
   - ☐ medium.
   - ☐ small.

B Circle the correct word.

1. I really like those (**cotton** / **gold** / **leather**) socks.
2. Your (**plastic** / **silk** / **silver**) tie is a beautiful design.
3. This (**gold** / **plastic** / **wool**) necklace is perfect for me. But it's $3,000!

C Complete the sentences with *this*, *that*, *these*, or *those*.

1. How much is ____________ watch? I can't find a price tag.
2. Look at ____________ purple jeans over there! Aren't they stylish?
3. I like ____________ gold earrings. They look great on me!
4. Excuse me. I like ____________ cap. Can I see it, please?

D Complete each sentence with the correct form of the adjective. Add *than* if necessary.

Example: That purple T-shirt is nicer than the pink one. (nice)

1. Are these boots ________________________ the ones over there? (large)
2. Silk is ________________________ cotton. (expensive)
3. Which dress is ________________________ , the red one or the green one? (pretty)
4. Leather jackets are usually ________________________ wool ones. (good)

E Circle the correct word.

1. Johnny Depp is my favorite actor. I like (**him** / **it** / **you**) a lot.
2. Music videos aren't very interesting. Do you like (**her** / **them** /**us**)?
3. My favorite TV program is *Survivor*. What do you think of (**her** / **it** / **me**)?

F Complete the sentences with *do*, *does*, or *would*.

1. A: __________ you like to see a movie tonight?
   B: Sure. What time does it start?
2. A: __________ you like horror movies?
   B: No, not really.
3. A: What kinds of music __________ your friend Ricardo like?
   B: Rock and classical, I think.

G Read the article. Then check (✓) the correct answers.

Audrey Tautou

Audrey Tautou is a young French actress. She has fans around the world. Here are some interesting things about Audrey's life and career.

1978 ....
Audrey is born in Beaumont, France.

1980s and 1990s ....
Audrey acts in plays (especially comedies) in high school. After that, she goes to acting school. She wins the prize "Best Newcomer" for her acting on French TV (1999).

2000-2002 ....
Audrey acts in many movies, including *Voyous Voyelle* (2000). Then she plays a young woman called Amélie in a movie of the same name. *Amélie* (2001) is in French, but the film is a big international hit. Audrey becomes popular in many countries, including the United States. Audrey also acts in a film called *God is Great, I'm Not* (2002).

2003 ....
Audrey has a big year. She acts in *The Spanish Apartment* and *He Loves Me, He Loves Me Not*. She also acts in *Dirty Pretty Things*. This is the first time she speaks English in a movie.

1. In high school, Audrey Tautou acts
   - ☐ in plays.
   - ☐ on television.
   - ☐ in movies.
2. Many Americans like the movie
   - ☐ *Voyous Voyelle*.
   - ☐ *Amélie*.
   - ☐ *God is Great, I'm Not*.
3. Audrey acts in three movies in
   - ☐ 2001.
   - ☐ 2002.
   - ☐ 2003.
4. In her movies, Audrey usually speaks
   - ☐ English.
   - ☐ French.
   - ☐ Spanish.

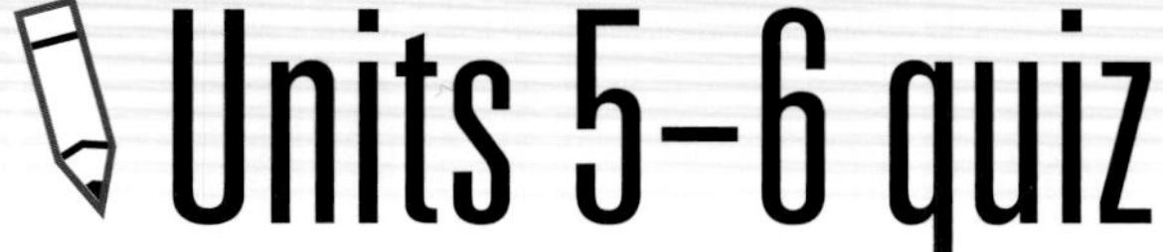

Units 5–6 quiz

Name: ______________________

Date: ______________________

Score: ______________________

A Listen to the conversations. Check the correct answers.

1. Catherine has __________ brothers and sisters.
   - ☐ four
   - ☐ seven
   - ☐ nine
2. Nowadays, Mark is living
   - ☐ at home.
   - ☐ with a friend.
   - ☐ with his wife.
3. Sharon usually goes to the gym
   - ☐ on Thursdays.
   - ☐ twice a week.
   - ☐ three times a week.
4. Some of the man's younger brothers and sisters
   - ☐ are in school.
   - ☐ have one child.
   - ☐ are working abroad.

B Complete the conversations. Use the present continuous of the verbs.

Example: A: You look nice, Jill. _Are you going_ (go) somewhere special?

B: Yes, I am. I'm on my way to a new nightclub downtown called The Mix.

1. A: How is your sister? ________________ (study) these days?

   B: No, she isn't. She ________________ (work) as a cashier at a grocery store.
2. A: Is that David over there? Who ________________(wait) for?

   B: His girlfriend, Maggie. She ________________ (come) in on the bus.

C Rewrite each sentence using *all*, *most*, *some*, *few*, or *no one*.

Example: In the United States, 0 percent of the people can vote before age 18.

In the United States, no one can vote before age 18.

1. Fifty-five percent of American mothers with small children work.

   ____
2. A small percent of Japanese families have more than three children.

   ____
3. In the U.S., 27 percent of young adults live at home with their parents.

   ____

D Circle the correct word.

1. Jay does (**yoga** / **football** / **jogging**) every morning before breakfast.
2. How often do you (**go** / **do** / **play**) swimming in the summer?
3. I sometimes play (**in-line skating** / **aerobics** / **baseball**) with my friends.

E Put the words in the correct order to make sentences or questions.

1. (dinner often TV I watch after)

____ .

2. (in you coffee the do drink ever evening)

____ ?

3. (very doesn't Jeff much exercise)

____ .

F Complete the conversations.

1. A: How ____________ do you work out?

   B: Every day. I'm a real fitness freak.

2. A: How ____________ do you play tennis?

   B: About average. But I'm getting better and better!

3. A: How ____________ do you spend at the gym?

   B: Just thirty minutes a day. Who has the time?

4. A: How ____________ are you at soccer?

   B: OK, I guess. It's not really my favorite sport.

G Read Ruth's letter. Then check (✓) four true statements.

Dear Ted,

Berkeley is a great city. I really like it here! There's always lots to do. Every day after class, I walk down Telegraph Avenue. I always like to go to my favorite coffee shop in the afternoon and meet my friends there for coffee. In the evening, there is always something interesting to do in town or near the university. For example, I sometimes see a foreign movie or listen to live music.

On Saturday, my friends and I usually take the bus to San Francisco for the day. I love the shops and restaurants, and it's a great city for jogging or in-line skating (I'm really getting good at it!) in Golden Gate Park. We always go to Chinatown to have lunch, and then we go walking or shopping in the afternoon.

On Sunday, sometimes I like to play tennis with friends, or we watch a sports event, like a football game or a basketball game, on TV. I think American football is very exciting!

Well, that's all for now. Take care. Hope to hear from you soon!

Love,
Ruth

☐ She walks down Telegraph Avenue every day after class.
☐ She meets her friends for coffee in the evening.
☐ She sometimes dances to live music.
☐ She enjoys going to San Francisco on the weekend.
☐ She doesn't like in-line skating.
☐ She goes shopping or walking after lunch on Saturdays.
☐ She plays tennis with friends every Sunday.
☐ She likes to watch football and basketball on TV.

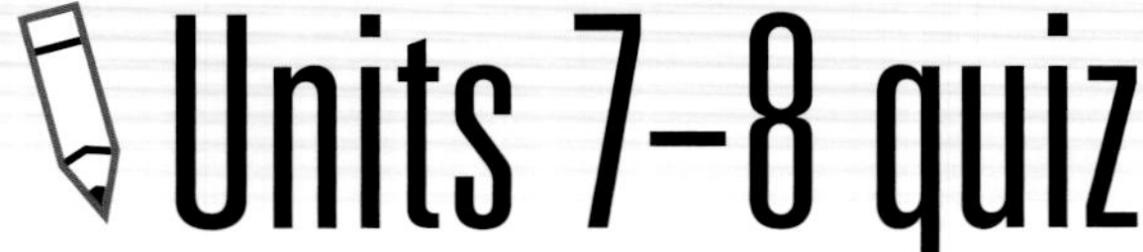

Units 7–8 quiz

Name:	
Date:	
Score:	

A Lisa and Peter are talking about vacations. Listen and check (✓) the correct answers.

Name	Country visited			Weather		
Lisa	☐ Australia	☐ Austria	☐ Korea	☐ good	☐ OK	☐ bad
Peter	☐ Indonesia	☐ India	☐ Italy	☐ good	☐ OK	☐ bad

B Complete the conversation. Use the correct form of the verbs.

A: *Did* you *stay* (stay) home last night?

B: No, I didn't.

A: What ________ you ________ (do)?

B: I ________ (go) dancing at the new club on Eighth Street. Suzie and Mike ________ (be) there, too.

A: Oh, really?

B: Yes, we ________ (have) a great time! But where ________ (be) you?

A: I ________ (be) in the laundromat all evening.

B: How boring!

A: Actually, no. I ________ (meet) my girlfriend there. We ________ (spend) the evening laughing and talking.

C Correct the mistake in each set of sentences.

Example: My hair was pretty long. I needed a haircut. So I went to the ~~theater.~~ *barber shop*

1. All my clothes were dirty. I wanted to wash them. So I went to the library.
2. I went to the post office. I was very hungry. I needed to buy food.
3. I went to the music store. I go to Singapore on Sunday. I need a plane ticket.
4. I don't have a computer. I wanted to send an e-mail. So I went to the grocery store.

D Circle the correct word or phrase.

1. A: Excuse me. Is there a gas station near here?
   B: Yes, there is. There's (**any** / **one** / **some**) around the corner.
2. A: How (**any** / **many** / **much**) hotels are there in this neighborhood?
   B: There are (**a few** / **a little** / **not much**).
3. A: Is there (**many** / **much** / **one**) public transportation near here?
   B: No, there isn't (**any** / **one** / **none**).

E Read Sarah's e-mail. Then check (✓) four things you can do in her neighborhood.

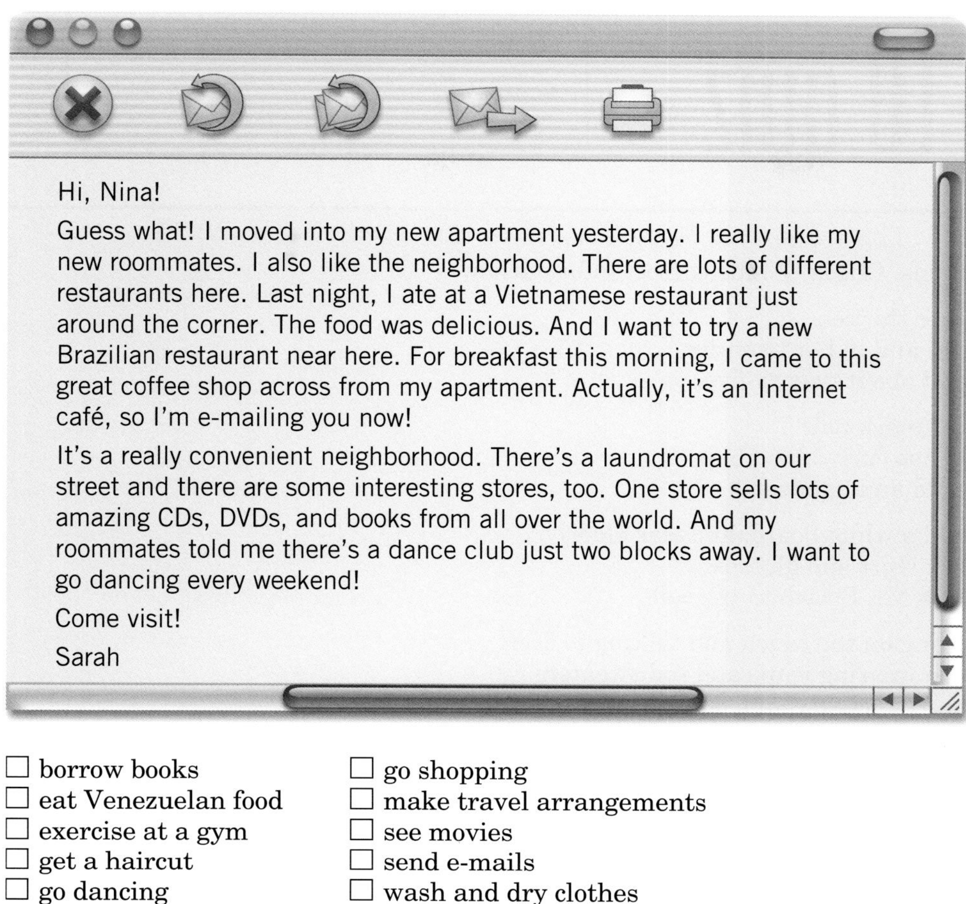

Hi, Nina!

Guess what! I moved into my new apartment yesterday. I really like my new roommates. I also like the neighborhood. There are lots of different restaurants here. Last night, I ate at a Vietnamese restaurant just around the corner. The food was delicious. And I want to try a new Brazilian restaurant near here. For breakfast this morning, I came to this great coffee shop across from my apartment. Actually, it's an Internet café, so I'm e-mailing you now!

It's a really convenient neighborhood. There's a laundromat on our street and there are some interesting stores, too. One store sells lots of amazing CDs, DVDs, and books from all over the world. And my roommates told me there's a dance club just two blocks away. I want to go dancing every weekend!

Come visit!

Sarah

- ☐ borrow books
- ☐ eat Venezuelan food
- ☐ exercise at a gym
- ☐ get a haircut
- ☐ go dancing
- ☐ go shopping
- ☐ make travel arrangements
- ☐ see movies
- ☐ send e-mails
- ☐ wash and dry clothes

Units 9–10 quiz

Name: ______________________

Date: ______________________

Score: ______________________

A Listen to the conversations. Check (✓) the correct information.

1. ☐ Emily is short and in her thirties.
   ☐ Emily is medium height and in her twenties.
   ☐ Emily is fairly short and about twenty-five.
2. ☐ Steve has blue eyes and black hair.
   ☐ Steve is really tall and has curly blond hair.
   ☐ Steve is only 29 years old and handsome.
3. ☐ The thief was short, had a white beard, and was elderly.
   ☐ The thief had on a black shirt and glasses.
   ☐ The thief had lunch with Mr. Brown in the café.
4. ☐ A.J. and Penny are sitting on the couch and talking to Tom.
   ☐ A.J. and Penny are both wearing jeans and red sweaters.
   ☐ A.J. and Penny are the attractive couple sitting on the couch.

B Circle the correct word.

1. My brother is (**in** / **about** / **at**) his twenties and goes to college in Arizona.
2. Tracy (**does** / **has** / **is**) short straight black hair and blue eyes.
3. Phil's nephew (**is** / **has** / **are**) 5 feet 8 and has a dark brown beard and mustache.

C Put the words in the correct order to make sentences or questions.

1. (is gorgeous thirties and Kristi her really in)

   ____ .
2. (wear mustache have Sam a does glasses and)

   ____ ?
3. (red Cindy height long has and is medium hair)

   ____ .
4. (on person next the Jason couch who's to sitting the)

   ____ ?

D Complete the conversations. Use the present perfect of the verbs.

Example: A: *Has* ______ Ann *called* ______ yet? (call)

B: Yes. She called a few minutes ago.

1. A: ______________ you ______________ to any good movies lately? (be)

   B: Yes, I ______________ already ______________ three films this month. (see)
2. A: ______________ he ever ______________ Thai food before? (eat)

   B: No, he ______________ never ______________ it in his life. (have)

E Circle the correct word.

1. Has Martin ever (**missed** / **climbed** / **lost**) an appointment?
2. How many times have you lost your (**classes** / **sports** / **cell phone**)?
3. Have you ever (**ridden** / **driven** / **drunk**) a truck?

F Complete the sentences with *for* or *since*.

1. I lived in Boston ____________ five years. I loved every minute I was there!
2. My wife and I have gone to Costa Rica every year ____________ 2001.
3. Patrick has studied Portuguese ____________ a long time. He's a good speaker now.

G Read the stories. Then write the correct title for each one.

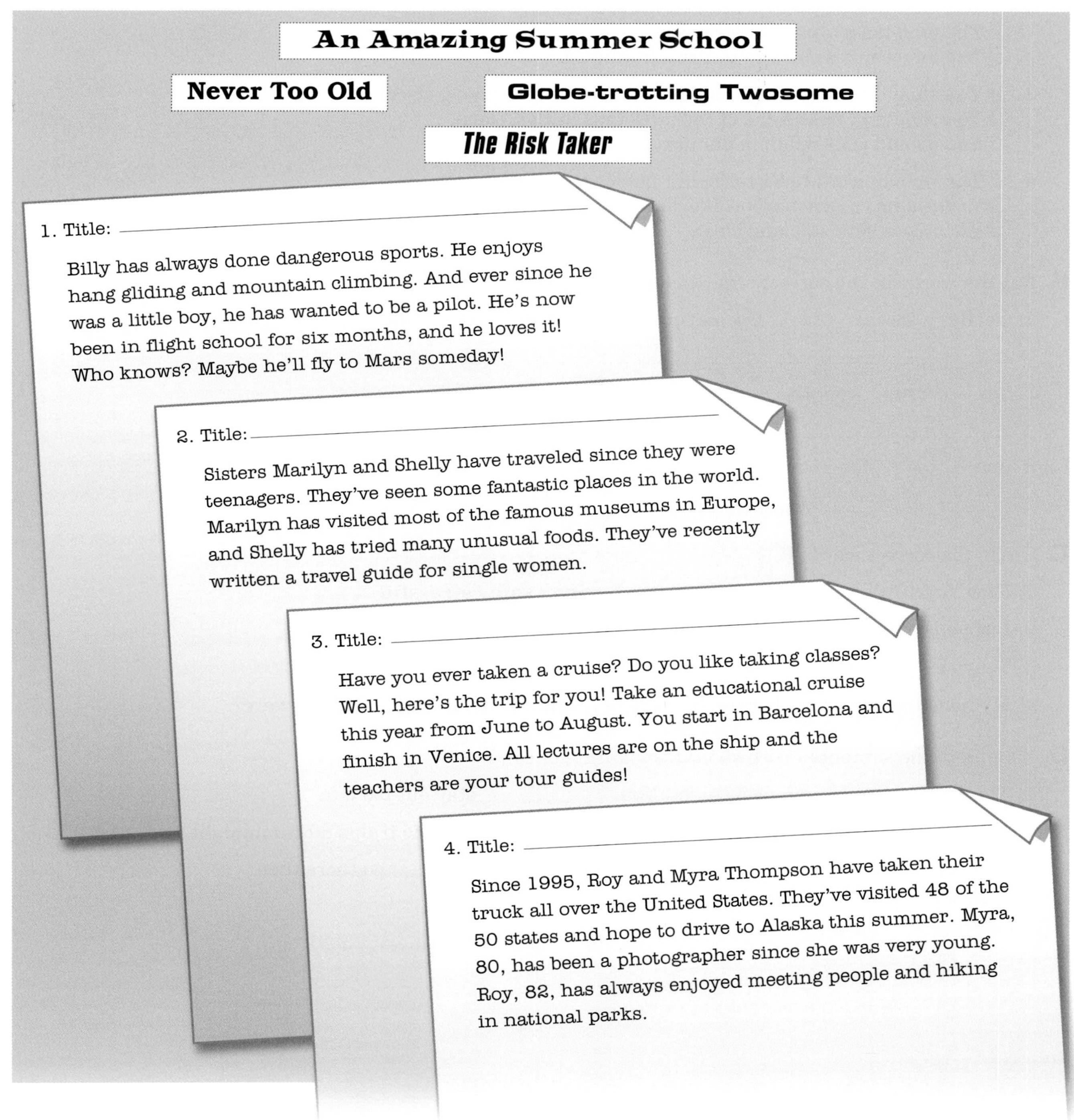

An Amazing Summer School
Never Too Old
Globe-trotting Twosome
The Risk Taker
1. Title: ____________
Billy has always done dangerous sports. He enjoys hang gliding and mountain climbing. And ever since he was a little boy, he has wanted to be a pilot. He's now been in flight school for six months, and he loves it! Who knows? Maybe he'll fly to Mars someday!
2. Title: ____________
Sisters Marilyn and Shelly have traveled since they were teenagers. They've seen some fantastic places in the world. Marilyn has visited most of the famous museums in Europe, and Shelly has tried many unusual foods. They've recently written a travel guide for single women.
3. Title: ____________
Have you ever taken a cruise? Do you like taking classes? Well, here's the trip for you! Take an educational cruise this year from June to August. You start in Barcelona and finish in Venice. All lectures are on the ship and the teachers are your tour guides!
4. Title: ____________
Since 1995, Roy and Myra Thompson have taken their truck all over the United States. They've visited 48 of the 50 states and hope to drive to Alaska this summer. Myra, 80, has been a photographer since she was very young. Roy, 82, has always enjoyed meeting people and hiking in national parks.

Units 11–12 quiz

Name: ______________________

Date: ______________________

Score: ______________________

A Listen to the conversations. Check (✓) the correct information.

1. ☐ The woman visited Hokkaido for the first time.
   ☐ The beaches in Hokkaido are not crowded.
   ☐ The woman thinks Hokkaido is pretty stressful.
2. ☐ The man had a great vacation in Paris last July.
   ☐ The man hasn't been to Paris yet.
   ☐ The man can't wait to go to Paris in August.
3. ☐ You shouldn't go to the Ramblas because it's a very long street.
   ☐ You shouldn't miss some of the museums in Barcelona.
   ☐ You should visit Spain in January.
4. ☐ The woman went to Victoria, but not Vancouver.
   ☐ Victoria has a nice harbor. It's dangerous, however.
   ☐ Victoria is both safe and clean.

B Put the words in the correct order to make sentences.

1. (really Seoul is fascinating city a)

   ____ .

2. (an Peru country interesting is extremely)

   ____ .

3. (me too for is Taipei expensive)

   ____ .

C Circle the correct word.

1. New York City is very exciting, but it's (**boring** / **safe** / **stressful**).
2. Lisbon is an interesting city, and it's (**beautiful** / **noisy** / **polluted**).
3. Tokyo is a safe city. It's (**clean** / **crowded** / **dangerous**), though.
4. My hometown is pretty boring. It's very (**expensive** / **relaxing** / **ugly**), however.

D Complete the sentences with *should*, *shouldn't*, or *can't*.

1. This city can be dangerous at night. You ____________ stay out too late.
2. You ____________ travel by subway late at night. There are no trains after midnight.
3. In Hong Kong, the weather is best in the fall. You ____________ go there then.

E Match the problem with the advice. Then use the information to write conversations.

Problem	*Advice*
✓a fever	use a heating pad
a sunburn	see a dentist
sore muscles	✓take some aspirin
a toothache	try this lotion

Example: A: What should I do for a fever?

B: It's sometimes helpful *to take some aspirin.* ______

1. A: ______

   B: It's a good idea ______

2. A: ______

   B: It's sometimes helpful ______

3. A: ______

   B: It's important ______

F Complete the conversations with *bottle*, *jar*, *pack*, or *tube*.

1. Customer: What do you have for a cold?

   Pharmacist: Take this ______ of vitamin C. Take one every day.

2. Customer: Can I have something for dry skin?

   Pharmacist: I suggest this ______ of hand cream. Apply some every morning.

3. Customer: May I have something for a toothache?

   Pharmacist: Of course. Try this ______ of special toothpaste.

4. Customer: Could I get something for a sore throat?

   Pharmacist: Sure. Here's a ______ of cough drops. They really work.

G Read the article. Then check (✓) four things people suggested the writer should do.

Too Much Advice!

Isn't it amazing? You have a health problem, and everyone gives you different advice. For several months, I felt tired all the time. Some people suggested I sleep longer, but others said I was sleeping too much. One friend told me I was working too hard, and she said it's important to relax. Another friend suggested that it's helpful to get a lot of fresh air. His advice was that I should go for a long walk every day after work. One co-worker told me, "You're not tired, just lazy!" Even different doctors give you different advice for the same problem! I visited one doctor, and she gave me some vitamin C. It didn't work. So I went to another doctor, and he simply suggested I take a vacation. That didn't work either. A third doctor told me to pick up some medicine from the drugstore. I felt even more tired! Finally, I went to a doctor of traditional Chinese medicine. He gave me some medicinal plants. He advised me to cook them in water and then drink the herbal mixture. It worked! Now, I'm never tired but I can't sleep at night! Who should I ask for advice this time?

- ☐ Ask someone for advice.
- ☐ Go on a vacation.
- ☐ Never sleep at night.
- ☐ Sleep less.
- ☐ Sleep more.
- ☐ See a doctor.
- ☐ Take some aspirin.
- ☐ Try some medicinal plants.
- ☐ Walk before work.
- ☐ Work longer hours.

Units 13–14 quiz

Name: ______________________

Date: ______________________

Score: ______________________

A A waitress is taking an order. Listen and complete the restaurant check.

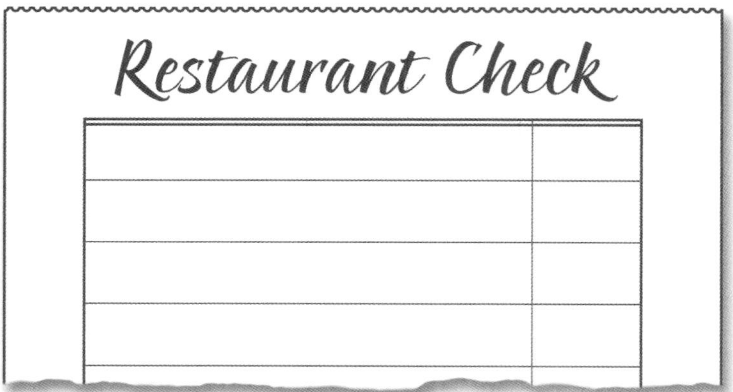

B Check (✓) the correct response.

1. I'm crazy about real spicy food.
   - ☐ I am, too.
   - ☐ Oh, I can't.
   - ☐ Neither do I.
2. I can't stand greasy fast food.
   - ☐ Really? I can't.
   - ☐ Neither am I.
   - ☐ Oh, I love it!
3. I like Indian food a lot.
   - ☐ So can I.
   - ☐ So do I.
   - ☐ So am I.
4. I'm not in the mood for pizza.
   - ☐ Neither am I.
   - ☐ I don't either.
   - ☐ Really? I can't.

C Circle the word or phrase that doesn't fit.

1. iced coffee / tea with lemon / vinaigrette / cappuccino
2. grilled salmon / spaghetti and meatballs / tuna sushi / shrimp curry
3. beef kebabs / cheese omelet / stir-fried tofu / fried bananas

D Complete the conversation with *would*, *will*, *I'd*, or *I'll*.

A: What ____________ you like to eat?

B: The fried chicken, please.

A: What kind of potatoes would you like?

B: ____________ have the mashed potatoes.

A: Anything to drink?

B: Yes, please. ____________ like some water.

A: Anything else?

B: No. That ____________ be all.

E Circle the correct word.

1. There are lots of beautiful trees in this (**sea** / **forest** / **waterfall**).
2. A (**desert** / **river** / **hill**) is a very hot and dry place.
3. A (**lake** / **mountain** / **river**) is always higher than a valley.

F Complete each sentence with the correct form of the adjective.

1. Which city is ______________________ , Buenos Aires or Lima? (crowded)
2. Is Disney World ______________________ amusement park in the world? (famous)
3. What is ______________________ river in the world: the Amazon, Danube, or Nile? (long)

G Read the article. Then answer the questions.

THE BIG ISLAND

Everyone knows that Hawaii is a beautiful group of islands in the middle of the Pacific Ocean. But did you know that "Hawaii" is both the name of the state and the name of the biggest island in the state? Yes, it's confusing, so most people call the island of Hawaii "the Big Island."

The weather on the Big Island is very interesting. It has 10 of the 15 kinds of climates in the world, including tropical, desert, mountain, and alpine. Sometimes it even gets snow on top of its two biggest volcanoes!

On the west side of the island, the weather in sunny Kailua Kona is almost perfect. It gets up to about 80°F in the winter and 87°F in the summer. It only goes down to 64°F in the winter and 69°F in the summer. The Kohala area in the north is the driest part of the island with only about 10 inches of rain a year.

Hawaiian Islands

On the east side, Hilo gets around 140 inches of rain per year. It's the wettest city in the United States! All that rain makes for some amazing waterfalls near Hilo.

Water temperatures are coldest in February and warmest in September and October. There is good snorkeling, great scuba diving, and wonderful fishing year-round. That makes the Big Island popular with people from all over the world anytime of the year.

1. What is Hawaii?
   - ☐ a city
   - ☐ a state
   - ☐ an island
   - ☐ a state and an island
2. What climate is NOT found in Hawaii?
   - ☐ arctic
   - ☐ tropical
   - ☐ mountain
   - ☐ desert
3. How hot does it get in Kailua Kona in the winter?
   - ☐ 87°F
   - ☐ 80°F
   - ☐ 69°F
   - ☐ 64°F
4. Where does it rain the most?
   - ☐ in the north
   - ☐ in the south
   - ☐ in the east
   - ☐ in the west

Units 15–16 quiz

Name: ______________________

Date: ______________________

Score: ______________________

A Listen to two telephone conversations. Check (✓) the correct information.

Name	Invitation	Excuse
Wes	☐ beach party ☐ birthday party ☐ dinner in a restaurant ☐ go swimming	☐ Amy and Terry are going to be there. ☐ He doesn't like going to the theater. ☐ He starts work at 6:00 P.M. ☐ None
Rita	☐ baseball game ☐ basketball game ☐ dance performance ☐ play	☐ She doesn't like sports. ☐ She isn't feeling well. ☐ She needs to study for a test. ☐ None

B Complete the conversations. Use the correct form of the verbs.

1. A: What __________ you __________ (plan, do) tonight?
   B: I __________ (want, stay) home. There's a soccer match on TV.
2. A: What __________ you and Dave __________ (go, do) tomorrow?
   B: We __________ (like, have) a barbecue on the beach, but it may rain.
3. A: What __________ you __________ (hope, do) after graduation?
   B: I __________ (love, travel) in Europe for a while.

C Circle the correct word or phrase.

1. Please (**tell** / **to tell**) Mary there's a school party on Saturday.
2. Would you ask Bill (**bring** / **to bring**) the concert tickets tonight?
3. Could you (**tell** / **ask**) Dana that the movie starts at 8:15?

D Look at each message. Complete the request using the name in parentheses.

1. The test on Thursday is at 1:00 P.M.
   Please tell ______________________________ . (Ken)
2. Meet me after class today.
   Would you ask ______________________________ ? (Alex)
3. There's a volleyball game tonight.
   Could you tell ______________________________ ? (Marcus)
4. Come to the picnic on Saturday.
   Please ask ______________________________ . (Paula)

E Check (✓) four statements. Then complete the sentences.

Example: ☑ I've gained a lot of weight.

I want *to lose about five kilograms.*

1. ☐ I don't like my job anymore.
   I want ____________________
2. ☐ I've moved to a new place, but I don't like it.
   I hope ____________________
3. ☐ I don't like my hairstyle.
   I plan ____________________
4. ☐ I really need some new clothes.
   I'd like ____________________
5. ☐ I spent too much money last month.
   I hope ____________________
6. ☐ I get bored on the weekend.
   I plan ____________________
7. ☐ Another English course starts soon.
   I'd love ____________________

F Read Nicole's e-mail. Then complete the chart with two recent changes in her life and two future plans.

Hi Stephanie!

How have you been? What have you done in the past year? Sorry I haven't written in a long time. It's been a crazy year.

I've been pretty busy. I was bored with my job, and my life was going nowhere. I had no real career and no boyfriend! I knew I needed to make some changes.

First, I found a new job. I now work for a travel agency. I love it, but it's a lot more stressful than my old job. I just got a raise, though.

Also, I told my friend Jackie that I wanted to go out, so last fall she and I went out more. Then last December she arranged a date between Patrick and me. Patrick is a student, and he hopes to graduate in the summer. Guess what? We're engaged now! Surprised? Patrick and I plan to get married next year. Then we hope to travel around Mexico for our honeymoon. We're very happy!

Looking forward to hearing all your news.

Nicole

Changes	Plans
____________________	____________________
____________________	____________________

Quiz audio scripts

Units 1–2 *[CD 1, Track 16]*

A Lucy, Michael, and Sylvie are talking. Listen and check the correct answers.

LUCY: Good morning, Michael.
MICHAEL: Hi, Lucy. How's it going?
LUCY: Pretty good, thanks. How about you?
MICHAEL: Great! Hey, who's your friend?
LUCY: This is Sylvie Marceau. She's from Canada.
MICHAEL: Hi, Sylvie. Nice to meet you. I'm Michael Morse.
SYLVIE: Hi, Michael. It's good to meet you, too.
MICHAEL: I'm sorry, Sylvie, but what's your last name, again?
SYLVIE: Oh, it's Marceau.
MICHAEL: How do you spell that?
SYLVIE: M-A-R-C-E-A-U.
MICHAEL: I see. So, you're from Canada. Are you from Toronto?
SYLVIE: No. I'm from Montreal. Where are you from, Michael?
MICHAEL: I'm from Chicago.
LUCY: You know, Sylvie and I are in the same chemistry class this semester.
MICHAEL: Oh, really?
SYLVIE: Yeah. And what do you do, Michael? Are you a student here, too?
MICHAEL: Yes, I am. Lucy and I are in the same math class.
SYLVIE: Oh? Is your class interesting?
MICHAEL: Yes, it is. It's very interesting.
LUCY: And the teacher is really good. By the way, he's from Canada, too!
SYLVIE: Really?
MICHAEL: Listen, I'm on my way to the cafeteria now. Are you free?
LUCY: Sure! Let's go and get some coffee. OK, Sylvie?
SYLVIE: Sounds great!

Units 3–4 *[CD 1, Track 31]*

A Ann and Ben are talking in a clothing store. Listen and check the correct answers.

ANN: Hey, those shirts look nice. What do you think, Ben?
BEN: Yeah, Ann, they do look nice. I really like the blue ones. And the green ones are nice, too.
ANN: Which ones do you prefer?
BEN: I think I like the green ones better. They're very stylish. Oh, but look at the price – $41. That's expensive!
ANN: The blue ones are only $29. That's more reasonable.
BEN: But they're polyester. The green ones are made of better material. They're cotton.
ANN: Say, Ben, what size are you? Small or medium?
BEN: I wear a medium.
ANN: But there aren't any medium ones in blue. They're all large or small.

Units 5–6 *[CD 2, Track 9]*

A Listen to the conversations. Check the correct answers.

1.

MAN: Tell me about your family, Catherine. How many brothers and sisters do you have?

CATHERINE: Well, I have four sisters – Annette, Sarah, Jill, and Liza.

MAN: Wow! That's great! And do you have any brothers?

CATHERINE: Yes, I have three brothers – Ed, Mark, and Sam. And we all eat dinner together each night – all my brothers and sisters *and* my parents.

MAN: How fun! It's like having a party every night!

CATHERINE: Yeah, I guess it is.

2.

WOMAN: Hi, Mark! Nice to see you again! Hey, where are you working now?

MARK: I'm working full-time for a newspaper. I'm a photographer there.

WOMAN: Wow! That's interesting! Are you still living at home?

MARK: No, I'm not. I'm living in an apartment with Jim. He's an old friend from school.

WOMAN: So, you're not married?

MARK: No, not right now, but I *am* getting married this summer.

WOMAN: Congratulations!

MARK: Thanks!

3.

MAN: How often do you exercise, Sharon?

SHARON: Well, I go jogging about twice a week.

MAN: Oh, really? And do you ever go to the gym?

SHARON: Yes, I usually go on Mondays, Wednesdays, and Fridays.

MAN: Wow! How long do you spend there?

SHARON: Hmm, around two or three hours each time I go there.

MAN: Well, you're not a couch potato!

SHARON: That's for sure!

4.

MAN: Listen to this, Kylie. It says here: "In Australia, most married couples have children."

KYLIE: That's true. My parents have two kids – my sister and me.

MAN: In my country, we have really big families. There are 12 people in my family.

KYLIE: That's amazing! And are they all living at home?

MAN: Well, some of my younger brothers and sisters are still in school and living at home with my parents. A few of us older ones are married with children.

KYLIE: Are you all living in the same town?

MAN: No, my two older brothers are single and working abroad, but the others live near our parents in the same town.

Units 7–8 *[CD 2, Track 24]*

A Lisa and Peter are talking about vacations. Listen and check the correct answers.

PETER: So, Lisa, where did you go for your vacation?

LISA: I went to Australia. It was my first time there.

PETER: Did you enjoy it?

LISA: Well, yes and no. I wanted to go surfing, but the waves were really scary. It was often very windy. The weather was pretty cloudy and cool, and it rained for two whole days.

PETER: That's terrible! So you didn't surf?

LISA: No, but I visited lots of museums and saw some movies. But what about you, Peter? How did you spend your vacation?

PETER: Well, I had a lot of fun. I went to Italy.

LISA: Wow! What did you do there?

PETER: I took a walking trip in the Alps.

LISA: How was the weather?

PETER: Both good and bad. The weather can change very quickly in the mountains. Some days were sunny and warm, perfect for walking. But other days were cold and wet. But I still loved the trip.

Units 9–10 *[CD 2, Track 38]*

A Listen to the conversations. Check the correct information.

1.

MAN: Excuse me. I'm looking for someone. I'm meeting her for lunch here. Her name is Emily Black.

HOSTESS: All right. What does she look like?

MAN: Let's see. She's about 25, I guess.

HOSTESS: Look over there. Is she the one with the long black hair?

MAN: Uh, no, that's not her. Emily's fairly short and has . . .

HOSTESS: Oh, I think I see her! Look, she's waving at you!

2.

WOMAN: Sara, did you hear that Judy has a new boyfriend?

SARA: No, I didn't! What's he like?

WOMAN: Well, his name's Steve, and he's very nice. And he's tall, really tall. He's over 6 feet tall!

SARA: What color is his hair?

WOMAN: His hair is blond and curly.

SARA: He sounds very handsome.

WOMAN: He is, and he's the same age as Judy.

SARA: So he's only 19?

WOMAN: Yes, that's right.

3.

OFFICER: All right, Mr. Brown. Tell me again what happened here.

MR. BROWN: Thank you, Officer. I told you . . . the man took my wife's purse from the back of her chair. We were at this table.

OFFICER: What did the thief look like?

MR. BROWN: I told you – he was elderly. He was maybe in his seventies.

OFFICER: And about how tall was he?

MR. BROWN: You mean, how *short* was he? He was *short* – only about 5 feet tall.

OFFICER: What else do you remember?

MR. BROWN: Well, he had on baggy pants and a red T-shirt. He also had a white beard.

4.

SHARON: Hi, I'm new here. My name's Sharon.

CHARLIE: I'm Charlie. Welcome to our school party. Do you want something to eat?

SHARON: Not right now, thanks. Actually, I'm looking for A.J. and Penny. I need their phone number. Which ones are they?

CHARLIE: They're that good-looking couple sitting on the couch.

SHARON: Oh, I see them, thanks. And one more thing. Is Clara here? I need to ask her a question about our homework for tomorrow.

CHARLIE: Let me see . . . oh, yes, I see her. She's wearing jeans and a red sweater. She's standing over there talking to Tom.

Units 11–12 *[CD 3, Track 15]*

A Listen to the conversations. Check the correct information.

1.

MAN: Where did you go for your vacation?

WOMAN: I went to Hokkaido, in northern Japan. It was my third time there.

MAN: Oh, really? I've never been there. Did you enjoy it?

WOMAN: I sure did. I love the mountains, and there are some beautiful beaches there.

MAN: Are the beaches crowded?

WOMAN: No, you can usually find very quiet beaches.

MAN: Sounds like it's an excellent place to relax.

WOMAN: Oh yeah. That's why I go there.

2.

WOMAN: Have you ever been to Paris?

MAN: Yes, I have. I went there last year in July.

WOMAN: How did you like it?

MAN: It's an amazing city! I had a really great time there.

WOMAN: And what about this year? Have you taken a vacation yet?

MAN: No, I haven't, but I plan to spend a week on a beach somewhere, probably in August.

WOMAN: Sounds good.

3.

MAN: Can you tell me a little about Barcelona?

WOMAN: Oh, my favorite city. It's so beautiful.

MAN: What should I see there?

WOMAN: Well, you should definitely visit some of the wonderful museums there, like Picasso's and Miro's. And you shouldn't miss the Ramblas.

MAN: The Ramblas?

WOMAN: Yes. It's a very long street. You can walk and stop for a drink or a meal there.

MAN: Sounds great! And when's a good time to visit?

WOMAN: Oh, I went there in June, and the weather was very nice. Don't go in the winter, though. It's pretty cold then.

MAN: OK. Thanks for your information.

4.

WOMAN: Did you enjoy your trip to Canada?

MAN: Oh, it was great!

WOMAN: What did you do there?

MAN: Well, I went to Vancouver and stayed there for a couple of days. And then I took a ferryboat to Victoria.

WOMAN: I don't think I know Victoria.

MAN: It's a really nice city on Vancouver Island. It has an interesting harbor with lots of sailboats.

WOMAN: Is it a safe place?

MAN: Oh yes, and it's not polluted at all. It's wonderful.

Units 13–14 *[CD 3, Track 29]*

A A waitress is taking an order. Listen and complete the restaurant check.

WAITRESS: Good afternoon. How are you doing today?
CUSTOMER: Just fine, thanks.
WAITRESS: May I take your order now?
CUSTOMER: Yes, I think I'll have a hamburger.
WAITRESS: One hamburger. And would you like cheese with that?
CUSTOMER: Uh, no thanks.
WAITRESS: OK. What else would you like with it?
CUSTOMER: A large order of french fries, please.
WAITRESS: All right. One large order of fries. And how about a salad?
CUSTOMER: That sounds good. A small green salad.
WAITRESS: What kind of dressing?
CUSTOMER: Vinaigrette, please.
WAITRESS: Anything else? Would you like something to drink?
CUSTOMER: Yes. Do you have iced coffee?
WAITRESS: No, but we have iced tea.
CUSTOMER: That'd be fine.
WAITRESS: How about dessert? We have pie, cake, ice cream . . .
CUSTOMER: I'll have some chocolate ice cream. And actually, I've changed my mind about the french fries.
WAITRESS: You don't want the fries?
CUSTOMER: No thanks.
WAITRESS: OK, that's fine. I'll bring your salad right away.
CUSTOMER: Thanks a lot.

Units 15–16 *[CD 3, Track 43]*

A Listen to two telephone conversations. Check the correct information.

1.

WES: [*phone rings*] Hello.
LAURA: Hi, Wes. This is Laura.
WES: Oh, hi, Laura. How are you?
LAURA: Pretty good, thanks. Listen, would you like to come to a beach party on Saturday? Amy and Terry are going to be there.
WES: Amy and Terry? Great! Uh, what time on Saturday?
LAURA: Well, we want to start around 6:00 in the evening.
WES: Oh, no! I start work at 6:00. I have a part-time job in a restaurant.
LAURA: Oh, that's too bad, Wes. Well, maybe another time.
WES: Yeah, I hope so. Thanks for thinking of me.
LAURA: Bye.
WES: Bye.

2.

RITA: [*phone rings*] Hi, this is Rita.
CHARLIE: Hey, Rita. This is Charlie. How're things?
RITA: Not bad. How are you doing, Charlie?
CHARLIE: Fine. Say, would you like to come to a dance performance this weekend?
RITA: I'd love to, but I'm pretty busy this weekend. I have to study for a test on Monday morning.
CHARLIE: Hmm. Are you going to study *all* weekend?
RITA: Well, no. I'm going to a basketball game on Saturday night with Lucinda. But I really have to keep some time on the weekend for studying.
CHARLIE: How about tomorrow evening? The tickets are half price midweek.
RITA: That's a good idea! Let's do it.
CHARLIE: Great! We could meet outside the Odeon Theater at about 7:45.
RITA: Excellent! See you there! Bye.
CHARLIE: Bye.

Quiz answer key

Units 1–2

A (4 points)
1. Lucy's friend
2. Marceau
3. really good
4. in the same school

B (4 points)
1. are
2. Is
3. is
4. Are

C (4 points)
1. your
   My
2. her
   Our

D (3 points)
1. do
2. does
3. go

E (3 points)
1. Carmen is a ~~salesperson~~ *flight attendant*. She works for an airline. She serves drinks to passengers.
2. I work for World Travel. I'm a ~~receptionist~~ *tour guide*. I take people on tours.
3. Sam and Jerry are in the entertainment business. They play music. They are ~~servers.~~ *musicians*

F (3 points)
1. until
2. late
3. on

G (4 points)
1. new friend
2. a full-time student
3. is Chris's friend
4. works with Daniel

Units 3–4

A (4 points)
1. green shirts
2. $29
3. cotton
4. medium

B (3 points)
1. cotton
2. silk
3. gold

C (4 points)
1. this
2. those
3. these
4. that

D (4 points)
1. larger than
2. more expensive than
3. prettier
4. better than

E (3 points)
1. him
2. them
3. it

F (3 points)
1. Would
2. Do
3. does

G (4 points)
1. in plays
2. *Amélie*
3. 2003
4. French

Units 5–6

A (4 points)
1. seven
2. with a friend
3. three times a week
4. are in school

B (4 points)
1. Is she studying
   is working
2. is he waiting
   is coming

C (3 points)
1. Most American mothers with small children work.
2. Few Japanese families have more than three children.
3. In the U.S., some young adults live at home with their parents.

D (3 points)
1. yoga
2. go
3. baseball

E (3 points)
1. I often watch TV after dinner.
2. Do you ever drink coffee in the evening?
3. Jeff doesn't exercise very much.

F (4 points)
1. often
2. well
3. long
4. good

G (4 points)
She walks down Telegraph Avenue every day after class.
She enjoys going to San Francisco on the weekend.
She goes shopping or walking after lunch on Saturdays.
She likes to watch football and basketball on TV.

Units 7–8

A (4 points)

Name	*Country visited*	*Weather*
Lisa	Australia	bad
Peter	Italy	OK/good *and* bad

B (8 points)
A: What did you do?
B: I went dancing at the new club on Eighth Street. Suzie and Mike were there, too.
A: Oh, really?
B: Yes, we had a great time! But where were you?
A: I was in the laundromat all evening.
B: How boring!
A: Actually, no. I met my girlfriend there. We spent the evening laughing and talking.

C (4 points)
1. All my clothes were dirty. I wanted to wash them. So I went to the ~~library~~ *laundromat*.
2. I went to the ~~post office~~ *grocery store*. I was very hungry. I needed to buy food.
3. I went to the ~~music store~~ *travel agency*. I go to Singapore on Sunday. I need a plane ticket.
4. I don't have a computer. I wanted to send an e-mail. So I went to the ~~grocery store~~ *Internet café*.

D (5 points)
1. one
2. many / a few
3. much / any

E (4 points)
go dancing
go shopping
send e-mails
wash and dry clothes

Units 9–10

A (4 points)
1. Emily is fairly short and about 25.
2. Steve is really tall, and has curly blond hair.
3. The thief was short, had a white beard, and was elderly.
4. A.J. and Penny are the attractive couple sitting on the couch.

B (3 points)
1. in
2. has
3. is

C (4 points)
1. Kristi is really gorgeous and in her thirties. / Kristi is in her thirties and really gorgeous.
2. Does Sam wear glasses and have a mustache? / Does Sam have a mustache and wear glasses?
3. Cindy has long red hair and is medium height. / Cindy is medium height and has long red hair.
4. Who's the person sitting on the couch next to Jason? / Who's the person sitting next to Jason on the couch?

D (4 points)
1. A: Have you been to any good movies lately?
   B: Yes, I have already seen three films this month.
2. A: Has he ever eaten Thai food before?
   B: No, he has never had it in his life.

E (3 points)
1. missed
2. cell phone
3. driven

F (3 points)
1. for
2. since
3. for

G (4 points)
1. The Risk Taker
2. Globe-trotting Twosome
3. An Amazing Summer School
4. Never Too Old

Units 11–12

A (4 points)
1. The beaches in Hokkaido are not crowded.
2. The man had a great vacation in Paris last July.
3. You shouldn't miss some of the museums in Barcelona.
4. Victoria is both safe and clean.

B (3 points)
1. Seoul is a really fascinating city.
2. Peru is an extremely interesting country.
3. Taipei is too expensive for me.

C (4 points)
1. stressful
2. beautiful
3. crowded
4. relaxing

D (3 points)
1. shouldn't
2. can't
3. should

E (3 points)
Answers in part A may vary.
1. A: What do you suggest for a sunburn?
   B: It's a good idea to try this lotion.
2. A: What should I do for sore muscles?
   B: It's sometimes helpful to use a heating pad.
3. A: What should I do for a toothache?
   B: It's important to see a dentist.

F (4 points)
1. bottle
2. jar
3. tube
4. pack

G (4 points)
Go on a vacation.
Sleep less.
Sleep more.
Try some medicinal plants.

Units 13–14

A (4 points)
hamburger
small green salad with vinaigrette dressing
iced tea
chocolate ice cream

B (4 points)
1. I am, too.
2. Oh, I love it!
3. So do I.
4. Neither am I.

C (3 points)
1. vinaigrette (all others are drinks)
2. spaghetti and meatballs (all others are seafood)
3. beef kebabs (all others are vegetarian)

D (4 points)
A: What would you like to eat?
B: The fried chicken, please.
A: What kind of potatoes would you like?
B: I'll have the mashed potatoes.
A: Anything to drink?
B: Yes, please. I'd like some water.
A: Anything else?
B: No. That will be all.

E (3 points)
1. forest
2. desert
3. mountain

F (3 points)
1. more crowded
2. the most famous
3. the longest

G (4 points)
1. a state and an island
2. arctic
3. 80°F
4. in the east

Units 15–16

A (4 points)

Name	*Invitation*	*Excuse*
Wes	beach party	He starts work at 6:00 P.M.
Rita	dance performance	She needs to study for a test.

B (6 points)
1. A: What do you plan to do tonight? / What are you planning to do tonight?
   B: I want to stay home. There's a soccer match on TV.
2. A: What are you and Dave going to do tomorrow?
   B: We'd like to have a barbecue on the beach, but it may rain.
3. A: What do you hope to do after graduation?
   B: I'd love to travel in Europe for a while.

C (3 points)
1. tell
2. to bring
3. tell

D (4 points)
1. Please tell Ken (that) the test on Thursday is at 1:00 P.M.
2. Would you ask Alex to meet me after class today?
3. Could you tell Marcus (that) there's a volleyball game tonight?
4. Please ask Paula to come to the picnic on Saturday.

E (4 points)
Answers may vary.
1. I want a new one. / I want to go back to school.
2. I hope to get a different place. / I hope to move out.
3. I plan to get a new style. / I plan to cut it short.
4. I'd like to go shopping later. / I'd like to buy something special.
5. I hope to save some this month. / I hope to spend less.
6. I plan to have a party. / I plan to do something fun.
7. I'd love to study more. / I'd love to have the same teacher.

F (4 points)

Changes	*Plans*
found a better job	to get married next year
went out more	to travel around Mexico

Workbook answer key

1 Please call me Beth.

Exercise 1
Answers will vary.

Exercise 2
2. A: What's your teacher's first name?
   B: My teacher's first name is . . .
3. A: Where is your teacher from?
   B: My teacher is from . . .
4. A: How is your English class?
   B: My English class is . . .
5. A: What are your classmates like?
   B: My classmates are . . .

Exercise 3
2. A: My name is Young Hoon Park.
   B: Nice to meet you, Young Hoon.
3. A: Hello. I'm a new club member.
   B: Welcome.
4. A: I'm sorry. What's your name again?
   B: Joe King.
5. A: How do you spell your first name?
   B: A-N-T-O-N-I-O.
6. A: What do people call you?
   B: Everyone calls me Ken.

Exercise 4
2. Jim: What's your last name?
   Bob: My last name's Hayes.
3. Jim: Who's that?
   Bob: That's my wife.
4. Jim: What's her name?
   Bob: Her name is Rosa.
5. Jim: Where's she from?
   Bob: She's from Mexico.
6. Jim: Who are they?
   Bob: They're my wife's parents.

Exercise 5
2. Our 3. your 4. He 5. My 6. Her 7. They 8. It

Exercise 6
Amy: Oh, they are on the volleyball team. Let me introduce you. Hi, Surachai, this is Lisa Neil.
Surachai: Pleased to meet you, Lisa.
Lisa: Nice to meet you, too. Where are you from?
Surachai: I am from Thailand.
Amy: And this is Mario. He is from Brazil.
Lisa: Hi, Mario.

Exercise 7
A

Name	*Where from?*	*Languages*	*Sports?*
1. Mario	Cali, Colombia	Spanish and French	volleyball
2. Eileen	Mozambique, Africa	Swahili and Portuguese	
3. Su Yin	Taiwan	Chinese and English	volleyball
4. Ahmed	Luxor, Egypt	Arabic and English	baseball

B
Answers will vary.

Exercise 8
Sarah: Pretty good, thanks. Are you a student here?
Rich: No, I'm not. I'm on vacation. Are you a student?
Sarah: Yes, I am.
Rich: And what are you studying?
Sarah: I'm studying Spanish.
Rich: Oh, really? Is Susan Miller in your class?
Sarah: Yes, she is. Is she your friend?
Rich: No, she's not. She's my sister!

Exercise 9
Tina: Hi. I'm Tina Fernandez.
Amy: Are you from South America, Tina?
Tina: Yes, I am. I'm from Argentina. Where are you and your sister from, Alex?
Alex: We're from Taiwan.
Tina: Are you from Taipei?
Alex: No, we're not. We're from Tainan. Say, are you in English 101?
Tina: No, I'm not. I'm in English 102.

Exercise 10
2. A: Are you free?
   B: No, I'm not. I'm very busy.
3. A: Are you from Spain?
   B: No, we're not from Spain. We're from Mexico.
4. A: Is your teacher Mr. Brown?
   B: No, my teacher isn't Mr. Brown. I'm in Ms. West's class.
5. A: Are Kim and Mika in your class?
   B: Yes, Kim and Mika are in my class.
6. A: Is it an interesting class?
   B: Yes, it's an interesting class.
7. A: Are they on the same baseball team?
   B: No, they're not on the same baseball team. They're on the same volleyball team.

Exercise 11

	Hello	*Good-bye*
How are you doing?	✓	
See you around.		✓
So long.		✓
How's everything?	✓	
Long time, no see.	✓	
See you Monday.		✓
Have a good weekend.		✓
Hi there!	✓	

Exercise 12
Answers will vary.

2 How do you spend your day?

Exercise 1
2. computer programmer
3. disc jockey
4. fashion designer
5. security guard
6. tour guide

Exercise 2
1. He's a computer programmer. He works in an office. He likes computers a lot.
2. She works in a nightclub. She's a disc jockey. She plays music.
3. He's a security guard. He works in a department store. He guards the store at night.
4. She works in a design studio. She creates beautiful fashions. She's a fashion designer.

Exercise 3
2. She works for a travel company and arranges tours. She's a travel agent.
3. He has a difficult job. He's a cashier. He works in a supermarket.
4. She's an architect. She works for a large company. She builds houses. It's an interesting job.
5. She works with computers in an office. She's a Web-site designer. She's also a part-time student. She takes an English class in the evening.

Exercise 4
Answers will vary.

Exercise 5
Tom: What does your husband do exactly?
Liz: He works for a department store. He's a store manager.
Tom: How does he like it?
Liz: It's an interesting job. He likes it very much. But he works long hours. And what do you do?
Tom: I'm a student. I study architecture.
Liz: Oh, really? Where do you go to school?
Tom: I go to Lincoln University. My girlfriend goes there, too.
Liz: Really? And what does she study?
Tom: She studies hotel management.
Liz: That sounds interesting.

Exercise 6
Victor: I work for American Express.
Mark: And what do you do there?
Victor: I'm in management.
Mark: How do you like it?
Victor: It's a great job. And what do you do?
Mark: I'm a salesperson.
Victor: Really? What do you sell?
Mark: I sell computers. Do you want to buy one?

Exercise 7
1. He's a chef.
2. He practices cooking new things, and then he writes cookbooks.
3. He makes TV programs about Thai cooking.
4. She's an electrician.
5. She finishes at eight or nine o'clock in the evening.
6. She loves it.

Exercise 8
Answers will vary. Possible answers:
2. Where does he work?
3. When does he start work?
4. How does he like his job?

Exercise 9
Everyone knows Pat at the hospital. Pat is a part-time nurse. He works at night on weekends. On Saturdays and Sundays, Pat sleeps most of the day and wakes up a little before nine in the evening, usually at 8:45 or 8:50. He has breakfast very late, around 9:30 or 10:00 P.M.! He watches television until eleven o'clock, and then starts work at midnight. Early in the morning, usually around 5:00 A.M., he leaves work, has a little snack, goes home, goes to bed, and sleeps late. It's a perfect schedule for Pat. He's a pre-med student on weekdays at a local college.

Exercise 10

			1 s	2 t	a	r	3 t	s	
				a			y		
	4 w	o	r	k	s		p		
	r			e		5 g	e	t	6 s
	i			s			s		e
	t								l
7 s	e	r	v	e	s		8 d		l
	s					9 g	o	e	s
							e		
	10 a	n	s	w	e	r	s		

Exercise 11
2. What does he do?
3. She serves food in a restaurant.
4. He goes to the university.
5. She stays up late.
6. He works part time.

Exercise 12
1. New York Hospital needs nurses. Work during the day or at night, weekdays or weekends, full time or part time. Call 614-555-1191.
2. Interesting job for a language student. Mornings only. Take people on tours. Need good English and Spanish. Call 917-555-3239.
3. No need to work long hours! Only work from 6:00 until 11:00 four evenings a week. Our restaurant serves great food! Work as our manager. Call 308-555-6845.

3 How much is it?

Exercise 1

Sam: The light blue ones over there. They're nice.
Rebecca: Yes. But I don't really like light blue.
Sam: Hmm. Well, what about that sweater? It's perfect for you.
Rebecca: Which one?
Sam: This red one.
Rebecca: Well, I like it, but it's expensive.
Sam: Hey, let me buy it for you. It's a present!
Rebecca: Oh, Sam. Thank you very much.

Exercise 2

2. A: How much are those bracelets?
   B: They're $29.
3. A: How much are these shoes?
   B: They're $64.
4. A: How much is that dog?
   B: That's *my* dog, and he's not for sale!

Exercise 3

1.	backpacks	7.	necklaces
2.	companies	8.	rings
3.	dresses	9.	scarves
4.	days	10.	sweaters
5.	gloves	11.	ties
6.	hairbrushes	12.	boxes

Exercise 4

Answers will vary. Possible answers:

2. That's cheap.
3. That's pretty expensive!
4. That's reasonable.
5. That's not bad.
6. That's cheap.
7. That's not bad.

Exercise 5

1. Clerk: It's $195.
   Luis: And how much is that one?
   Clerk: It's $255.
   Luis: Oh, really? Well, thanks, anyway.
2. Kim: Excuse me. How much are those jeans?
   Clerk: They're only $59.
   Kim: And how much is this sweater?
   Clerk: Which one? They're all different.
   Kim: I like this green one.
   Clerk: It's $34.
   Kim: Well, that's not bad.
3. Sonia: I like those sunglasses over there.
   Clerk: Which ones?
   Sonia: The small brown ones.
   Clerk: They're $199.
   Sonia: Oh, they're expensive!

Exercise 6

Cotton	*Gold*	*Leather*	*Silk*	*Plastic*	*Wool*
pants	bracelet	boots	pants	boots	pants
gloves	ring	pants	gloves	bracelet	gloves
shirt	necklace	gloves	shirt	ring	shirt
jacket		jacket	jacket	necklace	jacket

Exercise 7

1. A: These cotton gloves are nice.
   B: Yes, but the leather ones are nicer.
   A: They're also more expensive.
2. A: Those silk jackets look more attractive than the wool ones.
   B: Yes, but the wool ones are warmer.
3. A: This purple shirt is an interesting color!
   B: Yes, but the color is prettier than the design.
   A: The design isn't bad.
   B: I think the pattern on that red shirt is better than the pattern on this purple one.
4. A: Hey, look at this gold ring! It's nice. And it's cheaper than that silver ring.
   B: But it's smaller than the silver one.
   A: Well, yeah. The silver one is bigger than the gold one. But look at the price tag. One thousand dollars is a lot of money!

Exercise 8

Clothing	*Electronics*	*Jewelry*
athletic shoes	CD player	bracelet
cap	laptop computer	earrings
dress	television	necklace
sweater	video camera	ring

Exercise 9

Answers will vary. Possible answers:

2. Which cap do you like more, the wool one or the leather one?
   I like the wool one more. *or* I like the leather one more.
3. Which ones do you like more, the high-tops or the tennis shoes?
   I like the high-tops more. *or* I like the tennis shoes more.
4. Which one do you prefer, the laptop computer or the desktop computer?
   I prefer the laptop computer. *or* I prefer the desktop computer.
5. Which television do you like better, the 19-inch one or the 25-inch one?
   I like the 19-inch one better. *or* I like the 25-inch one better.

Exercise 10

A

1. b
2. c
3. a
4. d

B

1. False
2. True
3. True
4. True

C

Answers will vary.

4 Do you like rap?

Exercise 1
Answers will vary.

Exercise 2
Answers will vary. Possible answers:
2. Do you like Justin Timberlake? Yes, I do. I love <u>him</u>.
3. Do you like rap? No, I don't. I can't stand <u>it</u>.
4. Do you like Beyoncé Knowles? Yes, I do. I like <u>her</u> a lot.
5. Do you like reality TV shows? No, I don't. I can't stand <u>them</u>.
6. Do you like soap operas? No, I don't. I don't like <u>them</u> very much.

Exercise 3
1. Julio Iglesias is <u>a singer</u>.
2. The Rolling Stones are <u>a rock band</u>.
3. Oprah Winfrey is <u>a TV talk show host</u>.
4. Matt Damon is <u>an actor</u>.

Exercise 4
1. SARAH: Yes, I <u>like</u> it a lot. I'm a real fan of Garth Brooks.
   ED: Oh, <u>does</u> he play the guitar?
   SARAH: Yes, he <u>does</u>. He's my favorite musician.
2. ANNE: What kind of music <u>do</u> your parents <u>like</u>, Jason?
   JASON: They <u>like</u> classical music.
   ANNE: Who <u>do</u> they <u>like</u>? Mozart?
   JASON: No, they <u>don't</u> like him very much. They prefer Beethoven.
3. SCOTT: Teresa, <u>do</u> you <u>like</u> Christina Aguilera?
   TERESA: No, I don't. I can't stand her. I like Pink.
   SCOTT: I don't know her. What kind of music <u>does</u> she sing?
   TERESA: She <u>sings</u> pop songs. She's really great!

Exercise 5
Responses will vary.

1. <u>What kinds</u> of movies do you like?	I like comedies and musicals.
2. <u>What</u> is your favorite movie?	My favorite movie is *Star Wars*.
3. <u>What kind/kinds</u> of TV shows do you like?	I like game shows.
4. <u>Who</u> is your favorite TV actor or actress?	My favorite TV actor is Matt LeBlanc.
5. <u>What</u> is your favorite song?	My favorite song is "Let It Be."
6. <u>Who</u> is your favorite rock band?	My favorite rock band is U2.

Exercise 6
Answers will vary. Possible answers:
2. Which movies are more interesting, musicals or science fiction films?
   <u>Science fiction films are more interesting than musicals.</u>
3. Which films are scarier, horror films or thrillers?
   <u>Horror films are scarier than thrillers.</u>
4. Which films are more exciting, westerns or crime thrillers?
   <u>Crime thrillers are more exciting than westerns.</u>

Exercise 7

A

Listen to	***Play***	***Watch***
jazz	the piano	videos
music	the guitar	the news
CDs	the trumpet	a film

B
Answers will vary.

Exercise 8

A
1. Ahead of Time
2. House of Laughs
3. Coming Up for Air

B
1. a science fiction film
2. a comedy
3. a crime thriller

Exercise 9
2. A: Do you like gospel music?
   B. <u>I can't stand it.</u>
3. A: There's a baseball game tonight.
   B. <u>Great. Let's go.</u>
4. A: Would you like to see a movie this weekend?
   B: <u>That sounds great!</u>

Exercise 10

A
1. Yes
2. No
3. Yes
4. No
5. Yes

B
Answers will vary.

Exercise 11
1. KATE:Yes, I do. <u>I like</u> it a lot.
   ROBIN: There's a Dixie Chicks concert on Friday. <u>Would you like</u> to go with me?
   KATE: Yes, <u>I'd love to</u>. Thanks.
2. CARLOS: There's a French film tonight at 11:00. <u>Would you like</u> to go?
   PHIL: <u>I'd like to,</u> but I have to study tonight.
   CARLOS: Well, <u>do you like</u> Brazilian films?
   PHIL: Yes, <u>I do</u>. I love them!
   CARLOS: There's a great Brazilian movie on TV tomorrow. <u>Would you like</u> to watch it with me?
   PHIL: <u>I'd love to</u>. Thanks.

Exercise 12
2. Richard can't stand classical music.
3. I love horror films!
4. Celia is not a fan of country music.
5. Would you like to go to a baseball game?

5 Tell me about your family.

Exercise 1

Males	*Females*
brother	aunt
father	daughter
husband	mother
nephew	niece
son	sister
uncle	wife

Exercise 2

DON: No, I'm not. My brother and sister are staying with me right now. We go to bed after midnight every night.
JOEL: Really? What are they doing this summer? Are they taking classes, too?
DON: No, they aren't. My brother is on vacation now, but he's looking for a part-time job here.
JOEL: What about your sister? Is she working?
DON: Yes, she is. She has a part-time job at the university. What about you, Joel? Are you in school this summer?
JOEL: Yes, I am. I'm studying two languages.
DON: Oh, are you taking French and Spanish again?
JOEL: Well, I'm taking Spanish again, but I'm starting Japanese.
DON: Really? That's exciting!

Exercise 3

2. Peter is Liz's husband.
3. Frank and Liza are Isabel's grandparents.
4. We have a son and (a) daughter.
5. My father-in-law is a painter.
6. Michael is looking for a job right now.

Exercise 4

CHRIS: Wow! Do you like it?
PHILIP: Yes, I do. I like it a lot.
CHRIS: And is your brother still working in Hong Kong?
PHILIP: Yes, he is. He loves it there.
CHRIS: And how about your parents? Are they still living in Florida?
PHILIP: No, they aren't. They're living in New York these days. How about you and your family, Chris? Are you still living here?
CHRIS: Yes, we are. We really love San Francisco.

Exercise 5

1. This is my aunt Barbara. She lives in Rome, but she's visiting Chile this summer. She has a second home there.
2. And these are my parents. They work in London, but they're visiting my aunt in Chile this month.
3. And here you can see my grandparents. They live in New York, but they're staying at my parents' house in London now.
4. This is my brother-in-law, Edward. He wants to be a company director. He's studying business in Canada right now.
5. And this is my niece, Christina. She goes *or* She's going to high school. She likes mathematics, but she doesn't like English.

Exercise 6

Answers will vary.

Exercise 7

A

Answers will vary.

B

1. False: Many college students live in university housing.
2. True
3. False: Few young people in the United States live with their parents.
4. False: Nearly all university students live with their parents.
5. True
6. False: (Rents in the city are very expensive.) Many young people continue to live with their parents after they marry.

Exercise 8

1. all
2. nearly all
3. most
4. many
5. a lot of
6. some
7. not many
8. a few
9. few
10. no

Exercise 9

1. Many children start school before the age of 5. All children go to school after the age of 5.
2. Nearly all young people get a job after they finish high school. Only a few go to college.
3. Not many people over 65 have part-time jobs. Few people like to travel abroad. Many people like to stay with their grandchildren.

Exercise 10

In my country, some couples get married fairly young. Not many marriages break up, and nearly all divorced people remarry. Elderly couples often live at home and take care of their grandchildren.

Exercise 11

Answers will vary.

6 How often do you exercise?

Exercise 1

Team sports	*Individual sports*	*Exercise*
basketball	swimming	swimming
baseball	jogging	jogging
football	bicycling	aerobics
soccer	tennis	bicycling
volleyball	yoga	tennis
		stretching
		yoga

Exercise 2

2. They hardly ever play tennis.
3. How often do you go jogging?
4. We often do yoga on Sunday mornings.
5. Does Charlie ever do aerobics?
6. What do you usually do on Saturdays?

Exercise 3

2. A: <u>What do you usually do on weekends?</u>
   B: Well, I usually do karate on Saturdays and yoga on Sundays.
3. A: <u>Do you ever go to the gym after work?</u>
   B: No, I never go to the gym after work.
4. A: <u>How often do you exercise?</u>
   B: I don't exercise very often at all.
5. A: <u>Do you ever play sports on weekends?</u>
   B: Yes, I sometimes play sports on weekends – usually baseball.
6. A: <u>What do you usually do in your free time?</u>
   B: I usually play tennis in my free time.

Exercise 4

A

Answers will vary.

B

Answers will vary.

Exercise 5

JERRY: I always go jogging <u>at</u> 7:00. How about you, Susan?
SUSAN: I usually go jogging <u>around</u> noon. I jog <u>for</u> about an hour.
JERRY: And do you also play sports <u>in</u> your free time?
SUSAN: No, I usually go out <u>with</u> my classmates. What about you?
JERRY: I go to the gym <u>on</u> Mondays and Wednesdays. And sometimes I go bicycling <u>on</u> weekends.
SUSAN: Wow! You really like to stay in shape.

Exercise 6

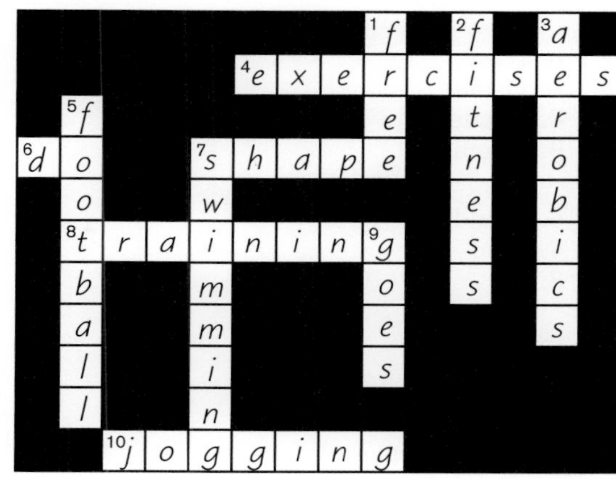

Exercise 7

B

	Hiking Club	*Adult Education Program*	*YWCA/ YMCA*
1. play indoor sports			✓
2. do outdoor activities	✓		
3. take evening classes		✓	
4. go dancing			✓
5. learn to cook		✓	
6. meet new people	✓	✓	✓

Exercise 8

2. A: How long do you spend in the pool?
   B: <u>About 45 minutes.</u>
3. A: And how well do you swim?
   B: <u>I'm about average.</u>
4. A: How good are you at other sports?
   B: <u>Not very good, actually.</u>

Exercise 9

2. A: <u>How often do you go</u> for a walk?
   B: Almost every day. I really enjoy it.
3. A: <u>How long do you spend jogging?</u>
   B: I spend about an hour jogging.
4. A: <u>How good are you</u> at soccer?
   B: I'm pretty good at it. I'm on the school team.
5. A: <u>How well do you play basketball?</u>
   B: Basketball? Pretty well, I guess. I like it a lot.

Exercise 10

2. Tom doesn't exercise very often.
3. Philip tries to stay in shape.
4. Jill often works out at the gym.
5. I always go jogging with my wife.
6. How well do you play tennis?

Exercise 11

Answers will vary.

7 We had a great time!

Exercise 1

A

2. enjoyed
3. invited
4. loved
5. studied
6. tried
7. visited
8. washed
9. watched

B

2. give
3. meet
4. see
5. sleep
6. spend
7. take
8. go

C

Answers will vary.

Exercise 2

2. Who did you meet at the party?
   I met someone very interesting.
3. What time did you and Eva get home?
   We got home a little after 1:00.
4. How did you and Bob like the art exhibition?
   We liked the art exhibition a lot.
5. What did you buy?
   I *or* We bought the new Madonna CD.
6. Where did Jeff and Joyce spend their vacation?
   They spent their vacation in the country.

Exercise 3

Answers will vary.

Exercise 4

A: What did you do?
B: Well, on Saturday, we went shopping.
A: And did you do anything special in the evening?
B: No, nothing special.
A: Where did you go on Sunday?
B: We went to the amusement park.
A: How did you like it?
B: We had a great time. In fact, we stayed there all day.
A: Really? What time did you get home?
B: We got home very late, around midnight.

Exercise 5

2. A: I stayed home from work all day yesterday. Did you take the day off, too?
   B: No, I didn't take the day *or* yesterday off. I worked all day until six o'clock.
3. A: I worked all weekend on my research paper. Did you spend the weekend at home, too?
   B: No, I didn't spend the weekend at home. I went out with friends.
4. A: I studied all weekend. Did you and John have a lot of homework, too?
   B: No, we didn't have a lot of homework. We finished our homework on Saturday.
5. A: Carl drove me to work yesterday morning. Did you drive to work?
   B: No, I didn't drive to work. I took the bus.
6. A: Kathy went to the baseball game last night. Did you and Bob go to the game?
   B: No, we didn't go to the game. We watched it on TV.

Exercise 6

2. d. He took a day off.
3. e. He did housework.
4. c. He didn't do the laundry.
5. a. He had people over.
6. b. He had a good time.

Exercise 7

A

Answers will vary.

C

	William	*Sue*
2. stayed for two days in Bangkok		✓
3. visited the floating market	✓	✓
4. bought fruit		✓
5. saw some historic ruins		✓
6. traveled on the river	✓	✓
7. loved the food the most	✓	
8. enjoyed everything		✓

Exercise 8

B: It was great. I really enjoyed it.
A: How long were you there?
B: We were there for two weeks.
A: Were you in Lima all the time?
B: No, we weren't. We were in the mountains for a few days.
A: And how was the weather? Was it good?
B: No, it wasn't good at all. The city was very hot, and the mountains were really cold!

Exercise 9

B: It was a great trip. I really enjoyed South Africa and Namibia.
A: How long were you in South Africa?
B: For ten days.
A: And how long were you in Namibia?
B: I was in Namibia for about five days.
A: Wow, that's a long time. How was the weather?
B: It was hot and sunny the whole time.
A: And what was the best part?
B: It was definitely the natural parks and wildlife in Namibia. And we saw some meerkats!

Exercise 10

1. I'm sorry I was late. I had to make a phone call.
2. My friends and I really enjoyed your party. We all had a good time.
3. I made some photocopies of the report and put them on your desk.
4. We didn't see very much in the mountains. The weather was very foggy.
5. I worked very hard in Switzerland last week. I was there on business.

Exercise 11

A

Answers will vary.

B

Answers will vary.

8 What's your neighborhood like?

Exercise 1

A

2. gas station
3. grocery store
4. Internet café
5. karaoke bar
6. movie theater
7. pay phone
8. post office
9. travel agency

B

2. A: I want to send an e-mail. Are there any Internet cafés near here?
   B: No, there aren't, but there are some near the university.
3. A: I want to send this letter. Is there a post office around here?
   B: Yes, there's one next to the laundromat.
4. A: I need to make a phone call. Are there any pay phones around here?
   B: Yes, there are some across from the library.
5. A: We need some gas. Are there any gas stations on this street?
   B: No, there aren't, but there are a couple on Second Avenue.
6. A: We need to make a reservation for a trip. Is there a travel agency near here?
   B: Yes, there's one near the Prince Hotel.

Exercise 2

Possible answers:

3. There's a laundromat on the corner of 1st Street and Oak in Avery, but there isn't one in Bailey. There's a hospital.
4. There's a grocery store on Elm Street in Bailey, but there isn't one in Avery.
5. There's a restaurant on the corner of 3rd Street and Oak in Avery, but there isn't one in Bailey. There's a drugstore.
6. There's a bank on the corner of 2nd Street and Oak in Avery, but there isn't one in Bailey. There's a department store.
7. There's a post office on the corner of 3rd and Birch in Avery, but there isn't one in Bailey. There's a movie theater.
8. There's a supermarket on the corner of 2nd and Elm in Avery, but there isn't one in Bailey.
9. There are some houses on 3rd Street in Avery, but there aren't any in Bailey. There are some apartments.
10. There's a barber shop on 4th Street in Avery, but there isn't one in Bailey. There's a coffee shop.

Exercise 3

Answers will vary. Possible answers:

2. Is there a post office near here?
   Yes. There's one on the corner of Lincoln Street and 3rd Avenue.
3. I'm looking for a drugstore.
   There's one opposite the gas station.
4. Is there a laundromat in this neighborhood?
   Yes. There's one next to the YMCA.
5. Is there a department store on Lincoln Street?
   Yes. There's one between the travel agency and the gym.
6. Are there any pay phones around here?
   Yes. There are some in front of the post office.

Exercise 4

Answers will vary.

Exercise 5

B

	Advantages	*Disadvantages*
Downtown	near the shopping center near the bus station	very noisy, streets full of people traffic is terrible parking is a big problem
Suburbs	safe a lot of parks good schools very little crime	too quiet not many shops, no clubs or theaters nothing ever really happens

C

Answers will vary.

Exercise 6

Count nouns		*Noncount nouns*	
bank	people	crime	pollution
hospital	school	noise	traffic
library	theater	parking	water

Exercise 7

2. How many buses are there? There aren't any.
3. How much traffic is there? There's only a little.
4. How many banks are there? There are a couple.
5. How many people are there? There are a few.
6. How much crime is there? There's a lot.

Exercise 8

ALEX: Sure. There are a lot. There's a great club across from the National Bank, but it's expensive.
LUIS: Well, are there any others?
ALEX: Yeah, there are a few. There's a nice one near here. It's called Sounds of Brazil.
LUIS: That's perfect! Where is it exactly?
ALEX: It's on Third Avenue, between the Royal Theater and May's Restaurant.
LUIS: So let's go!

Exercise 9

1. I'm going to the stationery store to get some birthday cards.
2. We're taking a long drive. We need to go to the gas station.
3. I live on the 8th floor of my apartment building.
4. Our apartment is in the center of the city. We live downtown.

9 What does she look like?

Exercise 1
2. light
3. young
4. short
5. tall

Exercise 2
A
2. fairly long
3. good-looking
4. medium height
5. middle aged

B
2. A: How long is his hair?
   B: It's fairly long.
3. A: What color is his hair?
   B: It's dark brown.
4. A: How old is he?
   B: He's middle aged.
5. A: How tall is he?
   B: He's medium height.

Exercise 3
JIM: And how long is her hair?
STEVE: It's medium length.
JIM: How tall is she?
STEVE: She's fairly tall.
JIM: And how old is she?
STEVE: She's in her early twenties.
JIM: Does she wear glasses?
STEVE: Sometimes. I think she's wearing them now.
JIM: I think I see her over there. Is that her?

Exercise 4
Answers will vary.

Exercise 5
1. George is in his late sixties. He's pretty tall. He has a mustache, and he's bald. He's wearing a shirt, jeans, and boots.

   He isn't bald. He has short, curly hair.
2. Sophie is about 25. She's very pretty. She's medium height. Her hair is long and blond. She's wearing a black sweater, a jacket, and tennis shoes. She's standing next to her motorcycle.

   She isn't wearing tennis shoes. She's wearing boots. She isn't standing next to her motorcycle. She's sitting on her motorcycle.
3. Lucinda is in her early twenties. She's pretty serious-looking. She has glasses and curly dark hair. She's fairly tall, and she's wearing a nice-looking jacket and jeans.

   She doesn't have glasses.
   She isn't wearing jeans. She's wearing a skirt.

Exercise 6
Formal	*Casual*
shirt	boots
dress	jeans
scarf	shorts
skirt	running shoes
suit	T-shirt
necktie	cap

Exercise 7
2. Alice is the woman talking to the man.
3. Mandy is the tall woman carrying a jacket.
4. Edward and Kate are the ones wearing sunglasses.
5. William is the one wearing a suit and tie.

Exercise 8
Possible answers:
2. A: Who's Carlos?
   B: He's the one behind the couch.
3. A: Who are Dan and Cindy?
   B: They're the ones dancing.
4. A: Which one is Angela?
   B: She's the one on the couch.
5. A: Who's Ken?
   B: He's the one with short black hair.

Exercise 9
2. A: Which ones are the teachers?
   Who are the teachers?
   B: They're the ones on the couch.
   They're the ones sitting on the couch.
3. A: Which one is Larry?
   Who is Larry?
   B: He's the guy wearing the coat.
   He's the guy in the coat.

Exercise 10
There's a middle-aged woman walking her dog, and a young guy using the pay phone. Two people are standing next to him. Hey! The one wearing a baseball hat is my classmate! Some people are waiting at the bus stop. A serious-looking woman is asking for directions. And hey, here comes a really cute girl carrying a backpack. Wait a minute! I know her. That's my old girlfriend. I have to go now! Bye.

Exercise 11
2. A: Who's Sam?
   B: The handsome guy near the door.
3. A: Is she the one on the couch?
   B: That's right.
4. A: How tall is she?
   B: Pretty short.

10 Have you ever ridden a camel?

Exercise 1

2. e. called
3. b. done
4. j. eaten
5. a. gone
6. h. had
7. f. jogged
8. g. made
9. c. seen
10. i. tried

Exercise 2

2. A: Has Sue gone running lately?
   B: Yes, Sue usually runs in the morning and evening.
3. A: How many phone calls have you made lately?
   B: I made only one – on my father's birthday.
4. A: How long have you had those sunglasses?
   B: I've had them for a few weeks.
5. A: Have you eaten at Rio Café?
   B: Yes, we've already eaten there. It's very good but a little expensive.
6. A: How many times have you gone shopping at the mall this month?
   B: Actually, I haven't gone at all. Why don't we go later today?

Exercise 3

A

Answers will vary.

B

Answers will vary.

Exercise 4

1. Damien has lived in Hong Kong since 2001.
2. I have been a nurse for several years.
3. Masayuki was an exchange student in Spain for a whole semester.
4. I'm so sleepy. I've been awake since 4:00 this morning.
5. Mr. and Mrs. Chang have been married for nearly 40 years.
6. Maggie has had the same hairstyle since high school.
7. How are you? I haven't seen you since your wedding.
8. Where have you been? I've been here for over an hour!
9. I haven't had this much fun since I was a kid.

Exercise 5

Answers will vary.

Exercise 6

B

1 stayed in the mountains
2 lost a wallet
1 enjoyed the view
1 and 2 got no exercise
2 spent time on a boat
1 waited for help
2 went swimming
1 and 2 had a terrible day

C

Answers will vary.

Exercise 7

2. A: Have you ever seen a sumo wrestling match?
   B: Actually, I saw a sumo wrestling match last month on TV. It was terrific!
3. A: Have you ever eaten oysters?
   B: No, I haven't. I've never eaten oysters.
4. A: Have you ever gone wall climbing?
   B: Yes, I went wall climbing on Friday night.
5. A: Have you ever been camping?
   B: No, I haven't. I've never been camping.
6. A: Have you ever ridden a motorcycle?
   B: Yes, I have. I once rode my brother's motorcycle.
7. A: Have you ever been to India?
   B: No, I've never been to India.

Exercise 8

Answers will vary.

Exercise 9

B: Yes, I lost my cell phone last month.
A: Have you found it yet?
B: No. Actually, I've already bought a new one. Look!
A: Oh, that's nice. Where did you buy it?
B: I got it at Tech Town last weekend. What about you? Have you ever lost anything valuable?
A: Well, I left my electronic address book in a coffee shop a couple of months ago.
B: How annoying! Maybe that's why you haven't called me for a while.
A: But you haven't called me in a long time. What's your excuse?
B: I told you. I lost my cell phone!

Exercise 10

2. A: Are you having a good time?
   B: Yes, really good.
3. A: How long did Joe stay at the party?
   B: For two hours.
4. A: How many times has Gina lost her keys?
   B: Twice.
5. A: What about a tour of the city?
   B: Sure. I hear it's great.
6. A: Have you been here long?
   B: No, just a few minutes.

11 It's a very exciting place!

Exercise 1

2. Rome is a beautiful old city.
   There are not many modern buildings.
3. My hometown is not an exciting place.
   The nightlife there is pretty boring.
4. Some parts of our city are fairly dangerous.
   They're not very safe late at night.
5. Athens is a very quiet city in the winter.
   The streets are never crowded at that time of the year.

Exercise 2

A: What's your hometown like?
B: My hometown? It's a pretty nice place and the people are very friendly.
A: Is it big?
B: No, it's fairly small, but it's not *too* small.
A: What's the weather like?
B: The winter is wet and really cold. It's very nice in the summer, though.
A: Is the nightlife exciting?
B: No! It's really boring. There are no good restaurants or nightclubs.

Exercise 3

2. Sapporo is a very nice place. The winters are terribly cold, though.
3. Marrakech is an exciting city, and it's a fun place to sightsee.
4. My hometown is a great place for a vacation, but it's not too good for shopping.
5. Our hometown is somewhat ugly. It has some beautiful old homes, however.

Exercise 4

2. ___ Restaurants are very cheap in Mexico.
3. _✓_ Copenhagen is a clean city.
4. ___ The buildings in Paris are really beautiful.
5. ___ Apartments are very expensive in Hong Kong.
6. _✓_ Amsterdam is a fairly crowded city in the summer.
7. ___ Toronto has good museums.
8. _✓_ Rio de Janeiro is an exciting place to visit.

Exercise 5

Ever-Popular London

London is Britain's biggest city. It has a very old capital and dates back to the Romans. It is a city of interesting buildings and churches, and it has many beautiful parks. It also has some of the best museums in the world. London is very crowded in the summer, but it is not too busy in the winter. It is a popular city with foreign tourists and has millions of visitors a year. The city is famous for its shopping and has many excellent department stores. London has convenient trains and buses that cross the city, so it is easy for tourists to get around.

Exercise 6

B

City	*Date founded*	*Population*	*Weather*	*Attractions*
Budapest	1872	2 million	very cold in the winter	the Danube nightlife
Los Angeles	1781	3.8 million	smoggy dry and warm	film studios Hollywood Boulevard beaches Disneyland
Taipei	18th century	2.7 million	humid not pleasant	museum shopping

C

2. Los Angeles has good beaches nearby.
3. Budapest was once two cities.
4. Los Angeles and Taipei were both founded in the eighteenth century.

Exercise 7

2. You shouldn't stay near the airport. It's too noisy.
3. You shouldn't miss the museum. It has some new exhibits.
4. You can take a bus tour of the city if you like.
5. You shouldn't walk alone at night. It's too dangerous.
6. You should get around by taxi if you're out late.

Exercise 8

B: You shouldn't miss Jogjakarta, the old capital city. There are a lot of beautiful old buildings. For example, you should see the temple of Borobudur.
A: Sounds great. Bali is very popular, too. Should I go there?
B: Yes, you should. It's very interesting.
A: Should I take a lot of money with me?
B: No, you shouldn't. Indonesia is not an expensive country to visit.
A: So when should I go there?
B: Anytime. The weather's always nice.

Exercise 9

Possible questions:

2. What can you see and do there?
3. What shouldn't you do there?
4. What special foods should you try?
5. What should you buy there?
6. What other interesting things can you do?

Exercise 10

2. The streets are always crowded.
3. It's a fairly ugly city.
4. When's a good time to visit the city?
5. You really shouldn't miss the weekend market.

12 It really works!

Exercise 1

A

Suggested answers:

2. a headache: take some aspirin
3. a bad cold: go to bed and rest
4. an insect bite: apply anti-itch cream
5. sore muscles: use some ointment
6. a burn: put it under cold water

B

Possible answers:

2. A: What should you do for a headache?
   B: It's helpful to take some aspirin.
3. A: What should you do for a bad cold?
   B: It's important to go to bed and rest.
4. A: What should you do for an insect bite?
   B: It's a good idea to apply anti-itch cream.
5. A: What should you do for sore muscles?
   B: It's helpful to use some ointment.
6. A: What should you do for a burn?
   B: It's important to put it under cold water.

Exercise 2

Possible answers:

2. For a sore throat, it's a good idea not to talk too much.
3. For a burn, it's important not to put ice on it.
4. For insomnia, it's helpful not to drink coffee at night.
5. For a fever, it's important not to get out of bed.

Exercise 3

Answers will vary.

Exercise 4

A

Answers will vary.

B

1. False
2. False
3. True
4. True
5. False
6. True
7. True
8. True

Exercise 5

A

Bottle	***Box***	***Can***	***Tube***
ear drops	cough drops	insect spray	anti-itch cream
eye drops	bandages	sunburn spray	muscle ointment

B

Possible answers:

2. Mary has a bad cough.
   She should get a box of cough drops.
3. David has a terrible earache.
   He should buy a bottle of ear drops.
4. Andrew and Carlos have a lot of mosquito bites.
   They should get a can of insect spray.
5. Manuel has dry, itchy skin.
   He should buy a tube of anti-itch cream.
6. Susan has a cut on her hand.
   She should get a box of bandages.
7. Jin Sook and Brandy got burned at the beach.
   They should get a can of sunburn spray.
8. Mark's shoulders are sore after his workout.
   He should buy a tube of muscle ointment.

Exercise 6

1. CUSTOMER: Yes. Can I have a bottle of aspirin?
   PHARMACIST: Here you are.
   CUSTOMER: And what do you have for a sunburn?
   PHARMACIST: I suggest this lotion.
   CUSTOMER: Thanks.
2. PHARMACIST: Hi. Can I help you?
   CUSTOMER: Yes. Could I have something for sore muscles?
   PHARMACIST: Sure. Try this ointment.
   CUSTOMER: Thanks. And what do you suggest for the flu?
   PHARMACIST: Try some of these tablets. They really work.
   CUSTOMER: OK, thanks. I'll take them. And could I have a box of tissues?
   PHARMACIST: Sure. Here you are.

Exercise 7

A: Wow, you don't look very good! Do you feel OK?
B: No, I think I'm getting a cold. What should I do for it?
A: You should stay at home and go to bed.
B: You're probably right. I've got a really bad cough, too.
A: Try drinking some hot tea with honey. It really helps.
B: Anything else?
A: Yeah, I suggest you get a big box of tissues!

Exercise 8

Possible answers:

2. I think I'm getting a cold.
   You should get a bottle of vitamin C.
3. I can't stop sneezing.
   Try and hold your breath.
4. I don't have any energy.
   I suggest some multivitamins.
5. I'm stressed out!
   You should work less and play more.

13 May I take your order?

Exercise 1

2. A: I really like healthy foods.
   B: So do I.
3. A I'm in the mood for Japanese food.
   B: I am, too.
4. A: I can't stand spicy food.
   B: Neither can I.
5. A: I don't like bland food very much.
   B: I don't either.
6. A: I think Italian food is delicious.
   B: I do, too.

Exercise 2

A

Answers will vary.

B

Answers will vary.

Exercise 3

A

Answers will vary.

C

	Trattoria Romana	*Dynasty*	*Beirut Café*
Food	Italian	American	Lebanese
Atmosphere	quiet and relaxing	boring	lively
Specialties	desserts	steak and potatoes	meze
Service	very good	slow and unfriendly	very friendly
Price/person	about $25	$22	about $18
Reservation	yes	no	yes

Exercise 4

Possible answers:

2. roasted lamb (others are seafood)
3. beef burrito (others are vegetarian)
4. garlic bread (others are potatoes)
5. grilled salmon (others are snacks)
6. sushi (others are drinks)

Exercise 5

WAITER: What kind of dressing would you like on your salad – French, Italian, or vinaigrette?
CUSTOMER: I'd like French, please.
WAITER: And would you like anything to drink?
CUSTOMER: Yes. I'll have iced coffee.
WAITER: With milk and sugar?
CUSTOMER: Yes, please.
WAITER: Anything else?
CUSTOMER: No, thanks. That'll be all.
WAITER: OK. I'll bring it right away.

Exercise 6

2. A: What kind of soda would you like?
   B: I'll have a cola.
3. A: Would you like anything to drink?
   B: No, thanks.
4. A: What flavor ice cream would you like?
   B: Vanilla, please.
5. A: Would you like anything else?
   B: That will be all, thanks.

Exercise 7

SHERRY: It's delicious! I like it a lot!
WHITNEY: I do, too. It's my favorite kind of food. Let's call Chiang Mai restaurant for home delivery.
SHERRY: Great idea! Their food is always good. I eat there a lot.
WHITNEY: So do I. Well, what would you like tonight?
SHERRY: I'm in the mood for some soup.
WHITNEY: So am I. And I think I will have spicy chicken and special Thai rice.
SHERRY: OK, let's order. Oh, wait a minute, I don't have any money with me.
WHITNEY: Neither do I. What should we do?
SHERRY: Well, let's look in the refrigerator. Hmm. Do you like boiled eggs?
WHITNEY: I can't stand them!
SHERRY: Actually, neither can I.

Exercise 8

2. Baked potatoes are less greasy than french fries.
3. Many people like dressing on their salad.
4. Some people rarely cook with spices. They prefer bland food.
5. Vanilla is a popular ice cream flavor.

14 The biggest and the best!

Exercise 1

A

2. b. forest
3. a. valley
4. a. lake
5. c. volcano
6. a. desert

B

2. Amazon River
3. Lake Superior
4. Mount Fuji
5. Mediterranean Sea
6. Angel Falls
7. Pacific Ocean
8. Sahara Desert

Exercise 2

2.	cooler	the coolest	7.	older	the oldest
3.	friendlier	the friendliest	8.	safer	the safest
4.	heavier	the heaviest	9.	smaller	the smallest
5.	nicer	the nicest	10.	wetter	the wettest
6.	noisier	the noisiest			

Exercise 3

IAN: Well, it certainly has some of the most famous cities in the world – Rome, Milan, and Venice.

VAL: Yeah. I had the best time in Venice. It's the most beautiful city I've ever seen. Of course, it's also one of the most popular tourist attractions. It was the most crowded city I visited this summer, and there weren't even any cars!

IAN: I've always wanted to visit Venice. What's it like in the winter?

VAL: Actually, that's the worst time to visit unless you want to avoid the summer crowds. Venice is one of the coldest and foggiest places in Italy in the winter.

Exercise 4

3. The highest waterfall in the world is in Venezuela.
4. The Suez Canal joins the Mediterranean and Red seas. It is 190 kilometers (118 miles) long. It is longer than the Panama Canal.
5. The Atacama Desert in Chile is the driest place in the world.
6. Mount Walialeale in Hawaii gets 1,170 centimeters (460 inches) of rain a year. It is the wettest place on earth!
7. The hottest capital city in the world is Muscat, in Oman.
8. The continent of Antarctica is colder than any other place in the world.
9. The Himalayas are some of the most dangerous mountains to climb.
10. Badwater, in California's Death Valley, is the lowest point in North America.
11. Mont Blanc in the French Alps is higher than the Matterhorn in the Swiss Alps.
12. The Pacific Ocean is deeper than the Atlantic Ocean. At one place the Pacific Ocean is 11,033 meters (36,198 feet) deep.

Exercise 5

A

Answer will vary.

C

1. False
2. False
3. True
4. False
5. False
6. False

Exercise 6

2. How far is New Zealand from Australia?
   a. It's about 2,000 kilometers (1,200 miles).
3. How long is the Amazon River?
   a. It's 6,437 kilometers (4,000 miles) long.
4. How cold is Antarctica?
   b. It gets down to -88.3 degrees Celsius (-126.9 degrees Fahrenheit).
5. How big is the Amazon Rain Forest?
   a. It's 6 million square kilometers (2.5 million miles).
6. How deep is the Grand Canyon?
   b. It's about 1.6 kilometers (1 mile) deep.

Exercise 7

Answers will vary.

Exercise 8

					1 c			2 s	m	a	l	3 l	e	s	t
					o							a			
			4 m		l					5 h		r			
		6 g	o	o	d				7 l	o	n	g	e	r	
			s		e					t		e			
8 b	e	t	t	e	r		9 b	e	s	t		r			
			c				i			e					
	10 f	a	r		11 h	i	g	h	e	s	t				
	a		o		o		g			t		12 w			
	m		13 w	e	t	t	e	s	t			o			
14 c	o	l	d				s					r			
	u		e				15 t	a	l	l	e	s	t		
	s		d									t			

15 I'm going to a soccer match.

Exercise 1

2. comedy act
3. dance performance
4. golf tournament/game
5. pop concert
6. soccer match/game/tournament
7. street fair/party/performance
8. volleyball game/tournament

Exercise 2

Possible answers:

2. On Monday, she's working overtime to finish the report.
3. On Tuesday evening at 7:00, she's seeing a play with Tony.
4. On Wednesday night, she's watching the tennis match with Kate and Sam.
5. On Thursday, she's having lunch with Candy at noon.
6. On Friday, she's staying home and watching the baseball game on TV.
7. On Saturday afternoon, she's going to the golf tournament.

Exercise 3

MARK: I'm going to go to a rock concert on Saturday.
MARTA: That sounds interesting.
MARK: Yeah. There's a free concert in the park. And how about you, Marta?
MARTA: Well, Brian and I are going to see a basketball game in the afternoon.
MARK: And what are you going to do in the evening?
MARTA: Brian's going to visit his mother in the hospital. But I'm not going to do anything really.
MARK: Well, I'm going to have some friends over for a barbecue. Would you like to come?
MARTA: Thanks. I'd love to!

Exercise 4

2. A: Do you want to visit the street fair with us tomorrow?
   B: Sure, I'd love to.
3. A: We're having friends over for dinner tonight. Would you like to come?
   B: I'm sorry. I'm working late tonight.
4. A: How about going to a movie on Saturday?
   B: Oh, I'm sorry. I can't.

Exercise 5

Answers will vary.

Exercise 6

Answers will vary.

Exercise 7

A

Answers will vary.

B

2. e
3. f
4. i
5. j
6. b
7. a
8. g
9. c
10. d

Exercise 8

Possible answers:

1. Could you ask her to bring the fax from New York?
2. Could you tell Mr. Alvarez that we need the report by noon? Please ask him to call Ms. James as soon as possible.
3. Would you tell Miss Lowe that the new laptop is ready? Could you tell her to pick it up this afternoon?

Exercise 9

Possible answers:

1. Please ask Michael not to meet me at the airport until midnight. Would you tell him that the plane is going to be late?
2. Please tell Lucy that we're meeting at Dino's house before the concert. Could you ask her not to forget the tickets?
3. Could you tell Christopher that the beach party starts at noon? Please ask him not to be late.

Exercise 10

SECRETARY: I'm sorry. She's not in. Can I take a message?
MS. CURTIS: Yes, please. This is Ms. Curtis. Would you tell her that I'm staying at the Plaza Hotel? The number is 555-9001, Room 605. Could you tell her to call me?
SECRETARY: OK, Ms. Curtis. I'll give her the message.
MS. CURTIS: Thank you very much. Good-bye.

Exercise 11

2. Could I ask her to call you back?
   Yes. My number is (303) 555-3241.
3. Who's calling?
   My name's Graham. Graham Lock.
4. Can I take a message?
   Yes, please. Could you tell him Roz called?
5. Could I speak to Paul, please?
   Let me see if he's in.
6. I'm sorry. She's busy at the moment.
   That's OK. I'll call back.

16 A change for the better!

Exercise 1

2. A: I haven't seen you for ages.
   B: I know. How have you been?
3. A: You know, I have three kids now.
   B: That's terrific!
4. A: How are you?
   B: I'm doing really well.

Exercise 2

1. Judy has moved to a new apartment. Her old one was too small.
2. Kim and Anna have stopped eating in restaurants. Now they cook dinner at home every evening. It's much cheaper.
3. Alex has started going to the gym. He looks healthier, and he has more energy.

Exercise 3

Answers will vary. Possible answers:

2. Elena doesn't wear glasses. *or* Elena wore glasses before.
3. Susan isn't a student now. *or* Susan was a student.
4. Eddie is thinner now. *or* Eddie lost a lot of weight.

Exercise 4

Possible answers:

2. James was heavier before.
3. Mary has changed schools.
4. Tess isn't married anymore.
5. My hair is longer now.
6. We quit working out.

Exercise 5

A

Answers will vary.

B

1. Aki c
2. Luis a
3. Rosie b

C

1. Aki
   Now I actually look forward to getting up early.
   I dress up now.
   My hair is shorter.
2. Luis
   I got married!
   My wife and I often have friends over for dinner.
   We're taking evening classes.
3. Rosie
   Now I work as a computer programmer.
   I've gained several kilos.
   I feel much happier and healthier.

Exercise 6

2. What career do you think you're most interested in pursuing?
3. I go to school, and I have a family and a part-time job. I have a lot of responsibilities.
4. Lucy wants to pay off her student loan before she buys a car.
5. Marie lost her job. Now she's broke and can't pay her rent.
6. I'd like to be successful in my first job. Then I can get a better job and a raise.

Exercise 7

LEO: I want to get a summer job. I'd like to save money for a vacation.
MELISSA: Really? Where would you like to go?
LEO: I'd love to travel to Latin America. What about you, Melissa?
MELISSA: Well, I'm not going to get a job right away. First, I want to go to Spain and Portugal.
LEO: Sounds great, but how are you going to pay for it?
MELISSA: I hope to borrow some money from my brother. I have a good excuse. I plan to take courses in Spanish and Portuguese.
LEO: Oh, I'm tired of studying!
MELISSA: So am I. But I also hope to take people on tours to Latin America. Why don't you come on my first tour?
LEO: Count me in!

Exercise 8

Answers will vary. Possible answers:

1. I hope to find a new job.
   I want to make more money.
   I plan to take a computer class.
2. I'm going to go to a gym.
   I'd like to eat healthier food.
   I'd love to get more sleep.
3. I'm going to join a singles club.
   I want to be more outgoing.
   I plan to find a hobby.

Exercise 9

2. Heather's salary is much lower than before. She had to take a pay cut.
3. After graduation, Jack plans to work for an international company.
4. This job is more stressful than my last job.
5. Mel hopes to move to a small town.
6. William and Donna got engaged last summer. The marriage will be in April.

Exercise 10

Answers will vary.

Appendix

Countries and nationalities

This is a partial list of countries, many of which are presented in this book.

Country	Nationality	Country	Nationality	Country	Nationality
Argentina	Argentine	Germany	German	Peru	Peruvian
Australia	Australian	Greece	Greek	the Philippines	Filipino
Austria	Austrian	Hungary	Hungarian	Poland	Polish
Bolivia	Bolivian	India	Indian	Russia	Russian
Brazil	Brazilian	Indonesia	Indonesian	Saudi Arabia	Saudi Arabian
Canada	Canadian	Ireland	Irish	Singapore	Singaporean
Chile	Chilean	Italy	Italian	Spain	Spanish
China	Chinese	Japan	Japanese	Switzerland	Swiss
Colombia	Colombian	Korea	Korean	Thailand	Thai
Costa Rica	Costa Rican	Lebanon	Lebanese	Turkey	Turkish
Ecuador	Ecuadorian	Malaysia	Malaysian	the United Kingdom	British
Egypt	Egyptian	Mexico	Mexican	the United States	American
England	English	Morocco	Moroccan	Uruguay	Uruguayan
France	French	New Zealand	New Zealander	Vietnam	Vietnamese

Irregular verbs

Present	Past	Participle	Present	Past	Participle
(be) am/is, are	was, were	been	make	made	made
bring	brought	brought	meet	met	met
buy	bought	bought	put	put	put
come	came	come	quit	quit	quit
cut	cut	cut	read	read	read
do	did	done	ride	rode	ridden
drink	drank	drunk	run	ran	run
drive	drove	driven	see	saw	seen
eat	ate	eaten	sell	sold	sold
fly	flew	flown	set	set	set
fall	fell	fallen	sit	sat	sat
feel	felt	felt	sleep	slept	slept
get	got	gotten	speak	spoke	spoken
give	gave	given	spend	spent	spent
go	went	gone	take	took	taken
grow	grew	grown	teach	taught	taught
have	had	had	tell	told	told
hear	heard	heard	think	thought	thought
keep	kept	kept	wear	wore	worn
lose	lost	lost	write	wrote	written

Comparative and superlative adjectives

Adjectives with *-er* and *-est*

big	deep	heavy	nice	small
busy	dirty	high	old	tall
cheap	dry	hot	pretty	thin
clean	easy	large	quiet	ugly
cold	fast	light	safe	warm
cool	friendly	long	short	wet
dark	funny	new	slow	young

Adjectives with *more* and *most*

attractive	dangerous	expensive	outgoing
beautiful	delicious	famous	popular
boring	difficult	important	relaxing
crowded	exciting	interesting	stressful

Irregular adjectives

good → better → best
bad → worse → the worst

Acknowledgments

Illustrations

Rob De Bank 11, 16, 17, 19, 32, 33, 42, 59, 81, 88, 100 (*bottom*), 102, 106, 107, IA9, SS3, SS9
James Elston IA12
Tim Foley 17, 20, 44 (*top*), IA6, SS12, SS16
Travis Foster 14, 68, 70, 71, 90, SS7
Jeff Grunewald 80
Adam Hurwitz SS8
Randy Jones *v*, 4, 9, 25, 39, 40, 44 (*bottom*), 47, 50 (*top*), 51, 56, 58, 60, 61, 85, 86, 91, 92, 93, 99, 108, 110, IA3, IA15
Eric Larsen IA2
Adolar de Paula Mendes Filho T-164
Jeff Moores 53, IA7
Tom Richmond 30, IA1, IA14
Andrew Shiff T-162, T-171, T-175
Dan Vasconcellos 8, 18, 76, 78 (*top*), 100 (*top*), 105, 113, IA16
Sam Whitehead 2, 3, 5, 31, 37, 50 (*bottom*), 53 (*bottom*), 64, 66, 67, 78 (*bottom*), 79

Photo credits

6 (*top*) © Veer; (*bottom*) © Jim Craigmyle/Corbis
9 (*left to right*) © John Riley/Getty Images; © Superstock; © Bruce Byers/Getty Images; © Dennis Hallinan/Getty Images; © Michael Krasowitz/Getty Images; © Bruce Ayres/Getty Images
10 (*top*) © Corbis; (*bottom*) © Jim Cummins/Corbis
11 © Peter Beavis/Getty Images
12 (*top*) © Walter Hodges/Corbis; (*bottom*) © Dex Images/Corbis
13 (*left to right*) © Stephen Schauer/Getty Images; © Lawrence Manning/Corbis; © Getty Images
15 (*top, left to right*) © Paul Redman/Getty Images; © Britt Erlanson/Getty Images; © Bill Frymire/Masterfile; © ImageState/Alamy; (*bottom*) © Chris Harvey/Getty Images
19 (*top, left to right*) © George Kerrigan; © istock; © istock; © Creatas; (*bottom, left to right*) © George Kerrigan; © Getty Images
23 (*top to bottom*) © Kevork Djansezian/AP/Wide World Photos; © Kevin Winter/Getty Images; © *Newsday* David L. Pokress Pool/AP/Wide World Photos
24 (*clockwise, from top left*) © Rufus F. Folkks/Corbis; © EPA/Javier Rojas/AP/Wide World Photos; © Wally Santan/AP/Wide World Photos; © Universal/The Kobal Collection; © Kevork Djansezian/AP/Wide World Photos
27 (*top to bottom*) © Laurent Rebours/AP/Wide World Photos; © *The Holland Sentinel* Dan Irving/AP/Wide World Photos; © Everett Collection
28 (*left to right*) © Alamy; © Alamy; © Istock; © Corbis; © Getty Images; © Corbis
29 © Robert Holmes/Corbis
31 (*left to right*) © Mitchell Gerber/Corbis; © Reuters/Corbis; © Steve Chernin/AP/Wide World Photos; © Carlos Alvarez/Getty Images; © AFP/Gerard Julien/Getty Images; © Lacy Atkins/AP/Wide World Photos; © Andrea Renault/Globe Photos; © Bob V. Noble/Globe Photos
34 (*top to bottom*) © Yang Liu/Corbis; © Chuck Savage/Corbis; © Pablo Corral V/Corbis
35 © Rob Gage/Getty Images
36 (*left*) © Ty Allison/Getty Images; (*right*) © Corbis
37 © Tim Pannell/Corbis
39 © Phil Cole/Getty Images
40 © Paul Loven/Getty Images
43 © Corbis
46 © Peter Ginter/Getty Images
47 © Ron Chapple/Getty Images
48 © Cliff Hollenbeck/Getty Images
49 (*top to bottom*) © Art Wolfe/Getty Images; © Robert Y. Ono/Corbis; © George F. Mobley/Getty Images
52 © Kelly Mooney Photography/Corbis
54 © Jose Fusta Raga/Corbis
55 © Dian Lofton
60 © Patrick Giardino/Corbis
61 (*left to right*) © Getty Images; © Age Fotostock; © Ryan McVay/Getty Images
63 © Punchstock
64 (*left to right*) © Zac Macaulay/Getty Images; © Kevin Fleming/Corbis; © Creatas; © Creatas; © Denis O'Regan/Corbis
69 (*top to bottom*) © Darryl Torckler/Getty Images; © Elan Sun Star/Getty Images; © David Madison/Getty Images
72 (*top to bottom*) © Scott Gog/Corbis; © Nik Wheeler/Corbis; © Bill Ross/Corbis
73 © Mark L. Stephenson/Corbis
74 (*top*) © Gary Yeowell/Getty Images; (*bottom, left to right*) © Reuters/Corbis; © Orion Press/Getty Images; © Trapper Frank/Corbis/Sygma; © AFP/ Patrick Kovarik/Getty Images; © Bohemian Nomad Picturemakers/Corbis
75 (*top*) © Don Klumpp/Getty Images; (*bottom*) © Poulides/Thatcher/Getty Images
76 © Getty Images
77 (*top*) © Zefa/Masterfile; (*middle*) © Corbis; (*bottom*) © Javier Pierini/Corbis
80 © Franco Vogt/Corbis
81 © Barros&Barros/Getty Images
82 (*top*) © Getty Images; (*bottom*) © Fotosearch
83 (*top*) © Brian A. Vikander/Corbis; (*bottom*) © Age Fotostock
86 (*top row, left to right*) © Getty Images; © Paul Webster/Getty Images; © Getty Images; © David Bishop/Getty Images; (*bottom row, left to right*) © Creatas; © Getty Images; © Creatas; © David Bishop/Getty Images
87 (*left to right*) © Stone/Getty Images; © Laurence Dutton/Getty Images; © Luis Castaneda/Getty Images; © James Jackson/Getty Images; © Alberto Incrocci/Getty Images; © Kenneth Mengay/Getty Images; © Richard Bachman
89 (*top*) © George Kerrigan; (*bottom*) © C.J. Gunther/AP/Wide World Photos
90 © Jose Luis Pelaez Inc./Corbis
94 (*left to right*) © Getty Images; © Getty Images; © Chabruken/Getty Images
95 © Paul A. Souders/Corbis
96 © Catherine Karnow/Corbis
97 (*top, left to right*) © Ed Pritchard/Getty Images; © Ariel Skelly/Corbis; courtesy of Philips Lighting Company; © Dian Lofton; (*bottom, left to right*) © Corbis; © Dian Lofton; courtesy of Niagara Conservation Corporation; © Kevin Laubacher/Getty Images
102 © AP/Wide World Photos
109 (*top to bottom*) © Robert Holmes/Corbis; © Superstock; © Sean Justice/Getty Images
112 © Cameron/Corbis
IA4 (*left*) © Vallon Fabrice/Corbis/Sygma; (*right*) © Lee Jin-man/AP/Wide World Photos
IA5 (*left*) © Rob Lewine/Corbis; (*right, top to bottom*) © Ariel Skelly/Corbis; © Ronnie Kaufman/Corbis
IA8 (*clockwise, from top left*) © Lee Snyder/Corbis; © Corbis; © Sandro Vannini/Corbis; © Phil Schermeister/Corbis
IA10 (*left*) © Corbis; (*right*) © Getty Images
SS5 © Ryan McVay/Getty Images
T-165 (*left column*) © Antonio Lacer/Newscom; (*middle column*) © Getty Images; (*right column*) © Getty Images
T-203 © Zuma Press/Newscom